Welcome to Clemson—
Best wishes
Jerry Reel

THE HIGH
SEMINARY

VOLUME
ONE

Tinted photograph of Thomas Green Clemson, ca. 1880.
Fort Hill Collection, Clemson University.

THE HIGH
SEMINARY

1: A History of the Clemson Agricultural College of South Carolina 1889-1964

JEROME V. REEL

CLEMSON UNIVERSITY
DIGITAL PRESS

Published by Clemson University Digital Press at the Center for Electronic and Digital Publishing, Clemson University, Clemson, South Carolina.

CLEMSON UNIVERSITY
DIGITAL PRESS

Works produced at Clemson University by the Center for Electronic and Digital Publishing include *The South Carolina Review*, its themed series, and monographs such as *Thomas Green Clemson* (2009), *Legacy of a Southern Lady, Anna Calhoun Clemson, 1817-1875* (2007), *Women and Clemson University* (2006), and *Integration with Dignity: A Celebration of Harvey Gantt's Admission to Clemson University* (2003). Online editions, previews, and purchase information may be found at our Web site: http://www.clemson.edu/caah/cedp.

Contact the Director, Center for Electronic and Digital Publishing, Strode Tower, Box 340522, Clemson University, Clemson, South Carolina 29634-0522. Tel: 864-656-5399.

The High Seminary, vol. 1: *A History of the Clemson Agricultural College of South Carolina, 1889–1964* was produced with the Adobe Creative Suite CS5 and Microsoft Word. This book is set in Adobe Garamond Pro and was printed by RR Donnelley.

Dust jacket design by David W. Dryden, Director, Creative Services
Editor and Managing Producer: Deborah G. Dunning, Manager of Editorial Services, Creative Services

Interior book design and layout by Charis Chapman, CEDP
Editorial Assistant: Christina Cook, CEDP

Table of Contents

LIST OF ILLUSTRATIONS

Plates

Figures

Charts

Maps

Preface

The land-grant university is a creation of American government that has changed the United States and many other parts of the world. It gathered the threads of traditional learning and integrated them into the fibers of continuing scientific evolutions and the strands of ever-quickening technological changes. All this was in the hopes of promoting liberal and practical education for a higher standard of living.

What emerged has been truly amazing. Fostered by the Morrill Land Grant Act of 1862 and advanced by a number of other federal statutes, the land-grant schools stand on several different types of foundations. Some rose on older public, traditional colleges in which the liberal arts dominated. Another smaller group was grafted onto older private colleges. Almost half were new creations, among them the Clemson Agricultural College of South Carolina.

For Clemson, the people who merged the land tract together form the first thread that runs through the entire history of the college. In the nineteenth century, the tract now considered the campus rested nearly alone in the northwest corner of South Carolina, isolated but with a geographic good fortune. Mountains that help seal the American East Coast from the lower half of the continent's rich river basin soften into "the great blue hills of God" northwest of the Clemson tract. The landscape smooths out to the west and southwest so that the nineteenth and twentieth century rail lines and then concrete ribbons could pass around what became the Clemson campus. For the years 1889 to 1964, these roadways formed the paths young people coming from Washington, D.C., or Birmingham, Alabama, or from Savannah, Georgia, and the South Carolina cities of Charleston, Conway, and Columbia, traveled when coming to Clemson.

Uncertainty and angst dogged the first thirty years (1889–1917) of Clemson's existence. Measured by the number of young men who enrolled, the college was successful. Measured by the successes in agriculture and engineering and by the successful expansion into textiles and architecture, the faculty performed admirably and grew stronger. Measured by the college's efforts to reach the white people of South Carolina, the whole school did well. The support the leaders of Clemson gave the state's African American higher education institution and the efforts to include the state's college for women marked a grace of decency. But the weaknesses in the school administration up until 1910, along with the economic conditions and political jostling in the state and region, caused the college to scramble beyond the state to maintain momentum.

Clemson's service to the nation in two world wars and its aid to the state in drought and depression (1917–1945) dominated its outreach during its second period of existence. At the same time, its student body doubled, its faculty increased, its reputation built (in spite of the shaky years 1920–1925). The magnificent commitment and sacrifice in World War II remain a precious part of the school's record.

America deepened its own commitment to its rhetoric of freedom and equality before the law, which would require true soul-searching and change for the nation, the state, and for Clemson. Openness, reorganization, and flexibility were required of Clemson: its faculty, its students, and its alumni. They met and even exceeded the challenges of these years (1945–1964) while holding fiercely to a deeper and richer heritage.

Yet, upon reaching that goal, Clemson still would have challenges. It was little like most of the other land-grant schools. It was small. It was heavily male. It was heavily white. But it had proved its capability both to change and to remain.

Acknowledgments

"**Y**ou're going to title the Clemson history *The High Seminary*?" Joe Turner half in jest asked, "That's a phrase from Mr. Clemson's will, isn't it?" "Yes," I replied.

"Well, how long should it take?"

My simple-minded reply was, "Oh, I should be able to have it done in four years." It took much longer. Joe and his wife, Cathy Campbell Turner, have been the closest of friends to my wife, Edmèe, and me for four of five decades here in Clemson.

Some years passed, and I received notice from Clemson University's Advancement Division that Joe and his business partner, Kelly Durham, had made a generous gift to the Clemson University Foundation to support my research and writing of the university's history. Kelly grew up in town and attended Clemson before a stint in the army. Joe also had served in the army after college. They became the "Tiger angels" for the project, and I am ever grateful to these men and their families.

So I, a British medieval historian, set to the task of thinking about a school founded as a land-grant college, one of the major contributions of the United States to the world's higher education tradition. Of course, as a medievalist, I had long realized that the origins of universities lay in the quest of the scholar for truth, whether presumed lost in the example of universal law or perhaps in the understanding of the divine. That meant that research was the first charge, so I began reading whatever I could find on the development of this particular type of institution, all the while keeping notes on what I read.

Fortunately, both my other research interests and my teaching took my wife and me regularly to many campuses in the United States, Great Britain, and Canada. Literally, we "collected" campuses. British friends kindly introduced us to the various forms of higher education in use there. My shared role as a professor and an academic dean brought me into regular contact with similar academic offices from a great number of schools—of great variety—in North America. Seeing higher education through the eyes of these economists, literary scholars, mathematicians, agriculturalists, and lawyers helped broaden my own view of this institution.

At home, we are fortunate to have known many Clemson faculty families whose association with the university stretched back into the second decade of the twentieth century. Through our church we knew Clemsonians whose ties to this place began before World War I. They befriended us, and when we were with them, they frequently told tales (some of which seemed quite "tall") that on occasion turned out to be verifiable. One of Clemson's longest-lived families was

xiv

that of Mr. and Mrs. Preston Brooks Holtzendorff Jr. "Mr. Holtzy's" memories of the YMCA enriched my feel for student life in the World War I and II eras. Our neighbors, the Ivy Duggans, fed us regularly, having as table companions their across-the-fence neighbors Roy and Edith Cooper. Mrs. Cooper came to Clemson as a toddler with her parents, Dr. and Mrs. William Hayne Mills, the first resident pastor of the Presbyterian Church. Readers will find that a few of these friendships and connections provide stories that color and even clear up some historical developments and points.

After I had been a faculty member long enough to be tenured, my first department head, Robert S. Lambert, whose studies focused on Loyalists in South Carolina, and Ernest M. "Whitey" Lander, a leading scholar in post-American Civil War southern history, joined me in proposing a short credit course on "Higher Education and Clemson." We taught it first in 1978 and were determined to keep the course on a strong and high path, meaning independent research for the students. For myself, I learned much (and still do) from these scholars, and as the years moved on, student interests in the forms of their research reports and their questions caused me to turn what I heard or read about Clemson many different ways.

Until the years of Clemson College President Walter Merritt Riggs (1910–1924), Clemson school correspondence was neither organized nor preserved. Riggs, however, was interested in history, as was his young assistant, James Corcoran Littlejohn. Littlejohn himself proposed to write a Clemson history, and he began assembling various documents. His secretary, Mary "Tootsie" Mills Ritchie, was a stickler for accuracy and worked to produce error-free transcriptions of critical items. Like her sister, Edith Cooper, she had a keen memory and maintained an alumni obituary file that proved to be a wealth of information to me. Besides an important preserver and conveyer of the written word, Littlejohn also used his reel-to-reel tape recorder to capture memories of James H. "Red" McHugh, the campus engineer and construction supervisor, and B. Rhett Turnipseed, a member of the first graduating class, and he elicited members of the early classes for their written memories. He also tape-recorded the memories of William Greenlee, who grew up on the Fort Hill grounds and whose stories go back to the last years of the university's founder, Thomas Green Clemson.

Eventually, Cornelia Graham, Clemson's third librarian, began gathering these and other resources together into the collection that came to be known as the University Archives. The Archives is part of a much larger collection of manuscripts, recordings, rare and/or unusual books, and artifacts tended by Michael Kohl, the Special Collections director. Mike's courtesy has opened the Special Collections reading room to my research and provided the space for my work. Directly overseeing the Clemson Archives is Dennis Taylor. He has been especially kind in helping me locate unusual letters that have borne on topics of my interest. The keeper of the photographs and artifacts that bear on Clemson, Susan

Hiott, has zealously and without murmur helped with selection and identification of photographs.

Other members of the Special Collections staff supported this work significantly. Linda Ferry, now retired, grew up in Clemson, and her memories of her father, mathematics professor John Lagrone, also a former mayor of the town of Clemson, enriched my knowledge of the community. Laurie Varenhorst, also the daughter of a professor and a member of the Special Collections staff, added as well to my accuracy. Carl Redd has shared his knowledge of the African American collection, which has helped my efforts in this study. Alan Burns, who specializes in the massive Strom Thurmond collection, helped guide me to the papers in that large group that bore directly on the university. Jennifer Bingham provided insight into some of the smaller sets of papers, and Virengia Houston used her contacts at the University of South Carolina library to expedite my requests to borrow and use some of the photographs in this book. Jim Cross, who has responsibility for the collections of the letters of the Clemson trustees, alumni, and public figures, also directed me to papers. For many of the athletic photographs, Tim Bourret, Clemson's Sports Information director, Sam Blackman, his assistant, and others in the Athletic Department provided knowledge and identification.

In the 1990s, Clinton Whitehurst, a professor of industrial management, proposed developing a collection of interviews of leaders of Clemson in the post-World War II era. Don McKale, a thoughtful and highly published historian of World War II, Class of 1941 Memorial Professor of History at Clemson, and the editor of *Tradition*, which studied the presidents of Clemson, conducted some twenty illuminating interviews for the project. I was privileged to use the DVDs of those interviews. They are housed in Special Collections.

The Clemson University Emeritus College Advisory Board expanded that idea, and emeritus faculty continue to interview other retired Clemson folk to aid in this montage. More than ninety people, many absolutely vital to Clemson's development, have been video-taped (or agreed to be) talking about each one's "personal Clemson," building a rich legacy of the school's more recent fifty years. The interviewers are listed in the bibliography with their subjects. My thanks to all. Vital to this effort was the audio-visual staff headed by Al Littlejohn and his assistant, the now-retired Fred Tuck. The people behind the cameras who frequently joined me on the road were Lance McKinney and Glenn Spake, while back at their offices Beverly Arp and Karen Blackman handled the permission paperwork, the disc preparation, and the business details of that enterprise.

Then, to manage the enormous amount of documentation and track down federal and state documents, deeds, writs, and court records, Andrew Land, Evan Nooe, and Alex Crunkleton, all graduate students in Clemson's History Department, were far more than "useful"—"essential" would be a better term.

Drew, currently a college faculty member in the Atlanta suburbs who did his undergraduate and graduate work at Clemson, developed the census tables, revealing the patterns of male-female, rural-urban, and black-white population splits in South Carolina over the past 130 years. Together, we discussed the data and worked to extract ideas.

Evan, an undergraduate from the University of Florida, was a wiz at identifying both federal and state statutes and regulations that pertained to all universities, all public universities, all land-grant colleges, or Clemson specifically. Evan is now pursuing his doctorate in history at the University of Mississippi.

Alex did his undergraduate work at Georgia Southern University and came to Clemson to study for his master's in history. He has worked most closely on the patterns of student, faculty, and staff backgrounds of degrees, gender, and ethnicity. From these data, he created charts and graphs to aid the reader, but the reader must understand that these data fluctuate on a daily, even hourly basis. We have attempted to identify the high mark in each year to demonstrate the workload placed on the teaching, research, faculty, staff, and facilities. Alex also helped with textual reading and the selection and captioning of pictures for this work.

My other regular research assistants included my grandson, Thomas Reel Adams, who helped work through a number of manuscript collections to identify materials for transcription or photographic copying. He was excellent! His mother, Helen Adams, my oldest daughter, is a member of the Advancement team and frequently helped with the contacting of alumni for this work. Stanley B. Smith, the university registrar, provided information on non-graduates who attended Clemson, while Robert Barkley, our admissions director, provided the contacts that led to Mrs. Kelly Traynham's gift of the George Washington Carver correspondence to Special Collections, a pleasant surprise that emerged from this project.

My beloved friend of seventy years and my loving wife of fifty of those years, Edmèe Reel, traveled with me by plane and car to Vermont, New Orleans, New York, Philadelphia, Auburn, Starkville, Chicago, Atlanta, Columbia, Anderson, Pickens, Walhalla, Charleston, and more where we worked side-by-side with archivists at libraries and depositories noted in the bibliography. But as the terra cotta chimney plaque at the Hanover House reads, "Peu à peu...."

My students in Creative Inquiry classes have aided me by studying aspects of leadership as manifested in the college's commandants, honors winners, student publications editors, and more. Faculty and alumni have offered memories, some captured on DVD, which have been given to the Special Collections, others in conversations, scrapbooks, letters, manuscripts, and papers. These are thanked in the footnotes.

Because I grew up in a benighted (or perhaps beknighted) age when girls took typing and boys took wood and machine shop, I do not type. But as a medievalist and a onetime frequenter of H. M. Chancery, the Public Record Office, I learned Caroline miniscule (*in extremis*) cursive hand, thus secretaries needed to translate the same into a court hand print. Mrs. Barbara Rogers and Mrs. Linda Bridges, two wonderful ladies of Clemson University, began the work of typing my handwritten documents, aided on a few occasions by Ms. Angie Keaton. However, Mrs. Paula Rahn Reel, my daughter-in-law, who helped with some of the deed research for this work, undertook the heavy typing, correcting, and improving, draft after draft. Her husband, Jerome "Jay" Reel, my son, served as the hanaper-courier, shifting chapters back and forth to their home in Anderson.

Deborah Graham Dunning, manager of editorial services in the Creative Services Department, has been the kindest editor a writer could have. In many ways, she shaped my ablative absolute-riddled prose into something far better. Reading behind her for historical accuracy was Rod Andrew Jr., professor of history at Clemson and author of two very well-received books in post-Civil War southern history. He was especially helpful in my understanding of the student walkouts between 1902 and 1925 and military discipline at the college. Michael Kohl, Special Collections director, also read the text and pointed my way to overlooked materials. As a reader, he brought a strong sense of chronology to the work. Don McKale, professor emeritus of history at Clemson, Class of '41 Memorial Professor of Humanities, and recipient of the Class of 1939 Award for Excellence, also assisted me as a reader. McKale, a highly published historian of World War II and author and/or editor of three studies on Clemson history, the history of Fort Hill Presbyterian Church, the study of Clemson's presidents (to which Michael Kohl also contributed a chapter), and a study of the Clemson Class of 1941, provided aid far too great to detail in such a limited space. To these four I owe much.

Other members of the Creative Services staff who have been critical to the production of this work are David Dryden, the director, who designed the dust jacket; M. Elizabeth Newall, editor of *Clemson World* magazine, who provided proofreading and editorial assistance along with office manager Arizona Black and Creative Inquiry students Taylor Reeves, Victoria Witte, and Laura Good; John Mounter, production manager, who served as our liaison with the printer; and Judith Morrison, *Clemson World* art director, who aided with layout and photography selection. Patrick Wright, Creative Services photographer and a man with whom I have worked on several projects, trudged across campus to capture the images in the color signature and others throughout the book. He alone got to ride in the bucket truck to snap the beautiful photos of the Rudolph Lee grotesques and tiles on Riggs and Sirrine halls, respectively. The identification of the former fell to Alex Crunkleton and me based on the information and photographs extant in the Special Collections. Mike Hubbard, professor emeritus of textile science, provided the explanations of the Sirrine Hall ceramic tiles. Charles Gooding, professor of chemical engineering, explained the molecule that Willard Hirsch depicted on Earle Hall.

At the Clemson University Digital Press, Wayne Chapman, the director and executive editor of the Press and the Clemson Center of Electronic and Digital Publishing, editor of the *South Carolina Review*, and professor of English at Clemson, oversaw the typesetting of Christina Cook and the specialized image manipulation and illustration setting done by Charis Chapman. Provost Dori Helms funded half the graduate assistant support for the work, while the Durham-Turner gift funded the other half and all the archive and travel costs.

Through the support of many people in Alumni Relations, I have made contact with and received help from many Clemson alumni scattered around the nation. Further, Alumni Relations has stood behind the financing of the publication of this book and its distribution to the Clemson Family.

Each of the above and others were important to this publication. I cannot thank each one enough. The dedication is the hardest part of a book to write, but this work truly belongs to four who genuinely exemplify the Clemson ethos—Joe Turner '71, Debbie Dunning '75, Kelly Durham '80, and Edmèe Reel '82.

Deo Gratia,
Jerome V. Reel

Abbreviations

#	number
A&M	Agricultural and Mechanical
AAU	Amateur Athletic Union
AB	Latin form of BA, Bachelor of Arts
ACC	Atlantic Coast Conference
AEC	Atomic Energy Commission
AEF	American Expeditionary Forces
AIA	American Institute of Architects
AM	Latin form of MA, Master of Arts
API	Alabama Polytechnic Institute
b	box
B.	born
BA	Bachelor of Arts
BLS	Bachelor of Library Science
BS	Bachelor of Science
ca.	circa
CAC	Clemson Agricultural College
Capt.	Captain
CMP	Cresap, McCormick and Paget
Col.	Colonel
CUA	Clemson University Archives
CUL	Clemson University Libraries
CUL.SC	Clemson University Libraries, Special Collections
D.	died
DAR	Daughters of the American Revolution
D.C.	District of Columbia
Dr.	Doctor
DVM	Doctor of Veterinary Medicine
ed(s).	editor or edited by
et al.	et alia ("and others")
f	folder
FHA	Federal Housing Administration
GEB	General Education Board
Gen.	General
GI	Government Issue and slang for a member of U.S. Armed Forces
GPA	grade point average
GPR	grade point ratio

ID	identification (used to indicate a special card)
IFC	Inter Fraternity Council
IPTAY	I Pay Ten A Year (original manifestation)
Jr.	Junior
LLB	Bachelor of Laws(s), the first professional degree taken by an aspiring lawyer
LSU	Louisiana State University and Agricultural and Mechanical College
Lt.	Lieutenant
M.	married
MA	Master of Arts
Maj.	Major
MD	Doctor of Medicine
MLS	Master of Library Science
Mrs.	Mistress
MS	Master of Science
MSS	manuscripts
NAACP	National Association for the Advancement of Colored People
NAB	National Accrediting Board
NCAA	National Collegiate Athletic Association
n.d.	no data
no.	number
OYA	One Year Agriculture
PhD	Latin form of Doctor of Philosophy
POW	Prisoner of War
P.R.C.	People's Republic of China
Prof.	Professor
PWA	Public Works Administration
RAC	Rockefeller Archive Center
Rev.	Reverend
ROTC	Reserve Officers Training Corps (1916)
RPI	Rensselaer Polytechnic Institute
S	Series
SACS	Southern Association of Colleges and Schools (also known as Association of Colleges and Schools of the Southern States)
SAT	Scholastic Aptitude Test
SATC	Student Army Training Corps
SC	Special Collections
SCA&M	Popular acronym for South Carolina State College
SCDAH	South Carolina Department of Archives and History
SCIAA	South Carolina Intercollegiate Athletic Association
SEC	Southeastern (Athletic) Conference
SIAA	Southern Intercollegiate Athletic Association

SLED	State Law Enforcement Division
SREB	Southern Regional Education Board
ss	subseries
St.	Saint
U.N.	United Nations
U.S.	United States
U.S.S.	United States (Steam) Ship
UDC	United Daughters of the Confederacy
UNC	University of North Carolina
USC	University of South Carolina
USDA	United States Department of Agriculture
USMA	United States Military Academy
v.	versus
vol.	volume
VPI	Virginia Polytechnic Institute (and State University)
VMI	Virginia Military Institute
WPA	Works Progress Administration
YMCA	Young Men's Christian Association

THE HIGH SEMINARY

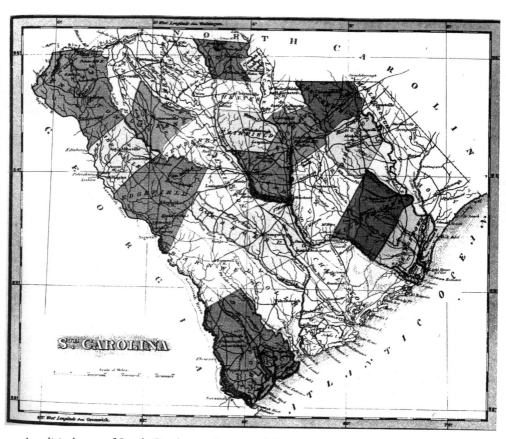

A political map of South Carolina at the turn of the nineteenth century. This topographic map is in the political cartographic scheme of dividing the state into districts. The Fort Hill property appears in the Pendleton District, in the northwestern section of the state. Map taken from Robert Mills, *Mills' Atlas of the State of South Carolina*.

CHAPTER I

The Land

S lowly but relentlessly across the eighteenth century, Europeans pushed into the land they had come to call South Carolina. Some came from the east, but many flooded down from British colonies[1] to the north. Those who came from the east usually entered South Carolina by Charleston. Because the government of South Carolina was willing to accept monotheists from all known European religions except Roman Catholicism, a mixture of European Protestants and Jews found their way into the colony. Among the religious who would play important roles were English Protestants, most of whom were Church of England families whose religious practices were what may now be described as "low." The Church of England was the established church and would dominate the few early charitable and educational facilities. Another significant religious tradition was the French Protestant Calvinist (called Huguenots) movement, whose adherents quickly became a major force in both the commercial and the agricultural life of the colony. Numbers of these families, including the Bonneaus, the DeSaussures, and the Boisseaus, would play significant roles in the history of Clemson. They had been dislocated by the revocation of the Edict of Nantes (the Bourbon French grant of limited religious toleration in 1598) on October 22, 1685, by Louis XIV. A third group of uprooted people were the southern European Jews (Sephardics), who also found refuge in South Carolina. Most of these came through Charleston, although some moved from other colonies.

Those from the northern territories also represented a variety of ethnicities and religions, but for the Clemson history, the major group was the Scots-Irish, a name given to Scottish Calvinist families who had migrated (or even been moved) into Ireland in the late sixteenth and seventeenth centuries. Their attachment to their dual heritages of Gaelic Scots and Scottish Calvinism and their desire for good, arable land caused them to move down the interior of the colonies, settling along the way in mid and western Pennsylvania, Virginia, and the Carolinas. Among those families were the Jacksons, the Pickenses, and the Calhouns (whose name was originally rendered Colquhoun, then Calhoun, Colhoun, or phonetically, Cahoon). Typically they landed at Philadelphia or another of the Chesapeake Bay or Delaware River ports. They might have traveled in a number of directions, but a favorite was to turn south following the "great wagon road" to the southern colonies.

The Europeans had driven the earlier inhabitants of the land, called "natives" or "Indians" by the settlers, into the west. By the 1760s, the European, or Caro-

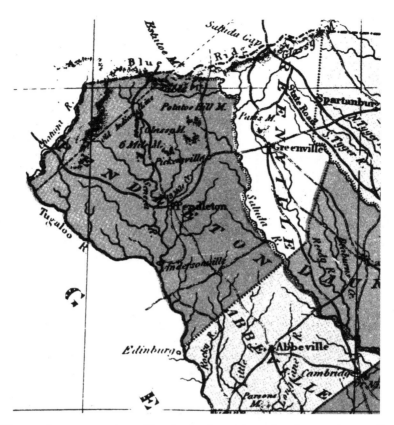

The northwestern section of South Carolina. Map taken from Robert Mills, *Mills' Atlas of the State of South Carolina.*

linian, settlers had made deep inroads westward along the Savannah River and the younger and less-settled Georgia colony. From east to west the South Carolina colony was a series of plateaus formed by the sea as it receded millennia earlier. It rose in steppes from coast level to 260 feet above sea level within 110 miles. The residual soil in the Coastal Plain region drained well into the river system and, containing a variety of minerals, was very arable and conducive to farming. Inland, the travelers would have encountered a sharp rise in elevation into a relatively small band of hills, the Sandhills. This soil, while good for some types of fruit trees, had limited farming (as then practiced) usage. Directly west lies the Piedmont, the entrance area of settlers coming from the north. The Piedmont occupies about a third of South Carolina. The land continues to rise to about 700 feet above sea level. Many thousands of years of decayed vegetation and matter built up a topsoil layer of about a foot or more deep, but the subsoil in the Piedmont is a compact clay, which is difficult to work. Toward the western end of South Carolina (about where the towns of Anderson, Greenville, and Spartanburg now sit in a crescent), the land rise becomes sharper, the valleys deeper, and the rivers swifter.[2]

This was the upper Piedmont, the land of the "lower town" Cherokees. Although these people were hunters, they also were well settled into four areas by the banks of the rivers. The Cherokees were the most "civilized" (that is, dwelling in reasonably well-settled communities) of the southern natives. Nine of these communities operated in 1775. Of these, Esseneca was the most populous, sited on the western side of the Keowee (now Seneca) River. Over the years, these Cherokees had become dependent on the military protection of the British from their enemy, the "over-hill" Creeks. In the years just prior to the French and Indian War (1756–1763), the British army (heavily composed of colonials with overseas officers) had built Fort Prince George, as much for the protection of the Cherokees as for the scattered colonials.[3] The fort, placed on the upper reaches of the Keowee River some twelve to fourteen miles north of Esseneca, helped keep the Cherokees tied very loosely to Britain, but not so closely that Cherokee bands occasionally raided colonial settlements. The British army abandoned the fort in 1768.

In the mid-1770s, tensions between the British government and some of the colonial leadership deepened, causing the government and loyal colonials to keep their ties close to the Cherokees. Then in June 1776, nine British warships attempted to force their way into the Charleston harbor. Upcountry men feared a coordinated attack by Cherokees from the west. Indeed, a series of raids by Cherokees and loyalist colonials disguised as Cherokees gave rise to a retaliatory sortie led by Col. Andrew Williamson against the Cherokees.[4] His company comprised a number of men from the Ninety-Six District, including Scots-Irish/Huguenot Calvinist Andrew Pickens, English-born Sephardic Jew Francis Salvador, as well as some of the Upcountry men. They fell on the Cherokees, routing and killing a number of them. Three of the militia died, among them Salvador, who became the first Jewish casualty after the Declaration of Independence.[5] The militia under Williamson moved on and thoroughly defeated a number of other lower towns. By 1777, the Cherokees sued for peace with the Revolutionary government of South Carolina and ceded more of western South Carolina.

Immediately after the battle at Esseneca, Williamson and his men built a fort on the eastern bank of the Keowee (Seneca) River. They named it Fort Rutledge, in honor of John Rutledge, then president of South Carolina. The fort burned down in 1780, but its role would be remembered in the name Fort Hill.[6]

The Neighbors

South of the site of the fort lay a tract of land dominated by a bluff overlooking the Keowee (Seneca) River. It would come to be owned by Andrew Pickens

(1739–1817). Born in Paxton Township, Pennsylvania, Pickens was from Scots-Irish and French Huguenot roots. His family moved southward as part of the general Scots-Irish migration, and they settled in the South Carolina Waxhaw region. At age twenty, Pickens began his long military career in the Cherokee War of 1759–1761.

Following that war, he moved to Long Cane Creek across the colony, where in 1765, he married Rebecca Calhoun, the daughter of Ezekiel Calhoun and Jane Ewing. She was the sister of John Ewing Colhoun and niece of Patrick Calhoun (the difference in spelling was an idiosyncrasy of John Ewing) and, thus, the cousin of John C. Calhoun.[7] In July 1785, Gen. Pickens obtained 573 acres, including the bluff to the south of Fort Rutledge, where he and his family (Andrew and Rebecca Pickens had twelve children) quickly built a log home. Named Hopewell by the Pickenses, the home still stands but has changed much over the centuries.[8]

Later that same year, the U.S. government commissioned Gen. Pickens, Col. Benjamin Hawkins of North Carolina, and Lachlan McIntosh to negotiate with the Cherokees, Chickasaws, Choctaws, and Creeks to move the boundary be-

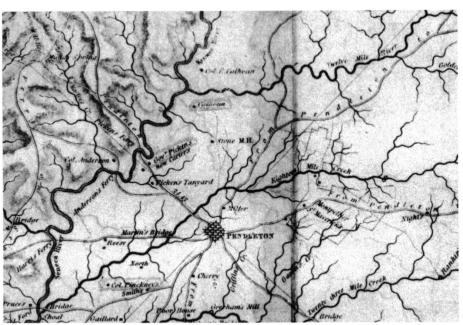

A close-up of the Mills Atlas of the Pendleton District, ca. 1825. This close-up of the Pendleton town area appears within the Pendleton District on the Mills Map of South Carolina. A careful observer should locate the Old Stone Church meetinghouse (marked as "Stone M. H."), the Andrew Pickens home (Hopewell), the site of the John C. Calhoun home (Fort Hill), and the site of the John E. Calhoun [sic] home (Keowee Heights). Map taken from Robert Mills, *Mills' Atlas of the State of South Carolina.*

tween the Europeans and their African slave peoples and the four "first nations" westward once again. This Treaty of Hopewell (1785) ceded most "first nations" land (now Pickens and Oconee counties in South Carolina) along with other "western lands" to the United States in exchange for farm implements, utensils, and supplies.

Directly north of Pickens's holding, Maj. Samuel Taylor owned a 640-acre plot of Keowee (Seneca) riverfront property on which Fort Rutledge's ruins were located.[9] Taylor and his descendants expanded the holdings for another generation.

North of Taylor's property and also on the river was a 504-acre tract obtained by Robert Tate in 1784.[10] Seized for nonpayment of a loan, the tract was leased for one year beginning April 1, 1789, to Henry William DeSaussure of Charleston. The parcel was then deeded to DeSaussure. To make the transfer secure, Robert Tate and his wife issued a quitclaim deed on April 30, 1789, in DeSaussure's favor.[11]

Henry DeSaussure (1763–1839) was the son of Daniel DeSaussure, a Huguenot, and Mary McPherson, a Scots-Irish. DeSaussure, a staunch American patriot, joined the rebels as soon as he could. He was taken prisoner in 1780 and exiled to Philadelphia. There he read law and was called to the Pennsylvania bar in 1784. A year later he returned to South Carolina to practice law. A Federalist, DeSaussure served in the South Carolina 1790 constitutional convention.[12] William McCaleb had purchased the 400-acre parcel to the east of the DeSaussure tract. McCaleb then conveyed the property to DeSaussure.[13]

In the meantime, a religious gathering, called Hopewell (Keowee) but later Hopewell (Seneca), had begun close by Hopewell House. Organized probably in 1788 or 1789, the gathering is first noted in the October 13, 1789, minutes of the Presbytery of South Carolina. The minutes state,

> A few of their number are wealthy and very forward to support the Gospel; among whom are General Pickens and Colonel [Robert] Anderson, both men of great influence in the State of South Carolina. Messrs. Calhoun and DeSaussure, two eminent lawyers in Charleston, have done themselves much honor by liberally subscribing to the assistance of this church.[14]

In 1802, after the pastorate of the Rev. Dr. Thomas Reese, who died in 1796, the congregation called the Rev. Mr. James McElhenney, who shared the pulpit with his son-in-law, the Rev. Mr. John D. Murphy. DeSaussure deeded the 504-acre tract to McElhenney on January 20, 1802.[15]

McElhenney, born in the Waxhaw region of South Carolina, obtained his basic education in the community before going to Dr. Joseph Alexander in Mecklenburg, North Carolina, to learn mathematics, geometry, and ancient languages. He then followed an older brother to study theology with a Dr. Hall before he was ordained, licensed, and began active teaching and preaching. Prior to accepting the call to the Upcountry, he held the Presbyterian pulpits of Johns Is-

Pedigree Chart for Anna Maria Calhoun

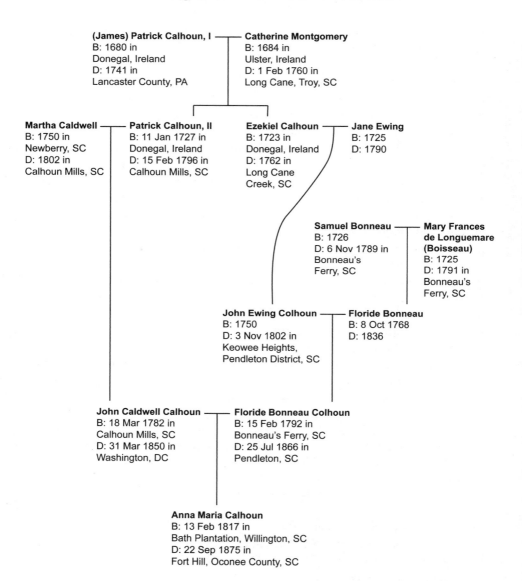

(James) Patrick Calhoun, I
B: 1680 in
Donegal, Ireland
D: 1741 in
Lancaster County, PA

Catherine Montgomery
B: 1684 in
Ulster, Ireland
D: 1 Feb 1760 in
Long Cane, Troy, SC

Martha Caldwell
B: 1750 in
Newberry, SC
D: 1802 in
Calhoun Mills, SC

Patrick Calhoun, II
B: 11 Jan 1727 in
Donegal, Ireland
D: 15 Feb 1796 in
Calhoun Mills, SC

Ezekiel Calhoun
B: 1723 in
Donegal, Ireland
D: 1762 in
Long Cane
Creek, SC

Jane Ewing
B: 1725
D: 1790

Samuel Bonneau
B: 1726
D: 6 Nov 1789 in
Bonneau's
Ferry, SC

**Mary Frances
de Longuemare
(Boisseau)**
B: 1725
D: 1791 in
Bonneau's
Ferry, SC

John Ewing Colhoun
B: 1750
D: 3 Nov 1802 in
Keowee Heights,
Pendleton District, SC

Floride Bonneau
B: 8 Oct 1768
D: 1836

John Caldwell Calhoun
B: 18 Mar 1782 in
Calhoun Mills, SC
D: 31 Mar 1850 in
Washington, DC

Floride Bonneau Colhoun
B: 15 Feb 1792 in
Bonneau's Ferry, SC
D: 25 Jul 1866 in
Pendleton, SC

Anna Maria Calhoun
B: 13 Feb 1817 in
Bath Plantation, Willington, SC
D: 22 Sep 1875 in
Fort Hill, Oconee County, SC

Note the common parentage of Ezekiel Calhoun and Patrick Calhoun II. This created a preexisting blood relationship between John C. Calhoun and Floride Bonneau Colhoun, first cousins, once removed. Chart prepared by Charis Chapman.

land and Wadmalaw. The Upcountry call included a dual ministry of Carmel and Hopewell (Keowee) churches, with two-thirds of McElhenney's time given to Carmel church and one-third to Hopewell. Because of Hopewell's stone structure, erected between 1797 and 1800,[16] the meetinghouse has come to be called Old Stone Church.

The arriving McElhenney household consisted of the pastor, his second wife, his daughter (probably by his first wife) and her husband, John Murphy, and McElhenney's three minor children. Murphy, licensed to preach by Orange Presbytery of North Carolina, acquired land to the east of McElhenney.[17] With community help, they built the four-room, two-story manse with separate kitchen on a knoll overlooking the site of old Fort Rutledge. The home, named Clergy Hall, would become part of Fort Hill house. The ground floor contained a common room, with a steep flight of stairs going up to the two bedrooms, and a small study used by McElhenney and Murphy. It also served as the community classroom where children were instructed in grammar, reading, writing, and arithmetic.

Aside from their pastoral duties, McElhenney and his son-in-law worked a small amount of the land. Church records indicate that they experimented with varied crops and that they built a mill and pond on a creek that flowed into the river. They also built and planted rice fields on the banks of the creeks and the river bottoms. But in the summer of 1812, malaria struck. Murphy's death preceded the death of forty-four-year-old McElhenney on October 4, 1812.[18]

Although McElhenney's place in the history of Fort Hill ended tragically, use of the land for teaching and serious agricultural experimentation began with him and his acquisition of the property in 1802.

The Calhoun Family

The land passed from the McElhenneys to the Calhouns, a family of Scots-Irish who migrated from Donegal, Ireland, in 1733. (James) Patrick Calhoun I (1680–1741) and his wife, Catherine Montgomery (1684–1760), first settled their family in Pennsylvania. Following Patrick Calhoun's death in 1741, the family moved to Virginia, where they stayed for a few years before political changes pushed them farther south into South Carolina. There they settled in the Savannah River Valley close to Long Cane Creek. The Cherokees attacked the small settlement in 1760, killing Catherine Montgomery Calhoun and a number of others. But the settlement revived and sixteen years later became the strong place from which Col. Andrew Williamson raised a number of men for a strike at the Cherokees, then British allies.

The Calhoun family's ties to the land that came to be called Fort Hill emerged with Catherine Calhoun's grandson, John Ewing Colhoun (b. 1750–d. November 3, 1802). On October 8, 1786, Colhoun (who had changed the spelling of his last name from Calhoun) married Floride Bonneau (1768–1836), the daughter of Mary Frances de Longuemare (1725–1791) and Samuel Bonneau (1726–1789), Huguenots from Bonneau's Ferry. Earlier, in 1770, John Ewing had enrolled in the College of New Jersey (now Princeton), where he studied under the Rev. Dr. John Witherspoon and earned his diploma in 1774. John Ewing read the law in Charleston, interrupting his studies to serve in Capt. Charles Drayton's company.[19] John Ewing and Floride had six children. Their first two children and their last child died very young. Their third child was John Ewing Jr. (1790–1853); fourth, Floride (b. February 15, 1792, in Bonneau's Ferry–d. July 25, 1866, in Pendleton), who would marry John Caldwell Calhoun, her first cousin; and fifth, James Edward (1798–1889).

John Ewing, prior to his marriage, had served as ordinary for the Ninety-Six District in 1783 and in 1796 was executor of his brother Patrick's will. Patrick was John Caldwell Calhoun's father.[20] Like many Upcountry white settlers, John Ewing was actively involved in land transactions, including in the Pendleton District.[21] His home place, acquired between 1783 and 1786, amounted to more than 3,000 acres and was served by the Keowee (Seneca) River and the Twelve Mile River.[22] It was to this large holding that John Ewing Colhoun brought his wife, Floride. The Colhouns named the house, which stood on very high ground, Keowee Heights. John Ewing lived there usually only in the spring and summer, while his wife and children typically spent summers in Newport, Rhode Island. During the winters, the whole family lived at Bonneau's Ferry (St. John's Parish) or in Charleston.

John Ewing was elected one of two U.S. senators from South Carolina for a six-year term to begin October 26, 1802.[23] He died just over a week into the term, however, on November 3, 1802, leaving his widow and four minor children. His will noted that his wife was "possessed in her own right of considerable real property," including a "house in Charleston, Santee lands in St. Stephens Parish, and one half western part of Lot #1 of the Ferry Tract." John Ewing Jr., his eldest surviving son, received Keowee Heights, the 3,700-acre plantation on Twelve Mile River. James Edward received 550 acres in Abbeville District and 640 acres on Twenty Three Mile Creek in Pendleton District. The third son named in the will, William Sheridan, died before he would receive the 540-acre Trotters Mill plantation on the Savannah River, an additional 200 acres three miles away, and 150 acres below that. Floride, John Ewing's daughter, received no real property but shared equally (one-fifth) in the African American slaves. A "minority and no legitimate heir devolution" clause passed the real property from brother to brother and, if necessary, eventually to Floride. The death of William Sheridan had the effect of increasing shares to John Ewing Jr. and to James Edward. The will named five executors and added a sixth just five days before John Ewing's death. Lastly,

John Ewing specified that the sons were also to "get collegiate education at some college of note and respectability."[24]

Mrs. John E. (Floride Bonneau) Colhoun did not remarry. She relied on De-Saussure and Ezekiel Pickens to act as her agents for most of the remainder of her children's minorities. And she prepared to live her life partly in the Upcountry. In October 1809, she asked the two agents to attempt to sell one of her Lowcountry tracts, the Ste[a]dman place, and to purchase a tract in the Upcountry. The choice was Clergy Hall from the McElhenneys. For whatever reason, McElhenney sold but continued to live there until his death.[25]

Clergy Hall as it appeared ca. 1825, artist unknown. Clemson University Libraries, Special Collections (hereafter cited as CUL.SC), Fort Hill Subject Series.

John Caldwell Calhoun

John Caldwell Calhoun, son of Patrick Calhoun II and nephew-in-law of Floride Colhoun, was born on March 18, 1782. He attended a boys' academy operated by his brother-in-law Moses Waddel (the spelling he seems to have used most), also a Presbyterian minister. The death of his father in 1796, however, required that John C. return home.

After managing the farm successfully for four years, during which time he read widely in his evening hours, Calhoun returned to Waddel's academy to study Latin and Greek. In 1802, at the age of twenty, Calhoun went north to Yale and enrolled in the third, or junior, year. Yale was still very much a Puritan institution, while Calhoun, although a "cradle Presbyterian," had allied himself with no denomination. Nonetheless, his serious personal temper led him to excel in schoolwork, so much so that he was elected to the Yale chapter of Phi Beta Kappa.

Following graduation (September 12, 1804), he joined John Ewing's widow, his aunt Floride Bonneau Colhoun, on Newport, Rhode Island, where he met his thirteen-year-old cousin, also named Floride Bonneau Colhoun. He returned to South Carolina in November and on December 24, 1804, entered the Charleston law office of DeSaussure and Ford. Henry DeSaussure, who two years earlier had sold the tract of land that would come to be called Fort Hill to the Rev. Mr. James McElhenney, was much impressed with young Calhoun. But Calhoun wanted to study law in a more formal setting, so he returned to Connecticut and on July 22, 1805, began a year's study at Judge Tapping Reeve's well-known school of law.

With his studies completed, Calhoun returned to DeSaussure's office and received a call to the South Carolina bar in the autumn of 1806. Writing of Charleston, however, he noted, "It was Cavalier from the start; we were Puritan." In 1807, he returned to the family home in the Savannah River Valley and opened a legal practice in Abbeville. He continued to court Floride Bonneau Colhoun, and much to her mother's joy, they were married in Bonneau's Ferry on January 8, 1811. He took the congressional seat, to which he had been elected in 1810, on March 4, 1811.[26]

On October 15, 1811, the Calhouns had their first child, Andrew Pickens Calhoun. The second, Anna Maria, was born on February 13, 1817, in Willington, Abbeville District. Within the year, Anna, Andrew, and their parents departed for Washington, D.C., for Calhoun to take up his post as secretary of war. The brood expanded. Patrick (1821) was followed two years later

John Caldwell Calhoun (1782–1850), noted writer, orator, and politician. This portrait depicts the South Carolina representative and senator, U.S. secretary of war and state, and seventh vice president of the United State as a young man. J. C. Littlejohn Series, CUL.SC.

(1823) by John Caldwell, whose poor health required the family to leave Oakly (now Dumbarton Oaks) in the Georgetown countryside for Clergy Hall, then the residence of Floride's mother, Mrs. Floride Colhoun. A second daughter, Martha Cornelia, who would be impaired in walking, was born in 1824.[27] Mrs. Colhoun had enlarged the home somewhat, but much needed to be done to accommodate two more adults and five children. Calhoun asked his cousin and brother-in-law John Ewing Colhoun Jr. to oversee the extensive work.[28] The rent amounted to $250 per year.[29]

The two older children were away at school, Andrew at Yale and Anna enrolled in the Edgefield Female Academy. But Andrew did not last long at Yale. He, along with about fifty other students, was dismissed for a student disruption. The editor of the Calhoun Papers commented, "It was the first of many disappointments he would receive from his five sons."[30] On the other hand, Anna did very well in Edgefield. She returned to the white house now called Fort Hill in 1829 and stayed there until 1831, when she went to Barhamville, a small village several miles out of Columbia, to attend the South Carolina Female Collegiate Institute. She stayed only one year, coming back to the "healthful" Upcountry at the end of 1832.[31]

John C. Calhoun returned to Washington in 1833. Anna, part of the traveling party, served as her father's confidential secretary in the winter of 1834. The Calhoun quarters were in Dawson's boarding house on Capitol Hill. In the same establishment lived South Carolina's other senator, William Campbell Preston, and his wife; Judge Mangum, one of Virginia's senators; B. W. Leigh, a senator from North Carolina; and Mr. Archer, a member of the House of Representatives. Living next door, but accustomed to taking his evening meal at Dawson's, was still another senator, Louis Linn from Missouri.

Over the next four years, Anna made her marks as a pianist and as a person skilled in political discussion.[32] She spent her winters in Washington serving as her father's secretary and her summers and autumns at Fort Hill. In March 1838, Anna met Thomas Green Clemson (1807–1888) of Philadelphia through her father's relationship with Senator Linn. Clemson, who had been visiting Linn concerning a lead mine venture in Missouri, fell deeply in love with Anna and pursued her intensely.[33]

Two years before this auspicious meeting, however, ownership of the Fort Hill land again changed hands. On April 26, 1836, Mrs. Floride Bonneau Colhoun, Anna's grandmother, had died. Property questions arose immediately. John C. Calhoun had little confidence in John Ewing Colhoun Jr. and urged James Edward to "take it in hand yourself & without delay. It is said that delay is dangerous. It is eminently so at law." The two brothers began talking about the estate, and John C. worried about the outcome.[34] Whatever last testament Mrs. Colhoun may have left had been declared invalid, and Calhoun wanted the issue

**Pedigree Chart for
Thomas Green Clemson**

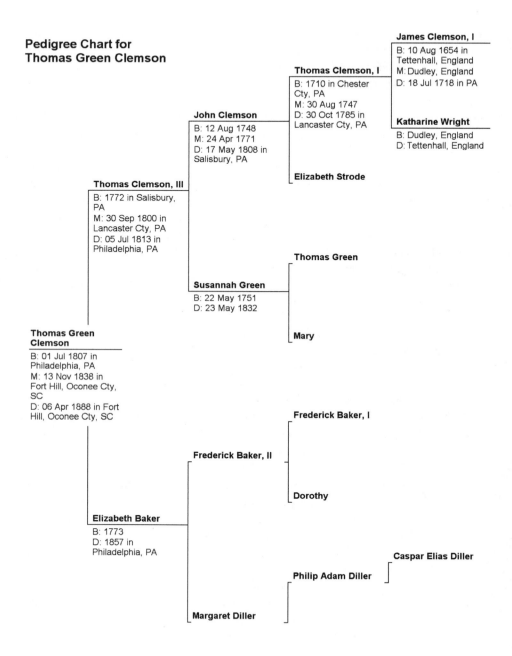

Prepared by Jerome V. Reel

settled before he returned to Washington in the winter.[35] Before October ended, the three had arranged it so that James Edward received 1,621 acres in Pickens County. It is important to note that John Ewing's wife and Floride, Calhoun's wife, both relinquished dower rights.[36] Then in turn, John C. Calhoun (and Floride, who once again renounced dower rights) and James Edward Colhoun released to John Ewing Colhoun the 1,900 acres known as Cold Spring.[37] On the same day (October 22, 1836), a third deed released Fort Hill, listed as containing 550 acres, and the Murphy tract, composed of 450 acres, to John C. and Floride, his wife. John Ewing's wife released dower rights.[38] In each instance, the recipient paid a token five dollars.

While the deeds do not reflect it, the properties belonged solely to Floride Bonneau Colhoun, not John Ewing Colhoun Sr., whose property had been distributed much earlier. Further, John C. Calhoun had no inherent rights to his mother-in-law's property, only those through his marriage to Floride. Regardless, by the autumn of 1836, John C. Calhoun was the master of Fort Hill.

This was the Fort Hill to which Thomas Green Clemson came in the late autumn of 1838 to claim his beloved Anna. They married on November 13, 1838, in the parlor of Fort Hill. The Rev. Mr. William Taylor Potter, rector of St. Paul's Episcopal Church from Pendleton, some three miles away, officiated. The newlyweds soon left South Carolina for Philadelphia to meet Clemson's family.[39]

The Clemsons of Philadelphia

The Clemson family had lived in Pennsylvania for over a century and was descended from James Clemson, born in Tettenhall near Birmingham, England. While some historians and biographers have noted the Quaker leanings of the American Clemson family,[40] Thomas III (Thomas Green Clemson's father) was expelled from the meetinghouse when he married Elizabeth Baker, an Episcopalian from Lancaster County, Pennsylvania. Thomas and Elizabeth Clemson had three sons: John Baker Clemson, who became an Episcopal pastor and served in a number of parishes around Philadelphia and in Delaware; Thomas Green Clemson, the husband of Anna Calhoun; and William Frederick Clemson, who married Susan Dorr. They also had three daughters: Catherine, who married George Washington North; Elizabeth, who married the Honorable George Washington Barton; and Louisa, who married Samuel Walter Washington, the great-nephew of President George Washington.

Thomas III died on July 5, 1813, leaving five minor children and his widow, Elizabeth Baker Clemson, who would deliver their third daughter seven months after his death. The Court of Orphans appointed a second cousin, John Gest, the guardian. Although little is known of Thomas Green's childhood, there is documentation showing that he attended first a grammar school operated by Tabernacle Presbyterian Church in Philadelphia, within walking distance of the Clemson home at Filbert and Ninth Streets, one block north of Market Street. It is possible that he attended a secondary school in Philadelphia.

In 1823, Gest sent fifteen-year-old Thomas to Norwich, Vermont, where Capt. Alden Partridge (1785–1854), a well-regarded headmaster, operated an experimental boarding school that emphasized science and military training. While there, Clemson developed an interest in science, especially chemistry and biology. After completing two years of schooling there, he spent two years working and writing in Philadelphia. In 1826, at the age of nineteen, he sailed for France to continue his scientific education at the Royal School of Mines in Paris.

Although he studied for three years at the Royal School of Mines, he found time to attend lectures at the Sorbonne, a college of the University of Paris. Later, in a court case in which he served as an expert witness, Clemson gave this statement of his qualifications:

> Before 1826, I was engaged in the acquisition of chemical information in the United States. In 1826 I went to Europe, and in the fall of that year I entered the practical laboratory of Mr. Gaultier De Clowbry; at the same time, I attended the lectures of Thénard, Gay-Lussac, and Dulong, as delivered at the Sorbonne, Royal College of France. In 1827 I entered the practical laboratory of Langier and Fiber and afterwards the private laboratory of Robiquet; after which I gained admittance to the Royal School of Mines. I was then examined at the mint, and received my diploma as Assayer. It is dated June 1831. I then came to the United States, where I arrived in the fore part of September, 1831.[41]

Lest it be thought that Clemson only studied while in Paris, a letter from a fellow student, Lefte Neal, a Canadian, written in 1831, tells more:

> Mr. Berthier, whom I saw on the 12th, regrets to see you leave. It was indeed willingly that this scholar, the greatest analyst of the century, gave you the certificate that you bear. For the way he spoke to me of his great pupil is worth even more than the certificate. I congratulate you with all my heart for the keen interest that you have inspired in all of your teachers....
>
> Your departure, my dear Clemson, is then irrevocably fixed; and for you to refuse your friends even the fifteen days of grace that they ask of you is bad, very bad; and not one of us can conceive why you do not wish to be present at the celebrations of July festival, you, one of the combatants of our three great days; you whom I can still see covered with sweat, coming from the firing, and taking, in order to return thither, a new strength at a wine shop on the corner of Mazarin and Guenegant streets at the foot of the barricade.[42]

This letter refers to the July 28–30, 1830, revolution, which succeeded in removing the reactionary Charles X (1757–1836) from the throne. Paris revolutionaries had hoped to establish a republic headed by Gilbert, Marquis de Lafayette (1757–1834), who Thomas Green Clemson apparently favored, but the liberals, anxious to create a constitutional monarchy, turned to Louis Philippe, Duke of Orleans (1773–1850), who accepted the throne. That same revolution spread to the Belgian (as now called) portion of the Netherlands, which then rebelled and established the independent Kingdom of the Belgians.

From 1832 to 1837, Clemson spent his summers touring Europe and, in particular, various types of mines. He returned to the United States as a chemical analyst, specially educated in mining, a field he would practice off and on through the American Civil War. During this period, he lived in Philadelphia, traveled frequently to Europe, and visited Washington, D.C., where he met his beloved Anna in 1838.

Thomas G. Clemson by Joseph Bayas Ord, ca. 1830. Oil on canvas, 33 ½ x 26 ¾ in. Fort Hill Collection, Clemson University. *Anna Maria Calhoun Clemson* by Jacobus Joseph Eeckhout, ca. 1848. Oil on canvas, 72 x 61 ¼ in. Fort Hill Collection, Clemson University.

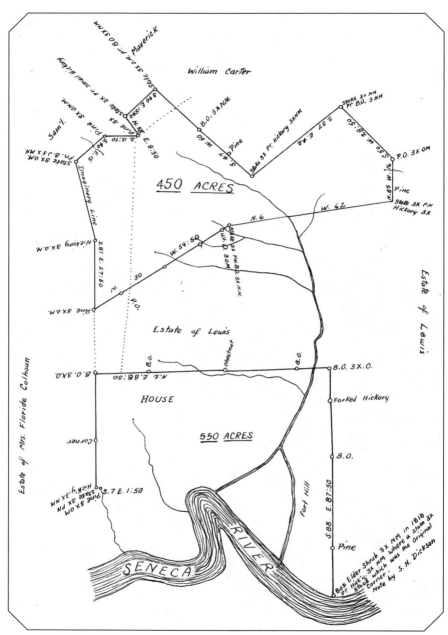

A map of the Calhoun lands surrounding Fort Hill, eastern orientation. Notice the lands are in two separate tracts, intersected by the Lewis land. Mr. Clemson would acquire much of that land for the Calhouns later. Recopied from the original hand-drawn maps and archived at the direction of James Corcoran Littlejohn. J. C. Littlejohn Series, CUL.SC.

Thomas and Anna Calhoun Clemson

The courtship that began in Washington, D.C., was sealed at Fort Hill, South Carolina, with the wedding of Thomas Green Clemson and Anna Maria Calhoun on November 13, 1838. Following a lengthy visit to Pennsylvania, Thomas and Anna Clemson returned to South Carolina in 1839 and settled in at the Fort Hill estate. The Clemsons' first years at Fort Hill were marked by the births of their first three children. Their first child, a daughter, died of a fever shortly after birth in 1839. During the next two years, the Clemsons had two more children: John Calhoun Clemson (b. July 17, 1841), called Calhoun, and Floride Elizabeth Clemson (b. December 29, 1842), sometimes called Lizzie.

During this same period, Clemson became involved in the coal mining operations in Cuba and in the gold efforts at O'Bar Mine in Dahlonega, Georgia, with his father-in-law, John C. Calhoun.[43] He also oversaw much of the day-to-day management of the Fort Hill plantation for Calhoun.[44] In their correspondence, Calhoun urged Clemson to acquire, in Calhoun's name, some of the land to the south of the Fort Hill estate. At the time, Andrew Lewis managed the land for his widowed mother. Initially, Lewis desired only to rent on an annual basis, but after many negotiations, Clemson purchased 275 acres from a Mill Creek branch to the Fort Hill property line for $1,658 (2009 equivalent $34,216.68). The papers, including a three-year mortgage, were signed and sealed on November 27, 1841.[45] In 1843, Clemson bought the Canebrake Plantation in the Edgefield District in what is now Saluda County. An overseer managed the plantation—including property, slaves, and equipment—for the Clemsons after 1844, and in 1856 they sold it to Albert Dearing.[46]

John C. Calhoun, besides having served as a member of the U.S. House of Representatives, secretary of war, a U.S. senator, and vice president of the United States, became secretary of state after an explosion on the *USS Princeton* killed then-Secretary of State Abel Upshur. Upshur had been a Calhoun supporter throughout his career. Clemson accompanied Calhoun to Washington,[47] and it was through Calhoun that President John Tyler (1790–1862) appointed Clemson chargé d'affaires to the Kingdom of the Belgians.

Anna, the two children, and one slave accompanied Clemson to Brussels, but Anna found court ceremony out of date and the economic plight of the poor worse, she thought, than American slavery. The family returned home on a brief furlough in the autumn of 1848 after the season of failed liberal uprisings in Europe that spring and summer.[48]

Clemson's service as chargé d'affaires lasted through the presidencies of John Tyler (1841–1845), James K. Polk (1845–1849), Zachary Taylor (1849–1850), and into the presidency of Millard Fillmore (1850–1853). During this last administration, the Clemsons were summoned back to the United States in 1851.[49]

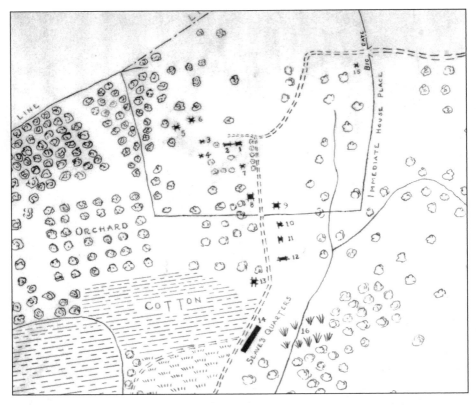

Above, Fort Hill Plantation, main house, and adjoining buildings in 1850 as drawn in the twentieth century, artist unknown. *Below*, close-up of map legend. Photographed by Patrick Wright, Creative Services, Clemson University. Map courtesy of Clemson University Map Collection, CUL.SC.

```
1 -  CALHOUN  MANSION
2 -  KITCHEN , STOREROOM ,& SERVANT'S  QUARTERS
3 -  SERVANT'S  QUARTERS
4 -  SMOKE-HOUSE  for  CUREING  MEATS
5 -  THREE  SERVANT  HOUSES
6 -  PIGEON  HOUSE
7 -  OFFICE  OR  LIBRARY ,  ICE-HOUSE  BENEATH
8 -  CARRIAGE  HOUSE
9 -  STABLES
10 - CARRIAGE  DRIVERS  QUARTERS
11 - GRAINERY
12 - SHEEP  SHELTER
13 - OVERSEERS  HOUSE
14 - 210  FOOT , STONE , FIELD HAND'S  QUARTERS
15 - TOM , THE  GATE-KEEPER'S  HOUSE
16 - RICE  GROWN  ONLY  FOR  HOUSEHOLD
17    WATER  MILL
18    DAM  AT  HEAD  OF  MILL  R..CE

      IT  IS  SAID  THAT  INDIANS  RETURNED  EACH
      WINTER  TO  CAMP  IN  THE  SOUTHERNMOST
      FIELDS  ALONG  THE  BANKS  OF  THE  RIVER
```

Right: Belgium-era portrait of Anna Calhoun Clemson in court attire. Oil on canvas, attributed to Henri Jean Baptiste Jolly (1812-1853). *Above*: Portrait of Thomas Green Clemson painted in Belgium. Oil on canvas; attributed in family tradition to Eugene DeBlock. Both paintings are in the Fort Hill Collection, Clemson University, and are gifts of Mr. and Mrs. Creighton Lee Calhoun.

This assignment allowed Clemson to continue to observe European scientific agriculture. When he returned to the United States, he brought back that acquired knowledge. The family also brought back portraits of Calhoun, Mr. and Mrs. Clemson, and the two children, rendered by the Belgian court portraitist, and a chair, which was the gift of King Léopold I.

A year before the Clemsons' return to the United States, however, on March 31, 1850, John C. Calhoun had died in Washington, D.C. The rights of his widow, Floride Bonneau Colhoun Calhoun, in her mother's estate passed back to her along with her dower share of John C. Calhoun's financially strapped estate. Fortunately, she received a substantial gift from South Carolina citizens who admired Calhoun. Mrs. Calhoun used the gift, originally meant for a restful sea voyage for Senator Calhoun, to pay off the indebtedness and to buy out shares from Anna, Martha Cornelia, and John. In 1854, Andrew, her eldest son, thinking his Alabama plantation had sold, contracted to buy Fort Hill, including fifty slaves, slave quarters, 1,341 acres, the home, and sundry outbuildings for $49,000 (2009 equivalent $1,160,353.67; note that this includes the price of fifty slaves). Mrs.

Calhoun moved to a Pendleton house she had purchased, Mi Casa, and Andrew's family moved into Fort Hill. When the anticipated Alabama plantation sale fell through, Mrs. Calhoun was forced to hold Andrew's note in mortgage.[50]

Meanwhile, the Clemsons settled in Bladensburg, Maryland. In 1855, Anna gave birth to their fourth child, Cornelia, who quickly became her father's pet. When Cornelia died of scarlet fever on December 20, 1858, Clemson became severely depressed.[51] Further, his mood did not improve when he failed to get another European appointment. Even in 1857 when King Léopold I specifically requested that President James Buchanan redispatch Clemson to Brussels, he met with failure.[52] To add to their sorrow, in 1860, Anna suffered a miscarriage. Some hopeful signs, however, existed.

Government Initiatives in Agriculture

Jacob Thompson, secretary of the interior, had moved the small agricultural unit from under William D. Bishop, commissioner of patents, to report directly to the secretary. And he selected Clemson, writing on February 3, 1860, "You are hereby appointed Superintendent of this Department to have charge of the Agricultural Division under my direction."

The *National Intelligencer* reported, "The Secretary of the Interior yesterday [February 7, 1860] responded by asserting to the request preferred and directing the affairs of the agricultural division of the Patent Office to be arranged for transfer as early as practicable." The *National Intelligencer* also noted that Thompson had appointed Clemson to the post and commented, "It is not doubted that the public will appreciate and commend what has thus been done, and rejoice in the selection for this position of a gentleman who will reflect honor upon it, and who is competent both to conceive and to execute its highest and most varied and beneficent design."[53]

Clemson went almost immediately to Europe "to gather seeds, plants, and shrubs." He reported that the Department of Agriculture consisted of the "Superintendent, four clerks, including a translator, the gardener and his assistants, and a $53,000.00 appropriation including the distribution of plants."[54]

Even earlier, in the mid-1850s, Clemson had used The Home, his Bladensburg, Maryland, farm, to continue his agricultural and fertilizer tests. He became active in agricultural societies both in Maryland and Washington, D.C. On occasion, he read papers at the Smithsonian Institute and to the agricultural societies and published observations in a number of scientific journals. Certainly, Clemson ranked among the more highly regarded agricultural chemists in the United States.[55]

During the decade of the 1850s, Clemson also became a strong advocate of scientific and agricultural education. He supported the efforts in Maryland to create an agricultural college, and he was one of five agriculturalists considered by some to be founders of the Maryland Agricultural College. The others were Simon DeWitt, Alden Partridge (Clemson's former schoolmaster), Jonathan B. Turner, and Justin Morrill. The Maryland Agricultural College opened in September 1859 where the University of Maryland now stands.[56]

Justin Morrill's (1810–1898) home place in Vermont lay relatively close to Alden Partridge's former school, and he and Partridge are thought to have exchanged frequent visits. In fact, in the late 1840s, Partridge had advocated using the western land to underwrite scientific education. In 1857, Morrill introduced the proposed "land-grant" bill in Congress. It cleared Congress, barely passing in the U.S. Senate in 1859. President Buchanan, as a strict constructionist, vetoed the bill. The veto was sustained, and for the moment, the land-grant bill was dead.

The bill had had Clemson's complete support. He wrote in *The Necessity and Value of Scientific Instruction* in February 1859,

> No one more than myself appreciates the blessings of our civilization which are greatly due to the classics, and I believe that they will continue to have a most happy effect for all time in their sphere—but at the same time it appears less clear that the sciences are destined to increase the amount of knowledge in the world, far beyond what imagination conceives. The want of adequate scientific instruction is everywhere felt more and more, and as population increases and our fertile lands are exhausted, it will become a necessity.[57]

With a modification in the requirements, the bill was reintroduced and passed both houses. President Abraham Lincoln signed it into law on July 2, 1862. This landmark law stands as one of the most important steps taken in the United States' expanding role in higher education. Entitled "An Act Donating public land to the several States and Territories which may provide colleges for the benefit of agriculture and mechanic arts," the act "appointed to each State a quantity (of public land) equal to thirty thousand acres for each Senator and Representative in Congress to which the States are respectively entitled by the appointment under the census of eighteen hundred and sixty..." to provide revenue through land sales to create "permanent" endowments, support, and maintenance of at least one college "where the leading object shall be, without excluding other scientific and classical studies, and including military tactics, to teach such branches of learning as are related to agriculture and the mechanic arts...." The act specifically excluded using the endowment and/or the income to erect buildings and further continued that states in "a condition of rebellion or insurrection against the Government of the United States shall not be entitled to the benefit of this act."[58] In 1862, South Carolina clearly had been in a state of rebellion for two years.

The Civil War

Almost immediately upon the 1860 election of President Abraham Lincoln, the S.C. General Assembly issued a call for a constitutional convention and for an election to select the delegates. On December 6, 1860, the general election was held, and on December 20, 1860, the S.C. constitutional convention voted to break ties with the Union. The Clemsons did not avidly support secession, but both hoped that South Carolina would not be forced into a war over secession and slavery.[59]

Mrs. Calhoun, who had been with the Clemsons in Maryland in 1860, had already made her way back to Pendleton. Mrs. Clemson and Floride had traveled with her but returned to Maryland after the firing on Fort Sumter and would remain in Maryland and Pennsylvania until late 1864. Just prior to Lincoln's inauguration, Clemson appropriately had tendered his resignation from the outgoing Buchanan administration. Clemson deeded all his Maryland property to Anna and traveled to South Carolina with Calhoun, their son. The Clemsons shipped the thirty-five oil paintings they had collected in Europe to Thomas's uncle Elias Baker in Altoona, Pennsylvania, where the paintings remained through the war.[60]

Floride traveled to Philadelphia to stay with her paternal kindred. In this, she followed the path that her brother, Calhoun, had taken before the war, when he went to Philadelphia to study with his uncle John Baker Clemson, the Episcopal minister. Floride enrolled there in her aunt Elizabeth Barton's finishing school. After Philadelphia, she traveled to great-uncle Elias Baker's home in 1863. She was baptized in the Episcopal Church there, with her uncle John Baker Clemson performing the rite. In December 1864, Anna and Floride began their journey across hostile war lines down to Pendleton to Mrs. Calhoun's home.

Calhoun Clemson had immediately enlisted in the South Carolina Rifles when war erupted in 1861 and served in the Confederate military forces. Thomas Clemson had volunteered for Confederate service in 1863 and oversaw the Iron Service of the Trans-Mississippi Department. Calhoun joined his father in the Confederate mining program but was captured on September 9, 1863, and spent the remainder of the war at a prison camp on Johnson's Island, Ohio. At the war's end, Calhoun was released from prison in June 1865, and Thomas Clemson returned from Shreveport, Louisiana, on June 9, 1865.[61] All five, the Clemsons and Mrs. Calhoun, reunited in Pendleton by midsummer 1865.[62]

Rebuilding

The first matter of business involved the Fort Hill place. Prior to the war, Mrs. Calhoun had sold the estate to her son, Andrew Pickens Calhoun (October 15, 1811–March 16, 1865). As he never paid her, she held the mortgage. When he

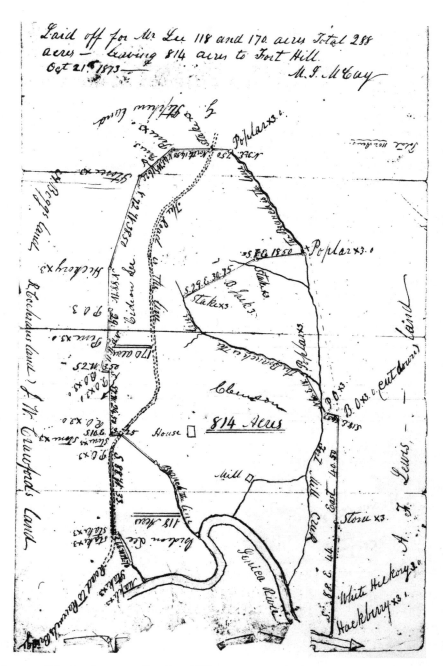

A map of the land surrounding Fort Hill, ca. 1875, including the land known as the Lee Partition. Some labels have been digitally rotated for easier reading. Map is easterly oriented. Thomas Green Clemson Papers, CUL.SC.

died of a heart attack in March 1865, Mrs. Calhoun filed a foreclosure bill against Andrew's estate. The case dragged on for several years. On July 25, 1866, Mrs. Calhoun died. Her will assigned one-fourth of the Fort Hill estate to her grand-daughter, Floride, and three-fourths to her daughter, Anna Maria. The widow of Andrew Pickens Calhoun challenged the will. Now it became the Clemsons versus the Calhouns. The Clemson lawyer was Edward Noble, a member of the Calhoun family through his great-grandmother Mary Calhoun Noble. It would not be settled until 1872, but when it was, Anna Maria received 814 acres, including the house, and Floride's share of the estate was 288 acres.[63]

Before that would happen, though, a double tragedy struck the Clemsons. Their daughter, Floride, had on August 1, 1869, married Gideon Lee, a New Yorker, who was a family friend and nineteen years her senior, and by him she had a daughter, Floride Isabella, born on May 15, 1870. On July 23, 1871, Floride Clemson Lee died unexpectedly of a lung ailment, possibly due to an earlier bout of tuberculosis. Her share of Fort Hill passed to her daughter, Floride Isabella. Seventeen days later, Calhoun Clemson died in a train wreck near Seneca. This marked the fourth, and last, death of the children of Thomas and Anna Clemson. The Clemson family now consisted of only Anna, Thomas, and one granddaughter.[64]

The Advocate for Scientific Education

Through the decade 1865–1875, besides his absorption with the Fort Hill estate, Clemson pursued his ownership of The Home in Maryland and his investments around the country. The Home title was cleared and the property sold after Clemson's death.[65] In addition, he continued his advocacy of scientific agriculture, made all the more timely by the condition of affairs in the Upcountry of South Carolina. In 1865, Clemson commented,

> This country is in a wretched condition, no money, nothing to sell. Existence is almost problematical. The Negroes utterly demoralized. Murders and robberies are common occurrences. I fear a long time must elapse before the country arrives at a settled state. Everyone is ruined, and those that can are leaving.[66]

Clemson envisioned scientific education as the only solution.

Clemson participated in the Pendleton Farmers' Society, one of the oldest of these societies in the United States, and the S.C. Agricultural and Mechanical Society. In 1869, he was selected president of the Pendleton Farmers' Society. His address, delivered at the Farmers' Hall, called for the creation of a scientific educational institution. The society appointed Clemson, R. F. Simpson, and W. A. Hayne to a committee to build support for this type of institution. They produced a circular setting forth the need and making the following appeal:

We, the committee, on behalf of the Agricultural Society, and our fellow citizens, now make this our earnest appeal to the well disposed of all classes and sects, for aid to found an institution for the diffusion of scientific knowledge, that our civilization may advance, and that we may once more become a happy and prosperous people....[67]

Besides wide circulation in South Carolina, the circular went to Prof. Joseph Henry of the Smithsonian with a request:

The Agricultural Society wishes to set the example of establishing an institution, which will in time secure permanent prosperity. I commend the purpose to your attention. Perhaps it may be in your power, through your correspondence, to have it published in England. There are persons in that land who can appreciate our effort.[68]

Henry, an old friend of Clemson's, did as Clemson requested.

The matter did not end here, though. Clemson wrote an article, "The Principles of Agriculture," in February 1867, which stated, "If we endure, if we retain our possessions, it will be done through those laws with which we have either had little acquaintance or neglected to apply. Multiply schools of science; make them gratuitous."[69]

At a meeting of the S.C. Agricultural and Mechanical Society in November 1869, Clemson called for a committee to determine the path to take. The committee members included Gen. Wade Hampton, B. F. Evans, J. D. Kennedy, G. W. Morse, and Clemson. The resolution appointing the committee carried several "resolves" that mark Clemson's thinking at the time. First, he envisioned that the county where the school would be located would be determined by the amount of the subvention it would give. Second, the federal government via the Morrill Land Grant Act and its successors would endow the school. The federal role was no more than an assumption because South Carolina's Reconstruction government would claim the land-grant opportunity for South Carolina College. At the same time, Col. J. E. Calhoun, the surviving son of John Ewing Colhoun, offered 1,000 Pickens County acres to the state for that purpose. The state did not respond.

Less than a year later, Clemson published an article in the *Rural Carolinian* that noted growing frustration over the "much indifference, such solid apathy to that kind of knowledge to which we owe all we have in civilization.... The Word says, 'Be ye skilful in all wisdom, and cunning in knowledge and understanding in science.'"

That appeal was repeated on July 4, 1870, when the Oconee Agricultural and Mechanical Society adopted the following statement:

The works of man are finite, of the earth earthly. Those of the Creator perfect and infinite. Familiarity with these works, and the laws which are inherent to and which govern all matters, coextensive with the universe, organizes and purifies the mind and elevates the soul to exalted aspirations. Progress is the spirit of civilization. Stagnation inevitably leads to conquest and death.

Little came immediately of these entreaties.

Anna Maria also furthered the idea of scientific education. She formed a committee of Ben Sloan, A. H. Cornish, the rector of St. Paul's Church in Pendleton, and others. The committee circulated a pamphlet written by William Henry Trescot endorsing the idea and necessity of scientific education. Clemson also supported that idea and proposed action. In an October 29, 1878, letter to his old friend W. W. Corcoran of Washington, D.C., Clemson noted that every effort to get a scientific institution established in South Carolina had come to naught. Corcoran, remembered in the twenty-first century for having built one of the famous Washington art galleries, was a friend of Clemson's, and Clemson purchased art for him in Europe. A well-known financier and quite wealthy, Corcoran sympathized with the South. He had been the U.S. government's agent, raising money in Europe to finance the Mexican War. Even earlier, he had co-founded the Riggs and Corcoran Bank. He also advised Clemson on financial matters and contributed financially to numerous churches and institutions.[70] Clemson wrote,

> The necessity is paramount, and I have been solicited again to use my feeble exertions to convert Fort Hill into such a purpose, and thus save from desecration that beautiful hallowed spot, and pass it down for future time for the diffusion and investigation of the laws of the Creator.
>
> When the subject was first agitated by Mrs. Clemson and myself we were willing to donate sixty or eighty acres and the plot was surveyed but it was thought that the entire place would be necessary to carry out the project in a manner commensurate with its importance.[71]

This effort produced nothing substantial.

Further, the text of the later federal lawsuit *Lee v. Simpson* notes a reference that after the deaths of Floride Clemson Lee and Calhoun Clemson, Mr. and Mrs. Clemson entered into "mutual wills one to the other, with the joint purpose that the survivor would donate the property to the state of South Carolina for the agricultural institution."[72]

Thomas Clemson Alone

Anna Maria Calhoun Clemson died on September 22, 1875, and the Fort Hill estate passed by her will into the hands of her husband, Thomas Green Clemson, joining his own investments and properties. He now lived alone at Fort Hill house with only a housekeeper, Mrs. Jane Prince, her daughter, Essie, and several African American servants.

After Anna's death, Clemson received visitors and made a trip to Carmel, New York, to see his granddaughter and his daughter's grave. In 1878, U.S. President Rutherford B. Hayes appointed Clemson the U.S. representative to the International Exhibition in Europe, and he made that extended trip. His lawyer, Col. James Rion of Winnsboro, visited as Clemson planned his will. Rion's last visit to Fort Hill was in the summer of 1886. Further, William Pinckney Starke, a frequent guest at Fort Hill who was beginning a biography of John C. Calhoun, died on October 12, 1886. Certainly, Clemson felt his own mortality.[73]

In 1883, Rion had drawn Clemson's next will after the possible 1870s document. Rion, very involved in South Carolina affairs, was both a graduate and a trustee of the University of South Carolina.[74] As a boy he had spent time at Fort Hill and during his school days was very much a Calhoun favorite. The 1883 will proposed the gift of Fort Hill to the state for a scientific college. Further, it required that there be departments of mathematics, geology and mineralogy, chemistry, and modern languages. It provided that if the state did not accept the will with its terms in seven years, the estate would be turned over to a society headed by Mrs. Rion and organized like the Mount Vernon Society group. The idea of a Mount Vernon-style arrangement originated from Anna's cousin Floride Noble Cunningham, who, in turn, was the sister-in-law of Ann Pamela Cunningham, the founder of the Mount Vernon Ladies' Association. The association, composed of prominent American women, formed to raise money, purchase Mount Vernon, the home of the adult George Washington, and then preserve and restore Mount Vernon as a permanent "shrine." But new winds stirred the small farmers of South Carolina, winds of great change.

Notes

1. For those who are conscious of chronology, the Royal Historical Society's *Handbook of British Chronology* (Fryde et al., eds.), 45, notes that "the phrase 'Great Britain' had been used on the great seal almost continuously since 1625."
2. Horton and Zullo, *Geology of the Carolinas*, 4–5.
3. McKown, "Fort Prince George," 1–14; and Sheriff, ed., *Cherokee Villages in South Carolina*, 104–108.
4. Edgar, *South Carolina*, 227–229.
5. Bass, "Francis Salvador," in *South Carolina Encyclopedia*, 833–834. Alan Schaffer, a former Clemson history professor, first noted Salvador to me. See also Rezneck, *Unrecognized Patriots*, 23–24. Richard Imershein brought this work to my attention.
6. Anderson *Independent*, March 12, 1961. A South Carolina historical marker and a small stone representation of the fort mark the site. Because South Carolina declared itself a republic on March 26, 1776, its constitution titled its chief executive "president." See also http://www.sciway.net/hist/governors/jrutledge.html (accessed September 15, 2010).
7. Salley Jr., "Calhoun Family of South Carolina," in *South Carolina Historical and Genealogical Magazine,* vol. 7, 81–98 and 153–169. This is the source of much of the Calhoun family information.

8. Clemson University Libraries, Special Collections, Clemson, South Carolina (hereafter cited as CUL.SC.) MSS 68 f 314. Occupied by the Cherry family almost continuously after they received it from Francis Pickens, Andrew Pickens Sr.'s grandson, the home and its land were acquired by the federal government in the land reclamation project during the Depression (1929–1940). It was leased to Clemson Agricultural College, which then received (via federal law in 1955) fee-restricted ownership.

9. Seaborn, ed., *Micheaux's Journey*. From *State Plats*, v. 5, 245. Seaborn used the plat with the permission of the S.C. Department of Archives and History (SCDAH). Fred Holder, who has been of great assistance during this study, provided the reference and a copy of the plat.

10. According to attorney William L. Watkins in a 1956 letter to J. C. Littlejohn, Clemson Agricultural College former business manager, the deed was recorded in Deed Book A, 27, and the plat is in Plat Book 5, 196 (Anderson Courthouse). Watkins was an attorney with Watkins, Vandiver, and Freeman, of Anderson, and served as legal counsel for Clemson Agricultural College beginning with the rise of the Hartwell Lake issue in the mid-1940s and remained legal counsel through the 1960s. In CUL.SC.MSS 68 f 26.

11. Willie, *Pendleton District, S.C., 1790–1806*, 2.

12. Gannon, "Henry William DeSaussure," in *South Carolina Encyclopedia*, 260–261.

13. Anderson County, South Carolina, Clerk of Court, Deed Book B, 262. Paula Reel aided in this research in the SCDAH.

14. Brackett, *Old Stone Church*, 87–94.

15. Anderson County, South Carolina, Clerk of Court, Deed Book L, 158–160.

16. Brackett, *Old Stone Church*, 116.

17. Anderson County, South Carolina, Clerk of Court, Mesne Conveyance Book L, 1810–1812; and Willie, *Pendleton District*, 211–212.

18. Brackett, *Old Stone Church*, 95–97. The estate papers of John Murphy were filed with Anderson County, Probate Judge, Estate Papers, Packets 417–452, c 1128, Packet 428.

19. Salley, "Calhoun Family of South Carolina," vol. 7, 81–85. Most of these lines will play roles in the history of the land and Clemson's purpose. The company roll shows he signed his last name "Calhone," 153. Ann Ratliff Russell, a former Clemson history professor, provided much of the Bonneau information. The information on Colhoun's education in New Jersey is in Green, *Our Honoured Relation*, 20–23.

20. Salley, "Calhoun Family of South Carolina," vol. 7, 89–90.

21. The area was called Pendleton District from 1786 to 1790. From 1791 to 1799, it was the Washington District, and was subdivided into two counties: Greenville and Pendleton. In 1800, the counties became districts. In 1826, Pendleton District was divided in two: Anderson and Pickens. It remained as such until 1868, when the districts were renamed counties and Oconee was created from western Pickens District. See http.//www.state.sc./schdah/guide (accessed October 13, 2009).

22. Abbeville County, South Carolina, Clerk of Court, Deed Book A, 8 and 258; Deed Book 2, Record 108; Deed Book 14, Record 305; and Deed Book 19, Record 393.

23. Salley, "Calhoun Family of South Carolina," 154.

24. Willie, *Pendleton District*, 22–31.

25. Simpson, *History of Old Pendleton*, 211. Simpson spelled the name "McElhanney." See also Green, *Our Honoured Relation*, 184–185.

26. Peterson, *The Great Triumvirate*, 18–27.

27. Lander, *Calhoun Family and T. G. Clemson*, genealogy chart, end papers.

28. Hemphill, ed., *Papers of John C. Calhoun*, vol. 10, 62–63; and Wilson, ed., ibid., vol. 11, 282.

29. Wilson, ed., *Papers of John C. Calhoun*, vol. 11, 283.

30. Ibid., 95–96.

31. Russell, *Legacy of a Southern Lady*, 3–5.

32. Ibid., 6–7.

33. Lander, *Calhoun Family and T. G. Clemson*, 5, 18–19.

34. Wilson, ed., *Papers of John C. Calhoun*, vol. 13, 277, 278, and 281 (ca. August 15–31, 1836).

35. Ibid., 295.

36. Pickens County, South Carolina, Deed Book D–1, 276–277. The deed was not recorded until September 29, 1840.

37. Ibid., Deed Book C–1, 252–254. This deed was recorded December 3, 1836. In some things, then, John Ewing acted with alacrity.

38. Ibid., 419–420. The deed was recorded August 22, 1837.

39. A valuable study of the life and career of Thomas Green Clemson is Alma Bennett, ed., *Thomas Green Clemson*. Much of what follows in this chapter is drawn from the research and writings that are contained therein. My thanks and appreciation go to each of my colleagues in turn.

40. Holmes and Sherrill, *Thomas Green Clemson: His Life and Work*, 1–2, 19.

41. CUL.SC.MSS 2 b 1 f 2; See Butler, "Thomas Green Clemson: Scientist and Engineer," in *Thomas Green Clemson*, 106.

42. Reel, "The 1807–1838 Life and Education of Thomas Green Clemson," in *Thomas Green Clemson*, 21.

43. CUL.SC.MSS 2 b 1 f 2; See Butler, "Scientist and Engineer," in *Thomas Green Clemson*, 114–115.

44. Kelly, "The Scientist as Farmer," in *Thomas Green Clemson*, 139–145.

45. The deed was recorded January 7, 1842, in Pickens County, South Carolina, Clerk of Court, Deed Book D–1, 453–455, and the mortgage in Pickens County, South Carolina, Clerk of Court, Deed Book D–1, 463–464.

46. CUL.SC.MSS 2 Oversize Box 1: Deeds; and Lander, *Calhoun Family and T. G. Clemson*, 151.

47. Russell, *Legacy of a Southern Lady*, 12.

48. Ibid., 13.

49. Cross and Godts-Peters, "The European Years," in *Thomas Green Clemson*, 56–70.

50. Lander, *Calhoun Family and T. G. Clemson*, 129.

51. Ibid., 130.

52. Grubb, "The Washington Years," in *Thomas Green Clemson*, 77–78; and Russell, "Anna Maria Calhoun Clemson," ibid., 32–38.

53. Grubb, "Washington Years," ibid., 92–93.

54. Ibid. The quotations are documented fully in Grubb's work.

55. CUL.SC.CUA. S 3 b 1 f 8.

56. Edmond, *The Magnificent Charter*, 20.

57. CUL.SC.CUA. S 3 b 2 f 23.

58. Kerr, *The Legacy*, 205–208.

59. Edgar, *South Carolina*, 351–353. On the secession attitudes of Thomas and Anna Clemson, see Lander, *Calhoun Family and T. G. Clemson*, 199.

60. Hiott, "Thomas Green Clemson: Art Collector and Artist," in *Thomas Green Clemson*, 203.

61. Lander, *Calhoun Family and T. G. Clemson*, 199–201.

62. Bartley, "Race, Reconstruction, and Post-Bellum Education," in *Thomas Green Clemson*, 169.

63. An interesting study of Floride during the Civil War is in *A Rebel Came Home: The Diary and Letters of Floride Clemson, 1863–1866* by E. M. Lander, Clemson history professor, and Charles McGee, Clemson English professor.

64. Lander, *Calhoun Family and T. G. Clemson*, 239.

65. Ibid., 179.

66. CUL.SC.MSS 2 b 5 f 2.

67. Lander, *Calhoun Family and T. G. Clemson*, 230.

68. CUL.SC.MSS 2 b 5 f 6.

69. Ibid., f 4.

70. Goldstein, "Washington and the Network of W. W. Corcoran," in *Business and Economic History: On Line*, 2007, 1–10.

71. Holmes and Sherrill, *Thomas Green Clemson: His Life and Work*, 147. The authors quote Clemson writing in the "Principles of Agriculture," reprinted in *The Land We Love*.

72. District of South Carolina, Fourth Circuit, *Lee v. Simpson*.

73. Holmes and Sherrill, *Thomas Green Clemson: His Life and Work*, 146–155.

74. Lander, *Calhoun Family and T. G. Clemson*, 245–251.

A map of the town of Pendleton as it appeared during the 1880s and 1890s. Ernest McPherson Lander Papers, CUL.SC.

CHAPTER II

New Winds, New Will

1886–1889

Autumn 1886 settled over the town of Pendleton as the westerly running train stopped at the depot to unload shipments from points to the southeast. Its crew needed to make only a few more stops before they would reach the terminus at Walhalla and rest before arising the next morning to begin their return run. Passengers had boarded and exited all along the line until the junction at Anderson. Here, the midstate line joined the westerly line to head west, and the passengers for Greenville and Spartanburg transferred and continued due north. At Pendleton, a few passengers, mostly from Anderson, left the train. Among them was a traveler from Trenton, a man with no sight in his left eye, who stepped from his rail carriage onto the platform. He was Benjamin Ryan Tillman, who had been making a reputation for himself as an opponent of the political forces that had controlled South Carolina since 1876. He was a stirrer of the new wind.[1]

South Carolina politics had been a seething cauldron since the death of Senator John C. Calhoun in 1850. Prior to the Civil War and divided unequally between secessionists and unionists, the white minority reunited in what many knew was an effort to preserve slavery and which many others understood as the defense of their homes. They put aside all the class divisions of puritans and cavaliers, yeoman and manorial masters in that cause. But their effort failed. The older leaders attempted to retain control with a slightly changed program of limited economic franchise for African Americans but almost no political participation for them. The Republican congressional leaders rejected that solution in what came to be called "congressional reconstruction." The congressional insistence that universal adult male suffrage be embedded in a state's constitution if it were to be readmitted to the Union led to the new South Carolina Constitution of 1868. It guaranteed males equal political rights and public (although not necessarily integrated in race and/or gender) education. South Carolina historian Walter Edgar has noted, "With the exception of one integrated school in Kershaw County and several in Richland County, the remainder of the state's public schools were segregated."[2]

White Reaction

After the ratification of the new South Carolina constitution, one unconscionable blow to many South Carolina whites was the appointment in 1869 of two

African Americans as trustees of what had been renamed the University of South Carolina (USC). Some faculty resigned, and students began to withdraw. The first African American student enrolled only in 1873, and by 1875, the student body was less than 10 percent white. Further, the government had opened an agricultural and industrial training institute in Orangeburg next to Claflin College, a school opened in 1869 by northern Methodists for African American students. To support these ventures, South Carolina would avail itself of the Morrill Land Grant Act endowment interest.[3]

White South Carolinians generally withdrew from public life, whether in politics or education. A number left and moved west. Others, however, realized that because the new constitution had transferred the weight of taxation from business transactions to land, they still held the strings of the public purse. They refused to pay taxes, thereby reducing the public treasury. At the same time, political corruption drained what public money there was into private purses. Edgar called it a "sordid record," noting the magnitude of the raid on the state treasury.[4] The national depression of 1873, which wiped out such bank savings as there were throughout the South and elsewhere, made the financial problems worse.[5]

The South Carolina gubernatorial and the United States presidential elections were scheduled in 1876. Even though many white South Carolinians wanted to seize state government by force, some Democratic Party leaders, particularly Wade Hampton III, urged the use of the ballot. The Democrats nominated Hampton, a constitutional unionist before secession and a Confederate general by war's end, for governor. He favored male suffrage, limited by an educational requirement.[6]

Prior to the elections, several other actions besides the integration of USC led to the inflamed public mood. First, even against the advice of Republican Governor Daniel Chamberlain, a Massachusetts native, the general assembly elected William J. Whipper and Franklin J. Moses, two men generally thought to be corrupt, as circuit judges in 1875. Second, eight months later in Hamberg, an incident between two young white men and the mainly African American militia resulted in gunfire and several deaths during the exchange. A hostile white mob gathered and overwhelmed the militia. After the whites had taken the African Americans captive, the captors murdered six of their new prisoners. In the crowd of white belligerents was the twenty-nine-year-old Benjamin Ryan Tillman.

At this point, Tillman was not a major player in South Carolina's political scene, but later he would boast of his participation in the crowd witnessing the killing of the six African Americans as a plank in the platform on which he stood. His deep contempt for African Americans, whom he later referred to as the "mudsill," has almost obliterated the memory of what reforms he helped produce in education, including his role in founding Clemson College, his contribution in the establishment of Winthrop College, and his frequently overlooked interest in public schools.[7]

The presidential electors and gubernatorial elections in late 1876, which were marred by violence and voting irregularities, left the outcome in South Carolina in great dispute. The U.S. House of Representatives finally ruled that the electors from South Carolina pledged to Republican presidential candidate Rutherford B. Hayes had been chosen. Hayes, after he took office, withdrew federal troops from South Carolina, effectively recognizing Wade Hampton III as governor. The new legislature and governor closed the University of South Carolina, ending that irritant to the white elite,[8] and a legislative committee began to sort through the shambles of the state treasury records. However, the legislative committee's report conveniently did not include the names of prominent white Democrats who also profited from the theft. That "sin of omission" appears to have contributed to the notion of the total and unselfish motives of the "Bourbon Restoration," so called because the chief counselors of Wade Hampton were "former Confederate generals" to whom, as Walter Edgar wrote, "land [was] still more important than commerce...." They were called "Bourbons (for the French royalists who resumed power after Napoleon and acted as if nothing had changed)...."[9]

The general assembly, after much debate, finally passed the bill to reorganize USC as a university with two campuses, one in Columbia called South Carolina College, and the other an institute dependent on Claflin College in Orangeburg.

James Henry Rion (1828–1886), friend, advisor, and attorney of Thomas Green Clemson, ca. 1885. George Valentine, photographer. South Caroliniana Library, University of South Carolina.

One board composed of four ex officio and voting members—namely the governor, the state superintendent of education, and the education committee chairs of the house and the senate—and seven legislatively elected trustees, who would serve four-year terms, would govern both schools. Further, the act directed that the trustees establish an agricultural department at the Columbia campus. The Act of 1879 (An Act to Provide for the State University), however, did not set a date for an opening.[10] That would not happen until late December 1879.

Then, in February 1880, the USC trustees created the college structure. A president would have, among others, two lead officers: the foreman of the farm and the foreman of mechanics. Trustee James H. Rion, who framed the structure, called for four chairs: chemistry and experimental agriculture; geology, mineralogy, botany, and zoology; mathematics and natural philosophy (physics); and English language, literature, and belles-lettres (the humanities). Initially, no diplomas were offered in either agriculture or engineering (mechanics). One could conclude that the trustees believed those fields ineligible for collegiate status. However, the majority of the funds used to pay the school's costs were derived from the Morrill land-grant funds.[11]

By 1882, critics, led by Tillman, decried this as fraud. If, in the Act of 1879, the legislature meant that agriculture and mechanics were to be taught, then to the critics, the fraud originated in 1882 when the trustees did away with the positions of foremen of the farm and of mechanics. Those positions were replaced with five new chairs: ancient languages, modern languages, agriculture and horticulture, history and political economy, and mental and moral philosophy.[12] Whatever else was meant, the changes greatly diminished mechanics. For agriculturists, however, the appointment of John M. McBryde as the agriculture professor was a good sign. McBryde had served as chair of agriculture at the University of Tennessee, was considered the best agriculturist in the South, and was an excellent administrator.[13] It was a hopeful signal to the state's agricultural interests.

From the autumn of 1882 to 1890, McBryde worked to broaden the college from the classical Anglo-American curriculum that was favored by the antebellum elite toward new and useful curricula. Not only were there three-year studies for the bachelor of arts, but extra time and study could lead to the master of arts degree. The bachelor of science degree was offered briefly but abandoned. As hopeful as the program sounded, the general assembly was neither able nor inclined to fund McBryde's vision. In fact, by 1884–1885, no certificates had been awarded in engineering, while the enrollment in agriculture and chemistry (for certificate and for short courses) numbered ten students. The total enrollment that year in all programs and at all levels was 213, while the total state appropriation was $20,700 (2009 equivalent $489,193).[14]

Rise of the Upstate

At the same time, two major developments rapidly moved South Carolina's economic bases from the Lowcountry to the Upstate. The first was in transportation. Railroads connected points of commerce, whether agricultural or industrial. The major lines connected the Sandhills to Washington, D.C., through Richmond to Columbia and on to Savannah or Augusta. In the Upstate, the Southern line, which also ended in Washington, D.C., had pushed through York, Spartanburg, and Greenville before crossing Georgia to Atlanta and on to New Orleans. Within the state, local lines began to connect smaller towns to the larger junctions. This development favored the lands above the sharply defined change from the Coastal Plain to the Sandhills, or the fall line.[15]

FARMERS SOCIETY HALL 1826   PENDLETON, SOUTH CAROLINA

A drawing of the Pendleton Farmers' Society Hall by Joseph L. Young, A.I.A. Young was a professor of architecture at Clemson from 1950 until his retirement. This presentation drawing is used with the kind permission of the Joseph Laurie Young estate.

Above the same fall line, the land rose rapidly toward the mountains and the eastern Continental Divide. Abundant water running downhill was the source of energy. And cheap energy meant good sites for textile mills. Two clusters of mills emerged in the early 1880s. The first appeared in Aiken, Lexington, Orangeburg, and Sumter counties. The second, in the Piedmont, clustered the mills more densely in Anderson, Greenville, Spartanburg, York, and Chester counties. These were the same two belts favored by the railroads. Further, in 1880, the investors in both regions were heavily South Carolinian.[16]

But to extend this prosperity required a more educated work force—both scientifically and technologically—than inhabited South Carolina. To keep abreast of mechanical improvements, a population that could translate oral or written instructions into lightly supervised actions was needed. Above that, a layer of instructors and supervisors had to manage and maintain the increasingly complicated machinery. As long as the colleges produced only lawyers, physicians, teachers, bankers, and classicists, as fine as these might be, desired economic growth would not occur. And although McBryde and a few in Columbia attempted to move education toward broad general improvements, the state lawmakers did not follow suit.

The average South Carolina family, however, was engaged in farming, the business of planting, tending, gathering, and selling products of the earth. It was clear that much of what was legislated or taught in Columbia made little change in their status. If anything, the changes since 1860 only made their lives more meager. Even nature seemingly conspired against those farmers, whose well-being depended directly on the harvest. From 1881 (or shortly after the triumph of the old Confederate elite), a succession of droughts and insect invasions had added to the farmers' misery.

Agricultural Societies in South Carolina

As Alexis de Tocqueville recognized, Americans were association makers. In agriculture, associations emerged already in the early Federal period. The S.C. Society for Promoting and Improving Agriculture and Other Rural Concerns, founded in 1785 by Lowcountry planters, was among America's oldest. In the Upstate, the Pendleton Farmers' Society (1815) had a wide array of members, most of whom were farmers. The membership included a number of holders of large properties, including Thomas Pinckney Jr. and John E. Colhoun; men whose holdings were more modest in size, including C. W. Miller and John Green; and those who shared farming with other interests, including John C. Calhoun's relative and teacher Moses Waddel.[17] In 1866, this society approved a pamphlet calling for a scientific educational institution. They printed and distributed the pamphlet, but nothing immediately happened.[18]

A broader demand for such an institution was needed. By 1871, the Patrons of Husbandry (the Grange), a midwestern, semi-secret farmers' association, opened a large number of Granges in South Carolina. However, the Grange did not embrace the sponsoring of political action, and almost as quickly as it appeared, it dissipated. In its place, several other types of organizations appeared. One, the S.C. Agricultural and Mechanical Association, had local groups. It drew members from both the older elite and from the mercantile and town leadership. The farmers' associations were another new voice. Locally organized, they were loosely bound to each other and were racially separated into "white" and "colored" alliances.

On August 6, 1885, a statewide meeting of the S.C. Agricultural and Mechanical Association convened in Bennettsville in conjunction with the remnants of the Grange. Tillman, the founder and president of the Edgefield Agricultural Association, delivered a speech, more accurately a challenge, that caused an informal split of the state white Democratic Party structure into two distinct groups. He launched an attack on the "planter-lawyer-businessman-ex-confederate officer clique," whom he characterized as the enemy of the yeoman farmer. He had multiple plans to aid the common farmer. Some were thinly disguised efforts to further himself or perhaps his oldest living brother, George Dionysius. Some, however, bore a resemblance to the land-grant concept. He would come to believe a separate agricultural college a necessity, pointing to the absence of progress at the Columbia institution. Also he demanded the establishment of agricultural experiment stations.[19]

Agricultural Experiment Stations

Using biological and chemical analyses to study and measure efforts to improve plants and animals was not new, but few instances existed of the use of public funds to finance such efforts. A European example generally cited was the 1852 Kingdom of Saxony combining laboratory investigations with a royally sponsored experiment station (*Landwirtschaftlich Versuchsstation*). The first use of this "practical research" in the United States appeared in 1857, when the Connecticut State Agriculture Society hired German-educated Samuel W. Johnson to analyze the claims of the makers of fertilizer, publish the results, and inform society members of the validity of the various claims.[20]

At about the same time, Thomas Green Clemson had sent a letter to the magazine, *American Farmer*, noting the results of a series of tests on the use of Peruvian guano (decomposed sea fowl dung) on his Maryland farm plantings. He concluded, attested to by neighboring farmers, that whether or not the reputed fertilizer was used, the crops produced showed no difference.[21] And just as the Civil War stopped Clemson's agricultural work, so it halted the work of Johnson in Connecticut.

A decade after the war, the state of Connecticut contracted first with Wesleyan College in Middletown and later with Yale at New Haven to host the newly created laboratories called the Connecticut Agricultural Experiment Station.[22] Within the decade (1877–1887), state-financed agricultural experiment stations opened in California (1877), North Carolina (1877), Massachusetts (1878), New York (1880), New Jersey (1880), Ohio (1882), Tennessee (1882), Alabama (1883), Wisconsin (1883), Louisiana (1884), and Maine (1885). It is no wonder that a similar idea appeared in Tillman's speech in August 1885.[23]

Benjamin Ryan Tillman (1847–1918), famed South Carolina politician and agrarian leader, as a young man. Benjamin Ryan Tillman Papers, CUL.SC.

Tillman also demanded increased funding for agricultural education and for a separate college for the teaching of agriculture. The idea of a college whose primary purpose was the teaching of agriculture, with the other disciplines offered in support, was also not singular to Tillman. Farmer dissatisfaction in Virginia, Michigan, Mississippi, North Carolina, Alabama, and Indiana had led to small farmers' demands that their states separate agricultural colleges from designated public colleges (in the instances of those just mentioned) or in some of the northeastern states, separate the agricultural schools from the private and usually denominational colleges that received state support.

Of course, Tillman's speech was a sensation and was carried, and widely commented upon, in most of the newspapers in South Carolina. Certainly, interested observers in Pendleton, including Thomas Green Clemson and members of the Pendleton Farmers' Society, such as R. F. Simpson's son, Richard Wright Simpson, read the speech. Another was Clemson's lawyer, J. H. Rion.

The Will of 1883

James Henry Rion had first entered Clemson's life when Rion's mother came to Pendleton to work as the housekeeper at the Pendleton Hotel in the early 1840s. Floride Colhoun Calhoun wanted a housekeeper for Fort Hill and contacted Mrs. Rion, who moved to Fort Hill with her son, James Henry. They lived at Fort Hill, where John C. Calhoun took an interest in the boy, helping to finance his education at South Carolina College. When James completed his studies, he read the law and, by 1853, was a practicing attorney. During the Civil War, he held the rank of major and took a very active part in the defense of Charleston, serving in the Seventh Infantry Battalion (SC). After the war, he and his family lived in Winnsboro.[24]

Rion had become one of Thomas Clemson's legal and financial advisors. Clemson kept all his stocks and bonds in Rion's office in Winnsboro, and in 1883, Clemson asked Rion to draft a will for him. After Clemson received the draft, which had been composed according to his instructions, he wrote Rion on April 27, 1883,

> I have received the draft of my will drawn up by you in accordance with my instructions, but after further consideration I have determined to make certain alterations in the form or draft sent me....Nothing contributes so much to the advancement of a people in civilization as a knowledge of the natural sciences and their application to the practical uses of life and it is my sincere desire to aid in such a laudable object by founding at Fort Hill a Scientific Institute embracing the following departments or schools, namely a department of mathematics; a second department of geology and mineralogy with especial reference to the art of mining; a third department of chemistry as applied to agriculture and the useful arts; lastly, a department of modern languages.[25]

Clemson considered the properly managed 800-plus-acre Fort Hill might be productive enough to support the school, but he added,

> the importance of such an institution in developing the material resources of the state by offering to the youth the advantages of scientific culture and that I do not underestimate the intelligence of the legislature of a State ever distinguished for its liberality in assuming that such appropriations will be made as may be necessary to supplement the fund resulting from the annual product of the estate.

Clemson then proposed to give the state (that is, the general assembly and the governor) seven years from the date of his own death to accept the conditional gift. Should the state refuse the terms of his will, then Clemson specifically by-passed his heir (granddaughter Floride Isabella Lee), his heir's guardian (Gideon Lee), and/or his heir's husband. (Because Floride Isabella was twelve years old and not married, the clause was only to foreclose future litigation.) The land, house, furnishings, and other appurtenances, if that were necessary, were to be given to an association of South Carolina women selected by Mrs. James H. Rion or, if she had already died, then by her daughter to preserve the memory of John C. Calhoun. Clemson's last set of instructions established a trust to aid his house-keeper, Jane Prince, and her daughter, Hester. Clemson signed the will on August 14, 1883.

One could see a few vague or unclear phrases in Clemson's concept for a college. First, when Clemson listed in his will the fields to be taught, the introductory "namely" might serve to limit the subject fields to those specified. Only two phrases provided real openings for change. The first was the phrase "useful arts," which could be construed to mean almost anything. The second was the phrase "modern languages," which eliminated the classical forms of Hebrew, Greek, and Latin but not the modern manifestations of them. Whether that vague wording could open the way to the study of literature and history could be the subject of legislative debates and suits and counter-suits. Another question involved who would govern or direct the "Fort Hill Scientific Institute." Did Clemson expect the legislature, the University of South Carolina trustees (who had jurisdiction over South Carolina College and the Agricultural and Mechanical Institute loose-ly attached to Claflin College), or some other body of legislative creation or designation to make the decisions?

The Meeting of 1886

In the summer of 1886, the trustees of USC apparently decided to award Clemson an honorary doctorate. Rion, who served on the USC board, must have recommended the degree. Was the honor a bit of honey or perhaps glue to keep Clemson and his wealth within the reach of those who might have dreamed of a multicampus university? The structure was in existence; the dual campus in Columbia and Orangeburg, the example. The closed normal school had partisans, and like agriculture, the need was obvious as a result of the current constitution.[26] That would leave the question as to the future of the Citadel issue to be resolved. Would it continue a separate institution or a part of the enlarged university?

Regardless, Clemson had taken an interest in Tillman's ideas about a separate college for the study of agriculture. As a result, he invited Tillman to Fort Hill to discuss the possibility. For that reason, Tillman had come by train to Pendleton, where he was met by Clemson's carriage, horse, and driver. It is hard not to imagine that the driver was the sixteen-year-old African American Bill Greenlee (1870–1972), who worked for Clemson, taking care of his carriage, carriage house, and the trappings.[27] The road from the Blue Ridge Railroad depot, located south of Pendleton's Main Street, carried the driver and his guest to Queen Street, past the Methodist parsonage, turning westward to pass Richard Wright Simpson's law office and Mrs. S. T. Sloan's home, and then toward Fort Hill.[28] The road was not good, and while most of the streams were shallow, Eighteen Mile Creek always presented a challenge to ford. The nearly four-mile road finally came to the

FORT HILL
HOME OF JOHN C. CALHOUN

CLEMSON UNIVERSITY
CLEMSON, SOUTH CAROLINA

A drawing of Fort Hill House by Joseph L. Young, A.I.A. Young was a professor of architecture at Clemson from 1950 until his retirement. This presentation drawing is used with the kind permission of the Joseph Laurie Young estate.

first of several gates that required opening, passage, and latching before proceeding. But Fort Hill finally came into view through the thicket.

Upon Tillman's arrival at Fort Hill, Clemson welcomed him while his luggage was placed in an upstairs bedroom. Mrs. Jane Prince had prepared the evening meal, and the two men dined. No doubt they talked about the meeting scheduled the next day; however, whatever else might have been discussed is lost. Tillman (1847–1918), at thirty-nine years of age, was by far the younger. Clemson was forty years his senior. This was the first and only time the two men would ever meet.

The next morning, the second guest invited to Fort Hill that autumn arrived, Daniel K. Norris (1846–1905). Only a year older than Tillman, Norris knew Clemson from the Pendleton Farmers' Society. Originally from St. Matthew's Parish in the Orangeburg District, he attended local schools there. During the Civil War, he served in the Second South Carolina Regiment under the command of Gen. Joseph Johnson. After suffering a wound at Bentonville (March 19–21, 1865), he remained in military service until Johnson's surrender on April 26, 1865. He married in 1877, and with his wife, Bessie Caldwell, from Abbeville, he moved to Anderson County in January of that year. A strong community leader, he had a large farm, Hickory Flat, just outside Pendleton.[29]

Daniel Keating Norris (1846–1905), an original member of the Board of Trustees of Clemson College, a friend and advisor to Thomas Green Clemson, and a renowned textile mill owner and planter. This portrait hangs in Sikes Hall at Clemson University and was made available through the Clemson University Artwork Photographs Collection, CUL.SC.

The third guest that day was Richard Wright Simpson (September 11, 1840–July 11, 1912). Simpson came from a family of lawyers. His father, Richard Franklin Simpson, practiced law and had bought 1,500 acres on Three and Twenty Mile

Creek. An overseer and slaves farmed the land. It was through the elder Simpson's wife, Mary Wells, that the Taliafero (pronounced "Tolliver") homestead in Pendleton came into Simpson's possession. Richard Franklin Simpson had served as a U.S. senator and signed the S.C. Ordinance of Secession. After the Civil War, he served on the Pendleton Farmers' Society committee with Thomas Clemson to draft an appeal for support of agricultural education.

Richard Wright Simpson was well educated. He attended Miss Mary's School in Pendleton until he was eight years old and then attended the Pendleton Male Academy. Upon finishing that course of study, he enrolled in Wofford College, a Methodist school in Spartanburg. While a student at Wofford, he became a Methodist and practiced that faith diligently all his life. Wofford had admitted Simpson as a sophomore with twenty-four other students in his class; he participated actively in the Preston (Literary) Society. Wofford awarded Simpson the AB degree in 1861. Almost immediately, he became engaged to his sweetheart, Maria (Mary) Margaret Garlington, whom he had known since he was seventeen.

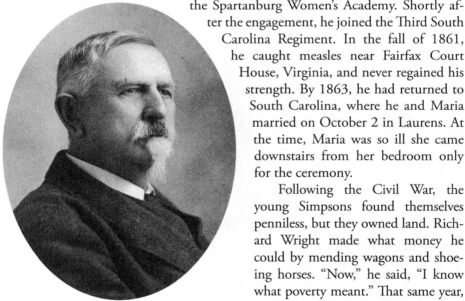

While Simpson was at Wofford, Maria had attended the Spartanburg Women's Academy. Shortly after the engagement, he joined the Third South Carolina Regiment. In the fall of 1861, he caught measles near Fairfax Court House, Virginia, and never regained his strength. By 1863, he had returned to South Carolina, where he and Maria married on October 2 in Laurens. At the time, Maria was so ill she came downstairs from her bedroom only for the ceremony.

Following the Civil War, the young Simpsons found themselves penniless, but they owned land. Richard Wright made what money he could by mending wagons and shoeing horses. "Now," he said, "I know what poverty meant." That same year, 1865, he made a "solemn obligation with my God, that I intended from there to devote myself to the amelioration of the poor." Simpson's wholehearted devotion to Clemson's legacy stemmed directly from this vow, for he virtually put his practice aside upon

Richard Wright Simpson (1840–1912), member and first president of the original Board of Trustees of Clemson College, longtime friend and advisor, and the attorney and executor for the estate of Thomas Green Clemson. Clemson University Photographs, CUL.SC.

Clemson's death and committed himself to fulfilling what Clemson wanted. And it was in his understanding of that vow that he formed the Democratic Club in Pendleton and aided in formation of similar clubs throughout the district. They were political and "military company" groups. By 1868, Simpson had prospered enough to buy the Frost place adjacent to his father's land. Because of his growing leadership in the county, he was elected to the state legislature in 1874.

The election of 1876 was hotly contested between the Republicans, whom Simpson called the "Radicals," and the reemerging "straight-out" Democrats, led by Wade Hampton, a former Confederate officer. When settled, Governor Hampton called a special session of the legislature. The Democrats controlled the house, and the Republicans controlled the senate. The state stood deeply in debt; Simpson, because of his business acumen, was named chair of the Ways and Means Committee.

Against the background of political maneuvering, the South Carolina College, which had operated as an integrated institution, closed. C. G. Memminger, a legislator from Charleston and part of a group Simpson described as the "low country set," proposed its reopening and that it be named the "Land Grant College." Simpson opposed the designation, which helped to defeat Memminger's bill. It would, however, pass into law in 1880. Simpson was not happy. In his memoirs, he noted his goal "to secure any permanent relief for the great mass of people," which

> must be obtained through education. I had devoted all my influence to secure the adoption of measures that were to establish an Agricultural College. I talked the matter over with some friends and they agreed to back and support me. My purpose was to establish this college in the upper part of the state amidst the white counties....It was necessary to make it different from the South Carolina College.[30]

He would eventually prevail.

Simpson further noted that when Tillman came to the forefront as the "leader of the Reform Movement and called a convention, I [Simpson] wrote him and urged him to drop every other plank in their platform but one: that one was a demand for an agricultural college." This he did, and the first battle was won. "The opposition would be furious, coming from many major state newspapers, the backers of South Carolina College," now retitled, "'The University of South Carolina,' the backers of the Citadel, and the supporters of the several denominational colleges in the state." Simpson continued to remember in memoirs he wrote for his children:

> Now I must go back a little. When the people were beginning to mutter against the selfish, class legislation for some years prevailing, and the Reform Movement

was beginning to take shape, Colonel Thomas G. Clemson, the son-in-law of John C. Calhoun, the owner of and residing upon Fort Hill, the homestead of Mr. Calhoun, invited me and several other gentlemen, one of whom was Tillman, to dine with him. After dinner, he handed me a paper and asked me to read it and see if there was anything wrong in it. (I had during these years quietly practiced law)....I was surprised to see it was a copy of his will.

When I read it, I told him there was something very wrong with it. He, in his will, had donated Fort Hill and his property to the State, to establish an Agricultural College. But Colonel J. H. Rion, Clemson's attorney...who wrote the will, had so worded the will, either by accident or intention I do not say, as to render it unlikely to establish such an institution.

Simpson cited two serious defects. First, the will specified a limited number of courses to be taught at the proposed college. While it did not prevent the teaching of other subjects, Simpson pointed out that some members of the state government probably would attempt to limit the teaching only to those fields. The second concern involved the fallback clause, which offered an alternative disposition should the state not receive the gift. The estate would pass into the hands of Rion's wife, who received the charge to select other ladies to manage the estate as a memorial trust. When Clemson heard Simpson's concerns, he asked Simpson to write a codicil. Simpson demurred and suggested that Clemson ask Rion to do it. The meeting ended and the guests left.

The Will of 1886

Simpson probably visited Clemson regularly over the next months, and Clemson's confidence in Simpson grew. But Rion had handled all of Clemson's investments besides his will, and Clemson decided to move them. Simpson, at Clemson's request, went to Rion's office to collect the various bonds, securities, and other investments, which Simpson remembered amounted to $100,000. Simpson drafted the new will, and Clemson asked Simpson to serve as its executor. Simpson felt it might be a conflict of interest, since he was serving as Clemson's financial manager. Clemson, however, disagreed, and Simpson concurred. Simpson also served as the lawyer for the Bank of Pendleton and Blue Ridge Railway.

Simpson delivered the will to Clemson, who signed it and had it witnessed on November 6, 1886. In the remaining year and a half of Clemson's life, he added one codicil on March 16, 1887. The new will specifically revoked the 1883 will. The new document urged that the school be "modeled after the Agricultural College of Mississippi." Clemson continued that he wished to "establish an agricultural college which will afford useful information to the farmers and the mechanics...." The college was to be governed by trustees. "I desire to state plainly that I wish the Trustees of said institution to have full authority and power to regulate all matters pertaining to said institution—to fix the course of studies, to make rules for the government of the same and to change them, as in their judgment, experience may prove necessary...."

The will appointed seven life trustees who acted as a self-perpetuating corporation, consisting of Richard Wright Simpson, D. K. Norris, B. R. Tillman (the only three men Clemson personally knew), M. L. Donaldson, R. E. Bowen, J. E. Wannamaker, and J. E. Bradley. If the state accepted the gift, then the legislature could name up to an additional six trustees who would serve for fixed terms. If after three years the state had not accepted the gift, then the seven named life trustees were to create a private school, "Clemson Scientific School" or "College."[31]

Even more extraordinary was what the will did not say. It did not limit admissions by state (South Carolina), by gender (male), or by race (white). This was most unusual given the era and climate in which the will was drafted, and it was unusual given the sentiments, at least, of Tillman.

For the remainder of his life, Clemson attempted to arrange for the writing of a biography of John C. Calhoun. Rarely did Clemson leave Fort Hill. Toward the end of his life, he took an interest in Christianity, a topic to which he had paid scant attention prior to this point. Clemson died on April 6, 1888; he was buried beside his beloved Anna in the churchyard of St. Paul's Episcopal Church in Pendleton.[32] Simpson handled the necessary arrangements. On April 20, 1888, Simpson carried Clemson's will to the courthouse in Walhalla for probate, and a bitter statewide argument ensued.

Notes

1. Andrew, *Wade Hampton: Confederate Warrior to Southern Redeemer*, 413.
2. Edgar, *South Carolina*, 390. Edgar's discussion of the African American and white activities during "radical" or "congressional reconstruction" is well worth reading. He notes the local white reaction to a racially integrated public school in Charleston.
3. Hollis, *The University of South Carolina*, vol. 2, 44–79.
4. Edgar, *South Carolina*, 394–395.
5. Ibid., 396–402.
6. Andrew, *Wade Hampton*, 312–313.
7. Kantrowitz, *Ben Tillman*, 64–71. The reader should note that Kantrowitz's study does not offer itself as a comprehensive study of its subject. Its purpose is to study Tillman's attitude and political actions toward African Americans.
8. Andrew, *Wade Hampton*, 408, 429–431.
9. Edgar, *South Carolina*, 407–411.
10. Hollis, *University of South Carolina*, vol. 2, 94–97. The title is An Act to Provide for the State University.
11. Ibid., 101–103.
12. Ibid., 103. Hollis cites the USC trustees' minutes, February (n.d.), 1882.
13. Ibid., 103–108.
14. Ibid., 119. The "per student" appropriation was $96 (or $2,300 per student in 2009 dollars).
15. Edgar, *South Carolina*, 426–427.
16. Ibid., 455–462.

17. Newman and Stribling, *Pendleton Farmers' Society*, 18–19, 125–126.
18. Ibid., 72.
19. CUL.SC.MSS 80 S 5 b 1. Tillman's files contain, among other things, his scrapbooks. Many of these contain newspaper clippings, some of which are reported transcriptions of speeches. Box 1 contains five scrapbooks, numbered I–V. Given the acidic nature of newspaper, the copy is very clear. Volumes I and II contain material beginning in the spring of 1885. The text of Tillman's August 6, 1885, Bennettsville speech (vol. II) sets out his proposal: 1. To create an experimental farm; 2. Make the "South Carolina University" board follow the law and establish a practical agricultural college with teachers prepared to teach practical agriculture; 3. Put farmers (as opposed to planters) on the college board; 4. Ensure an agricultural commission composed of farmers selected from the various regions of the state; and 5. County and state farmers' institutes supported by the state treasury.

     Needless to say, Tillman received criticism to which he responded with an attack on the S.C. Agricultural and Mechanical Society (Charleston *News and Courier*, November 30, 1885). D. P. Duncan of Union County, president of the society, struck back in a somewhat testy fashion in the *News and Courier* dated December 11, 1885. After a vitriolic response by Tillman in the same journal (December 18, 1885), the editor declared a truce, which did not hold. Tillman continued stumping the state addressing the Clarendon Agricultural Society and helping orchestrate the summoning of another farmers' convention for April 29, 1886. A. B. Williams, the editor and proprietor of the *Greenville Daily News* (March 18, 1886), commented, "Mr. B. R. Tillman shows a good deal of hard, horse sense in his reply to the attack made on him by Secretary of State Lipscomb." Williams then supported Tillman's basic plans. As to be expected, Tillman was the main speaker at the April Farmers' Convention in Columbia, widely carried in newspapers (for example, see the Newberry *Observer*). The Winnsboro *News and Herald* speculated that the entire program was to propel George Dionysius Tillman (1826–1902), B. R.'s older brother by twenty-one years, into the governor's office. In the meantime, B. R. Tillman sent his address to Stephen D. Lee, then the president of Mississippi Agricultural College, whose response was highly supportive of the effort to establish a separate agricultural and mechanical college. Tillman had taken that stand December 9, 1885, in a letter to the Charleston *News and Courier*. In it he used Ohio as the example.
20. Kerr, *The Legacy*, 3–5.
21. Grubb, "The Washington Years," in *Thomas Green Clemson*, 83.
22. Kerr, *The Legacy*, 11–16.
23. Ibid., 16–17.
24. Lander, *Calhoun Family and T. G. Clemson*, 80.
25. CUL.SC.MSS 2 b 5 f 21. This and the following transcription are from Clemson's holograph. I have extended the abbreviations, placed careted phrases with the text and have ignored stricken words or phrases. Further, in the interest of brevity, I have not presented the entire three-page letter but have summarized those intervening passages.
26. The post-Reconstruction government in the Act to Provide for the State University in Section 25 stated, "It shall be required, and it is hereby made the duty, of the Trustees of the University to open and establish an Agricultural Department in said University." See Hollis, *University of South Carolina*, vol. 2, 89.
27. *The Tiger*, December 4, 1964, an article by Luke C. Hamilton, Clemson's Cooperative Extension information specialist, based on Greenlee's memories. The death year is from Social Security records as shown on Ancestry.com.
28. CUL.SC.MSS 280, oversize folder: map of Pendleton, South Carolina.
29. Garlington, *Men of The Time*, 332–333; and Reynolds and Faunt, *Biographical Dictionary of the Senate*, 1206–1207. In addition, I wish to thank William Norris of Greenville, the great-grandnephew of D. K. Norris, who helped me gain access to several family-published and unpublished compendia, including Gilmore, *Two Great-Grands: A Factual Story*, 114–127.
30. CUL.SC.MSS 96 f 41: typewritten memoir of Richard Wright Simpson. Also is a draft holograph of the "Rion" August 1883 unsigned Clemson will commencing with Item 6. The items that addressed the school would have been items 1, 2, and 3.
31. See the will in the appendix.
32. Lander, *Calhoun Family and T. G. Clemson*, 234.

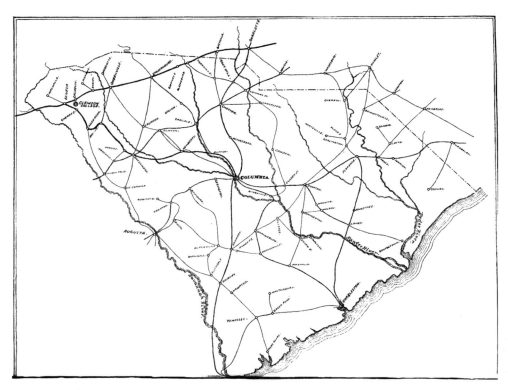

A Map of the South Carolina Railroad System drawn by Thomas Grayson Poats, early Clemson professor of mathematics and civil engineering. Taken from the 1898 *Catalogue of the Clemson Agricultural College of South Carolina.*

CHAPTER III

The Founding

1888–1889

R ichard Wright Simpson probably boarded the Blue Ridge rail line close to his home in Pendleton on the morning of April 20, 1888, two weeks after Thomas Clemson's death. The rail crossed the Seneca River at Cherry's Crossing, about two miles south of Fort Hill, just north of Hopewell, once the Pickens family home. From Hopewell, the line ran to the town of Seneca, which was founded in 1873. Seneca was well-placed on a crossing of the Blue Ridge and the Southern lines. The Southern line crossed the Seneca River above Ravenel's Bridge. In consequence, Fort Hill was well-situated near the major developing north-south line (Washington, D.C., through Atlanta, Georgia, and on to New Orleans, Louisiana) and South Carolina's major east-west line (Charleston to Columbia and on to Walhalla).[1] From Seneca, the Blue Ridge line moved northwest toward Walhalla, the seat of Oconee County, the county in which Fort Hill was located. Walhalla, a nineteenth century German settlement, hosted the county courthouse.

Simpson's wooden briefcase contained the will of Thomas Green Clemson, the codicil of 1888, and other documents associated with the estate. Simpson entered the will for probate at the Wallhalla courthouse. The will was a remarkable document, not only for its own time, but for the wisdom it carried into the future. At its heart, the 1886 will established for the proposed college a Board of Trustees composed of seven life trustees, all of them named in the document. Should one or another of the life trustees die or resign, the remaining life trustees would select the replacement. It further provided that should the state of South Carolina accept the will in toto, the S.C. Legislature would be empowered to select up to six trustees who would serve for fixed terms.[2] If the legislature and the state did not accept the will in toto within three years after Mr. Clemson's death, then the life trustees would establish a private school. The terms of the will required legislative passage, the governor's signature, and the approval of the S.C. Supreme Court chief justice.

Besides the unusual governance, the will granted the trustees broad authority. They were to "fix the courses of study, ever mindful of the needs of the farmers and mechanics." And they functioned as the sole governors of the school. They could set and change the curricula, approve any and all changes, and never lose their powers.

Further, the will did not require that the students wear military uniforms. Nor did the will specify that the college admit only South Carolinians, men, or whites, although such restrictions commonly existed throughout the nation in the decades after the Civil War. In the South and Southeast toward the end of the nineteenth century, three other southern colleges—two private, Vanderbilt and Rice, and one, a private takeover of a "sort of" public university, Tulane—were heavily endowed by philanthropists from the Northeast. Each of those establishing documents had gender, racial, or other inherent characteristics as requirements for enrollment.[3]

The Will and the Life Trustees

When he returned to Pendleton, Simpson summoned the other six life trustees to a meeting at Fort Hill on May 2, 1888. They all accepted the obligation that Clemson imposed on them. Over the next nearly two decades, the trustees worked to ensure the well-being of Clemson Agricultural College. Of course, Benjamin Ryan Tillman and Daniel Keating Norris, having been at the very important Fort Hill meeting in the autumn of 1886, knew what to expect. The other four men who came to Fort Hill in May 1888 were knowledgeable probably only through their newspapers and their correspondence.

John Edward Wannamaker, from the lower region and the agrarian community of St. Matthews, joined them. Born on September 12, 1851, in Poplar Springs, he attended Wofford College, graduating in June 1872. Less than a year later, he began the Aeolian Hill Farm two miles east of St. Matthews. He was an early supporter of a separate college of agriculture, speaking forcefully for it in the Democratic State Convention of 1888. He also supported the state experiment stations. He later served on the Clemson College board's committees on agriculture and the state fertilizer board of control. A lifelong Methodist, he had married Martha Duncan. Wannamaker would serve as the president of the Clemson Board of Trustees from 1929 to his death in 1935. His sister, Anna, married Thomas W. Keitt, a future professor of English at Clemson. Their son, Thomas, would become a Clemson Agricultural College agronomist. Wannamaker's public service was not limited to Clemson. He chaired the World War I Liberty Bond drive for Orangeburg County and pioneered study in the science of seed breeding. He died on March 6, 1935.[4]

The fifth life trustee, John E. Bradley, was born in Indian Hill Township (lower Greenville District) on December 25, 1839. He received his early education at Clear Springs Academy, after which he enrolled in Erskine College, a school of the Associate Reformed Presbyterian Church in Due West. Bradley left Erskine in 1861 to join the First South Carolina Volunteers. During the Civil War, he served in Butler's Brigade, and after the war, he was a member of the local vigilance committee. Bradley worked actively in the Grange, the Farmers' Alliance, and the association of Tillman supporters known as the Farmers' Movement. He was elected to the S.C. House of Representatives and served one term.

In scientific agriculture, Bradley worked as an amateur soils engineer, experimenting with irrigation. This interest carried over into his service as trustee. He advised J. P. Lewis, the Clemson College farm manager, on agricultural practices. In addition, he aided in the selection of clays used to make the bricks with which the Chemistry Building (now Hardin Hall), the Main Building (now Tillman Hall), the Hardin residence (now Trustee House), and Barracks Number One (no longer standing) were built.

Bradley married Sarah Margaret Wideman in late 1865, and they had six sons and two daughters. One son, Mark Bradley, graduated from Clemson Agricultural College and later joined the faculty. John Bradley's grandson, also named Mark, was a Clemson alumnus as well as a career military officer. He retired from the U.S. Army after World War II a four-star general. John Bradley died on April 18, 1907, and is buried in the Long Cane Associate Reformed Presbyterian Cemetery in Troy.[5]

Robert Esli Bowen served as the sixth life trustee. He was born on September 8, 1830, on George's Creek near Briggs Post Office in Pickens County, where his Welsh-Irish family had settled around 1785. Bowen was educated in common school and apprenticed to his father, from whom he learned surveying. In 1853, he moved to Texas and taught school there for five months. He then traveled extensively in Texas before returning to superintend the family farm.

Bowen, too, served in the Confederate army. He was at Appomattox Court House at the surrender of the Army of Northern Virginia on April 9, 1865, and ended his service with the rank of colonel. Bowen married Martha Oliver and they had two children, James Oliver, who died in 1908, and Esli Elvira, who never married. Bowen's father had given him the tract of land on which he and his wife lived.

Bowen was elected to the state house in 1872 and to the senate from 1874 to 1878, where he served on the committee to investigate the financial condition of South Carolina's government. He probably worked closely with Richard Wright Simpson on the difficult inquiry. In the 1880s, Bowen was involved in several railway ventures as president of the Atlantic and French Broad Railroad (1881–1883) and first director (1883–1886) and then president (1886–1889) of the Carolina, Cumberland Gap and Chicago Railroad. Neither proved successful, but the contacts he gained would aid the college.[6] Like Bradley, Bowen served as a Presbyterian elder. After he died, Clemson College morning chapel on January 11, 1909, was given over to a memorial service. He is buried in the old Pickens Presbyterian churchyard.

The final original life trustee was Milton Lafayette Donaldson. Born on July 29, 1844, to a family of farmers and mechanics in the Greenville District, he attended the Williamston School (1858–1862). At the onset of hostilities between the United States and the Confederacy, he enlisted in the Confederate army and remained in it until the war's end. On January 23, 1866, he married Margaret Louisa Ware.

Like several of the trustees, Donaldson served in the S.C. House of Representatives (1878–1880 and 1884–1886), where he probably knew Simpson. He also served in the senate from 1888 to 1892 and played an instrumental role in steering Thomas Green Clemson's bequest through that body. Further, he was a strong Tillman supporter. Active in farming movements, Donaldson served as president of the S.C. Farmers' Alliance from 1891 to 1892. His agricultural research led to a series of articles published in national farming journals. He also served in the National Democratic Executive Committee from 1890 to 1894. The Donaldsons were active members of Greenville's Pendleton Street Baptist Church, which he served as a deacon. Donaldson and his wife had no children. He died on September 3, 1924, and is buried in Springwood Cemetery in Greenville.[7]

While Mr. Clemson ultimately chose the seven initial life trustees, the fact that three had served in the legislature during the time that Simpson also served suggests that Simpson played a leading role in Mr. Clemson's selections. Only one trustee came from a town of any consequence, and the remainder were from the rural areas of the state. All seven came from agricultural backgrounds, although two had industrial interests as well. Four trustees had attended college; three went to Wofford and one to Erskine. Five came from the Upstate and two from the Lowcountry, although one of the Lowcountry men, Norris, had his career in Pendleton. Finally, they all had religious backgrounds in the Methodist, Presbyterian, and Baptist churches, and five might be called strong churchmen.

When Simpson summoned the other life trustees to meet him at Fort Hill on May 2, 1888, they met under a large oak tree on the east side of the home. Bowen acted as temporary chair and Norris as temporary secretary. The life trustees organized formally, selecting Simpson president and Wannamaker secretary. There being no further business required until the fate of the Clemson-offered gift to the state was determined, the life trustees adjourned.

Reaction to the Will

As harbingers of the public attitudes concerning the Clemson will, newspapers provided insights into the opinions of literate citizens. At first, newspapers noted the death of Thomas Clemson as the death of a prominent citizen.[8] However, in the press the terms of the will were open to speculation. Shortly thereafter, at least one newspaper reported that J. M. McBryde, professor of agriculture and president of the University of South Carolina, had spoken to the Farmers' Club of Orangeburg and detailed the importance of experiment stations. Prior to the passage of the Hatch Act in 1887 by the U.S. Congress, the S.C. Legislature had authorized the creation of two stations, one in Darlington and the other in Spartanburg, to provide reports on climatic and soil variety in research studies. These operated under the direction of the renamed University of South Carolina. Ironically, McBryde remained that evening with the Farmers' Club while it adopted a resolution stating, "Teaching of a more progressive and economical mode of farming...cannot be acquired in an institution devoted to mixed literary and agricultural courses." The same newspaper also noted the emergence of the Farmers' Alliance, which pledged "to labor for the education of the agricultural classes in the science of economical government in a strictly nonpartisan spirit."[9] McBryde contended, with good justification, that South Carolina could not afford to fund the public (Citadel and USC) colleges and the agricultural and mechanical institute at Claflin. He noted that Cornell and California were conducting the best mechanical and agricultural work.[10] But neither Cornell (founded 1865) nor California (1868) was comparable. In neither case were the scientific or technological fields being added to an older, existing classical college. In many places where that had been attempted, such as the University of Louisiana (now Tulane), the University of Mississippi, the University of North Carolina, or the University of Virginia, the effort had not been successful and had led to the formation of separate land-grant schools. Some, Tennessee and Missouri, did work, but beginning with Michigan Agricultural College (an 1855 pre-Morrill Land Grant Act foundation) or with Kansas State (1863), the first school founded as a land-grant college, separate foundations were the trend.[11]

Tillman exploited the fact that USC had taught young men and boys from the more prosperous families, and he used the Farmers' Alliance conventions, which he had called for and which he frequently attended and addressed, to build support. Only a year earlier, the legislature had funded USC in excess of its request and had given its trustees an appropriation greater than it requested.[12] Tillman was so disgusted that he sent a farewell letter to the Charleston *News and Courier*.[13] However, Mr. Clemson's death reinvigorated his determination, his audacity, and his caustic comments.

The Elections of 1888

By April 19, terms of the Clemson will were becoming known. The *Laurens-ville Advertiser* published a letter from Norris to G. W. Shell of Laurens that detailed the governance and predicted, "Our college is a certainty; our cause is strengthened and we will go into the canvass with victory perched on our banners." But on the same day, the *Pickens Sentinel* predicted that Gideon Lee, in behalf of his daughter and Thomas Clemson's granddaughter, Floride Isabella Lee, would contest the will. And also on that day, the Rock Hill *Herald* printed a letter from "Pike" entreating, "Let me beg the farmers not to become disheared; don't give up the fight." By April 23, the Charleston *Sentinel*, in an editorial, opposed the plan for Clemson's school if it required "the suppression or strangulation of any institution of learning which has been established by the State and is now in existence."[14]

The Floride Lee issue also emerged rapidly. She and her father, Gideon Lee, traveled from New York to meet with Simpson at Fort Hill. The terms of the will still seemed a matter of speculation.[15] Six days after the will was entered for probate at the Walhalla Courthouse, its terms became public. The Charleston *Sentinel* urged caution[16] and later in the same paper noted, "It is not safe, we think,

This picture, entitled "Leaders of the Farm Movement in South Carolina," portrays (*left to right*) George Washington Shell, an Upcountry legislator; Benjamin Ryan Tillman, self-appointed spokesman for South Carolina farmers; and John Laurens Manning Irby, lawyer and South Carolina state representative, as the three heads of the agrarian movement in South Carolina in 1890. Clemson University Photographs, CUL.SC.

to take it for granted that Mr. Lee will not contest the will of Mr. Clemson."[17] A week later, the *Sentinel* reported that Mr. Lee "claims he was misled as to the value of the Clemson Estate by the Representatives of the Executor and Trustee—was Mr. Clemson of 'Sound and Disposing mind.'"

Lee also raised the issue of fairness to Clemson's granddaughter when he noted to the press that in a codicil to his will, Clemson "revokes and cancels all legacies made by him to his grand daughter, even the portraits of her mother and grandmother, if she or I, as her guardian should contest the will." He concluded, "Now, I came down here to seek justice for my daughter."[18]

By May 2, 1888, the Charleston *News and Courier* printed a letter from Norris in which he restated the Farmers' Association's position on agricultural education, experiment stations, and the Citadel, South Carolina's military college, which was to continue its operation. The very next day, the Pickens *Sentinel* carried Tillman's address to the farmers and other citizens. It called the efforts to mix practical and literary training an utter failure. "The Executive Committee of the Farmers' Association, has two goals:" one to force the hand of the state in accepting the bequest of Mr. Clemson, and second to "safeguard white supremacy."[19] On the same day, in the same newspaper, and also on the front page, Gideon Lee's letter to the *News and Courier* was repeated in its entirety. In it he reminded the readers that his daughter was the only surviving descendant of Thomas Clemson and was the great-granddaughter of John C. Calhoun.

Two days later, the *News and Courier* interviewed Simpson, who stated, "The law makes it my duty…to defend the will and carry into effect the purposes of the testator as set forth therein.…I have concluded that both prudence and proper regard for my duties as executor imperatively require me…to refrain from anything like a newspaper controversy over matters soon to be litigated."[20] Simpson also felt that Clemson had provided for Floride Lee in the will in a satisfactory manner.

On page 6 of that same edition, the *News and Courier* reprinted editorials from around the state. The Edgefield *Monitor* raised the issue of the structure of the Board of Trustees, suggesting that the state would be unable to control a board divided into seven life trustees and six legislative appointments. The anticipated Lee versus the Will (known as *Lee v. Simpson*) would not begin until January 7, 1889, when the court appointed J. E. Hagood as special master in equity, the court's office designated to enumerate and protect an estate during a transition.[21]

As the journalistic arguments heated up, the Democratic county conventions and the county farmers' organizations began their regular meetings. The Newberry County farmers' club called on farmers to demand that the legislature accept the gift.[22] Three days later, the same paper noted that the Lancaster Democratic Convention resolved that the state should accept the bequest.[23] The Anderson County Democratic Convention added that it hoped the state would add to Mr.

Clemson's gift, the Morrill legacy, the Hatch Act funds, and the inspection fee on fertilizer to fund the new college.[24]

To the issues of other educational institutions, the claims of Gideon Lee, and the structure of the proposed Board of Trustees, the *News and Courier* raised the question of the suitability of the controversial Tillman, both as a life trustee and a potential government official. "About the only thing they (the farmers) cannot accomplish, in the direction of reform, is to make Mr. Tillman a safe friend and judicious counselor. The sooner he is unloaded, the sooner will the farmers reach the goal of their desires."[25]

An article in the Charleston *World* reflected the growing political tensions. On July 3, 1888, the paper suggested that the new school need not be built on the financial support heretofore going to the Citadel and the University of South Carolina.[26] By July 10, 1888, Governor John P. Richardson addressed the Clarendon County Democratic Convention. In his speech, he attempted to straddle the growing chasm between supporters and opponents of Clemson's proposed new college but with little success.[27] In response to Richardson at a Democratic Party gathering in Charleston, Tillman pointed to the lack of agriculture graduates from USC and also from the Citadel. Newspapers continued the arguments throughout the end of summer and most of the harvest season. [28]

The Legislature and the Will

With public opinion mixed about the legacy of Thomas Clemson, the will went to the legislature. Simpson, as a result of his service in the legislature and particularly the leadership he had given to the Hampton Democrats, worked well with many of the legislators. In the elections in the summer of 1888, a goodly number of "Tillmanites" had been chosen for the house, but Tillman had much less influence in the senate. Simpson, as executor, officially apprised the legislature of the bequest on December 4, 1888. The governor had addressed a joint session of both chambers and had cautioned against destruction of existing institutions.[29] In the house, William Benet of Abbeville, who quickly became the leader of the pro-will group, introduced the bill to accept Clemson's gift to the state. The bill also made its way to the Judiciary Committee and the Agriculture Committee. Lawyers comprised the first; farmers dominated the second, which also held several physicians/farmers and a few planters. Besides the division of the two committees by occupation, a geographic division would play a role also. The thirteen-member Judiciary Committee had two Upstate lawyers, William Benet from Abbeville and W. B. McCaw from York County. The other eleven were from the eastern and southern counties. The strongest opposition to the Clemson proposal centered in those same counties in part because the planter culture was predominant. Graduates of South Carolina and the Citadel were predominant here as well. The Agriculture Committee had fourteen members; ten were farmers, one a physician, another a lawyer, yet another a physician/lawyer, and the last a planter from Richland County (the Midlands). Those who had collegiate backgrounds were attached to one or another of the Upstate denominational colleges, although one went to South Carolina College. The Judiciary Committee members opposed acceptance, while those of the Agriculture Committee favored acceptance.[30]

On the same day (December 4, 1888) the *News and Courier* carried a report from D. K. Norris and J. E. Tindal. The Farmers' Association had sent the two to inspect the Mississippi Agricultural and Mechanical College. They provided thoughts concerning finances, student labor, fertilizers, research, and the impact the college, under the direction of its president, Gen. Stephen D. Lee, had on the state of Mississippi.[31] Lee, a South Carolinian, had been second in command in the Confederate defense of Vicksburg, Mississippi, in 1863.

In the house, the bill to accept Clemson's gift was read for the first time and again on December 4.[32] The joint Judiciary and Agriculture Committee met on December 9 and reported the bill out on Thursday, December 13.[33] It issued a negative majority report, supported by most members of the Judiciary Committee, and a favorable minority report, basically from the Agriculture Committee.

After the second reading of the bill, Walter Hazard, a lawyer from Georgetown, moved to strike the section of the bill that stated that the senate and house expressly accepted the Clemson gift (Section 1). Simply, that would defeat the bill. No one could have accurately predicted the outcome of that vote. When the vote was taken, Hazard's motion was defeated. But that did not mean that the bill of acceptance had passed; it merely had not been killed. Then William Brawley, a lawyer from Charleston and a member of the Judiciary Committee, moved to continue the bill to the next session. There was one strategy in play with the motion. This delay would use another year in the three-year deadline imposed by the donor, leaving about a year and five months for the chief justice of the state Supreme Court to certify that all the terms of Mr. Clemson's will had been met. Thus, a representative could vote for continuance, postpone consideration, but still not have voted against acceptance. This would be the crucial vote in the house.

One hundred twelve representatives voted. Fifty representatives voted to continue until the next session. Twenty-nine were lawyers, eleven farmers, two planters, five physicians, two merchants, a carpenter, a miner, and one unknown (some reported more than one occupation). Sixty-two members voted against continuance. Thirty-seven were farmers, three planters, ten lawyers, four merchants, a teacher, two physicians, a millwright, an accountant, a manufacturer, a clergyman, and three whose occupations were not recorded. The clustering of lawyers voting to continue and farmers voting against continuance is strengthened when one considers home county. Forty-two of the positive votes for continuance were from representatives from the Lowcountry and the Midlands, including all but two of the farmers, while six of the eight positive Upstate votes were lawyers. The negative voters were more evenly scattered across the state, with most of the farmers and the lawyers in the Upstate and the Midlands. No doubt some of the negative voters had personal or political ties to Simpson or to Tillman.

Such an examination suggests that occupation and geographic area of representation disposed some of the representatives how to vote on the issue. What could not be known was whether the vote was truly representative of beliefs held about the newly proposed school or if some of those who voted nay opposed the school and thought there were enough votes to defeat it in that session.

By Friday, December 14, the house defeated the motion to strike out the enacting words by a vote of sixty-seven to forty-eight. This clearly indicated that the earlier vote fairly represented the disposition of the members. The next day, the house heard the third reading, after which its version of the Bill of Acceptance passed and was duly sent to the senate.

The senate worked simultaneously on the bequest. The offer of the gift had been sent to the Committee on Education on Saturday, December 8. The first reading was given before the bill was committed. It was reported out Saturday, December 15, with no recommendation.[34] Consideration was to begin the following Monday.[35] On that Monday, the bill was taken up, with Senator E. B. Murray moving to discharge the bill on Tuesday, December 18. That process was agreed to, and the next day the will was read for a second time. Senator C. St. G. Sinkler from Eutawville moved to continue the bill to the next session. This prompted the crucial voting in the senate. The roll call ended with sixteen senators voting yes and sixteen voting no. W. L. Mauldin of Greenville, the lieutenant governor serving as president of the senate, then cast a nay vote, and the maneuver was thwarted.

Just as the issue in the house produced a geographic difference, geography was a factor in the senate. Three senators from the Midlands and thirteen from the Lowcountry voted for continuance. Two senators from the Lowcountry, five from the Midlands, and nine from the Upstate voted nay. The lieutenant governor was from the Upstate.[36] The second reading then passed seventeen to fifteen. Later the next day (December 19), the bill received its third reading, which occurred after a series of procedural motions designed to kill the bill had been defeated. The bill to accept the Clemson gift passed!

There were some differences between the house and the senate versions, namely the specification that finance issues brought to the Clemson Board of Trustees would require a nine-vote majority for passage. The two houses met in joint session Monday, December 24, 1888, and, at 3:45 a.m., the bill was reconciled, approved, and sent to the governor. Because of the almost immediate adjournment of the general assembly, the governor did not act upon the bill until the beginning of the next session, scheduled to convene on November 27, 1889.

When he recalled the autumn of 1888, Simpson wrote that passage of the bill in the house was actually more difficult than in the senate. However, he noted that to get the bill through the senate required him to convince Augustine T. Smythe of Charleston (who had substantial influence on coastal senators) merely to vote against the bill and not to urge fellow senators to do likewise. Simpson had asked Smythe to serve as one of his lawyers in the judicial battle for the will.[37] Smythe later served as a legislative trustee of the new Clemson Agricultural College.

Still, Simpson had two looming problems. The first was Governor Richardson's approval or veto. Nothing but time would answer that. Second, Gideon Lee, the father of Floride Lee, Thomas Clemson's granddaughter, had filed suit in federal court contesting the legality of Mr. Clemson's claim to sole ownership of the Fort Hill plantation.

The Lees and the Will

Governor Richardson, in his message to the general assembly, had noted that the state should not accept the Clemson bequest unless and until the will "is clearly established and before it is ascertained that the institution [Clemson's proposed college] shall 'forever remain under the supreme and sole control of the state.'"[38] Many officials felt that the *Lee v. Simpson* litigation would last three to four years, which, if the state were to wait until that was clear, would have the effect, under the terms of the will, of causing the executor and the life trustees to organize the school privately.[39] On December 11, the Charleston *News and Courier* reported that Mr. Clemson's estate was worth $106,179.61, of which $25,000 consisted of real estate and the remainder of personal worth (2009 equivalent $2,503,084.78).[40]

The pending Lee lawsuit had been in the press for almost the whole year. On April 19, 1888, the Pickens *Sentinel* reported that Gideon Lee had come south to contest the will.[41] Lee wrote a lengthy letter explaining his grounds for the suit and delivered it to area newspapers.[42] In the same edition, an editorial commented, "Mr. Lee's statement...upsets all the calculations that have been made in relation to the founding at Fort Hill of a great college for the farmers."[43] In May, Lee sent a lengthy letter to the *News and Courier* stating that he (Lee) had been in error when he calculated the "estate to be worth $40,000 or possibly $50,000."[44] Lee continued,

> An old man of four score years, weak in body and almost imbecile [*sic*] in mind, living alone with only his housekeeper and her daughter to care for him, and with considerable property to dispose of, made an unnatural and unjust will, in which he practically disinherits his granddaughter and sole living descendant for the sake of erecting a monument to his vanity, a posthumous one, to be called Clemson Agricultural College.

Lee consulted with a lawyer, R. A. Childs of Pickens, who refused to take the case.[45] Lee then hired Leroy F. Youmans as his legal consultant,[46] and Youmans directed Lee to seek J. P. Carey to serve as the trial lawyer. For the defense, Simpson selected Augustine T. Smythe and James L. Orr, a very well-known Upstate lawyer.

The Lee suit began in the state courts, which quickly held that the will was valid. Lee's suit contended that Fort Hill had been willed to Anna Calhoun Clemson for life, and upon Thomas Clemson's death, the estate was to pass to her granddaughter, Floride Isabella Lee. The state court gave its opinion in the autumn of 1888.[47] By December, Lee had appealed the case to the U.S. Circuit Court for the District of South Carolina.

Simpson was the defendant as well as the executor of the will of Thomas Green Clemson. He selected four attorneys to work with him, the Charleston firms of Smythe and Lee and Wells and Orr. Interestingly, Smythe, as a state senator, had not favored the creation of the separate agricultural school, and Orr, in the state house, had supported the college's creation. Each later served as a trustee for the Clemson Agricultural College.

The defense set forth tracing the property from Mrs. John C. Calhoun's sale of Fort Hill to her eldest son, Andrew Pickens Calhoun. Because Andrew's worth was tied up in an Alabama plantation, Mrs. Calhoun held his mortgage on the property. Mrs. Calhoun drew a will on June 27, 1863, in which the property bequeathed to her daughter, Anna Maria, consisted of a life interest in Mrs. Calhoun's Pendleton

Gideon Lee Jr. (1824–1894) and his daughter, Floride Isabella Lee (1870–1935), granddaughter of Thomas Green Clemson, the chief plaintiffs in the case *Lee v. Simpson*. Both pictures are used courtesy of the Fort Hill Collection, Clemson University, and are gifts of Mr. and Mrs. Creighton Lee Calhoun.

house (Mi Casa), a vacant lot, and the furnishings within Mi Casa, all of which upon Anna Maria's death would pass to Anna's daughter, Floride Clemson (Mrs. Gideon Lee), and, if Floride were dead, to her child (Floride Isabella Lee).

The bulk of Mrs. Calhoun's estate—including the mortgage she held of Andrew, a share in a Dahlonega gold mine, an interest in the estate of her deceased son, Patrick, and another interest in the estate of her daughter, Cornelia—was deeded so that one-fourth of the property would be in life trust for Anna, and upon her death, to Anna's daughter. The remaining property, a three-fourths share, she divided between Floride E. Clemson and Mrs. Calhoun's daughter-in-law, Kate P. Calhoun.[48]

On January 22, 1866, owing to the effects of the Civil War, Mrs. Calhoun changed her will. To Kate she gave the Pendleton house and property, which in 1863 she had directed to Anna. The rest of the property would be divided, with one-fourth going to Floride Elizabeth Clemson and three-fourths going to Anna "with the exception and alteration, that my daughter, Anna is hereby authorized and empowered by a last will and testament duly executed by her to dispose of this bequest of three-fourths of said bond and mortgage debt as she pleases. If she does not thus dispose of it, at her death, I give and bequeath it, the said three-fourths, to her daughter Floride." This was the arguing point in the Lee lawsuit. Had Mrs. Clemson made a valid will? The remaining one-fourth would go to Floride Elizabeth Clemson and her child.[49]

Mrs. Calhoun's will used the other portions of the estate to pay her debts, with the remainder to be divided in thirds. Two-thirds would go to her grandsons—J. C. Calhoun, A. P. Calhoun, and W. L. Calhoun—and one-third to Anna C. Clemson, who could dispose of her share as above. In sum, the codicil grants to Anna "three-fourths of the bond and mortgage due by A. P. Calhoun, certain furniture and other personal property, one-third of the residuary estate after debts would be settled."

In the passage of time, four deaths had occurred. Mrs. Calhoun died on July 25, 1866; Floride Clemson Lee died in 1871 leaving one child, Floride Isabella; John Calhoun Clemson died in 1871, seventeen days after his sister, Floride Lee; and Anna C. Clemson died on September 22, 1875. Thus, all of Anna Clemson's adult children died before she did. In the meantime, Anna substituted her husband, Thomas Green Clemson, as her trustee in place of lawyer Edward Noble, her relative. On September 2, 1871, after the deaths of her two adult children, Anna Calhoun Clemson executed her last will and testament.

Simpson then introduced several witnesses who testified to the longtime wish of the Clemsons to found an agricultural and scientific institution in South Carolina. Catherine Cornish, the widow of the rector of St. Paul's Episcopal Church in Pendleton, asserted that after the deaths of Floride C. Lee and J. Calhoun Clemson in 1871, Mrs. Clemson was heartbroken and wanted the Fort Hill land to be used to benefit the Upstate, particularly for an agricultural college.[50] Mrs. Cornish stated that Mrs. Clemson wanted the Calhoun family silver to go to her only grandchild, Floride Lee, along with the one-fourth share in Fort Hill.[51] Further, Mrs. Cornish understood that the Clemsons had made mutual wills to create the agricultural college from their estates.[52]

The Rev. Mr. H. W. McLee, pastor of the Pendleton Presbyterian Church who had known the Clemsons quite well since 1866, filed the next deposition. He testified that Anna Clemson clearly wanted an agricultural college supported by the Clemson estate and by the state of South Carolina. Mr. Clemson, after Mrs. Clemson's death, had continued their desire to create the school.[53]

Other property was also in question, most notably the home and farm in Bladensburg, Maryland, which Thomas Clemson had purchased in 1856. With the onset of the Civil War, he transferred ownership of that property to his wife, Anna, who stayed in Maryland. In 1864, she conveyed the property to Elias Baker, the brother of Thomas Clemson's mother. Baker's estate returned the property to Mrs. Clemson in 1869, and she immediately transferred ownership to her husband. Again, the argument centered on Mrs. Clemson's intent, which was that the property belonged to her husband. In sum, then, the court found that Thomas Green Clemson had inherited all rights and all the property, real and chattel, that had been Anna's at the time of her death.[54] Lee appealed the decision to the U.S. Supreme Court, which denied the appeal.[55]

The Governor and the Will

The S.C. Legislature reconvened on November 27, 1889, and received a message that Governor John P. Richardson had signed the bill accepting Clemson's gift of land and his money to the state for the establishment of an agricultural college. The bill has come to be known as the Act of Acceptance and the date as Acceptance Day. The Charleston *News and Courier* proclaimed the issue was the most important decision of the legislature in that two-year session.[56] With the governor's signature, the Clemson Agricultural College of South Carolina was alive.[57]

Governor John Peter Richardson III (1831–1899), eighty-third governor of South Carolina, whose signature made the Act of Acceptance law on November 27, 1889. South Caroliniana Library, University of South Carolina.

Notes

1. The paths of the rail lines are from maps of South Carolina in CUL.SC.MSS Map Files and *South Carolina in 1888*, a twenty-page pamphlet. Besides some railroad data, the pamphlet contains other agricultural and production data. The Pendleton depot was about 400 yards from Simpson's house on Elm and Queen streets in Pendleton.
2. The will and the codicil are reprinted in an appendix. Alumni Distinguished Professor Emeritus Bruce Yandle has studied the establishing documents of public higher education institutions in the United States and has found four—the University of Alabama, Purdue University, the University of Delaware, and Clemson University—which have charters that call for some or all the trustees to be lifetime. Clemson has a majority that are lifetime and self-perpetuating.
3. The thorough discussion of this is in Kean, *Desegregating Private Higher Education*.
4. Columbia *State*, March 6, 1935, a clipping in CUL.SC.CUA. S 30 ss I b 2 ff 24 and 25 and S 28 f Keitt. I also appreciate the assistance of J. Keitt Wannamaker II of St. Matthews, Clemson 1980.
5. CUL.SC.CUA. S 30 ss I b 1 f 8.
6. Ibid., f 7; Garlington, *Men of the Time*, 40–41; and Reynolds and Faunt, *Biographical Directory*, vol. 1, 163–165.
7. CUL.SC.CUA. S 30 ss I b 1 f 21; *Senate Biographical Directory*, vol. 1, 400–401; and Hemphill, *Men of Mark*, vol. 3, 139–140. M. L. Donaldson had written Tillman on February 6, 1886 (not the first letter that Donaldson sent to Tillman), in which he noted he had written "parties in Spartanburg, Anderson, York & Marion counties" seeking support. Donaldson noted that the editors of the *Greenville News* and the *Baptist Courier* are favorably disposed to Tillman's ideas. And Tillman heard (February 20, 1886) from E. T. Stackhouse. See also CUL. SC.MSS 80 S 2 b 1 f 1.
8. Charleston *Sunday News*, April 8, 1888; and Charleston *News and Courier*, April 9, 1888. The *Sunday News* printed epitomes from papers from around the state.
9. Rock Hill *Herald*, April 12, 1888.
10. Hollis, *University of South Carolina*, vol. 2, 139.
11. Http://en.wikipedia.org/wiki/History_of_Cornell_University; http://berkeley.edu; http://en.wikipedia.org/wiki/Kansas_State_University; and http://en.wikipedia.org/wiki/History_of_Michigan_State_University (accessed August 15, 2010).
12. Hollis, *University of South Carolina*, vol. 2, 145.
13. Charleston *News and Courier*, January 26, 1888.
14. Charleston *Sentinel*, April 23, 1888. The other letters or summaries are reprinted in the Charleston *Sentinel*. Some of these quotes follow through the paragraph.
15. Greenville *Daily News*, April 14, 1888.
16. Charleston *Sentinel*, April 26, 1888.
17. Ibid.
18. Ibid., April 25, 1888.
19. Pickens *Sentinel*, May 3, 1888.
20. Charleston *News and Courier*, May 5, 1888.
21. CUL.SC.MSS 68 b 18 f 329. The other newspapers are clipped and filed.
22. Charleston *News and Courier*, May 12, 1888.
23. Ibid., May 15, 1888.
24. Ibid.
25. Ibid., May 19, 1888.
26. Charleston *World*, July 11, 1888.
27. Charleston *News and Courier*, July 11, 1888.
28. Charleston *World*, August 4, 1888.
29. Charleston *News and Courier*, November 28, 1888.
30. The committee memberships are in the *Journal of the House of Representatives*, second session 1888; and the membership backgrounds are available in Bailey, Morgan, and Taylor, *Biographical Dictionary*.
31. Charleston *News and Courier*, December 4, 1888.
32. *Journal of the House of Representatives*, 123.

33. Charleston *News and Courier*, December 8, 1888.
34. *Journal of the Senate*, 112 and 69–70, 97–98, and 105.
35. Ibid., 119.
36. Bailey, Morgan, and Taylor, *Biographical Dictionary*, vol. 11, 1072–1080.
37. CUL.SC.MSS 68 b 18 f 331.
38. Charleston *News and Courier*, November 28, 1888.
39. Ibid., December 10, 1888.
40. Ibid., December 11, 1888; and http://www.westegg.com/inflation. This latter source is used throughout this study.
41. Pickens *Sentinel*, April 19, 1888.
42. Charleston *News and Courier*, April 26, 1888.
43. Ibid.
44. Ibid., May 2, 1888.
45. Ibid., May 3, 1888.
46. United States Circuit Court: District of South Carolina, Charleston, December 1888: *Lee v. Simpson* as noted in *37th Federal Reporter* and filed in CUL.SC.MSS 68.
47. Charleston *Sunday Budget*, November 11, 1888.
48. Lander, *Calhoun Family and T. G. Clemson*, 207–226.
49. CUL.SC.MSS 68 b 96.
50. Ibid., "*Lee v. Simpson* brief," *Fourth Circuit Court of Appeals*, 7–8.
51. *Fourth Circuit Court of Appeals*, 9.
52. Ibid., 10.
53. Ibid., 11–15.
54. *Cases Argued and Decided in the Supreme Court of the United States in October 1889*, vol. 134, 1038–1047.
55. CUL.SC.MSS 68 b 93.
56. Charleston *News and Courier*, November 26, 1889, and November 27, 1889.
57. Charleston *World*, November 28, 1889.

An early photo of the Board of Trustees of the Clemson Agricultural College of South Carolina, dated 1894. *Seated, left to right*: J. R. Jeffries, D. K. Norris, B. R. Tillman, J. H. Hardin. *Standing, left to right*: M. L. Donaldson, P. H. E. Sloan, R. W. Simpson, J. E. Bradley, D. T. Redfearn, J. E. Tindall, R. E. Bowen. *Inset photos, left to right*: H. M. Stackhouse, E. B. Craighead, J. E. Wannamaker, W. H. Mauldin. Clemson University Photographs, CUL.SC.

CHAPTER IV

Building the School

1889–1893

With Governor John Richardson's signature on Act No. 166 (the Act of Acceptance), the Clemson Agricultural College of South Carolina received its second charter, this one from the S.C. General Assembly and the governor. Thomas Clemson's will now directed that "the legislature may provide, as it sees proper, for the appointment or election of the other six trustees...." (Item 2). The general assembly now set about doing so.

The Legislative Trustees

The legislature elected the six legislative trustees for staggered terms: James L. Orr, B. W. Edwards, J. H. Hardin, E. T. Stackhouse, James E. Tindal, and Alan Johnstone. Orr was born in the Abbeville area on August 29, 1852, and educated at King's Mountain Military Academy, finishing in 1869. From there, he went to the University of Virginia from 1870 to 1872 to study law. Later he served as a colonel in Wade Hampton's gubernatorial staff. He prepared the *Lee v. Simpson* case for use in the courts. Besides his career as a lawyer, he worked with the Orr Mills, Piedmont Manufacturing, and other industrial pursuits. As a prominent citizen, he served on the boards of the Medical College of South Carolina, Converse College, and Christ Episcopal Church in Greenville. He died in Greenville on February 27, 1905.[1]

The second legislative trustee was Berryman Wheeler Edwards. Born on January 27, 1824, in Spartanburg County, he attended South Carolina College from 1846 to 1850, after which he studied law and then graduated from the Harvard Law School. He married Anna M. Coker on January 1, 1857; they had nine children. Edwards served in the Ninth South Carolina Regiment in the Civil War. In 1886, he was elected to the state senate from Darlington County and was instrumental in moving the Act of Acceptance through that body. In December 1889, he introduced what became Act No. 188, Clemson's basic funding act. He died on June 11, 1890.[2]

The general assembly also selected as trustee Jesse Havries Hardin, a farmer from Chester County. Born on April 11, 1829, he married Joanna Smith, also from Chester; they had seven daughters and three sons. After serving in the Confederate infantry, he raised fine horses. Hardin was serving in the state house (1889–1892) when first elected as a Clemson trustee. A Baptist, he was reelected as a legislative trustee on Clemson's board and served until his death on August 27, 1910.[3]

Eli Thomas Stackhouse, born in Little Rock, Dillon County, on March 27, 1824, was educated in the community school. In 1847, he married Elizabeth Ann Fore of Marion County, with whom he had three sons and five daughters. He served in the Army of Northern Virginia, attaining the rank of colonel before the Appomattox surrender. Elected to the S.C. House of Representatives in 1862, he remained there until 1868. Stackhouse served as the president of the S.C. Farmers' Alliance and served one term in the U.S. House of Representatives (1891–1892). He was a legislative trustee from 1890 to 1896.[4]

The fifth legislative trustee, James Ezra Tindal, was born in Clarendon County on February 1, 1839. By age 15, he worked as an assistant teacher. That same year, he enrolled at Furman, graduating in 1858, after which he went to Europe and studied at the University of Bonn. The outbreak of the American Civil War called him home, where he served in the Army of Northern Virginia to the end of hostilities. His first wife, whom he married in 1861, died in childbirth, and the infant died shortly thereafter. Tindal remarried in 1866 and with his second wife had three daughters and three sons.

Tindal's first public speech (1866) indicated him in a position close to that of Wade Hampton when he said, "We cannot suspend the negro between slavery and citizenship. We should set a qualification for suffrage and let him vote when he attains to it under our tutelage or he will get manhood suffrage and ruin the state."[5] He was shouted down and not allowed to finish the speech. Active in all aspects of education, he campaigned to reopen the Citadel and South Carolina College. At the same time, he called for an agricultural college connected to a farm. Because of his outspoken advocacy, he had been with the delegation that the Farmers' Association had sent to inspect the Mississippi Agricultural and Mechanical College in 1888 to examine the effort there.[6]

Alan Johnstone, born in Newberry on August 12, 1849, lived in the home of his birth all his life. Educated at the Newberry Male Academy, he had prepared to join the Confederate army at age sixteen, but the war ended before he enlisted. He enrolled at Newberry College and then at the University of Virginia. In 1875, he married Lilla Kennedy, also of Newberry, and they had five sons and five daughters.

Johnstone worked actively in local politics, serving as town warden and then on the county school board. In the latter capacity, he turned the local private academy into a public school for white children and opened a public school for African Americans. He organized the Newberry Farmers Oil Mill. A member of

Aveleigh Presbyterian Church, he served as an elder and a commissioner to the General Assembly of the Presbyterian Church (U.S.).

He served one term as a legislative trustee for Clemson, but the next legislature, with a strong Tillmanite group, did not return him; however, when D. K. Norris died, the other life members elected Johnstone as a life trustee. He served in that capacity until his death in 1929. When Richard Wright Simpson announced that he would no longer serve as president of the board, Johnstone was elected and served until his death.

Johnstone was a leading spokesman for the agricultural extension movement and hosted the national "Father" of the extension movement, Seaman Knapp, and his son Bradford in Johnstone's home. South Carolina Governor Richard Manning asked Johnstone to fill the U.S. Senate seat made vacant by B. R. Tillman's death and later urged Johnstone to run for governor of South Carolina. He declined both because they would take significant time away from his farm and from Clemson.

Later, Clemson cadets thought highly of Johnstone. At the dedication of Riggs Hall (1928) when he and the other trustees emerged from the onetime Prof. M. B. Hardin home, which the school converted into a lodge for the trustees, the cadets broke into spontaneous cheering. Further, several trustees suggested he be named as Riggs's successor. He died on January 5, 1929. Members of the board and Clemson President Enoch Sikes served as honorary pallbearers. Johnstone's widow told President Sikes, "He went to heaven but he went by Clemson College on the way."[7]

The legislative trustees mirrored the characteristics of the life trustees and, for that matter, the state's voting population in that they were white, male, and Protestant. This made them little different from the boards of most educational institutions throughout the nation. White, male Protestants dominated the boards of almost all public higher education institutions. And Clemson's original legislative trustees fit the pattern of most of the Morrill land-grant institutions in that their economic interests were predominantly agricultural. In their geographic distribution, however, they were mostly Upstate men, mirroring the split in both the farming and slowly emerging industrial interests of South Carolina.[8] Edwards died too soon to have much influence on Clemson's policies, while both Tindal and Johnstone favored education for African Americans, albeit separate.

Legislative Financing

While at one point Mr. Clemson had expressed the thought that properly managed, his estate might by itself sustain the college, when he signed the will, that was no longer his plan. He concluded in his four-paragraph introduction of the will:

I trust that I do not exaggerate the importance of such an institution for developing the material resources of the State by affording to its youth the advantages of scientific culture, and that I do not overrate the intelligence of the legislature of South Carolina, ever distinguished for liberality, in assuming that such appropriation will be made as will be necessary to supplement the fund resulting from the bequest herein made.

In Item 1 of the will, Mr. Clemson expected that the state's acceptance as confirmed by the votes of both houses of the legislature, the signature of the governor, and the judgment of the state supreme court's chief justice should signal a period in which the erection of the school's buildings, hiring of faculty, and admitting of students should commence. Further, in Item 3, which formed a fallback option, Mr. Clemson stated that even if the state rejected his offer, the trustees should use no more than $5,000 of his gift for the building of the school. That represented less than 5 percent of the legacy.

In Act 188, the legislature began its funding. First (or Section 1), the Morrill land-script **endowment** [bold face editorial] was shifted from the University of South Carolina ($191,800) and divided evenly between the African American institute adjacent to Claflin College in Orangeburg and the to-be-elected six legislative trustees of Clemson Agricultural College. The state treasurer issued a certificate of stock to the six trustees ($95,900) to be the base of a perpetual endowment that would pay 6 percent per annum in semiannual payments to the six legislative trustees. By Section 2, the annual $15,000 federal Hatch Act grant would also go to the legislative trustees to provide for the experiment station. An appropriation of $15,000 annually from the state government for the building and maintenance of the college (Section 3) was part of the financing.[9] This funding would not continue long. These actions and those that followed clearly identified Clemson College as South Carolina's Morrill Land Grant Act of 1862 institution. Making Clemson a land-grant school formed the third charter, joining the Clemson will and the Act of Acceptance as the basis of funding and authority of the Clemson trustees.

The thirteen trustees could expect about $5,000 per year from Mr. Clemson's bequest, another $20,754 from federal revenues (1862 Morrill interest and 1887 Hatch Act), and from the state a total of $3,000, of which $1,500 could be spent on buildings at Fort Hill until the resolution of *Lee v. Simpson*. The other $1,500 could be spent for tools, implements, and farm animals (Act of Acceptance, Section 6).

The general assembly next turned to a definitive statement of financial arrangements in Act 188. Signed on December 23, 1889, Act 188 set the fiscal date of July 1, to commence July 1, 1890. Section 1 respected the Morrill 1862 endowment and specifically repealed the prior designation to USC. Section 2 provided a due delivery date of November 1, 1890, and repeated the Hatch 1887 designation transfer. However, in Section 3 the general assembly began its real appropriations for building and maintaining the college. Therein, the general assembly provided $15,000 from the state general revenues. Section 4 dealt with the fertilizer tag sales fees, which the act referred to as the "privilege **tax** [bold face editorial] on fertilizers."[10] The section designated that an already-collected $10,000 be transferred on the board's order to the Clemson board treasurer for building and maintenance. And from the fertilizer tags revenue collected between November 1, 1889, and October 31, 1890, the law provided an additional $15,000 for Clemson.

Section 5 required the directors of the state penitentiary to furnish, on the request of the Clemson board, up to fifty "able-bodied convicts…for preparation of the grounds and the materials" and for the "work connected with the erection of the buildings" of Clemson Agricultural College. In turn, the Clemson board was to pay transportation of the convicts to and from the penitentiary and their medical costs, food, and lodging. For plans, estimates, building costs, and maintenance of the buildings, an immediate transfer of $3,000 would be made from the state to Clemson's treasurer (Section 6), who must be bonded (Section 7).

With Governor Richardson's signature, this funding arrangement, Act 188, became law on December 23, 1889. For building purposes, the trustees had approximately $28,000 (not counting the Hatch or Clemson funds, which totaled about $20,000 annually). For annual operations, the trustees could use the Morrill endowment interest of $5,754 and such Clemson interest and Hatch annual appropriations not used for building. Of course, the state treasurer would handle the Clemson endowment.[11]

The general assembly had completed creating Clemson's Board of Trustees. The time had come for the full board to meet. Simpson, serving as president of the life trustees, convened the first meeting at Wright's Hotel in Columbia on January 20, 1890. The trustees elected Simpson to a two-year term as president and J. E. Wannamaker as secretary-treasurer. They directed Wannamaker to obtain a corporate seal as authorized in Act 166 of 1889 (Section 4). Recognizing the need for close supervision, the trustees established an executive committee holding limited power. Composed of Simpson, Norris, Orr, and Johnstone, the executive committee acted as needed between board meetings. Made up of two life and two legislative trustees, the committee composition demonstrated the entire board's determination not to differentiate between the two groups. Further, proximity to Fort Hill might have played a role in the choice of committee members. The executive committee was charged with arranging for tentative designs of the desired college buildings and with calculating the estimated costs for them. In addition, it purchased necessary equipment. If that were not enough, its charge even included securing options on neighboring lands if such were possible. The Calhoun family asked for and received permission to erect an iron fence around the family graves on what would come to be known as Cemetery Hill.[12] The fence, however, would not be built for some years.

The Curricula

To establish the two curricula for agriculture and mechanics, as mandated by Mr. Clemson's will and the Morrill Land Grant Act of 1862, the trustees established a five-member committee composed of Edwards, Tillman, Donaldson, Tindal, and Wannamaker. Obviously, the board also recognized that a truly useful college needed connecting with the public schools; thus, it made a note that the new college's first president would be instructed to contact South Carolina's teachers' association to determine what it recommended as best for Clemson's involvement in agricultural and industrial education. This idea occurred thirty years before enactment of the federal Smith-Hughes Act, which placed this responsibility on the land-grant colleges. The trustees also envisaged special summer courses to attract women and men, a possibility that demonstrated the flexibility of the will. Finally, the trustees selected P. H. E. Sloan, a Pendleton pharmacist and onetime friend of Mr. Clemson, as the trustees' salaried and bonded secretary-treasurer. With that, the meeting concluded, and the trustees departed.[13]

Bradley and Edwards did not attend the board's second meeting on April 17, 1890, which Simpson convened in the Masonic Hall in Pendleton. Simpson announced that only ten days earlier (April 7, 1890), the U.S. Supreme Court had ruled favorably for the college (and Simpson) in *Lee v. Simpson*. Arguments for the appellant, Gideon Lee, had been presented by Youmans and Carey, who were supplemented by lawyer A. C. King. S.C. Attorney General Joseph H. Earle presented for the state. The Honorable Justice Samuel Blatchford of New York read the court's decision.[14]

For the new colleges like Clemson, the land-grant acts of 1862 and 1887 set forth the two major goals of teaching (1862) and economic research (1887), established the curricula (agriculture and mechanics as laid out in the Act of 1862), and permitted all other subjects (the Act of 1862 had been specific in that regard). Also, the 1862 law mandated the teaching of military tactics. No other subjects had to be excluded. In addition, Mr. Clemson's will provided for the greatest flexibility in the subjects taught at his college. It stated that the decisions as to what would be taught were to be left to the trustees and no other body. Concerning both the composition and the authority of the trustees in curricular matters, the will and the Act of Acceptance were in full conformity. In Section 3, the act declared "a Board of thirteen Trustees, composed of the seven members nominated by said will and their successors and six members to be elected by the Legislature in Joint Assembly...."[15] Just as did the will, the Act of Acceptance granted curricular authority to the board in the phrase "shall prescribe the courses of study" and directed that such curricula must include "all branches of study pertaining to practical and scientific agriculture and other industries connected therewith...." But the same paragraph allowed the trustees to institute other such "studies as are not inconsistent with the terms of the said will." This would be their authority. It should be noted, however, that while the trustees could implement such fields or studies, the state incurred no obligation except that to which it agreed (Section 4).[16]

The Campus

Upon the announcement of the Supreme Court decision, Simpson deeded the property to the state and transferred $81,528.80, Mr. Clemson's cash worth, to the state treasurer. Norris and Simpson made arrangements for harvesting timber and cultivating the land. Under supervision, convicts cut trees and dressed the fallen timbers while the Pickens firm of Mauldin and Glospie set up a sawmill to prepare the lumber for structural timbers. Scrap was reserved for burning bricks. Some three million bricks were estimated as needed. The Poole Company of Newberry won the bid for producing the bricks and moved its equipment to Fort Hill.[17]

After deliberation, the trustees awarded the architectural contract to Bruce and Morgan, an Atlanta firm, to lay out the campus and design the principal buildings. Of the homes for faculty, two were of the highest priority: one for the head chemist, who was critical for the fertilizer analysis, and a second for the president. Other buildings included the Chemistry Building, the Main Building (classrooms, library, and administration), the barracks, other faculty residences, and Mechanical Hall. Chemistry was the highest priority; the work there would provide much of the all-important revenue from the college's fertilizer tag sales. Mechanical Hall had the lowest priority because it would not be used until the year after classes began.[18]

When the Poole Company delivered the first order of one million bricks, the bricks proved improperly fired and were crumbling. The board's executive committee rejected the shipment and canceled the entire order. The board then purchased Poole's brick-making machine, requested an increase in the number of African American convicts, and ordered many more wheelbarrows and shovels. The legislature authorized a total of 150 convicts (Act 448 of 1890). Trustee J. E. Bradley came to Fort Hill to supervise the selection of clay. Immediately, the convicts began digging, hauling, mixing, drying, and firing. Working the mule teams, the laborers hauled the new bricks from the Mill Creek (now Hunnicutt Creek) to the building sites.[19]

Even as the old plantation slave quarters' granite was being used in constructing the foundations of the chemistry laboratory and several faculty houses, the trustees counted their financial resources. They considered delaying further con-

The original Hardin Hall, ca. 1893, the first academic building constructed on Clemson's campus, the original chemical laboratory, and the current home of the Department of History and Geography and the Department of Philosophy and Religion. Note the construction rubble still present on the grounds. Clemson University Photographs, CUL.SC.

struction for two years, but even with that they feared they would be $10,000 short. By February 1891, to keep the convicts fed and medically fit, the trustees began paying the bills out of their own pockets, receiving undated promissory notes that accrued no interest. Mules needed to be fed, materials purchased, and the various supervisors and other workmen paid.[20]

The First Officers

A question since the passage of the Act of Acceptance was, "Who will be the president?" The trustees considered nine people. After a nomination by Wanna-maker and support from Bradley, the trustees offered the position to Gen. Ste-phen Dill Lee (1833–1908), a South Carolinian and graduate of West Point.[21] Lee garnered fame when in April 1861 he had transferred the orders of Gen. P. G. T. Beauregard to the batteries near Fort Sumter to commence firing on the federal troops at Fort Sumter. Lee served later as second in command of the Confederates at Vicksburg and completed the surrender there on July 4, 1863.[22] He had mar-ried a Mississippian and managed her large plantation in Noxubee County, just south of Columbus and Starkville.[23] Lee was serving as president of the Agricultural and Mechanical College of Mississippi, the school named as a model in Mr. Clemson's will. The Clemson trustees offered Lee the Clemson post with a salary of $2,500 (2009 equivalent $58,935) and a house.

With that offer, which far exceeded Lee's Mississippi salary, Lee met with the Mississippi trustees. After much discussion, they counter-offered Lee $3,000, a 50 percent increase, and a new house.[24] Lee declined Clemson's offer, noting that he had business complications in Mississippi and also that his wife's health would make the move to Clemson College very difficult.[25]

Clemson's trustees, after further deliberation, extended an offer to the second person on their presidential list, Henry Strode. Strode, at the time a professor at the University of Mississippi, seemed to know the details of Clemson's offer to Lee. He answered the trustees that the offer made to him was less. Clemson's trustees answered Strode, pointing out that his offer included a salary, a house, and a supplement of $1,000 as director of the agricultural experiment station. Strode accepted.[26]

Clemson's First President

Born in Fredericksburg City, Virginia, on February 14, 1844 (his tombstone reads February 6), Strode was educated first at the Edgehill School in Virginia. At the age of sixteen, and lying to make himself eighteen, he enlisted in what ultimately became Braxton's Brigade in the Confederate army. Some suggest he fired the shot that killed U.S. Gen. John F. Reynolds at Gettysburg. Paroled at Appomattox, he worked for a time before entering the University of Virginia in 1867 to study Latin, Greek, and mathematics. In the last subject, he received the Courtenay (green) medal. After graduation, he had charge of the preparatory division at the University of Richmond. The following year, he headed the mathematics department at the McCabe School in Petersburg before returning to Virginia for advanced work in mathematics and chemistry. He married Millie Ellis, daughter of Col. J. E. Ellis, killed in Pickett's Charge at Gettysburg; they had six daughters and two sons. He then was employed as the mathematics instructor at William Cabell's Norwood Prep School on the

Henry Aubrey Strode, the first president of Clemson College, from 1890 to 1893. Clemson University Photographs, CUL.SC.

James River. Strode purchased a large home in Amherst County, Virginia, which he and his wife renovated into a young men's preparatory school called Kenmore. They welcomed the young men, their hunting dogs, and guns for seventeen years before Strode accepted the chair in mathematics at the University of Mississippi.

At Kenmore, Strode had contact with a number of South Carolinians, including C. G. Memminger, a state legislator, and R. I. Manning, a later Clemson trustee. Upon acceptance of the Clemson offer, his main responsibilities involved development of the curricula, working on the requests of young men to enroll in Clemson, and with Simpson and Norris, attending to the building of the school. And he played the major role in identifying and hiring the faculty.[27]

When Strode and his family arrived at Fort Hill, they lived in the former plantation house, convenient to the construction of the school. Convicts dug the foundations of several faculty homes and the Chemistry Building. Bruce and Morgan had hired W. B. Beacham to provide the materials for construction of the needed buildings. By August 15, 1890, Beacham had delivered the limestone arch for the Chemistry Building, with the raised letters "Chemistry," the decorative terra cotta plaque with "1890" on it, and the tin for the roof flashing and slate for the roofing.[28]

Col. Mark Bernard Hardin, first faculty member and original director of the chemical and fertilizer testing laboratories who served from 1890 until retirement in 1910. Clemson University Photographs, CUL.SC.

The trustees and Strode had selected Mark Bernard Hardin as the first chemist. A fifty-two-year-old graduate of Virginia Military Institute, Hardin had served in the Confederate artillery during the Civil War. After its conclusion, he worked from 1865 to 1867 as an analytical chemist in New York City and was a member of the Lyceum of Natural History and of the American Chemical Society. He then returned to Virginia Military Institute as a faculty member. From there he came to Fort Hill as the professor of chemistry.[29]

Each of the major disciplines at Clemson had one professor. Strode, besides serving as president, was the professor of mathematics, just as Hardin was the professor of chemistry. Others, assigned titles of associate or assistant, would be added if needed. Chemistry, because of the college's obligation to analyze fertilizers sold in the state, would also include other chemists who helped in instruction as needed, although they had no regular teaching assignments.

Meanwhile, the late autumn-winter 1890–1891 session of the general assembly met in Columbia. In the new legislature, the state's white, small farmers had strengthened their hand, and a new governor, Benjamin Ryan Tillman, had achieved the position he had sought.[30] But whatever might have been feared for the future of USC and the Citadel by the traditional "straight-out" Democrats, that did not come to pass. No colleges would be closed. Rather, the reform, so far as it affected the public colleges, was somewhat limited.

The general assembly in Act 461 abolished the state agriculture department along with the commissioner, transferring such power to the Clemson board. Financially, the most important aspect of the change directed the Clemson board to "supervise and enforce…all laws respecting the sale of commercial fertilizers within this State." To aid them in this task, they were to appoint the inspectors of fertilizer (Section 4). To cover such costs, the law ordered that "all the privilege tax on fertilizers now required…shall in the future be paid to the Treasurer of the State, subject to the order of the Board of Trustees of the Clemson Agricultural College of South Carolina; and so much of the money so received as shall be necessary to defray the expenses of the Board in performing the duties now, by this Act, devolved upon them shall be thus used…." For Clemson, the crucial phrase followed. "…And the balance [of money received from those fees] shall go to the Clemson Agricultural College of South Carolina for its erection and maintenance" (Section 6).[31]

As the winter of 1890–1891 deepened, the first wagonloads of commercial fertilizer arrived. The Chemistry Building, although not finished, served to store the bags, and Strode, who held a certificate in chemistry, joined Hardin in the work of analyzing the fertilizer. Even today the old building where chemistry resided for fifty-six years shows on its exterior the marks of the old bricks and the wavy courses of unraked mortar, signs of the work of the African American convicts. Also their work can be traced in the other two surviving original buildings, now called Trustee House and Tillman Hall.[32] At about the same time, Hardin and his family moved into the brick two-story house located between the Chemistry Building and Fort Hill house. Campus wags insisted that the house's placement enabled Hardin to notice any night fires or explosions in "his building."

Even while the building of the college moved ahead, the curious came to see Fort Hill and the progress of construction. John Adger McCrary, Clemson 1898, grew up in the Lebanon community, a few miles south of Pendleton. He and his parents occasionally visited the school. McCrary, in a later letter to Clemson business manager J. C. Littlejohn, remembered,

> My first visit to Clemson College, known at that time as "Fort Hill," was to the sale of property, such as wagons, plows, manure spreaders, cattle, hogs, etc. This was possible before or soon after the state of South Carolina had accepted the Clemson bequest.

At that time the road from Pendleton was a very sorry dirt road with a few fields on each side to about where the road to Old Stone Church branches off to the west. From here the road to the Calhoun Mansion was in dense woods, with trees overhanging. There were three gates to open, the first two, I think, were the largest gates I had ever seen up to that time. The first gate was about where the present stone posts are located at the entrance from Pendleton. The second gate was about where the present library [now called Sikes Hall] is now located. The third gate was at the entrance to the Mansion yard proper about 100 yards to southeast of the front porch.

On the Fort Hill property there was no cleared land towards Pendleton except the old broom sedge field where the Main College Building and the first old Dormitory are now located. The farm lands were to the west and southwest and this of course included the river bottoms, which were very fertile, but were subject to overflow of the Seneca River.[33]

As the Chemistry Building and the first faculty homes were finished, some convicts excavated the site for the Main Building. Bruce and Morgan's on-site junior architect and building supervisor, both who had rented rooms in the vicinity, kept careful oversight of the work. The architects had experience with the design of other college campuses, most notably Georgia Tech, so there was a striking relationship, particularly at Clemson College in the massing and the towers of the main buildings. The use of brick and the steep roofs in conjunction with the rounded archways gave a strong Romanesque feeling to both scientific and technological schools and gave them a distinctive identifying style. While the colonial style of Dartmouth and William and Mary created one aura, as did the Greek revival style favored by the early nineteenth century state schools such as South Carolina and Virginia, the Clemson/Georgia Tech style seemed to reflect the fortress/castle frontier life.

The numbers of convict laborers rose and fell over the years. The stockade that housed them was located in a large ravine at the college, which by 1990 contained the Outdoor Theater, the large pool and fountains, the Robert Muldrow Cooper Library, and the Strom Thurmond Institute. P. H. E. Sloan, the board secretary-treasurer, remembered that during the first Christmas season (1890), a convict had disappeared after the evening roll call. Following an unsuccessful search, "The authorities decided he had made good his escape and thought no more of it. As soon as Christmas had passed, however, he came to the stockade and knocked at the door. When the guard opened it, he was surprised to see the escapee. The fellow said, 'I've come back. I only went home to spend the Christmas holidays, and I had a good time. I've come back, now you see.' The guard let him in, and he returned to work."[34]

The convicts did many kinds of work. Some gained skills in masonry and others in carpentry. Today—when the size of the Main Building (Tillman) is considered; or the barracks, located directly to the west of the Main Building, is

An African American convict at work on the campus. This photo typifies the work done by African American convicts, by whose labors Clemson's original campus and buildings were built. Clemson University Photographs, CUL.SC.

re-visualized from the surviving photographs; or the no-longer-existent kitchen and bathroom wing for the barracks is considered; or when the brick homes for the president, the professors, and the commandant are added, not to overlook the fireplaces and chimneys on the wooden homes of the associates and assistants—one can see that the number of bricks made for the construction was astounding. McCrary, who became a regular visitor, recounted,

> I saw bricks being made down in the river bottoms where there was plenty of good quality of brick clay and it was here that I saw my first brick making machine into which the clay and water was dumped and bricks came out pressed and ready for the kilns where they were burned. State convicts did most of the work, all handwork and hauling the clay by mule teams. I saw the foundations being laid and the walls going up on the other visits. All of this was going on over a period of two or three years.[35]

The largest number of convicts reached 150, and in the years between 1890 and 1896, the convict population averaged about forty-seven. Besides the labor on the public buildings, they constructed support buildings. Holding pools for the water supplies were dug and, with wells and subterranean clay tile pipes, routed from the reservoirs to the emerging campus. The coal-burning electric power generator and the heating plant were constructed. The architects and the trustees had decided to electrify and steam heat the buildings and fit the campus for indoor plumbing. By 1900, only 4 percent of all the United States had electricity and indoor plumbing. This made Clemson College quite unusual.[36]

Another piece of federal legislation and several state decisions also provided aid to these educational projects. The federal statute was the Morrill Land Grant Act of 1890. It directed more federal money to strengthen the educational effort. However, the act also recognized by federal statute the practice in southern and border states of establishing separate land-grant schools for whites and for African Americans. It ordered federal appropriations be divided equally:

> That no money shall be paid out under this act to any State or Territory for the support and maintenance of a college where a distinction of race or color is made in the admission of students, but the establishment and maintenance of such colleges separately for white and colored students shall be held to be a compliance with the provisions of this act if the funds received in such State or Territory be equitably divided as hereinafter set forth.[37]

Although Governor Tillman was quite hostile about this required division, by 1895, this opportunity for additional funding came to South Carolina.[38]

The regular arrival of fertilizer samples kept Hardin and Strode busy across the winter of 1891 and demonstrated the need for more chemists. Therefore, a new faculty member was hired, Richard Newman Brackett, a twenty-eight-year-old PhD (*Philosophiae Doctor* or doctor of philosophy) in chemistry. Born in 1863 in Richland County, he had lived at various times in Rowan, North Carolina, and in Winnsboro before his father accepted the pastorate of Second Presbyterian Church in Charleston when Richard was nine. Brackett spent summers with family in Newton, Massachusetts, and in the western North Carolina mountains. Brackett graduated from Davidson College in 1883.

Brackett, who had shown interest in Greek, poetry, and science, then attended the seven-year-old Johns Hopkins University, one of the first research higher education institutions in the United States. Modeled on the University of Berlin, it granted the doctorate of philosophy and made the word "university" nearly synonymous with

Richard Newman Brackett, professor of chemistry at Clemson from 1893 to 1937 and successor to Col. Mark B. Hardin as the director of the chemistry and fertilizer testing laboratories. Clemson University Photographs, CUL.SC.

the granting of that degree and the expectation of original research by its faculty.[39] Brackett received the PhD in 1887. Immediately employed as the chief chemist with the Arkansas Geological Survey, he remained there until he accepted Clemson's offer and arrived in South Carolina in November 1891. Brackett and his research partner, J. Travers Williams, had discovered two minerals in the kaolinite group (newtonite and rectorite). By then, Brackett had married Bessie Brandon Craig, daughter of a Presbyterian minister. Brackett, his wife, and their infant son, Richard Brandon, moved into their home, named the Hollies, on the Clemson campus.[40]

When Simpson and the other trustees reported to the general assembly on October 31, 1891, the college's financial situation was dire. The state treasurer had not paid the bills charged to the fertilizer fee, and the balance remaining of the initial appropriation was $3,707.40. To keep the convicts fed and the carpenters paid, the trustees again borrowed money ($27,944.91), using their real and chattel properties for securities. At the same time, unpaid bills for delivered materials amounted to approximately $12,000, so that the total had reached $39,944.91. Across the year 1891–1892, the total fertilizer privilege fee revenue brought in only $35,000 instead of the projected $56,000. Because of the recession of the mid-1890s, the legislature had retracted the originally appropriated and anticipated revenue from the proposed sale of the Agricultural Hall and fishpond in Columbia. Also, the projected February 1893 opening of Clemson had to be delayed. To add further pressure on Clemson, Simpson reported that Strode had received and acknowledged "up to 1000 applications" from prospective Clemson students.

Meanwhile, four carpenters directed the labor of the convicts, although some convicts worked in the college's farm fields. After the college fed the convicts and the mules, the surplus produce was sold. From that income, the direct farm expenses, medical care of the convicts, and carpenters' wages were paid, leaving the farm showing a small profit.[41] Such farm activity was separate from the experiment farm.

The Agriculture Experiment Station

Established by the legislature in 1886, the South Carolina Experiment Farm, originally located in Spartanburg and Darlington, operated initially under the management of USC. However, Section 2 of Act 188 (1889) had withdrawn the farm from USC and lodged it with the legislative trustees of Clemson. Clemson's board had designated Strode director of the school's experiment farm. For the day-to-day management of the farm (or station), the trustees sought and hired, through Strode, two men: James Stanley Newman and J. F. Duggar.

Col. James Stanley Newman, professor of agriculture and horticulturalist at Clemson from 1891 to 1894 and from 1897 to 1905. Clemson University Photographs, CUL.SC.

Born in Orange County, Virginia, Newman had attended the University of Virginia. After the Civil War, he settled in Georgia, where he established a boarding school for teenage boys. An avid farmer, his greatest interest involved growing fruits. He had helped organize the Georgia State Horticultural Society. In 1875, he joined the Georgia State Department of Agriculture as vice-director of the Georgia Experiment Station. His responsibilities there included planning and conducting the farmers' institutes and writing agricultural bulletins. His research eventually led to five books on agriculture. When the state of Alabama established the experiment station at Alabama Agricultural and Mechanical College (now Auburn), the school offered Newman the directorship of the station in 1883. He was very successful and opened its first branch in Uniontown, in the heavy black soil belt. As successful as that was, when offered the position of associate director of the South Carolina Experiment Station at Clemson working with his fellow Virginian, Strode, he accepted in the autumn of 1891.[42]

Aiding Newman as assistant director was J. F. Duggar, who had joined the faculty in October 1890 as the manager of the dairy. He received a starting salary of $1,200. Clemson named Duggar assistant director of the station and assistant professor of agriculture on July 29, 1891. The strain of ever-changing instructions, however, led to his resignation on September 15, 1892.[43] Another specialist who joined the staff on July 29, 1891, as a station horticulturalist, was the self-taught J. F. C. DuPre. He worked very closely with Newman in laying out and planting the experiment station.[44]

During the first year, enough corn, hay, peas, and vegetables were harvested to feed the convicts, the mules, and the cattle and to erect a cannery to set aside food for the upcoming winter. With the help of a small crew of convicts, Newman and DuPre planted 265 apple, 241 pear, 311 peach, 170 plum, 24 fig, and 12 quince trees. Fruits and berries, including currants, gooseberries, and mulberries (for the hogs), were also planted along with other trees: 6 chestnuts, 12 filberts, 20 walnuts, and 100 pecans. Over 1,000 grape vines were trellised during the autumn. Along Pendleton Road, corn yielded 308.3 bushels per acre. Most of the cornfields lay in recently cleared woodlands. The old fields were "ornamented with gullies, galded clay spots, Bermuda grass, and quartz rock," according to Newman. These were terraced and turned under, planted, or left fallow. In addition, the farm produced beets, turnips, cantaloupes, watermelons, cucumbers, tomatoes, cabbage, onions, and legumes; however, some was lost to a drought and to insects. The college sold surplus that could not be preserved. In addition, fertilizer use tests began.[45] The fertilizer board, led by Trustee Tindal, noted a decline of 32 percent in fertilizer inspections and in fees collected, owing in great part to a decline in cotton acreage. This type of erratic production, along with, or perhaps caused by, the rapid decline in the per pound cotton price, would block the trustees' efforts to project long-term improvement projects into the 1930s.[46]

With all of this activity, John Adger McCrary remembered,

> The next few years after my first visit I made several others on sight-seeing trips. At one time I remembered going on a school picnic (Lebanon School), about 150 or 200 in the crowd going in wagons and buggies. This trip I recall quite vividly because of a small accident that occurred which might have resulted in something more serious had it happened in another room of the Calhoun Mansion. We were more or less crowded into the large room to the West[47] looking at the old relics, when without any warning the floor beams gave way and the center of the floor fell about 2 feet with a crash. This particular room had no cellar and that is why the accident was not more serious.[48]

Perhaps McCrary stood among the crowd of 2,000 who assembled on July 28, 1891, for the ceremonial laying of the cornerstone for the main college building. "Carriages, buggies, vans, wagons and carts brought the hundreds of pilgrims to the Mecca of the farmers of the state." Of the audience, the same source noted, "A stern face here, a bearded farmer there, a prosperous merchant there, a saucy belle from the city here, and a quiet, subdued face of some pretty girl from the hills and valleys, made up a diversified picture, pleasant to see and to describe."[49]

The Faculty Arrive

Gradually, the college added the remainder of the faculty; most of them would have their classrooms in the main college building. It, like the Chemistry Building, had classes from the very first day the school took in students. Strode, whose office was in the Main Building, had an assistant in teaching mathematics, J. G. Clinkscales. A second assistant professor in mathematics projected in 1891 (J. W. Perrin) did not accept the offered post, and by 1893, Augustus Shanklin filled the position.

The professor of English was Charles Manning Furman, son of the Rev. Dr. J. C. Furman, born on July 8, 1840. Educated at Furman University in nearby Greenville, where his father was president, he graduated in 1859. In college, he belonged to Chi Psi Fraternity. Afterward, he moved to Charleston and read law in the firm of Whaley and Lord. When the Civil War commenced, Furman enlisted as a private on May 9, 1861. This was a new life for him because until then, he read voraciously and hunted; he "never did a day's work with his hands until he

The earliest, best photo of the faculty of Clemson College, ca. 1894. These men make up the backbone of the fledgling college's faculty discussed in this chapter. *First row, left to right:* Furman, Hardin, Pres. Craighead, Strode, Morrison, Welch. *Second row, left to right:* Harrison, Hook, McGee, Sims, Secretary/Treasurer P.H.E. Sloan, Smith, Clinkscales, Bowman, Welch. *Third row, left to right:* Hart, Shanklin, Shiver, Clinton, Lytton, Blythe, Wright. Clemson University Photographs, CUL.SC.

Charles Manning Furman, a professor in and director of the English program at Clemson from 1891 to 1913. He was also a grandson to Richard Furman, founder of Furman University; a son of Dr. James C. Furman, Furman University's first president; and the father of both Clemson's first librarian, Charles M. Furman Jr., and Alester G. Furman, the founder of the Furman Co. Insurance Brokerage. Clemson University Photographs, CUL.SC.

entered the army." He rose to the rank of captain. In February 1864, he married Fannie Garden; they had six children. After her death, he married Sallie Villipigue, and they had three children. For a short time after the Civil War, Furman taught mathematics at Bethel College in Kentucky.[50]

At Clemson, Thomas P. Harrison served as Furman's associate in English. The third professor in the area, eventually titled the Academic Department, was William Shannon Morrison. From Winnsboro (born in 1853), he graduated from Wofford College with distinction in 1875. Morrison established the Wellford (Spartanburg County) High School in 1876 and taught there until he was asked to organize and superintend the Spartanburg city schools.

William Shannon Morrison, professor in and chair of history and political economy program at Clemson from 1892 until his death in 1922. Clemson University Photographs, CUL.SC.

In 1886, the city of Greenville hired him to do the same for Greenville, which he did until 1892. At that point, he joined the Clemson faculty.[51]

The Campus

The Main Building dominated the landscape. Of campus-made brick, it rested on a rusticated granite stone foundation. Its main entrance, on the eastern façade, was through a large Romanesque arch placed in a tower that rose to a decorated limestone band and frieze of running vines, above which the open arches of a belfry and a pyramidic cap stood. The eyes for the campus clock remained vacant until the 1900s. (The trustees could not see their way clear to purchase the clock face, the clockwork, or the bell until the twentieth century.) Over the Romanesque portal, constructed in granite, were the words "Clemson College."— which indicated an abbreviation of the name "The Clemson Agricultural College of South Carolina."

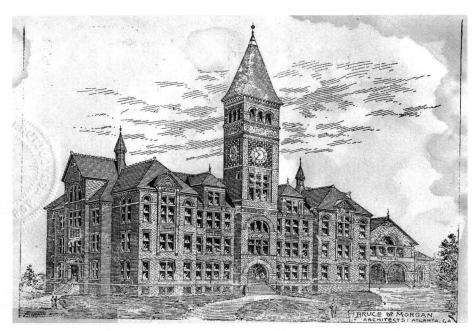

Bruce & Morgan Architect's rendering of the original plans for the Main Building, today's Tillman Hall. Clemson University Photographs, Fort Hill Subject File, CUL.SC.

Called the Main Building or the College until the 1940s, it contained eighteen classrooms, a library, a biology laboratory and specimen museum space, meeting rooms for the anticipated literary societies, an office for the president, and a smaller outer office for the college's secretary-treasurer. The south portal led under a terra cotta plaque bearing the legend "Agriculture" onto granite steps that led down to the "small parade ground," where the flagpole carried the U.S. flag. Directly south and ahead stood the Mechanical Hall. This view encompassed the three required subjects of the Land-Grant Act of 1862.

In the opposite (northern) direction lay the Norman-style Memorial Chapel, a distinct space yet part of the mass. The porch, at the level of the first floor of the Main Building, was approached through twin arches divided by a handsome deep-rose marble column. Smaller, unglazed arched openings flanked the entrance archways. On the north side of the porch existed a *porte cochere* to receive guests arriving by carriage. The auditorium was laid out on an east-west axis with a large arch framing the platform at the west end. The wooden ceiling rose in a naved style with brackets and elaborate wooden spindle arches and strainers. The entire space sat about 900 persons with an east-end loft. On the façade in raised stone appear the word "Memorial" and a red star painted in the gable. To what or to whom the memorial, raised in 1891 and 1892, was dedicated is not included in the trustees' minutes.

Probably because of the responsibility for testing fertilizer, the faculty involved in it already had notoriety in the state. Hardin was the professor and Brackett was the associate. C. W. Sims and Frank Shiver assisted on occasion in the laboratory instruction, although their primary duties lay in fertilizer analysis. These men were grouped together in the Chemistry Building. Built of solid brick and heart of pine, the building contained a full basement, most of it used for storage. On the main floor were five rooms for the fertilizer analysis and for the experiment station. Because federal experiment station funds could be used for buildings and because of the fertilizer tag sales revenue, the college completed and equipped this building (much like Hardin's home) first. A balance room, an advanced laboratory, and an office existed also on the main floor. The second floor had five rooms.

Mechanical Hall lay at the south end of the main knob of the large ridge. The school finished it last among the three classroom buildings, in part because of the money flow, which dictated a staggered start. Further, while the shops, which formed wings of the mechanical building, would be needed early, formal instruction was not planned until the second year. The mechanical building had a three-story main unit (including dormers) made of plastered brick, several prominent towers, and a slate roof. Three wings, one of two stories and two of one story each, stretched east and south. One wing was for forge and foundry, the second for woodworking, and the third for the electrical laboratory. Here the newly recruited professor of mechanics, S. Tompkins, taught after the opening year. Williams Welch taught drawing; W. M. Yager, mechanical drawing; and R. T. V. Bowman, forge and foundry works. In addition, several tutors and two foremen worked on the mechanics staff.

The three-story barracks was sited on the west side of the Main Building. The rapid westerly fall of the terrain disguised its bulk, but the ground floor contained the mess hall and the upper two stories the sleeping space. Each of 160 bedrooms was equipped with three iron single cots, mattresses, a table, chairs, wardrobes, and a mirror. The bathrooms, containing flush toilets, bathtubs, and sinks, were attached on the west side of the building. As in the other main buildings, steam heat, electric lights, and cold spring water ran through these barracks.[52]

Mrs. John F. Calhoun served as the mistress of the barracks. Her husband, John Francis Calhoun, was the bursar of the mess hall. John Francis (August 29, 1831–November 13, 1897), the grandnephew of John C. Calhoun, had been hired for $600 and his wife, Rebecca Noble Calhoun (a distant cousin of her husband), for $200. They also received board and "a house on the grounds free of rent." Shortly thereafter, the trustees raised their salaries to $900 and $300, respectively. At that point, the last four of their eleven children still lived at home, and their seventh child, daughter Rebecca, had married Frank S. Shiver, one of the chemists in the fertilizer laboratory.[53] Calhoun supervised a small staff of cooks, all of whom were African Americans. Most of the cooking staff lived in campus-owned wooden cottages located in the western valley (now Death Valley) that lay north of the Calhoun family cemetery.

A wooden infirmary building sat on the southeastern side of the major cluster of buildings, sufficiently removed both for quiet and sanitation. The physician, Alexander May Redfern (early Clemson records spell his last name "Redfearn"), born on March 21, 1862, in Anson, North Carolina, received his early education in North Carolina and Chester-field, South Carolina. For a short time, he studied at Furman and then at Wake Forest College, from which he graduated in 1884. Then he enrolled at the Long Island College Hospital. Graduating valedictorian, he continued studying in the New York Graduate Hospital and then in the Tulane University of Louisiana Polyclinic. After a peri-od of practice in Chesterfield County, he joined Clemson as the college physician. His wife, Annie Strayhorn Redfern, and their two small daughters accompanied him.[54] Redfern's father, David Town-ley Redfearn, a Confederate veteran and a farmer, had served in the S.C. House from 1874 through 1880 and then the senate from 1882 to 1885 and 1890 to 1893. Coincidentally, D. T. Redfearn was elected a legislative trustee on March 4, 1891, and served until his death on June 11, 1902.[55]

Dr. Alexander May Redfern, Clemson's first physician from 1893 to 1920 and a son of D. T. Redfearn, South Carolina state legislator and early trustee of Clemson College. Clemson University Photographs, CUL.SC.

By mid-1892, some unhappiness had emerged in several powerful quarters over the school's delayed opening. On June 3, 1892, Governor Tillman, as a life trustee, moved that Strode's salary as president cease being paid on July 1, 1892, and not be reinstated until the college opened or until the board asked him to re-sume the post. The motion passed.[56] Tillman knew better than most that Strode's 1891 request to the legislature for supplemental funding had been denied despite Tillman's support. Orr, perhaps attempting to avoid this unpleasantness, had of-fered a substitute motion that delayed the salary suspension until October 1, 1892. It had been defeated. Regardless, and in spite of what appeared to be a halt in the payment of his salary, Strode's correspondence, particularly with those seek-ing information about the college or asking for admission, did not lessen.

Then unexpectedly in late November 1892, Strode tendered—and the trust-ees accepted—his resignation as president, as of December 31, 1892, although not his professorship of mathematics. Robert S. Lambert, in his study of Strode's presidency, noted several possibilities for Strode's decision. One possibility cen-tered on the division of the board between those who supported Tillman and

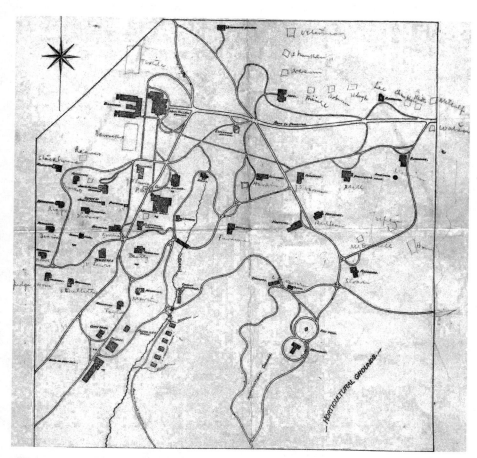

The campus as it would have appeared in 1893, with the exception of the hotel, added in 1894, and the additions of 1895 and 1896, faintly penciled in by the draftsman, Thomas Grayson Poats, early Clemson professor of mathematics and civil engineering. Taken from the 1896 *Catalogue of the Clemson Agricultural College of South Carolina.*

those who favored the more moderate posture of Orr (or perhaps Simpson). Other signs of such a rift existed, particularly in the correspondence of Strode in the early autumn of 1892, when he offered to mediate between Tillman and Orr. Or perhaps Strode's illness led eventually to the insistence of trustees that he resign completely on January 22, 1896.[57]

Another possibility is that Strode diverted his interest from the presidential duties. Unknown until recently, Strode had involved himself in a land business that could have conflicted with the interests of the college. But, in fact, the business, Cold Springs, a large holding that lay north of Fort Hill, had been purchased by the Calhoun Land Company, the officers of which included David Blassingame Sloan of the Calhoun community and Nelson Poe of Greenville. D. B. Sloan and P. H. E. Sloan were first cousins once removed. Strode served as president of the company, and the son of P. H. E. Sloan, the Clemson board's secretary-treasurer, was to be the land company's secretary-treasurer. Within a year, Strode became disgusted with what he took to be stalling by Poe, and he had turned to Orr for advice. Whether Strode's resignation resulted from his growing interest in land cannot be confirmed. However, he had involved the Clemson board through young Sloan himself.[58]

While Mr. Clemson may have thought of Fort Hill as an Eden-like paradise, his will provided the pollen that would attract many bees in the hopes of making golden honey. Part of the attraction was the patronage that the college afforded. Simpson, the real leader in the founding movement,[59] certainly looked after his own. P. H. E. Sloan, the father of Simpson's son-in-law, served as the paid secretary-treasurer of Clemson's Board of Trustees. And the Board of Trustees had selected Simpson's wife's relative, Capt. Ernest A. Garlington,[60] as the college's first commandant. Only a military assignment kept him from accepting the offer.

In 1892, the legislature, even while the issue of Strode emerged in public, strengthened the role of Clemson's trustees. First, it described the municipal jurisdiction of the trustees as a swath of land whose radius of five miles was to be circumscribed from the Main Building.[61] Then, to enforce the trustees' rules, the legislature granted them authority "to license or prohibit the sale of goods, wares and merchandise of any kind whatever on the grounds belonging to said College, as are not repugnant to the laws of the State; and also to appoint peace officers or policemen, who may arrest at any time any and all parties guilty of disorderly conduct or of any violations of the laws of the State and carry them before the nearest Trial Justice for trial."[62]

At the same session, the state created the nearby town of Calhoun, whose boundary limits formed a circle with the radius of one-half mile "from the depot of the Air Line Railroad Company...." Perhaps in deference to the college, "the sale of spirituous, malt or intoxicating liquors" was prohibited within the corporate limits of the town.[63]

The young Calhoun community readied itself for its new role as one of two entranceways to the new college. At the rail depot, James Carey served as the postal official. Incoming mail arrived by train, just as bags of outgoing mail were handed up to the clerk on the postal car. A college employee carried the mail back and forth to the Fort Hill campus post office, which had been established in 1892. Jeptha P. Smith served as the Fort Hill postmaster. In addition to the mail arriving from the Calhoun post office, he received from the Pendleton post office mail coming from the east via the Blue Ridge road.[64] Both lines were vital to the growth and health of the college. The Blue Ridge granted access to the Midlands and much of the Lowcountry, while the Southern line provided entrance for much of the Upstate, North Carolina, Virginia, and points further north. Over the years, these gave Clemson geographic diversity.

The Pendleton rail station did not expect an increase in boarding and exiting passengers because the college instructed cadets to disembark at Cherry's Crossing. However, the Calhoun Station expected and got potential cadets bounding off their trains. And on the campus, not every building was quite finished, nor were the odd piles of bricks and other building materials cleared away.[65] However, the ninety-year-old manse and its grounds had been fitted out to return to the teaching, research, and contemplation with which it had begun.

Notes

1. CUL.SC.CUA. S 30 ss I b 2 f 1.
2. Ibid., b 1 f 24.
3. Ibid., f 32.
4. Ibid., b 2 f 14.
5. Hemphill, *Men of Mark*, vol. 3, 427.
6. CUL.SC.CUA. S 30 ss I b 2 f 23.
7. Ibid., b 1 f 34.
8. The conclusion is based on a reading of some of the major studies of higher education institutions in the nation. See, for example, the following authors listed in the Bibliography: Ballard; Dyer, John; Dyer, Thomas; Hollis; Kinnear; and Webb.
9. South Carolina, *Acts and Joint Resolutions of the General Assembly*, 1889, no. 188, 299–302. This shall be referenced as "Act of Acceptance," and the specific section referred to by section number, there being no introduction and nine sections.
10. For one state to tax a product made in another was, A. T. Smythe would argue, a violation of the United States Constitution. The correct term, he claimed, was a "fertilizer inspection fee."
11. *Acts and Joint Resolutions*, 1890. Resolution 442, 0. 662.
12. CUL.SC.CUA. S 30 v 1, 3.
13. Ibid., 2–4. The earliest minutes of the 1888 meeting and the first 1890 minutes were formally engrossed in ink. Later they were transcribed in type. Both sets are preserved at Clemson in Special Collections and are available. I have used the bound and typed set.
14. Ibid., 5.
15. CUL.SC. MSS 68 b 18 f 329. This collection of James Littlejohn (Clemson 1908) contains many pieces of Clemson correspondence that are part of the history of Clemson. Littlejohn served as a Clemson instructor, then assistant to presidents Riggs, Earle (acting), and Sikes. Sikes created the business manager's post for him, a post he held late into the Poole administration. Littlejohn planned to write a history of Clemson Agricultural College. In his office, where Clemson's files were kept, he and his secretary, Mrs. Ritchie, who was a daughter of the Rev.

Dr. William H. Mills, the first resident Presbyterian minister and an important faculty member, extracted significant correspondence and refiled them with the papers and photographs he considered of historical importance.

16. *Acts and Joint Resolutions*, 1889, no. 166.
17. CUL.SC.CUA. S 30 v 1, 5.
18. Trustees of the Clemson Agricultural College of South Carolina, *Report to the General Assembly*, 1890. Bound in *Reports and Resolutions of the General Assembly*. This annual report, required by the Act of Acceptance, will be cited as *Clemson Trustees' Report to the General Assembly* with the appropriate year.
19. Ibid., 1890.
20. CUL.SC.CUA. S 38 f "Hardin;" and Hemphill, *Men of Mark*, vol. 4, 126–128.
21. CUL.SC.CUA. S 30 v 1, 10–13.
22. Tulane University of Louisiana. Joseph Merritt Jones Library, Manuscript Collection: MSS 130 b 10 f 35.
23. Mississippi State University. University Archives. Stephen Dill Lee Correspondence, May 1890.
24. Betterworth, *The People's University*, 102.
25. Lee's letter declining the offer is filed in CUL.SC.MSS 68, Photographic album, v 1, leaves 2 and 3. The letters are dated June 18 and June 28, 1896.
26. CUL.SC.MSS 68 b 18 f 329.
27. Lambert, "The Builder of a College: Henry Aubrey Strode, 1890–1893," in *Tradition*, 20–30. For the acceptance letter, see CUL.SC.CUA. S 50 b 1 f 1.
28. CUL.SC.CUA. S 30 ss ii b 7 f 1.
29. Ibid., S 38 f "Hardin;" and Hemphill, *Men of Mark*, vol. 4, 126–128.
30. Kantrowitz, *Ben Tillman*, 147–152.
31. *Acts and Joint Resolutions*, 1890–1891, no. 461, 705–706. For a recent study of South Carolina's phosphate industry, see Davis, "Coosaw Rock Alchemy," in *South Carolina Historical Magazine*, October 2008, vol. 109, no. 4, 269–294. Of special interest, Davis presents the data compiled by Rogers, *The Phosphate Deposits of South Carolina*, 219 and 292.
32. CUL.SC.MSS 68 b 12 f 244.
33. Ibid., b 18 f 329.
34. Ibid.
35. Ibid.
36. Twelfth Census of the United States, 1900: Census Reports v. II Population Part II: Section 11, Tables 95–104 Dwellings and Families at http://www.uscensus100.
37. United States Act of August 30, 1890, ch. 841, 26 Stat. 417, 7 USC 322 et seq. at http://www.csrees.usda.gov.
38. Kantrowicz, *Ben Tillman*, 216–219; and Chapter 6 footnotes 42, 43, 44, and 41, 353–354.
39. *Acts and Joint Resolutions*, 1890–1891, no. 460.
40. Hemphill, *Men of Mark*, vol. 4, 35–36; and conversations with Helen Waddell Comer of West Columbia, granddaughter of Brackett. She lent me her collection of Brackett papers, photographs, and memorabilia to be scanned and placed in Clemson University's Special Collections, for which I am very grateful.
41. *Clemson Trustees' Report to the General Assembly*, 1891; a full report in the 1892 Report, 511–514; and *Acts and Resolutions*, 1892–1893, no. 36.
42. Foscue, "J. S. Newman," in *Highlights of Agricultural Research*, vol. 9, no. 2, 4.
43. CUL.SC.CUA. S 28 f "Duggar." This series includes a large series of index cards created by A. B. Bryan during his years as editor for the South Carolina Agricultural Experiment Station.
44. Ibid., f "J. F. C. DuPre."
45. *Clemson Trustees' Report to the General Assembly*, 1892, 516–526.
46. Ibid., 530–533.
47. This was in the 1803 part of Fort Hill, now functioning as the room with the personal artifacts on display.
48. CUL.SC.MSS. 68.
49. Bryan, *Clemson*, 37–38.
50. Garlington, *Men of the Time*, 148–149; and Hemphill, *Men of Mark*, vol. 1, 126–129.

51. Garlington, *Men of the Time*, 321–322.
52. *Record of Clemson Agricultural College of South Carolina* 1893–1894, 2–4; 25–28. Consultation of the initial prospectus of 1893, the *Trustee Reports* of 1891 and 1892, the *Record*, along with the *Announcements of 1894–1895* and the P. T. Brodie "Map of Part of Clemson College Grounds" form the bases of the descriptions. The reflections are based on my thoughts.
53. CUL.SC.MSS 68 b 1 f 14.
54. Hemphill, *Men of Mark*, vol. 4, 295–296.
55. Bailey, et al., *Biographical Directory of the South Carolina Senate*, vol. 3, 1346–1347.
56. CUL.SC.CUA. S 30 Board Minutes v 1, 63.
57. Lambert, "The Builder of a College: Henry Aubrey Strode, 1890–1893," in *Tradition*, 20–32 and in particular 30–32.
58. CUL.SC.MSS Poe Papers b 1 ff CLC1 and CLC2. Michael Kohl, the Special Collections librarian, obtained this material and sped its acquisition. He brought the collection to my attention, for which I thank him very much.
59. Certainly this statement can be debated. Tillman would claim the title quite loudly, and he had great partisanship in the persons of his sons. However, it seems to me that Simpson, who also claimed "pride of place" in his private memoirs, is far more involved and in more critical ways. He wrote the will and was, with Clemson, responsible for selecting four of the seven life trustees. He was the executor of the will. And, using his network of legislative colleagues and friends, he guided the acceptance bill through the house and senate, converting Augustine T. Smythe to the college's side. No doubt, Tillman's brash oratory kept the agrarian flames bright, but even when he was governor, he was unable to convince the legislators, who were mostly his partisans, to grant the monetary relief Strode requested. Simpson, as a member of the four-trustee executive committee, made most of the building, hiring, and financial decisions that kept the college breathing in its early years.
60. Garlington, *Men of the Time*, 153–154.
61. *Acts and Joint Resolutions*, 1892, no. 35, 85–86.
62. Ibid., no. 37, 88–89.
63. Ibid., no. 252, 343.
64. US Post Office Department, Office of the First Assistant Post Master General, July 19, 1892.
65. *The Tiger*, September 18, 1941. The reprint of a letter from B. R. Tillman Jr.

The very first students of Clemson College, assembled on the grounds roughly where McCabe and Holmes halls are today, preparing to enter the school in their civilian clothes, ca. July 1893. Clemson University Photographs, CUL.SC.

CHAPTER V

First Graduation

1893–1897

The Blue Ridge Railroad came to a halt at Cherry's Crossing by the old Pickens homestead. Whether coming from east or west, the trains had picked up boys as young as fourteen and young men in their twenties bound for the new "farmers' college," Clemson. They were deposited beside the tracks. No depot and no shelter awaited them. Four miles to the north on the line variously called the Danville and Richmond, the Airline, or the Southern, the new students got off in the comfort of a small depot, a two-story brick general store, and a small number of homes. The sign declared the town to be Calhoun.

These two rail lines would be very important to the growth and development of Clemson Agricultural College. The Blue Ridge line, which began at the Atlantic Ocean coastline, had terminal stations in Savannah, Georgia; Port Royal, Charleston, Georgetown, and Conway, South Carolina; and Wilmington, North Carolina. These roads converged at Columbia, the state's capital, then fanned out to Chester, Carlisle, Clinton, and Greenwood. The heavily traveled Greenwood line continued west by northwest to Anderson, Pendleton, Cherry's Crossing, and then to Seneca and Walhalla. The local lines fed the trunk (or main) line so that, except for the northwestern third of South Carolina, all were within an easy train ride of the college. The Southern line served the northwestern third of the state. It stretched conveniently (for people having business at the college) from New Orleans, Louisiana (a major port); through Birmingham, Alabama (a large industrial town), and Atlanta, Georgia (an emerging commercial center); and then stopped at Calhoun. Then the line moved on to two emerging South Carolina textile centers at Greenville and Spartanburg before crossing into North Carolina, Virginia, and Washington, the nation's capital. So the college, although isolated in the immediate region, was at a southeastern crossroads. For at least a century, student enrollment and alumni dispersion patterns followed these railroad lines. Nearly one hundred years later, when asked by a Philadelphia lawyer, "Where is Clemson?" a grinning Clemson undergraduate explained Clemson's 120-mile separation from Atlanta, Charlotte, and Augusta and then concluded, "Clemson's centrally isolated!"

At both Cherry's Crossing and Calhoun, mule-drawn wagons with African American drivers waited to load the new students' luggage to the new college. Steamer trunks, carpetbags, pillowcases, and makeshift clothes carriers filled the wagons. Members of the faculty met the new cadets, quickly formed them into small units, and began to march them toward the college as the luggage wagons rumbled along with them. From Calhoun the march was a bit under a mile and a half, but the road formed little more than a dirt track, and it ran uphill. The road from Cherry's Crossing was better defined, up and down, but it covered two miles.[1]

Local young students-to-be arrived in wagons at the college from their farming homes scattered across the rolling Piedmont. Their family wagons were joined by those of the simply curious who drove over to see the college opening from July 3 to July 6, 1893. Like many of the other inquisitive and hopeful, John Adger McCrary and his father had ridden over to witness the activities. He recalled,

> On the way home my father asked me if I would like to go to school at Clemson, and I remember his reply very characteristic of him, which was always quick and to the point. When my answer to his question was "yes," he said, "Get your clothes and things together and I'll take you up on Monday morning," and he did.[2]

J. T. Bowen had arrived on July 3, 1893, the very first day. He remembered,

> We were all up early the next morning for everyone seemed to be more or less excited....
>
> A number of faculty that afternoon [July 4] proceeded to Cherry's Crossing to meet the gang and pilot them over to the college. The members of this piloting committee, as I remember them were Professors Furman, Moncrief, Morrison, Chris Welsh and William [sic] Welsh. A crowd was gathered at the south entrance to the main building when the head of the column came in sight led by the above mentioned members of the faculty.

This line stretched from the Main Building south portal, above which was cast in terra cotta the word "Agriculture," all the way to the wood-frame infirmary. Waiting beneath the terra cotta plaque was the commandant, Lt. T. Q. Donaldson Jr., who had been detailed from the Seventh Cavalry by the U.S. secretary of war to serve at the new land-grant college in Clemson. Bowen continued, "Finally Lt. Donaldson took charge and the boys were herded into the barracks and room assignments were undertaken. Trunks were trammeled along the halls practically all night and there was very little sleeping."[3]

The new students ranged in age from their early twenties down to fourteen. While the trustees had set no maximum age, on March 4, 1891, they established the minimum age of fifteen, except if two brothers applied. Then, if one were fourteen and the other fifteen or older, both could be admitted. At the same time, Trustee James Orr's curriculum committee recommended, "The government shall be military and each student shall be required to purchase a prescribed uniform of cadet grey." In addition, for placement in the freshman class, the young man needed to demonstrate, through a test, proficiency in arithmetic, geography, and history of the United States, and "a fair knowledge of grammar." But just as the uniform guaranteed a sense of economic and social equality, the trustees did not intend to send inadequately prepared young men home to community shame. Therefore, they had directed that the faculty develop preparatory classes. Neither of these approaches was unusual. Other southern (and a few midwestern and mid-Atlantic) land-grant colleges had taken similar paths, indicating a genuine concern for personal feelings and family sensitivity.[4]

The next morning after breakfast, the young cadets, not yet in uniform, assembled in the chapel for introduction of the faculty, those trustees present, and Edwin Boone Craighead, Clemson's second president. Craighead had only just been selected president on June 21, 1893; however, he was traveling to Clemson barely sixty miles from Wofford College, where he held a professorship in classics.[5] Born in Missouri in 1861, Craighead spent his early years helping his widowed mother manage the family's small farm. In addition to the experience of farm work, he attended Central College, a small Methodist school in Missouri. His best subjects were English literature, Greek, and Latin. He pursued advanced studies at Vanderbilt and in Germany and France. His gift for languages paralleled, to some extent, that of Thomas Green Clemson's. Craighead had taught at Emory and Henry College in Virginia and then at Wofford College, so that until he came to Clemson, all the U.S.

Edwin Boone Craighead, the second president of Clemson College from 1893 to 1897. Clemson University Photographs, CUL.SC.

institutions in which he studied or taught were affiliated with the Methodist denomination. But, unlike Strode, he had no experience in any management. The noncompatibility of his academic field of study, given that he had studied classics, and his lack of a managerial record would mar his administration.[6]

The 442 students who comprised Clemson College's first class sat for an entrance examination designed to test each student's knowledge of algebra, literature, general science, and United States history. Copies of the entrance examinations survive in the university archives and show the test's rigor. The determination of most of the trustees and most of the faculty to maintain high academic standards would be a point of contention between the college and some members of the state government and the general public throughout Clemson's history. But Richard Wright Simpson, while planning and building the school, once declared,

"We are building in the forest a college, which one day will be the equal of any in the South, including Vanderbilt!"[7]

Just the vision of electrification was heady enough. Bowen remembered,

> The electrical lights were quite a novelty to most of the boys and there were several amusing incidents due to their unfamiliarity with electric lamps. I wonder if Johnny Simpson, now a prominent electric [sic] engineer, remembers the fact that he was sent with a basket to Prof. Tompkin's office for a supply of incandescent lamp wicks?[8]

Cadet Life

After the grading of the placement tests, 277 students were enrolled in the college, and 165 entered in the hastily cobbled together "fitting" school[9] (referred to formally as the "preparatory class") placed under the direction of William Shannon Morrison. No doubt Morrison's extensive experience with creating school systems in several large Upstate towns aided him. Two other faculty assisted him. The fitting school raised another issue with the general public.[10]

Cadet life was tightly organized. Reveille was sounded at 6:30 a.m., and the cadets had fifty minutes to clean their rooms, bathe (baths were required twice weekly), shave (a point of confusion among the younger cadets who had no reason to shave nor shaving gear), dress, and be in formation in time for their officers to march them to breakfast. The officers were selected from among the cadets who transferred from other colleges. Full roll call came at 8:10 a.m., with daily chapel at 8:15 a.m. It consisted of a morning prayer, Scripture reading, hymn, and announcements. The cadets attended classes from 8:30 a.m. until 12:30 p.m. Dinner, again by companies, was served family style at 1:00 p.m., with classes, laboratories, and practical work (forge, wood shop, or field work) followed by military drill. Retreat then followed a half hour for recreation. Supper, which was not as heavy a meal as dinner, followed. Usually at 6:30 p.m., the cadets were dismissed to their barracks rooms for study until 10:00 p.m. Taps sounded at 10:30 p.m., followed by "lights out." The last was easily enforced by having the main switch turned off at the power station.[11] Auxiliary lamps and lights (for that matter, any flame) were prohibited in the barracks.

Throughout the day, from breakfast until recreation, the cadet remained in his dress uniform. These were of 24-ounce West Point gray wool (both cut and color) with trim and cap. Brass buttons had "C.A.C." embossed on them, although button designs and uniform cut and style changed over the years. At recreation, however, the young men could slip out of the woolen garments into their denim fatigues (the trustees' minutes use the term "salem jeans," which identified the weight).[12]

For cadets in the regimental band, however, recreation time involved band and drill practice. The band students brought their instruments from home. The

The majority of the Class of 1896 in front of Hardin Hall. *Visions* Collection of Professor Alan Schaffer, CUL.SC.

trustees annually appropriated between $100 and $175 (2009 equivalent $2,448 to $4,284) for music for the band.[13] A band (or at least a drum and bugle corps) formed an essential communications group for any military unit, as did the color guard. The band and the flags conveyed orders for unit or troop movement. It was no surprise that USMA and the Norwich Academy, which Thomas Clemson attended when young, both had bands. However, the teaching of music was not part of the regular curriculum. The band operated as a separate company and was among the early intramural and sports teams and other extracurricular activities.[14]

Saturday morning was given to rigorous room inspection in which cadets removed bedclothes and took them to the laundry, and rolled the mattresses to the end of the iron bedstead. They cleaned and polished shoes and arranged them beneath the beds. One of the three roommates had been designated the orderly for the month. Ultimately, dust on the lintel of the door or on the top of the wardrobe, or a cloudy shaving mirror, or a dirty pitcher, washbasin, or footbath would be charged to him. Responsibility for the bed, springs, and all other matters fell to the assignee. In a ten-month term, each student in a three-person room served as the orderly for three nonconsecutive months. Even the supervisor of the barracks came from the older students. Students handled the laundry collection and delivery and the cleaning of the bathrooms at the west end of each floor.[15]

Saturday morning inspection in a typical room in the barracks of Clemson College. J. C. Littlejohn Collection, CUL.SC.

On the ground floor of the barracks was the mess hall, scoured daily by the kitchen staff. The kitchen at the west end remained clean, thanks to the African American kitchen staff. Procurement of food was the duty of P. H. E. Sloan, secretary-treasurer of the board, although Augustus Schilletter, a German immigrant and former baker, made the actual choices. Schilletter joined the staff in 1893 and held the position until 1919.[16]

Saturday after dinner at 1:00 p.m. was reserved for the meetings of the college's two literary groups, the Calhoun and Palmetto societies. By the second year, the Columbian Society had also been formed. These served as opportunities for students to improve their writing skills through set essays critiqued by other students. Members also gave speeches and regularly practiced debate. Each club had its own room in the Main Building, and during the first three years, each acquired its own parliamentary guide, a gavel, and black gowns for the society's officers. The officers changed each term, which allowed a large number of cadets to prepare for community leadership. Membership in the societies was by application and majority vote of older members. Students not in any of the literary societies convened at the same time each Saturday to write or declaim before faculty critics.[17] The students were forbidden to establish any Greek letter or secret societies at Clemson such as existed at many of the other schools in the area.[18] Later in the afternoon, the cadets had free time for recreation, which usually involved sports of one form or another.

Sunday mornings were for corporate worship in the Memorial Chapel. Visiting ministers from the available denominations preached (all came from the four main Protestant denominations). Cadets excused from this service had to remain quietly in their barracks rooms. The denominational surveys, printed in each year's *Record*, indicated the vast majority of the students came from Baptist, Methodist, Presbyterian, and Episcopalian families. Presbyterians distinguished Associate Reformed separately from the Presbyterians (U.S.). A few other denominations, including Lutherans, were noted among the students. The first Roman Catholic students received listing in 1895, and Jews, counted as Israelites, in 1896–1897.[19]

The cadets formed a student Christian association in the winter of 1894. Prof. T. P. Patterson, an English instructor, served as the faculty sponsor. Later in the year, F. S. Brockman, the state secretary of the Young Men's Christian Association, met with the group, and it formed into the YMCA. Over the first sixty years of the history of the student body, the "Y" took second place only to the cadet corps in its importance to and impact on Clemson's student body.[20]

Athletics

By the spring of 1896, pickup games of baseball had moved from occasional to intramural by companies. The competition was vigorous. The college formed a team, and the players prevailed on R. T. V. Bowman to serve as coach. Bowman taught forge and foundry, a skill required of all the students. Originally from Charlottesville, Virginia, he had studied at the Miller School and had also taken course work at the University of Virginia. The Miller School, created by the will of Samuel Miller, opened in 1878 as a boarding school for orphan boys (it became coeducational in 1884). The school taught the basics of reading, writing, and arithmetic, followed by the classics, agriculture, metalwork, and woodwork. The Miller School fielded its first baseball team in 1882, winning its first interschool match over Fishburne Military School 55–0.[21] Thomas Grayson Poats, another early Clemson faculty member who had been a member of the Miller team, served as Bowman's aide.[22]

That first Clemson baseball team had few more than ten or eleven players, and they played only two matches with Furman University, thirty-five miles away in Greenville. The first game was at Clemson and played on the relatively flat field to the northeast of the Main Building. The second was on the Furman campus. The Furman Purple Hurricanes won both games. (Natural phenomena were very popular team mascots at the end of the nineteenth century. Think of the Crimson Tide, the Green Wave, or the Golden Cyclones.) Clemson fielded no team in 1897. Bowman coached the 1898 season, which would be his last, to a two-win and four-loss season.[23] "Physically unable to take any considerable part in athletic games he helped by his counsel and presence whenever practicable," remembered then-President Henry Hartzog when he announced in chapel on Sunday, April 16, 1899, that Bowman had died two days earlier.[24]

The 1898 Clemson College baseball team, the earliest known and dateable photo of any of the college's baseball teams. Professor and Coach Randolph T. V. Bowman, the man for whom Bowman Field is named, is marked with the number 3. Photo taken from the June 1899 issue of *The Clemson College Chronicle*.

The 1896 session also saw the arrival of a young engineering instructor, Walter Merritt Riggs, who climbed down from a Southern Railroad northbound carriage at the Calhoun stop. "The depot," he recalled later, "was about the size of a French box-car, unlighted and uninhabited, and there was no halo of light where might lie sleeping the college [I] had to serve." He remembered that he walked the muddy red clay road for about a mile and a half uphill carrying his luggage to the college. "When I reached the campus," he continued, "I felt beneath the forest primeval. There were many trees and much underbrush, and miles and miles of bad roads, but only a few buildings."[25]

Riggs came to Clemson from Alabama Polytechnic Institute (API) at Auburn. Born in Orangeburg on January 24, 1873, of a Connecticut father and South Carolina mother, Riggs worked with his father on Saturdays and during the summers in the family's lumber mill and paint shop. He proved himself adept at building miniature machines based on the real ones in his father's shop. Riggs finished high school and in 1890 entered API.

An active student at API (now Auburn), he became a member of Phi Delta Theta Fraternity, was a champion orator, the captain and catcher for the baseball team, and left end on the football team. Although he had not joined any church, he was reared a Presbyterian and attended Fort Hill Presbyterian while at Clemson. He was a strong supporter of "muscular Christianity," a popular all-denominational movement that emphasized physical fitness and competition. Riggs graduated from API in 1893 and immediately became a postgraduate assistant in English literature during 1893–1894. The next year he served as an instructor in physics. During the summer of 1894, Riggs studied electrical physics and mechanics at Cornell. He arrived at Clemson from Auburn in the winter of 1896 as an instructor in electrical engineering.[26]

Given his great interest in student sports, Riggs might well have watched the Clemson-Furman baseball game the next April (also in 1896). In that spring, the students, Bowman, Riggs, and a few other faculty formed the Clemson Athletic Association and, through President Craighead, asked the trustees to designate some land for their use. The trustees took no action, except to direct the question to the president.

In the early autumn of 1896, the students formed a football team and asked Riggs to serve as the coach. He agreed. The question of the team's colors and mascot arose. The colors selected were red and blue, and the mascot was the Tiger. As the years progressed, many people said the Tiger mascot and the colors came with Riggs from Auburn. However, R. G. Hamilton, the captain of the first football team, remembered, "The mascot of the Tiger was first used by a student named Thompson, who claimed it was based on Princeton's mascot."[27] Red and blue colors did not come from Auburn, whose colors were orange and blue.

The 1896 Clemson College football team, the first squad fielded by the college in that sport. Professor and Coach Walter Merritt Riggs is the man in black at the center. Clemson University Photographs, CUL.SC.

Clemson's football Tigers defeated Wofford and Furman before falling 12–6 at the State Fair to the South Carolina College Jaguars, who sported garnet and black. All three games were played away from Clemson, as would be the games of 1897. Clemson played its first home football game in 1898, when it defeated Bingham Military School from North Carolina. The game was played, as with baseball, on the large parade ground (first called Bowman Field after R. T. V. Bowman's death in April 1899) near the Main Building. Besides baseball and football, it served until 1915 as the site of home track and field meets and some basketball games.[28]

New Trustees

During the years 1893–1897, the legislature elected two new trustees to replace those scheduled either to be reelected or replaced. This presented Governor (and life trustee) Benjamin Ryan Tillman an opportunity to strengthen his position on the board. The continuing legislative trustees were J. E. Tindal, J. H. Hardin, D. T. Redfearn, and E. T. Stackhouse. The legislature elected new trustees W. H. Mauldin and J. R. Jeffries.

William Henry Mauldin, son of the Rev. Mr. Benjamin Franklin and Adeline Hamilton Mauldin, was born on January 15, 1839, near Anderson. He attended the Wesley Leverette private school at old Calhoun, near Belton, and then the Williamston public schools. He married Lenora Connors of the Slab-town community, and the couple had two sons and three daughters. The family settled in the Hampton community in the new county carved out of the Orange-burg District. While serving in the S.C. Senate, he became a close colleague of B. R. Tillman. An active Baptist and a Mason, Mauldin was elected a legislative trustee on January 10, 1894, and served Clemson until his death on December 26, 1900.[29]

The legislature chose John Randolph Jeffries as its second new trustee. Born in the Elbethel community in Union County (now in Cherokee County), he was educated in public schools. He attended Furman University but did not gradu-ate. He had served in the Confederate army and attained the rank of captain. After the Civil War, he married Mary Henrietta Allen of Cedar Springs on No-vember 1, 1866. A large landholder and farmer, Jeffries involved himself in ag-ricultural improvement and public education and affairs. He served as a lecturer for the Farmers' Alliance and as a member of the S.C. House of Representatives, where he too had become a close friend of Tillman. Jeffries was elected trustee on the Clemson board on December 7, 1893. He served only two months; on his way home from the early February board meeting, he fell ill and died in a friend's home in Jonesville on February 10, 1894. He is buried in the Elbethel Baptist churchyard.[30]

With this legislative trustee election, Tillman strengthened his influence on the board somewhat, while practical farmers, whether in crops or in lumber, con-tinued to have the most influence. Both new trustees were born in the Upstate. Even with Tillman's increased influence, the genius of the makeup of the board allowed the college to grow steadily without the convulsive shifts in one or an-other direction.

But with the unexpected death of Jeffries, the legislature had another seat to fill. It selected W. H. Ellerbe, who had served as the S.C. comptroller in 1890 and who at the time of his selection as a legislative trustee was a member of the "Tillmanite" group. Born in Sellers (Marion County) on April 7, 1862, Ellerbe was educated by private tutors and then at the Pine Hill Academy. A Methodist, he attended Wofford College from 1880 to 1882 and then Vanderbilt, although bad health ended his enrollment there. After recovery, he married Henrietta Rog-ers on June 21, 1887, and they had one daughter and five sons. A merchant and farmer with an interest in horses, Ellerbe was elected governor in 1896 and again in 1898. He died on June 2, 1899.[31]

College Issues

In the summer of 1893, the trustees asked J. S. Newman to begin a search for a resident veterinary surgeon to serve at the experiment station, oversee its cattle and other livestock, and supervise the college's dairy herd that provided milk and butter for the mess halls. Because funds for these areas came from two different federal laws and from student fees, the finances had to be accounted for separately. Thus, the veterinary surgeon's position would have a "split appointment." Further, the veterinarian also taught in the second- and third-year agricultural curriculum.[32]

However, a number of trustees and others worried that the most prominent teaching part of the college was the Academic Department to the detriment, they feared, of the Agricultural Department and the Mechanical Department. In 1895, a trustees' committee composed of R. W. Simpson, M. L. Donaldson, and E. T. Stackhouse formed to address this concern and propose remedies if needed. Obviously, if this turned out to be the case—inasmuch as the trustees established and changed the curricula at will, hired the faculty, and set the salaries of individual faculty—the fault could lie only with the trustees themselves. And, indeed, in self-fulfillment, the committee report found the concern warranted. It noted that the Agricultural Department had no "full professors," the Mechanical Department had only one, but the Academic Department had three "full professors and two associates the latter paid $1500.00 each." But in arriving at its conclusion, the committee overlooked the particular assignment of M. B. Hardin full time to the fertilizer laboratory (drawing his salary from fertilizer tag sales), even though he shared (unequally) teaching with R. N. Brackett, the associate professor with less experience but the only holder of the doctorate. The trustees considered chemistry an agricultural subject. The other "full" professors were in mathematics, English, and physics in the Academic Department, and mechanics in the Engineering Department. At that point, W. S. Morrison, who held the "full" professorship in history, received assignment as headmaster of the "fitting school."

The trustee committee then recommended that the chair of physics be transferred from the Academic Department, his "chair" canceled, and his salary reduced. His teaching assignment would be changed from physics to electrical or mechanical engineering. The committee also recommended that the board ask the professor of mathematics, H. A. Strode, to resign. The same report also proposed that E. L. Litton, foreman of the wood shop, resign because his "education [was] lamentably deficient." Other instructors in the Mechanical Department—R. T. V. Bowman in forge and foundry, T. W. Wright in the machine shop, W. M. Yager in mechanical drawing, and Williams Welch in drawing—were told to spend their noninstructional time attending an advanced study school to improve their academic credentials.

The committee submitted its report on December 12, 1895, and by the following January 22, during the winter break, the board had taken action. Strode had submitted his resignation, and J. G. Clinkscales filled his professorship in mathematics. The board set the president's salary at $2,700, while Hardin, as professor of chemistry, received $2,500. Although the position was vacant at the time, the professor of agriculture's salary would be $2,000.[33]

This reordering resulted from a number of factors not necessarily related to the committee "preamble" noted above. The trustees' ire seems to have been focused on Strode and Christopher Welch. The Strode problem likely involved his growing lethargy and loss of interest in his work. The committee's concluding comments urged the board to "retain only those professors who manifest by their acts a genuine love for their work and a hearty interest in all their pupils...."[34]

Nor was there any obvious reason for Welch's dismissal, but given the remainder of the board's decisions that day, his poor teaching may have been the cause. Welch resigned, replaced by Riggs.[35]

Even though the trustees had strong feelings about the direction the college should take, they were anxious to hear, in a systematic fashion, from the people. In their bylaws, they created a Board of Visitors, an independent body that would report to the trustees. The trustees selected the members of the board, composed of one citizen from each of South Carolina's congressional districts. Each member served a two-year term. The board visited the campus to observe the "working condition" of the college and suggest improvements.[36]

Adversity

Of course, occasional unexpected troubles arose. The first for Clemson was the death of H. A. Powers, an orphan cadet from Georgetown who died of measles. Brackett arranged Powers's funeral, and the college paid for it, according to a decision by the board in January 1894.[37]

A second unexpected misfortune happened during the night of May 22, 1894. Fire began on the third floor of the Main Building. Fueled by the alcohol used as a preservative for zoological specimens, the fire spread rapidly through the building. Students, faculty, staff, and convicts fought the blaze. Firemen from several nearby communities joined them, but in spite of all, the interior of this classroom, museum, and library building was lost. Destroyed were almost all of John C. Calhoun's books, particularly his annotated volumes on law. Fortunately, his personal papers had remained at the Calhoun office behind Fort Hill house. The trustees had hired his nephew, John F. Calhoun, to arrange the papers in chronological order. Mr. Clemson's papers also were not there. Richard Wright Simpson, as Mr. Clemson's executor, had not yet placed them at the college. However, the Main Building held Mr. Clemson's entire library, and those books were lost.[38]

Within two days, eight trustees had gathered at Clemson. The Main Building was vastly underinsured (insured for $20,000, it cost nearly $50,000 to clean and rebuild). To rebuild would require the trustees to borrow $15,000 on their

Main Building aflame on May 22, 1894. Note the students, evacuated from the barracks that sat adjacent to Main, watching the terrifying spectacle with their worldly possessions gathered around them. Clemson University Photographs, CUL.SC.

The shell of Main Building after the fire. Clemson University Photographs, CUL. SC.

personal signatures. Simpson arrived on the morning of May 26, and he took charge of the board's meeting (raising the number of trustees present to the nine required for monetary business). The four principal buildings, along with the farm buildings, twenty faculty homes (eight brick and twelve wood), servants' quarters, barns, the infirmary, and the college-owned furnishings and equipment were insured for $97,550 (2009 equivalent $2,386,782). Mr. Clemson's oil paintings were covered for $800 (2009 equivalent $19,584), and Fort Hill house for $1,000 (2009 equivalent $24,480). The Main Building would not be insured until rebuilt.

The board ordered the installation of hydrants, the purchase of more fire hoses, the organization of a volunteer fire brigade, and the installation of a sprinkler system. The firm of Bruce and Morgan had already sent a superintendent at Simpson's request to oversee the rebuilding. And ads were placed in the Charleston *News and Courier*, the Columbia *Record*, and the *Greenville News* for bids for the rebuilding.[39]

Opportunity

But even in the midst of those difficulties, the opportunity to acquire land loomed large in the minds of some of the trustees. The general assembly was also interested, particularly in the land at Fort Hill that had come into the possession of Floride Isabella Lee, Mr. Clemson's granddaughter. Partitioned to her upon the 1871 death of her mother, Floride Elizabeth Clemson Lee, the plot cut two triangles on the north side of Fort Hill with their apexes touching at the point where the trail from Calhoun reached the Greenville-Central-Seneca road. The Lees had offered the 288 acres for $12,000 (2009 equivalent $293,760), but on April 19, 1893, the trustees turned down the offer.[40] They then made a counter-offer of $10,000, appropriated by the general assembly in 1894. Miss Lee and her advisors agreed to be paid in five annual installments as the general assembly proposed.[41] The resulting extra river frontage and the experience of the spring floods along the Seneca River persuaded the trustees to build a dike along the east bank of the river.[42]

The trustees now held municipal authority for the college that extended to approximately 1,100 acres (not including the jurisdiction of a five-mile radius from the Main Building tower). They appointed Joseph B. Watson as policeman for the college and J. N. Hook, the secretary of the agricultural experiment station, as trial justice.[43]

Resulting from the fire, a wood-frame hotel was built on the hill to the east of the Main Building. Classes met there until the reconstruction of Main. The other place used for classes (but only early in the day) was the schoolhouse that had been built on the campus for the children of the small community.[44]

A General Attack

At least one more challenge confronted the new college before Craighead's presidency had run its course. Enrollment was quite erratic, in part because of the rigid military discipline, in part because of the difficulty of academic standards, and, by the second year, in part because of the culture of hazing that first appeared in the autumn of 1894. At the time, some of the college students presented a petition to the trustees asking that they replace Craighead as president. The students stated that he was frequently absent from the college and that when he was in his office he was too busy to visit with them. Craighead met with them, but the parties reached no resolution. Although the enrollment in late July 1894 began with 635 cadets, by August 3, 1894, 190 cadets and preparatory students had withdrawn.[45]

The student displeasure continued to fester so that by the winter of 1897, total enrollment had shrunk to only 330 students.[46] George Tillman, the brother of life trustee and then-U.S. Senator Benjamin Tillman, launched a series of attacks. He argued that the school paid too much attention to English and not enough to agriculture and engineering, which seemed to echo the trustee committee's statement of a year earlier. There was a difference, however. The former Simpson committee had worried that, given the acute shortage of revenue, the salary scale reflected an imbalance in the faculty ranks. George Tillman argued that too much of the teaching time focused on the "academic" subjects. His brother, the senator, replied that Clemson graduates needed preparation to lead the people of their communities and to contend in writing and speaking with the best in the state. George Tillman also claimed that the military studies and drilling distracted from agriculture and engineering. In that, he had a point. Even though military strategy and tactics was a third subject requirement of the Morrill Land Grant Act of 1862, the idea that the college should operate as an all-male military college seems to have come from the trustees, from local culture, and from the other southern land-grant institutions.[47]

Agricultural Experimentation

George Tillman also made a valid point with his criticism that Clemson's agriculture benefited the state only through its graduates because all the experimentation remained confined to the Fort Hill campus. The initial trustee decision to centralize agricultural experimentation made sense in 1890–1891, when all attention and all revenue were needed simply to get an experimental farm and the college founded and operating. The decision to make the college president the director of the agricultural experiment station worked only because Strode had a strong background in chemistry. That did not carry over to Craighead, whose academic field and interests lay in languages and English. Further, Craighead and Newman clashed over a number of issues, especially over the management of the two farms (that is, the farm that helped supply food to the students and the experimental farm).

Newman had also ignored, in part, a board directive to build an extra reservoir for the college water supply. Instead, and without notifying the trustees or explaining his reasons (to provide water pressure enough to reach the top floor of the barracks for daily use and in case of fire), Newman built a standpipe. So irritated were the trustees that they asked him to resign on November 30, 1893.[48] Newman responded but received no immediate rejoinder. When the board met in Clemson on January 10, 1894, Newman wrote and requested an audience. It was granted, and he spoke. The trustee minutes record nothing of his statement, but he resigned that day.

To move the experiment station work forward, the trustees established a Board of Control for the Experiment Station. D. K. Norris served as the chair and two other trustees, M. L. Donaldson and R. E. Bowen, as members. All three life members were from the region and could travel to the campus relatively quickly. Also the Fertilizer Control Board was part of the agricultural experiment station. Its membership included trustees J. E. Tindal, J. E. Wannamaker, and B. R. Tillman.[49]

By March 18, 1896, the Clemson board concluded that the experiment station needed to expand its outreach in the state. Rather than the occasional printed bulletins for distribution to farmers that had marked the first years, the trustees now directed the agriculture and horticulture departments to issue no fewer than six bulletins each year and to send no less than 30,000 copies of each to farmers.[50] At the same time, the station, now awaiting a new vice director, planned a farmers' institute in each of the state's six congressional districts. The first institutes were held in Orangeburg, Darlington, Manning, Fairview, Walhalla, and Anderson. Professors William L. McGee of agriculture and Mark Hardin of chemistry attended along with President Craighead.[51] Even though no member of the board (other than B. R. Tillman) chose to answer George Tillman's charges, he had obviously goaded the board into activity.

While much of a positive nature happened at Clemson, signs of unrest still centered around the leadership of Craighead. The lines of communication among the students, the president of the college, and the board remained tightly intertwined. The disciplinary relationship between the college president and the students was the irritant. The board promoted the idea that individual students had the freedom to appeal the president's decision to the full board. Of course, the board did not meet continuously, and the created "lag time" between its meetings allowed even minor problems to fester. Articles published in the Columbia *State* reporting unhappiness magnified each complaint.[52] Six students replied to the paper's reports, noting that no student would admit to providing negative information to the *State*. One faculty member admitted to making "damaging statements." The six students wrote the *State*, challenging the reporter to name his sources or "stand branded by faculty and students as a liar and a slanderer." One of the six students, W. W. (Wee Willie) Klugh, eventually married one of Richard Wright Simpson's daughters and joined the Clemson faculty, while a second, L. A. Sease, became a trustee (1901–1908). As expected, the reporter refused to name sources.[53] This was, by no means, the last time the *State* and Clemson College would cross swords (or pens).

To investigate the rumors of unrest, the trustees appointed a committee composed of Tillman, Simpson, and Donaldson. Tillman said that the Mechanical Department had not yet evolved into what the trustees envisioned.[54] He insisted that the problem lay not with the existing faculty. He pointed out that some of the difficulty resulted from the college not having a large enough teaching staff to cover all the subjects adequately.[55] By September 9, the committee reported, "No facts had been found which would warrant the charges of misadministration and incompetence made by the *State* reporter."[56]

The Columbia *Register* suggested a coverup and quoted from Gilbert and Sullivan,

> I am right, and you are right
> And all is right as right can be.

The *State* agreed.[57] In the aftermath, a faculty member, Williams Welch, who admitted to anonymous public complaining, obeyed the board directive and resigned.[58]

Welch was not the only employment change in the spring of 1896. *The Peoples' Journal* reported on Thursday, May 21, that Peter Lindsay, a local person and not an employee of the college, shot W. D. James, foreman of the Clemson farms, on May 12. James died on the thirteenth, and Lindsay went to jail.[59] J. P. Lewis filled James's position.[60]

During the spring of 1897, Craighead submitted his resignation, given, he wrote, to accept an offer to serve as president of his alma mater.[61] He also served later as president of Missouri State Normal College, Tulane University, and the University of Montana.

George Tillman had been named chairman of the Board of Visitors, which did not blunt his attacks on the college. Shortly before the graduation in December 1896, he visited the campus and wrote a series of articles for the *State*. It was, he thought, beyond the means of the state to have a first-class polytechnic institution. His criticism has had supporters throughout the history of the school.[62]

The First Class Finishes

Although C. C. Newman, who had transferred from Alabama Polytechnic Institute, finished his class work earlier, the first graduation, which was of the students who had transferred in 1893, was set for December 1896. Planning began on August 5, 1896, when a trustee committee composed of Tindal, Donaldson, and Ellerbe conferred with the faculty on the appropriate processes for awarding the degrees and the ceremony. They also heard from the candidates about the festivities. In addition to the ceremonies, the seniors wanted a banquet, reception, and dance, all to be held in the Main Building. The trustees approved everything except the dance. Not to be quickly turned aside, the seniors proposed a "hop" in some other location. The trustees relented.[63]

The events began with a baccalaureate chapel service Sunday afternoon, December 13, 1896, with a sermon delivered by the chancellor of the University of Georgia, W. E. Boggs. All cadets, except the freshmen, attended as did the faculty, trustees, and guests. The guests were quartered in the barracks in space vacated by the freshmen, who had been sent home. Monday began with a military review and the awarding of honors. In the afternoon, athletic competitions preceded a glee club concert. Public speaking filled Tuesday morning. Wednesday, graduation was held in the chapel. Fourteen of the thirty-seven graduates addressed the audience on their senior theses, while the remaining twenty-three submitted their papers. They received their diplomas, signed by the professors, president, and trustees.

After the graduation ceremony, the graduates met and formed the Clemson Alumni Association. They elected T. H. Tuten of Hampton, who had graduated in engineering, as the president of the alumni and W. W. Klugh from Abbeville as secretary. Fortunately, Klugh was one of a number of seniors who remained at Clemson on the faculty, which aided in the survival of the alumni association minutes.[64] Besides Klugh, Rudolph Lee (engineering) and L. A. Werts (agriculture) stayed at Clemson as tutors. C. M. Furman Jr., son of the English professor, served as Clemson's librarian, while J. M. Blaine and J. T. Bowen remained as postgraduates. Ten other graduates became teachers, four farmers, three merchants, five engineers, two lawyers, one a chemist, and two enrolled in medical school.[65]

After the graduation, the mess hall was made ready for the hop. Years later, Frank Breazeale, one of the graduates, remembered the day well:

> On that memorable day…our class divided up—the sheep and the goats. The "ladies men," or the "sheep" decided to throw a dance, while we goats, who did not have any girl friends, thought we would have a feed. The goats were in the majority. The faculty, many young people from Anderson, Greenville and Sen-

A composite of the Class of 1896, Clemson College's first graduating class. *Top row, left to right:* E. P. Earle Jr., P. G. Langley Jr., W. W. Klugh Jr., T. H. Tuten, P. N. Calhoun, B. R. Tillman Jr., J. F. Breazeale, T. W. Cothran, L. A. Sease. *Second row, left to right:* A. J. Tindal, J. G. Simpson, P. H. Gooding, A. M. Chreitzberg, F. L. Bryant, G. P. Boulware, B. F. Sloan, J. T. Bowen, L. A. Werts. *Third row, left to right:* G. W. Hart, F. G. Tompkins, G. Dowling, J. B. Blain, T. S. Moorman Jr., R. G. Hamilton, J. H. Moore, B. F. Robertson, W. W. Wardlaw. *Bottom row, left to right:* J. F. Folk, J. E. Hunter, O. M. Pegues, L. M. Mauldin, W. H. Carpenter, R. E. Lee, B. M. Aull, J. T. Bradley, C. M. Furman Jr., B. R. Turnipseed. *Visions* Collection of Professor Alan Schaffer, CULSC.

eca, and members of the lower classes, went to the dance, but we boys had only one guest at the banquet—good old Doctor Sloan.

He then remembered some who went to the dance: "Will Klugh went and took 'Miss Simpson,' she was R. W. Simpson's daughter. He married her afterwards, and out-married himself when he got her." Breazeale must have chuckled as he recalled,

> Joe Wertz went, but he had to stag it. Joe was awfully bad about trying to put his arms around every girl who would let him. I don't know what happened, but it was a little dark in the hall, and in about two minutes they reappeared, the girl looking very indignant, and Joe looking much the worst for wear.

In a few moments, Breazeale remembered the banquet:

> Lawrence Sease and I were on the committee to get the refreshments. We went to Greenville for a tub of oysters, and we bought Worcestershire sauce, pickles, and jams and other things at Sloan's store. Shorty (Schilletter) furnished the vegetables and coffee, and we bought a jug of wine from somewhere. Doctor Sloan sat at the head of the table and we pulled Schilletter in by the apron strings.[66]

Although the school year had one more term, the college was a success—at least for Tillman, Norris, and Simpson, and probably for the faculty, parents, and other trustees. But they planned no graduation for 1897. While the school year was a success, the experimental calendar, which ran the school year from late February to early December, was not. Clemson would move to the traditional calendar, starting the year in late summer with vacations in June, July, and August. For this transition to succeed, however, the college held its next graduation February 6–9, 1898.[67]

Notes

1. CUL.SC.CUA. S 3 b 1 f 8.
2. CUL.SC.MSS 68 f 69.
3. Columbia *State*, July 13, 1893.
4. CUL.SC.CUA. S30 v 1, 37–39. On the sectional differences among the land-grant colleges, see Andrew, *Long Gray Lines*.
5. CUL.SC.CUA. S 30 v 1, 93.
6. Idol, "The Controversial Humanities Professor: Edwin Boone Craighead, 1893–1897," in *Tradition*, 34–51. I am thankful for Idol's thoughtful analysis.
7. CUL.SC.MSS 96.
8. Columbia *State*, July 13, 1893.
9. CUL.SC.CUA. S 30 v 1, 93.
10. Idol, "The Controversial Humanities Professor: Edwin Boone Craighead, 1893–1897," in *Tradition*, 48.
11. CUL.SC.CUA. S 30 v 1, 82.

12. Ibid., 80.
13. Ibid., 164.
14. *Chronicle*, vol. 1, no. 8, 44–45.
15. CUL.SC.CUA. S 30 v 1, 83; and CUL.SC.MSS 304 Cassette 3, Dr. Barnwell Rhett Turnipseed to J. C. Littlejohn.
16. CUL.SC.MSS 68 f 23.
17. CUL.SC.CUA. S 30 v 1, 101.
18. Ibid., 93.
19. *Record*, 1893–1894, n.p.; 1895–1896, 6–7; and 1896–1897, 7.
20. CUL.SC.MSS 68 f 189; and Anderson *Daily Mail*, April 24, 1944.
21. Http://www.millerschool.org. This material was located and prepared by Paul Alexander Crunkleton, my graduate research assistant, 2009–2010.
22. Webster P. Sullivan Jr., Clemson 1965, furnished me photographs online of the Miller School baseball team, in which his ancestor, Bowman, and Poats are clearly identified.
23. Bourret, *Clemson Baseball 2009*, 176. The word "campus" is Latin for "field." Its attachment to college or university land is an American early nineteenth century development at the College of New Jersey, now Princeton.
24. CUL.SC.CUA. S 25 ff 9 and 15.
25. Ibid., S 17 f 370.
26. Hemphill, *Men of Mark*, vol. 4, 301–303.
27. Anderson *Independent*, March 6, 1934. The account credited Maj. William T. Brock, who died that year, with the mascot and association. Entering in 1894, he played football on the teams and was quarterback in 1897. Capt. Hamilton concurred and noted that the mascot was borrowed from Princeton, noting Princeton's national football prominence, having finished 11–0 in 1893, 8–2 in 1894, and 10–1–1 in 1895. Princeton also had five of the consensus All-Americans in 1893, two in 1894, and two in 1895. However, southern schools found the Tiger a popular mascot. The University of the South, Missouri, and Louisiana State University were and are the Tigers. LSU may have the oldest claim, traced to the Louisiana regiments who, in the Mexican War (1849–1850), fought in striped Zouave uniforms earning them the name Bengal Tigers. Alabama Polytechnic Institute (Auburn), now frequently called the Tigers, was usually called War Eagles after one faculty member's pet eagle. The school still maintains an eagle, and Auburn's school song begins,
    War eagle fly down the field,
    Ever to conquer, never to yield.
    However, Auburn's earliest "official" printed reference to the Tiger is a cheer in the 1898 edition of *Glomorata*, 119,
    Tiger 'rah! Tiger 'rah!
    Tiger, Tiger, 'Rah! 'rah! 'rah!
    'Rah! 'Rah! 'rah, Heisman!
28. Bourret, *Baseball 2009*, 168; Bourret, *Football 2009*, 202; Bourret, *Track and Field 2004–05*; and Bourret, *Basketball 2009–2010*, 198.
29. CUL.SC.CUA. S 30 ss 1 f "Mauldin."
30. Ibid., f "Jeffries."
31. Ibid., f "Ellerbe."
32. Ibid., v 1, 84; 90–91.
33. Ibid., 154–158.
34. Ibid., 156.
35. *Record*, 1893–1894, n.p.; and 1895–1896, 6–7.
36. CUL.SC.CUA. S 30 v 1, 111.
37. Ibid., 103; and Craighead, "President's Report," November 1, 1893, in *Clemson Trustees' Report to the General Assembly*, 1893, 13.
38. CUL.SC.CUA. S 30 v 1, 102. Besides the loss of Mr. Clemson's books, which represented a collection of the library of a nineteenth century American gentry man, were the law books of John C. Calhoun. Fortunately, the papers were not there.
39. Ibid., 119–121.
40. Ibid., 87.

41. Ibid., 103, 116.
42. Ibid., 117.
43. Ibid., 136. Incorporation of the government of Clemson Agricultural College would be completed January 22, 1895.
44. Ibid., 120. On the school, see ibid., 95.
45. Columbia *State*, August 4, 1894.
46. *Record*, 1896–1897.
47. Andrew, *Long Gray Lines*, 40. Andrew has dated the establishment of the military regimen at each of the southern land-grant colleges. See also McCandless, *The Past in the Present*. On 82, McCandless noted that, as early as 1871, the act establishing the Arkansas Industrial University was to be opened to all qualified youth "without regard to race, sex, or sect." At the school's opening in January 1872, one woman was among the seven students who matriculated there. Alabama Polytechnic opened to women in 1892. And the University of Tennessee opened to women in 1893. Although not a land-grant foundation, South Carolina College (now USC) admitted thirteen women in 1895. (See McCandless, 86–88.) The George Tillman citations are from the Columbia *State*, August 21, 22, and 23, 1896.
48. Idol, "The Controversial Humanities Professor: Edwin Boone Craighead, 1893–1897," in *Tradition*, 38.
49. *Record*, 1894–1895, 9.
50. CUL.SC.CUA. S 30 v 1, 162.
51. Ibid.
52. Ibid., S 37 f "Faculty 1890–1908."
53. Ibid.
54. Ibid., S 30 v 1, 168.
55. Ibid., 166.
56. Ibid., 159.
57. Columbia *State*, September 21, 1896.
58. CUL.SC.CUA. S 30 v 1, 151.
59. Pickens, *People's Journal*, May 21, 1896.
60. Ibid., July 6, 1896.
61. CUL.SC.CUA. S 30.
62. Columbia *State*, January 7, 1897.
63. CUL.SC.CUA. S 30 v 1, 166, 168.
64. *Record*, 1897–1898, 92.
65. Ibid, 87.
66. CUL.SC.MSS 68 f 69.
67. *Record*, 1897–1898, 88.

The 1897 football team, dubbed "state champions" for that season, posed with Coach
Walter Merritt Riggs (at center with the boutonnière on his lapel), a man identified only
as Coach Williams to Riggs's left, and chief referee and Coach Randolph T. V. Bowman
on the back row at the extreme left. Observe the nose guard suspended around some
players' necks. Also note the "tiger" striped hose on at least six players and the heavier skin-
protecting leggings on one and one-half players. A keen eye will observe the melon-shaped
football being cradled. Clemson University Photographs, CUL.SC.

CHAPTER VI

First Walkout

1897–1902

The 1897 school year opened in the autumn with a new September-to-June school calendar in effect, which the trustees had adopted in the early winter of 1897. A total of 449 students—some fitting school students, a few special students, twelve in the two-year agriculture program, and twenty-one postgraduates—made up the student body. Most were from South Carolina, but six came from North Carolina, five from Georgia, and one each from Tennessee, Florida, and the District of Columbia. Clemson's first foreign student, E. Ferreta, had arrived from Rome, Italy, a year earlier, so almost from its opening, Clemson had students from other cultures. This was the second largest class in the school's five years, surpassed only by the 635 who entered the second year.[1]

The Faculty

The trustees had not yet selected Clemson's third president, so Mark Hardin, the head of chemistry and the acting president for five weeks, greeted the students. The trustees returned on September 15, 1897, and the next day elected Henry Simms Hartzog as Clemson's new president, freeing Hardin to return to his chemistry laboratory.[2] Born in 1866, Hartzog was only thirty-one years of age. The son of a prosperous farmer in Bamberg, he studied in local schools before he won the county scholarship to the South Carolina Military Academy (the Citadel), where he studied mathematics and civil engineering. No doubt the trustees were delighted to have selected a South Carolinian with an agricultural background and solid technological training. After his graduation, Hartzog taught in public schools, served as principal of Allendale High School, and then on the urging of the young lady he was court-

Henry Simms Hartzog, the third president of Clemson College from 1897 to 1902. Clemson University Photographs, CUL.SC.

ing, he enrolled in Southern Baptist Seminary (Louisville, Kentucky). He received the bachelor of divinity degree in 1889, and in 1891, he married Cornelia Harley with whom he had six sons. For the Clemson trustees, Hartzog's connections with the state's public schools, particularly the secondary schools, was a bonus.[3] Both B. R. Tillman and M. L. Donaldson, who approved of his agricultural, engineering, and military background, backed Hartzog's selection for the presidency.

Other new faculty joining the Clemson contingent in 1897 included J. S. Newman, who had been Clemson's first agriculture professor in 1891. While his return emphasized the break in agricultural programming during the Craighead administration, it actually resulted from the death of William L. McGee. McGee had been elevated to the rank of professor of agriculture in February 1896 at age thirty-six. Eight months later, while demonstrating a new corn husking and shucking machine to the agriculture seniors, he was caught in the machinery and so badly injured that he died four hours later.[4] The next year at Hartzog's request, Bowman carved a memorial tablet in McGee's memory and a second tablet remembering Strode. These marble pieces were placed in the Memorial Chapel. Perhaps this placement is the answer to the earlier question asking for whom or to what this memorial is dedicated.[5]

With the forced resignation of the physics instructor and the movement of its teaching into the engineering program, Capt. Ezra B. Fuller (USMA), professor of military science, began teaching physics. The trustees were ecstatic. Because the Department of War paid much of his salary and covered his housing, Fuller's pay from the college amounted to much less than a full stipend. By surviving accounts, Fuller was an excellent physics teacher. An assistant professor, P. T. Brodie, a mathematician who had earlier served as principal of Lexington's high school, joined Fuller in the strengthened engineering program. Brodie's undergraduate education had been at Furman University, and he had done advanced work at the University of Virginia.

J. G. Clinkscales taught mathematics. Like W. S. Morrison, he was an alumnus of Wofford College. Four young men served as tutors or assistant instructors: Gus Shanklin, a graduate of the South Carolina Military Academy, in mathematics; Rudolph Lee, the assistant instructor in drawing; and Williston Klugh and LeRoy Werts, both general tutors. Lee, Klugh, and Werts all had graduated from Clemson in December 1896. Werts stayed a very short period, but Klugh and Lee both spent the greater part of their professional careers at Clemson.

During Hartzog's administration, the number of faculty with advanced degrees increased. By Hartzog's last year, the college's thirty-six faculty (including the president) held the following degrees: Twenty had finished their schooling with a single baccalaureate, five held two or more baccalaureates, six held master's degrees, and four had doctorates (one medic who taught hygiene, one veterinarian teaching veterinary medicine, and two doctorates of philosophy). Richard

Brackett's PhD was in chemistry, and A. P. Anderson held his in entomology from the University of Munich. In this regard, Clemson's faculty began moving away from intellectual insularity.

Another view of the changing faculty is to look at the locale of the final institution from which a faculty member graduated before coming to Clemson to teach. One studied in Europe and thirty-two in the United States, of which nine were not from the South. Seventeen were from South Carolina, including seven who were Clemson alumni. The faculty, therefore, remained heavily provincial. The roster of the South Carolina-educated men formed the teaching backbone of the school for decades.[6]

The Trustees

The trustees remained too close to the college and too quick to involve themselves personally and individually in the workings of the school. Occasionally, a trustee's position bordered on the presumptuous. For example, Senator Tillman, when prevented from attending a trustees' meeting by governmental obligation, telegraphed Board President Simpson that because he was unable to be present, he would send the governor in his place. The other trustees, prior to the arrival of the proxy, drafted a reply informing Tillman that he did not hold his position ex officio, but rather in his person, for which absence no proxy privilege existed. When the governor arrived at the meeting, he was welcomed as a guest and cordially asked to address the others. After his impromptu speech, which the board applauded and Simpson commented on, the governor was thanked and excused.[7]

The brief slump in school popularity turned around when the school year opened. In part, however, that resulted from the planned calendar transition. Nonetheless, the trustees worried about overcrowding in the barracks, as the college had to resort to three-man rooms again. The trustees had received a report from the State Board of Health calling attention to a statement from "eminent physicians in neighboring counties," which claimed that the college dairy was the locus of a fever the Board of Health had pronounced as malarial. Part of the problem, the health board members suggested, was that the dairy barn sat on a filled-in pond into which fouled water from the toilets was leaching.

The trustees had been worried about student health, particularly during the summer, and had rearranged the calendar to avoid those pestilential months, partially on the advice of Dr. Redfern, the campus physician. Further, the board had asked Dr. Redfern to give the buildings and grounds a thorough inspection. His full report contained several recommendations. The first urged a major enlargement and retiling of the drain fields below the campus. The second suggested making improvements to the drainage, heating, and ventilation of the barracks. Part of the problem was the dumping of the slop bowls out of the barracks windows;

the implication was that these contained more than washing and shaving water. Upon hearing the report, the trustees directed Redfern, P. H. E. Sloan, himself an MD, and Hartzog, the new president of the college and a civil engineer, to carry out the reforms. Even while the trustees made the decision, they knew the cost would come from the fertilizer money, setting the date for construction of a second barracks further in the future.[8]

Although he had begun his trustee service in 1895 when he served as comptroller general of South Carolina, William Haselden Ellerbe of Marion County had been elected governor in 1896. A farmer and a merchant, he had been a member of the Farmers' Alliance, but his membership was suspended because of his mercantile interests. Although part of the Tillman political cadre, Ellerbe did not receive Tillman's endorsement for governor in 1894. His second term as governor ended prematurely with his death on June 2, 1899. Although more moderate and open than Tillman toward townsfolk, he was a rigid racial segregationist.[9] His concern for cadet health led him to insist that the surgeon general of the U.S. Marine Hospital Service send an experienced sanitation engineer to inspect Clemson's water and sewage system. That was done, and the recommendations carefully followed.[10]

Textiles Added

In 1900, the general assembly elected Augustine T. Smythe of Charleston to serve as a Clemson trustee. Although Smythe was the first truly urban figure on the board, the latter could hardly have had a more acceptable person. His role in defending the will against the challenge of Gideon Lee, Mr. Clemson's son-in-law, had persuaded the Tillmanites to consider him an ally. Further, his involvement in the growing cotton mill industry won much favor in the Sandhills and the Upstate.

No industry was more acceptable to the white people of the Upstate than textiles. Prof. Stonewall Tompkins (mechanics and engineering), on the request of Trustee D. K. Norris, attended the board meeting on July 7, 1897, to make an "exhaustive argument on textile education."[11] At the September 15 meeting, a committee was charged to report on the advisability of the college entering into textile education and to report on the cost of constructing and equipping a textile building. Norris served as chair, and the three-man team received $300 for its expenses.[12] The committee reported on March 2, 1898, that it favored establishing a textile program. On the same day, the board approved moving forward with construction of a building for it, although to get the ninth vote, a full poultry program also received support because it was the dream of Trustee Donaldson.[13] At about the same time, Georgia Institute of Technology's (Georgia Tech) president, Lyman Hall, planned to create a similar program. The first to open would be the

Textiles Building as it appeared shortly after its construction. Notice that the right half of the building appears to be "missing," due to the fact that it was originally a one-wing building. *Note*: the upper left-hand corner of this picture was torn off, so it has been digitally repaired, accounting for the cloudiness there. The glare from the building's windows could not be removed to enhance the quality of the photo, however. Clemson University Photographs, CUL.SC.

Textiles Building after the completion of its second wing in 1901, the look it retains to this day as Godfrey Hall. Clemson University Photographs, CUL.SC.

first in the South.[14] Clemson had the advantage of the fertilizer tag sales revenue for building, equipping, and staffing. Further, the trustees did not have to seek outside approval. Therefore, when the trustees made the decision to establish the program, a contract could be signed with J. D. Elliott, an Upstate builder experienced in the construction of textile mills. Norris, who had built two successful textile mills, agreed to supervise the construction. Modeled after a typical textile mill, the two-story structure with walk-in ground floor was planned and built in two sections, the south wing and water tower first, and then, after the program began, the north wing.[15]

The first textile students began their textile studies as juniors in the summer of 1898, having moved from the engineering program. The curriculum, designed by Norris and William H. Boehm, the professor of mechanical and electrical engineering, enabled students to spend the first two years in engineering (later termed "mechanical engineering") before moving into textiles with its heavier chemical emphasis. Boehm had received his bachelor's degree from Rose Polytechnic Institute and his master's in mechanical engineering from Cornell University. The first textile faculty member, J. H. M. Beatty, had an undergraduate degree from South Carolina College and experience in the textile industry. He was joined by F. D. Frissell, a specialist in dyeing and weaving who had studied at the Philadelphia Textile Institute.[16] Hartzog announced with no little pride in September 1898, "Today the doors of the first textile school in the South are thrown open to students."[17]

Needless to say, the Clemson announcement surprised Lyman Hall, the Georgia Tech president. He wrote Hartzog asking how the program opened so quickly. Hartzog's reply of October 8, 1898, was a model of barely concealed pride.[18] During the spring, Georgia Tech announced its program; it opened with fifty-eight students and four faculty.[19] The next year, the president of the Mississippi Agricultural College opened its textile building, which still remains on the campus.[20] However, by 1911, the Mississippi program had closed.[21]

On December 26, 1900, William Harrison Mauldin, a legislative trustee since January 10, 1894, died. When the general assembly convened in 1901, it selected Lawrence Andrew Sease as the replacement. Born in Lexington County in 1868 to J. R. N. and Frances Hook Sease, he received a strong education beginning in the Sease community rural school. Afterward, Sease studied engineering at Clemson and was a member of the first graduating class. From Clemson, he attended UVA for graduate work in English literature, after which he studied at Cornell. A devout Lutheran, he married Frances Leonora Hunter of Prosperity, where he taught until 1908. Sease was the first Clemson graduate to serve as a trustee upon his election on March 1, 1901.[22]

Also Sease had become a close friend of Clemson English professor David Wistar Daniel, born in Mount Gallagher in 1867. Daniel did his undergraduate work at Wofford College, where he belonged to Sigma Alpha Epsilon fraternity.

After Wofford, he attended Vanderbilt and received an MA in English. He spent time as a public schoolteacher, and he also studied at the University of Chicago. At the time he joined the Clemson faculty in 1898, he was serving as the principal of the Central (South Carolina) High School. His first Clemson duties involved teaching in the preparatory school. In his many years at Clemson, Daniel had a marked influence on the cadets.[23]

The third trustee chosen during the Hartzog administration was John Sam Garris. He, like Sease, graduated from Clemson, but in agriculture in 1898. While at Clemson, Garris wrote for the *Chronicle*, the college's first student publication. The magazine began as a record of the graduating class and a conveyor of Clemson news. The yearbook, *Taps*, grew out of it as did *The Tiger*, the weekly newspaper, eventually leaving the *Chronicle* as a literary and humor magazine. Garris went from Clemson to Georgetown University, where he received a bachelor of laws degree in 1900. He moved from his home in Smoaks, Colleton County, to Spartanburg to practice law. At the time of his election as a trustee, he married Leila Small, also from Smoaks. Garris died on March 28, 1903, and his body was returned to Smoaks for burial.[24]

The Spanish-American War

The first American war after the founding of Clemson College was the conflict with Spain (April–August 12, 1898). A brewing issue for some time, the conflict erupted over the sinking of the *USS Maine* (February 15, 1898), which U.S. President William McKinley had sent to Havana, the capital city and major harbor of Spanish Cuba, during an independence uprising of the Cubans against Spain. McKinley said he sought to protect U.S. interests and U.S. citizens there. Young Clemson alumni, graduates, and cadets quickly offered to join the conflict. The War Department advised the young men to wait at home until called. Eventually, three 1896 graduates—Thomas S. Moorman (a lieutenant), I. M. Maulding, and George P. Boulware—along with other Clemson men—Newberry Comb, Marion B. Leech, Frank Parrott, Junious Parrott, J. Leland Kennedy, and J. W. Gray—saw service in the war. Others may have served, but none were reported as killed. After the war ended in December 1898, a number of young graduates worked in the former Spanish territories of Puerto Rico, Cuba, and the Philippines as agricultural and engineering agents for the federal government. Others served in the armed forces in those islands.[25]

Buildings

Demand for enrollment at Clemson continued to build[26] and was felt the most in the need for classroom buildings; enough money had accumulated from

Barracks Two, built in 1904 and torn down in 1954. The trees in front of the building are of note as well. They are magnolias planted by the Norris family in the late 1890s to commemorate the founding of the Textiles Department and the construction of the Textiles Building. They remain standing on Clemson's campus, in front of the Edgar A. Brown Student Union and Johnstone Hall, to this day. Clemson University Photographs, CUL.SC.

the fertilizer tag sales to begin construction of new buildings. Because of the ability to use federal Hatch funds for some agricultural buildings, the college added a small extension to the one-story wooden experiment station located where the Pendleton road divided (the location of Sikes Hall at present). The addition provided storage for back issues of extension bulletins. By April 1899, the college had also completed the veterinary hospital and teaching facility.[27]

Early in 1900, the trustees designated $3,000 to build a much-needed addition to the Chemistry Building. Willis F. Denny, an Atlanta architect, designed the wing. Denny broke with the Romanesque style of the older building and moved to the then-more-fashionable *beaux-arts* style. He retained the dusky red brick, however. The new space added five laboratory rooms for upper division classes and a lecture/demonstration laboratory hall that sat 200 cadets. It would open in 1901.[28] In addition, the demand for textiles was strong enough for the planned north wing of that building to be built within two years of the program's opening.[29]

By then, too, the trustees felt financially secure enough to begin the much-needed new barracks. Senator Tillman proposed to start construction on April 2, 1901. For the board's decision, Secretary-Treasurer Sloan wrote for and received back written votes. That took forty-eight hours. (The college had one telephone line, which ran from Sloan's desk in the president's office to the Southern railroad depot in Calhoun.) As soon as Sloan had the votes in hand, the work began. Housing eighty-six rooms and more than 200 beds, the barracks was built by skilled craftsmen and laborers using convict-made brick. It opened fourteen months after the trustees had decided to build it.[30] Although that happened after Hartzog had left Clemson, the achievement of first getting the teaching space together before moving toward the obvious bed space was the work of a mind that kept priorities well in order.

At the same time, the trustees, anxious to preserve their record, "suggested" that the college have portraits of the original thirteen trustees painted and displayed. Their first choice for display was the chapel and second was the library, then located in the Main Building. The library already displayed Mr. Clemson's thirty-four European oil paintings.[31] There is no record of those portraits being executed, although a number of trustees or their families have presented portraits as gifts to the institution. During the 1930s, an artist subsidized by the federal government created a representation of the May 2, 1888, first meeting of the life trustees.[32] Also the college received a portrait of Justin Morrill, once a representative and then U.S. senator from Vermont and author of the Land Grant Acts of 1862 and 1890.[33]

In addition to the two new buildings and additions to other buildings, the empty clock eyes and silent belfry on the Main Building reminded all of the unfinished features of the young campus. The trustees asked Hartzog to investigate the cost. To fit the clock's eyes, the faces had to be eight feet in diameter, and for

Cadets on parade in front of Main Building in 1899. Notice the eye of the clock tower covered by boards due to the inability of the Clemson College Board of Trustees to purchase a clock! Clemson University Photographs, CUL.SC.

major use, a striking mechanism had to connect to a bell with sufficient audio power to be heard for a one-mile radius. Two firms bid. Seth Thomas Company bid $635 and the Meneely Bell Company, $500. For some reason, probably financial, the trustees did not order the clock, mechanism, and bell.[34] The wooden boards painted to resemble clock faces continued to fool visitors and serve as a running jest among the folks in the little hamlet forming to the north.

Community

While the campus provided space for housing most faculty, all students, and a few staff, the Calhoun Land Company owned most of the land directly north of the school. One of the hopes of the trustees in the first decade was to build a spur train line from the Southern line depot into the campus. It would pass between D. B. Sloan's store and the dentist's office, coming onto the campus and running alongside the Trustee House. By the time the fertilizer revenue had reached a level to support the venture, however, the price of land had escalated, and the trustees abandoned the notion.[35]

Nonetheless, the trail that Riggs had followed to campus in 1896 began to attract businesses, homes, and other establishments. Mr. Clinkscales had built a livery stable slightly north of Sloan's general store, while a few steps farther, Leonard Keller had opened a men's store. Each played a significant role in the development of the community, but none became more of an institution than Keller's. Keller came to Clemson as a student in 1893. He brought with him a home-acquired talent as a tailor and quickly established a small barracks-housed business in alterations of cadet uniforms. Given the ages of the cadets (fifteen years and older) and remembering the rapid growth spurts of those years, one can only conclude that Cadet Keller was a busy young man. After he left the college, Keller opened the town shop. The commandant had called in a new student for not wearing his uniform, and the cadet responded that the uniform did not fit properly. The commandant ordered the young man to go to Keller's to be fitted and added that Keller would be the judge as to whether or not the uniform fit. The "Judge" title stuck, and over a hundred years later, students, faculty, staff, and townsfolk still refer to "Judge Keller's."[36]

After the Presbyterians had settled in their church, the Episcopalians were next to build close to the college. While the college chapel, the place of daily services and Sunday morning worship, required attendance of all cadets (Sunday service was not required of Roman Catholic or Jewish students), and while most faculty and their families attended that service, both denominations were active close to the campus. The Presbyterian church had operated since 1895. For Episcopalians, the closest church was St. Paul's in Pendleton. Established in 1820, St. Paul's is said to be "the first entrance of the Episcopal Church into the distinctly up-country of South Carolina."[37] By 1893, the Rev. Mr. Octavius T. Porcher, rector of St. Paul's, had begun holding services twice each month on Sunday afternoons in Fort Hill (then the mailing address of the college). On the first Sunday afternoon, service was in the convict stockade; Porcher held the third Sunday afternoon service in one of the finished parts of the Mechanical Hall. Two years later, Porcher also held services at Old Stone Church; the Presbyterians "kindly allowed its use for mission services," the Episcopal bishop of South Carolina noted. By April 1899, the diocesan officers gave permission for property sale and purchase of a lot close to the campus. The building began, and on December 3, 1899, Bishop Ellison Capers of the Diocese of South Carolina consecrated the new chapel, called Holy Trinity. He wrote, "The Lord's Table, made by Dr. McCollough and one of his grandsons, out of native woods, is one of the handsomest in the Diocese...." The chapel drew its permanent membership heavily from the faculty families who had attended St. Paul's.[38] Certainly the unity of the primary mission to the students by the young congregations in the community gave rise to the comity of the religious meetinghouses of the town. And when the testimony the former Pendleton pastors and their wives gave in the *Lee v. Simpson* case is remembered, the ties to the college are certainly strong.

Students

During the years 1897–1902, student enrollment rose slowly from 449 to 500 (11 percent). With the new barracks nearly finished, Clemson's future looked very bright. By this point, it was the largest state college in South Carolina, a position it held until World War II.

Hartzog continued the practice begun by Strode of handling the admissions correspondence personally. Students were admitted at any point before or during the first half of the academic term.[39] The student's minimum age for admission also generated much correspondence, as Hartzog stayed firmly with the board's minimum of fifteen years of age.[40]

Eventually for the 1898–1899 school year, all places, some would say "beds," at Clemson were filled, and no one else could be admitted.[41] Of course, not all new enrollees had success at school. For example on September 15, 1898, a student was sent home as too "puny" to withstand the rigors of military life. But the military was not required of everyone. Exceptions could be made, but such students had to obtain housing separate from the barracks.[42] And parents were quick to write the president. One wrote asking for directions from Crocketville (near Augusta, Georgia) to Fort Hill.[43] Another parent complained about hazing. Hartzog responded on September 22 that hazing was illegal and noted the student had not complained.[44] Hazing was practiced even if allegedly not known by the president.

Tuition and scholarships also occupied the president's time. Rather than attempt to determine at Clemson whether or not a student qualified for tuition remission by reason of parents' lack of means and resources, the determination was made locally by the county auditor.[45] Also, questions arose of course placement for students. Usually the entrance examinations determined this. But during the first week or two of the term, as achievement levels became clearer, students were moved in their classes, causing consternation for the parents.[46]

The *Chronicle*, Clemson's first student publication, emerged as a monthly journal in October 1897 with Arthur Buist Bryan of Barnwell as the editor-in-chief. Its sponsors were the Calhoun, Columbian, and Palmetto literary societies, and the staff was drawn from the three. An effort to establish a student publication two years earlier had failed for lack of sufficient financial backing. However, the *Chronicle* was successful and would, for many years, appear irregularly. Funding came from a combination of advertising from merchants in the region and a few national firms and from student, faculty, and friends' subscriptions. Bryan, after his 1898 graduation in agriculture, went away to Peabody College in Nashville, Tennessee, for a bachelor of letters degree and then returned to teach initially in Clemson's Preparatory Department. He would teach English in Clemson's Academic Department from 1904 to 1918. Because of his excellent writing skills and his agricultural knowledge, he served as editor (and principal writer) of the Clemson Extension Service and the S.C. Agricultural Experiment Station. He retired in 1947.[47]

Intercollegiate Sports

With no spring baseball season in 1897, the students had to wait until the autumn to renew rivalries on the football gridiron. Again, all games were played away from Clemson, and all but South Carolina were played out of state. Clemson lost two, the opener to Georgia and the contest with North Carolina, and won two, a game with the Charlotte (North Carolina) YMCA and the return clash with South Carolina. Clemson's team continued to call itself the Tigers but no longer had the colors red and blue. Perhaps these were too close to South Carolina's garnet and black. Whatever the reasons, the new colors chosen fluctuated among orange and gold for one color and purple and blue for the other. Accounts of the games for over a half century routinely referred to orange and purple or purple and gold. Orange and purple emerged as the more frequent combination.[48] The use of blue seemed a temporary solution to a problem with the hue instability of the available purple dye. Clemson won the four games with South Carolina between 1897 and 1900. No game was played in 1901; officials at both schools could not agree on the terms.[49]

In 1899, the second year Walter Riggs coached the football team, the Clemson team won four matches, beating Davidson (the game was played in Rock Hill)

34–0, North Carolina State 24–0, and Georgia Tech 41–5 (the game was played in Greenville); the Tigers lost to Georgia and Auburn. The latter, a 34–0 drubbing, goaded Riggs to action. He talked with Hartzog about hiring a "professional" coach, a direction not always considered "gentlemanly." He assured the president that the effort would cost nothing. After thought, Hartzog agreed, and Riggs proposed to the students, faculty, and community the formation of the Foot Ball Aid Association. After formation, the group named Riggs the hiring agent. Riggs tracked down John Heisman, whom Riggs had met in 1895, and convinced him to move to Clemson.[50]

Born on October 23, 1869, in Cleveland, Ohio, Heisman grew up and learned football in Titusville, Pennsylvania. He studied law, receiving a two-year certificate from Brown University (1887–1889), then moved to the University of Pennsylvania, where he played football and graduated with a law degree in 1891. He coached football at Oberlin (1892, 1894) and Buchtel (1893, now the University of Akron). From Oberlin he went to Auburn, where he stayed five years, earning a 12–4–2 record. He accepted Riggs's offer and arrived at Clemson in late spring 1900.

His four-year record at Clemson was nothing short of spectacular. Clemson had an undefeated season in 1900, winning the Southern Intercollegiate Athletic Association Championship. Led by captain J. Norman Walker of Appleton (Barnwell County), the Tigers played their second-ever home game, this against the Davidson Wildcats. They went on to defeat Wofford (21–0), South Carolina (51–0), Georgia (39–5), Virginia Tech (12–5), and Alabama (35–0).[51] The Davidson game was played on Bowman Field, the large parade ground so-named shortly after R. T. V. Bowman's death.[52] National rankings did not exist then, although Clemson was one of seven undefeated, untied college teams.[53] The 1901 season opened October 5 with a 122–0 rout of Guilford on Bowman Field. The one loss, to Virginia Tech, was in Charlotte, North Carolina.

John W. Heisman (1869–1936), the legendary football coach, guided Clemson College's football teams from 1900 to 1903. Photo taken from the 1903 edition of the *Clemson College Chronicle*.

In baseball, after Bowman's final season in 1898, the next two years (1899: 4–3; 1900: 8–2) the Clemson team had no coach. So Heisman coached baseball the next three years, amassing a 28–6–1 (.814) record, the best multiyear coach's record in Clemson history. Although most opposing teams were local, Cornell and Hobart both appeared on Clemson's schedule.[54]

Outreach

Clemson held its second graduation on February 9, 1898. Twenty-five men graduated. Several joined the faculty either immediately or after some additional study. J. H. Hook, who had majored in engineering, was asked to stay as the secretary and librarian of the agriculture experiment station. Much of his correspondence dealt with the bulletins sent "franked" (postage-free) to the newspapers of record and to farmers who had requested them. In 1897, the station issued eight bulletins, two by the veterinarian related to illnesses in horses, mules, and swine and a third on treatment of animal wounds. Hardin issued two bulletins on commercial fertilizers, while the chemist, F. S. Shiver, worked exclusively on sweet potatoes. Newman, who joined the staff during the year, provided instruction on improving worn soils. The fertilizer board examined an increase of 14 percent in fertilizer samples, indicating the economic depression of 1893 had retreated. That trend continued through the 1901–1902 school year. The growth also could be seen in the frequency of issuing bulletins. The titles rose from five to eight or nine each year. By 1901, the bulletins included information on experimentation and tests of rice, still a desired crop in the state's low coastal region.

A second mode of outreach was through the experimental farm. Clemson had come under increasing pressure to open branch farms, usually referred to as "stations." The most persistent requests came from the Charleston area, and particularly from the Agricultural Society of South Carolina (founded in Charleston in 1795), which wrote the U.S. commissioner of agriculture requesting the creation of an experiment station in Charleston County, specifically to study rice. The commissioner directed them to ask Clemson for help. Although the rice industry had partly revived after the Civil War, the cultivation of rice and the inefficient methods of harvesting it along with the labor costs rendered Carolina rice noncompetitive with the Louisiana and Texas fields. Clemson agreed to help. Initially, the station was located on the outskirts of Charleston on the site of the South Carolina Interstate and West Indian Exposition (December 1, 1901, to June 20, 1902). Clemson Agricultural College had an exhibit on the exposition grounds (now Hampton Park and the Citadel campus), so that site became the South Carolina Experiment Station branch, the Coast Land Experiment Station. With W. G. Garrison as the new branch's coordinator, tests began on producing crimson clover, field peas, millet, and Texas bluegrass. However, the site was smaller than needed, and the Agricultural Society and Garrison searched for a larger tract.[55]

During the period 1896–1902, Clemson's agricultural visits to many rural communities were very important. Clemson's agents generally traveled by railway. The two major rail systems, the Southern and the Coastal, had links to miles of lines of local rail companies. For example, in 1899, 7,080 farmers with their spouses and their offspring attended Clemson-organized local institutes.[56] One year later, the legislature passed and the governor signed the act giving the Clemson Board of Trustees the authority of a state entomology board. The trustees now found themselves in the vector biology business.[57]

Cadets in Trouble

In spite of all intentions, the cadets, whose average age in 1900 was eighteen, could cause problems. Early conduct rules prohibited roughhousing, fighting, possessing alcohol, playing cards, gambling, or using any tobacco in the barracks. While almost all the rules reflected the moral (and in some cases, legal) tone of the white population of the Piedmont, tobacco use in barracks was a fire hazard. Outside the barracks, cadets could smoke pipes and cigars during their recreational time. Cigarettes were considered inappropriate for men (this is not to suggest that they *were* appropriate for women).[58]

But adolescent and young adult male fighting happened everywhere in the country.[59] Clemson cadets were little different. Students disrespectful to the faculty were dismissed. In a literary society meeting, for example, one cadet "rebuked" another. A fight ensued, and the shamed student drew and opened his knife, threatening his verbal harasser. Other society members subdued them. The faculty suspended the knife-wielder for the remainder of the term. Still another student found drunk on campus was dismissed. All student discipline charges were brought to the faculty, who heard both sides (each with counsel if so chosen, selected by the students from the faculty, the military, or the cadets), asked questions, and then rendered an "opinion." The "opinion" was sent to the president for final judgment and execution.[60] The president, in cases of suspension or dismissal, wrote the cadet's parents an explanatory letter.

Some few cases of alleged academic dishonesty were handled the same way and were almost always initiated by a faculty member. That type of issue brought the 1901–1902 academic year to a confusing end. The winter session began with the theft of a turkey from Prof. W. S. Morrison's poultry pen. The college charged a senior with the theft and tried him before the faculty, who found him guilty. Because the young man was scheduled to graduate, many of the seniors and some others petitioned the faculty, requesting leniency for him. Perhaps swayed by the pleas, the faculty vote, while confirming the guilt, did not have the necessary three-fourths vote to recommend dismissal, which was permanent dishonorable separation. The senior was thus suspended by the president and missed being eligible for June graduation.[61] Other thefts occurred, and Hartzog and the trustees hired a private detective to ferret out the culprits. He had little success.

In this atmosphere, R. N. Brackett charged E. A. Thornwell with taking a test tube from the chemistry laboratory cabinet to his laboratory bench without permission, an issue of academic dishonesty. Hartzog saw the case as theft

Edward Allison Thornwell, the person whose disciplining resulted in the 1902 student walkout, as he appeared as a senior in the 1904 Clemson College annual, *The Oconeean.*

because Thornwell had not asked Brackett's permission to take the test tube anywhere. The faculty voted to suspend Thornwell for the remainder of the term. Both Brackett and Hardin, however, voted against the suspension.

Reaction was immediate. Student petitions noted that the practice engaged in by Thornwell had gone unpunished in the past, and that, wrong though Thornwell's action was, the punishment far exceeded the alleged offense. The faculty met on April 28, 1902, to consider a petition from the sophomore class to reinstate Thornwell. The faculty refused, and the next day sixty-nine of the seventy-four sophomores packed their bags and left Clemson by train. The seniors first and then the juniors and freshmen supported the sophomore action and prepared to depart.

Trustee President Simpson had two strong memories that seemed to inform him. The first was the negative correspondence that filled newspapers (see Chapter V). But even more compelling was the uproar around the "Cantey affair" at the Citadel. Samuel O. Cantey, a Citadel cadet in 1898, had reported that five other cadets had broken garrison, which led to their suspension. Seventy other cadets attempted to force the student informant out of school.[62] A near tragedy was averted when one faculty member, Col. Coward, barred the angry seventy from entering Cantey's room. Under advice from Coward, Cantey left the Citadel, staying first in a hotel in Charleston before going home to Summerton. But it took a squad of thirty Charleston policemen to restore order. The Citadel Board of Visitors was immediately summoned; Governor Ellerbe and Adjutant General Watts attended the meeting. The board decided to expel seventy-four of the cadets (eventually, the number dropped to sixty-four). Twenty additional cadets "announced their intention of withdrawing," which would have left about fifteen cadets in the Citadel.[63] The names and hometowns of the expelled students were published in a local newspaper.[64] The upperclassmen were given leave to reapply, but the first-year and second-year men were given no hope. Some of these applied to Clemson; Hartzog would not budge. Without an honorable discharge from the Citadel (or any other school), the applicants would not be accepted at Clemson.[65]

Hartzog's role in Thornwell's suspension and the resulting walkout was less clear. On April 28, a sophomore delegation had visited Hartzog and asked to appeal the faculty decision. Hartzog replied that he would present the students' petition to the board. Apparently, the students did not trust him, and the sophomores left campus. The trustees then met and heard the case, deciding to forgive Thornwell and reinstate the students who had left campus on the condition that they make up missed academic work.[66] Hartzog resigned, but the trustees refused to accept the resignation. Hartzog resigned again in June 1902 to accept the presidency of what is today the University of Arkansas, and Hardin again acted for a time as chief executive.[67]

Mark Hardin had voted against the harsh penalty against Thornwell, so perhaps one reason for his selection as temporary president was his sense of mercy and fair dealing. As had happened earlier when Hardin had served as acting president between Craighead and Hartzog, little occurred during his 1902 tenure. He had a record of meticulous attention to the affairs of the college, and his membership in the American Chemical Society in 1876 and in the Lyceum of Natural History of New York, now the New York Academy of Sciences, added to his credibility. All these reasons may have motivated the trustees' confidence in him. In addition, from time to time during Hartzog's absence, he chaired the faculty meetings, which governed faculty support for the choice.[68]

Hartzog's youth and inexperience, and certainly the close involvement of the trustees in the day-to-day operation of the college, produced some truly rough moments for Clemson College. However, the foundation of the textile program, which was Hartzog's great achievement, would become a driving force in the boom of the textile industry in the Midlands and Upstate.

Notes

1. Student statistics have been garnered from the annual Clemson *Record* and from the annual *Report of Board to the General Assembly*, 1897, 16, 17. Undergraduates who helped with the initial efforts were James Tyrell, Lindsay Tapp, Greg Miller, and Brian Parsons. History graduate student Paul Alexander Crunkleton carried out the final gathering, refinement, categorization, and graphing.
2. CUL.SC.CUA. S30 v 1, 166; and Pickens *People's Journal*, September 23, 1897.
3. Kohl, "A Youthful Administrator: Henry Simms Hartzog, 1897–1902," in *Tradition*, 52–67. Hartzog's family home is still standing just north of the Bamberg County seat and outside of Barnwell.
4. *Record*, 1895–1896.
5. *Report of Board to General Assembly*, 1897, 15. On the marble plaques, see *Chronicle*, vol. 2, no. 8, 346.
6. *Record*, 1897–1898; 1899–1900; and 1901–1902.
7. CUL.SC.CUA. S 30 v 1, 102.
8. Ibid., 175–180.
9. Andrew, "William Haselden Ellerbe," in *South Carolina Encyclopedia*, 295–296.
10. CUL.SC.CUA. S 30 v 1, 181–182.
11. Ibid., 175.
12. Ibid., 188.
13. Doggett, "History of the Textiles Department at Clemson," an unpublished paper in CUL. SC.CUA. S 37 f "Textile Education, 1890s–1920s."
14. Georgia Institute of Technology archives: Lyman Hall Papers, vol. 1, January 7, 1898.
15. CUL.SC.CUA. S 37 f "Godfrey Hall."

16. *Record*, 1899–1900, 7–8.
17. Gage, "A History of the Textile School of Clemson College," *Textile History Review*, vol. 4, January 1963, no. 1.
18. CUL.SC.CUA. S 25 f 4.
19. Georgia Tech, *Announcements*, 1898–1899, 14.
20. Mississippi State University Archives: President John Hardy Correspondence, January 4, 1901.
21. Betterworth, *People's University: The Centennial History of Mississippi State*, 88–89, 118–121.
22. CUL.SC.CUA. S 30 ss I b 2 f 43; and S 30 ss I b 2 f 6.
23. Ibid., S 6 f 6.
24. CUL.SC.MSS 68 f 140.
25. *The Tiger*, April 21, 1939; and CUL.SC.CUA. S 37 "Alumni, 1896–1909." For an alumnus' memory of the Philippines, see *Chronicle*, vol. 3, no. 1, 22–26. For a student's pro-annexation of the Philippines, see same issue, 27–33.
26. *Report of the Board to the General Assembly*, 1901, 11; for example, see *Record* 1896 through 1900.
27. CUL.SC.CUA. S 30 v 1, 205.
28. Ibid., 214; and CUL.SC.MSS 68 f 272.
29. CUL.SC.CUA. S 30 v 1, 214.
30. CUL.SC.MSS 68 f 244.
31. Hiott, "Thomas Green Clemson: Art Collector and Artist," in *Thomas Green Clemson*, 187–222. Hiott has presented a study of the paintings and their travels from Europe to the United States and their movement from Maryland to Pennsylvania and then to South Carolina. He has reproduced Anna Calhoun Clemson's catalog, indicating those that are missing. It is an excellent study of the taste of a nineteenth century European-educated gentleman.
32. Commissioned for the first purpose-built federal post office in 1940, it was removed when the federal post office moved to a second building in the town. Then it was moved to the main administrative building (Sikes Hall), where the Board of Trustees had its meeting room. However, the number of non-board members attending increased, causing the board to move its meetings, and the will-named life trustees Depression-art painting was moved again in 2002 to the newly renovated Hardin Hall.
33. Morrill's portrait was moved from the Memorial Chapel when that facility was renovated in 1979–1980 and hung in Sikes Hall. At the moment, it is displayed in the entrance of Sikes Hall.
34. CUL.SC.CUA. S 25 f 1.
35. Ibid., S 30 v 1, 219 and 230.
36. Leonard Keller Jr. to Farrell Brown.
37. Skardon, *A Brief Informal History of Holy Trinity Episcopal Church, Clemson, South Carolina, 1899–1999*, 1–10.
38. Ibid.
39. CUL.SC.CUA. S 25 b 2 ff 13, 27 and 37.
40. Ibid., f 2, ff 2, 22, 23, 47, and S 3 f 28.
41. Ibid., ff 41, 71, and 75.
42. Ibid., f 4.
43. Ibid., b 3 f 89.
44. Ibid., b 2 f 100.
45. Ibid., b 3 ff 93 and 98.
46. Ibid., ff 218, 287, and 292.
47. Atlanta *Journal and Constitution*, May 18, 1959.
48. Matthews, ed., *Clemson Foot Ball: An Historical Sketch of Football at Clemson College*, 31; and *Chronicle*, vol. 1, no. 2, 35 (orange and blue); vol. 2, no. 3, 166 (orange and purple).
49. Griffin, *Carolina vs Clemson: Clemson vs Carolina*, 23.
50. Matthews, *Clemson Foot Ball*, 55.
51. Bourret, *Clemson Football 2009*, 202.
52. *Record* 1898–1899, 14.
53. MacCambridge, *College Football Encyclopedia*, 1144.
54. Bourret, *Clemson Baseball 2010*, 176.

55. Murray, *This Our Land: The Story of the Agricultural Society of South Carolina*, 170–176.
56. *Record* 1900, 14.
57. Ibid., 1901, 16.
58. CUL.SC.CUA. S 37.
59. Ballard, *Maroon and White: Mississippi State University*, 60; and Horowitz, *Campus Life: Undergraduate Cultures from the End of the Eighteenth Century to the Present*, 5 ff.
60. CUL.SC.CUA. S 36 b 25 f 10.
61. Ibid., Bound Faculty Minutes, January 22–23, 1901.
62. Charleston *Evening Post*, April 5, 1898.
63. Ibid., April 8, 1898. In his work, *Long Gray Lines*, Rod Andrew addresses the Cantey episode in detail on pages 68–69. I am indebted to him for his help with this entire project.
64. Ibid., April 9, 1898.
65. CUL.SC.CUA. S 25 b 2 ff 2, 51, 83, 84, 149, 150, and 202.
66. Kohl, "A Youthful Administrator: Henry Simms Hartzog, 1897–1902," in *Tradition*, 52–67. Kohl has done thorough research on the Hartzog administration, and his analysis is excellent.
67. CUL.SC.MSS 68 b 1 f 79.
68. Also see Bryan, *Clemson*, 64–67.

The faculty of Clemson Agricultural College during the administration of President Patrick Hues Mell (1850–1918). Mell, the fourth president of Clemson College from 1902 to 1910, is on the far left of the first row (to the left of the uniformed commandant of the college). Clemson University Photographs, CUL.SC.

CHAPTER VII

Challenging Years

1902–1910

For Clemson College, the eight years from 1902 to 1910 provided a challenge. The new president was the best qualified; faculty quality rose steadily; the experiment station expanded; and outreach to the state increased. But the conflict between the trustees and the president came squarely into public view, and the public confidence in Clemson sagged.

Patrick Hues Mell

By September 9, 1902, the new president, Patrick Hues Mell, had assumed office. Like Strode, the first president, Mell was an older man, born on May 24, 1850. He enjoyed a distinguished career as a scientist and had served in the faculty of the Alabama Polytechnic Institute (now Auburn University).[1] He received the bachelor's degree in 1871 from the University of Georgia, where his father served as chancellor.[2] Natural science was his real strength and the out-of-doors his favorite workspace. After receiving degrees in chemical engineering in 1872 and mining engineering in 1873, he won the doctorate of philosophy degree from Georgia in 1878. He then served as the state chemist for the Georgia State Department of Agriculture, analyzing soils and fertilizer. The latter work made him very attractive to Clemson's trustees because the fertilizer tax brought Clemson its main source of revenue. His administrative abilities had also earned him offers for the president's post at Mercer in 1893 and at North Georgia Agricultural College in 1897, neither of which he accepted. When he took over the Clemson presidency in 1902, he was a mature scholar and administrator.[3] The minutes of the Clemson Board of Trustees meeting show that the board chose Mell, whom Tillman had nominated, after three ballots.[4]

Athletics

Mell's administration, the longest at that point, was vexed by the interrelationship between the school's obligations in teaching textiles and engineering and teaching and research in agriculture, and by the roles that the military and intercollegiate athletics would play. These problems confronted most schools. Yet athletics (or sports) had an infectious quality about them. Collegiate football was by far the greatest attraction in the 1900s. While the earliest "official" southern intercollegiate football contest was the October 18, 1888, victory of Wake Forest over UNC played in Raleigh, North Carolina,[5] Walter Merritt Riggs had remembered his first collegiate game when on February 20, 1892, Alabama Polytechnic met the University of Georgia. It was API's first game and Georgia's second. George Petrie coached API, and Charles Hertz, Georgia. Riggs later recalled, "I believe foot ball [*sic*] stands today as the greatest man-making game on the American continent. View it from any standpoint you please—the physical, the mental, the moral—I am prepared to say, and attempt to prove, that it excels them all."[6]

Football could be particularly brutal, however, and most collegians resisted any padding, except nose and genital protectors. By 1894, concerned over the lack of conformity in equipment and in players' relationships to the institutions they represented, Vanderbilt, at the time a leading athletic and academic southern institution, invited nineteen other schools to meet them in Atlanta. There they formed the Southern Intercollegiate Athletic Association (SIAA), a rule-making and monitoring athletic group.[7]

The principal issues centered on the eligibility and injury of the student athletes. The most flagrant eligibility abuses happened in the northeastern states, where young men frequently hired out on a week-by-week basis to one school and then another, spending the weeks working in mines, mills, factories, and docks. They moved with the money, usually provided by zealous alumni and supporters, and were called a variety of names, such as "tramp" or "gypsy athletes." Travel distances and difficulties and the lack of abundant cash minimized the practice in the South. There, the more likely sources of abuse involved farm or mill youth or postgraduate students "continuing" their training in programs such as law, pharmacy, or even medical fields, some of which frequently had no undergraduate requirements. To ensure true eligibility, the SIAA agreed to a freshman ineligibility rule.[8] Clemson joined the association in 1896, and Riggs remained a staunch advocate of the rule throughout his life.[9]

Injury, by far, proved the more serious issue. Many of the rules were created to lessen the incident of injury. However, as the number of schools playing football increased, the number of deaths from football injury reached such a level that in 1905, President Theodore Roosevelt summoned the presidents of a number of football-prominent colleges (Clemson was not included) to the White House to discuss ways to eliminate the deaths. The meeting led to the formation on March 31, 1906, of the Intercollegiate Athletic Association, which became the nucleus of the National Collegiate Athletic Association (NCAA).[10] Clemson would not be a member institution during Mell's presidency. At the state level, Riggs served as president of the S.C. Intercollegiate Athletic Association (SCIAA) from its founding in 1900 until his death in 1924. For years, the SCIAA promoted the tennis, wrestling, boxing, cross country, track and field, and golf state champion-ship tournaments. Riggs also served as an officer in the SIAA from 1901 until his death.

During Mell's presidency, John Heisman coached baseball from 1901 through 1902, ending with an impressive .814 record. After Heisman, John McMakin amassed a three-year losing percentage of .457. Over the next four years, four dif-ferent coaches led the Tigers to an even more mediocre .455 percentage victory rate.

Fred Harvey Hall Calhoun (1873–1959) as a young man. Calhoun, known as "Doc Rock" or "Rock" to his friends and his students, was a longtime fixture of the Agricultural Department during his tenure as professor of geology and mineralogy from 1904 to his retirement as dean emeritus of the Agricultural Department in 1947. Clemson University Photographs, CUL.SC.

Also Clemson students established a track program led by Fred Harvey Hall Calhoun. Joining the Clemson faculty in 1904, Calhoun had come from Illinois College, where he taught from 1902 to 1904. He had received his PhD in geology from the University of Chicago in 1902. Born in Elbridge, New York, in 1874, he finished high school in Auburn, New York, in 1893. Calhoun attended the University of Chicago, completing his bachelor's degree there in 1898. He was a member and captain of the university track team and a member of the Chicago chapter of Phi Delta Theta Fraternity. Riggs was also a "Phi Delt." While teaching at Illinois College, a Congregational-Presbyterian school in Jacksonville, Illinois, Calhoun met and later married Grace B. Ward. Shortly after Calhoun arrived at Clemson, he found an existing Clemson track team. By 1905, the track team, of which he became the coach, joined baseball, football, and the cadet corps in the use of what by then had been named Bowman Field.[11]

Football, the most popular sport, was coached by John Heisman, who pre-pared to begin his third season at Clemson.[12] In 1900, Heisman's first season, the Clemson Tigers went undefeated and captured the SIAA championship. Heis-man's years at Clemson (1900–1903) saw him developing deceptive plays and lobbying Walter Camp's committee to sanction the forward pass. Walter Camp (1859–1925), a Yale University undergraduate (1888–1892) and then briefly the

Stanford University football coach, chaired a voluntary membership rules committee that began the development of standard football rules.

During the 1902 football season in the annual Big Thursday battle, South Carolina upset Clemson 12–6, South Carolina's first win over the Tigers since 1896. Excited students from South Carolina held an impromptu victory parade in Columbia, carrying a banner displaying a tail-twisted Tiger surmounted by a crowing Gamecock (by then no longer Jaguars). The Clemson cadets objected, insisting that the banner not be displayed again the next night—a Friday night. But it was, and it inflamed the Clemson cadets, who participated in the parade in uniform, bearing rifles (no ammunition) with bayonets and sabers. After the Friday night parade ended at the statehouse, the cadets were dismissed, but they reassembled at the boundary to the South Carolina campus. Wright Bryan, whose father taught at Clemson, remembered the confrontation as dangerous when from the cluster of outnumbered South Carolina students came a call, "McKissick, are you armed?" South Carolina student J. Rion McKissick had a loaded gun, and the voice called again, "McKissick, make every shot count." Disaster was averted when a South Carolina volunteer assistant coach, Christie Benet, jumped to the wall and offered to fight any two cadets. That break lasted just long enough to allow the police to arrive and separate the two groups.

Ironically, McKissick later served as editor of *The Greenville Piedmont* and then president of the University of South Carolina, and he was a good friend of Clemson Agricultural College. The irony was doubled by the fact that Christie Benet's father had been one of Clemson's ardent legislative sponsors at the time of the college's founding, and Christie Benet served, at the end of his long and productive life, as president of the Clemson Board of Trustees.[13]

Following that near disaster, there was no game between the Clemson eleven and South Carolina for the next six years. This produced the second break in the series.[14] In January 1908, the South Carolina Athletic Council proposed that the game be renewed. Clemson responded that it had nearly completed the 1908 schedule, which left no room to meet the South Carolina team on the gridiron. Further, Clemson preferred not to play on Thursdays or always in Columbia.[15]

The loss to South Carolina in 1902, however, did not end Clemson's season. Clemson still had to play Georgia, Auburn, and Tennessee. Georgia played at Clemson, the Bulldogs' first venture into the South Carolina Upstate. Clemson played the other two games at Auburn and Tennessee. While not allowing any one of the three to score, the Tigers racked up 11 points on Tennessee, 16 on Auburn, and 36 on Georgia. The Tigers won the SIAA championship for the second time in three years.[16]

The 1903 season was also blemished by a single defeat, an 11–6 loss to UNC. However, the campaign opened with a 29–0 win over Georgia. In the give and take after the game, the two teams struck up a wager focused on Clemson's next opponent, Georgia Tech, and with no concern for which team won. If Clemson did not score 29 points on Tech, for each point less than 29 not scored, the Clemson team had to send the Georgia team a bushel of apples. Should Clemson score more than 29, then the Georgia players would send a bushel of apples to the Clemson team for each point over 29.

On Friday, October 16, 1903, the Clemson coach, some of the faculty, the twenty-piece regimental band, and a large number of the cadets who had leave to attend the game in Atlanta (this took the place of the Big Thursday Columbia excursion) boarded the Southern train at Calhoun. After the many stops, the train pulled into the Atlanta station. Many passengers disembarked. Greeting the Clemson cadets was a group of young Georgia Tech alumni, identifying themselves as the "official welcoming committee," who gathered up those cadets carrying the sparse equipment (jerseys, pants, and shoes). The cadets were treated to an evening of merriment (and alcohol) before they were sent to bed.

But Heisman had taken the team off the train at Lula, Georgia, to spend a restful night. They arrived in Atlanta at the playing site, and when the fray was finished, the scoreboard read Georgia Tech 0, Clemson 73. There is no record that the Georgia players ever sent the forty-four bushels of apples.[17]

Following the five-game season, Clemson and Cumberland, who tied for the lead of the SIAA, met on Thanksgiving Day in Montgomery, Alabama, in what was Clemson's first postseason game. The teams played to an 11–11 tie, thus sharing the championship.[18]

Almost immediately, Georgia Tech hired Heisman away from Clemson, with a substantial raise, 30 percent of the gate receipts (Clemson had no such monies to offer), and no other duties than to coach football. The *Chronicle* wept, "He has left us." Indeed, Clemson football was without its genius, and so was the baseball team. The Clemson glee club had lost a strong baritone and the local theater group, its leading man. However, there is more to the story of his going. R. E. DeSpain, one of Heisman's biographers, suggests that Heisman's real reason involved his 1903 marriage to Evelyn McCollum Cox, a widow with one son. They met in summer stock theater, and Atlanta provided many more venues for actors.[19]

Shack Shealy followed Heisman as Clemson's head football coach, the only Clemson player to serve in that capacity. Shealy coached one year and was followed by Ed Cochems, who also stayed only one year. Then Bob Williams, who had coached the 1902 USC team, led Clemson in 1906, 1909, and 1913–1915. Frank Shaughnessy, who also coached the 1907 baseball team, coached football until February 1908, when the Clemson Athletic Council terminated his contract.[20] The council members included Riggs, four other faculty, and four cadets, one from each class.

Student Honors

During Clemson College's early years, Richard Wright Simpson began offering a medal for the "best drilled cadet" as determined by the commandant. Because no other qualifications for the medal existed, at times a freshman received it, and on several occasions, a cadet won the medal several years in a row.

The second honor, the Oratorical Medal, originated in the inordinate success Clemson students achieved in intercollegiate oratorical competition. Among the earliest of all intercollegiate contests, oratory and debate ranked among the most popular in the latter years of the nineteenth and early decades of the twentieth centuries. The rapidly growing reach of the railways eased the opportunities for competition. Clemson's relative geographic isolation, with few other forms of campus enter-

W. Lionel Moise, winner of the South Carolina Inter-Collegiate Oratorical competition in 1899, president of the Palmetto Literary Society in 1899 and 1900, and winner of the Southern Intercollegiate Oratorical Competition. Clemson University Photographs, CUL.SC.

tainment, combined with the high faculty-student relationship to create a natural breeding ground for this competition.

In 1896, the three literary societies held an open oratorical contest immediately before graduation. The victory was its own reward, and the honor accrued to the society of which the winning student was a member. The first real success came in the spring of 1899 in the contest held by the S.C. Inter-Collegiate Oratorical Association in Due West. Besides Erskine College, the host institution, teams came from Presbyterian College, Furman University, Wofford College, and Clemson College. Clemson entered W. Lionel Moise, from Sumter, who at sixteen had finished public schooling and worked in Savannah. In the fall of 1896, he enrolled as a "rat" at Clemson and by 1899–1900 was a senior and president of the Palmetto Literary Society.[21] From the state competition, Moise went on and won the Southern Intercollegiate Oratorical Competition on the campus of the University of the South (Sewanee).[22] The *Chronicle*, in an editorial frame of mind, commented,

> The fact that a Clemson student has won this distinction, [*sic*] will go far toward upsetting the idea entertained by a great many people that Clemson is merely an aggregation of laboratories and shops. We take this signal victory to indicate that while the literary work at Clemson is not so extensive as at literary colleges it is thorough and for practical purposes equally as good.[23]

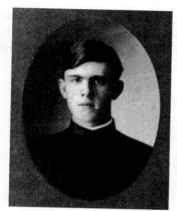

Wilson Parham Gee received the first Norris Medal award upon his graduation in 1908. He would go on to be a widely published and noted entomologist and applied economist. This is Gee's senior portrait from the 1908 edition of the Clemson College annual, *Taps*.

A year later, W. G. Hill, the rising president of the Palmetto Literary Society, won the second honor medal in the South Carolina contest.[24]

In an effort to reward and strengthen the oratorical programs at Clemson, in March 1903 the trustees offered a gold medal to the best orators within the literary societies. The *Chronicle* applauded the action and hoped it would stimulate "more interest" among the society members. The first recipient was Henry C. Tillman, the senator-trustee's second son.[25]

D. K. Norris, an original life trustee named in Mr. Clemson's will, created the third medal. When he died on January 23, 1905, he left stock in his cotton mill company to establish a medal for the best all-around student, as chosen by the college faculty. After much discussion about what Norris might have meant by "best all-around," with Mell holding out for the "best all-around textile student," the trustees decided to give the award to the "best all-around student without regard to the academic field of study."[26]

The first recipient of the Norris Medal was Wilson Parham Gee, who received the award in 1908.[27] After graduation, Gee enrolled at South Carolina, where he earned an MA, and then traveled to California for a PhD in agriculture and statistics. Some years later, he joined the faculty of the University of Virginia, and there in the 1920s he created the Institute for Research in the Social Sciences. He attracted a gift of $27,500 from the Laura Spelman Rockefeller Foundation, which is credited as the "primary impetus to research" at Virginia. Considered by faculty at the University of Virginia as "egotistical" and "somewhat dictatorial," Gee nonetheless received the honor upon his retirement in 1959 of having the rural economics and sociology department named for him.[28]

Alumni

While all Clemson alumni were not as successful as Gee, they nevertheless felt a strong tug of loyalty toward their alma mater. Some returned in June for the annual commencement and election of the new alumni president. A faculty member, himself an alumnus, usually served as the general secretary.

Clemson alumni also began to form clubs and to meet. The Greenville alumni had twelve members, while the Pittsburgh, Pennsylvania, association counted fifteen. Given the prominence of the Clemson family name in the area (a second cousin of Thomas Clemson was a vice president in the Carnegie Corporation), one can only wonder if Thomas Clemson's family ever crossed paths with any of the alumni of the college he founded. The New York City Club claimed twenty-two members. The strongest outpost was the Washington, D.C., chapter, also with twenty-two active members, where a regular attendee at meetings and associate member was U.S. Senator Tillman.

To keep up with the growing number of alumni, A. G. Shanklin, the Clemson registrar, served as the alumni recording secretary. The Clemson *Record* published his lists of alumni at irregular intervals. The 1906–1907 *Record* listed 388 graduates and five known to have died. Even though all had received military training, only six were then serving in the U.S. armed forces. Eighty-eight worked in America's growing power industries, many in major New York, Massachusetts, and Pennsylvania companies. Some 10 percent worked directly in production agriculture, while another 10 percent had jobs in transportation, much of which involved agricultural products. Still another 10 percent had careers in business, most of them local. Textile machinery and production involved slightly over 8 percent of the alumni. Another 8 percent worked in other forms of engineering and construction. The next largest group (6 percent) taught in public schools and higher education. Twelve alumni served in the medical professions, seven were lawyers, another seven in mining, and the remainder scattered in banking and government at local, state, and national levels.

The alumni had begun to fulfill Thomas Clemson's charge to the trustees:

> Always bear in mind that the benefits herein sought to be bestowed are intended to benefit agricultural and mechanical industries. I trust that I do not exaggerate the importance of such an institution for developing the material resources of the State by affording to its youth the advantages of scientific culture...." (Will: Introduction, fourth paragraph).

Accepting the intimate connections among agriculture, engineering, and transportation, there could be no doubt that the college was realizing Mr. Clemson's hopes and vision for "affording to its youth the advantages of scientific culture...." But where did South Carolina's "youth" exercise these "advantages"? Forty-two percent, including most who entered production agriculture, stayed in South Carolina. Almost half of the young electrical and mechanical engineers who went to work for the power industry migrated to up- and mid-state New York, while other Clemson alumni in the state involved themselves in some form of finance. New York claimed 9 percent of the graduates to rank second. Following in third place, Georgia's share was 7.2 percent, while Pennsylvania (again in power) and the District of Columbia (departments of War, Agriculture, and the Interior) each had 6 percent. North Carolina, Alabama, and Virginia had 4.5 percent. Also twenty-two states and six other nations or overseas U.S. territories had a sprinkling of the young Tigers. When the large corporations (including the power plant production factories such as General Electric and Westinghouse) hired Clemson graduates one year after another, keeping the seasoned and bringing in more from the same source, one could only conclude that industry's satisfaction with the teaching at Clemson remained strong.

Military

The other major student enterprise at Clemson was the military system and its demands. The Board of Trustees policy mandated that the commandant, usually an officer assigned from the U.S. War Department, would oversee campus discipline, but only the president could suspend or expel students for misbehavior.[29] The commandant disciplined cadets by assigning them demerits. Commandant E. A. Sirmyer contended that he had so much work with such matters that it left too little time to teach military strategy and tactics, which he calculated at three and one-half hours per week.[30] Further, when football or baseball was in season, with practice and games held on the parade grounds, he could not use the grounds with any regularity.[31] Mell calculated the available hours for military instruction at nine and three-fourths per week, which, if accurate, exceeded that of a large number of the military colleges.[32] The War Department recommended a total of five hours a week.[33]

This contention between the president and commandant continued throughout Mell's administration, bubbling up again during the tenure of the commandant, Capt. Charles D. Clay.[34] Clay began very successfully as the professor of military strategy, but his nagging wounds from the Spanish American War soon hindered his usefulness. He had resorted to drugs and alcohol to ease the pain. His problem emerged especially in the spring semester of 1907. A large number of students took April Fools' Day as a holiday and, while chastised, avoided most punishment.

Student exuberance erupted again on the night before commencement, when the seniors, having been released from military discipline by Clay, paraded on campus, serenading faculty homes and generally creating an uproar. Clay had the seniors arrested and proposed withholding their diplomas the next day. Neither the president nor the board concurred, and Clay found himself isolated on the issue. He wrote a long letter to the U.S. adjutant general. Mell also wrote the adjutant general, and Clay resigned on June 28, 1907. Clay recommended no further posting of a military officer to Clemson because of the two outbreaks of cadet unruliness and the unwillingness of the college administration to uphold his discipline. Of course, the administration had the Citadel 1898 suspensions and expulsions and the Hartzog conflict as part of the background to the incident with Clay.

When the War Department appeared to consider Clay's recommendation seriously, a delegation of Clemson leaders, including Mell, called at the department in Washington, D.C., to press it to appoint a new commandant. Mell pointed out that Clay could not name the student or students who deserved the withholding of diplomas, and the college refused to withhold diplomas from all of the students.[35] The War Department responded by naming J. C. Minus the new commandant. Minus, a South Carolinian from the Lowcountry, had attended the Citadel and graduated from West Point. He, it was hoped, would be a better match for Clemson.

Other Problems

But that was not the end of Mell's difficulties. In mid-July 1907, the *Farm and Factory* newspaper of Seneca published a column attributed to an unnamed faculty member whom the paper quoted as saying,

> We are not fighting Clemson College. We want her to take the highest place of any institution of learning in the South, and we believe she will when she is cleansed. But we are going to fight inefficiency in the Faculty; tyranny and partiality in the Board of Trustees, and rottenness wherever we find it....If things go on here getting worse like they have for the past three years, I believe the college cannot stand six months. I don't know what they will say to me, nor do I care. Someone has got to be sacrificed to put Clemson where she belongs, and if they call that treason let them make the most of it.[36]

The article upset both Simpson and Mell, who asked that the person who gave the interview come forward. A number of faculty wrote Mell to say that they had nothing to do with the article. Trustee Alan Johnstone assumed the faculty member was John N. Hook, with the experiment station, but that was never proved. The Board of Trustees established a special committee to investigate. Unexpectedly, H. D. Howse, the instructor in botany and bacteriology, resigned with no reason given. There the matter rested.[37] Senator Tillman wrote to record his displeasure with the way the entire affair had been handled.[38]

Hazing especially posed a constant problem. One parent, in 1907, wrote to report that her freshman son and his friends had taken to sleeping in the woods to avoid the almost round-the-clock physical and other harassment by the upperclassmen.[39] Mell denied the charge. On another occasion, a cadet's uncle complained about hazing.[40] And again, a mother claimed that freshmen were forced to carry loaded steamer trunks up and down the barracks stairs. Trustee R. E. Bowen also complained about the hazing. Student guards reported that some of the mis-behavior in the dormitories was caused by the presence of illegal "visitors."[41]

But a most serious and deadly accident occurred. A cadet, Reaves, expressed his fear of heights and worried about scrambling down a dormitory rope ladder in the event of fire. Several nights later, Reaves fell from his bedroom's window fifteen feet above ground and died the next day. A coroner's inquest termed the death accidental, probably caused by sleepwalking. When the boy's body was sent home to Latta, a detail of uniformed cadets accompanied it. The father expressed his thanks for the school's kindness and thoughtfulness.[42] Nonetheless, the Seneca *Farm and Factory* newspaper wondered if the death had resulted from hazing.[43] Nothing seemed to curb the problem.

The Walkout of 1908

The famous Pendleton Guards, the instigators of the 1908 walkout, in April Fools' Day "costume." Clemson University Photographs, CUL.SC.

Student flaunting of rules occurred once more when, on April Fools' Day 1908, many of them left campus without permission to parade to Pendleton. They left the college from 7:40 a.m. to 6:00 p.m. Because of this event, the college sent 305 students home.[44] Later, Mell mused to A. E. Gonzales, editor of the *State*, that the parade to Pendleton was an expression of a deeper problem, which he described as "the vastly more important question of who shall rule at Clemson. When I came here in 1902, I found that the answer to this would have to be made at some time in the future...."[45]

Even state Attorney General J. Fraser Lyon asked for a copy of the orders dismissing the cadets from the school. On May 20, 1908, Mell sent him a copy of the charge citing the rule violation.[46] By June, a number of the expelled cadets applied for readmission. The college denied most of the applications because the expelled said their loyalty to their school class was more important than their loyalty to the college.[47] These would be known as the "Pendleton Guards."[48] Most eventually were readmitted and received their degrees.

Riggs would later reminisce on the 1908 affair to students on the eve of another April 1:

> It was a beautiful day just as it is today, nor was there a cloud upon the sky of the college. All was going well. But that morning at breakfast some light-headed leader (he was a good friend of mine and a good football player) raised a cry in the mess hall to cut classes and go to Pendleton, and under his foolish leadership 306 men disobeying the personal orders of the Commandant, marched away.
>
> From the porch of my home I watched them go by, with yells and laughter, and I thought to myself, what a tragedy for Clemson. I saw them that afternoon as they came silently back, without a song or a cheer, with the impending doom hovering over them....And then comes to mind the saddest picture of all—the last Sunday service in chapel...when those who were to return home met for the last time with corps of cadets. I can never forget the scenes of parting between comrades and condemned students and their friends upon the faculty.[49]

This continued turbulence, along with the anger mingled with jealousy over the issue of the fertilizer tag sales revenue, led to an issue that persuaded the next governor, Coleman Blease, to propose a radical restructuring of the college.

Buildings

Besides difficulties with military discipline and student behavior, the college's physical plant provided more concern. The student population had grown from 442 in 1893 to 539 in 1902, and the school turned many applicants away. Of those, 102 enrolled in the fitting school. In the same period of time, the faculty grew from nineteen to forty-four. Crowding resulted in the barracks and laboratories. The Chemistry Building was enlarged in 1900 by an addition, which among other new rooms included a lecture hall that seated 200 students and included a large laboratory display table.

Perhaps the development most symbolic of such changes was the addition of the clock and the bell to the tower on the Main Building. The Seth Thomas Company received the bid to do the work. With it came the obligation of supervising the casting and installation of the bell. The McShane Bell Foundry cast the great bell in the pitch of F.[50] When both arrived by train at Calhoun, they were hauled up the hill to the college. The boards with the fake clock faces and hands were removed, and the equipment and machinery hoisted up and into the tower.

The main tower with its clock was the central symbol of Clemson…and, it might be noted, the locus of student pranks. Almost annually on April 1 at sunrise, carriages, phaetons, and victorias appeared on the great roof, while the mules and horses could be found tethered around the base. As the years passed, carriages became motorcars, and the campus mules appeared patiently waiting and sporting coats dyed in many colors.[51]

Also the campus badly needed an addition to the laundry. The water supply had reached capacity, but heat and electricity were barely adequate. The trustees authorized the construction of a new power plant. Riggs designed the structure and the production, and Lee, the façade.

Clemson, with the largest percentage agriculture student body in the American land-grant college system, desperately needed a new Agricultural Hall.[52] Permission to build it was given, the architecture firm of Edwards and Walter of Columbia was selected to design it, and a million bricks, limestone, and granite were ordered.[53] By November 1903, the convicts began digging the foundation space.[54] Mell worried that the laying of the cornerstone would have all the right feel to it. The date chosen for it, January 19, 1904, a literary society day and Robert E. Lee's birthday, assured a good audience. Tillman was asked to speak along with Mell.[55] By completion date of the new Agricultural Hall, it was estimated that the physical plant now had a net worth of some $250,000. If one added in farm buildings and homes for faculty, staff, and laborers, the replacement cost amounted to $325,000.[56]

Agricultural Hall, now known as Sikes Hall, as it appeared in the 1910 edition of the Clemson College annual, *Taps*.

The president and trustees worked to make the campus as beautiful as possible. They contracted a Connecticut-based landscape architect to produce a master plan. Tillman was elated. When the architect fell ill, Mell sought a replacement, this time from Boston. After entering into a tentative contract, Mell was "hung out to dry" when the trustees voided the contract. They disapproved of the cost.[57]

Experiment Stations

Agricultural experiment work also proved challenging. In 1904, a legislator introduced a bill establishing an experimental farm in every county. While the bill did not pass, the sentiment that Clemson needed experiment station representation throughout the state was significant. The seacoast presented the first real opportunity for Clemson to concern itself with the state's rice crop.[58] As part of the growing desire for more agricultural experiment stations, the coast also raised the issue of the hay crop.[59] Clemson named W. D. Garrison director for a coastal station.[60]

In 1906, Southern Railway offered land adjacent to a rail line west of Charleston for the site of a coastal station.[61] This gift, including three large lots, amounted to approximately 300 acres lying between Summerville and Jedburg.[62] Initially, the Agricultural Society offered to buy the land and deed it to Clemson, but the railway willingly gave the college the land. The low-lying land had some marshes on it; therefore, drainage created a problem.[63] If properly drained, the property would be a fine plot of coastland. The trustees remained wary, but in the end, they established the station there.[64] It supplied much-needed research on grasses, hay, sea-island cotton, and rice, all aimed at identifying and removing pests in the crops. The station had the name Drainland.[65]

Extension

Extension work had not yet been federally articulated as a mission of the land-grant colleges, but some land-grant schools engaged in extension work as part of the experiment station program. Clemson involved itself in a number of extension activities. First, it produced brochures, which by 1905 it sent to some 12,000 permanent addressees and distributed elsewhere as requested. In all, the college sent out about 300,000 yearly.[66] Also, it produced a weekly fertilizer bulletin for farmers and agricultural businesses.[67] The state veterinarian, a member of the experiment station staff, noted that regular inspections of livestock plus bulletin "seventy-five" accounted for the dramatic decrease in Texas fever in cattle.[68] To produce and distribute bulletins more rapidly, Clemson established its own print shop at a cost of $3,685 for the building (an extension to the experiment station) and the press.[69]

The bulletins contained much more than information solely about crops and livestock. Some of the most important information involved drainage and sanitation. Extension bulletins and later home visits by extension agents offered advice on the placement of water sources such as wells and ponds. Other brochures dealt with the placement of feedlots and cattle sheds. The placement, construction, and maintenance of human waste closets (privies or outhouses) were stressed in brochures and on the extension visits in the state. These played an important role in the improvement of rural and community life in South Carolina.[70]

Direct contact worked especially well. Clemson used the railroads, engines, baggage cars, and coaches for faculty traveling on special "extension trains." Such trains traveled throughout the state, stopping at preannounced places where extension faculty made presentations. The rail companies lent the rolling stock to the college.[71] The trips were scheduled between the two major (winter and spring) quarter breaks. At the end of 1905, the train stopped in thirty-nine sites between November 21 and January 6 of the new year.[72] About 8,400 persons visited the 1905 fall tour. The winter 1906 train stopped thirty-seven times and had 6,300 visitors.[73] The winter tour in 1907 was of about the same length, but had an unparalleled attendance of nearly 15,000.[74] There were minor logistical problems. Southern Railway officials noted after one winter tour that many of the oil lamps in the coach car had disappeared and that the seats had suffered damage. Within three days, Clemson administrators documented that the coach had been in disarray when the college received it. Mell, anxious to keep the goodwill of this major contributor, offered to pay for repairs.[75] By 1907, an economic crisis in the South and the resultant shortage of money from the fertilizer tag sales led Clemson to cancel the extension winter train for 1908. Other avenues would be sought.[76]

The extension train that ran on circuits throughout the state three times a year, late autumn, winter, and spring (always between the college's academic sessions). Staffed by twelve to fifteen of Clemson College's faculty, the extension train was a novel way of reaching out to the communities of South Carolina. Clemson University Photographs, CUL.SC.

During the summer of 1909, "extension" faculty held four-week farmers' institutes in Edgefield, Barnwell, Aiken, Lexington, Saluda, Greenwood, Abbeville, and Lancaster, and one-week institutes at Newberry and Winnsboro.[77] Clemson clearly moved in the direction of taking good agricultural practices based on accurate research in a decentralized fashion to the farmers.[78] It had already attracted attention of Seaman A. Knapp, the "father" of the Cooperative Extension Service.

The number of farm families reached by the "extension" program—borne by the Federal Hatch Act, the Second Morrill Act, other congressional actions, the state of South Carolina, and Clemson's fertilizer tag sales revenues—contributed significantly to the dietary health and financial improvement of the state's citizens. This effort at public service had supporters across the nation and formed part of an emerging network of private groups, such as the various "benevolent and protective societies," semiprivate organizations like "scouting," and public-supported services such as the early public health agencies that sprouted up in the United States. In South Carolina and many other places, the initial social separation of the races continued and expanded the legal segregation of the late nineteenth century.

The largest agricultural operation, however, was the Clemson campus. It was divided into two major parts: the teaching campus and the experimental farm. There existed, from time to time, two farms: the college farm (sometimes called the "home farm") and experimental farm or station. The trustees, the president, and the secretary-treasurer could not agree on whether the farms should be managed and reported on separately or as one. The heart of the issue involved accounting for the officers' stewardship not just of federal or state funds, but also for "cadet funds," the money the cadets, their parents, or some other private source paid for teaching, room, board, laundry, and other expenses, such as uniforms.

Knapp's visit to Clemson led to the appointment of J. Phil Campbell, from Georgia, as director of Clemson's extension demonstration work. Work with farm families, particularly in food safety and preservation, led A. L. Easterling, school superintendent in Marlboro County, to establish the Boys' Corn Club, a movement that began in the Midwest. The Corn Clubs sought to teach future farmers new methods of planting, fertilizing, and harvesting. It paid off quickly, for in 1909, Jerry Moore, a Corn Club member from Florence County, produced the world's record for bushels of corn per acre. A scholarship to Clemson and his graduation in 1917 were well-earned rewards. Then in 1910, Marie Cromer (Seigler), who taught in Talathia School in Aiken County, organized the Girls' Tomato Canning Club, the first of its kind in the nation. These two efforts led to the formation of the 4-H Clubs, which still flourish. Within the year, the work with white boys and girls in the state fell under the formal direction of Clemson; however, the college did not begin programming for African Americans at that time.

The most important of these public activities was the annual summer institute held at Clemson in July and August. Regularly attracting 600 to the campus, the institute featured speakers and some entertainers. The families stayed in the barracks while the speakers were housed in the college's hotel. The barracks dining rooms served meals. The institute hired cadets as workers, but all faculty and staff were considered full-time employees and, unless given permission for study leave by the trustees, had duties with the institute.

Invariably, the college received complaints about the institutes. Regular criticism was sent, usually to the president and frequently with a copy to a legislator. Four issues appear most prevalent in the criticism: quality of the food, lack of faculty availability, poor cleanliness of toilets and baths (which were communal), and cleanliness of bedrooms. Much of the displeasure was the result of Clemson's modern draining and flushing equipment, which many guests found unfamiliar. Regular scrubbing and spraying helped. But for food, the problem arose from its mass preparation. As for the availability of faculty, Mell had to explain that professors had to set up and take down experiments, rework lectures, and research answers to questions.

Jerry Moore as a member of the South Carolina Boys' Corn Club, a precursor to 4-H. Moore was the national champion of corn production per acre, for which he won a scholarship to Clemson. Clemson University Photographs, CUL.SC.

However, when the institute attendees were on campus, and even though they were guests of Clemson's experiment station, they saw themselves as guests of Clemson College. Therefore, if a foodstuff were in short supply, the mess staff often "borrowed" from the "home farm" to feed the guests. The bookkeeping was exceptionally difficult. To complicate matters and to keep overhead down, one person, P. H. E. Sloan (and his successors), was allowed to order, purchase, receive, and distribute all goods and animals. In this system, the trustees found it tempting to ignore Mell and direct employees such as Sloan without conferring with the president.

When it came time to appoint a chief of the Dairy Department, for example, Mell turned to Maj. Henry E. Alvord, the chief of the USDA Dairy Division, to recommend a candidate. At Tillman's request, which the latter did not communicate to the rest of the Board of Trustees, Alvord in 1902 recommended a mature, though mild, man, C. O. Upton of Cornell, for the position.[79] The cattle herds consisted of Guernseys, Herefords, polled Angus, Shorthorns and Jerseys. Alvord also helped build the herds by selecting cattle, frequently from Kentucky, and having them shipped by rail to Clemson. Tillman, who had a deep interest in agriculture, also recommended buying Kentucky mules, jackasses, and jennies for breeding to keep the plow teams strong.[80] Mell requested from the board permission to hire Tillman's candidate as professor of animal husbandry to supervise the herds of beef, registered, and commercial cattle. Fortunately, they concurred. The Dairy Department also produced milk, cheese, and butter, and in 1904 Clemson added the manufacturing of ice cream.[81] A tradition began.

In fact, the regular involvement of the trustees in direct contact with the college faculty and staff proved to be a problem, a common theme at Clemson. J. S. Newman, the vice director of the experiment station, who had returned to Clemson after his first resignation, again resigned on August 3, 1904. The cause was the individual trustees' circumventing their own announced administrative chain of command as seen in ordering foodstuffs, shipping cattle, and selecting staff without securing board approval or involving the vice director and the president/director.[82]

Fertilizer Revenue

The fertilizer tag sales revenue was another constant worry. The income from the tag sales fluctuated widely but offered a juicy plum for the legislature. Sometimes the general assembly's goal was to move the tag revenue to the state treasury and at other times use portions of it for support of other academic institutions, usually Winthrop College.[83] In January 1905, Trustee Augustine T. Smythe, a board member from 1900 to 1906, sent to the administration and the board a lengthy legal opinion based on federal court rulings that prohibited a fee such as the fertilizer tag sales from going into the state's general revenue. He based his well-reasoned paper on Section 10, Article 1, of the U.S. Constitution.[84]

Smythe, a former state senator and opponent of the Act of Acceptance of 1889, had served as Simpson's counsel in the *Lee v. Simpson* case. He was a Charlestonian, born in 1842. Educated first locally and then at South Carolina College, he served in the Confederate army from 1862 to the end of the war. He married Louisa McCord in 1865, and they had six children. For fourteen years (1880–1894), he served in the state senate and as a trustee of South Carolina College from 1890 to 1894. In 1900, the legislature elected Smythe to fill the seat on the Clemson board made vacant by the death of Governor W. H. Ellerbe (1895–1899). An active citizen, he held memberships in the Delta Kappa Epsilon Fraternity, Hibernian Society, Charleston Yacht Club, Washington Artillery,

South Carolina Society, Second Presbyterian Church of Charleston, Scottish Rite Masonry, and Knights of Pythias. Despite all those interests, he was one of the very dedicated trustees of Clemson Agricultural College.

Smythe also had Upstate connections. His brother, Ellison Adger Smyth (the use of the final "e" varied from branch to branch as well as branch to twig), was one of several Charleston businessmen who, with Francis J. Pelzer, founded the Pelzer Manufacturing Company in 1881. Ellison Smyth served as the firm's first and only president. The company built the mill and village of Pelzer.[85] Smythe, the trustee, invested in the Pelzer enterprise and, with his brother, owned Connemara (now identified with Carl Sandberg), in Flat Rock, North Carolina. Augustine Smythe also owned Woodburn, the plantation home outside of Pendleton, where he raised fine horses and cattle.[86]

The Library

Clemson College's original library in Main Building. Clemson University Photographs, CUL.SC.

Although Mell likened the college library to the "institution's central laboratory," it remained far smaller than desired by the faculty. Further, neither the space nor the collection (estimated at 8,000 items) was really adequate. The library tried to obtain a copy of the newspaper of record for each county in the state, but those arrived haphazardly. The real research library existed as part of the agriculture program and was scattered among its three main buildings: Agricultural Hall (1904), the Experiment Station, and the Veterinary Building.

The college allocated money annually for library books and journals and received regular private contributions, frequently from Senator Tillman. By far the largest number of contributions came from the U.S. government. By 1904, the library desperately needed a professional librarian. Prior to that point, a single secretary presided in the library, which was located in the Main Building (now Tillman Hall). Mell took the trustees' suggestion to seek a professional librarian. He corresponded with a number of land-grant presidents whom he knew through the land-grant college association. The president of the Nebraska Agricultural and Mechanical College recommended a young woman who had trained in the college library, and Mell began a correspondence with her.[87]

Eventually, he offered her the position, she accepted, and he informed the trustees. They reacted quickly. On August 11, 1904, they insisted that Mell seek a man for the post. Mell had to write the young woman, who had already resigned her current position and begun preparing to move. She protested on August 17, and ultimately Mell sent her $100 to close out the contract on September 9. She agreed to the settlement on the twelfth.[88]

Again the board undercut Mell. Unable to find a man for the post, the trustees continued the contract of Susan Sloan, a secretary and daughter of P. H. E. Sloan, who resigned on December 9, 1905. Richard Wright Simpson asked the board to hire Katherine Trescot (1850–1934), a South Carolinian and a daughter of Henry Trescot, a warm supporter of Clemson Agricultural College.

Thus, the first woman professional had joined the college staff. Prior to Trescot's arrival, several women had served as "matrons": Mrs. John F. Calhoun in the barracks and Mrs. J. A. Fitzgerald in the infirmary. It is doubtful if the cadets made a distinction among female clerical staff, matrons, and professionals. The board's reaction to Mell's selection of the Nebraska female as librarian suggests that the place of origin might have been as much of a stumbling block as gender.[89]

The Community

Slowly a semblance of a community began to spring up between the college campus and the Southern railway. The first resident member of the clergy in the community was the Episcopal minister, the Rev. Mr. Benjamin McKenzie Anderson; his title was rector of St. Paul's, Pendleton, and missionary-in-charge of the "mission of the Holy Trinity at Clemson College." Families who transferred membership from St. Paul's to Holy Trinity included J. S. Newman, senior warden, and P. H. E. Sloan, treasurer of the mission. The constituency of the mission, usually referred to as a "chapel of ease"—that is, a separate place for worship within the "bounds" (or jurisdiction) of the parish church—exceeded that of St. Paul's, the parish church.

In 1902, the Rev. Mr. Kirkman George Finlay replaced Anderson, whom the diocese had, on Anderson's request, dismissed. Finlay would remain with St. Paul's-Trinity until 1907, when he was called to Trinity Church in Columbia. Young and married, Finlay physically helped build the rectory. When his infant son died in 1907, Finlay asked his good friend the Rev. Mr. William Hayne Mills, the new resident pastor of Fort Hill Presbyterian Church, to lead the committal service in the Christ Church yard in Greenville.[90]

After sharing a pastor with the Pendleton Presbyterian Church, Fort Hill needed to build a manse. Consequently, in 1905, the Fort Hill Presbyterians contracted with Frank Milburn, a Columbia architect, to design the structure. Built on the south side of the church's property and including porches and a section for classrooms, the manse accommodated a good-sized family. In September 1906, the presbytery confirmed the call of the Fort Hill session and congregation, and Mills, who was from Winnsboro and had preached at Fort Hill several times, came to the community. He, his wife, Louise, and their daughter, Edith, settled in by Thanksgiving. Subsequently, they had other children, several of whom played roles in the development of Clemson College. Mills started a weekly Sunday school for the convicts on campus, a monthly ministry at Old Stone Church, and a weekly chapel in the Ravenel community across the Seneca River.[91]

By April 1907, a group of Baptists in the college had also organized and, within two months, established a church, with Mell presiding. The congregation used supply preachers until 1909, when their first full-time pastor, the Rev. Mr. Thomas V. McCaul, a graduate of the University of Virginia, joined them. With the second largest number of adherents (the Methodists had the most) among the student body, Baptist students formed an organization almost immediately.[92]

The community benefited also from improvements made to the road connecting the college to the Calhoun train depot. Macadamized with "crusher-run" granite, the road had a surface of a mixture of granite chips and granite dust as a binder. As the road proceeded north from the campus, it passed Sloan's store, a general store that sold some packaged food items, candies, tobacco, toiletries, and various men's clothing. Then came the dentist's office (open one or two days a week) operated by Dr. Burgess, and next Frank Clinkscales's livery stable. There, William Greenlee, who had driven Mr. Clemson's carriage, now drove the drayage wagon, which doubled as the garbage scow.[93] Across the road, L. Cleveland Martin, a licensed pharmacist, opened a drugstore in 1902. After a brief period, Martin, who also had a store elsewhere, hired Pickens McCollum, a graduate of the Southern College of Pharmacy in Atlanta, as the resident pharmacist. In a short period of time, McCollum owned the store.[94] Initially, the college attempted to handle textbook sales but by 1900 had contracted the New York firm of Hines and Noble to get the books.[95] The company needed a local bookseller, and McCollum stepped forward and created a relationship selling books that lasted into the 1950s.[96]

Student Life

Campus activities for the cadets also expanded. The Agricultural Hall had a large two-story wing on the south side outfitted as a gymnasium, and it was slowly equipped with the latest exercise equipment. This gymnasium also provided a new space for dances. The regimental band now had nineteen members, and the string orchestra, which specialized in popular dance music, had seven instrumentalists.[97] The latter played for most of the dances, while the regimental band added to the din at sports events. Joining the bands in performances were the glee and minstrel clubs, which included faculty and staff. Riggs served as president of the glee club, and until he left, Heisman was an officer in the theater club. The *Chronicle* reported that annually the theater group gave performances in nearby communities.

The gymnasium room of Agricultural Hall, today's Sikes Hall, set up for a junior class dance in 1916. Benjamin Gaillard Sitton Scrapbook, CUL.SC.

From 1897, the *Chronicle*, published by the three campus literary societies, annually gave over one issue to the graduating class. By 1901, the senior class had taken matters into its own hands, and it published a separate hardcover yearbook entitled *Clemsonian*. It was not repeated. After the lapse of one year, the seniors, led by electrical engineer W. E. G. Black from Florence, published *Oconeean*.[98] That publication repeated in 1904 and carried pages of clubs. While some, such as the Salons De Cercle, were dedicated to social self-improvement, others were a bit of merriment, such as the Epicurean Club, whose motto was "Eat, Drink, and Be Merry—For Tomorrow You Might Flunk," and whose purpose was "To

Make Things Disappear!"[99] The next effort for a hardback yearbook was *The Annual of Clemson College* in 1906 and 1907. Then in 1908, the annual entitled *Taps* appeared with William Otis Pratt, a senior civil engineering student from Greenwood, as editor in chief. Nicknamed "Ote," he had served as the editor in chief of *The Chronicle*. Except for the years 1944, 1945, and 1946, during and immediately after World War II, *Taps* has remained the end-of-the-year annual publication.

Meanwhile, the *Chronicle* continued as a monthly magazine, combining campus news with student and alumni essays. An interesting feature was the "Exchange," which commented on the literary output of other colleges. These were accompanied by comments from other schools' editorial staffs. Clemson, the "cow college," fared rather well.[100]

However, the students and others on campus desired more frequent and up-to-date news. In the winter of 1907, a weekly newspaper, *The Tiger*, first appeared. The editor was Samuel Roseborough Rhodes, a twenty-five-year-old senior born in Darlington in 1881 and educated in Florence. He had graduated from Furman (twice) and served briefly in the Lees and Williston public schools as an administrator before entering Clemson in September 1905 to study engineering. With both a bachelor of arts degree in English and a master's in mathematics, he attracted other men interested in the arts and the sciences and who formed the core of the proposed *Tiger* staff. The first issue of the weekly came off the commercial press in January 1907. The cadets, the faculty, and some alumni took great interest in the paper, and many subscribed to it.[101] From its beginning, *The Tiger* was a success.

Student "Rebellion"

With a creative and energetic student body, intercollegiate athletics, intramural teams, dance clubs, publications, and clubs for almost anything, not to mention the strict daily schedule and the classes, the cadets still found time on their hands. Even though college regulations forbade nighttime "horsing around," it existed aplenty. Spring was the "dangerous season." The walkout of 1902, although set off by a student misstep, had longtime consequences. Favorite pranks included "breaking quarters" and roaming the campus, raucously serenading faculty homes. In such instances, the commandant and his staff had to restore order. So the cadet focus on the "spoilsport" always characterized the military structure. Fortunately, that unit had a reasonably high turnover of federal officers, thus the frustrations and ire rarely became personal.

However, one instance of student mischief in 1904 had the potential for causing serious consequences. The commandant, Capt. Edgar A. Sirmyer of the Eighth U.S. Cavalry, had come from Michigan and graduated from West Point. He had just married the sister of Walter Riggs's wife. The outburst occurred on March 12, 1904, at the morning raising of the American flag. The detail brought forward the large red, white, and blue trifolded ensign, attached it to the lanyard, and drew it upward. The breeze caught the flag, and as it broke free, Capt. Sirmyer saw not Old Glory but the Stars and Bars.[102] He leapt forward and grabbed the lanyard to halt the flag's ascent, but the cadets raising the banner had the momentum and advantage. Both the flag and Sirmyer began their journey upward. At three or four feet off the ground, the captain jumped free. What happened next is unclear, except for the text in the printed record that declared, "March 13, 1904 'Next morning at inspection—everybody burnt—trouble around the flag pole!'"[103]

This is the only known picture of the "Student Rebellion of 1904," in which the student flag detail raised the Stars and Bars banner of the Confederacy rather than the American flag. This photo appeared in the 1904 edition of the Clemson College annual, *The Oconeean.*

Graduations and the Clemson Ring

From the very first graduation in 1896, a Clemson symbol of graduation was a ring. Initially in 1896, the gold ring had an unmarked stone with chasing on the shank. By 1901, the "C," palmetto, and year appeared. The student ring committee in 1906 added the eagle with a blank shield to the shanks. Committee member F. Raymone Sweeny, an electrical engineer, is credited with the design.

Some older alumni declared that the eagle represented a student disavowal of the flag incident, which had occurred a year earlier. In the first graduation after World War I had begun in Europe, the United States shield, swords, tiger head, and star were added to the ring. In 1916, the ring also bore the S.C. state seal with both faces and rifles, and in 1927, the school's name appeared on it. For men, the ring has remained unchanged since then, except for the graduation year cut into the onyx or cast on the gold and the name changes of the school. The trustees made the ring the only official one in 1939.

During Mell's administration, the number of graduates annually from Clemson grew from 68 in 1902–1903 to 268 in 1908–1909, an increase of nearly four times. While the general enrollment grew, it did not increase by that magnitude. Clemson was becoming ever more effective and efficient in teaching if persistence to graduation is a measure.

Trouble at the Top

Clemson, the largest of the state's schools, enjoyed a broadening popularity. However, by the middle of Mell's term as president, complaints about him and others became more pointed. In August 1906, a letter to the school attacked Simpson directly, while two weeks later a state senator wrote of "serious charges preferred against the management of the college."[104] Smythe replied publicly:

> It is charged that the life trustees practically run the college and that because they are in the majority they act together as a closed corporation. This is entirely a mistake. During the entire time of my service as a trustee, I never once saw the line drawn between the life trustees on the one side and state trustees on the other. Our discussions were earnest and frequent, and as in all deliberative bodies, there were differences of opinion, sincerely and honestly entertained. The votes were sometimes close, but I never saw a cleavage along the line of state or life trustees.[105]

Another charge said that the trustees received a per diem, which was false. Still another held that the faculty received food supplies originally designated for the students. Again, the charge had no truth to it. On that issue, faculty and staff were not allowed to purchase or receive supplies from the home farm. They raised their own or purchased needed items from the general store, about a mile away in Calhoun, or from merchants in Pendleton. And still again, the cry arose that the fertilizer tag revenue should go into the state treasury. The college's response followed Smythe's legal reasoning that it was part of police powers not tax powers of the state. The response cited two North Carolina cases tried in federal courts. State Senator Blake complained about the absence of faculty at the summer farm and home institute. Mell responded that nine faculty had served as the greeting party and all other faculty had worked in laboratories to demonstrate their recent research findings.

In some instances, it appeared that critics coordinated their letters to the newspapers. An anonymous writer in the *Greenville News*, a Mr. Hance in the Lancaster *News*, and a Mr. Major in the *State* all complained about the institute. A candidate for governor, Mr. McMahan, furthered the attack in a speech made in Greenville.[106] The criticisms, however, did not decrease the demand for places at the college. While 852 applied, the school had space for 624 only.[107]

Nonetheless, because of the growing political and other clamor, Mell invited the governor and the general assembly to visit the campus in 1907 and arranged a railroad coach for them. The trip was a success, partly as a result of Mell's giving each of the 250 guests an advanced student as an escort.[108]

During the 1907–1908 year, Richard Wright Simpson decided to step down as president of the Board of Trustees. The board elected Alan Johnstone of Newberry as its new president.[109] Simpson would remain a life trustee until his death in 1912.

Also elected a legislative trustee was Coke D. Mann of West Union, replacing Robert Aldrich. Mann, a Methodist minister, had attended rural schools in Abbeville County before he received admission in 1871 to the S.C. Methodist Conference. He continued as a minister until 1903 and farmed in the Walhalla area. As a member of the S.C. House of Representatives from 1906 to1908, he was elected a trustee in 1908. Prior to Mell's resignation, Mann published several letters attacking Mell as president.[110]

By the spring of 1909, some of the trustees concluded that Mell's usefulness to the college had ended. Tillman, for example, wrote Riggs on April 26 stating he would support him for the presidency.[111] Riggs became increasingly certain that Mell planned to resign. Riggs told Tillman, however, that he did "not want the Presidency of Clemson," which may have been false. But he continued that money was of little interest. He felt content in his present position as professor and director of the Engineering Department. "Why," he continued, "should I risk this contentment and exchange it for an office beset with difficulties and trials and responsibilities and heartache." He asked, "What is my duty to the College and its welfare?" Obviously unhappy with the strained relationship between Mell and the board, he raised the telling question:

> Do you believe the Board wants one-man rule at Clemson? That is what I believe in....Are they willing to give him absolute control in their absence, and that overshadowing authority which no President has yet exercised, and make him responsible for *results* without dictating the ways and means by which he shall attain it?...And that reminds me of another objection—that I am not a churchman, although I affiliate with the Presbyterian Church....Heaven send us deliverance from anymore experiments in the Presidential office.[112]

In the meantime, Trustee Mann had launched the public attack on Mell, causing the latter to write Smythe, then no longer a trustee, "Of course I feel very keenly the injustice of this outrageous attack on me particularly when a member of the Board does so far forget his relationship as a member of the Board to undertake such outrageous steps through the newspapers of this state."

By June 1909, Simpson was convinced that Mell was preparing to resign, and he asked Riggs about his future plans. Riggs responded that he was not a candidate for the presidency and that Tillman had not "directly or indirectly mentioned such a thing to me," which proved untrue.[113] In July, Mell considered responding to Mann through the press, but Henry Tillman offered to get his father to talk with Mann. But the pressure on Mell mounted. On July 9, he submitted his resignation, which the board accepted on August 14, 1909. One newspaper, commenting on the resignation, urged that Mann be forced from the board.[114]

In October, a strong supporter of the college wrote Riggs, urging him to accept the presidency for the sake of the school. And a month later, J. Moore McConnell, a professor at Davidson College, urged Riggs to accept the office.[115] Early in December, Riggs informed Hartzog of the board's impending meeting to select a president. Riggs hoped it selected someone with stature and that it gave the new chief executive liberty to manage the institution. On December 4, President Thatch of Auburn urged Riggs to accept the job. The trustees turned first to Hardin, who refused to serve as acting president yet another time, citing his age. Riggs responded to Thatch that Hardin was "unwilling to accept the burden." On December 8, the board, in a unanimous vote, chose Riggs president pro tempore. Riggs shared the news with his aged mother, who lived in Orangeburg, and he informed Trustee Rawl that he fully intended to govern.

Although Riggs had said on several occasions that he did not want the president's post, he had been clear that if he did become Clemson's president, he fully intended to be "the" president. Whether he was dissembling earlier when he asked whether or not he should "risk this contentment and exchange it for an office beset with difficulties and trials and responsibilities and heartache" is hard to judge. However, when the trustees selected him, they should have known what his style would be.

The troubles and challenges that brought an end to the presidencies of Hartzog and Mell included, of major importance, the question of student discipline, which vexed both administrations. Underlying that was the tendency of the board, or at least some of its members, to circumvent the president of the college in dealing with student discipline and in dealing with the faculty. A shortage of funds caused by the decline of the annual sum derived from the fertilizer tag revenue added to the pressure felt by the president of the college and the board.

When Mell left, he wrote a long letter to three members of the general assembly detailing his view of the school's problems. Foremost was the board's interference "with the duties of administration, including student discipline, budget, and other attendant matters." He also wrote, "Nepotism is a serious drawback to good and efficient growth in the college, and there should be some remedy for this evil." He noted that five trustees had family in the staff and faculty and that the board overrode his hiring decisions to advance less-qualified friends to places on the staff. Even his secretary was related to a board member. The indictment was powerful.

Notes

1. CUL.SC.CUA. S 25 f 13.
2. Green, "A Scholar's Turmoil: Patrick Hues Mell, 1902–1910," in *Tradition*, 78–97. The biography is a model of concision.
3. Ibid., 80–81.
4. CUL.SC.CUA. S 30 v 1, 327–328.
5. MacCambridge, *College Football*, 600.
6. Matthews, *Clemson Foot Ball*, 7–9.
7. Conklin, *Gone with the Ivy*, 137–141.
8. Ibid.
9. MacCambridge, *College Football*, 216.
10. Sam Blackmon, March 8, 2010, to J. V. Reel. Blackmon is on the staff of the Clemson University Sports Information Office.
11. Hemphill, *Men of Mark*, vol. 4, 59–60.
12. Umphlett, *Creating the Big Game: John W. Heisman*, 14, 18, 61, and 255.
13. Bryan, *Clemson*, 76–77. The full newspaper account is clipped (without citation evidence) and pasted into Mell's scrapbooks in CUL.SC.CUA. S 18.
14. Hollis, *South Carolina*, vol. 2, 192–193.
15. Bourret, *Clemson Football 2009*, 202.
16. The major features of the tale are extracted from newspaper clippings in CUL.SC.CUA. S 18 Mell Scrapbooks. These are from the Atlanta *Journal*, October 17 and 18, 1903. I have followed this tale, adding the story of the unpaid bet from the University of Georgia's football program, September 27, 1969 (Clemson game). It is also told slightly differently and dated a year earlier by R. E. DeSpain Jr., in *Life and Career of Heisman*, 75–76.
17. Bourret, *Clemson Football 2009*, 202.
18. Umphlett, *Creating the Big Game: John W. Heisman*, 65; and DeSpain, *Heisman*, 77.
19. Bourret, *Clemson Football 2009*, 170–171.
20. *Chronicle*, June 1899, vol. 2, 418.
21. Ibid., June 1900, vol. 3, 47–49.
22. Ibid., June 1899, vol. 2, 419.
23. Ibid., June 1900, vol. 3, frontispiece.
24. Ibid., June 1903, vol. 6, 320; CUL.SC.CUA. S 30 v 1, 221; and Bryan, *Clemson*, 273.
25. CUL.SC.CUA. S 30 v 1.
26. Bryan, *Clemson*, 271.
27. Dabney, *A History of Mr. Jefferson's University*, 82, 166–167, 415; and CUL.SC.CUA. S 28 "Gee."
28. CUL.SC.CUA. S 30 v 1, 112. In the same year, the faculty awarded a second Norris Medal to Clarence Albertis McLendon; see Bryan, *Clemson*, 271.
29. Ibid., v 2, 263.
30. Ibid., S 25 b 2 f 9.
31. Ibid., S 28 f 4.
32. Ibid., S 25 b 12 f 13.
33. Ibid., S 18 f 50.
34. Ibid., ff 47 and 50.

35. Ibid., f 47.
36. Ibid., f 49.
37. Ibid., S 8 f 50.
38. Ibid., f 52.
39. Ibid., f 12.
40. Ibid., f 22.
41. Ibid., f 35.
42. Ibid.
43. Ibid., S 18 f 43.
44. Ibid., f 63.
45. Ibid., f 64.
46. Ibid., f 65.
47. Green, "A Scholar's Turmoil: Patrick Hues Mell, 1902–1910," in *Tradition*, 91.
48. CUL.SC.CUA. S 17 f 364.
49. Ibid., S 18 f 1.
50. Ibid.; and *Chronicle*, May 1903, vol. 6, 377.
51. CUL.SC.CUA. S 18 f 2. See also the *Annual* 1907, 119–120.
52. Ibid., f 3; and *Reports and Resolutions*, 1904, 1131. The *Reports and Resolutions* for each of these years contains reports on the numbers of convicts but little or nothing about tasks.
53. CUL.SC.CUA. S 18 f 3.
54. Ibid., f 4.
55. Ibid., f 59.
56. Ibid., f 3.
57. Ibid., f 27.
58. Ibid., f 18.
59. Ibid., f 27.
60. Ibid., f 33.
61. Ibid., f 34.
62. Ibid., f 35.
63. Ibid., ff 39, 41, 42, 43, 52, 55, and 56.
64. *Clemson Trustees' Report to the General Assembly*, 1904, 523–659.
65. CUL.SC.CUA. S 18 f 26.
66. Ibid., f 69.
67. Ibid., f 8.
68. Ibid., f 46.
69. Fite, *Cotton Fields No More*, 16.
70. CUL.SC.CUA. S 18 f 18.
71. Ibid., f 24.
72. Ibid., f 35.
73. Ibid., f 41.
74. Ibid., f 45.
75. Ibid., f 57.
76. Ibid., f 73.
77. Ibid., f 78.
78. Ibid., S 2 f 13.
79. Ibid., S 18 f 1.
80. Ibid., f 8.
81. Ibid., f 11.
82. Ibid., f 15.
83. Ibid., f 26.
84. Baker, "Ellison Adger Smyth," in *South Carolina Encyclopedia*, 886.
85. Hemphill, *Men of Mark*, vol. 3, 409–412.
86. CUL.SC.CUA. S 18 f 5. Michael Kohl, Special Collections librarian at Clemson, on a visit to colleagues at the University of Nebraska, located this file, had copies made, and, with permission, placed the copies of this sad correspondence in the Clemson University archives. The first

full-time employee assigned to the library was C. M. Furman, son of the English professor and 1906 graduate. He was succeeded by Miss L. Lewis in 1902 and Miss Sloan in 1903.

87. Ibid., f 12.
88. Ibid., f 3.
89. Ibid., f 67.
90. Skardon, *Holy Trinity*, 9–16.
91. McMahon, *Country Church and College Town*, 47–61.
92. Arrington, *History of Clemson Baptist Church*, 5, 7, 8, 16, and 21.
93. *Chronicle*, vol. 10, no. 7, 449, 458.
94. Lindsay-McCollum papers; and Clemson *Messenger*, June 22, 1977.
95. CUL.SC.CUA. S 18 f 55.
96. Ibid., S 38 f "McCollum."
97. *Oconeean*, 1903, 96 and 100.
98. Copies of each of these are in the Special Collections of the Clemson University Libraries.
99. *Oconeean*, 1904, 151–156.
100. *Chronicle*, see the "Exchange" section in the monthly issues.
101. *Clemson Slipstick*, May 1954, 8–9, 22, and 27.
102. *Oconeean*, 1904, 71, is a picture of the event, and it is captioned "Raising the Stars and Bars." The flag is limp at the top of the pole, thus it is impossible to tell whether or not it was the Stars and Bars (the first national flag of the Confederacy) or the now more recognized battle flag, usually called "the star-crossed banner." The former with its canton of blue with a circle of white stars and its three horizontal red-white-red bars is more easily confused with the U.S. Stars and Stripes.
103. Ibid., 78. The story of the Confederate flag was retold a number of times. In the February 22 and 29, 1948, edition of the Columbia *State*, which is the source of much of the text, Sirmyer reported the "insurrection" to the Department of War. The story got to the folks at the Carnegie Foundation, who may or may not have been considering the gift of a library building to Clemson. Purportedly, they refused to consider the idea any further. The *Greenville News* of June 21, 1958, added that the plan was set by a group of four cadets over a month's time. Perrin Cothran made (or caused the making of) the flag. In 1958, he claimed to know where the banner was hidden. Cothran had retired as vice president of Phoenix Insurance Co. in Hartford, Connecticut. Another plotter was J. Frank Wilson, who went on to own Sumter Dairies. They were joined by O. M. Roberts, who owned an electric contracting firm. The fourth was J. D. Tarbox, an engineer and inventor who lived in Philadelphia. A year later, the Anderson *Daily Mail* (June 21, 1959) noted even the perpetrators could no longer separate fact from fiction.
104. CUL.SC.CUA. S 18 f 34.
105. Ibid.
106. Ibid., f 35. This speech and letter will be addressed in the next chapter.
107. Ibid.
108. Ibid., f 41.
109. *Clemson Trustees to the General Assembly*, 1908–1909, 485.
110. Ibid., S 30 ss 1 ff "Bradley" and "Coke D. Mann."
111. Ibid., S 18 f 70.
112. Ibid., f 80.
113. Ibid., f 72.
114. Ibid., f 80.
115. Ibid., f 75.

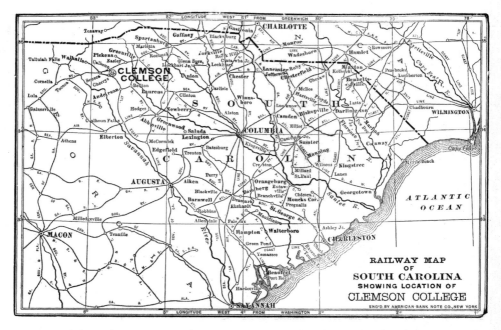

A map of the railroad system of South Carolina in the second decade of the twentieth century showing location of Clemson College. Taken from the 1917–1918 *Clemson College Catalog.*

CHAPTER VIII

Stability, Stress

1910–1918

In the autumn of 1910, the enrollment at Clemson Agricultural College of South Carolina reached 703. Of these, eighty students enrolled in the preparatory course, twenty in the two-year short courses, some in agriculture, and others in textiles. The freshman class had 243, the senior class, eighty-seven. South Carolinians numbered 691 with all counties represented except Allendale and Jasper. In addition, five students were from North Carolina, two each from Kentucky and Georgia, and one each from New York, Nebraska, Virginia, Tennessee, Alabama, Florida, and the District of Columbia.

By 1912, Latin American students were in the student population, hailing from Panama, Brazil, Cuba, and Jamaica. All but two had Latin surnames. Two of the three Brazilians bore distinctly Anglo Celtic surnames, causing wonder if they were missionary sons (one listed Rio de Janeiro as his hometown) or even descendants of Confederate émigrés. In 1913, the first student at Clemson then considered "nonwhite" was a Japanese student enrolled in textiles.

South Carolina had growing and changing demographics; the state's population had increased from 1,340,316 in 1900 to 1,515,400 in 1910 (a 13 percent rise). The African American population increased by 7 percent, while the white population grew by 21 percent. In addition, the state's urban population rose 2 percent as the rural dropped to 85.2 percent (urban meant here as a village or town with a population of 2,500 or greater). The two trends of population growth and the drift to towns continued at least until 1990.[1] The relative decline in the African American percentage resulted in part from the decline of the agrarian economy, the increased severity of both de jure and de facto segregation, and the greater difficulty African Americans had in obtaining jobs in towns throughout the southern textile states.

South Carolina's "textile boom" was centered in the Upstate, and the years when the opening of new mills was at its greatest coincided with the start of Clemson's textile program. Further, the new mills no longer turned out only yarn or unfinished cloth as production of usable or "finished" cloth began. While Upstate investors became wealthy from the textile business, the industry created a strong separation in the white population in the towns. Generally, African Americans received little benefit from this industry, and their migration from South Carolina intensified. By 1911, as Riggs took office, the Upstate was the hub of this industry,

James Corcoran "Mr. Clemson" Littlejohn (1889–1959) held at different times the varied posts of electrician, instructor, registrar, assistant to the president, and business manager for Clemson College. Here we see Littlejohn (marked by an arrow) as a member of the engineering instruction staff with professors Thomas Grayson Poats to his left and Frank Townes Dargan seated in front of him. J. C. Littlejohn/Mary Katherine Littlejohn Scrapbook, Littlejohn Family Papers, CUL.SC.

driven as it was by cheap power, cheap labor, and good transportation. By the end of Riggs's presidency in early 1924, the Upstate dominance was firmly entrenched. Clemson Agricultural College was both benefactor and beneficiary.[2]

Clemson remained one of the largest of the southern land-grant colleges, with 281 students in various agriculture courses, 271 in engineering, and the remainder in textiles. A key person in the enrollment of students, James Corcoran Littlejohn served variously as assistant to the college's president and as registrar. Littlejohn, born in Jonesville in 1889, had enrolled at Clemson in 1904. Graduating in 1908 in "mech-elec" (a student term for mechanical and electrical engineering), he stayed after graduation, working as the campus electrician. Then he served as an instructor in woodworking and mechanical engineering, and by 1911, as registrar and assistant to the president. He held the latter posts until 1926.[3]

The students were representative of the white males of the state. The majority of the students came from villages under 2,500 and from the country, and most were sons of farmers. The average age of all the students had risen to 19.5 years. Organized as a military corps, the students were subject to military or, as Walter Merritt Riggs said, "semi-military" discipline. Riggs, named acting president on the resignation of Patrick Hughes Mell on December 3, 1909, took office immediately. On January 1, 1911, the trustees appointed him president.[4]

Walter Merritt Riggs (1873–1924), the fifth president of Clemson College, longtime professor of engineering, and father of Clemson football, as he appeared around the midpoint of his presidency in the 1918 edition of the Clemson College annual, *Taps*.

The Faculty

In 1910, the faculty, all males, numbered fifty-four, of whom four held PhDs and two, the doctor of veterinary medicine degree. The campus physician held a medical degree and taught hygiene as a part of military instruction. Of the remaining faculty, thirty-two had attained the bachelor of science or arts degree, one held a master's in engineering, and thirteen held the traditional master of science or arts. Two listed no degree. The staff numbered twenty-one: sixteen men and five women.

Almost all the faculty lived on campus. Generally, the professors (one per subject) lived in two-story brick homes. F. H. H. Calhoun, associate professor of geology and chemistry professor, one of the four PhDs and first track coach, and his bride, Grace Ward Calhoun, lived in a two-story wood-frame house with large porches, front and back. On the back porch was a well. The house had seven large rooms, one closet, a pantry, and a bath. Even though the classroom buildings and the barracks were fully plumbed and electrified, faculty residences were not all plumbed, although all were electrified.[5]

The Community

At about the same time that the local Baptist congregation was being formed, the Pendleton circuit of the Methodist church proposed the establishment of a congregation near the college. Three years passed, and in 1905, Maj. Samuel Maner Martin (b. 1875), a mathematics instructor at Clemson, pressed the Methodist conference for a church near the college. After graduating from the Citadel (1896), he taught in Johnston (Edgefield County). Joining the Clemson faculty, he served as assistant commandant of the Clemson cadet corps under A. G. Shanklin when most of the regular army officers served in the Spanish-American War. He married Elizabeth Conway Simpson, one of R. W. Simpson's daughters. The cadets gave Martin the honorific title of "Major," by which he was known for the rest of his life.[6]

Samuel Maner "Major" Martin (1875–1959) near the beginning of his 50 years of service at Clemson College. Between 1898 and 1948, Martin served as a major and assistant commandant, professor of mathematics, director of the Mathematics Department, and acting director of the Academic Department. Taken from the 1903 edition of the Clemson College annual, *The Oconeean*.

In December 1907, the S.C. Methodist Conference gave the Rev. Mr. John Hagan Graves the task of organizing a Methodist congregation at the college. He joined the preaching rotation for the college Sunday chapel services. In February 1908, the conference appointed a Clemson Methodist board of trustees and registered a congregation of eighteen members. Graves spent much of his time appealing to other area Methodist congregations for support. The conference transferred him in 1909 and replaced him with the Rev. Mr. Melvin B. Kelly.

Buoyed by the conference-wide support and by the stipend the college trustees paid to the congregations with resident pastors for their counseling services to the cadets, the Methodists prepared to purchase a lot, next to Holy Trinity Episcopal Church, on which to build their church. A two-story frame house was re-sited and converted into the parsonage. F. Raymone Sweeny, a 1906 Clemson graduate and instructor in the engineering faculty, designed the church in brick Gothic with an offset entrance tower and steeple. By October 1912, with construction of the church nearly finished, the pastorate of the Rev. Mr. Philip A. Murray also ended.[7]

With 87 percent of the cadets belonging to one of the four denominations physically represented by the churches in the community (4 percent belonged to some other Protestant denomination, such as Lutheran, Universalist, or Quaker, and one found very few Roman Catholics, Jews, or nonaligned), President Riggs announced on April 1, 1913, that students or parents would select one of the four town churches to attend each Sunday, and that roll would be taken at the church. Those who chose not to select a church remained quietly in their barracks, rejoining their squad at Sunday midday mess.[8] The college administration was able to discontinue its Sunday service and could disentangle itself from the thorny problem of selecting the preacher each week.

Adult social life revolved around the campus. The president's wife organized the weekly sewing meeting held at the president's home. By the time Riggs became the president (January 1, 1911), his family was well established in a Queen Anne style home, which he had purchased through Baker and Klutz, a Tennessee-based architecture firm noted for its "fine homes plan books." Riggs had paid for the purchase and erection of the home on college "bequest" land in 1906. When he became president, he chose not to move into the smaller, eighteen-year-old president's home next door. The college converted it into a four-apartment dwelling, and it served as such until the 1950s. The Riggs home remained a campus landmark until its destruction in 1976.[9] When Riggs died, the board recompensed his widow for the house. It became the home for President and Mrs. Sikes and in 1940, the Poole family home. It was located west of the current (2011) president's home. When demolished, the college built a low-rise residence hall in its backyard.

The sewing circle met regularly and became the nucleus of the Clemson Woman's Club of which Mrs. Lula Riggs served as the president. The Woman's Club adopted a set of organizational and procedural guidelines, but when a suggestion was tendered to join a nascent federation by its first chapter in Seneca, the club did not do so. While the Woman's Club developed into a unique Clemson College organization, the men had formed a Masonic lodge. A number of the faculty, such as Maj. Martin, became very active locally and in the lodge's regional structure.

Besides belonging to the sewing group, most of the women joined the Daughters of the American Revolution (DAR), the local chapter of which was named for Andrew Pickens. The DAR marked the graves of Revolutionary soldiers, which attracted the chapter's attention to the Old Stone Church yard. In turn, a number of early Clemson faculty were vitally interested in the Old Stone Church, although their involvement with it did not seem to have been connected to that of the Daughters or Sons of the American Revolution. As early as 1893, Dr. O. M. Doyle of Seneca and J. Miles Pickens of Pendleton had issued a call that led to the creation of the Old Stone Church and Cemetery Improvement Association, which adopted a constitution and bylaws on December 4, 1893.[10] By 1899, the association had created an endowment fund and in 1902 began its preservation efforts by erecting a stone wall around the cemetery at a cost of $516.66 (2009 equivalent $13,147.34).[11] The wall enclosed the burial places of three veterans of the American Revolution,[12] two veterans of the War of 1812,[13] and twenty-five veterans or casualties of the American Civil War.[14] At the time of the wall's construction, two Clemson cadets, E. M. Rembert (October 1, 1874–September 9, 1894), an orphan, and Wade H. Martin (March 18, 1877–March 13, 1896), leaving his widowed mother alone, were both buried there.[15] R. N. Brackett served as the early historian of both the church and yard.

Many women of Clemson also joined the United Daughters of the Confederacy (UDC). Their local chapter was named for John C. Calhoun, and they took on the task of marking the graves of Confederate veterans as well. Some years later, the UDC, led by Mrs. Alester Holmes, acted as a critical force in the first major restoration of Fort Hill. Members of the John C. Calhoun Chapter gave many hours as the hostesses at the house, a task held previously by members of John F. Calhoun's family.

While the local stores carried some food items, a meat wagon arrived at Clemson from Pendleton once a week, causing the women (faculty and staff, black and white) to race to it to buy desired cuts. Local farmers brought in produce in seasonal rounds. Poultry and vegetables were raised on campus, usually in kitchen gardens, and some households kept a milk cow and calf. As housing space got tighter, this lessened. The availability of milk, eggs, and other products for sale from the college's "home farm" vacillated both by policy and productivity.[16]

Trustees

Of the four men who met together in the autumn of 1886, now only Richard Wright Simpson and U.S. Senator Benjamin Ryan Tillman remained. They, along with Robert Esli Bowen, M. L. Donaldson, and John E. Wannamaker, were five of the original seven life trustees named in Mr. Clemson's will. Alan Johnstone, the president of the Board of Trustees, had been chosen by the surviving six to fill the vacancy caused by the death of Daniel Keating Norris in 1905. Then on January 11, 1909, toward the end of Mell's administration, Bowen died.

The life trustees selected Richard Irving Manning (b. August 15, 1859, at Homesly Plantation in Sumter County) to take Bowen's seat. Educated at the University of Virginia, he had joined the Delta Kappa Epsilon Fraternity. In 1881, he married Leila Bernard Meredith of Richmond, Virginia. The farmer-turned-banker served in the S.C. House from 1892 until 1896 and then in the senate from 1899 to 1904. His wife, their eleven sons, and two daughters moved to Columbia, where they were active in Trinity Episcopal Church. Manning also served on the national boards of the Episcopalian Church. In 1915, he was elected South Carolina's governor and was reelected in 1917. He would be the second sitting governor (after Tillman) to serve on Clemson's board. Interestingly, prior to his enrolling in the University of Virginia, Manning attended the Kenmore school operated by Henry Strode prior to his becoming Clemson College's first president. In his political posture, Manning ranked as a "progressive," and much of his governorship (and his positions on the Clemson board) reflected his deep concern for education. As governor, he would use his authority to secure the passage of South Carolina's first county-option compulsory school attendance law.[17] He firmly supported Walter Merritt Riggs.

The last of the life trustees, Alan Johnstone of Newberry, had been one of the first legislative trustees elected, but he had not been reelected when his first term had ended in 1894. When Daniel Keating Norris died in 1905, the other life trustees selected Johnstone to succeed him on January 23, 1905. This action alone suggests the waning of Tillman's influence, given that the "Tillman" legislature was responsible for Johnstone's "non-reelection." Johnstone's election as the second president of Clemson's board, upon the resignation of Simpson from board presidency (although not from the board), was a continuing sign of the fading Tillman presence. Certainly, some part of that was due to Tillman's preoccupation with federal work as a member of the Senate Naval Committee during the era of the naval arms race, which embroiled the British Empire, the Japanese Empire, the Russian Empire, the German Empire, and those in the United States with imperial ambitions in the building of the battleships.[18] However, much was the result of Tillman's declining health.

There were several other major changes in the makeup of the board. First, Richard Wright Simpson died on July 11, 1912. Seventeen months later, Paul Hamilton Earle Sloan, secretary-treasurer to the Board of Trustees, resigned as of January 1, 1914. Samuel Wilds Evans replaced Sloan.

Evans, born on June 21, 1882, was the son of recently deceased Trustee W. D. Evans and Mary Pegues Evans. A Clemson alumnus, he also attended Draughan's Business College. On July 1, 1908, he joined Clemson's very small business staff. Three years later (April 12, 1911), the Rev. Dr. W. H. Mills married Samuel Wilds Evans to Rosa Calhoun, born on December 25, 1875, the daughter of John Francis and Rebecca Noble Calhoun, at Fort Hill Presbyterian Church. The Evanses had two daughters. Selected on January 1, 1914, as secretary-treasurer to the board, Evans served in that role until June 30, 1947. He died on December 30, 1950.[19]

Two of the legislative trustees died in 1910: J. H. Hardin, elected in the first selection of those trustees in 1890, and John Gardiner Richards, first elected in 1908. One successor was the thirty-two-year-old Eddings Thomas Hughes. Upon Hughes's graduation from Clemson in agriculture in 1901, South Carolina's U.S. Representative Asbury Francis Lever added him to his Washington staff. Hughes attended Columbian University (in the District of Columbia) and received a bachelor of laws degree from South Carolina College in 1905. He married Mary Edna Carmichael of Marion, where he practiced law, and they had one son and one daughter. When Hardin's term expired, Hughes was reelected for a full four-year legislative term (1912–1916), focusing on his main interest, agriculture.[20]

The other elected successor was S. T. McKeown, chosen by the legislature in 1912 from Cornwell in Chester County. He would be reelected in 1916. A farmer, McKeown served on the Fertilizer Committee (1913–1919), which regularly proposed the precise proportions of the elements used in fertilizers sold in South Carolina. Clemson chemists recommended these elements and examined closely the work of scientists at the experiment stations in South Carolina and in other states with similar soils and climates. This in turn was supported by the fertilizer tag sales revenue. Besides the Fertilizer Committee, McKeown served on the Crop Pest Committee (1913–1919), created to meet the threat of the boll weevil.[21]

In 1912, early in Riggs's administration, the surviving life trustees selected Asbury Francis Lever, a U.S. representative from Lexington County, as a life trustee to replace Simpson on his death. Lever was an honors graduate of Newberry College. After a short stint in teaching, he joined Congressman J. William Stokes in Washington. Lever studied law at Georgetown University, from which he received the bachelor of laws degree in 1899. He spent one year in the S.C. House of Representatives and, in 1901, at the age of twenty-seven was elected to the U.S. House, where he served on the Agriculture Committee. Immersing himself in agriculture, he quickly became the major intellect of the committee. When the Democratic Party gained control of the U.S. House, Lever was elected chair of the House of Representatives Agriculture Committee. There he helped to shape American modern agriculture.[22]

Asbury Francis Lever (1875–1940), South Carolina state representative and federal congressman, Clemson College life trustee, and co-author of the 1914 Smith-Lever Act, which established the Cooperative Extension Service. Clemson University Photographs, CUL.SC.

The first of the legislative trustees to leave the board in the Riggs era was Coke Danley Mann. Mann's rather "touch and go" health, which had taken him from his pulpit ministry, turned downward again, and in early 1912 he resigned his trusteeship.[23] On March 12, 1912, the general assembly selected as trustee Ransom Hodges Timmerman, a farmer and physician, to replace Mann. Born in Edgefield County on June 29, 1865, Timmerman attended Furman University for two years before going to the Medical College of South Carolina, from which he graduated with his MD in 1888 at twenty-three years of age. That same year, he married Charlotte Thompson of Dillon County; they had two daughters. He stayed in Dillon practicing medicine before moving his family across the state, first to Aiken County and then to Edgefield County and Batesburg. Very civic-minded, he served in the state legislature from 1896 to 1900 and practiced medicine until 1949. In his sixty-two years of practice, he served actively in the Philippi Baptist Church and helped establish a bank and a hospital. He would serve on the Clemson board until 1928.[24]

Between 1913 and 1918, three more legislative trustees stopped serving for one reason or another. The first was William DeWitt Evans, who died on April 10, 1913. Born in 1849, he began his adult life managing his father's plantation in Marlboro District. He did not attend college. In 1873, he married Mary Elizabeth Pegues, with whom he had seven daughters and four sons. He was in the state house from 1886 until 1889 and the senate from 1890 to 1893. Evans was active in the state Democratic Party, as state president of the Farmers' Alliance, and president (1899–1900) of the state Agricultural and Mechanical Society. Not only was he active in agricultural (and state fair) issues, but he also served as a trustee for South Carolina College (and the University of South Carolina) from 1890 to 1898 and Columbia Female College from 1893 to 1896. On

March 6, 1901, the governor appointed Evans to the Clemson board to replace the deceased H. M. Stackhouse. He was then elected to three successive terms. Of Evans's work for Clemson, A. B. Bryan wrote, he "gave devoted service to the College and its affairs in the formative period."[25] His son, S. W. Evans, a book-keeper in P. H. E. Sloan's college business office, became the board's secretary-treasurer following Sloan.

The other two legislative trustees elected in April 1914 were Josiah James Evans, another son of W. D. Evans, and William Duncan Garrison. Josiah Evans was born in Bennettsville in 1885. After local schooling, he attended Clemson and the South Carolina law school. At barely twenty years of age, he was called to the bar on December 7, 1904. Settling back in Bennettsville, he worked as a farmer, attorney, and public official. At twenty-seven, he entered the state house for two terms before his election to the senate. While in the house, the legislature elected him a Clemson trustee four times from 1914 to 1930. He served in the state general assembly intermittently until 1950. Evans also served as a member of the S.C. Public Service Commission (1933–1944) and the State Development Board (1945–1947). A Methodist, he married Amanda Louise Gillespie on December 7, 1940, and they had one daughter. Evans died in 1960.[26]

William Duncan Garrison had also graduated from Clemson. Born in 1878 in Anderson County, he married Alice Gertrude Seabrook in 1908. After he graduated from Clemson in 1903, he worked with the S.C. Experiment Station and remained devoted to the station's needs and progress until his death in 1918. The legislature chose him when he had left the station and worked as manager of the Charleston Farms Corporation. When he returned to the experiment station, he resigned from his position on the board.[27]

The legislature filled Garrison's board position in 1916 with another Anderson County resident, Samuel Anderson Burns, born in 1876 in Sandy Springs. Following his education in the local schools, he married Sally McClure, also of Anderson County. Burns and his first wife had four sons: George, Pierce, Leon, and Ralph, who all would be Clemson graduates, and one daughter, a Winthrop graduate. In late 1919, he moved to Talladega, Alabama, and resigned his board position. He died on December 31, 1951.[28]

As prominent as many of these trustees were, few, other than Tillman, Lever, and Manning, achieved the level of regional influence that Trustee Bernard H. Rawl reached. Born in Lexington on May 2, 1876, Rawl graduated from Clemson in agriculture in 1900 and then attended Pennsylvania State College. In 1902, he returned to Clemson as a worker in the Dairy Department, which he combined with studies at the University of Wisconsin until 1904. He returned to Clemson as an assistant professor in dairy science and department head. In 1905, the U.S. Department of Agriculture hired him to head its Dairy Division in the South, a position that took him to Washington, D.C. In 1909, he headed the USDA

Dairy Division and in 1918, served as assistant head of USDA's Bureau of Animal Husbandry. He resigned in 1921 to become involved in California's growing dairy industry. He had married Mary Dandridge Bunting from Petersburg, Virginia; they had no children. A Lutheran, he attended the Episcopalian Church with his wife. Rawl, elected to the Clemson board in 1909, resigned on July 13, 1921, when he moved to California.[29]

Difficulties for the Board

Given the issues that faced Clemson, the college was fortunate to have such an accomplished board to guide it. The board's structure remained politically problematic. Although objections to the independent structure of the Clemson Board of Trustees arose from almost the first day the details of Thomas Clemson's will were made public, a major test for the board occurred on September 1, 1905, when Dr. John Hopkins, who held property on the Seneca River, sued Clemson Agriculture College for damages to his land.

The trustees, in an effort to hold back the regular spring flooding of the river, had consulted in April 1894 with Col. W. A. Neal, superintendent of the state's penitentiaries, on using some of the convict labor to build dikes protecting the college bottom lands from flooding. The agreement was made and work began.[30] There were few mentions of the dikes until June 5, 1905, when the trustees "raised and widened the dyke [sic] so that it will absolutely protect the low ground from overflow."[31] Apparently this action caused flooding of Hopkins's land and persuaded him to file suit.[32] In December 1905, the board authorized an independent survey of the dike and the alleged damage.[33] The issue dragged on for years.[34]

The suit specifically asked for destruction of the dike, restoration of the damaged land, and an assessment on Clemson of a penalty of $8,000 (2009 equivalent $188,758). Clemson responded that it acted as an agent of the state, which owned everything. The state had approved every step, and as a state it had sovereign immunity. The two parties agreed that this question of jurisdiction had to be settled first. Judge James Aldrich of the S.C. Circuit Court found in favor of the Clemson board on April 25, 1906. Hopkins appealed to the S.C. Supreme Court, which on January 27, 1907, concurred with the lower court.

Dr. Hopkins appealed to the federal courts on the applicability of the Eleventh Amendment and the legal principle of sovereign immunity. The U.S. Supreme Court accepted the case on December 7, 1910, and gave its ruling on May 29, 1911, reversing the lower court's decision. The ruling found that "the Fort Hill place is not subject to levy and sale, it does not follow that the institution may not now or hereafter own property out of which a judgment in plaintiff's favor could be satisfied." Thus, the damages could be assessed, but the embankment was, in essence, a part of the real property so not subject to that type (destruction) of remedy. The land (at least that deeded), therefore, belonged to the state, but the trustees, at least the seven life trustees, are not part of state.[35] Although not the principal issue of the court action, the ruling recognized the authenticity of the peculiar (if not "unique") nature of the structure of the board.

At almost the same time, John J. McMahan, a candidate for S.C. governor, also levied an attack on Clemson and directly on the trustees. On August 12, 1906, the Charleston *News and Courier* reported his Greenville speech in which he said, "But the entire organization of Clemson is wrong. It is supported by a tax on farmers, which some years far exceeds the usual income.…The fertilizer tax should go into the state treasury and Clemson should be supported as the other institutions of the State by annual appropriations from the treasury."[36] That suggestion, which was neither unreasonable nor immoral, was nonetheless considered unconstitutional or, at least, illegal according to then-Trustee Smythe in his August 29, 1906, letter to Trustee J. E. Wannamaker.[37] Smythe probably wrote it in response to McMahan's speech.

McMahan also challenged the board structure because the majority was a self-perpetuating unit. He observed, "No State institution should be beyond State control. Trustees become old, become antiquated in their ideas, or for other reasons may be out of joint with the progress and demands of the times." He went on to observe that "Clemson College is a close [*sic*] corporation, largely officered by the kinsmen and other favorites of these life trustees.…"[38] Certainly the last statement, as it related to kinsmen, was true as Mell declared in his letter to the governor. It is not hard to understand why the legislature, during the final months of 1909, launched an investigation of Clemson organizational and financial practices.

One of the more outspoken legislators was the Rev. Mr. J. H. Archer, a clergyman from Spartanburg, who considered himself a representative of the denominational schools. When he first came to public attention in 1897, he was described as "a tall, slim, wiry-looking man, with a scrub of a beard and a tangle of iron gray hair"[39] and as a real opponent of Tillman (at least in pursuit of political power). By 1910, Archer focused his aim on Clemson, its finances, its generosity to its trustees (according to the attackers), and the quality of the education received.[40]

With that as a background, the general assembly authorized a legislative "committee to examine into and report on the affairs of the various institutions of learning fostered by the State." Composed of Senator T. I. Rogers and representatives John J. McMahan and A. Vanderhorst, the committee submitted a report to the legislature on January 29, 1911. The committee chose not to examine spending practices of the five institutions.[41] While its report basically spoke favorably to the teaching at all five institutions, it raised an earnest question about cost per student, noting the cost per student was $128.75 (2009 equivalent $2,928) at

the Citadel, $150 (2009 equivalent $3,411) at Winthrop, $178.41 (2009 equiva-
lent $4,057) at USC,[42] and $241.06 (2009 equivalent $5,254) at Clemson. The
sums included only the state-"appropriated" funds or, in Clemson's case, the fertilizer tag fee. The investigators removed from the appropriations and (it would
be hoped) from the fertilizer tag fee the cost of permanent campus improvements.
But they did not take into account that the education (at that time) in mathematics or Latin required little beyond chalk, writing supplies, and library texts, while
animal husbandry required animals and electrical engineering required the most
up-to-date generators.

A second issue that they raised was coordination among the state schools.
This, they reasoned, required two steps: first, establishment of an unpaid commission to visit states that had unified educational authority, and second, for the
commission to present a plan for creating a coordinating authority. The legislators recommended that the governor and the state superintendent of education
be on every higher education board. The report pointed out that every board
except Clemson's had one or the other officer, if not both. Inasmuch as the general assembly elected more than two to each Clemson board at whatever term it
chose to set, then it might be assumed that the legislature chose not to do such.
The committee also noted that the Citadel, Clemson, and USC all taught civil
engineering, "which might be united in one, and with better results through
concentrated effort."[43]

The legislators did not ask, however, a pertinent question: "What is South
Carolina's need in civil engineers?" Nor did they address the fact that Clemson's
federal charter, so accepted or designated by the state government, assigned "agriculture, mechanics, and military training" to Clemson, although not necessarily
exclusively. Nor did they note that the state government was capable (as it had
shown earlier) of assigning the "land-grant fields" exclusively to the land-grant
schools. But they were not capable of forbidding those same fields to those land-
grant schools. Instead, in the twelve-page document, they spent nearly one-third
in generalities; about one-sixth on USC, the Citadel, Winthrop, and the State
College for Negroes; and about one-half on Clemson, some of which was an hon-
est attack on "nepotism."[44] And in fairness, the committee assigned no blame to
any "nepotistic" hire in the performance of duties. On the other hand, given the
racial and gender attitudes of the era and the available population in the region
that fit the racial and gender attitudes of the state, the "nepotism" might well have
been a political "necessity."

The risk in placing on a board any state official simply because of his office
appeared almost immediately upon the election of Coleman Livingston Blease
(1868–1942) from Newberry as governor of South Carolina. Educated at Newberry College and USC, he graduated in law from Georgetown University in
1889. Admitted to the bar and elected to the S.C. House in 1890, he served as

speaker pro tempore from 1892 to 1894. After a period of time in local politics, he won a seat in the state senate in 1905. Senator Blease's committee received several reports that decried the independence of the Clemson board and its supposed extravagance with the fertilizer revenue. Archer's (the Spartanburg legislator) attack, much of which was focused on such "extravagance," continued to resonate with Blease, who in the 1910 gubernatorial campaign became the champion of the textile workers.[45]

Blease won the election of 1910 on the basis of class warfare, and his attack on perceived privilege came full in his efforts to champion white textile workers against all others, especially African Americans. He aimed his first fury against Thomas E. Miller, the president of the Colored Institute (hereafter South Carolina State), who had voiced his opposition to Blease's candidacy. After Blease's election, he demanded that Miller resign. Miller responded, "Because I opposed your election to the Chief Officer in the gift of our beloved state, you have demanded my resignation, stating that you will not permit the State Colored College to do any business until my resignation is in your hand....I counted the cost before I opposed you, hence, I am prepared for the blow of your official act."[46] Of Miller, the founding president of South Carolina State, the legislative report that Blease would receive said, "...a president who had displayed excellent judgment and admirable ideals in his conduct of this institution."[47]

Blease's mean-spiritedness turned against higher education in general in April and May 1911 when the Peabody board was considering the distribution of much of the Peabody estate. His interference, which a Winthrop University historian called "racist," added to the financial difficulties both Winthrop and South Carolina State bore.[48]

Blease's anti-higher education thrust, however, was greatest against Clemson, in part perhaps because of Tillman, who, once Blease's "captain," now lay weakened by a stroke and appeared as the "dying chieftain." Blease had fractured the Tillman coalition by singling out the textile "operatives" (as mill workers were called) for his attention. Blease's opportunity came in the person of Floride Isabella Lee, Mr. Clemson's granddaughter. Shortly after the sale of her share of Fort Hill to the state of South Carolina and into the demesne of the Clemson College campus and the death of her father, Gideon Lee Jr., she married her second cousin, Andrew Pickens Calhoun II (August 14, 1895), with whom she bore four children.[49] She had also met John C. Calhoun of New York City.[50] Together they proposed a scheme to Governor Blease, who was in the last year of his second gubernatorial term. They urged that the state now reject the Act of Acceptance, which should, they reasoned, pass the property back to Floride Lee Calhoun, who then would give the property to the state for the agricultural college, which would continue with all legislative trustees and with the name changed to Calhoun University. John C. Calhoun of New York stated that be-

**Descendant Chart for
Anna Maria Calhoun and Thomas Green Clemson**

Prepared by Jerome V. Reel, Jr.

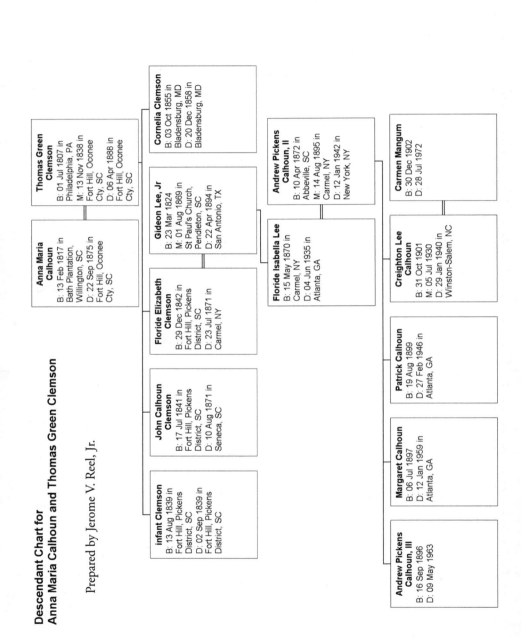

tween all the other Calhouns, their many (and wealthy) friends, and the many admirers of John C. Calhoun, millions upon millions of dollars would be raised to endow the school.[51]

Blease took the idea and incorporated it into his message to the general assembly.[52] *The Tiger* reacted quickly, suggesting that before the state government ventured too far down this path, John Calhoun's family and friends should produce legal, dated, verified, and collectable bank notes as a guarantee.[53] It was not long before the S.C. attorney general pointed out that the will itself had a fallback clause in the event the state rejected the conditional gift or attempted to modify any of the conditions. Further, he noted that *Lee v. Simpson* already had placed the will before the U.S. Supreme Court, which had found for the will (Simpson). There the matter ended, and Blease stopped his scheming.[54] But the issue would come up again and again.

Buildings

Left to right: Barracks Three, Two, and One and the Main Building, ca. 1913. Clemson University Photographs, CUL.SC.

Regardless of the various attacks on the school's governing structure, the students (703 in 1910) remained crowded into the barracks. Barracks Two had opened in the spring of 1903 and allowed a 13 percent enrollment increase, which, when coupled with the cessation of the lower preparatory grade, raised the overall graduation rate. The increase was a sign of the slow addition of grades nine, ten, and eleven in some public schools and improvement in some high school standards. Nonetheless, a 1910 report claimed that, of the 166 public and private high schools in South Carolina, only thirteen were judged to be adequate. The thirteen (all white) included two private schools and graduated 250 students the previous year.[55] Nonetheless, the pressure to enter Clemson grew.

Fortunately, the fertilizer tag sales had allowed continued accumulation of funds by the Clemson trustees so that a new barracks for 200 more cadets could be authorized by the board.[56] Rudolph Lee designed Barracks Three with a col-

The Dairy Building as it appeared in 1916. Clemson University
Photographs, CUL.SC.

onnaded portico, which recalled the north porch on the 1904 Agricultural Hall.
With the addition of a like entrance to Barracks Two, the style of all three barracks
was similar, including the granite ground floor and red brick upper stories. Even
though the styles moved from Romanesque to *beaux-arts*, the harmonies of the
materials and the pitches to the roofs added to a sense of unity on the growing
campus.

Two smaller buildings had been constructed along the drive that moved south
from Bowman Field. Both were on the east side of the still-unsurfaced road. First
came the greenhouse, all in glass and steel, reminding the few who traveled of
the royal botanical greenhouses at Kew in Great Britain. Then came the enlarged
Chemistry Building, in which the venerable Prof. Mark Bernard Hardin labored
and taught until his retirement in 1911.[57] Next to Chemistry, a new fertilizer
laboratory designed by Lee continued the architectural language of Chemistry,
while its basement became the campus post office.

In 1911, all the barracks—including Barracks One with a new fourth story
and set of bathrooms, a slightly redecorated Barracks Two sporting its portico,
and the almost new Barracks Three—greeted 804 cadets. The corps had increased
by 23 percent since 1908.[58] Even the main building, now called Old Main (in
use for eighteen years), felt more spacious. With the agricultural programs transferred to the 1904 Agricultural Hall and with the YMCA moved into space in the
enlarged Barracks One, the college library (in Main) doubled in space. That was
fortuitous because in 1907, the U.S. Congress designated all land-grant college
libraries as federal government depositories. Class space for the academic subjects
allowed a bit of flexibility in scheduling. The basement was improved for the registrar and the business office.[59]

The growth in students dictated an increase in the number of faculty, who were
usually young and brought children with them. That led to the construction of a

new schoolhouse to accommodate the children of the faculty and staff and of the few others who built homes on the hotel hill. The cadets called them "hill folk."[60]

On the college farm, the milk production barn, which provided milk for the cadet mess hall, was refitted, and the teaching part of the dairy operation moved into a "half dairy barn" with a calf barn attached. Despite legislative criticism, which charged that the milk herd had been degraded as a result of inbreeding, milk production (measured in pounds) and quality (measured in fat content) had steadily risen. Sales of surplus products allowed the design by Lee and construction of a neoclassical and early art deco Dairy Building across the major north-south ravine. The sale of ice cream to the cadets led them to beat down a path up and down the ravine to the Dairy Building.[61] A Clemson tradition had begun.

Agricultural Directions

The expansion to meet the economic needs of South Carolina continued in the era 1910 to 1918. Recognizing that agriculture remained the business of a large majority of the people of South Carolina and the Southeast, the Clemson faculty determined that one direction in growth would be in agriculture, with chemistry separate from it. By 1910–1911, the faculty instructing and doing non-experiment station research grew to three, where it remained in 1918. The animal departments' faculties grew from six in 1903 to ten in 1918. Poultry and dairy had new appointments, as Clemson helped coax the Southeast slowly from row crops to more diversified agriculture. One of the interesting areas Clemson explored was to add a basic course in forestry in 1903. President Theodore Roosevelt (in office 1901–1909), in his domestic policy, focused on bringing large corporations under the control of the federal government and on conservation. While president, he designated four national game preserves, five national parks, eighteen national monuments, twenty-one reclamation projects, and 150 national forests, which set a "seal" of federal protection on about 230 million acres. His biographers noted that acreage equaled all the Atlantic seaboard states. Given this national movement toward conservation, it was unfortunate that neither Clemson's trustees nor the S.C. Legislature was prepared to invest in a full-fledged forestry program that early in the state's modern history.[62]

Extension

The broadening of teaching received two federal stimuli in the years 1910–1918. The first was to some extent home-grown. The efforts of the early advocates of formalized extension, including Seaman Knapp, had led to a variety of ideas, including the creation of county agricultural societies, county fairs, and county experiment farms. The first two, while useful, met too infrequently to deal with immediate issues such as infectious diseases and invasive pests, while experimental farms were almost too sedentary to be truly effective.

Since the 1890s, Clemson had considered extension to be a regular part of the school's activities. As has been noted, a variety of methods were developed for extension activity. Much of this "unmandated" work was funded through the fertilizer sales. The most useful included farmers' institutes scattered throughout the state, regular publication of research result brochures, youth work, and short and correspondence courses.[63] The institutes took teams of specialists by train to well-located towns for two- and three-day meetings. Also a summer multiweek institute brought farmers and their families to the campus. Research bulletins were published in lots of 10,000. The separate courses for boys in raising corn and cultivating cotton, for girls in canning tomatoes, and for women in sanitation and food preservation helped to achieve better health and production.[64]

The Smith-Lever Act

The extension work received no regular support from the state or the nation. While support for Clemson's extension work came to a goodly extent from the college's regular revenues, including the federal and state allotments through the Hatch Act and its subsequent legislative enhancements, the largest nongovernmental source was the General Education Board, a group that oversaw the distribution of some of the wealth accumulated by the Rockefeller family.[65] But between 1910 and 1914, pressure from agricultural interests mounted for development of a federal "public service" side of agricultural policy. As early as the 1860s, northeastern states' legislatures supported the local farm institutes. By 1904 in Texas, resident agents began to travel from farm to farm offering practical and up-to-date advice and instruction under the direction of the Texas Agricultural and Mechanical College. Clemson experimented with and modified the Texas model.

Eventually, Life Trustee A. F. Lever, a member of the U.S. House of Representatives and chair of the House Agricultural Committee, and Hoke Smith, a U.S. senator from Georgia, introduced an act written by Lever that provided federal money for agricultural extension work. The model Lever and Smith selected to use was the Clemson way of attaching the extension work to the land-grant college research system. As members of the college staff, the agents had disciplinary expertise and, by affiliation with the various agricultural experiment stations, were knowledgeable in local soils, crop and livestock problems, and new plants.

Each state operated its own program determining local needs. To support such, the federal government provided an annual appropriation through the Department of Agriculture and an annual "Smith-Lever" grant, which would have to be more than matched by the state. The amount of the grant was determined by the size of the agricultural population in each state.[66] Some states attempted to

Richard Irvine Manning III (1859–1931), South Carolina state representative and senator, governor, and Clemson College life trustee. South Caroliniana Library, University of South Carolina.

attach the resident agents to the state departments of agriculture rather than the land-grant college. In addition, in the seventeen states practicing educational racial segregation, the added issue of the "1890 Land Grant Institutes," authorized by the Morrill Act of 1890, was a complication. They were not specifically mentioned in the Smith-Lever Act.[67]

By the spring of 1914, the "extension bill" had passed both houses of Congress and sat on the U.S. president's desk. Clemson President Riggs prepared to meet with the governor to clear the way for the bill. The S.C. Democratic primary had just named Richard I. Manning, a Clemson life trustee, to succeed Coleman L. Blease as governor. Manning took the leadership role in drafting appropriate legislation to submit to the general assembly, and in July, Riggs, with the approval of the Clemson Board of Trustees, signed the extension contract with the USDA.[68] Still to be determined were the questions about serving African American farmers and the home and family aspects of the law.

The federal statute was clear. The Cooperative Extension Act clearly assigned the responsibility for the outreach to the institution designated as the agent for the agricultural experiment station, and Clemson served that role in South Carolina. But in South Carolina, pieces of the curricular foundation issues were divided among Clemson, Winthrop, which the state had created as the "teachers" college along with other fields, and South Carolina State at Orangeburg, which the state government had not yet authorized to grant the bachelor's degree. At this point, Riggs had formed a good working relationship with Winthrop's president, David Bancroft Johnson. Winthrop faculty and staff had been a part of the "Clemson extension train" since 1910.[69] It was no surprise then when in June of 1914, Clemson's business officer at Riggs's direction established a salary line for home demonstration agents to be housed, supervised, and evaluated by Winthrop but paid by Clemson.[70] Mary E. Frayser became the Winthrop officer through whom Clemson operated.[71]

Riggs's ability to work with other presidents also could be seen in the close working relationship/friendship he had with the new president of South Carolina State, Robert Shaw Wilkinson (1865–1932). From Charleston, Wilkinson was nominated to West Point (one of the first African Americans to be so nominated), but he obtained the BA from Oberlin. Afterward, he joined the faculty of the State University of Kentucky at Louisville, where he received the PhD in 1898. There he taught physics and chemistry until 1911, when he was selected as the

Robert Shaw Wilkinson (1865–1932), second president of South Carolina State College. Frank C. Martin, et al., *South Carolina State University, The College History Series.*

second president of South Carolina State. He and Riggs worked closely together in an era when other college presidents in South Carolina scarcely noted State's existence, aided by the fact that Riggs traveled frequently to Orangeburg to visit with his (Riggs's) elderly mother.[72] To help save money for the Orangeburg college, Riggs personally drew up several of the plumbing, heating, and electric plans for buildings.[73]

Riggs preferred that the African American agents he hoped to hire be a part of Clemson's staff; however, the Board of Trustees pressed to arrange for the African American extension workers to be supervised through South Carolina State.[74] The board's stance probably resulted from the racial attitudes of some (or perhaps, most) of its members, and they feared further antagonizing Governor Blease and the vocal Clemson critics in the state general assembly, the public, and some of the press.

Even before the passage of the Smith-Lever Act of 1914, Clemson had placed agents in every county. Once arrangements were made with Wilkinson in 1912, officials at South Carolina State hired African American agents, assigned them to the designated counties, and evaluated them. However, Clemson's secretary-treasurer drafted the paychecks. The African American extension staff received considerably less salary than its white counterparts.[75] No one offered a reason for the reduced African American pay scale.

On the other hand, this set of decisions, which dodged bullets of political criticism, carried positive benefits for President Wilkinson and South Carolina State, as a legitimization of their equivalent status when the legislature, the governor (who was on the South Carolina State board), and several of the other public higher education entities in the state seemed to have ignored the Orangeburg institution.[76]

W. L. English of the USDA served as national superintendent of the Division of Extension Work and Farmers' Institutes, and also as land-grant school extension director agent for the Farmer's Cooperative Demonstration work, all part of the Smith-Lever Act.[77] Passage of the Smith-Lever law also brought a third federal revenue stream to Clemson, which combined with the state and county matching funds did improve Clemson's financial position, although it did not completely fund the total extension cost. To add to the financial problems, once the federal government began funding the Smith-Lever program, then the General Education Board (GEB) ended its independent funding. President Wilkinson appealed directly, asking for a continuation of the annual gift of $2,500 from the GEB, but within a few days he received an unfavorable letter from Wallace Buttrick, GEB secretary. Buttrick pointed out that the Smith-Lever Act specifically "excluded contributions from without the state where the work was done."[78]

The U.S. Department of Agriculture determined that fieldwork was the only extension work funded by the federal government. Riggs felt that theoretical work by researchers, when immediately concerned with statewide problems, should also be funded. The practical issue was in administrative ties. For the USDA, Bradford Knapp, son of Seaman Knapp, wanted the agents under the control of the state director of extension, who in South Carolina was W. W. Long, a Clemson faculty member. Riggs, and perhaps Long, favored ties to researchers for solutions to problems with coordination by the state director. From 1914 to 1918, the issue of the relationship of extension to research continued to arise in correspondence and in face-to-face meetings. In 1918, Riggs conceded. The toll on Long pushed him to take a leave of absence. He returned later and remained director until he died in 1934.[79]

Smith-Hughes Act

Another new federal initiative appeared: the education of agricultural and industrial teachers for the lower schools and the supervision of such work. Introduced into the Congress as the Smith-Hughes Act (signed into law February 23, 1917), which the S.C. General Assembly accepted and the governor signed on February 28, 1917, the act, in the placing of the work, set up potential conflicts with the state superintendent of education. In addition, Winthrop's president, D. B. Johnson, raised the issue of Winthrop's role as did Wilkinson for South Carolina State. Riggs recommended that inasmuch as the state Department of Education was the lead organization, it should make the assignments within the framework of past arrangements. The program was trifurcated among South Carolina State for African Americans, Winthrop in home economics for non-African American females, and Clemson in agriculture and industry for non-African American men.

But the Smith-Hughes Act was clear on what it intended, and Clemson's leader was Verd Patterson, professor of agricultural education. The Board of Education accepted the decision on September 14, 1917.

Other Public Service

During Riggs's first eight years, the state also designated Clemson as the S.C. Crop Pest Commission. Again, the legislature assigned the task to Clemson but appropriated no funds. Prof. A. F. Conradi served as state entomologist, and his superior, H. W. Barre, as state pathologist. In this, there was a potential challenge from the federally established Institute for Entomology located at the University of South Carolina. The land-grant tripartite mission of teaching (Morrill Act of 1862 and of 1890), research (Hatch Act of 1887), and extension (Smith-Lever Act of 1914) would guide Clemson for much of the rest of its history. The series of laws marked the apogee of federal leadership in agriculture.

The S.C. (Clemson) Experiment Station and the Extension Service produced a number of successes. Among them were elimination of hog cholera and bovine tuberculosis and tick control. To centralize the work and speed delivery, the state veterinarians (all Clemson faculty) and the supply center for the serums were both located at Clemson's Sandhill Experiment Station at Pontiac near Columbia.[80] This effort stripped the campus of its small professional veterinary staff, which ended the teaching of veterinary medicine at Clemson beyond some elementary courses in poultry science and animal husbandry.

Engineering Studies

Almost as early as 1900, Mechanical Hall began demonstrating that it was too small for the number of students who wanted to study engineering in its various forms. Small additions to the building occurred throughout its years of service.[81] With the resignation of Prof. William H. Boehm as head of the Mechanical Department and from the college on September 1, 1901, the trustees elected Riggs as the head, and it was during this tenure that Riggs attracted Samuel Broadus Earle to the Clemson faculty.

Sam Earle was born in Gowensville in 1878, a son of a Baptist minister. Fortunately, because of his father's calling, he and his four older brothers attended Furman at a discount. Apparently, "college" agreed with him, because after receiving the bachelor's degree in 1898 (at age twenty), he stayed on to earn a master's in language and mathematics. With that in hand, he went to Cornell University (as had Riggs) and then returned to South Carolina to join Clemson's engineering faculty, serving under Riggs. In accepting Clemson's offer in 1902, he turned aside offers from General Electric and West-

Samuel Broadus Earle (1878–1978) served as a professor of mechanical engineering, director/dean of engineering, and acting president (1919, 1924–1925) during his tenure at Clemson, which began in 1902 and ended with his retirement as dean emeritus in 1950. Clemson University Photographs, CUL.SC.

inghouse. Earle soon began courting a young Clemson College librarian, Susan Sloan, one of the ten children of P. H. E. Sloan (the Sloans and the Earles were already distant kin), the secretary-treasurer of the Board of Trustees. They married in 1908. When Riggs was named Clemson's fifth president, Earle became the director of the Engineering Division.[82] Earle began taking students to visit large industrial plants, especially near Birmingham, Alabama, which was only a five-hour train ride on the Southern line.[83] The close rail connections between the college and regional centers of business and industry helped strengthen the Clemson presence in the development of the "new South."

Architecture

For some few years, the Clemson faculty had discussed the creation of a curriculum in architecture.[84] Riggs, while director of engineering, had formed a small committee to determine the need and, if it were genuine, then to design a program and a course of study. He designated Rudolph E. Lee committee chair. Lee, born in Anderson in 1876, was the son of Thomas B. Lee, a well-known civil and mechanical engineer, and Miriam Earle Lee (a distant relative to Samuel B. Earle). Lee attended the Citadel from 1891 to 1893 and transferred to Clemson when it opened that year. He graduated with the first class in 1896 and was hired as a tutor for the entering class in the autumn of 1897. He also did advanced studies during summers at the Zanerian Art College (1898), Cornell University (1901), and the University of Pennsylvania (1903). At Clemson, Lee rose from assistant instructor in drawing (1897–1899) to instructor in drawing (1899–1903) and associate professor of drawing in 1903. At that rank, he chaired the faculty committee on architecture.[85]

The committee concluded that the region needed a program in architecture with an emphasis on the construction aspects. The result was that the trustees

Rudolph Edward "Pop" Lee (1876–1959) began his lengthy career at Clemson in 1897 as a tutor in the Preparatory Department but quickly moved on to become an instructor and then professor of drawing and architecture. He retired as the head of architecture in 1948. This photograph was taken in 1923, around the time he designed three significant academic buildings on campus. Clemson University Photographs, CUL.SC.

approved a curriculum solidly rooted in practical design and use. Students began their studies as engineering students with grounding in physics (and the areas of electricity, water, and materials) before proceeding into design and construction.[86] The first class of architecture students began in 1913, and the first two graduates were in 1915. By June 1918, Clemson had graduated eleven architects.[87]

Lee focused his attention on the design of rural schoolhouses, with great care lavished on fire safety, good lighting, ventilation, and sanitation. Limited to one-story buildings easily expandable and adaptable, these structures were designed to be locally built. Lee's ideas on community schools appeared in several cooperative extension bulletins. He also rode the extension trains, encouraging and organizing local school communities. Although many of the simple buildings have disappeared, their memories remain in the rising literacy and numeracy rates as surely as the young teachers educated in the state's religious and public colleges who did their important work in these structures.[88]

The Rockefeller Gift

Besides Lee's work on the power plant, enlargement of Barracks One, portico for Barracks Two, exterior of Barracks Three, Dairy Building, and Fertilizer Building, his greatest architectural contribution of these years was his design of the YMCA building. But the idea for the building and its funding belongs to others. Bits of discussions about the need for a student activities and club center had been part of the conversation for some time among faculty and staff. Who originated the idea of approaching John D. Rockefeller (1839–1937) about a gift for such a YMCA facility for Clemson College is not clear.

On April 7, 1913, Riggs asked the Board of Trustees for permission to ask Rockefeller if he would consider providing a gift of $50,000 to erect a Young Men's Christian Association building at Clemson. Rockefeller had recently made similar gifts to Georgia Tech and Mississippi State. The trustees agreed to Riggs's proposal. Briefly in a letter to Rockefeller, Riggs outlined the isolation of the college and the relatively large number of students enrolled. Rockefeller received the letter, read it, and asked one of his secretaries to find out a bit more, particularly if Clemson was a "state institution, the same as the other A & M Colleges, and also if you would give me your views as to the propriety of helping them...."[89] Given the unusual arrangements of the land-grant colleges in the Northeast (Cornell, for example) and Clemson's name (CAC), Rockefeller's questions made sense.

The secretary's response must have been favorable because Riggs met soon with Clemson College division heads, and they suggested that the YMCA building be placed on a line north of the Textile Building. Lee went to work almost immediately with a plan. The building would face east (onto Bowman Field), and taking advantage of the lay of the land, it would include a basement (with daylight entering from the north, west, and south sides) and two upper floors. The plan included 36,000 square feet of floor space for a basketball court (Clemson had begun playing basketball in 1912 on Bowman Field and, in the winter, played the sport in the rear space in the Agriculture Building), two bowling alleys (and space for a third), a swimming pool, a private dining room, and a room for a quick lunch. The pool measured twenty-one by sixty feet (then the standard length for amateur competition). The building also contained an auditorium with a stage and two dressing rooms. The auditorium seated more than 400 people. On the second floor were nine bedrooms for visiting speakers, alumni, and guests. Rudolph Lee's design went through several critiques, but he had taken the time to visit a number of YMCAs and so had produced advanced designs and facilities.[90]

Riggs sent Lee's architectural plans to Rockefeller, and on January 17, 1914, the wealthy oil man and philanthropist wrote to say that if a few legal questions could be clarified, then he would commit two-thirds of the cost up to $75,000, to be delivered when the other one-third was secured. While Lee began making his building program final, Riggs contacted the trustees. Lee had help from Earle, Riggs, and advanced students in mechanical and electrical engineering and in architecture in getting the presentation plans together. The trustees met on April 15, 1914, and decided to request $50,000 from Rockefeller. They guaranteed that the site would be "held by the Board of Trustees of the College in trust for the social and religious work of the students of the institution." Other resolutions emphasized that the YMCA would direct the work in the new building so long as it and Clemson's trustees were satisfied with the impact the YMCA had on Clemson's students. Finally, the trustees pledged to have $25,000 cash in hand for the other third by January 1, 1915.

Riggs took the resolutions, the general program, and the architectural drawings to New York in February 1914. There he met with the Rockefeller Foundation secretary and with the YMCA southern secretary; they discussed the documents and made a few suggestions. Riggs returned and presented the very slight modifications to the trustees. They adopted the entire package, which Riggs then sent to Rockefeller's secretary. The positive reply was dated May 5, 1914.[91]

The full extent of the Lee-Riggs plan can still be seen or easily imagined. Lee's original darker brick was not available, so a change was made to a lighter buff. The red clay tile roof and the bracketed eaves marked the building as Renaissance style. The capitals to the columns of the building bore the triangle, the *chi rho*, and the reference to John's gospel, while the quarry tile, terrazzo, the frontal mosaic roundels, and pine flooring added to the Italianate feel.

When the building was finished and furnished, Rockefeller had given $50,000; the Clemson board, $15,000; and the students, faculty, alumni, staff, and friends, $13,000 for a total of $78,000 ($75,000 for the building and $3,000 for the furnishings). The very next year, Preston Brooks Holtzendorff Jr. (1903–1979), a graduate of the University of Georgia, arrived to become the general secretary of the C.A.C. YMCA. He became a strong positive force through his many years at Clemson.[92]

The YMCA building, now known as Holtzendorff Hall, as it appeared shortly after its construction in 1916. It is the oldest surviving building designed by Rudolph Lee on campus today. Clemson University Photographs, CUL.SC.

West of the building lay a full football field and a track, which looped around the field. The field ran east to west, with permanent stands on the south side. Behind the south stands as the ridge rose to form a knoll, the ground was leveled for tennis courts. Continuing west from the football field was the baseball diamond and bleachers that would be moved as needed from one playing site to another. The basement of the Textile Building served as the sports dressing room and office, and since the stairs to the track were not in a direct line to the field, it became customary for the players to enter the field running down the southeast corner onto the depressed playing field.[93] Another tradition began.

Student Life

With fully one-quarter of the students playing on Clemson's intercollegiate sports teams,[94] and with Clemson playing a wider array of colleges, Clemson found it ever more important to align itself with the emerging and rapidly growing National Collegiate Athletic Association. It did this in 1912.[95]

Football remained the most popular sport, although the brilliance of the Heisman years had departed. Frank Dobson, the head coach, a graduate of Lawrenceville, had come to Clemson from Georgia Tech. Clemson's captain, William Henry "Bill" Hanckel, had the nickname of "Coach." A student in animal industries, born in Pendleton but who moved with his family to Charleston,[96] Hanckel played every minute of every game at the position of right end. The sixteen-cadet team finished the 1911 season with six wins and two losses. The team lost to Auburn and Georgia Tech, and two of the wins were over South Carolina and Georgia.[97]

Coaches changed over the seven years. The team grew to twenty-five players, two coaches, and three managers. The 1912 record remained 6–2 with the two losses at the hands of Auburn and Davidson. But a 21–13 win over South Carolina and a 55–7 victory over Florida played in Jacksonville were highlights.[98]

Baseball also enjoyed popularity. Frank Dobson, the football coach, also coached the sixteen-cadet baseball team. While the team had break-even records across the 1911–1918 years, baseball was one of Clemson's better sports. During the same years, track was by "Doc Rock" Calhoun with the assistance of Murray S. Gardiner, assistant professor of agronomy, who had been a track champion at Purdue. The team was undefeated in its dual meets and amassed the most points both in the Southern IAA and the Southern AAU. Clemson first played basketball in 1912 and posted an undefeated season. The lone home game against Wofford, played on Bowman Field, ended Clemson 56, Wofford 13. Seven men composed the team.[99]

Among the favorite students was Frank Johnstone Jervey, a 1914 graduate from Charleston. As a cheerleader, he roamed the sidelines, whipping up enthusiasm with yells and school songs. One of his favorite songs warned,

> Don't send my son to Auburn,
>   The dying mother said;
> Don't send him down to Georgia Tech,
>   I'd rather see him dead;
> Send him to dear old Clemson,
>   It's better than Cornell,
> But rather than to USC
>   I'd see my boy in _ _ _ _ . ("Yale" is a suggested fill-in.)[100]

During the era, another of Clemson's standout students was John Furman Ezell, a 1912 graduate. From Cherokee (Springs), Spartanburg County, Ezell majored in agriculture. He held the college hammer throw record in 1912, won two Southern Intercollegiate Athletic Association medals, and lettered in football. He served also as business manager of *The Tiger* and won the Trustees' Oratorical Medal.[101]

The Norris Medal, selected by the faculty, honored the best all-around student in the senior class. The choice for 1915 was Wallace Bruce Wannamaker, a son of Trustee John Edwards Wannamaker. He was the fifth of seven children born on Aeolian Hill in St. Matthews. "Dickery" studied animal husbandry and after college returned to work at the college with the cattle herds. When an undergraduate, he had joined the Senior Bulls, which he served as secretary-treasurer, and the Calhoun Literary Society. Sadly for the Wannamakers, Wallace Bruce died in 1920 from a brain tumor.[102]

A second Norris Medal winner was Thomas Stephen Buie in the Class of 1917. Born in 1896 in Marlboro, one of five children, he had joined as a Clemson student the Palmetto Literary Society. Buie was also active in the Methodist church and served as a reporter for *The Tiger*. He majored in soils and became the regional director for the USDA Soil Conservation Service. Buie received his PhD from Iowa State College at Ames. Further, he wrote a number of books on cotton, including a career-capping volume, *Soil Conservation in the Southeast, 1933–1953*. A scholarship was created at Clemson in his name.[103]

The School's Reputation

After the harsh buffeting that Clemson had undergone by the politicians and the press during the years 1907 to 1914, Riggs sought to present as positive an image of Clemson as possible. This not only meant keeping a steady flow of positive news streaming to the press, the legislature, and the public, but also, where possible, solving unfavorable issues quietly and quickly. One major in-house matter arose in 1912.

Early in his presidency, Riggs had become concerned about financial matters in the mess hall. He contacted a private detective from Atlanta to investigate. Rather than seek trustee permission to contract and pay the costs, Riggs paid for the investigation himself. The detective later reported to Riggs that Augustus Schilletter, steward of the mess hall, had stolen between "five and eight thousand dollars a year"[104] (2009 equivalent $109,743.32 to $175,589.31). Riggs called Schilletter to his office, presented him the evidence, and told him that if he stopped the stealing, he could continue to work. Any breach of behavior or effort by Schilletter "to stir up dissension among the students out of revenge," Riggs warned, would result in Schilletter's forced resignation. Schilletter agreed, since he did not resign until 1919.

There is no way to explain completely Riggs's action except to note that Schilletter had held the position since the college opened in 1893, and he was well-liked by students and remembered kindly by alumni. Riggs, in only his second year as president, perhaps

Augustus Schilletter (1865–1929), steward of the mess hall and former bursar for the college. Clemson University Photographs, CUL.SC.

feared that an immediate resignation might likely lead to a public revelation or struggle that could have been the "final straw," particularly with the legislature.[105]

The Coming War

Certainly a part of the counterbalance to any negative publicity came in the strengthening of cadets' preparations for national defense. The experiences of the commandants during the Mell administration had not been good. The flag incident and several other pranks, each amusing in its own way, were collectively corrosive of the school's reputation. Commandant J. C. Minus had written a letter to the *State* concerned about Mell's "loose management" that, he felt, "broke down discipline and condoned grave infractions of the rules." He pointed to Mell's willingness to give "almost anything requested or demanded."[106]

Riggs took a more aggressive stance with the army officers assigned to Clemson. He and Trustee President Johnstone participated actively in the selection process, letting the candidates know that he was the final authority on discipline. Also he worked through Johnstone to remove the trustees individually and collectively from the disciplinary process. Riggs's imperatives were first, support the military system when it was fair, and second, provide an orderly way for the president to be involved in the system when needed.[107]

A second major issue involved the growing sense of looming change in the student body as difficulties in Europe continued to grow in the first half of Riggs's presidency (1910–1918). While the almost continual flareups on the Balkan Peninsula, along with the naval arms race, did not affect the cadets, European politics reached the explosion point in the June 28, 1914, murder of the heir to the Austrian throne when he was on a state visit to Serbia. The division of Europe into two large and hostile army camps led to a series of war declarations beginning with Austria's declaration of war on Serbia on July 28. In the United States, Woodrow Wilson had become U.S. president in 1913 and had pledged to keep the United States out of Europe's wars. But as World War I deepened, the American public, with large numbers of the citizenry of German stock and many others holding deeply felt British, Belgian, and French sympathies, became increasingly inflamed, and the federal government had a hard time maintaining neutrality.

Congress passed, and President Wilson signed, the National Defense Act of 1916, which established the collegiate Reserve Officers Training Corps (ROTC) among other features.[108] The base for the law was the work in "military tactics and strategy" as specified in the Morrill Act of 1862. The Act of 1916 permitted the establishment of military training units in colleges other than the land-grant institutions and junior units in secondary schools.

For Clemson and its cadets, the act was both favorable and (perhaps) unfavorable. On the former, benefits included access for Clemson at federal expense to up-to-date sidearms, including the relatively new .45-caliber Colt automatic pistol, the heavy knife bayonet, and vastly improved Springfield rifles. A second favorable aspect of the law was federal financial support for the ROTC cadets. A third was a potential army commission for graduates who successfully completed the ROTC regimen. On the negative side, at the end of the cadet's sophomore year, passing a fairly rigorous physical examination was essential for the cadet to progress into advanced ROTC. Those who failed the examination at Clemson remained in uniform and participated in all formations and general drills, but they had no access to federal summer camp, newer weaponry, or the modest federal student financial allotment. While this was not the first division in the corps (there had been "day cadets" prior to this), it did tend to split the student body.

The summer camps, at first held in Plattsburg, New York, soon became a *rite de passage*. For many it provided their first experiences outside the South; for most this meant their longest trip from home; and for others, as the infirmary reports suggested, the visit to the military camps produced unfortunate encounters with venereal diseases.[109]

Cadet Stephen Wayne Graham as a senior in the 1917 edition of the Clemson College annual, *Taps*. In April of his senior year, he moved that the senior class report for duty following the United States' Declaration of War on the Second German Empire.

However, before anyone went away to ROTC summer camp, a series of German decisions to resume submarine attacks on all ships, both war and merchant vessels, and to involve Mexico, which had been in a protracted state of civil war for a number of years, in the war against the United States led President Wilson on April 6, 1917, to summon Congress to declare war on the Second German Reich. The U.S. would not declare war on Germany's major ally in the war, Austria-Hungary, until December 7, 1917.

News of U.S. entry into the war was announced to the cadets on Monday, April 9, 1917. Immediately, a cadet, Maj. Wayne Graham, noted for his oratorical skills, having already proposed at a Sunday class meeting that the class notify President Wilson that they were ready to go as a unit "over there," so moved. The motion was met by cheering assent. Clemson's commandant, Col. Allen Jones, U.S. Army, Twentieth Infantry, had received instructions from the War Department that the cadets (and all ROTC units) were to remain in school and await additional instructions. This forestalled a mass exodus of Clemson cadets. By May 2, 1917, fifty-four seniors had been called to service, prompting one senior cadet, M. M. Brice, to write,

But some we may never see again,…
To part with our classmates forever.
And then, when you're serving for flag and your country
In no matter what land or scene,
We will know you are holding aloft the high honor
Of Clemson and old "Seventeen."

Forty-eight seniors left by train for Camp Oglethorpe on Friday, May 3, after breakfast in the mess hall, and *The Tiger* began to publish deployment news of older alumni.[110]

The college prepared for graduation in June, but the question arose, "What about the seniors serving in the armed forces?" The trustees, at their April 4, 1917, meeting, adopted the statement, "that the faculty be authorized to graduate ahead of the usual time any members of the Class of 1917, who may be called into the service of the United States between this date and Commencement, provided the record of such student is satisfactory to the faculty."[111] Including the young men who went to the U.S. armed forces, 110 Clemson men received diplomas, three times the number in the first graduating class in 1896. Missing from the graduation platform was Richard Wright Simpson, confidant to Mr. Clemson, true author of the will, and president of the trustees for nineteen years. Of the men who had met with Mr. Clemson in the autumn of 1886, only Tillman survived.

Notes

1. *Record*, an individual volume issued for each Clemson academic year from 1910 to 1918. Graduate assistant Paul Alexander Crunkleton has developed these data in detail. The federal census was supplied through the Geostat Center of the University of Virginia Library Systems.
2. Edgar, *South Carolina*, 456–459.
3. Anderson *Independent*, October 1, 1954.
4. CUL.SC.CUA. S 30 v 2, 622 and 730.
5. Clemson *Messenger*, May 20, 1956.
6. Ibid.
7. Lambert, *South Carolina Methodists in Mission: A History of the Clemson United Methodist Church, 1908–1998*, 3–9.
8. CUL.SC.CUA. S 17 f 380; and S 30 v 2, 879–880.
9. Fred Holder, an independent scholar, has done much research on the early buildings of Clemson University. He provided this information.
10. Brackett, *Old Stone Church*, 1–3.
11. Ibid., 11, 13–17.
12. Ibid., 130: James A. Garvin, Andrew Pickens, and John Rusk. The remains of Gen. Robert Anderson were moved here during the filling of Hartwell Lake in 1960–1962. Since Brackett's study, continued research has increased the numbers and names in notes 12, 13, and 14.
13. Ibid., 132: James A. Garvin and Andrew Pickens Jr.
14. Ibid., 133: J. N. Alexander, J. C. Cherry, Dr. O. H. Doyle, John Frazier, B. F. Gantt, William Goodman, John Harris, Robert Harris, G. Hopkins, Col. Kilpatrick, James Lanier, David

Lewis, Earle Lewis, Robert Lewis, Col. Livingston, Edmund McCrary, J. S. McElroy, J. F. Miller, W. C. Rochester, Ed Sharpe, E. B. Sloan, A. C. Stevens, Harvey Swords, Verner White, and John White.

15. Ibid., 135.
16. Calhoun, "Long, Long Ago." A manuscript of a talk given is filed in the Littlejohn papers (CUL.SC.MSS. 68 f 70). It has been printed at least once and developed into a dramatic monologue delivered by Mrs. William Ballinger of Clemson. "Millie" Ballinger's monologue has been recorded on DVD by Lance McKinney of the Clemson University's Audio Visual Service Department, and a copy is in the Clemson University Special Collections.
17. CUL.SC.CUA. S 30 ss 1 f "Manning"; Hemphill, *Men of Mark*, vol. 1, 248–253; and Moore, "Richard Irving Manning III," in *South Carolina Encyclopedia*, 589–590.
18. The interpretation is based on Tillman's waning health, his occasional absence from board meetings, and his extensive speaking schedule.
19. CUL.SC.CUA. S 30 v 6, 191; S 6 f 9; and S 38 f "Evans."
20. Ibid., S 30 ss 1 f "Hughes."
21. Ibid., f "McKeown."
22. Ibid., f "Lever." See also the introduction to the A. F. Lever Manuscript Collection in Special Collections in the Clemson University Libraries.
23. Ibid., f "Mann"; and Green, "A Scholar's Turmoil: Patrick Hues Mell, 1902–1910," in *Tradition*, 92–94.
24. CUL.SC.CUA. S 30 ss 1 f "Timmerman."
25. Ibid., f "Evans."
26. Ibid., f "Evans"; and Bailey, *Biographical Directory of the South Carolina Senate*, vol. 1, 487–488.
27. CUL.SC.CUA. S 30 ss 1 f "Garrison."
28. Ibid., f "Burns."
29. Ibid., f "Rawl"; and Bernard H. Rawl, *Journal of Dairy Science*, vol. 8, no. 1, January 1925, 1–3.
30. CUL.SC.CUA. S 30 v 1, 135–137,157, 162, 167, 178, 199. By January 22, 1895, it seems the dikes (frequently spelled "dykes") were not finished.
31. Ibid., 397.
32. Ibid., 412–413.
33. Ibid., 414.
34. Ibid., 526.
35. CUL.SC.MSS 68 ff 71 and 72; Columbia *State*, May 30, 1911; and Columbia *Record*, May 30, 1911, speculates that "the decision differentiates Clemson college [*sic*] in this respect from the other colleges maintained by the State; it is not a State college in the sense that the University of South Carolina, Winthrop and the Citadel are...."
36. Charleston *News and Courier*, August 12, 1906, filed in CUL.SC.MSS 68 f 71.
37. CUL.SC.MSS. 68 f 103.
38. Ibid., f 71.
39. *New York Times*, March 6, 1897.
40. Charleston *News and Courier*, an undated newspaper clipping in CUL.SC.MSS 68 f 68.
41. The Citadel, Clemson Agricultural and Mechanical College, the State College for Negroes, the University of South Carolina, and the Winthrop Normal and Industrial College are so named, several incorrectly, in the report. The document decries (correctly) the omission of the "Institution for the Deaf and Blind." State law classified this school with the state's "penal and charitable institutions."
42. A grueling fight led by partisans of the denominational colleges and joined by friends of the Colored Institute (at Orangeburg), the Citadel, and Winthrop prevented South Carolina College from receiving the "title" of "university" from the general assembly in 1905. A much more circumscribed bill won easy acceptance on February 17, 1906. See Hollis, *University of South Carolina*, vol. 2, 202–205.
43. CUL.SC.MSS 68 f 156, the third section entitled "Weakness Through Dissipation."
44. Ibid., f 161, a typescript copy made by Mary Mills Ritchie for Littlejohn.
45. Edgar, *South Carolina*, 472–73.

46. South Carolina State University Archives: President's files: Miller. A full text can also be read in the Columbia *State*, January 29, 1911.
47. CUL.SC.MSS 68 f 156; and *Carologue*, vol. 12, no. 4, 8–13.
48. Webb, *Winthrop University: The Torch is Passed*, 62–63.
49. Floride Isabella Lee Calhoun's husband, Andrew Pickens Calhoun II, was the grandson of John C. Calhoun's son Andrew Pickens Calhoun. The son of Duff Green Calhoun, Andrew Pickens Calhoun II was born on April 10, 1872, in Abbeville, and he died on January 12, 1942, in New York City. Their children were Andrew Pickens Calhoun III (September 16, 1896–May 9, 1963; no offspring); Margaret Calhoun (July 6, 1897–January 12, 1959; no offspring); Patrick Calhoun (August 19, 1899–February 27, 1946; no offspring); and Creighton Lee Calhoun (October 31, 1901–January 29, 1940; one son). The one heir (and Mr. Clemson's last heir), Creighton Lee Calhoun Jr. (b. February 11, 1934), married Edith Thompson on December 2, 1956. They have an adopted son, Andrew Duff Calhoun, born on July 16, 1959.
50. John Caldwell Calhoun of New York City (1843–1918) was a grandson of John C. Calhoun, the great-grandfather of Floride Isabella Lee Calhoun. She and this man were first cousins once removed.
51. *The Tiger*, February 14, 1914.
52. *Reports and Resolutions to the General Assembly*, 1913.
53. *The Tiger*, February 14, 1914.
54. CUL.SC.MSS 68 f 244.
55. Edgar, *South Carolina*, 463. He cites Hand, "The Sad State of the High Schools in 1910," in *Perspectives in South Carolina History*, 305–315.
56. CUL.SC.CUA. S 30 v 1, 448.
57. Ibid., S 38 f "Hardin." The daughters were Mrs. C. C. McDonnell (Washington, D.C.); Mrs. Edgeworth M. Blythe (Greenville); Mrs. J. W. Gantt and Mrs. T. E. Keitt (both of Clemson College); and four sons: Dr. Laurie Hardin (Washington, D.C.); William Hardin (New Orleans); and George H. and Mark B. Hardin (New York City).
58. *Record*, 1911–1912.
59. CUL.SC.CUA. S 37 "Library History."
60. Ibid., S 30 ss 2 b 7 f 1.
61. Ibid.; and *The Tiger*, October 17, 1911.
62. *Record*, 1903–1904 and 1910–1911; http://www.theodoreroosevelt.org/life/biotr.htm; and http://en.wikipedia.org/wiki/Theodore_Roosevelt (accessed October 29, 2010).
63. CUL.SC.CUA. S 17 f 95.
64. Ibid., f 374; f 382; and Anderson *Daily Mail*, January (date on clipping unclear), 1911.
65. Rockefeller Archive Center, General Education Board (hereafter cited RAC, GEB). S 1.1 b 129 f 1178.
66. Kerr, *Legacy*, 57–58.
67. Ibid., "Act of 1890," 211–213.
68. CUL.SC.CUA. S 30 v 2, 940–941.
69. Webb, *Winthrop University*, 49.
70. CUL.SC.CUA. S 17 f 322; and Webb, *Winthrop University*, 35–36.
71. Webb, *Winthrop University*, 34–35.
72. Hine, "Robert Shaw Wilkinson," in *South Carolina Encyclopedia*, 1028–1029.
73. CUL.SC.CUA. S 17 f 55.
74. In his skillful essay on Riggs, C. Alan Grubb notes that the Riggs correspondence with Bradford Knapp, the federal Department of Agriculture (they knew each other quite well), director of the extension service before (and after) the passage of the Smith-Lever Act of 1914, more than suggests that the board was an internal source of objection to Clemson's direct supervision of African American agents. Grubb, "The Master Executive: Walter Merritt Riggs, 1910–1924," in *Tradition*, 99–111, and especially footnotes 23 and 25. See also CUL.SC.CUA. S 17 ff 49, 51–54; Potts, *A History of South Carolina State College, 1896–1978*, 63; and Hine, "South Carolina State College" in *Agricultural History*, vol. 65, no. 2, 153.
75. Harris, *Blacks in Agricultural Extension in South Carolina*, 6–10. The Clemson trustee vote came on January 5, 1912. See also CUL.SC.CUA. S 30 v 1, 831–832.

76. When USC (then SCC) celebrated its 100th anniversary, South Carolina State did not take part, nor was President Thomas Miller invited to join with the other institutional presidents when they met together in Columbia in 1906.
77. CUL.SC.CUA. S 17 f 53.
78. RAC.GEB. S 1.1 b 129 f 1178.
79. Bryan, *Clemson*, 230–231.
80. CUL.SC.CUA. S 17 ff 203–204.
81. Ibid., S 30 ss ii b 8 f 12.
82. Ibid., S 38 "Earle."
83. See also Smith, "Herculean Task," in "Cemetery Chronicles," in *Clemson World*, Fall 2002, 19. Theodore Sloan of Covington, Tennessee, a member of the Sloan family of Pendleton, gave me a very large genealogical chart of the Earle family. I have given the chart to the Special Collections of the Clemson University Libraries. Mr. Sloan in turn received the chart from Clemson Professor Emeritus of Landscape Architecture Donald Collins, who found it in the back of a file cabinet purchased from the architectural firm of which Samuel Broadus Earle Jr., Clemson 1930, and son of Susan Sloan and Samuel Broadus Earle, was a member. I am grateful to all these for their help. "Tim" Sloan has been particularly kind.
84. *The Tiger*, March 28, 1907.
85. CUL.SC.CUA. S 38 f "Lee."
86. Ibid., S 30 v 2, 840–841.
87. *Record*, 1915, 1916, 1917, and 1918.
88. Lee, *Rural School Buildings*, Clemson Agricultural College: Extension Work Bulletins, vol. 10, no. 2, April 1914. A new set was then issued as vol. 8, no. 3, July 1917. Part of the cost was borne by the South Carolina State Department of Education.
89. RAC. Rockefeller Fund, April 12, 1913.
90. Lee, "A Young Men's Christian Association Building for Clemson College," in CUL.SC.MSS 68 b 9 f 191.
91. Ibid.
92. Bryan, *Clemson, An Informal History*, 87–89; and Clemson *Messenger*, February 4, 1979.
93. Conversation with J. Roy Cooper at Ivy Duggan's home 1971.
94. CUL.SC.CUA. S 17 f 357.
95. CUL.SC.MSS Reel Collection f "Athletics."
96. *Taps*, 1911, 33.
97. Ibid., 204–205.
98. Ibid., 1918, "Athletics" section, unpaginated.
99. Ibid., 1912, 169–192.
100. Ibid., 1911, 227.
101. Ibid., 1912, 42.
102. CUL.SC.CUA. S 367 f "1915-Wannamaker." Clemson student Blair Bolen researched this in 2010. Keitt Wannamaker, Clemson 1980 and a Pi Kappa Alpha, furnished family information.
103. Ibid., f "1917." Clemson student Kimberly Stockwell researched this in 2009.
104. Quoting from Grubb, "The Master Executive: Walter Merritt Riggs, 1910–1924," in *Tradition*, 108; and CUL.SC.CUA. S 17 f 60.
105. Grubb, "The Master Executive: Walter Merritt Riggs, 1910–1924," in *Tradition*, 109.
106. Columbia *State*, April 19, 1909.
107. CUL.SC.CUA. S 30 v 2, 739–740.
108. Http://www.history.army.mil/books/AMH-V1/ch16.htm, 381–383.
109. On the camp, see Ibid., 366. On infirmary reports, see Redfern to Riggs in CUL.SC.CUA. S 17 ff 191, 205.
110. *The Tiger*, April 11, 1917; May 2, 1917; May 30, 1917; and June 6, 1917.
111. CUL.SC.CUA. S 30 v 2, 103–104.

You are cordially invited
to attend the
Second Home Coming
of
Clemson Tigers
at the Old Lair
July 30th, 31st and August 1st.

W. M. Riggs,
President Clemson College.

An invitation to the second Clemson Homecoming, July 30–August 1, 1920. Attached to this card, which was in possession of President Walter Merritt Riggs, was his own badge from the event. The Walter Merritt Riggs Presidential Records, Series 17, CUL.SC.

CHAPTER IX

Riggs's Last Years

1917–1924

As the World War I guns and cannons fell silent at 11 a.m. on November 11, 1918, various international peacemaking agencies, including the Young Men's Christian Association, began preparing for European rebuilding and for the rehabilitation of combatants and their reinvolvement in civil societies. The war had swept away many of the European imperial and royal families. As the old empires disintegrated, the emerging nationalities, ethnic groups, and linguistic groups, some with great religious differences, made separate armistices with the victorious Allies. The war had cost about ten million lives. For the United States, which entered the war late, the war dead numbered about 115,000.

World War I

The Clemson Agricultural College service flag honored 698 who served in the war, including 317 graduates.[1] The Gold Star flag honored twenty-seven who died. Among the casualties in land combat was Augustus Massenburg Trotter, Clemson 1915, who died in the Battle of Belleau Wood, France, fought June 1–June 26, 1918. His schoolmate Lt. Mell Glenn wrote home, "I have just received news that a South Carolinian, a close friend of mine and a member of my regiment, Lt. Trotter of Camden, gave up his life while leading his men against a German machine gun nest....If any more of us have to go, may we be permitted to go as he has gone—our face to the enemy, in lead of others, urging them to press on." Trotter was awarded the Distinguished Service Medal.[2]

Harry Clyde Horton, Clemson 1919, was killed on September 13, 1918. His commanding officer said, "Harry was worth all the rest of us together." Horton, before he died, wrote his parents, "Don't worry about me; just remember what we are fighting for. One could not choose a more glorious way of closing the book of life."[3] In October 1918, Henry A. Coleman, Company C, 306 Field Signal Battalion, Eighty-First Division, was killed near St. Die. A comrade wrote, "I have wished so often that I had been given such a happy disposition and the faculty of being optimistic like Hal under the most trying ordeals." One day before the armistice, Lt. Richard H. Johnson, Clemson 1915, was killed as he led his men in an assault on enemy lines near Metz.[4]

Others died at sea, including Seaman 2nd Class Frank R. Stewart on a mine-sweeper that was completely destroyed on August 21, 1918. Another from the Class of 1915, John A. Simpson, died in the sinking of the *Ticonderoga* on September 30, 1918. And 1st Lt. Claude Stokes Garrett in the Army Air Corps was shot down by a German aircraft while reconnoitering the German lines.

Two men, Ensign Daniel Augustus Joseph Sullivan and Sgt. Gary Evans Foster, one who had attended Clemson and the other who attended later, received the coveted Medal of Honor. Ensign Sullivan of Charleston was aboard the *U.S.S. Christabel* when it entered into battle with a German submarine. A depth charge severely shook the *Christabel*, setting live depth charges free on deck. Sullivan threw himself on top of the charges, secured them, and saved his shipmates and the ship. He lived on until January 27, 1941. Sgt. Foster of Spartanburg was advancing against the enemy in his company when an enemy machine gun nest concealed in a submerged road opened withering fire. One officer and Foster moved forward. The officer was wounded, but Foster, using pistols and hand grenades, continued killing several and taking eighteen prisoners.[5]

The result of these efforts was a valiant attempt to rebuild Europe on more democratic lines. In that regard, the international YMCA asked President Riggs to go to Europe and help direct the educational efforts of the American armed forces. Because of the early success of the effort, the U.S. War Department assumed control of the program in April 1919. Originally dispatched to Paris, Riggs asked to be closer to the troops, and he applied for a transfer to Beaune, France, where the War Department had established a school to teach some 20,000 Americans skills in agriculture and elemental mechanics. Interestingly, like Thomas Green Clemson, he met the king and queen of the Belgians when he visited Chaumont, the headquarters of the American commander, Gen. John J. Pershing.[6]

By war's end, the best figures list 698 former students (both graduates and nongraduates) who had been in uniform. However, Clemson, like many other schools (particularly land-grant colleges), also had a wartime program, the Student Army Training Corps (SATC), which placed large numbers of young men who were not Clemson students but who were billeted at Clemson on campus. Created and partially funded by the War Department, SATC was subdivided into two parts. The first, called Section A (at Clemson, at least), provided an accelerated officer-preparation program in which candidates received training and commissioning in three months' time. Reading and writing were basic; emphases were on mathematics and military and leadership training. Section B students received eight weeks' training to become mechanics, electricians, blacksmiths, wheelwrights, carpenters, radio operators, topographical draftsmen, and other vital, skilled support soldiers. All manner were prepared at Clemson, and many would think of themselves as "Clemson men" until they died. Therefore, counts of Clemson men in World War I and Clemson men who died in that war (and for that matter, other wars) vary.[7]

Other consequences of the war included the outbreak of a devastating form of influenza. First appearing in military encampments in Kansas, it spread with the troops to the American East and on into Europe. Several Clemson men died from it both in America and in Europe. And with the large number of young men coming into Clemson for SATC training, it was nearly inevitable that the influenza (variously called the "Spanish flu" or the "Spanish lady") broke out at Clemson. Cadets, SATC trainees, some faculty, and others became sick. State officials contemplated closing the college until they realized that the result would spread the illness statewide and beyond. Barracks One served as a sick ward, while the chapel and the upper floors of instructional space of Textile Hall became the space for the severely ill. Under Dr. Redfern's direction, and with the help of several regional physicians and the town pharmacist, Mr. McCollum, the women of the campus, including the few stenographers and the wives of faculty and staff, nursed the sick of both the college and community. A very few died, among them the infant child of Mr. and Mrs. William W. Routten, an assistant professor of woodworking, and (the second) Mrs. Ben F. Robertson, whose husband graduated in the first class and was a chemist in the fertilizer laboratory.[8]

Faculty

Women had taken several other new roles both in the community and the college. In 1916, Mrs. Riggs converted the women's informal sewing circle into the Clemson Woman's Club. The idea was not original. The club faded away in the mid-1920s and was revived in the 1940s.[9]

The war directly depleted the emerging group of young potential college instructors, calling them into military service as it did young men in most fields. Clemson was not alone. The first woman to join the teaching and research faculty was Mary Hart Evans, an assistant professor of botany. Evans married assistant pro-

Left to right: Mary Hart Evans, Rosamund Walcott, and Katherine Trescot, early women involved in teaching at Clemson College. Clemson University Photographs, CUL.SC.

fessor of botany William Aull, and she remained on the faculty until the couple left for other employment. When her brother was called to military service in 1918, Rosamund Walcott was invited to join the architecture faculty. She stayed for a year before entering private practice. A third woman, Mabel Stehle, came to Clemson to teach entomology, and she also took over French instruction. These women joined the librarian, Katherine Trescot, whom the cadets called the "Goddess of Wisdom." Trescot was not a faculty member but was classified as a member of the professional administrative staff, with the small spending authority as the division heads had.[10]

The entire faculty had expanded greatly between 1910 and 1918, driven in part by the new barracks space and in part by the Smith-Lever Act of 1914. Some forty-five persons comprised the faculty in 1910, while the 1918 faculty roster included seventy (a 55 percent increase). All five divisions (Agriculture, Academics, Chemistry, Engineering, and Textiles) increased in number, while the greatest percentage (2.2 times) was in Agriculture, clearly driven by the additional research and program professionals located at Clemson on the experiment station staff. The county demonstration agents had been resident in every county of South Carolina since 1912.[11] Bradford Knapp, the USDA director, noted that South Carolina and Clemson had achieved that mark first among the American states and territories; the achievement was accomplished two years before the Smith-Lever Act passage (that is, two years before the federal government began dispensing extension funds). The revenue for the county agents came from the fertilizer tag sales.

In 1919, a large number of former students began returning from military service. The faculty also welcomed back a few men who had been called into service. One was Maj. Joseph M. Cummins, previously Commandant Lt. Cummins when he left in 1916. Marked as a rare officer who showed no partiality when dealing with his charges and as a rare colleague, he was called "a good scout." A border-stater, he had attained the AB degree from the University of St. Louis and remained at Clemson until 1922.[12]

Riggs and Mills in Europe

The United States (and most other belligerents) had made few plans for the demobilized young soldiers. The country's first effort was to create on-site vocational and academic education. The YMCA initiated the project, but it quickly came under the aegis of the U.S. armed forces and became the American Expeditionary Forces (AEF) University in Beaune. Staffed by military personnel and civilian academics recruited from the United States, the school enrolled men for short-term courses before they returned home.

Among the academic leaders who joined this effort were President Riggs and William Hayne Mills, the faculty rural sociologist. Mills came from Winnsboro, where his father had served as pastor of the Presbyterian church. Mills, educated at Davidson College, was a member of Kappa Sigma and Phi Beta Kappa fraternities there. Following his graduation, he attended Columbia Theological Seminary, receiving the bachelor of divinity degree in 1897. He had married and held several rural pastorates when, in 1903, he received a call to serve as a Presbyterian missionary to the mill families of the Horse Creek Valley. Moved by the plight of the child workers in the mills, he led a campaign for the passage of child labor laws. Indeed, South Carolina's first such law is generally credited to him. Mills then accepted the call of Clemson's Fort Hill Presbyterian Church. His wife, Louise Pressley, and their daughter, Edith, moved into the manse beside the church. His dynamism in the pulpit increased the size of the congregation and caused the church building to be enlarged. The Millses knew the joy and sorrow of family, having a son and three other daughters, two of whom died in early childhood. In 1917, he resigned his pastorate to create the field of rural sociology at Clemson. One year later, he received an appointment to teach rural economics and sociology at the AEF University at Beaune, the same institution to which Riggs was also attached. From there, Mills returned to Clemson and took charge of the vocational rehabilitation program.

At Clemson, student enrollment dropped in January 1919 to 662, fewer than the Clemson men still in U.S. uniforms. The military discipline continued, SATC ended, and ROTC quickly reestablished. Students, returning from the Christmas holidays or from military positions and camps, were back in cadet uniform "giving substantial monetary aid to all cadets."[13]

While Riggs was in Europe, and on his recommendation, the trustees designated Samuel B. Earle to serve as acting president, which he did from February 13, 1919, until Riggs returned six months later.[14] Riggs left a lengthy, detailed memorandum for Earle, who followed his instructions closely. The six-month period was marked by continuing cases of influenza, although not of the magnitude of the fall of 1918. There were more student disciplinary problems, and Earle and Commandant McFeeley were very nervous as April 1, April Fools' Day, approached. Riggs would later note, "The mass-psychology of the student body was unsatisfactory. It has been so in the session before and during the spring of 1919; while I was in France, an open rebellion against the military discipline under Captain McFeeley was barely escaped."[15]

New Directions

Riggs returned to Clemson in midsummer and took up the reins of duty again. His first concerns were for the curricula. Even as agriculture across the state had diversified, sometimes with Clemson's leadership, the curriculum needed changing. Specialization in one of the four branches: animal industry, which included livestock and poultry; plants; agricultural chemistry; and agricultural education, a part of the Smith-Hughes Act, moved from the student's junior to the sophomore year.

Industrial education, a second part of the Smith-Hughes requirement, had received approval by the Board of Trustees in July 1918, having been recommended by the faculty. Charles S. Doggett, director of Clemson's Textile Department, was appointed supervisor. That same July, the college and the S.C. Board for Vocational Training signed a memorandum of agreement. The agreement designated Doggett as the state supervisor who oversaw work in agriculture, trades, industries, and home economics. Doggett, a Massachusetts native, was educated at Oberlin College. After graduation, he worked for five years in the textile industry, increasingly focusing on textile chemistry. Once he decided his special field, he attended Yorkshire College (now the University of Leeds), where he received first prize as the best student. While in the United Kingdom, he married Sarah Ann Verity of Bramley (Yorkshire).

Charles Stebbins Doggett (1858–1929), long-standing professor of textile chemistry and dyeing, supervisor of the Industrial Education Department, and director of the Textile Department at Clemson from his arrival in 1905 until his retirement in 1927. Clemson University Photographs, CUL.SC.

They went to Europe, where he studied at the Federal Polytechnic in Zurich, the University of Munich, the Royal Prussian Polytechnic in Aschen, and in Lyons. Upon returning with his family to the United States, he lectured at Massachusetts Institute of Technology and worked in industry until he accepted President Mell's offer in 1905 to come to Clemson as head of the textile program. Thirteen years later, he accepted the offer to begin the industrial extension program.

Doggett spent most of the autumn of 1918 and the spring of 1919 with mill superintendents and owners developing a program that, modeled on agricultural extension, placed about thirty classes a year in the mills directly training the workers in such fields as mathematics, design, and technical aspects of the industry. By the summer of 1919, the program was set to begin.[16]

As soon as the college opened in September, Riggs again took a leadership role in American higher education. Early in his presidency, he had displayed a strong interest in the growth and development of the state's African American college for agriculture, mechanics, and teacher education in Orangeburg, Riggs's hometown. He was a southern progressive. His father had come from New England, and his mother from Charleston. Riggs's older brother had served in the Confederate army, and he had cousins and uncles in the Union army during the Civil War.[17]

In an address on July 30, 1919, in Orangeburg, he said, "A great gulf of experiences yawns between the colored soldiers who have lived in France and their brothers at home." He noted that racial prejudice was not confined only to white southerners, but also to most white Americans. Even as he spoke, the great migration of young African Americans had begun from the southern agricultural states to northern and midwestern industrialization cities. Either Riggs did not realize what was happening, or he thought it not good, for in the same speech, he noted, "Education of all people, white and colored, must help solve the great race problem, which in the shade of ignorance assumes the outline of a menace." Then he spoke in a manner typical of the southern (and perhaps from elsewhere) region, "Education will teach the negro that his natural home is in the land of cane and cotton, that his natural calling is the one which lies nearest to Mother Nature's heart, that his interests are *identical, not antithetical, with those of his white neighbors*, and that in the South after all resides affection for him that nowhere else is to be found."[18]

As condescending as these words sound in the twenty-first century, they represent a most open-minded strain of white attitudes toward African Americans at that time, particularly in the South. Rather than viewing blacks as a dangerous threat who had no legitimate place in American life, Riggs apparently believed that the potential of the "negro" was as yet unknown and that blacks might benefit greatly from more and better education and white assistance.[19]

Long-Range Changes

After the World War, the Clemson College student body increased. Eight hundred eighty-six students came from every county in the state and from eleven other states.[20] Not only was the makeup of the student body changing, but so was the population of South Carolina. Its inhabitants had grown from 1,515,400 in 1910 to 1,683,724 in 1920, an increase of 10 percent. More striking, the African American population dropped from 55.2 percent to 51.4 percent of the state's entire population. Urban population rose from 14.8 percent to 17.5 percent. The latter figure is a bit misleading, however, because villages with a population of 2,500 and over were still classified as urban.[21]

After 1920, the two population trends were hastened by a natural phenomenon, a long, slow excruciating drought punctuated by rare, plummeting rains. The drought and the winds depicted in *The Grapes of Wrath* began in an area that stretched from a Montana-Texas line eastward, following the Missouri-Ohio River Valley lines to the East Coast and south to the Gulf Coast. The West would suffer worse than the East, clay subsoils worse than gravel, and rough land worse than plain.[22]

In many places, those whose holdings were small were more apt to be forced off their land. Whites, if they owned the land, generally reduced tilled acreage, and the males sought employment in nearby villages. Black landowners, barred from most town jobs, at first intensified planting efforts but fell deeper and deeper into the slavery of debt. Eventually, younger African Americans migrated to the rapidly expanding assembly line industries of the upper Midwest. Most of the people, particularly in rural areas, suffered from malnutrition. Of African American children in the South, the rate was 71 percent, while for white children, 41 percent.[23]

For Clemson Agricultural College, an institution whose revenue depended on agriculture, and particularly on revenue based on the sale of fertilizer, this sword was double-edged. Many consumers gave up the product; others left farming. Over the first ten years of Riggs's presidency (1910–1919), the fertilizer revenue fluctuated sharply from a high of $286,721.68 (2009 equivalent $3,044,113.10) to a low of $155,859.76 (2009 equivalent $1,654,751.11). The average was $236,787.58 (2009 equivalent $2,513,964.67).

Two problems faced the Board of Trustees. First, what really caused the wide revenue fluctuation? And second, what financial tactic should the board take to stabilize revenue? On the first issue, the answer was simple. South Carolina, although still rural (in a 1919 speech in Orangeburg, Riggs referred to South Carolina's occupation as 80 percent agricultural), now moved toward a nonagricultural economy, and the fluctuating fertilizer revenue resulted from crop prices and the climatic wet and dry patterns.

At the time, Clemson's revenue stability could conceivably come from one source only—the state. In the shortfall of 1914–1915, the state lent Clemson $62,400, which the college repaid in three years. Consecutive shortfalls in 1920–1921 and 1921–1922 led to state loans amounting to $262,842.11, which took longer to repay. The case was made. Beginning in the 1922–1923 fiscal year, the general assembly began regular appropriations to Clemson, in addition to the fertilizer revenue and the appropriations as part of the agreements between the state and federal government.[24]

Curricular Changes

Besides the change in revenue sources caused by weather and demographic shift, a second major change was in curricula. Because he served as registrar, J. C. Littlejohn functioned as a gatherer of alumni statistics. He noted the frequency with which Clemson graduates led the classes at the Medical College of South Carolina. He reported this information to Riggs, who assembled a small group of faculty, including R. N. Brackett and Riggs's traveling companion, William Mills, along with others. Together they put together a block of courses that included biological sciences, chemistry, rural sociology, rural economics, American history, and nutrition.[25] This was a first venture for Clemson in a premedical program, but it was not a curriculum.

The need, therefore, was for a general science curriculum in which to place a premedicine "course." The trustees approved it on December 7, 1921. Brought forward at the same time were courses, also called "groups," in the mathematical and natural sciences, modern languages (German and/or Spanish), and education.[26] The choices of the courses did not reflect, necessarily, the existing strengths of Clemson's faculty as much as they did perceived needs of South Carolina, particularly in its just-emerging secondary school system. At the time, the trustees considered that the natural sciences included the biological and chemical sciences. This decision continued the trustees' concern for the overall educational condition of all the white people of the state that dated back before the college's opening.

To understand the benefit against cost of the preparatory program, Riggs asked L. A. Sease, then headmaster of the school, to assemble the data and frame a recommendation.[27] Sease concluded that since 1900, 1,299 young men and boys had begun Clemson as preparatory students. Of those, 504 moved forward to the first collegiate year. In all, forty-six had graduated, twenty-seven were currently freshmen, and eighteen were sophomores or juniors. There were no seniors, but forty-nine were then in the preparatory program.[28] The resources the program required were two instructors ($3,800 per year in salaries in addition to their housing in the hotel), one classroom, and sixty-five beds in the barracks. With that information in hand, Riggs recommended that the trustees "abolish" (his word) the preparatory program. The trustees concurred, and the preparatory program ended on June 31, 1914.[29]

The president, the trustees, and some of the faculty shifted their efforts to enhance South Carolina's two major economic pillars of the early twentieth century, namely agriculture and textiles, by increasing one- and two-year curricula in those fields. Almost devoid of any but course work that bore directly on improved production, the two paths nonetheless included some instruction in leadership, such as parliamentary procedure.[30]

On January 5, 1912, the trustees fulfilled (almost) Prof. Rudolph Lee's dream by authorizing the curriculum in architectural engineering. Lee had hoped for a separate program, but the president and the board concurred with the faculty committee by making the curriculum a sub-unit within engineering. The first year was common with the other engineering "courses," while the divisions in the second year introduced freehand and architectural drawing.[31] Clemson announced the new program immediately. Two students began the program as sophomores in the autumn of 1913. Both graduated in 1915. In that year's southern schools of architecture competition, which included graduates of Auburn, Clemson, Georgia Tech, and Tulane, one of Clemson's two graduates received first place. By graduation 1918, eleven students had graduated in that field.[32]

Taken together, these stirrings belonged to the beginnings of the technical and community college movements and the beginnings of Clemson's arts and sciences programs. Much of this work was carried on in the summers, and, in some nonlaboratory subjects, the Clemson faculty took the course work out to clusters of students, particularly in more remote areas of the state.[33]

The college's agriculture faculty had long recognized the importance of forestry. In 1903, Prof. Haven Metcalf taught the first forestry course at Clemson. Metcalf was a native of Maine, who had degrees from Brown (AM 1896), Harvard, and Nebraska (PhD 1902) in botany and bacteriology. From that beginning, forestry had been taught regularly, and with the South Carolina rural landscape gradually depopulating, the faculty turned to forestry as an alternative that helped maintain and slowly improve the soil. The college taught forestry continually into the 1930s. However, there were two impediments. First, the college needed to hire at least one more forestry professor, and second, it needed to acquire considerable additional land for good experimental forests, probably attached to the experiment stations. These needed a request from the Board of Trustees and appropriations by the legislature, neither of which happened.[34]

Nonetheless, the faculty had moved in the important direction of soil conservation. The federal government had signaled more than a mild interest with the creation of the national parks in 1872 and the designation of the national forests in the late nineteenth century. And on July 12, 1893, at the Chicago Columbian Exposition, University of Wisconsin Prof. Frederick Jackson Turner proposed to American historians his "frontier thesis" in which American innovation was generated on the "edges" of American civilization. The land frontier was closed; therefore, no more land or natural resources were thought to be available. As stewards of the land, public agencies had the obligation to use the resources wisely. Of course, without that as a clearly stated goal, the governments (federal, mainly, and states, occasionally) had tended in that direction. The educational set-aside land under the Northwest Ordinance (1787) was a major example of the wise use of land for the general public good as had been the Morrill Act of 1862. In that "chain of congressional acts," the creation of Yellowstone National Park, during Grant's presidency, was another landmark. Enacted on March 1, 1872, the reserve consisted of 3,472 square miles. Yellowstone was under the jurisdiction of the U.S. Army from its creation until 1917.[35] The federal government, through the Forest Reserve Act of 1891, in the presidency of Benjamin Harrison, created national forests within the Department of the Interior. Prior to that, the special agent in agriculture was assessor of the quality and conditions of all forests in the U.S.

With Harrison's placing of 20,300 square miles in federal status and McKinley's adding nearly 11,000 square miles, the concept was well established.[36] In 1905, during the presidency of Theodore Roosevelt, the (by then) Bureau of Forestry transferred from the Department of the Interior.[37] Thus, Clemson's entrance into forestry was well timed nationally even though the hopes were not soon realized.

In the same year that the Clemson faculty called for a new interest in forestry as part of an overall agricultural program, the faculties at Iowa State College, the University of Georgia, and the University of Minnesota initiated forest studies at the graduate level. Yale began its School of Forestry in 1900.[38] The Biltmore School of Forestry and Cornell University's program followed shortly. The USDA had begun collecting forest data also in the late nineteenth century, and by 1905, the U.S. Forestry Service was established. Unfortunately, neither the S.C. Legislature nor the Clemson trustees took the action necessary to create such a program at the college.

Athletics

Even though Riggs strongly supported all intercollegiate athletics, he did not emphasize the sports to the detriment of either academics or the military. In the years leading up to U.S. involvement in World War I (1910–1917), football was a break-even sport in its won-loss record, with thirty-one wins, thirty-one losses, and four ties. The second half of the Riggs administration (1918–1923) resulted in little improvement, although during Ed Donahue's four-year coaching stint (which straddled the two Riggs periods, running from 1917 to 1921), the team turned in three successive winning seasons (1917–1918, 6–2; 1918–1919, 5–2; 1919–1920, 6–2–2) and Donahue's last and only losing season (1920–1921, 4–6–1). This was so heartening that when, in 1920, Heisman, who found himself involved in an unpleasant divorce in Atlanta, wrote to inquire about a job back at Clemson, Riggs responded indicating that Clemson contemplated no change.[39] During the last phase of Riggs's presidency (1918–1924), football posted twenty-six wins, twenty-two losses, and six ties (1918–1924) for a 53.7 winning percentage.[40]

Basketball fared just as minimally. The team had five different coaches between 1911 and 1918, posting twenty-nine wins, twenty-three losses, and two ties (55 percent). Between 1918 and 1924, five coaches (two who had coached the teams earlier) led the cadets on to forty-two victories and forty-four losses (48 percent). The most successful season was 1918–1919, when the Tiger team, after opening with three wins and one loss, was forced to cancel the remainder of the campaign because of the influenza epidemic.[41]

Clemson's oldest sport, baseball, fared reasonably well in the first Riggs years (1911–1918) with 103 wins, sixty-four losses, and one tie for a very respectable 62.3 percent winning rate. Then from 1919 to 1924, the baseballers went into a slump. They posted only thirty-eight victories and two ties out of ninety-six games for a woeful 24.5 percent winning record. Some recovery began in 1922 and 1923, but the record was hardly strong.[42]

Famed botanist, scientist, inventor, and educator George Washington Carver (1864–1943) with cadet Kelly Traynham in 1933. The connections between Carver and Clemson, begun during his 1923 visit to campus, lasted well into the 1930s. Clemson University Photographs, CUL.SC.

The other sports showed somewhat greater success. Track, after several weak years, had successes in 1921, 1922, and 1923, while the other popular sports included cross-country, tennis, and swimming. The last had been made possible by the building of the YMCA, which contained a (then) regulation-sized indoor pool.

Clemson "Integrated"

Sure signs of other slight changes also showed in the later Riggs years. One was a visit and chapel speech by George Washington Carver, the great agricultural chemist and senior research professor at Tuskegee Institute in Alabama. The students, who greeted him warmly, welcomed his appearance as the first African American intellectual to visit and speak at Clemson College. P. B. Holtzendorff, director of the YMCA, served as Carver's host and introduced him to the cadets.[43]

In the 1924 class, the first non-Caucasian graduated from Clemson. A textile engineering student, Yukata Tsukiyama, had arrived at Clemson from Hiroshima, Japan, in 1922. He acquired a nickname, "Sooky." Not a cadet, nonetheless he lived in the barracks and was a veritable whiz at table tennis, or ping-pong.[44]

The first non-Caucasian student to graduate from Clemson, Yukata Tsukiyama, a textile engineering student from Hiroshima, Japan. Taken from the 1924 edition of the Clemson College annual, *Taps*.

Discipline

Student discipline and student activities changed greatly after the war. Two factors helped increase the change: a veterans' job training program sponsored by the federal government and the rising age of the regular students. The federal program was the more immediate and, therefore, greater shock. The AEF University idea could not be sustained in France. The federal government "contracted" with the land-grant colleges to teach, feed, and house numbers of veterans, but every land-grant college was not expected to offer all fields of academic study. Clemson was designated to prepare farmers and a small number of civil engineers. Just like any group so selected, the veterans came from around the nation. They lived together in the barracks, and they wore their U.S. uniforms. But their educational backgrounds ranged from some high schooling to illiteracy. They rejected college discipline as childish (having already accommodated the military regimen), drank a great deal (it was the era of Prohibition), left campus at will, gambled, and fought. In their roaming, they found women with whom to dance and have "intimate relations." A frustrated Riggs called in private detectives as he had done a decade earlier to try to sort out the problems of Schilletter and the mess hall. Neither Riggs nor the detectives were successful.[45]

Regular student discipline also suffered. Cigarette smoking, although still prohibited, was more widespread. That, too, resulted mainly from the war. The ability of any enemy to draw a nighttime sighting on a glowing pipe bowl or the lighted end of a cigar was so great that as early as autumn 1914 all combatant agencies replaced most other forms of tobacco with cigarettes. Smoking them became the youthful style.[46] On one occasion, Winslow Sloan's store, which sat across the Greenville highway (now Old Greenville Highway) from Bowman Field, was reprimanded for selling cigarettes to cadets.[47]

Hazing remained a continuing problem. E. A. Verner, a state legislator from Richland County, and Riggs corresponded extensively concerning it.[48] And in a letter to M. J. Yeomans, a parent from Dawson, Georgia, Riggs confessed, "We had tried a great many experiments in order to eradicate hazing, but it is largely composed of boys' nature. I doubt if it will ever be completely eliminated."[49]

With the opening of the school year 1919–1920, Riggs appointed David H. Henry, a Clemson graduate of 1898 and professor of chemistry, as director of student activities, replacing the commandant. Henry coordinated the student clubs, the class dances, and cadet travel to college sports events. The first dance, given by the senior class, did not please Riggs. He noted that the seniors were selling "dope," the slang for Coca-Cola and sometimes other soft drinks; he worried about accounting for the money the seniors collected from sale of the refreshments. Further, Riggs thought that the lights were too low, preventing the chaperones (faculty and faculty spouses) from seeing what was happening. And he asked whether or not Henry had published and posted a list of prohibited dances.[50] By May 1922, Riggs seems to have resigned himself to these new ways, for in speaking to the cadets and their dates at the Junior-Senior banquet, he noted, "In the mystic domain of the jazz, youth shall seek affinity with youth, and we older lookers-on shall pretend to sigh for the good old days of long skirts and long hair, for unplucked eyebrows and uncovered ears."[51]

Amid the changes, more sexual issues came to Riggs's attention than before the war. These were due in part to the rising age of the regular students (finishing tenth grade now was common and eleventh grade an emerging option) and to enrolled veterans returning from the war and seniors returning from summer camp experiences. In 1922, one regular student imported a "woman of pleasure" from Greenville on more than one occasion. He managed to sneak her into his barracks room where she would "entertain" him and then, for pay, entertain other cadet friends (frequently at least ten) of his. Riggs had the cadet arrested for operating "a bawdyhouse, which was frequented by immoral persons of both sexes for the purpose of prostitution...." Riggs also dismissed the cadet from the college, admonishing him to tell his father the reason, because Riggs was sending the young man's father a full explanation (a procedure Riggs followed for all dismissed cadets). The ex-cadet returned within the week, begging Riggs for mercy. The father had insisted that if his son was "like that," he would have to get married. His girlfriend (not the "woman of pleasure") and family had consented; the date was set. But the "miserable offender" feared that the impending trial for operating the bawdyhouse and publicity would ruin both their lives. Riggs had the charge withdrawn.[52]

The Third Walkout

The serious trouble began in the mess hall in March 1920. For a school that had student troubles in 1902 and 1908, and for Riggs, who had feared that trouble might erupt during his overseas absence in 1919, the problem that then ensued proved more than embarrassing. The typical winter daily menu started with a breakfast of fried bacon, fried potatoes, grits, gravy, wheat bread, corn bread, cane syrup, milk, and coffee. On March 9, 1920, the midday meal (called dinner) consisted of boiled ham, steamed rice, pork and beans, baked macaroni and cheese, mashed potatoes, gravy, bread pudding with cream, wheat bread, corn bread, and cane syrup. For supper that day, boiled ham appeared again with creamed potatoes, grits, gravy, pineapple preserves, wheat bread, corn bread, and cane syrup. Butter and milk were served at every meal. While adults might complain about the absence of vegetables and fruits, the younger cadets were more upset with the order of serving.

Freshman cadets were hired at the beginning of each term to serve as waiters. They picked up the filled platters and bowls in the kitchen and brought them to the long tables arranged perpendicularly to the wall; the circulation aisle ran between the files of tables. The company sat at the table with the seniors at the head on the serving aisle, then by class (junior, sophomore) with the freshmen at the foot closest to the wall. By this point, the freshmen were no longer "rats," having survived the season and having received their "rat dips" ("rat diplomas"). The waiters placed the serving dishes at the head, and usually the food disappeared fast; waiters were loudly summoned to fetch refills until all cadets were filled or the supply of food exhausted. One freshman wrote home that all he had three times a day was a combination of cornbread, grits, and cane syrup, a concoction the cadets labeled "zip," because, one said, "It zips right through you!"[53]

The life of a waiter, although compensated financially, was one of great harassment. Thus, on the morning of March 9, 1920, when Commandant McFeeley learned that influenza had reduced the wait staff by six, he ordered (not "asked for volunteers" nor even "asked") six other freshmen to take up the positions. No pay was mentioned, and several freshman cadets refused. Demerits were issued. A sympathy demonstration began, and some students sported red "Bolshevik" badges. Riggs met almost immediately with the junior and senior committees. They stated that there were three real problems: the mess hall food, both in quality and quantity, about which they had protested before but to no avail; the strict military discipline in which demerits were continually increased by the commandant without notice; and the presence of the war veterans, who chafed under the discipline and sowed the seeds of rebellion. The younger students met by classes and both voted to "walk out," which many did. Some upperclassmen joined them.

Then Riggs responded. Food would be improved in quantity and quality, although it required an increase in food expenses and subsequent charges in the coming autumn. The students who took part in the two-day demonstrations, and who had been suspended and sent home, and those who had walked out, could return and apply to the Board of Trustees for reinstatement. Riggs promised to support their individual appeals, but he held firm that Clemson would remain military for all its students. Parents of all the cadets received a letter from Riggs setting forth his perspective and his offer. The freshmen and sophomores who had not taken part in two days of the strike were also sent home from March 12 to March 21 to let passions cool.[54]

The Clemson Board of Trustees met immediately and stayed in session for a number of days. Meanwhile, other land-grant colleges such as North Carolina State, Massachusetts A&M, and Ohio State University had student unrest also, suggesting that whatever the issue, food served as a convenient "whipping boy." At USC, a meeting of students asked its Board of Trustees and the governor to oust President William Spenser Currell. The student body president delivered the request to the board.[55] It was taken under advisement. Riggs, of course, met with Clemson's board. He tendered his resignation to them. They turned it aside.[56] Meanwhile, Riggs received letters and telegrams of support variously from the presidents, faculties, and trustees of Winthrop, South Carolina, Auburn, Iowa State, North Carolina State, and Colorado State. Clemson's Board of Trustees reinforced Riggs by inviting all students to return on March 21, requiring all who had participated in the demonstration and/or the walkout to apologize and agree, with their parents' written approval, to abide by the discipline. Riggs also wrote again to the parents.[57]

Some parents were angry with Riggs and made efforts to hold meetings around the state. At most gatherings, attendance was slight, suggesting that many parents understood the problems of Riggs and the trustees.[58] At a meeting in Columbia, the participants voted to ask the trustees to let their sons return and let them develop a common set of grievances.[59] State Rep. D. L. McLaurin of Marlboro was reported as saying that Clemson was a "prison military camp.... The usefulness of Clemson, in my humble opinion, has been ruined....These boys ...have no confidence in the president of it; this is not a new thing...." Then he seized the opportunity to open old issues, at least two of which had been settled in S.C. and federal courts.

> Unless we get rid of the life trustees and make Clemson a state institution in fact as well as in name, I am in favor of cutting the fertilizer tax and establishing a college that can and will be run in the interest of the farmers of this state; we do not care much for the military feature, we want a college that will feed our boys plenty of good wholesome food, take care of them when sick, treat them like human beings, and then require them to obey sensible regulations.[60]

There was truth to some of his complaints about the military discipline and food. One can only conclude that, in the absence of any complaint about the education the students received from the faculty in class, the laboratories, the library, and the fields, teaching and learning were doing well.

But the unhappiness continued. Riggs appointed a student committee with faculty advisors to meet with the board; the committee had very strong support from the other cadets. While many alumni wrote supporting the college administration's position, all were not positive. Joseph N. Tenket wrote from Florence, "You [Riggs] have built up the college wonderfully—but many of your dealings with students have been worse than high-handed; they have been unscrupulous. The sessions of the discipline committee in my time were a veritable 'star chamber proceeding.'" One day later (April 6, 1920) T. C. Haddon, Clemson 1914 and employed by Winthrop College, wrote Riggs, "We boys of then doubt as to whether you really tried to see things from our points of view, although you would assure us that you did."[61]

Riggs moved carefully. The four student committees organized by class were abolished, and Riggs announced that he would involve himself more in the daily life of the cadets. Cadets could have a faculty member of their choice serve as their counsel at sessions of the discipline committee. Student life was moved from the commandant's jurisdiction and placed under Prof. D. H. Henry of chemistry.[62]

Food quality and quantity improved, but mess hall problems persisted. At the end of the 1920 spring semester, in examining and settling the accounts, the commandant discovered that Mrs. Middleton, the matron of the mess hall who was responsible for the cleanliness of the hall, serving platters, and table utensils as well as the student waiters, had been "padding" the payroll in her favor. Riggs, who had trouble with the matron before, called her to his office and reprimanded her; however, he did not fire her.[63] This would prove to be a mistake.

Finally, graduation day arrived. One hundred twenty-six students were awarded diplomas. Almost half (fifty-six) were in agriculture, fifty-one were in engineering, eleven in textiles, two in architecture, and six in chemistry. The graduation was somewhat subdued, but the occasion passed with no incidents.[64]

Summer Sessions

Summer session began shortly after spring commencement. To continue to support schoolteachers, the college offered two sessions: one for six weeks and the other for four. Eighteen classes were held on campus with housing available for single men, single women, and for families including their children. The state Department of Education took part in the programming.

In 1921, T. H. Quigley, regional agent for the department's industrial education service, recommended that all students studying textiles take vocational education courses so that they might start night schools in the mill villages. Thus, the outreach that began as summer institutes for farming families nearly a quarter of a century earlier expanded into the rapidly growing textile industry to broaden both the skill and knowledge bases in South Carolina.[65]

While teachers made up the majority of the summer enrollees, there were also a small number of deficient students and new students who had been tested and found lacking in English and/or mathematics. F. H. H. Calhoun served as the summer school director, which he had done since the origin of the effort. The use of the campus and its facilities by such a wide group of South Carolinians—including farming families and clubs, public schoolteachers, conditional admittees, and continuing students who had failed one or another of their past year's courses—had remained a characteristic of Clemson since its founding (and many other colleges and universities, particularly those in the land-grant tradition).[66]

To provide summer campus facilities, the college opened and operated all laboratories, and made the library, still in the Main Building, available. All meals, even for families, were in the mess hall. Regular students who lived in the area, along with some of the enrolled students, were hired as waiters. In addition, the YMCA offered several different moving pictures each week. This remained the pattern throughout the last of the Riggs years and on through the acting presidency of Earle.[67]

Gauging Opinions

When the 1920–1921 school year began, the enrollment rose to 1,007 regular students and about thirteen one-year agriculture (OYA) students. Clemson offered a series of intense courses in agriculture and textiles. The first was moderately successful, but the second did not last very long. "One year agriculture" gold rings were available for the men who completed the year. Those men were frequently a bit older; they did not live in the barracks, nor did they don the grey wool uniforms. Some roomed in one or another of the communities. The federally requested rehabilitation program also continued, but because the number of enrollees dwindled, it was not renewed.

Before the regular school year opened, Riggs directed Commandant Cummins to be particularly vigilant against hazing even if it meant locating "additional officers in the barracks."[68] Cummins complied and assigned two unmarried military instructors to live in each barracks with the cadets. Cummins's reports in November stated that hazing complaints appeared to be lessening.[69] This practice continued for the remainder of Riggs's presidency. In 1923, freshman Harold Carlisle wrote his mother, "If you see any accounts and I guess you've already done so of hazing in the papers don't believe a word."[70]

All of these changes led to a rise in student academic response. For example, the winter session of 1921 found 95.5 percent of those students who composed the fall 1920 student body and who did not graduate in January back in school.[71]

Riggs was not certain the reforms and additions would smooth "the bristling fur of his young Tigers." In the summer of 1921, he sent a survey to "select" members of the just-graduated alumni asking their opinion on a number of issues. First, he sought to gauge their thoughts about possibly abandoning the Clemson traditional four-year military program in favor of a new two-year Reserve Officer Training Corps model, which would allow juniors and seniors who had completed two years of required military training to decide whether or not to pursue two more years and be commissioned at the end of their studies. The alumni responded unfavorably. They liked the camaraderie of the military regimen, and they liked Commandant Cummins. Second, Riggs asked for suggestions. The newly graduated alumni proposed lengthening the senior visitation privileges. These proposals were implemented, and as part of an easing of the military discipline, marching to class on weekdays and to church on Sundays was eliminated.[72]

At the time, four churches existed in the white community: Presbyterians, Episcopalians, Methodists, and Baptists. The Presbyterian ministers held Jewish Sabbath services. The number of Catholic students in the community increased and outgrew the offering of the Mass in the President's Office. To accommodate their needs, the liturgy and Eucharist, led by the Rev. Mr. Mackin of the Anderson parish of St. Joseph, were moved to the YMCA. General Secretary P. B. Holtzendorff, like Riggs an active Presbyterian, greeted them warmly and ensured that the cadet worshippers had coffee and toast after Mass.[73]

A more widely distributed survey, apparently to continuing students, asked about the new infirmary physician, Dr. Heath. Not all students were favorably disposed toward him. Many found him detached and a strict disciplinarian, often too clever to let the infirmary be used as a way out of the regular school and drill day. He did not stay at the college long.

Student Life

The Clemson students who were intercollegiate athletes and who participated in enough games or meets earned large "C" letters called "varsity" letters. ("Varsity" is an abbreviated or slang form of the word "university.") The literary societies had increased in number to six, but nationwide their attraction had faded. Their success at Clemson likely resulted from the lack of social fraternities at the college. Dance clubs and newer academic discipline clubs were taking the place of the social fraternities and beginning to replace the literary societies. Among the oldest was the student chapter of the American Institute of Electrical Engineers. Many disciplines had such societies that brought faculty and students together in less formal settings. The World War I veterans formed the American Expeditionary Force Club, which remained active during the years 1919–1923. Regional, county, and town clubs functioned fitfully. The closest group to a fraternity, the Square and Compass consisted of young men who were Masons.[74] Some of the groups were local to Clemson, but others were broader, which helped break down the college's insularity.

Besides the various clubs and societies, the creation of Clemson's alma mater provided an unexpected addition. These are serious songs, even hymns, lauding and thanking the school for serving as a "nourishing mother," which is the meaning of *alma mater*. Over the quarter-century of Clemson College student life, several young authors had penned such songs, but none had taken hold. That changed in the summer of 1918, when 165 Clemson cadets attended ROTC camp at Plattsburg, New York, along with ROTC collegiate units from around the country. For evening activities, the military staff held a school night, and each unit was called upon to sing its school's alma mater. Clemson did not have one, although it had cheers in abundance. So cheers it would be.

Albert Cleveland Corcoran, member of the Class of 1919 and author of the words to Clemson's alma mater. Taken from the 1919 edition of the Clemson College annual, *Taps*.

When he returned to campus, A. C. "Allie" Corcoran from Charleston wrote lyrics for a proposed alma mater. Written when the school was all-male, military, and in the shadow of World War I, the words reflected those aspects. Corcoran had the four stanzas printed in *The Tiger*. The glee club practiced it using the tune of the Cornell University alma mater, which had not originated with Cornell and was used by many other schools and fraternities. It was an Irish melody called "Anna Lisa" or "Amici." Presented to the cadets in chapel, Corcoran's proposed alma mater received loud cheers. The cadets loved it, learned it, and adopted it. They sang it to that borrowed tune until the summer of 1950.[75]

The major student publications also remained highly important. These included the *Chronicle*, *The Tiger*, and *Taps*. One of the cadets immersed in the publications was Ben F. Robertson Jr., a second-generation Tiger and a "townie" from nearby Liberty. Known as a great jazz pianist, he was a horticulture major, active in the dance clubs, editor-in-chief of *Taps*, and a junior editor of the *Chronicle*. Like most of the cadets, he received a nickname, "Millie," which he carried the rest of his life. From Clemson, Robertson went to graduate school in journalism at the University of Missouri.[76]

Engineering Efforts and Problems

Nationally, the Association of Land Grant Colleges met in two large sections, agriculture and engineering. Riggs was active in both areas, serving for a time as chair of the engineering section. The group recommended that, to stimulate manufacturing, Congress should create a funded engineering experiment station attached to the state land-grant colleges. The problem with the concept was that in at least one state, Georgia, the state-supported school of engineering did not reside on the same campus with agriculture. And for that matter, agriculture

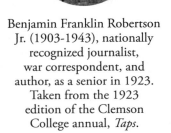

Benjamin Franklin Robertson Jr. (1903-1943), nationally recognized journalist, war correspondent, and author, as a senior in 1923. Taken from the 1923 edition of the Clemson College annual, *Taps*.

was fragmented. To gain the support of Senator Hoke Smith of Georgia, Riggs urged the other land-grant presidents to include Georgia Tech in the bill, but the land-grant executive committee refused to do so.[77] U.S. Rep. and Clemson Life Trustee Frank Lever actively supported the bill. Riggs did not give up, helping to form a national committee of practicing engineers and engineering deans to support the concept. But some schools opposed the idea because the program would be managed by the U.S. Department of Commerce. Eventually, when the Republicans gained control of Congress, the idea died.[78]

In South Carolina, three public schools—Clemson College, the University of South Carolina, and the Citadel—offered engineering. The latter two offered civil engineering, and USC also offered electrical engineering. Some legislators were concerned about the multiplication of expensive programs in the state's schools. In an effort to determine the extent of replication in state educational programs, the general assembly formed a Legislative Committee on Economy and Consolidation with Fred Telford as the chief investigator. Telford and the committee visited the three institutions, meeting with the presidents, the program heads, and the faculties. At Clemson, Riggs told Telford that he had no desire to consolidate the programs to Clemson. He believed that the other schools did "creditable" work in civil engineering, in part because it was not heavily laboratory oriented.[79]

Telford compared the three schools' curricula to each other and to "leading civil engineering schools." He concluded that Clemson should reexamine its requirements for wood shop and foundry. He also contacted well-known engineering professionals at a number of schools to garner their opinions on the merits of each of the three schools. Some of those contacted had no opinion, but most who did were positive about Clemson. C. M. Spofford, professor in charge of civil and sanitary engineering at Massachusetts Institute of Technology, wrote Telford, "It would seem to me that the only one of the three colleges prepared to give a reasonably complete course in civil engineering is Clemson College, which has a considerable instructing staff in the various branches of engineering and in the sciences and mathematics upon which engineering is based."[80] Ultimately, the legislative committee recommended that all graduate work in the state in engineering and agriculture be housed only at Clemson.[81] It would not happen.

State Economy

Even though the state's economic base had diversified, adding textiles to its large occupations, the agriculture sector remained the major portion. And research was vital. A new experiment station, Sandhill, opened at Pontiac, giving much help to the farmers of the Midlands. In post World War I, their research demonstrated that diversification, particularly in dairy herds, hogs, and beef cattle, could be profitable. In 1920, the livestock division began successfully eradicating cattle fever ticks and initiated a tuberculosis prevention program. It also gave much attention to hog cholera control and poultry pullorum.

The experiment stations also determined that adding limestone to the soil helped with growing Irish potatoes, soybeans, tobacco, corn, and cotton. The Pee Dee Station through these years reintroduced grapes as a commercial crop, but the crop required much hand labor, including at least three sprayings of the disease controls during growing season besides the hand harvesting. Also under study were peaches, plums, and pears. These were much more successful, and large orchards, particularly of peach trees, appeared in the Sandhills along the ridge. By 1922, the diversification allowed the railway shipping of 14,000 train carloads of S.C. fruits and vegetables to the Northeast.[82]

Riggs's Last Journey

The Clemson Agricultural College of South Carolina underwent radical reformation during Walter Merritt Riggs's fifteen-year presidency. Through his strong personality and vigorous leadership, the Board of Trustees withdrew from its previous role of close involvement in the daily operations of the college and the cadets. Further, the faculty, especially in the sciences and technologies, grew in qualifications and diversity. And Riggs's active role in national advocacy and associations began to break down the provincial isolation that characterized most southern institutions.

It was that advocacy and his growing national reputation that called Riggs to Washington, D.C., on January 20, 1924. He traveled alone by train to meet with other members of the land-grant association's executive committee. Members of that committee recalled that Riggs was in a jocular mood. The group of college presidents began their meeting in preparation to meet with the U.S. secretary of agriculture. After lunch the group walked the near mile to the office building. Raymond A. Pearson, then-president of Iowa State College, remembered that Riggs walked slower than the other members. After their meeting

An undated photograph of President Riggs near the end of his career. Clemson University Photographs, CUL.SC.

with the secretary and other staff, the committee returned to their hotel. After dinner they met to prepare for the meeting scheduled for the next day with President Calvin Coolidge.

Two days later, the group gathered again except for Riggs, who did not feel well. The others met with the president and then went to Congress to meet with the U.S. House Committee on Agriculture. After those engagements, the committee returned to the hotel to see Riggs, whom they found awake and very interested in the results. But Pearson noted a blood-stained towel on the bed. Through the afternoon and evening, the hotel's house physician and another physician attended Riggs almost constantly.

About 8:30 p.m., the outside physician proposed moving Riggs to a hospital for X-rays. Riggs's breathing was rapid, although he seemed to have no pain. At 9:25 p.m. on the evening of January 22, 1924, Walter Merritt Riggs died, surrounded by land-grant college presidents from across the nation.[83] A telegram was sent immediately to Clemson to Samuel Earle and James Littlejohn. They called on Mrs. Riggs, who made plans to go to Washington to accompany her husband's body home. She asked to go alone.

The inside of Memorial Chapel, displaying President Riggs's casket and the flowers sent in his memory from around the nation. Clemson University Photographs, CUL.SC.

Littlejohn, who served as both registrar and assistant to the president, sent telegrams to the trustees and other major state leaders notifying them of the death. When President Wilkinson of South Carolina State received his telegram, he penned in his desk day calendar, "Today my dear friend Dr. Riggs has died." Wilkinson, a devout Episcopalian, then took from his shelf *The Book of Common Prayer*.[84]

At Clemson, Mrs. Riggs prepared for her train ride. When she arrived in Washington, she was met at the train by President Brizzell of Texas A&M and Frank Johnstone Jervey, Clemson 1914, World War I veteran, staff member of the Department of War, and president of the Washington Clemson Club. They attended Mrs. Riggs, received her husband's body, and accompanied both back to Clemson.

In tribute to the importance of his life's work, the S.C. Senate recessed for fifteen days. In a memorial editorial, the Columbia *State* noted, "The state college for Negroes in Orangeburg, so often forgotten, has lost in him a friend that it will surely miss."[85]

Clemson held Riggs's funeral in Memorial Chapel on the campus. The legislative delegation included Alan Johnstone, chair of the Senate Finance Committee, and the presidents of almost all the colleges in South Carolina. The small town's clergy participated in the rite, which the Presbyterian minister conducted. The college's class presidents served as active pallbearers, and the entire corps of cadets in full uniform served as the military escorts. Riggs's body was borne to Woodland Cemetery on a western ridge of the campus, where he became the first servant of "dear old Clemson" laid to rest there.[86]

The funeral cortege of Walter Merritt Riggs as it left Memorial Chapel and passed in front of the Chemistry Building (now Hardin Hall). Clemson University Photographs, CUL.SC.

Notes

1. CUL.SC.CUA. S 37 f "Cadet Corps 1893–1929" and f "Alumni 1910–1919"; S 10 f 187; also see note 7.
2. CUL.SC.CUA. S 10 f 208.
3. Ibid., f 208.
4. Ibid., f 207.
5. Ibid., f 187.
6. Ibid., S 17 f 198.
7. As a part of the Clemson Corps's efforts to erect the Scroll of Honor Memorial (2006–2010) and to obtain a more accurate list of Clemson students who died in military service, a small group of undergraduate students (Christopher Alderson, Brian Ammons, Lyndsey Banks, Anna Lee, M. Heath, Jeffrey Metzler, and Charles Polly) undertook painstaking research into the individuals listed by the War Department and its successor as casualties in the American wars. Alex Crunkleton, graduate student, aided the work on the Medal of Honor recipients. Clemson Registrar Stan Smith and his staff assisted in their research. Nancy Cook Fisher, Clemson 1974 and a professional genealogist, provided the students a series of demonstrations and a bibliography (Web-based); she also corresponded with individuals about specific problems. Special Collection Librarian Michael Kohl and his staff worked directly with the students as well. The Office of Undergraduate Studies, through Associate Dean Jeffrey Appling, provided support for copying and for travel to depositories. Generous staffs at depositories including the USC Caroliniana Library and the S.C. Division of Archives and History helped the student scholars in their quests.
8. Barry, *The Great Influenza*. The book needs to be read closely to gain an understanding of the level of medicine in 1918.
9. Reel, *Women and Clemson University*, 7.
10. Clemson *Record*, various 1918 to 1924.
11. CUL.SC.CUA. S 17 f 374; and Anderson *Daily Mail*, March 24, 1912.
12. *Clemson Alumni*, vol. 2, 10.
13. CUL.SC.CUA. S 22 b 8 ff 91 and 92.
14. *Board of Trustees to the General Assembly*, 1918, 21.
15. Duffy, "The Conservative Caretaker: Samuel Broadus Earle, 1919 and 1924–1925," in *Tradition*, 127–129.
16. "Clemson President's Report," *Report of the Superintendent of Education*, 1921, 6. On Doggett, see the bibliography by his daughter, Marguerite Doggett, in CUL.SC.CUA. S 38 f "Doggett, C.S."
17. CUL.SC.CUA. S 17 f 198.
18. Ibid., f 367. The italics are mine.
19. Williamson, *A Rage for Order*, 70–79.
20. Clemson *Record*, 1922–1923.
21. U.S. Census Bureau and the Geostat Center of the University of Virginia Library system website accessed October 20, 2005, by Andrew C. Land, Clemson BS 2005 and MA 2007.
22. Woodruff, *Rare as Rain*. The argument is the subject of this study.
23. Fite, *Cotton Fields No More*, 38, 108–111.
24. *Board of Trustees to General Assembly*, 1925–1926, 18–19, gives an 18-year run of the revenue derived from fertilizer tag sales. This helps judge the health of the previous agriculture year (1909–1910 through 1926–1927). The revenue for 1919–1920 (reflecting the last year of World War I) was the highest ($313,472.54), and the lowest was 1921–1922 ($126,118.07). The state lent Clemson $150,000 that year to cover the shortfall.
25. CUL.SC.CUA. S 17 f 246 and S 30 v 3, 185.
26. Ibid., S 30 v 3, 185–189.
27. CUL.SC.CUA. S 17 ff 6 and 56.
28. Ibid., f 358.
29. Ibid.
30. Ibid., S 30 v 2.
31. Ibid., 840–841.

32. Clemson *Record*, 1915, 1916, 1917, and 1918.
33. CUL.SC.CUA. S 10 f 180.
34. Ibid., S 49 b 20 f 13.
35. Http://www.earlyamerica.com/earlyamerica/milestones/ordinance (accessed November 17, 2010); and http://en.wikipedia.org/wiki/yellowstone_national_park (accessed November 17, 2010).
36. Http://en.wikipedia.org/wiki/forest_reserve_act_of_1891 (accessed November 17, 2010).
37. Http://en.wikipedia.org/wiki/national_forest_service (accessed November 17, 2010).
38. Http://www.environment.yale.edu (accessed June 3, 2010); and http://www.fs.fed.us (accessed June 3, 2010).
39. CUL.SC.CUA. S 17 f 247.
40. Bourret, *Clemson Football 2009*, 203.
41. Bourret, *Clemson Basketball 2009–2010*, 198.
42. Bourret, *Clemson Baseball 2010*, 176–177.
43. *The Tiger*, November 28, 1923.
44. The story of Tsukiyama was gleaned from the *Chronicle* and *Taps*.
45. CUL.SC.CUA. S 22 b 8 ff 91 and 92.
46. It was interesting to quantify the types of tobacco advertisements in the Anderson and Greenville papers and in the student-operated *The Tiger*. All revealed the shift to cigarettes, although *The Tiger* moved that way more quickly.
47. CUL.SC.CUA. S 22 b 9 f 10 and S 17 f 218.
48. Ibid., S 17 ff 67–68, 71–73, 205–209.
49. Ibid., f 209.
50. Ibid., f 205.
51. Ibid., f 364.
52. Ibid., ff 253 and 320.
53. At least a dozen alumni from the late 1920s, 1930s, 1940s, and 1950s have thus defined the potage for me.
54. CUL.SC.CUA. S 17 ff 212 and 213.
55. Columbia *State*, March 23, 1919.
56. CUL.SC.CUA. S 17 f 213.
57. Ibid., S 30 v 3, 21–33.
58. Ibid., S 17 f 213.
59. Ibid., S 30 ss ii b 9 f 8. Box 9 contains most of the documents concerning the walkout of 1920.
60. Ibid., S 17 f 213.
61. Ibid., f 216
62. Ibid., S 22 b 10 f 15.
63. Ibid., S 17 ff 219 and 220.
64. *Record*, 1919–1920; and CUL.SC.CUA. S 30 v 3, 77.
65. CUL.SC.CUA. S 17 f 228.
66. Ibid., ff 238 and 242; and S 36 f 11.
67. CUL.SC.CUA. S 10 f 180.
68. Ibid., S 17 f 222.
69. Ibid., f 225.
70. Letter of Howard Carlisle in a typescript made by John Robert Carlisle, Clemson 1953, and sent to me by Jerry F. Carlisle on October 21, 2003. The typescript has been deposited in the Clemson Library Special Collections.
71. CUL.SC.CUA. S10 f 230.
72. Ibid., f 237.
73. Ibid., f 235.
74. The sources of the information are the annual memberships and lists published in the annual *Taps*. The *Chronicle* was the source for group activities.
75. *The Tiger*, February 20, 1919.
76. *Taps* and the *Chronicle*, 1919–1924, are the sources of this Robertson information.
77. CUL.SC.CUA. S 17 f 204.
78. Ibid., f 206.

79. Ibid., f 210.
80. Ibid., f 247.
81. Ibid., f 248.
82. Ibid., f 247; and Agricultural Experiment Station, *Miscellaneous Publications*, no. 27, 13–30.
83. CUL.SC.MSS 68 b 3 f46.
84. S.C. State University Archives, President's Papers: Wilkinson.
85. Columbia *State*, January 30, 1924.
86. *Greenville News*, January 25, 1924.

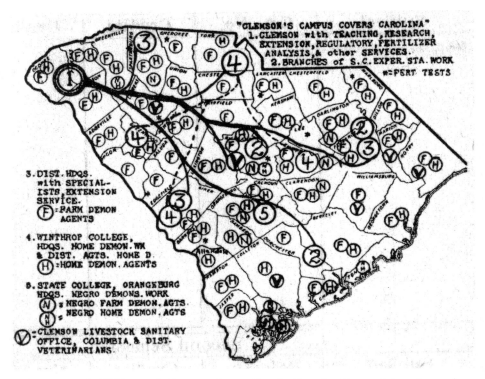

A map entitled "Clemson's Campus Covers Carolina" marks Clemson's location and the locations of its experiment stations—an important support structure for the state in the era of the Great Depression—showing how in this period, Clemson covered South Carolina. Taken from the 1928 *Clemson University Handbook*, published by the campus YMCA.

CHAPTER X

Gathering Resources

1924–1940

Earle's Second Watch

While the trustees gathered for Riggs's funeral in January 1924, they asked Samuel Broadus Earle, who had served as acting president during Riggs's post–World War I service in Europe, to return to that leadership position. Some board members considered proposing Earle for permanent president, but Earle, who had weathered a tense spring in 1919, was not interested.[1] He served as the director of the college's Engineering Division, a position he had held since Riggs became the sixth president in 1911. In that capacity, he had responsibility also for water, power, and heat for the entire campus and for the small community of several stores, a few homes, the four churches, and several other establishments, notably on the Greenville-Seneca highway and north of that roadway and west of the main road to Calhoun. The Board of Trustees gave Earle unqualified support during his time as acting president from January 1924 to July 1925.

Accreditation Denied

The most pressing issue that drove the brief Earle administration was accreditation. The Association of Colleges and Schools of the Southern States, now called the Southern Association of Colleges and Schools (SACS), had been formed in 1895 by a number of public and private liberal arts colleges and universities. It had not been hospitable toward accepting schools that emphasized science and technology. Thus, the University of Georgia, which taught agriculture and also offered classics and the bachelor of arts degree, held membership in SACS, but Georgia Tech, which offered no bachelor of arts degrees, had been refused membership. Apparently SACS was unique in that attitude among the emerging regional academic accrediting associations.

By itself, membership in SACS was of little consequence in the 1900s. However, the federal government had begun to link the opportunity for citizens to stand for civil service entry examinations and opportunities for upgrades to graduates of institutions approved by regional accrediting associations. Auburn was the first of the traditionally agricultural and mechanical land-grant schools in the South to gain accreditation from SACS. The faculty and trustees had created a strong lower school education preparation program and a bachelor of arts degree in general studies within which a number of curricula could serve as major fields. Virginia Tech followed Auburn in 1923, using the same strategy. Texas A&M and Clemson both applied for membership and accreditation in 1924. Clemson created the general science program but did not strengthen its education program nor add the bachelor of arts degree. Thus, SACS denied the application, prepared by Trustee W. D. Barnett.[2]

The Fourth Walkout

Despite the disappointing decision of the accreditors, Clemson College opened again in September. Then unexpected trouble flared up on Monday, October 13, 1924. A group of seniors who said they spoke for all seniors complained to Earle that the chicken served on the preceding Saturday and the sausages served on Sunday were spoiled. Earle listened to the disgruntled students and then directed the commandant to investigate. The senior committee waited on the commandant.

R. F. "Butch" Holohan, president of the 1924–1925 senior class, captain of the Clemson Tigers football team, and root cause of the walkout that President Earle faced in October 1924. Taken from the 1923 edition of the Clemson College annual, *Taps*.

During his meeting with the senior committee, the commandant said he smelled alcohol on the breath of R. F. "Butch" Holohan, president of the senior class and captain of the football team. The "Big Thursday" game with USC loomed on October 23. The team had a 2–1 record, and the students were already excited. The commandant summoned the disciplinary committee, which noted that Holohan had been excused earlier on a previous alcohol charge because of inconclusive evidence. The disciplinary committee then suspended Holohan for one year on the current charge. Holohan left school and did not return.[3]

Within the hour, the senior class vice president met with Earle and asked permission to hold a meeting in the chapel at 1:00 p.m. Earle agreed to the meeting but set it at 6:30 p.m. so as not to disrupt the midday meal and afternoon classes and laboratories. Defying Earle, the senior class met at 1:00 p.m. on Riggs Field and developed four complaints. The class officers delivered them to Earle. The seniors asked that the mess hall matron be retained, the mess hall director be replaced, the food improved, and Holohan reinstated. Earle agreed to look into food improvement but said "no" to the others. The matron, Mrs. Middleton, had been a sore spot in the dining services dating back to the walkout of 1920; no amount of "discussion" convinced her to change. On the other hand, the mess officer, who had come to Clemson in 1920 to replace Augustus Schilletter, who resigned in 1919, was James D. Harcombe. He came to Clemson from the Port of New York Army Hospital, where he had served as chief mess officer feeding the wounded soldiers returning from European battlefields. The complaints against him involved hemp allegedly found in apples and a fly in the syrup. The matron's behavior had a lengthy pattern, while the charge against Harcombe remained unproven and represented, if it happened, a single incident.[4]

The seniors responded that they "were walking," and some members of lower classes joined them. About 250 left campus without permission. Earle announced quickly that seniors who stayed away more than forty-eight hours would be dismissed and that lower classmen who did not return before forty-eight hours elapsed would be suspended for the remainder of the academic year. Thus, the issues reduced themselves to two. What, if anything, was wrong in the mess hall, and were announced punishments too harsh?[5]

Earle wired Board of Trustees President Alan Johnstone to inform him of the crisis. Meanwhile, the grumbles continued. Ham, scrambled eggs, and hominy, along with biscuits, milk, and coffee, were served for Tuesday's breakfast. The cadets still on campus complained that they found the eggs spoiled. At Earle's directive, Harcombe immediately sent remaining eggs and ham and the still-to-be-scoured utensils to R. N. Brackett, professor of chemistry, for analysis. After completing tests on the food, Brackett wrote Harcombe, with a copy to Earle, "We have carefully examined the sample of ham and eggs which had been sent to this laboratory from the mess hall. We find the specimen attractive in appearance, pleasing in odor and taste." He also tested the pots, pans, and utensils. "Furthermore, we have carefully examined the vessels used in cooking the eggs and find them in fine condition, and also find that there is no danger of metallic contamination."

Alan Johnstone called for the trustees to meet on Monday, October 20. Apparently at Johnstone's request, Dr. Hayden of the State Board of Health arrived and began a detailed inspection of the mess hall, its kitchens, and storage. Almost simultaneously, E. L. Tully, the State Board of Health's sanitation engineer, who had completed his routine semiannual inspection the Friday prior to the complaints, delivered a just-completed copy of his report to Earle. He wrote that the entire facility was thoroughly cleaned three times a day and that the cooks and food handlers were inspected twice yearly for disease.

At chapel on Wednesday, the fifteenth, a large number of younger alumni spoke to the remaining cadets, urging them to stay and "stand by the College." The students voted 302 to 157 to remain, conduct themselves in an orderly fashion, and await the outcome of the upcoming trustees meeting. At evening mess, the cadets were told "that all classes will be resumed as usual at long roll tonight, October 15, 1924."[6] The next morning after chapel, about 100 cadets threatened not to attend classes. The Rev. Mr. John McSween, pastor of Fort Hill Presbyterian Church, who took his charge as pastor to students very seriously, met with the dissident cadets. They listened to him and then went to class.

Shortly thereafter, Dr. Hayden reported to Earle, Johnstone, and some of the other arriving trustees that the food was always purchased from reputable sources. He added that although the number of cadets had increased by 11 percent in the two years, meat cooked, served, and consumed increased 16 percent, eggs 16 percent, and grits 52 percent. Two separate examinations found nothing amiss with the food, and an inspection of the facility also revealed close attention to cleanliness. So the problem was not one of quality or quantity. Word spread soon throughout the state of the baselessness of the cadets' complaints. Parents began bringing their sons back to the college. Earle greeted each family and urged the parents to eat a meal in the mess hall. Many did.

The Board of Trustees met on Monday morning, October 20, and continued meeting through Friday morning, the twenty-fourth. At their request, McSween stayed with them. The board interviewed each senior, whether or not he had "walked." Lower classmen who had left campus were also interviewed individually. On Friday afternoon, the board met with the cadets and gave them its decisions. Seniors absent more than forty-eight hours were dismissed. Seniors absent less than forty-eight hours also faced suspension through commencement of June 1925. Juniors and sophomores absent longer than forty-eight hours were suspended through commencement June 1925. Juniors and sophomores absent less than forty-eight hours would walk "60 extras" (that required the student to march with his usual equipment a regular path for one hour for each "extra" demerit) and have all privileges (most of which involved barracks room visitations) canceled through commencement in June. However, if all went well through the remainder of the first term, the president and the commandant could restore privileges. Freshmen who returned were permitted to continue, but each would walk "40 extras." With that, the Board of Trustees adjourned.[7]

The Fire

But the travails of Earle's administration had not yet ended. On the night of April 1, 1925, the Agricultural Hall, only twenty years old, caught fire and was gutted. The fire was so intense that one of the eight great limestone columns that stood across the northern front broke and the top third shattered.[8] Earle asked H. W. Barre, then head of the Agricultural Research and Service Division, and F. H. H. Calhoun, head of Agricultural Instruction, to meet with him and discuss the

Agricultural Hall in the aftermath of the fire that ravaged it on April 1, 1925. Clemson University Photographs, CUL.SC.

future. They concluded that the building, if reconstructed, would no longer suffice for agriculture. The addition of extension and agricultural education, along with the great expansion that the legislature added to Clemson's regulatory tasks without commensurate financial support, had rendered the *beaux-arts* building, highly reminiscent of Harvard's Widener Hall, far too small. Enough insurance money existed, however, to rebuild it for another purpose. So a needed expansion for agriculture was not possible. That was the administrators' first decision; second involved determining the most important need for the new building.

The SACS report denying Clemson accreditation pointed the way to the answer. Earle recommended a new library to the board, which spent a great deal of time considering the recommendation. By September 23, 1925, they decided to reconstruct the building according to Rudolph E. Lee's plans, which called for reserving one section for agricultural extension and the remainder for the library. Lee also created a three-story steel stack in the south wing and a large airy reading room that received filtered, indirect light from the east and the west and reflected light from the north, which he and others considered ideal for reading. Six limestone blocks were placed in the north porch wall, which bore the engraved names of academic subjects, such as "History." An oval balcony ran three-quarters of the way around and looked down on the reading room, providing handsome space for Mr. Clemson's collection of European art and memorabilia and antiquities. The balcony rail and the stairway rails were made in the college's forge and foundry shop and integrated the letters "C. L." for "Clemson Library." The creation of the molds and fabrication of the ironwork were the first and second year students' tasks in the autumn of 1925.[9]

Graduation in 1925 (including winter) saw the awarding of baccalaureate degrees to two former cadets who, after three successful years at Clemson, had gained admission to the Medical College of South Carolina, where they had received the MD degrees, and were now eligible for the Clemson degree.[10] The June commencement illustrated the growing geographic distribution of the student body. The graduates included several North Carolinians, a Floridian, a few Georgians, a New Yorker, and an Oklahoman.[11] Prior to the graduation, the fifteen-person Clemson Concert Orchestra led by Cadet Guy Hutchinson presented a program that began with the "Triumphal March" from Verdi's *Aïda* and concluded with Charles Gounod's reflective overture from *Faust*.[12]

On July 14, 1925, in the presence of the college's new president, Enoch W. Sikes, the board thanked Samuel Broadus Earle for his "herculean task performed with a grasp of detail." Probably with relief, Earle returned to the directorship of the Engineering Division, and Sikes took up the presidential mantel.[13]

"Ploughboy" Sikes

Enoch Walter Sikes was the son of John C. and Jane Austin Sikes, born on May 19, 1868, in Union County, North Carolina. He grew up on his parents' farm with an older sister and six brothers. Like them, he fed the farm animals, hoed, hauled wood, and plowed the fields. The last task gave him a peculiar gait and would earn him the nickname of "Ploughboy" from the Clemson cadets. His hard-working and thrifty parents, to Sikes's advantage, believed in giving their children as much education as each could absorb.

Lower school was a one-room log house. From there Sikes entered a boarding school that had one schoolmaster. Later, Sikes judged the master not very broadly educated. Some of his schoolmates were bright, and those became Sikes's "chums." They corrected each other's spoken and written English and systematically enlarged their vocabularies, relying on an abridged dictionary. On Friday afternoons, they read or declaimed their week's work. After supper, the debating societies met and debated, sharpening their logic and rhetoric. In his later writings, Sikes noted nothing about arithmetic, mathematics, or laboratory sciences.

All of his friends were determined to go to college. Sikes chose Wake Forest College, a Baptist school. He roomed with his childhood friend, Walter Brickett.

Enoch Walter "Ploughboy" Sikes (1868–1941), sixth president of Clemson College from 1925 to 1940, guided the college through the stormy periods of the Great Depression and the buildup to World War II. The viewer may note the characteristic gait that earned him his nickname. Clemson University Photographs, CUL.SC.

Their mothers had been childhood friends, and their fathers had served in the same unit of the N.C. Confederate regiments. Sikes chose his college friends carefully, remarking years later, "One's life is largely determined by his associates and the kind of people he likes." While at Wake Forest, he competed at debate and played varsity football.[14]

After graduation, he stayed as athletic director and chose his friends from among his former teachers. These men recognized Sikes's strong interest in history and economics and urged him to do advanced study at Johns Hopkins. He studied under Henry Adams and Woodrow Wilson and in 1897 received the PhD in history and economics from Hopkins.

Wake Forest called him back to teach history and economics. In 1900, he married Ruth Wingate, daughter of the college president, and they had one daughter and one son. In his nineteen years as a college professor, Sikes played an active role in Democratic Party politics and served as a senator in the N.C. Legislature from 1910 to 1911. Wake Forest named him dean of the college in 1915.

In 1916, he accepted the presidency of Coker College in Hartsville, South Carolina. He was successful there, increasing the enrollment, improving and enlarging the curriculum, and succeeding in getting Coker accredited by SACS, only the second college to receive such in South Carolina.[15]

The Clemson Faculty

In accepting the Clemson presidency in 1925, Sikes knew the challenge he faced. The teaching faculty included a few women and mostly men, many of whom lacked terminal degrees in their fields, and most had not prepared for lengthy illnesses or for retirement. Almost all rented their homes from the college. A number of the academic buildings needed renovation, reconstruction, or expansion. Clemson required more barracks if it was going to meet the needs of

South Carolina, its citizens, farms, industries, and schools. Intercollegiate and intramural facilities begged for expansion. The military program had to be lightened and improved. Much had to be done.

In 1925–1926, six faculty held the PhD degree and one a doctorate in veterinary medicine (DVM). Sixteen held the master of science degree and eight the master of arts. Two held professional engineering degrees. The highest degree held by thirty faculty was the bachelor of science, ten the bachelor of arts, one the bachelor of chemistry, and one the bachelor of divinity (of a denomination that required an undergraduate degree before entrance into seminary). But a number of faculty held no degree at all.

By the end of 1928–1929, PhD faculty had doubled to thirteen (16 percent), the combined number of master's degrees declined, and professional engineering degrees dropped to one. The important development was that nondegreed faculty dropped to seven. And by the end of 1939–1940, Sikes's last year as president, the change was even more profound. There were now thirty-one PhD's and one DVM. Twenty-six faculty held the MS and a like number the MA. Two held the bachelor of architecture, a five-year terminal degree. Seven had professional engineering degrees. The number of bachelor's degree faculty, however, had grown to fifty, and those without any degree had dropped to two.[16] This phenomenal change resulted to a great extent from Sikes's study-leave program for continuing faculty and a changed policy he developed and enforced in hiring better-educated faculty.

Medical care for faculty, staff, and their families presented a major problem. Dr. Lee W. Milford directed the college infirmary and medical service. Born in Anderson County in 1892, he was educated at Furman University and, in 1917, graduated from Emory Medical School. Dr. Milford, a founder of the Southern College Health Association, joined the Clemson staff in 1920. At Clemson, he was an active Baptist and a longtime member of the college Athletic Council. He retired as director of student medical services in 1956 and lived on in the community until his death in 1980.[17]

Although the college staff (secretarial, maintenance, and agricultural) had increased since 1893, it by no means grew in proportion to the student body and the faculty and their households. The infirmary handled all student ailments, even minor surgery. Faculty and others received treatment for a modest fee. Most other problems, including childbirth, were treated elsewhere. The Fellowship Club, an all-denominational Christian community men's club that had been created by the new Presbyterian minister, the Rev. Dr. Sydney J. L. Crouch, sponsored a free clinic for any and all, held weekly at the Fertilizer Building and later at Fort Hill Church.[18] There were some medical services in Seneca, nine miles away, or the patient was taken to Anderson by train or later by bus for planned visits or by automobile for emergencies. Anderson lay over twenty miles away, with the road to it anything but good.

Retirement posed a greater problem. The state had no pension plan, and even after the creation of Social Security, federal employees were not included, and each state would have to elect for its employees to participate, which South Carolina did not do. The problem was compounded by the fact that only a small, but slowly increasing, number of Clemson faculty and other employees owned their homes off college property. Sikes and Littlejohn investigated a number of retirement possibilities with representatives of large life insurance companies with the hope of establishing group annuities. From 1926 on, a number of companies made proposals, but, in part because of the pay reductions made necessary by the Depression, many faculty never elected to participate.[19]

Reorganization

College organization also needed rethinking, both to save money and to simplify and clarify internal reporting. Midway through his first year, Sikes asked W. W. Long, director of extension, to chair a committee that included H. W. Barre, director of the experiment station; Commandant Lt. Col. Otis R. Cole; S. W. Evans, secretary to the board and to the fertilizer committee; and J. C. Littlejohn, registrar, to study the structure and organization of the college. Neither the curriculum nor student discipline fell under the committee's work.[20]

The committee met almost daily, and, in a little over three months, Barre delivered its recommendations to Sikes. It proposed a dean for the college to whom the resident instruction directors would report, a business manager reporting to the president, and several other administrators reporting to the president: the extension service director, the experiment station director, and a full-time director of athletics and physical education. This reduced the total reporting to the president down to five. At the instructional level, the group proposed to create a poultry department separate from animal husbandry; a Division of Arts and Sciences that would merge into it the nondegree science fields; the upgrading of the faculty qualifications in textiles; and a hiring plan for acquiring new instructional faculty members, each with at least two years of professional education beyond the baccalaureate degree. The total annual additional cost was estimated at $11,700 per annum.[21] Sikes made a few minor changes and presented the plan to the trustees. They concurred with all.[22] Lamentably, Sikes, having filled all the other positions, never nominated or appointed a dean of the college, so in organization, the total of college officials reporting to the president was eight. The number of those reporting continued to increase for the next thirty years.

Sikes then began announcing a series of changes. He named J. C. Littlejohn business manager, with supervision over all money, including athletic and fertilizer revenue, power, coal, water (relieving Earle of this responsibility), and all build-ing, maintenance, and renovation costs (relieving Rudolph Lee of those chores). Textiles was moved under engineering. Prof. Doggett, the former head, would continue at his same salary, and a year later H. H. Willis was elected head of the Textile Department. Prof. W. H. Washington of the education program replaced Littlejohn as registrar. Without a dean of the college, the registrar, responsible for admissions, answered to the president, raising the total reporting to him back to nine, or nearly double the recommendation of the reorganization committee.[23]

The Great Depression

The worldwide Depression began in the United States with the October 29, 1929, crash of the Wall Street stock market. South Carolina began to feel the effects seriously during the 1930–1931 fiscal year. Clemson's administration re-duced nonprofessional costs. Of course, some costs such as cattle feed and gasoline could not be cut quickly, and these were worsened by the successive intermittent droughts from 1920 to 1936. The fertilizer tag revenue dropped sharply as more fields were abandoned to encroaching brambles and pine trees. By 1931–1932, on direction from the state treasurer, the entire college budget, including salaries, was reduced by 3 percent. Indeed, these were hard years.[24]

New Buildings

Academic buildings came next among Sikes's many concerns. With the con-version of Agricultural Hall to the library nearly finished, Lee asked Sikes, at the Board of Trustees' direction, to select the words to be incised in the stone plaques on the northern porch. The movement of the books, periodicals, government documents, manuscripts, and paintings allowed Miss Marguerite Doggett and her staff of three to move from the Dewey Decimal classification to the Library of Congress arrangement.[25]

Miss Doggett had joined the Clemson Library as a faculty professional on September 1, 1923, and Miss Katherine Trescot stayed on for several years as her assistant. Miss Doggett was one of Prof. Doggett's three daughters. Unlike her sisters, she remained unmarried and had finished college with an AB degree. The professional library science field had begun in 1887 at Columbia University. The founder of the field there was Melvil Dewey, who had pioneered a uniform library item catalog system named for him. Doggett accomplished a number of major tasks at Clemson. Two stood out above the rest. First, she organized and converted the college library from the older Dewey Decimal system to the much more advanced and more easily expandable Library of Congress system. She also directed the cadets in moving books, journals, paintings, and artifacts from the

Main Building to the new library in the former Agricultural Hall. She, her staff, and the cadets had completed both tasks by February 1926.[26]

Almost fifty years later, J. W. Gordon Gourlay, then library director at Clemson, remembered Doggett's accomplishments. "I am always very grateful to her for having had the wisdom and foresight to change the book classification of this library from Dewey Decimal to Library of Congress. This was a decision so far in advance of most other libraries in the country that even today [1974] some libraries are but now beginning to make the change." Miss Doggett resigned from Clemson on August 31, 1931, to return to graduate school at Columbia.[27] Miss Cornelia Graham, who had served as assistant librarian, filled her position.[28]

The building of the new library left the Clemson Agricultural College without an agriculture building. In the late autumn of 1925, appearing before the legislature's Ways and Means Committee, Sikes declared that Clemson was the only agricultural school he had ever heard of without an agriculture hall, and he requested $123,654.36 to construct a new hall to replace the one that burned. That request was turned down, but Sikes refused to let the issue go. Two years later, the general assembly authorized the Clemson board to borrow $250,000 to construct the sorely needed building. Before the necessary documents were created, however, the Depression intervened.[29]

Then in the summer of 1926, Life Trustee Richard Manning (1859–1931), S.C. governor from 1915 to 1919, secured a gift of $25,000 (2009 equivalent $306,210) from a donor, who wished to remain anonymous, to build the poultry farms, laboratory, and plant. While this did not begin the poultry industry in South Carolina, the research results from Clemson's work with poultry nutrition and disease have helped make this a major component of the economy. The donor was the South Carolina-born financial wizard Bernard Baruch.[30]

Yet Another Fire

Earlier, in May 1926, Mechanical Hall and some of its shops were totally destroyed by fire. It was the second major fire in slightly over a year. One of the fire departments that answered the distress call was from the Greenville district, and unfortunately, one of its firemen, J. C. F. Burns, was killed fighting the fire. Sikes asked the trustees at their June meeting to establish a scholarship for Burns's sons, which they did. Littlejohn reported that the hall had been insured for $75,000 and the equipment for $43,000. This fell $12,332 short of reconstructing and equipping the shops, while Earle estimated the total replacement would cost about $300,000. The state lent the difference, which Clemson repaid. Work began immediately on the shops. The displaced faculty in engineering and architecture were housed in the just-vacated library space in the Main Building.

Classes were taught across the Greenville-Seneca highway in the "old" Methodist church. Lee began the design of the replacement building.[31]

By June 30, 1927, W. H. Washington, the registrar, reported that through the years of the college's operation, the institution had enrolled 9,835 cadets and graduated 2,488, a bit under 25 percent. On the same day, Littlejohn noted that, including the experiment stations, the college held 3,224 acres in South Carolina, a fourfold increase since Mr. Clemson's bequest of his land and money for the school. W. W. Long, director of extension, informed Sikes that the college had seventy-four professional extension agents. Barre added that almost all the professional experiment station researchers held advanced degrees, and nine veterinarians were soon to be housed in the new Sandhill Station.[32]

Accreditation Gained

With these indicators of multiple improvements, Sikes and the division chairs prepared a new application to the Southern Association of Colleges and Schools. The college filed the application with SACS in November 1927. On the question of the holdings of the new library, a total of 30,000 items, including bound volumes, the modest manuscript collections, and journals, were held centrally. The report regarding the number of volumes on campus stated that the separate agricultural holdings, chemistry holdings, and classroom/office holdings added about 5,400 volumes. It did not indicate who owned the latter books. It observed that some 1,100 volumes were lost in the Mechanical Hall fire. All were insured and would be replaced with the newest editions when the new building was complete.

The application to SACS also noted 1,215 undergraduates enrolled at the college, but it reported no graduate activities. Graduate work was done as part of the summer outreach program. The campus instructional faculty numbered ninety-four. Half held advanced degrees, and most of the baccalaureate faculty had done advanced work. The college's annual income for the preceding year totaled $1,819,058, and expenses were less, leaving no indebtedness. In curricular matters, the addition of a BS degree in general science now allowed cadets to graduate with majors in fields such as botany, zoology, and English. One month later, Clemson received the SACS accreditation.[33]

New Construction

In the spring of 1928, Sikes recommended to the trustees that five new buildings be erected on the campus: an agricultural hall, for which the state had agreed to bonded indebtedness, a textile hall, a physical education building, a hospital, and barracks (no number specified). Even though some of the trustees worried about obtaining the money for that much new construction, they concurred. Lee,

Riggs Hall, new home to the engineering programs of Clemson College. Taken from the 1931 edition of the Clemson College annual, *Taps*.

Littlejohn, the agricultural directors, Earle, and R. A. McGinty, who had come from Colorado Agricultural College to replace C. C. Newman as director of campus grounds, began planning.[34]

The new engineering and architecture building, funded by insurance money and a state loan, was ready for dedication. The trustees named the building for Riggs, although some sentiment existed to name it for Alan Johnstone, the just-deceased president of the board and life trustee. This began the custom at Clemson of naming major classroom buildings for faculty or presidents. The trustees elected J. E. Wannamaker, the last surviving life trustee named in Mr. Clemson's will, to replace Johnstone as board president. The trustees prepared to dedicate Riggs Hall, the new building with its workshops that turned out magnificently. With the steel-reinforced concrete framing and subflooring, the hall continued the Renaissance style Lee first introduced in the YMCA building. Its tapestry bricks were laid in Flemish bond, and it faced north toward the Main Building but lay farther south than old Mechanical Hall. The main door and window above were framed in Palladian style limestone. Limestone also framed two principal windows and enclosed two identical tympana that depicted the tools of architecture to the left and those of engineering to the right, separated by the "Spirit of Electricity" with lightning bolts radiating from behind the spirit. The latter, of course, was an allusion to Riggs's own field of study. In a touch of whimsy,

Lee designed protruding grotesques (sometimes mistakenly called "gargoyles") between the third-story windows. The eaves were supported by brackets, guttered and flashed with copper, and roofed with red clay tiles.

The dedication was held during commencement week in June 1928. All land-grant colleges, most colleges in the Southeast, and most major engineering firms throughout the nation were invited to send representatives to attend the ceremony. Clemson engineering and architecture graduates as well as the editors of major national newspapers and all editors of newspapers in South Carolina received invitations. The editors also received a pamphlet describing the new facility and its equipment and features. Beyond the corps, the Clemson "family," and the graduates and their families, some 150 special guests attended.[35]

The new Physical Education Building (now called Fike Field House) was also designed by Lee. The new Department of Physical Education was placed under Athletic Director J. C. "Mutt" Gee, Clemson 1917. The college hoped to secure money for the building from alumni donations. This would be the school's first solicitation of the alumni for financial assistance. In the first months, donations received were meager.[36] Sikes turned to J. H. Woodward, one of his assistants, to lead the campaign. In the first four months, $8,000 was raised from one mail solicitation. Needing to do better, Woodward took to the road, visiting Florence, Marlboro, Marion, and Dillon counties, and also Augusta and Washington, Georgia. He returned home bearing $18,400. By January 1928, the fund held more than $150,000 in cash, land, and pledges.[37] No doubt alumni spirits were much improved because the new head football coach, Josh Cody, had guided the Tigers to a 5–3–1 season, the first winning campaign and the first win over USC since 1923.[38]

That was enough money to begin the building, but to complete Lee's plan, work continued until 1940. The first section, the "big gym," was dedicated on January 7, 1930, at the Furman-Clemson basketball game.[39] The administrative and visitors' housing unit was completed next, and the "little gym" finished in 1940 with most of the cost borne by the Federal Works Progress Administration.[40] The tapestry brick Renaissance style with bracket-supported eaves and the red clay tile roof marked the building as a creation of Rudolph Lee. Over the northern entrance loggia, A. Wolfe "Abe" Davidson, Clemson student and Russian émigré, modeled a bas-relief of a football moment. He based the main figure on one of Clemson's greatest athletes, "Bonnie" Banks McFadden, Clemson 1940, twice football All-American and once basketball All-American.

The Works Progress Administration, Enoch Sikes, J. C. Littlejohn, and Rudolph Lee teamed up seven times more during the 1930s to add to Clemson's growing architectural character. One added the theater wing of the YMCA. It terminated on the west with a lower arcade and two roundel plaques with the

The Physical Education Building—today's Fike Recreation Center—and entrance hall as they appeared shortly after the second phase of completion in 1940. Clemson University Photographs, CUL.SC.

The new Agricultural Hall, or Long Hall on today's campus, completed in 1937. Clemson University Photographs, CUL.SC.

watchful heads of two tigers, also molded by Davidson, looking down over Riggs Field. Daniel Construction Company of Greenville did the work.[41]

Also, Sikes fully intended to increase college enrollment. The biggest obstacle was the lack of student (and faculty and staff) housing. Consequently, he appealed to the federal government for financial help, emphasizing the school's record of preparation of officers for the army. Pressure from the War Department—led in part by alumnus Frank Johnstone Jervey, the weight of U.S. Senator and Clemson friend James Byrnes, and Life Trustee Frank Lever—encouraged the government to help complete the large barracks (now Norris Hall) and four new barracks on the north side of campus west of the Textile Building. Taking advantage of the roll of the land, four three-story units with full and useful basements were arranged along an alley on the high ground above Riggs Field. They were constructed in Lee's style, and Daniel Construction Company carried out all of the interior design and building. The exterior ornamentation consisted of heraldic escutcheons above each of the entrance loggias. The escutcheons were quite plain, suggesting the tight finances. These were completed and dedicated together with a full dress parade of cadets, and the principal "lobbyists" in Washington, D.C., were honored guests. Among the first men to move into the new barracks was Walter Thompson Cox Jr., Clemson 1939.[42]

A new agriculture hall was next. The general assembly had authorized the Board of Trustees to borrow $250,000 to construct a new agriculture hall in 1929.[43] Finally, with a generous grant of $800,000 from the Public Works Administration (PWA) in 1936, construction began.[44] In Lee's design and style, the words "Agriculture," "Instruction," and "Research" were incised over the three main portals. Lee's design of the central (north) portal, although in the Renaissance idiom, created capitals and cartouches from the major agricultural products, including cotton, grains, and other crops from the state. The eastern protrusion displayed a farmer driving a team of oxen pulling a moldboard plow, while its western mate portrayed a farmer atop a modern gasoline combine. The message was clear: Increased results from the same time invested equaled progress. All the sculpture was in the art deco style. At the May 12, 1937, dedication, Sikes, in the name of the trustees, presented forty-four honorary degrees to major national and state agricultural leaders. The trustees named the building Long Hall, in memory of the recently deceased director of extension.[45]

The last of the major Lee buildings erected on campus was Textile Hall (now Sirrine Hall). Here the "C" shaped footprint used in Riggs, Fike, and Long halls was turned over, creating an entrance forecourt. As in the other buildings, limestone and tapestry brick were used. The ornamentation on new Textile Hall included the incising of the names of great inventors in the history of textiles: Sir Richard Arkwright (British, 1732–1792), who in 1769 invented the mechanical spinning machinery to create yarn; Eli Whitney (American, 1765–1825), inventor of the cotton (en)gin(e) in 1792; the Rev. Mr. Edmund Cartwright (British, 1743–1823), creator of the power loom in 1794; and Sir William Henry Perkin (British, 1838–1907), the discoverer in 1856 of the first synthetic dye, mauveine, a new deep purple aniline-based color.[46] A series of polychromed tiles beneath the eaves displayed a variety of textile images such as a cotton boll, cotton bale, spinning wheel, distaff, and textile knot. The Lee signature, a copper-flashed red clay tile roof, crowned the building.[47] Although this was the last of the buildings Lee designed and completed, he also designed an office building for agriculture planned for location behind Long Hall. World War II intervened, and the building was scrapped. He also drew a façade of a chemistry building. In sum, the extensive building campaign of the 1930s essentially doubled the college's student capacity; from 1925–1926 to the 1939–1940 year, enrollment had grown to 2,227.[48]

New Resources

During the 1930s, in proof that progress can be made despite economic hardship, Clemson College took four major steps forward, besides the previously discussed building program. Two involved hard cash, and two involved land.

The first was the creation of the Clemson College Foundation. Although the idea had been discussed for some years, the Alumni Association finally approved establishing the foundation at the association's annual reunion on June 5, 1933. The initial plan called for alumni to obtain life insurance policies from New York Life Insurance Company and, while paying the annual premiums, thus guaranteeing the final payout, the holder would assign the annual dividends to the foundation.

The foundation would also receive such annual contributions from alumni and others as the corporation elected to deposit. In addition, personal and corporate donations were to be welcomed. The foundation elected Cecil L. Reid, Clemson 1902, as president. Within six months, the foundation received a gift of $10,000 (2009 equivalent $163,947.25) from Lydia and Alexander P. Anderson. Anderson (b. November 22, 1862, in Featherstone, Goodhue County, Minnesota – d. May 7, 1943) received a BS (1894) and MS (1895) from the University of Minnesota and a PhD from the University of Munich (1896). He joined the Clemson faculty in 1897 and re-

Alexander Pierce Anderson (1862–1943), onetime professor of botany at Clemson and inventor of the technique used to produce puffed grains, made the first contribution to the Clemson Foundation, a generous gift of $10,000. Clemson University Photographs, CUL.SC.

signed from Clemson in 1901 to become the curator of the herbarium at Columbia University (NYC). While on the Clemson faculty, he accidently discovered the process that causes grain such as wheat and rice to puff. He received the patent for "expanding starch material in cereal grains" in 1902 and went to work as a researcher for Quaker Oats Company. Anderson's timely gift remembered his years at Clemson.[49]

The second fund-raising unit focused on athletics. The concept appears to have begun during the 1932 football season. It was the first season for Coach Jess Neely, a Vanderbilt law graduate. Capt. Jervey remembered sitting in a car with Neely in Florence following Clemson's 6–0 loss to the Citadel. At that point, Clemson had just suffered its second loss in a season marked by a 0–0 tie with Presbyterian, a win over NC State, and a 42–0 thrashing by Tennessee. Jervey asked Neely how much he estimated it would take per year to build a strong team through athletic grants-in-aid, an idea tried in the Midwest to help alleviate and regulate the practice of alumni of eastern private schools of hiring players. Neely answered that it would cost $10,000 per year (2009 equivalent $155,586). Jervey attempted to generate interest in establishing a $50 (2009 equivalent $778) per year contributor's club. While the idea produced interest, given the Depression, it did not produce money.

Consequently, Dr. Rupert Fike, Clemson 1908 and a former football manager, had received a solicitation letter and was disappointed in the lack of results. He had brooded on the school's record since his graduation. Following a conversation with Jack Mitchell, Clemson 1912, and Milton Berry, Clemson 1913, Fike called a meeting of Clemson's alumni in Atlanta in August. Nine men attended, and from that ensued a secret fund-raising society named IPTAY. Its officers were the Bengal Tiger (president), the Persian Tiger (vice president), and the Sumatra Tiger (secretary). The group abounded in acronyms. IPTAY itself meant "I Pay Ten a Year," because the group established $10 (2009 equivalent $159) for annual membership dues.[50]

Dr. Rupert Fike (1887–1956), alumnus of the Clemson Class of 1908 and the man credited with creating IPTAY. Clemson University Photographs, CUL.SC.

Still, it was hard raising the money. Alan McCrary Johnstone, grandson of Life Trustee and Board President Alan Johnstone and the founding captain of Clemson's golf team, received a solicitation from his employer, also a Clemson man.

Johnstone begged off, saying he did not have $10 to spare. The employer "kindly" said he would pay for Johnstone and simply deduct $1 a month from Johnstone's salary. And so he did. Johnstone kept his membership in IPTAY until he died.[51]

During the first year, 162 persons contributed $1,623.70 to IPTAY, but by 1939, the membership had grown to 1,131 and the contributions to $13,416.55. Dr. Fike served as president from 1934 until 1954, and Hoke Sloan and R. R. Ritchie (professor of animal husbandry) served as volunteer secretaries.[52]

The land acquisitions included the creation of the fourth "off-campus" experiment station, the Edisto Station located between Williston and Blackville. The land came from college and state funds, while the federal government, through the PWA, aided in erecting the buildings. The station had two hundred acres, three researchers, a tractor, and six mules. While much of its work involved researching and raising cattle, it was also a site for growing bamboo, tested for use in the reinforcement of concrete.[53] This brought the number of experiment stations to four: Coastal (Drainland and Truck); Pee Dee (Florence); Sandhill (Pontiac); and Edisto (Williston-Blackville). Additionally, a relatively small experimental farm existed at Fort Hill.

The Fourth Resource

The federal government's drought and depression plan after 1933 included purchasing devastated land in many parts of the stricken nation. In South Carolina, much of the ruined land existed in the Piedmont. A Clemson agricultural economics professor, George H. Aull, had taken a leave from Clemson from 1934 to 1936 to serve as a senior administrative officer in the Land Policy Section of the Agricultural Adjustment Administration. Aull, born in Pomaria on October 16, 1899, served in the U.S. Army in 1918 and graduated from Clemson in 1919. He taught in secondary school from 1919 until 1921 and then joined the Clemson Agricultural Experiment Station as assistant director of research (1921–1933).

George Hubert Aull (1899–1988), alumnus of the Clemson Class of 1919, professor of applied economics and rural sociology at Clemson from 1922 to 1963, the director of the Department of Agricultural Economics from 1934 to 1963, and the father of the Clemson Land Use Project (the Clemson Experimental Forest). He was, to some, the greatest economic mind in South Carolina in the twentieth century. Clemson University Photographs, CUL.SC.

During that time, Aull received an MS in economics from Virginia in 1928 (he studied with Clemson alumnus Wilson Gee) and would be awarded his PhD by Wisconsin in 1937.

In his work with the Land Policy program in Washington, D.C., Aull proposed that several thousand acres of ruined land in the Piedmont of South Carolina be placed in the care of Clemson Agricultural College for restoration and redevelopment. His original proposal would have placed about 8,500 acres in the Fant's Grove Community, most of which lies south of the old campus, in Clemson's care. But the request was returned in 1934, labeled "too small," so Aull resubmitted a second proposal for about 35,000 acres. After more negotiations, the final acreage placed in Clemson's hands amounted to 27,469 acres. At this point, Aull was placed on leave to manage the project, which involved lake and pond building, tree planting, and design and construction of recreation facilities.[54]

Clemson's agriculture, civil engineering, and architecture students developed the plans. The Works Progress Administration supplied the labor along with the Civilian Conservation Corps and the National Youth Agency. At the pay of $.35 per hour, a number of young male laborers earned enough money to attend Clemson. The first area developed was the Issaqueena Forest in the Lawrence Chapel community. It provided recreation land and is frequently called North Forest, which includes other holdings such as the major site of Keowee Heights, the onetime home of John Ewing Colhoun. Wright Bryan recorded George Aull's reflections:

> We built six one-acre fish ponds, now covered by Lake Hartwell. We built Lake Isaqueena [sic] dam which backed up a substantial lake, and we stocked it with fish. We constructed about a dozen picnic shelters and recreational sites, including one which was a fully equipped boat house with boat landing and docking facilities. We planted approximately 10,000 acres of mostly loblolly pine and we built miles and miles of roads and nature trails.[55]

Supervision of the project, as described in Clemson's agreement with the federal government in 1935, rested with the extension service, but both Sikes and Littlejohn were uneasy with the college taking on such a burden, and the Clemson Board of Trustees regularly debated the whole concept of such land reclamation for nearly five years until July 7, 1939, when they finally approved the long-term lease. Aull's later contribution to the affairs of Clemson Agricultural College, the community, the state, and the nation are all part of the continuing Clemson saga.[56]

For Them

Sikes and his closest advisors always kept in mind that all these resources had been brought together for two goals, one of which was the general well-being of the people of South Carolina. However, these teachers knew that the second goal was the broad education of Clemson students, who produced a wide-ranging impact beyond the boundaries of South Carolina. But these students were different from the eager school chums of Sikes's youth, just as they were different from the young "rebellious" cadets of 1902, 1904, or 1908.

Sikes was well equipped to handle those changing cadets. His experiences as a college dean at Wake Forest and president at Coker College taught him a great deal about students, faculty, accreditors, and alumni, while his legislative experiences made him aware of the need for statewide support. Nothing was clearer than his deft way of working with students.

The cadets of 1925 were older than those of a decade earlier, and their sense of connectedness to the world was broader in scope than were those not yet dazzled by the "lights of Gay Paree!" Theirs was the age of the radio, which erased the

With the restoration of the State Fair trip announced by Sikes in 1925, the students boarded the train to Columbia, marched through the streets of the city (*above*), erected their tents on the fairgrounds (*below*), and participated as spectators on Big Thursday game against USC. Taken from the William David Craig Scrapbook (MSS 276), covering his years here from 1926 to 1930, CUL.SC.

limits of county, parish, and congregation. Theirs was the rise of the phonograph, bringing with it the splendors of the New York Philharmonic, Puccini, and Caruso nearly on demand, along with the intriguing world of jazz, whether Dixieland, or Chicago, or New York. And this was the age of the automobile, with the new freedom and license that came with it. And youth, in its freedom, rebuked government restrictions such as alcohol prohibitions.[57]

Everywhere in America, the response of colleges and universities was to broaden their involvement in the non-academic life of students, a holistic approach whose origins may well have been at Miami University (Ohio). The general approach was for the institutional president to be more involved in the day-by-day life of his students, particularly as schools grew in size. The president delegated many administrative tasks to others.[58] Of course, Riggs had begun many of these steps and details during his administration. For example, Riggs had appointed D. H. Henry director of student activities and made the commandant responsible for discipline and the barracks behavior, while the president focused more on the larger problems of legislative relations, financial resources, and intercollegiate activities. However, Riggs was not comfortable with total delegation. Sikes seemed more comfortable with a closer but almost avuncular attitude toward the students and was willing to increase their "liberties."

Almost Sikes's first action toward his cadets was to reinstitute the practice of taking all four classes to the State Fair for the USC game, a treat suspended in 1917 because of the war and not reinstituted afterward for financial reasons. The announcement was met with cheering by the cadets in chapel.[59] Sikes saw this as a way to display the manly, well-disciplined cadets, offsetting any lingering unfavorable public thoughts stemming from the 1924 walkout.

And even though the cadets really had only the YMCA canteen to repair to, Sikes abolished the requirement that the cadets dine three meals a day in the mess hall.[60] Shortly thereafter, he granted the glee club permission to go on a ten-day performance tour.[61] One month later, he convinced the Board of Trustees to do away with guard duty, wherein each student, fully uniformed and armed, marched a segment of the campus at regular, prescribed times.[62] It must have seemed to the cadets that this plump, bald, bespectacled, cigar-smoking North Carolinian was a herald of heaven.

The miracles continued after the Christmas break in the spring of 1926. Dr. G. D. Heath, the resident physician, who was an able medical doctor but aloof, resigned and was replaced by Dr. Lee Milford, who related very easily to cadets and to the community. And at almost the same time that he introduced Milford to the cadets, Sikes also announced that the cadet regimental band would take a state tour as had the glee club.[63] By his second year, Sikes changed mandatory chapel from five days a week to twice weekly (Tuesday and Thursday) and from early morning to the noon hour.[64]

The literary societies had shrunk from six to the three founded between 1893 and 1895. And the ratio of literary society members to the entire student body fell by 25 percent, both indications that the influence of the societies was weakening. The societies still combined their forces in the publication of the *Chronicle*, which was underwritten by the three societies from their dues, subscriptions, advertisements, and contributions solicited from alumni. In 1926–1927, the editorial staff included J. E. Youngblood, a senior horticulture major from Elko (Barnwell County) and senior class president, as the editor; Gilbert C. Dupre of Columbia as the business manager; and twelve other cadets. With the sports well covered by the two other publications, the *Chronicle* simply stopped.[65]

Taps appeared annually and, in 1936, began including the individual photographs of all the young men regardless of class. These almost always were taken after the first-year-to-be cadets had taken their placement examinations but before they had matriculated (easily observable by the length and fullness of their hair).[66] Because some number of freshmen simply packed up and returned home after receiving the placement results, persons searching for forebears are occasionally misled to believe someone attended classes at Clemson and, thus, was an alumnus when in fact he had chosen not to join the student body (matriculate).[67]

John Dewey Lane (1898–1968), popular and gifted professor of English at Clemson from 1924 to 1961, known as a "one-man journalism department" for his advisorship of *The Tiger*, Clemson's student newspaper, and his immense contributions to the careers of several nationally recognized journalists. Clemson University Photographs, CUL.SC.

The weekly newspaper, *The Tiger*, was financed through the student activity fee, advertisements, and subscriptions, mainly from alumni. Even though *Taps* exhibited excellent craftsmanship and became a reliable record of the individual careers of the seniors and a very good, trustworthy account of club, corps, and sports activities, *The Tiger*, under the advisorship of Prof. John D. Lane, achieved real prominence. Born in 1898 in Lamar (Darlington County), Lane received his AB (the BA when awarded with a Latin diploma) from Newberry College in English (1920). After teaching history and mathematics at Newberry (1920–1923), Lane studied for and received the MA from the University of Virginia in June 1924. He joined the English faculty at Clemson in

1924, and, except for 1928–1929 when he was in the advanced program in English and drama at Columbia University (New York City), he remained in the Clemson English faculty until his resignation for reasons of health in June 1961 at age sixty-three. In 1932, Lane married Bessie Mell Poats, daughter of Prof. Thomas G. Poats.[68] They had four children. Lane died on January 8, 1968.[69]

During Sikes's presidency, a number of remarkable student editors, with Lane's guidance, led *The Tiger*. W. Wright Bryan, the son of A. B. "Old Baldy" Bryan, served as editor of *The Tiger* in 1926–1927. Bryan studied civil engineering at Clemson and served as vice president of Clemson's student chapter of the American Society of Civil Engineers (ASCE). After graduation and a few weeks on a South Carolina highway road crew, he followed Ben F. Robertson Jr. to the School of Journalism at the University of Missouri. After a year there, he joined the staff of the Atlanta *Journal* as a reporter, where he worked from 1927 to 1935. He married Ellen Hillyer Newman on October 12, 1932. Together they had two daughters and one son. Bryan was city editor of the Atlanta *Journal* from 1935 to 1940 and managing editor from 1940 to 1943. He was the World War II correspondent for the *Journal* and for National Broadcasting Company (NBC) in Europe, broadcasting the first eyewitness account of the western Allied June 6, 1944, D-Day invasion of Normandy. Captured by the German army in September 1944, he was released in 1945. After the war, he returned to the Atlanta *Journal*.[70]

A second of John Lane's men was George Chaplin. Born in Columbia in 1914, Chaplin became a freshman studying textile chemistry in 1930, but in his senior year (1933), he was chosen editor of *The Tiger*. By graduation, he had changed his life's work and became a reporter for the *Greenville Piedmont*. While in Greenville, he married a Charleston girl, and in 1940, Chaplin won a Nieman Fellowship at Harvard University. When World War II began, Chaplin served as a captain in the U.S. Army. The army sent him to Honolulu as editor of the Pacific edition of the *Stars and Stripes*.[71]

John Lane's third journalist jewel was Harry Ashmore of Greenville. Born in 1916, he was the younger of two brothers. Like his brother, he attended Clemson, enrolling in 1933 and graduating in 1937. A member of Kappa Phi Fraternity, he joined *The Tiger* staff and worked his way up to editor. Upon his graduation, Ashmore joined the *Greenville Piedmont* but soon moved to the *Greenville News*. In 1941, he became a Nieman Fellow at Harvard University. That pursuit was cut short by the bombing of Pearl Harbor. Ashmore immediately reported for duty and was assigned to the Ninety-fifth Infantry Division, which was part of Gen. George Patton's Third Army. It saw heavy fighting and participated in the capture of Metz.[72]

The fourth of these gems was Earl Mazo. Born in Warsaw, Poland, in 1919, he and his family immigrated to Charleston in 1922. After school there, he entered Clemson in 1936 and served as editor of *The Tiger* in 1939–1940. Mazo became the president of Gamma Alpha Mu, an honor fraternity composed of Clemson's best writers, and he was invited to join Blue Key and Tiger Brotherhood. Mazo was inducted into the U.S. Army air program, where he served as a B-17 bombardier. After military service, he became a war correspondent for the European edition of the *Stars and Stripes*.[73]

The Student Body

President Sikes also sought more student diversity. By his last year, the cadets came from all counties of South Carolina, twenty-seven states, Puerto Rico, the Canal Zone, and the District of Columbia. But the Asian war had cut off Asian students who had been enrolling primarily in textiles, and the European strife, which had begun in earnest in the Spanish Civil War and which spread with the joint invasion by Germany and Russia of Poland in 1939, reduced the foreign countries represented in the student body down to Cuba and Austria.[74]

Another avenue of diversity was the issue of gender. The Depression gave Sikes an opening. He convinced the trustees to allow fourteen young women from the area to enroll as day students. All were sophomores or better, so there would be no strain on the more crowded freshman classes. Most of the women were daughters of faculty and others in the community. The move helped the women continue their education during the worst of the Depression, and Clemson's enrollment remained strong. The young men had few objections, although an editorial in a September 1932 issue of *The Tiger* groused,

This is all very well and good as a temporary measure and there is nothing we can do about it except submit gracefully....If we have women trailing over the campus after this year, it is up to the Corps to see that their hair is removed in the usual freshman manner, that they wear uniforms, live in the barracks and drill with Springfield Rifles. We love our masculine freedom and superiority.[75]

Sikes was very pleased with the presence of the women, and he wrote, "For a long time, it was questioned whether a woman could do as well as a man in higher education. It has been put to the test that has clearly demonstrated that she can."[76] Toward the end of the school year, Sikes recommended that the college integrate fully in gender. The trustees turned down the recommendation.[77]

Another sign of diversity was the occasional nonwhite student in the graduating class. This was a continuation of an earlier sign of diversity. The June 1926 commencement witnessed the trustees awarding one hundred bachelor's degrees. Besides the large number of graduates from South Carolina, graduates came from Georgia, North Carolina, New York, and China. Textile industrial education student Ko Chia Li of Manchuria had begun his American schooling at Lowell Textile School in Massachusetts in 1922, followed by work at NC State before entering Clemson. Called "Whang" by his Clemson friends, he played tennis and ping-pong and was described as "witty" and tremendously "girl shy." *Taps* wrote, "Here's to you, Ko Chia, we who have known you shall not like to see you part, but, when we do part, our best wishes for your success go with you."[78]

By 1929, the June commencement saw 164 seniors receive degrees, which demonstrated that Sikes's policy of enlarging the college, driven first by Littlejohn and then by Littlejohn and Washington, was taking effect. Twelve had studied architecture, fourteen arts and sciences (the new designation for general science), fifty-nine agriculture, sixty-four engineering, and fifteen textiles.[79] By spring 1931, total enrollment had grown to 1,348. While the large majority came from South Carolina, students also hailed from twenty-two other states, the District of Columbia, and Nicaragua. Over 500 were from farming families, nearly 100 from families in manufacturing (including textiles), about seventy-five from families in transportation, about 300 from mercantile families (most of them from small rural towns), and others from a broad array of occupations.[80]

The growth was such that in the spring of 1940, Sikes's last year, the registrar reported an enrollment of 2,281, an increase from 2,227 the previous fall and from 1,087 in 1925.[81] Of these, 1,981 were South Carolinians from every county. Other states represented in the student body included Alabama, California, Colorado, Delaware, Florida, Georgia, Illinois, Kentucky, Louisiana, Maine, Maryland, Massachusetts, Michigan, Minnesota, Mississippi, New Jersey, New York, North Carolina, Ohio, Pennsylvania, Tennessee, Texas, Virginia, Washington, West Virginia, and Wisconsin. The District of Columbia, the Canal Zone, and Puerto Rico also sent students. The enrollment included 450 in agriculture, 70 in chemistry, 440 in arts and sciences (still occasionally called general science), 350 in textiles, 360 in vocational education (including agriculture, textiles, and industry), and 800 in engineering. Twenty-six students had enrolled in special and graduate studies.[82]

But the growth was not without its consequences. At its Memphis meeting in 1939, SACS, which had increased its accrediting standards, placed Clemson on the "starred" list, citing the college for deficiencies in faculty preparation, faculty salaries, and library expenditures. The former was the most critical, and SACS had recommendations that Sikes presented to the trustees in June 1939. They unanimously approved three regulations. First, the college generally would employ new faculty with advanced degrees only. Second, Clemson teachers forty-five years of age or under would be required to secure an "advanced degree within the next four years from a well-established graduate school," and unless done, would "receive no further promotion in title or salary." Third, salaries improved for most faculty.[83]

Three dance clubs each offered one dance, occasionally with a band, per semester. Although only the two other dance clubs were invited, many other cadets and some non-Clemson youth attended, which produced periodic discipline problems. Prof. D. H. Henry, who still served as director of student affairs, handled the scheduling, but discipline remained the responsibility of the commandant.[84] The Board of Trustees, as an economy move, abolished the student affairs director's post and moved Henry to the post of secretary to the Fertilizer Control Board. As a chemist, he seemed a logical choice to replace H. M. Stackhouse in 1929. In 1932, the Board of Trustees requested that W. M. James and Associates of Greenville audit the accounts, and they found a $16,262.50 discrepancy between tags sold and revenues reported to the state treasurer. Although no one filed charges in the matter, Henry resigned, and the college replaced him with J. Woodward. Shortly thereafter, in a tragic end to his life, Henry committed suicide.[85]

A concert band, directed by engineering Prof. E. J. Freeman, enrolled forty-eight cadets. A concert orchestra, which included a string section, had twenty-five members, including faculty and spouses. Edwin Jones Freeman Jr. had entered Clemson as a freshman in 1919 after serving in the American Expeditionary Forces (U.S. Army Sixty-first Artillery). Reared in Spartanburg (although born in Lawrenceville, Virginia), he graduated from the local high school and worked for one year before enlisting. His three years as a cadet found him director of the glee club and the orchestra. He was the student chairman of ASME and treasurer of AIEE. The other cadets

Edwin Jones Freeman (1896–1969), professor of mechanical/industrial engineering at Clemson from 1924 to 1961, Clemson band leader and composer, and forerunner of today's modern football cinematographer on the Clemson campus. Freeman Hall stands today as a monument to his dedicated service. Clemson University Photographs, CUL.SC.

called him "Mr. Wizard" because of his proficiency with musical instruments and power tools. He was also a cheerleader and a member of the Block-C Club. After graduation in 1922, he taught one year in a military academy and a second in a public school. He returned to Clemson in 1924, and except for graduate school at Virginia Polytechnic Institute, he stayed at Clemson until he retired in 1961. Freeman Hall is named in his memory. In the 1930s, he composed "Tiger, Rah!" a fight song that is still used occasionally. Freeman was also a cinematographer, and beginning with his friendship with Jess Neely, he filmed almost all the football games in the 1930s and 1940s for coaching analyses.[86]

Cadet Wayland A. Strand led the glee club, consisting of thirty cadets. Also, the Jungaleers, a nine-person student band, played popular music for some of the dances. Between 1934 and 1937, the Jungaleers hired out as a dance orchestra in the summers to entertain voyagers on transatlantic crossings and to play in a few popular nightclubs in London and Paris. Among the leaders of the Jungaleers was Bob "Puff" Banister on the saxophone. Banister would return after World War II to serve in the engineering faculty.[87] Music of a different sort was provided by a forty-seven-member regimental band, which played for weekly dress parades and football games at home and on Big Thursday. The regimental band increased in size as the student body did. Following his graduation, the drum major, J. Roy Cooper, joined the staff of the college's YMCA. Also, a drum and bugle corps had twenty-four cadets.[88]

In addition to all this activity, during the Sikes years, forty or more county and town clubs in South Carolina, a Georgia state club, and a general out-of-state club provided cadets with other social outlets. A dozen other clubs of various names and purposes, or perhaps with little or no purpose, also existed.[89]

By May 1927, the government of South Carolina repealed early twentieth century legislation that prohibited Greek-letter groups—scholarly, social, academic, or any other—from operating at the state's colleges.[90] Almost immediately, the Clemson College trustees approved the establishment of local and national, honorary and professional, Greek-letter and otherwise-named fraternities and societies. During the 1927–1928 academic year, Phi Psi, a professional textile arts and sciences fraternity founded at the Philadelphia College of Textiles and Sciences in 1903, established its ninth (Iota) chapter at Clemson. Its appearance on the Clemson campus as the first national Greek-letter fraternity of any type reflected clearly Sikes's desire to broaden the students', and for that matter the faculty's, horizons. R. C. Harrington served as the first Phi Psi president.[91] Also in 1928, engineering faculty and students created a local group that became the first chapter of Tau Beta Pi in South Carolina. Named South Carolina Alpha, it was the fifty-first chapter of the national society.[92]

During the same year, President Sikes and a group of faculty selected nineteen seniors to serve as the first "cubs" of Tiger Brotherhood. Together they drafted a public code of ethics that pledged "to meet others in every walk of life fairly, to be on one's honor at all times, to help make a great Clemson, and to be a loyal son of Clemson." While the effort appears to have grown out of Sikes's failed attempt to establish a student government, the organization was designed as a local leadership, service, and honorary fraternity. The faculty involved in helping found Tiger Brotherhood included Mark Bradley, Aura M. Carkuff, W. W. Klugh, John Lane, John Logan Marshall, and Augustus M. Shanklin. Marshall, with Bradley's help, wrote the ritual.[93]

One year later, James G. "Mutt" Gee, professor of physical education and director of intercollegiate athletics, received a letter from B. C. Riley, founder and national president of Blue Key, a leadership and service honorary society founded at the University of Florida in October 1924, expressing an interest in establishing a chapter at Clemson. Gee sent the letter to Sikes, but nothing happened immediately.[94] Several years later, in 1932, a group of twenty students and some honorary members from alumni, faculty, and staff received a charter. The first chapter president was James Edgar Barker, and its student charter members included Olen B. Garrison, later head of the S.C. Agricultural Experiment Stations, and Patrick Noble Calhoun, a descendent of John Francis Calhoun, John C. Calhoun's greatnephew and Clemson College's first bursar. Pat Calhoun, later a major North Carolina financier, served as a Clemson life trustee. Seven men connected closely with Clemson were also on the charter roll, including Sikes, mess officer Capt. J. D. Harcombe, Col. Frank J. Jervey (then in the U.S. Army Ordnance Department in Washington, D.C.), Prof. W. W. Klugh, J. C. Littlejohn, commandant Col. Fred L. Munson, and Textile Dean H. H. Willis. Four years later, Blue Key inducted U.S. Senator James F. Byrnes.[95]

The last of the Sikes era service societies, Alpha Phi Omega, received its charter as the Gamma Lambda Chapter in the spring of 1940. The fraternity originated in 1925 at Lafayette College. Rooted in the Boy Scouts of America, APO is today the largest of the national collegiate service fraternities.[96]

Two years earlier, in 1938, Phi Kappa Phi, the national scholastic honorary society open to academically qualified students and faculty, was chartered at Clemson. It had no restrictions on area or field of study, nor did it have restrictions on gender, race, or religious persuasion. The Clemson chapter was Phi Kappa Phi's forty-ninth. The fraternity, founded at the University of Maine in 1897, had the strong support of the Maine University president, who, through the land-grant association, encouraged the presidents of the University of Tennessee and Pennsylvania State College to establish chapters on their campuses. The fraternity generally recruited the chapter officers from among its faculty members.[97]

Sikes's loosening of the grip on student organizations allowed for the emergence of five local social fraternities. The earliest noted in *Taps* in 1928 was named

Sigma Phi. Because one of the oldest existing college social fraternities with chapters on several college campuses bears that same name, some have claimed an affiliation between the two. That does not seem to have been the case. Another local organization, Beta Sigma Chi, which limited its membership to cadets who lived within a fifty-mile radius of Charleston, sometimes presented itself as a regional club. The remaining three were Alpha Chi Psi, Sigma Epsilon, and Kappa Phi. The five groups produced many members who went on to outstanding careers, including one Pulitzer Prize winner, one Medal of Honor winner, two major newspaper editors, and one university president.[98]

Religious Life

Student religious affiliations were heavily mainline Protestant, but 2.2 percent were Catholic, 1 percent Jewish, and 2 percent claimed no affiliation. Over 90 percent of students attended the four town churches, and Catholic students continued under the care of St. Joseph's parish in Anderson. With the blessing of Sikes and the commandant, Catholic cadets went to Anderson on Easter Saturday, spent the night with parish families, and attended Mass on Sunday. Following Easter dinner with their hosts, the cadets returned to campus.[99] As the number of Catholic students grew, the diocese of South Carolina, acting on a generous anonymous gift, built a chapel in Clemson. Constructed in Gothic style of local granite, the chapel was fitted with very lovely stained glass windows. It served not only the students, but also Catholics in the community.[100] The Rev. Dr. Sydney Crouch, the new pastor of Fort Hill Presbyterian Church, held Friday Sabbath service usually at the YMCA and the Sabbath meal for Jewish students and loaded those young cadets into his station wagon to drive them to High Holy Day services in Greenville or Anderson.[101] In addition, the growth in the student body and the community during the 1930s required the four older churches to expand their facilities.[102]

Crouch, an Australian who became a Presbyterian after he immigrated to the United States, strengthened the sense of community between the small village and the campus in many ways. One was the founding of two men's clubs, the Forum (1929), made up primarily of faculty and initially focused on foreign affairs, and the Fellowship (1936), composed of churchmen. Both continue to flourish. Before either club existed, Crouch, in his first year at Clemson, worked with the other three pastors, President Sikes, and Commandant Otis R. Cole (lieutenant colonel, U.S. Army, Infantry), to sponsor the first Clemson Mother's Day, May 9, 1926. Each cadet personally invited his mother to come to campus for church at one of the churches, while the families of the campus and community opened their homes for overnight guests. The guest mothers attended church wearing flowers provided by the college greenhouse and then sat with their cadet sons for

1. A 1915 aerial view of the core of Clemson's campus. Clemson University Photographs, CUL.SC.

2. The irregular bricks of Hardin Hall (old Chemistry Building), like those of Tillman Hall (old Main Building), were hand-pressed from the clay of the campus.

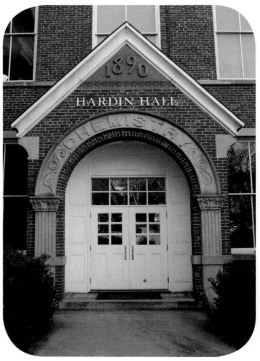

3. The "Chemistry 1890" porch on Hardin Hall.

4. Archway of Hardin Hall's side porch.

5. A close-up of the "Chemistry 1890" porch capital, highlighting the stylized palmetto leaves.

All color photographs are courtesy of Patrick Wright, Clemson University Creative Services.

6. Tillman Hall, perched atop its hill, on a winter's day.

7. The eastern, or front, entrance to Tillman Hall with the "abbreviated" name for the college above it, hence the period (.).

8. The southern entrance to Tillman Hall with a terra cotta plaque above it marking the building's original purpose, agricultural instruction.

9. The cannons "Tom and Jerry," installed in 1951, keeping watch over Bowman Field with downtown Clemson in the background.

10. A tile mosaic on Holtzendorff Hall, reminiscent of the YMCA triangle of "a healthy spirit, mind, and body" and a representation of the Holy Trinity.

11. A sketch of Holtzendorff Hall, the original YMCA, courtesy of University President James F. Barker, FAIA.

HOLTZENDORFF HALL   J. BARKER 12/26/00

12. The carved head of a tiger, created by A. Wolfe Davidson, on the western side of Holtzendorff Hall.

13. Two of the carved capitals that support Holtzendorff Hall, depicting the symbols of the YMCA: the Chi Rho, the opening letters of the Greek word for Christ; the double triangle, with the outer one representing the Trinity and the inner one representing the trinity within men; and the Bible in the center, open to the intercessory prayer of Christ in John 17:21. These symbols rest upon carved palm fronds, the Christian symbol of victory.

14. An aerial view of the central part of Clemson's campus in 1941. Clemson University Photographs, CUL.SC.

15. The northern side of Riggs Hall with the tympanum and grotesques *in situ*.

Introduction to Grotesques

"Being life-size bas-reliefs of human heads carved from limestone blocks… bearing emblems characteristic of each department of engineering…these fantastic exaggerations smile down in unholy glee or frown with devilish intent upon all who pass by, and seem to issue a flagrant challenge to the unwary student to meet and overcome the obstacles in his chosen profession.

"The clay models for these figures were made by Professor R. E. Lee, of the college faculty of the class of 1925, and J. B. Burts, and carved by the H. R. Hupffman Co., of Atlanta."

—*Tiger* Vol. XXIV, No. 24, April 10, 1929

16. Electrical engineering grotesque, marked by dynamo and electric flashes. The author guesses that the model is Frank Townes Dargan, who taught at Clemson from 1901 to 1929.

17. Radio grotesque, marked by earphone, strap overhead, and wires below. The model is probably William Emera "Monk" Godfrey, professor of physics at Clemson from 1919 to 1947 and advisor to the first radio club on campus.

18. The mechanical engineering grotesque, represented by a gear wheel and a piston of an engine. Due to limited photographs of faculty from that era, we can only guess that the model was one of these men, all of whom taught mechanical engineering at Clemson between 1922 and 1925: Samuel Broadus Earle, Edward Leroy Carpenter, and Dennis Kavanaugh.

19. The Academic Department grotesque, marked by the book and quill. The author guesses the model to be Samuel Maner "Major" Martin, professor of mathematics at Clemson from 1898 to 1947.

20. The architecture grotesque, complete with a capital of a column. The best guess for the model is Rudolph Edward "Pop" Lee, the architect of the college and professor in that subject from 1896 to 1948.

21. The physics grotesque, represented by the triangular prism with a beam of light passing through and dividing. Due to limited photographs of faculty from that era, we can only guess that the model was one of these men, all of whom taught physics at Clemson between 1922 and 1925: William Emera Godfrey, Austin Lawrence Hodges, Horace Arthur Sherman, Oliver Philip Hart, William Emanuel Muntz, Henry Ashby Rankin, William C. Phebus, and Henry Madison Davis.

22. The free drawing, or architectural drawing, grotesque, marked by the presence of the art palette and brush. Due to limited photographs of faculty from that era, we can only guess that the model was one of these men, all of whom taught free drawing at Clemson between 1922 and 1925: David Niven Harris, David Christoph Lange (architectural), Rembert Gary Allen (architectural), and Maurice Siegler.

23. The mechanical drawing grotesque, represented by the triangle and T square. The author's best guess is that the model is Williston Wightman "Wee Willie" Klugh, who taught the subject at Clemson from 1896 to 1948.

24. The structural engineering grotesque, represented by the I-beam and steel angle. It is most likely Howard Emmit "Pop" Glenn, who taught the subject at Clemson from 1924 to 1961.

25. The civil engineering grotesque, marked by the presence of the theodolite (surveyor's target) and telescope of a level. Probably, it is modeled on Elwyn Lorenzo "Will Rogers" Clarke, who taught civil engineering at Clemson from 1921 to 1951.

26. A polychrome tympanum on Riggs Hall that displays the arts and technologies taught within the building. On the left side are the architectural arts, and on the right side, the engineering and technological sciences. The Spirit of Electricity, representing Walter Merritt Riggs, the college's first electrical engineering faculty member and the building's namesake, unites them in the middle.

27. A downspout on Riggs Hall with "1927," the building's dedication date, prominently displayed on either side of a knight's shield and helmet. A broadsword and battle-axe and two arrows cross behind another smaller shield with the duogram "C.C." raised upon it, a stylized coat of arms for the college.

28. The eastern doorway into Sikes Hall. The finial at the top of the broken pediment is an acorn. The cornucopia and the swags are filled with the fruits and flowers of South Carolina. The rosette on the ionic capitals is a dogwood.

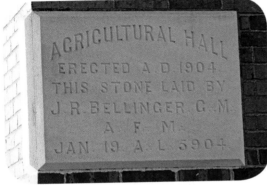

29. The cornerstone of Agricultural Hall (now Sikes Hall) laid by the Masonic Grand Master. Note the *Anno Domini* (A.D.) and *Anno Lucis* (A.L.) dating.

30. A frieze depicting the "old way" of agriculture—the plow and oxen—at the time of Long Hall's construction in 1937.

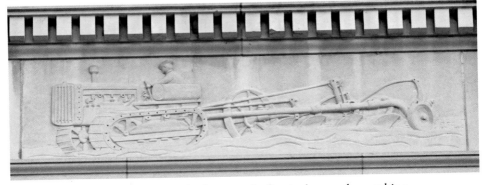

31. A frieze depicting the "new way" of agriculture—the combine— at the time of Long Hall's construction in 1937.

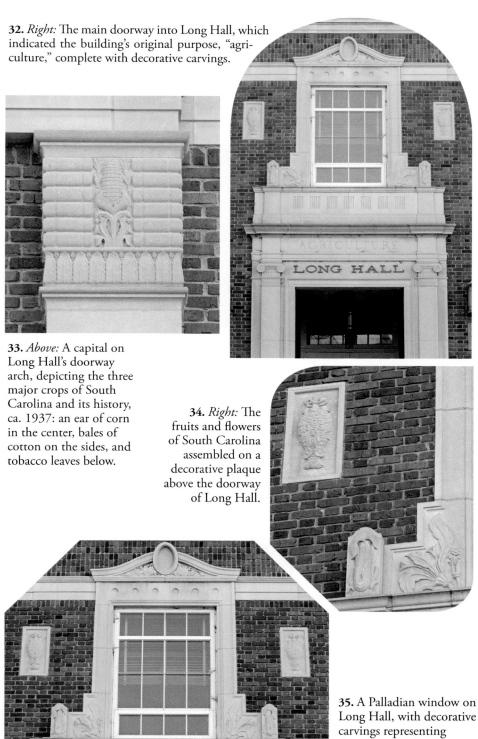

32. *Right:* The main doorway into Long Hall, which indicated the building's original purpose, "agriculture," complete with decorative carvings.

33. *Above:* A capital on Long Hall's doorway arch, depicting the three major crops of South Carolina and its history, ca. 1937: an ear of corn in the center, bales of cotton on the sides, and tobacco leaves below.

34. *Right:* The fruits and flowers of South Carolina assembled on a decorative plaque above the doorway of Long Hall.

35. A Palladian window on Long Hall, with decorative carvings representing the crops and flowering and fruit-bearing plants of South Carolina.

36. The low-relief above the entranceway to Fike Field House. Created by A. Wolfe Davidson, it is a stylized interpretation of football, reimagining it in a classically Greek way.

37. A mosaic in the foyer of Olin Hall mapping out the distribution of soil and clay types in the state of South Carolina.

38. The Willard Hirsch Tiger in front of the Clemson House.

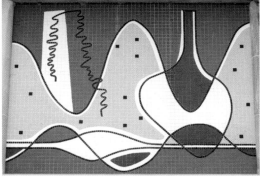

39. The mosaic above the entrance to Olin Hall, home to ceramic engineering.

40. The sculpture by Willard Hirsch on the side of Earle Hall, a depiction of a slide rule and an isobutylene bromide molecule, an important gas used in chemical engineering, the program housed in Earle Hall.

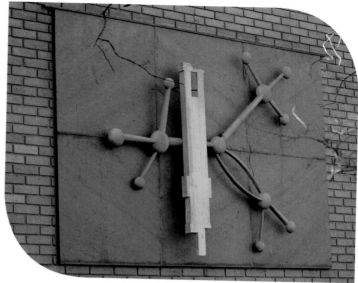

41. A sculpture by Willard Hirsch depicting a bull's head, a bush, and a beaker, the subjects studied in the Plant and Animal Sciences Building in the Robert F. Poole Agricultural Center (informally called P&A or Poole Hall).

42. A ceramic tile on Sirrine Hall depicting a cotton boll ripe for the picking.

43. A ceramic tile on Sirrine Hall showing a bale of cotton cut to pull staple.

44. A ceramic tile on Sirrine Hall depicting a spinning wheel preparing material to be drawn into yarn.

The Sirrine Hall tiles were modeled by Professor Rudolph E. Lee and identified for the author by Professor Emeritus "Mike" Hubbard.

45. A ceramic tile on Sirrine Hall depicting a weaving cone, or bobbin.

46. A ceramic tile on Sirrine Hall depicting a loom, gear, and spindle. The gear represents the mechanical spinning frame, while the other items are for filling yarn quills for shuttles.

47. A ceramic tile on Sirrine Hall depicting a weaver's knot.

48. An aerial view of Clemson's campus in the 1950s. Clemson University Photographs, CUL.SC.

49. The mural done by Gilmer Petroff (1913–1990) as it appeared in the Sabre Room of the Clemson House. A "free" interpretation of the mural appeared in the 1952 edition of *Taps*. Beginning at the left, the mural depicts the life of a Clemson cadet upon arrival as a bewildered freshman civilian and the gradual transformation into a more worldly collegian and military officer. Clemson University Photographs, CUL.SC.

50. An aerial view of campus on a football game day in 1962.
Clemson University Photographs, CUL.SC.

Sunday dinner in the mess hall. At 3:00 p.m., all gathered in the YMCA auditorium for a program honoring mothers. Cadets and town youth spoke or sang. After the program, the regimental band, positioned on Bowman Field, offered a concert. Mother's Day commemoration continued at Clemson for over a quarter of a century.[103]

The Trustees

As Sikes approached the end of his career, the trustees appeared determined that the gains in the college's reputation made during his presidency would not be lost. Unlike all the presidents before Sikes who had at least two of the three confidants of Thomas Green Clemson—that is, D. K. Norris, R. W. Simpson, and B. R. Tillman—advising and watching their every move and deed, Sikes had none.

Four years after Tillman's death, the remaining life trustees replaced him with Bennette Eugene Geer, a forty-nine-year-old textile executive born in Anderson County on June 9, 1873. After a local education, he studied at Furman University, receiving his AB and then in 1896 the AM degree. While an undergraduate, he was initiated into Sigma Alpha Epsilon Fraternity. After receiving his master's degree, he attended the University of Wisconsin and then the University of Michigan. He returned to Furman to teach English until 1911, when he resigned to serve as an assistant to his brother, John M. Geer, the chief executive of several textile mills. In 1913, Westervelt (later Judson) Mills first elected B. E. Geer its treasurer and then president. James B. Duke was the major stockholder in the mill, which produced "fine and fancy goods." Geer had frequent contact with Duke.

On November 3, 1922, the Clemson trustees elected Geer one of their life members. Interestingly, Geer's mother, Mary Malvenia Holmes (wife of Solomon M. Geer), a granddaughter of Jane Calhoun and William Holmes Jr., made him the second cousin twice removed of Anna Calhoun Clemson. When the James Buchanan Duke Foundation was established in 1925, it named Geer one of its trustees, a position he held until his death. That position led him to resign from the Clemson board on October 26, 1928.[104]

Prior to Geer's resignation and shortly after Sikes's presidency had begun in 1925, Paul Sanders was elected by the Clemson board to fill the trusteeship of M. L. Donaldson, who had died in 1924. Sanders, born in Beach Hill Plantation, Colleton County, on December 1, 1872, had received a private education. Primarily a farmer, he had a diverse business interest also in saw-milling, merchandising, banking, and rural real estate. In government he served on the draft board in World War I, the State Farm Labor Advisory Committee, the State Agricultural Adjustment Administration, and the U.S. Inland Waterways Commission, all of which helped him aid the Clemson board in making effective decisions for the good of South Carolina. Sanders served on the Clemson board until 1960. He married twice and fathered four sons and a daughter.[105]

The person chosen to replace Geer, following his resignation, was Joseph Emory Sirrine of Greenville, born on December 9, 1872, to George W. and Sarah Rylander Sirrine in Americus, Georgia. Educated at the Greenville Military Institute and at Furman University, he received a BS degree in 1890 at eighteen years of age. He learned engineering working for Poe Manufacturing Company and then joined Lockwood, Greene and Company in 1909. In 1928 with a partnership of friends, he formed J. E. Sirrine and Company, a general industrial engineering firm that specialized in textile engineering, aluminum, and shipyards, especially in the South and New England.

Throughout Sirrine's board membership, he concentrated on making Clemson's textile program world-renowned. To provide for that, he created the J. E. Sirrine Foundation, which supported textile research and education primarily at Clemson. Professionally very active, J. E. Sirrine held memberships in the American Society of Civil Engineers, the American Society of Mechanical Engineers, and the American Institute of Electrical Engineers. As the student chapters of those societies formed at Clemson, he supported them financially and with his occasional attendance. An active Mason and Knight Templar, he founded the Sirrine Children's Ward in Greenville General Hospital and supported liberally Greenville Shriners Hospital for Crippled Children. His gifts to his alma mater and to the Greenville public school system were also generous. He and his wife, Jane Pinckney Henry, had no children. Sirrine involved himself extensively in the federal World War I and II committees on textiles.[106]

When Alan Johnstone, president of the board since 1907, died in 1929, J. E. Wannamaker, the last of the will-named life trustees, took over as board president. The full thirteen members elected the president, and any trustee, life or term, was eligible. However, the post of life trustee had to be filled through an election by the six remaining life trustees. For this vacancy, the life trustees' choice was Christie Benet. The son of William C. and Susan Benet, he received his education in his hometown of Abbeville, then at South Carolina College, the College of Charleston (AB 1900), and the University of Virginia (LLB 1902). There he earned membership in Phi Beta Kappa. He returned to Columbia to practice law, serving also as a volunteer football coach for the South Carolina Gamecocks. Benet married Alice Yeveren Haskell in 1906, and they had two children, Christie Jr., who died in 1928, and Alice Benet, active in the Episcopal church, served on the vestry of Trinity Church, Columbia, and on the board of Kanuga, one of the denomination's recreational camps. On the state level, he served as secretary to the Democratic Party Executive Committee. Governor Manning appointed him to the U.S. Senate to fill the remainder of Tillman's term. He did not serve long, volunteering instead for the American Expeditionary Forces. He also led war bond and Red Cross drives. Before he joined the Clemson board, he had served on one of UVA's boards.[107]

Two life trustees were selected from existing legislative trustees. The first was Robert Muldrow Cooper. Elected a legislative trustee in 1922, he was in one way a perfect choice (he was a farmer), and in another way an unusual choice (he had graduated from USC in 1909). Nevertheless, his contributions were legendary. Born in Wisacky (Lee County), he was serving in the S.C. House when the general assembly chose him as a legislative trustee. In 1923, he was elected a state senator and served as such until 1934. In those bodies, he displayed his agricultural talents on the two agricultural committees, while at home on his 960-acre farm, he raised cotton, oats, tobacco, flax, cattle, and hogs. "Mr. Bob" also served on senate banking, manufacturing, roads and bridges, and education committees. He once noted that when elected to the Clemson board, some of his college chums asserted that Clemson was but a "pimple on the path of progress." Despite their efforts at humor, Cooper served as a conscientious, extremely well-informed trustee, and it was to the good for South Carolina when the other life trustees selected him as a life member of the board in 1935.[108] He remained a life trustee until his death thirty years later.

The next of the new life trustees was Thomas Benton Young. Born in Florence on June 12, 1882, he received his education in the Florence County schools and at Clemson College, graduating in agriculture in 1903. Young married three times and had three sons and two daughters. The S.C. Cooperative Extension Service published his graduation thesis on tobacco culture as a bulletin for the state's farmers. He was employed as a research scientist by USDA until 1920. He then joined the extension service, with which he stayed for five years. His successes included the introduction of red pepper as a viable commercial crop. Seeing a need for better marketing of crops, he created such agencies as the Planters Produce and Supply Company (1920), the S.C. Sweet Potato Growers (1922), the S.C. Peach Association (1924), the S.C. Dewberry Association (1926), and the S.C. Cooperatives Consolidated (1927), for which he served as one of the directors. Ill health forced him to retire from active participation in these agencies in 1933. The legislature chose him as a Clemson trustee on February 1, 1932, and on January 24, 1935, he was selected a life trustee to fill the vacancy that resulted from Governor Manning's death.[109]

During the administration of President Sikes, the Clemson board added six new legislative trustees. Frank Elmo Cope from Cope (Orangeburg County) served in the S.C. House from 1925 until 1928. While a representative, he was elected to the Clemson board and subsequently reelected until 1946. Cope, a 1905 Clemson graduate, was a farmer and an active Methodist. He and his wife, Irene Louise Rumph, had two daughters.[110]

In 1930, the general assembly chose Samuel Hodges Sherard from Ninety-Six as a trustee; he served continually until his death on July 5, 1947. Born in 1886 in Laurens, he attended the Ninety-Six schools and Clemson, from which he graduated in agriculture in 1908. His interest in animal husbandry led to active membership in the Canadian Veterinary Science Association of Ontario, from which he received a veterinary science degree. In 1911, he married Louise Lipscomb, and they had three daughters. Prior to his election as a state trustee, he served with the USDA in the Philippines and then as a county agent in Florida and Georgia. He returned to South Carolina in 1918 and served a term in the state house. He also served as a district officer of the Farm Security Administration.[111]

The next legislative trustee selected was state Senator Edgar Allen Brown. Born in 1888 on a farm near Aiken, Brown attended local schools and then Graniteville Academy. At sixteen, he studied shorthand in Augusta, Georgia. After a brief period as a public reporter, he served as a law clerk and then received admission to the bar in 1910. In 1914, the Barnwell County Democratic Party chose Brown, at age twenty-six, as its chairman, a position he held until his death in 1975. Elected to the S.C. House in 1920, he allied himself with the "Progressive" wing of the state and national Democratic Party. He then ran unsuccessfully in 1926 for the U.S. Senate against Ellison D. "Cotton Ed" Smith, the sitting senator since 1908. Brown was elected to the state legislature in 1928, and in 1934 the legislature elected him a Clemson trustee. Married, Brown was a Methodist.[112]

Also William Dickson Barnett served as a legislative trustee. Born in Oconee County on August 12, 1889, he enrolled in Clemson's preparatory course in 1905 and graduated in textiles in 1910. After teaching in Oconee County for a year, he enrolled in USC in law, receiving his LLB in 1913. He settled in Columbia and married Nellie Aycock Caughman; they had two daughters. Barnett was very active in Columbia public affairs, the Presbyterian church, and the life of Clemson College. The legislature elected him to the board in 1920, and he served through the presidency of Enoch Sikes.[113]

Another Clemson alumnus who served in the general assembly and also on the Clemson board (1934–1938 and again 1947–1957) was Ben Tillman Leppard. Born in Greenville County in 1892, he attended Clemson until May 1918, when he enlisted in the U.S. Army, which sent him to its training camp at Plattsburg, New York. (Leppard was one of the Clemson cadré who, with Allie Corcoran, had to offer school yells because Clemson had no songs.) He received the BS in agriculture from Clemson in 1919 and later attended Furman University's law school. He was admitted to the bar in 1930 and served in the S.C. House 1933–1934. He served in the senate from 1937 to 1940. Active in the Methodist church, he married Ella Cooley of Greenville in 1928, and they had two sons.[114]

On March 27, 1936, the general assembly elected a highly regarded Anderson County farmer to Clemson's board. Joseph B. Douthit lived in the Lebanon community and had received a BS in agriculture from Clemson. When he began farming in 1914, he had a Clemson-learned passion for soil conservation and promoted it through his entire career. Early on he moved the family farm from cotton into cattle and diversified crops and earned a reputation for the quality of his corn seed. He was named supervisor of the Upper Savannah Soil Conservation District. He married Mary Broyles, and they had one daughter.[115]

William Clyde Graham was the last of the legislative trustees elected during the Sikes administration. Born in the Pee Dee in Florence County on December 31, 1897, he graduated from Clemson in 1918. As a commissioned ROTC graduate (his was the first class to complete the advanced ROTC training), he left the college for his final training at Plattsburg, New York. However, he was not called to active service and in 1919 served as the agricultural teacher in Batesburg and then returned to Coward (Florence County). For a brief period (1921–1922), he was involved with his brother in a drug company. In 1923, he returned to teaching in Pamplico, where he also operated a business.[116]

Athletics

Helping to raise the spirit and morale of both Clemson students and alumni, the Sikes era saw a real upswing in the fortunes of intercollegiate sports. For football, Sikes dealt with Coach Bud Saunders. His team of 1924 had a 5–2–1 record, while during Sikes's first two years (1925 and 1926), Saunders's Tigers compiled three wins and thirteen losses. Such a performance was not tolerated by the former Wake Forest football letterwinner, and by January 1, 1927, he had appointed Josh Cody the new coach. By the end of the season, the team posted a 5–3–1 record. For the four seasons Cody coached the Tigers, the team won twenty-nine, lost eleven, and had one tie. On September 19, 1928, Clemson abandoned the traditional drab jerseys for orange ones with purple numbers.

There was also a change in the schools that Clemson scheduled and where the games were played. Old in-state rivals such as Presbyterian, Wofford, the Citadel, and USC remained on the schedule. Less competitive teams were dropped. Clemson defeated Auburn all three times the two land-grant schools played. NC State defeated Clemson in 1927, but the Tigers won the next three. And the Tigers swept South Carolina four times in a row. By 1929, Mississippi, Florida, and Kentucky, all of whom later entered the SEC as charter members, were on the schedule. Clemson played not only in Columbia and Charleston, but also in Florence against NC State, whom they later met in Charlotte in 1930. They played Virginia Military Institute in Lynchburg and Norfolk, and Florida once in Gainesville and twice in Jacksonville. While it was the standard for Clemson to play only three or four games at home a year, the exposure of the college to other southern cities outside the state began to move athletic finances into the black and, at the same time, enhance Clemson's name recognition.[117]

But the Depression intervened. The cuts the general assembly made were initially taken at Clemson by working to decrease nonpersonnel costs. First, the school froze salaries, but then as revenues from the fertilizer sales, tuition, and state appropriation all fell across the summer of 1930, Sikes and the administrative leaders, at the direction of the general assembly, had to reduce salaries. Clemson cut all salaries, with no exceptions, reducing Cody's from $6,500 to $6,000. After discussions with Sikes and others, Cody submitted his resignation on November 26, 1930. *The Tiger* pleaded to keep him, and he briefly reconsidered. But nothing changed, and, as the new year began, on January 2, 1931, Cody made plans to coach at Vanderbilt, his alma mater.[118] His resignation left Clemson without not only its football and basketball coach, but also athletic director, a position Cody had assumed when Gee resigned as basketball coach. Cody led the Clemson basketball players for five years, two of which, 1928–1929 and 1929–1930, were winning seasons.[119]

Some of Clemson's greatest football players came from the Cody years. O. K. Pressley, from Chester County, played center and linebacker from 1926 to 1928. In 1928, he earned all-state and all-Southern Conference honors and third team All-American.[120] Other standouts included Covington "Goat" McMillan, who later served as an assistant coach at Clemson from 1937 to 1964; Bob "General" Jones, who played both basketball and football from 1927 to 1930 and then served at Clemson as a football, boxing, and golf coach for forty-four years; and Henry Asbill, who played from 1927 to 1929.

Faced with the loss of Cody, Sikes, Barre (who chaired the Athletic Council), and Littlejohn fortunately hired Jess Neely as head coach before the month of January ended. Neely had played for Vanderbilt and after graduation continued there in school for a law degree. He coached at Southwestern Presbyterian College in Clarksville, Tennessee (now Rhodes University in Memphis), and coached at Alabama when he accepted the Clemson offer. He brought with him Frank Howard, an Alabama alumnus, and Joe Davis, who served also as basketball coach from 1931 to 1940.[121]

Football continued its improvement. The 1934 season ended 5–4, and the next two seasons broke even. Of great importance, the Tigers defeated USC all four years. Tulane, then a southern powerhouse, joined the schedule, and the Tigers traveled to New Orleans each year through 1940. The 1939 Tulane game was Clemson's only loss of the year 7–6. It was a terrific game; Banks McFadden's punting record that day remained unbeaten in the Tulane Sugar Bowl Stadium.

Clemson, which won its first Southern Conference title in 1939, received an invitation to play in the 1940 Cotton Bowl. Held in Dallas, Texas, the bowl

Jess Neely (1898–1983), Clemson head football coach from 1931 to 1939 and College Football Hall of Fame inductee in 1971. *Left to right*: Don Willis, Red Pearson, Bob Bailey, Dan Coleman and Neely. Clemson University Sports Information Department.

"Bonnie" Banks McFadden (1907–2005), letterman in three Clemson sports (football, basketball, and track), the 1939 Associated Press Athlete of the Year, member of the 1940 Brooklyn Dodgers (NFL), World War II veteran, 1959 inductee into the College Football Hall of Fame, Clemson football coach (1941, 1946–1969), head basketball coach (1946–1956), charter member of both the Clemson Athletic and South Carolina Athletic Halls of Fame, charter member of the Clemson Ring of Honor (1994), and director of Clemson's popular intramural sports program (1969–1984). He remains the only Clemson athlete to have a jersey number retired in two sports and to win an All-American citation in two sports in one year (1939). Clemson University Photographs, CUL.SC.

matched Clemson against Boston College, which, coached by Frank Leahy, was favored to win. The day before the Clemson team and others departed for Dallas, one of the regional newspapers noted, "Picture a student body of 2,200 that believes in Santa Claus, a football team that wept at the chance to play together once more, and a Southern conference basketball team that joyfully sacrificed its greatest individual star, Banks McFadden. There you have a picture of Clemson College upon acceptance of the Cotton Bowl bid."[122]

Thirty-one players, the coaches, the eighty-member regimental band, and the senior platoon drill team boarded six chartered buses on December 10, 1939, for the forty-eight-hour trip to Dallas. There they separated. The coaches and players were taken to the Hotel Adolphus, where the fans, who arrived shortly before New Year's Eve, joined them. Meanwhile, the band and drill team stayed in much less elegant quarters. They had been arranged by Marvin "Slick" Ellison, Clemson 1924, then a prominent member of the Dallas business community, who had urged the Cotton Bowl committee to invite Clemson and its band and drill team, all of which were highly regarded. Ellison had received "orders" from "Uncle Jake" Woodward, the alumni secretary, to keep the cost low. Slick served as the president of the Dallas Clemson Club, and he and his wife, Katharine, played social hosts for Clemson's band and drill team.[123]

Once the game began, Boston College struck first with an early second quarter field goal. But Clemson's defense and Banks McFadden's kicking kept the Golden Eagles well jessed. McFadden kicked nine times, averaging forty-three yards. His longest punt carried sixty-seven yards. Late in the second quarter, the game's and Clemson's only touchdown was set up by McFadden's return of an Eagle punt to Boston's 33-yard line. Then Charlie Timmons from Abbeville ran the ball into the end zone for the winning score.[124] In the stands of the Cotton Bowl sat S.C. Governor John G. Richards, U.S. Senator and Mrs. James F. Byrnes, President and Mrs. Sikes, and most of the Clemson trustees.

Clemson ended the season nationally ranked twelfth, and McFadden received All-American honors. Earlier, officials at Rice Institute, one of the southern private college football powerhouses in Houston, Texas, had begun negotiating with Neely. They were successful, and Neely left Clemson with Davis. Neely offered to take Assistant Coach Frank Howard also, but Howard elected to stay, whereupon Clemson named him its head football coach.[125] Howard always claimed later that he had seconded the motion to hire himself.

Basketball also improved so that by 1935 it had a 15–3 record. In 1939, Clemson won the Southern Conference and was led by Banks McFadden, who was named a basketball All-American. He remains today the only Clemson athlete named football-basketball All-American in one year.[126]

During Sikes's last half decade, the other sports also enjoyed a number of successes. Track, coached by Frank Howard, won the state championship every year.

One of the team's leaders was F. H. H. Calhoun Jr., the son of "Doc Rock" Calhoun, the first Clemson track coach in 1905. Bob Jones coached boxing, and the squad won several state championships, the Southern Conference in 1938–1939, and finished fourth in the 1939 Sugar Bowl match. Thus, the boxers were the first intercollegiate team to represent Clemson in the growing Christmas season bowl world. Baseball was Jess Neely's assignment, and the team responded with state championships from 1936 to 1938.

In March 1930, Sikes reported to the trustees that a faculty petition for a golf course had been referred by the agricultural committee to three trustees: Cooper, Sanders, and Sirrine. In August, that group reported favorably to the entire board, which adopted the motion unanimously. The new course was to be co-located within the meadow where "sheep did safely graze." The college's buildings and grounds unit had the charge to build the course, and $500 was allocated for it. The college business manager had the assigned responsibility for overseeing building and maintenance. Prof. Ed Freeman designed the course and supervised the construction. It was ready for play by the spring of 1931. A student team formed, and by the mid-1930s, Bob Jones coached them to regular break-even seasons. The first team captain was Alan McCrary Johnstone, grandson of deceased Trustee President Alan Johnstone.

Preston Brooks "Mr. Holtzy" Holtzendorff (1894–1971), general secretary for the Clemson YMCA from 1916 to 1959 except the years he served in World War I with the Army Air Corps. He founded the Clemson intramural sports program in 1931, coached freshman football for five years and swimming for twenty-seven, and served three terms on the national YMCA Board while helping establish the South Carolina State Conference of YMCAs. Taken from the 1930 edition of the Clemson College annual, *Taps*.

Different members of the military faculty coached riflery, and the team garnered regional and national honors. Mr. Holtzy coached swimming, ably assisted by Carl McHugh, Clemson engineering professor and star of the school's swimming teams in the mid-1930s. The team garnered ten state championships and set records in a variety of individual events. Because the tennis courts, located between Riggs Field and the barracks, were displaced to make room for new barracks, the college had no team in 1936. Teams, coached by alumnus A. Hoke Sloan, resumed play in 1937 and finished the decade with a state second place in the conference in 1938 and an 8–3 record in 1939. F. Kirchner coached intercollegiate soccer. Begun as a varsity sport in 1933, it also had success, with winning seasons all the years and in 1938 posted an undefeated, one tie season. So all the sports finished the 1930s showing great strength.[127]

Also Clemson men made names for themselves and for Clemson in professional baseball. Third baseman Norm McMillan played at Clemson from 1915 to 1917. He played for the New York Yankees, Boston Red Sox, and St. Louis Browns before ending his professional career in 1929 with the Chicago Cubs. Flint Rhem pitched for three different teams: the Philadelphia Phillies, Boston Braves, and St. Louis Cardinals.[128]

On the worldwide arena, Clemson's first claim to an Olympic medal occurred in the 1932 Los Angeles Olympics. John W. Wofford, who had attended Clemson for three years before his appointment to the U.S. Military Academy in 1918, rode for the U.S. Show Jumping Team, which won the silver medal.[129]

Thunderheads Gathering

Throughout the Sikes years, international conflicts were almost continuous and almost worldwide. Conflicts broke out in Asia, Africa, and Europe. With the strengthening of radical elements in Italy, Japan, Spain, Russia, Germany, and others, internal armed conflicts spilled across borders.

Earlier, the introduction of air travel had attracted the attention of young people everywhere. Among the pioneer aviators were two South Carolina brothers with Clemson ties. John Tarbox, who graduated from Clemson in 1904, and Gurdon Tarbox, his younger brother who attended Clemson from 1913 to 1915 but graduated from NC State, made aviation history when they flew the first airplane in South Carolina on July 12, 1911, out of Georgetown.[130]

Then in the late 1920s, James Sams Jr., Clemson 1924, urged Clemson College, whose young alumni from electrical and mechanical engineering had made paths in aeronautic design, to open a program in automotive and aeronautical engineering. When Sikes brought the idea to the board, one trustee quipped that there was a greater need for auto mechanics. Growing out of this youthful fascination with air power, seven young cadets formed the Clemson Aero Club, and Prof. John Logan Marshall agreed to serve as the advisor. In winter and early spring of 1929, the club members built an aircraft, "Little 372." It flew successfully that April at the Greenville airport.[131] One and a half years later, the Clemson Glider Club built and flew its first glider.[132]

Faced with the growth of worldwide violence and armed conflict, U.S. President Franklin D. Roosevelt (1933–1945) signed legislation to allow the federal

John Logan Marshall (1885–1975), professor of forge and foundry work and wood work from 1917 to 1959, a founder of Tiger Brotherhood, and director of the construction of "Little 372," the first successfully flown airplane built within the state of South Carolina. Here we see him standing to the right of student Dallas Berry Sherman, Aero Club member and 1929 Norris Medal winner, in front of "Little 372" on Bowman Field. Clemson University Photographs, CUL.SC.

government to finance the teaching of aeronautics in "civil aeronautic pilots" programs at the land-grant colleges. Sikes placed the program under the guidance of John Logan Marshall.[133] But on September 1, 1939, Adolf Hitler, the German *Fuehrer*, and Josef Stalin, the Soviet dictator, coordinated a two-front attack on Poland. Poland's allies, Great Britain and France, almost immediately declared war on the aggressors, and World War II had begun. In October 1939, the federal government brought civil aeronautic pilot training under the Army ROTC. Clemson Commandant Herbert Pool selected forty cadets to begin the training program.[134]

Coming from this decade of interest in aviation at Clemson were a number of men who made marks in the air frontier. From the "Little 372" adventure, Dallas Sherman graduated in 1929 and began working as an architect. In 1932, he joined the Army Air Corps, received pilot training, and served in the corps until 1937. In 1942, he was called to active duty and served in Europe, Africa, and the Middle East. After the war, he joined Pan-American Airways. A second Clemson graduate, Theodore J. Boselli, also entered the Army Air Corps and served as navigator of Roosevelt's plane that flew the president in 1945 to the Yalta Conference. A number of other Clemson alumni served in both the army and navy air forces.

Sikes's Legacy

Sikes tendered his resignation for June 30, 1939, but the trustees asked him to remain president while they searched for his successor. He agreed somewhat reluctantly. His fifteen years had been an unparalleled success. At the center of the "monument" he had produced, stood the library, which had its own building and was vastly improved. The college had also joined the ranks of schools accredited by SACS. New barracks sat on campus. Riggs Hall, Long Hall, and Sirrine Hall provided new space for engineering, architecture, agriculture, and textiles. A new field house also graced the campus. The land holdings had increased eighteen fold. New experiment stations now existed, leading the state into the soft fruit industry. The extension service had acted as a major force that led South Carolina through four droughts and helped ameliorate suffering and problems arising from the Depression. The student body had doubled and continued to diversify. The Clemson College Foundation and IPTAY had begun. Truly, it was a remarkable record.

Of course, some opportunities remained lost. At least three were curricular. Clemson had seen the need for a forestry curriculum early in the 1920s and again in the 1930s. But the suggestions and requests for it were turned down by the state government. The other two curricular issues involved automotive and aeronautic engineering. These were discussed with the trustees, but nothing else happened. Each would have been quite expensive. Further, the trustees turned down administrative streamlining in the late 1920s as well as Sikes's Depression-based proposal to open the college to female students.

By the time he closed his office door on June 30, 1940, Enoch Walter Sikes had left an indelible stamp on Clemson Agricultural College, South Carolina, and, to a degree, the nation. He died unexpectedly on January 8, 1941, and was interred in Woodland Cemetery next to Riggs. Almost his closing written words were drawn from the Sixteenth Psalm: "The lines have fallen to me in pleasant places" (KJV).[135]

Notes

1. CUL.SC.CUA. S 30 v 3, 391.
2. Ibid., S 16 f 24.
3. Holohan, in a 1980 noncommittal letter to Robert McPherson "Mac" Burdette, avoided the issue of whether or not he had been imbibing. Mac, a former student (BA; MA History; MCRP Clemson) and a good friend, gave the letter to the Special Collections of the Clemson University Library and a copy to me.
4. CUL.SC.CUA. S 38 f "Harcombe, J. D."
5. Ibid., S 17 f 297.
6. Ibid., S 30 v 4, 1–23.
7. Ibid., 22, 23, and 29.
8. *The Tiger*, April 8, 1925.
9. Ibid., September 23, 1925.
10. CUL.SC.CUA. S 30 v 4, 29.

11. Ibid., 50 and 51.
12. *The Tiger*, April 22, 1925.
13. CUL.SC.CUA. S 36 v 4, 50 and 51.
14. Ibid., S 2 b 1 f 8.
15. Ibid., S 16 f 35.
16. *Record*, 1925–1926; 1928–1929; and 1939–1940.
17. *Greenville News and Piedmont*, January 6, 1980.
18. CUL.SC.CUA. S 37 f "Fellowship Club."
19. Ibid., S 1 b 4 ff 5 and 37.
20. CUL.SC.MSS 68 f 3.
21. CUL.SC.CUA. S 1 b 1 f 4.
22. Ibid., f 9; and S 30 v 4, 87.
23. Ibid., S 1 b 2 f 9; b 63 f 22; and S 30 v 4, 87.
24. Ibid., S 30 v 4, 452–454.
25. Ibid., S 16 f 35.
26. Ibid., S 38 f "Doggett."
27. Ibid., S 74 ss 1 b 62 f 11.
28. Ibid., b 47 f 2.
29. Ibid., S 1 b 1 f 8.
30. Ibid., ff 4, 7 and 9; and b 2 f 11.
31. Ibid., b 1 ff 10 and 13.
32. Ibid., f 9; and b 2 f 13.
33. Ibid., b 4 ff 34 and 35.
34. Ibid.
35. Ibid., b 5 f 53.
36. Ibid., f 55.
37. Ibid., b 1 f 4; b 2 f 115; b 3 f 20; and b 4 ff 31 and 40.
38. Bourret, *Clemson Football* 2009, 203.
39. *The Tiger*, April 25, 1940; CUL.SC.CUA. S 37 f "Fike"; and CUL.SC.MSS 68 f 190.
40. CUL.SC.MSS 68 f 190.
41. CUL.SC.CUA. S 37 f "Y.M.C.A."
42. Walter T. Cox Jr. to Donald McKale, Class of 1941 Alumni Memorial Professor of History, DVD made under the auspices of the Strom Thurmond Institute (STI).
43. CUL.SC.CUA. S 32 b 107 f 1.
44. Ibid., S 37 f "Long Hall"; and *Charleston News and Courier*, February 12, 1936.
45. CUL.SC.CUA. S 37 f "Long Hall."
46. In order, *Dictionary of the National Biography, 1885–1900*, v. 2; *The New Georgia Encyclopedia*, http://www.georgiaencyclopedia.org; http://www.bbc.co.uk/history/historic_figures/cartwright_edmund.shtml; http://en.wikipedia.org/wiki/william_henry_perkin (all accessed November 21, 2010).
47. CUL.SC.CUA. S 37 f "Sirrine Hall."
48. *Record*, 1939–1940.
49. The biographical details on Anderson were developed by P. A. "Alex" Crunkleton, Clemson graduate research assistant, using the Clemson *Record*, 1897–1902, and CUL.SC.CUA. S 38 f "Alexander Pierce Anderson"; *The Tiger*, June 6, 1933, and July 27, 1933; and CUL.SC.MSS 68 f 207.
50. Arbena, *IPTAY: The First Fifty Years*, 7–11.
51. Alan McCrary Johnstone to J. V. Reel, DVD.
52. Arbena, *IPTAY*, 68.
53. CUL.SC.CUA. S 15 f 222; and S 30 v 5, 343.
54. Ibid., S 38 f "Aull."
55. Bryan, *Clemson*, 118–121.
56. CUL.SC.MSS 255 b 1 f 9; and S 37 f "Aull."
57. Hale, "Years of Transition," 1–2.
58. John S. Brubacker and Willis Rudy, *Higher Education in Transition*, 266–267.
59. *The Tiger*, September 30, 1925.

60. CUL.SC.CUA. S 1 b 6 f 49.
61. Ibid., b 1 f 1.
62. Hale, "Years of Transition," 52.
63. SCHS 3–9–9.
64. CUL.SC.CUA. S 1 b 2 f 11.
65. *The Chronicle*, October 1926; and *Taps*, 1927, 47, 103, and 248–249.
66. For example, see *Taps*, 1937, 134–144; and *Taps*, 1940, 174–183.
67. "Alumnus" means "one who is nourished" just as "matriculate" means "to be officially admitted and placed on the membership roll." This latter Latin term is derived from "mater" ["mother"]. And "alumnus" and "alumna" both derive from "alma," which means "nourishing."
68. CUL.SC.CUA. S 28 f "Poats."
69. CUL.SC.MSS 79 b 2 f 30.
70. CUL.SC.CUA. S 28 f "W. W. Bryan."
71. CUL.SC.CUA. S 38 f "George Chaplin."
72. Http://encyclopediaofarkansas.net/encyclopedia (accessed November 29, 2010).
73. *Greenville News*, March 22, 1942, and January 29, 1967.
74. *Record*, 1939–1940.
75. *The Tiger*, September 22, 1932.
76. CUL.SC.CUA. S 3 f 1.
77. Reel, *Women and Clemson University*, 20.
78. *Taps*, 1926.
79. CUL.SC.CUA. S 30 v 4, 319–321.
80. *Record*, 1924.
81. Yandle, "The Plowboy Scholar: Enoch Walter Sikes, 1925–1940," in *Tradition*, 141–158.
82. CUL.SC.CUA. S 10 f 14. The enrollment numbers, which fluctuated daily (and still do), are rounded up.
83. Ibid., S 2 b 1 f 8.
84. Ibid., S 1 b 2 ff and 16; and E. Doss, *War Classes: Social and Institutional Change at Clemson and the Citadel*, 6–7.
85. CUL.SC.CUA. S 1, b 3 f 28; S 2 b 2 f 21; and S 15 f 140.
86. *Taps*, 1922, 41; and CUL.SC.CUA. S 28 f "Freeman." Edwin J. Freeman to J. V. Reel, DVD. The information on "Tiger, Rah!" was provided by Freeman, the son of the composer and also a member of Clemson's faculty. Dr. Mark Spede reintroduced the song with the Tiger Marching Band in 2003. They also recorded it.
87. *The Tiger*, October 28, 1937.
88. *Taps*, 1926, 169–171 and 256–257.
89. Ibid., 265–319.
90. CUL.SC.CUA. S 1 b 2 f 24.
91. Robson, *Baird's Manual of College Fraternities*, eighteenth edition, 53 and 534.
92. Ibid., 651–653.
93. *The Tiger*, February 29, 1928, and June 5, 1928; and *Taps*, 1929, 286.
94. CUL.SC.CUA. S 1 b 7 f 74.
95. Ibid., S 37 f "Blue Key."
96. Ibid., f "Alpha Phi Omega."
97. Ibid., f "Phi Kappa Phi."
98. *Taps*, 1929, 1932, and 1939, all in the sections labeled "Clubs and Organizations." *Taps* was not always paginated.
99. CUL.SC.CUA. S 1 b 3 f 20.
100. Ibid., S 37 f "St. Andrews."
101. Ibid., S 503 b 1 f 1; and S 1 b 3 f 20.
102. McMahon, *Country Church and College Town*, 101–105.
103. CUL.SC.MSS 118 b 2 f 24, b 1 f 11 (Forum Club), and b 1 f 10 (Fellowship Club).
104. CUL.SC.CUA. S 30 ss 1 f "Geer." The relationship of Trustee Geer to Anna Calhoun Clemson was brought to my knowledge by John Geer, a friend and executive of Duke Energy Company. I thank him for his help. Trustee Geer and his wife, Reba McGee Rice, married on December 20, 1900, had six children: Rachel (Mrs. J. C. Jr.) Keys of Greenville; Sarah (Mrs. R. F. Jr.)

Gayle, Richmond, Virginia; John M. Geer, Leaksville, North Carolina; Robert A. Geer, Cedar Mountain, North Carolina; B. E. Geer Jr., Washington D.C.; and S. E. Bradshaw Geer, Marietta, Georgia.
105. Ibid., f "Sanders."
106. Ibid., f "Sirrine"; "Mr. J. E. Sirrine Passes," *Bobbin and Beaker*, Fall 1947, vol. 3, 20; and *Greenville News*, September 1, 1971.
107. CUL.SC.CUA. S 30 ss i f "Benet."
108. Ibid., f "Cooper."
109. Ibid., f "Young."
110. Ibid., f "Cope."
111. Ibid., f "Sherard."
112. Bailey et al., *SC Senate Biographical Dictionary*, vol. 1, 201–205.
113. CUL.SC.CUA. S 30 ss i f "Barnett"; Columbia *State*, December 12, 1940; and personal information supplied by W. D. Barnett's grandniece, Michelle Barnett, a Clemson alumna and Chi Omega.
114. Bailey et al., *SC Senate Biographical Dictionary*, vol. 2, 914–915.
115. CUL.SC.CUA. S 30 ss 1 f "Douthit."
116. Ibid., f "Graham."
117. Bourret, *Clemson Football 2009*, 203.
118. CUL.SC.CUA. S 30 v 4, 446. The correspondence on the Cody salary issue is scattered in a number of folders. First, the football total revenues for 1930 were 20 percent lower than projections (CUL.SC.CUA. S 103 b 1 f 1). With that damaging report, Sikes recommended no raises (and, in some cases, reductions), noting that the president and the board were contemplating an across-the-board salary cut. The Athletic Council asked for a clarification of its relationship to the Board of Trustees. Bradley answered for the board, reminding all that the Athletic Council was appointed by the president and the president was appointed by the board. Ultimately, Cody was paid for the time and work he did before he left, perhaps because the authority to set his salary was unclear.
119. Bourret, *Clemson Basketball 2009–10*, 198–199.
120. Bourret, *Clemson Football 2009*, 58.
121. Blackman et al., *Clemson: Where the Tigers Play*, 28–31.
122. CUL.SC.CUA. S 37 f "Athletics 1939."
123. The Ellison correspondence and newspaper clippings were lent to me by Brig. Gen. Chalmers Rankin "Happ" Carr, Clemson 1960 and nephew of the now deceased Katharine Carr Ellison. Gen. Carr has donated these papers to Clemson University.
124. *Greenville News*, January 2, 1940.
125. Blackman et al., *Clemson*, 39.
126. Bourret, *Clemson Basketball 2009–2010*, 167.
127. CUL.SC.CUA. S 30 v 4, 347 and 380; and *Taps*, 1931–1940 Sports and Minor Sports sections.
128. Bourret, *Clemson Baseball 2010*, 122–123.
129. *The Tiger*, September 22, 1932.
130. *The Alumni*, NC State University, 1952, 15.
131. *The Tiger*, April 10, 1929.
132. Ibid., September 17, 1930.
133. Ibid., January 12, 1939.
134. Ibid., October 5, 1939.
135. CUL.SC.CUA. S 3 f 29.

After President Poole announced President Roosevelt's declaration of war against Japan and Germany, Clemson cadets put a sign reading "Back to Berlin" on the World War I Howitzer that was placed in front of the Main Building. The Howitzer then was given to a United States scrap metal drive as part of Clemson's contribution to the war effort. *Left to right:* Cadets Earle Roberts, Chuck Tebeau, T. C. Moss, Bob Brooks, Dick Morrow, and Walker Gardiner. Clemson University Photographs, CUL.SC.

CHAPTER XI

Back to Berlin

1940–1945

Frank Poole

Robert Franklin Poole (1893–1958), Clemson's seventh president, took up his position promptly on July 1, 1940. As in the selection of Poole's predecessor, Enoch Walter Sikes, the Clemson Board of Trustees had time to search for a new president without the pressures of time shortened by resignations, unexpected or urged. They considered a number of persons before offering the post to Poole.

In some ways, Poole's background resembled closely the men who had preceded him as the college's president. He was southern born and educated through his undergraduate years, although he went north for his graduate work. Like Hartzog and Riggs, he was a native South Carolinian. Born in Gray Court, Laurens County, on December 2, 1893, he was the eldest of four boys and three girls born of Ula Barto and Lila Yeargin Poole. The family had a farm in South Carolina's Piedmont, which made Poole different from the other two South Carolinians from the Lowcountry. His ancestors had settled the land in 1788 and involved themselves actively in agricultural, educational, and religious enterprises.

Unlike any of his predecessors though, Poole spent his baccalaureate years at Clemson Agricultural College, where he studied agriculture. He was the first alumnus to serve as president of Clemson. He did not stray from his background when he entered the pursuit of botany. Through his childhood and youth, he had his share of farm chores. And like most southern rural children, he basically lived out-of-doors, working, playing, walking to school, and hunting, fishing, and gardening. The last three "loves" he carried throughout his life. His mother died when he was thirteen, requiring Poole and his siblings to take on additional household and farming chores. Like many rural youth, he earned his first dollar from the farm. In his early teens, he also earned money driving his uncle, a physician, on his medical rounds.

Having also participated in high school sports, Poole quickly joined the Clemson Tiger football team in 1912, his freshman year. In playing college football, he was like Riggs and Sikes. The 1912 team, coached by Frank Dobson, had a four-win, four-defeat season. Of course, as a freshman, Poole did not play. For 1913, Clemson changed head coaches, bringing in Bob Williams, who would remain through Poole's football career. In those three years, Clemson's team record was 11–11–3, with highlights of two victories and one tie with South Carolina and a headline-grabbing 3–0 upset of Tennessee in Knoxville in Poole's senior year.[1] Poole saw action in his senior year.

When Poole graduated from Clemson in 1916, he enrolled at Rutgers, New Jersey's land-grant college, where he began studying for a master's degree in plant pathology. But research toward his thesis was interrupted by the United States' entry into World War I. As an army sergeant first class, he went overseas in the winter of 1918 in the U.S. Army to Chatillon-sur-Seine, France, where he did aerial photographic work. At the end of hostilities (November 11, 1918), he then served in occupied Western Germany, a tour that lasted four months.

After World War I, he returned to Rutgers and began work toward his PhD. His research on the sweet potato won him recognition, and, in 1920, he obtained an appointment as assistant plant pathologist in the N.J. Agricultural Experiment Station. Rutgers granted him the PhD in 1921. This made Poole only the third Clemson president to earn the research doctorate and the only one from a non-southern (if Johns Hopkins is included in the South) university. Within the year, he became the experiment station's associate plant pathologist, where he remained until 1928.

President Robert Franklin Poole (*left*) and Trustee James Francis Byrnes on the porch of the Trustee House. Poole, the first alumnus (Clemson 1916) to be selected Clemson College president, served in World War I, earned his doctorate at Rutgers, and served as NC State's director/dean of graduate studies. He served as Clemson's seventh president from 1940 to 1958. Byrnes (1882–1972) was a Clemson life trustee and an active aid for arranging housing for returning veterans to Clemson in his position as director of the Office of War Mobilization. Byrnes was also a U.S. representative (1911–1925), U.S. senator (1931–1941), associate justice of the U.S. Supreme Court (1941–1942), U.S. secretary of state (1945–1947), and 104th governor of South Carolina (1951–1955). Clemson University Photographs, CUL.SC.

And importantly, on February 29, 1922, he married Sarah Margaret Bradley of Abbeville. She was the daughter of James Foster and Lillian Vernon Bradley, the niece of W. W. Bradley, a life trustee of Clemson Agricultural College from 1907 to his death in 1948 and president of the Board of Trustees from 1935 to 1948. Bradley had been elected to follow his father, J. E. Bradley, a will-appointed life trustee (1888–April 18, 1907). Another uncle, Mark Edward Bradley (1878–1971), served as professor of English at Clemson from 1901 to 1950.[2] Margaret and R. F. Poole brought five children—Robert Franklin, Thomas Bradley, Margaret Lillian, Mary Marcia, and William James—to the large Queen Anne style home of the president of Clemson.

But years before, Poole had joined NC State College in 1926 as an associate professor of plant pathology, continuing his research and publications. His inquiring mind, interest in plant research, and ability to write led him during his career to produce 130 articles, mostly in scholarly journals, and some published as USDA bulletins during the early years of his experiment station career. An additional thirty-six more general articles and twenty scientific papers contributed to his reputation as a leading plant scientist in the nation. Two years after his appointment to the NC State faculty, his department promoted him to professor, and just two years after that, he became director of the committee directing graduate instruction there, a position that in later years evolved into dean of the graduate school.

Poole's leadership in scholarly work contributed to his selection as president of the Southern Phytopathological Society and to active membership in the American Phytopathological Society and the American Mycology Society. As a college administrator, he served in 1938 as vice president of the Association of the Deans of Southern Graduate Schools. As a faculty member, he was a locally active member in the American Association of University Professors. He also served in a number of state and local professional organizations.

All scholarly and professional achievements aside, Poole was not a "shoo-in" for the post of Clemson's leader. There were other candidates. Some, such as J. C. Littlejohn, had many Clemson connections, while others possessed strong, but no better, scholarly records. But Poole, unlike the others, had an enviable résumé of academic administration. Further, with the exception of Littlejohn, he knew Clemson's cast of decision makers and was known by them better than any other candidate. Finally, his field of agriculture fit well with the economic needs of South Carolina. Thus, Board President W. W. Bradley announced with real pleasure that Poole would assume the presidency on July 1, 1940.[3]

Clemson in 1940

The Clemson that Poole received from Sikes was a far different place than the one he had left twenty-four years earlier. The college was nearly four times the size in students, faculty, and staff, and certainly stronger in faculty attainments, more diverse in degrees and courses offered, and much larger in land owned and/ or managed around all of South Carolina. Many of its buildings had been erected in the past fifteen years, others extensively renovated. The laboratories and the library were greatly improved. Social and intellectual outlets for the 2,381 students had grown immensely. Of those, 1,904 came from South Carolina; Clemson now enrolled one out of every thousand South Carolinians. The 1940 student enrollment also included 477 from twenty-five other states, the District of Columbia, U.S. territories, and foreign countries. Academically, 565 majored in agriculture, 1,007 in engineering, 327 in textiles, 189 in sciences, 149 in general science (mainly mathematics, sciences, and a few humanities fields), 14 in education, and the remainder in agricultural and industrial education. Thus, Clemson clung very closely to the original subject matter of "agriculture and mechanics" of the Land Grant Act of 1862 and to a close interpretation of the will of Thomas Green Clemson. The total enrollment in 1940 remained Clemson's all-time high until 1946–1947.[4]

Compared to the other "stand-alone" southern land-grant colleges—Virginia Tech (VPI), North Carolina State, Auburn (API), Mississippi State, and Texas A&M—Clemson was fourth in size (although first in percentage of in-state students when compared to total state residents and in the other measurable characteristics). It trailed its fellow land-grant institutions in developing new fields, such as forestry and automotive and aeronautical engineering, and in creating and sustaining advanced degrees and faculty research. Such basic problems remained until at least 1955, having to await solutions until well after another most destructive and costly global war.

The Spreading War

Those war clouds had been building in Asia since 1931 and in Africa and Europe for almost as long. The broadened European conflagration finally erupted in early September 1939 after Adolf Hitler's Germany had signed a nonaggression treaty with Soviet Russia on August 23. Poland was Nazi Germany's first military victim. Hitler, Germany's dictator, and Stalin, Russia's dictator, agreed to divide Poland between them. But even though Great Britain and France had guaranteed Poland's security, neither made any major military move until after Poland surrendered less than a month following the start of Germany's invasion.

The European conflict widened. Britain hoped to establish the sort of naval blockade that had been so effective in World War I. But to work this time, Britain had to interrupt the industrial trade between Sweden, a declared neutral, and Germany. To prevent such, Germany attacked Norway on April 9, 1940, and, although Great Britain landed troops there, German submarines torpedoed British

Clemson's Civil Air Patrol moved under the jurisdiction of the Army ROTC in October 1939. Clemson University Photographs, CUL.SC.

ships. Norway fell to the Nazis, and a puppet government was installed there. A month later, Germany invaded Western Europe. The Netherlands surrendered in five days. Belgium resisted until late May. France surrendered on June 10, 1940, and Britain managed to evacuate some 220,000 of its Expeditionary troops from Dunkirk. Such was the European condition when Poole became Clemson's seventh president.

During these years of threats and war, a strong isolationism dominated the American public and government. However, using authority derived from the National Defense Act of 1920, the government of Franklin D. Roosevelt began planning for agricultural, industrial, and economic security. These quickly involved America's land-grant colleges, including the experiment stations, whose concerns included food safety and productivity, and the extension services, which shared the same concerns, but also dealt with food distribution and the replacement of manpower taken from productivity for military needs.

Military personnel needs were harder to initiate. After the September 1938 Munich crisis, President Roosevelt had invited military and other American public leaders to the White House on November 14. As a result, the War Department developed the Protective Mobilization Plan, which by July 1, 1939, increased the active army to nearly 190,000 troops. Of those, about 50,000 were stationed overseas. In addition, the National Guard had some 200,000, and the reserves held another 110,000. Then, in October 1939, the land-grant college civil air patrol training units were moved into the Army ROTC.[5] With the German invasion of Poland, increased military strength was approved, although it took the German success in Western Europe in May and June 1940 for the U.S. Congress to approve induction of the National Guard and pass the Selective Service Act, which Roosevelt signed on September 23. Because it took time to build new and expanded training bases, few Americans were inducted until January 1941.[6] Registration for the selective service initially involved all male citizens between the ages of twenty-one and thirty-six. This changed to ages twenty to forty-five on December 20, 1941, shortly after Japan bombed Pearl Harbor and the United States entered World War II.[7] Colleges and universities felt the impact initially, until late 1942, only in losing to the draft older students, particularly graduate students, and younger faculty. The Clemson graduates of June 1941 barely had time to savor the moment. Many of them recalled later, "We received our diplomas on one side of the stage and military orders on the other, wondering what was in store for us."[8]

Clemson Students

Student life at Clemson College remained "usual" from 1940 through July 1, 1943. The Board of Trustees formalized the graduation ring design to take effect July 1, 1940. Early that year, the board also approved a student-requested $75 (2009 equivalent $1,175) per student per annum lyceum fee for "name" lectures and for first-class musical productions. Within the first year, the musical productions, called the Concert Series, achieved great popularity with both the students and the community. The initiative for the program had begun in the junior class during the spring of 1940.[9]

Other student activities continued. *Taps* from 1941 to 1943 provided an excellent record of them, as did *The Tiger* for the weekly news. Other publications, including the *Agrarian* and the *Bobbin and Beaker*, also appeared. The campus-wide scholastic honorary society, Phi Kappa Phi, remained influential. Academic societies in various subjects grew in prestige. Among them were the oldest, Phi Psi (textiles), whose president was W. H. Carder, and the eighteen-member Tau Beta Pi (engineering) led by Wilson C. Wearn, who became a leading figure in South Carolina's communications industry in the second half of the twentieth century.

The student leadership societies prospered. The eldest, Tiger Brotherhood, had a membership of forty-one students. After the death of former President Enoch Sikes, Tiger Brotherhood resolved to place a wreath at his grave each year on the anniversary of his death. Blue Key, inspired by the recently published biography of Thomas Green Clemson, co-authored by Prof. Alester G. Holmes and former Prof. George Sherrill, coordinated a fund-raising drive among the student organizations to erect a statue of Clemson. The sculptor was A. Wolfe Davidson, a Clemson alumnus. Donations to this effort came also from alumni. The monument, located

A. Wolfe Davidson (1903–1981), a Russian émigré and a Clemson student for one year, with an early model of the statue he created of Thomas Green Clemson. The statue was a gift of all the students and some alumni to the college in 1941. Clemson University Photographs, CUL.SC.

in front of the Main Building, was dedicated during Farm and Home Week in the summer of 1941.[10]

Graduations also continued but with a basic downward trend in numbers: 359 in 1940–41, 300 in 1941–1942, and 329 in 1942–1943. This mirrored a slight decline in overall Clemson student enrollment from 2,381 in fall 1940 to 2,322 in fall 1942, a decline of approximately 2.4 percent.[11] The national decline during that same period was 9.2 percent, or about four times Clemson's. Most of the decline nationally was caused by uncertainty or enlistment rather than draft. Clemson, in that period, would have only seventy-one students withdraw to enter military service.[12]

Academics

Between 1940 and 1942, the faculty fell slightly in numbers from 173 males in September 1940 to 171 (including one female, Marie Porcher Jones) by June 1943. However, between 1943 and 1945, forty-three faculty were on military leave, for reasons varying from combat service to government-funded scientific work (a faculty decrease of 26 percent). To cover the losses, Poole retained eleven faculty and nine administrative staff who had passed retirement age. Remaining faculty, most between the ages of forty and sixty-five, taught more class sections and more students per section. Given the ages of most of the academic facilities, it was nearly impossible to increase the number of laboratory sections or the number of student spaces in them.[13]

Curriculum offerings neither expanded nor contracted. Poole hesitated to move the college more into graduate work, believing that laboratory and library resources along with faculty research records were not sufficient to sustain such a program. Nor was he open to curricular innovation. To the National Fertilizer Association's June 1941 meeting, he deplored the impregnating of the curricula with sociology, economics, psychology, and other subjects. "We wish to stop them," Poole said. Some Clemson faculty, including George Aull, were appalled at the president's words.[14]

But for the other missions of research and service, the food-growing crisis produced by the war-induced manpower shortage found the work pace hastening. In experiment work, regional canneries were erected to help farm families, particularly women, improve food safety and extend shelf life.[15] Clemson's scientists continued enhancing strains in vegetables such as cucumbers and sweet potatoes.[16] And with support from the Williams-Waterman Fund of the Research Corporation of New York, the S.C. General Assembly, and the Bell Laboratories, the experiment station developed corn meal with vitamin B-1, which eliminated the pellagra scourge.[17]

All of this took time and was reinforced by memoranda from Claude R. Wickard, secretary of agriculture, which placed the responsibility for stopping food waste and for developing better systems of food use and preservation on both the local communities and a number of federal agencies. Because of its local distribution and relationship with the community, much of this effort passed to the land-grant colleges' extension services. The food supply itself would only become critical with the full entrance of North America's nations into the war.[18]

This in no way diminished the other roles that extension services continued to play around the nation, including in South Carolina, without adequate government support. One was the rapidly enlarging 4-H program, designed initially to educate pre-college boys and young men in the newest and best agricultural methods of increasing agricultural production while conserving resources. By 1933, the first South Carolina 4-H Camp, named Camp Long in honor of W. W. Long, Clemson Cooperative Extension Service director, was built through the efforts of Monson Morris, a New York winter resident in Aiken. Federal funds were used to extend the camp substantially. By 1936, conservation camps for white youth were being held there. A second camp, now named for Robert Muldrow Cooper, a Clemson trustee and an official of the Santee-Cooper Authority, was donated to the extension service by Santee-Cooper. By 1942, the first African American 4-H Club Conservation Camp was held at SC State College, the 1890 land-grant institution in South Carolina.[19] All of these capital and annual expenses were not covered adequately in federal or state monetary distributions. Donors frequently made up the deficits in food and materials, particularly as programming expanded more completely.

By September 1940, Clemson Extension Director D. W. Watkins served on the State Agricultural Planning Committee, as chair of the State Nutrition Committee, and as a major director of the conference that developed a southern states nutrition program.[20] Other responsibilities that fell to the extension service included peach pit retrieval for gas mask filtration war use, neighborhood leadership programs, and rural electrification, increasing the miles of strung electrical wire in South Carolina between 1935 and July 1942 by twenty-five times. Civil engineers educated at Clemson, USC, and the Citadel did much of this work.[21]

Increased Academic Opportunities

In preparation for the coming war, land-grant schools and a number of other institutions began offering nondegree extension courses in industrial skills. Usually, the education involved faculty in mathematics, industrial education, textiles, and engineering going to rapidly expanding industrial and factory sites to teach workers to read technical instructions and master production skills. Clemson, with its long commitment to vocational upgrading opportunities, operated short course education in agriculture and textiles and had helped with faculty staffing for the early (1914) pioneering programs of Wil Lou Gray. The state government incorporated her approach in 1921 in the South Carolina Opportunity School (which, in 1976, the legislature renamed the Wil Lou Gray Opportunity School). Other faculty went to public schools and county extension stations to teach women, men, and youth—black and white—to read and thus be able to join the industrial work force. In addition, a number of women in the area came to the Clemson campus regularly for short courses in welding, using the new electric welding tools made possible by the transformer invented by Thomas Hunter, Clemson 1909. The women, and other newly trained workers, went to the shipyards and the factories around the nation to help in the building of armaments. When the number of faculty traveling warranted it, the teachers would go by rail, reminiscent of the travel at the turn of the past century, and would usually be gone from the campus for two days and nights. Their campus work was handled by the remaining faculty.[22]

Forestry provided another area of expansion at Clemson. Landholding had begun moving from labor-intensive farming to less-intensive tree farming in the early 1920s. The efforts of President Sikes, agricultural planners, and some alumni to establish forestry programs in teaching, research, and extension over the years, but particularly in the 1930s, had been discouraged by legislative leaders and some Clemson trustees and upper level administrators. Even after the land management arrangement developed by George Aull provided more-than-adequate forestry research land, the efforts appeared stymied.

However, in most European societies, forests and woodlands had been considered, in part, under the management of the central authority, regardless of how small the unit. Great Britain provided the essential model for the United States, and it had a long tradition of royal forests with their divisions into woodlands, chases, and parks. The prerogative of the royal agents to "mark" suitable trees for building or naval use was one of the complaints of colonists everywhere. It is of more than passing interest that about the time of the "closing" of the American frontier, extension, protection, selective harvesting, and reforestation moved to the forefront. By 1911, the efforts toward management and control authorized the enlargement of the national forest system. In 1924, the Clarke-McNary Act extended the authority of USDA to work with owners of forestlands on refor-estation. In addition, the act encouraged states to create forest agencies ranging from schools of forestry to forest extension units within the existing extension divisions. This had been the impetus for President Sikes and others to urge the trustees and the legislature to establish and help fund a forestry program at Clem-son, which they did not do. By 1937, the federal government, now involved in land reclamation, sought through the Norris-Doxey Act to extend the productive forestlands. Although Clemson College had taught forestry courses since 1903, in 1926, using funds provided by the Clarke-McNary Act, the college hired H. H. Tryon as the first extension forester. After his resignation in 1927, the position had been left vacant.[23]

As the government of South Carolina also became more aware of the impor-tance of timber to the state's economy, it created the State Forestry Commission, whose chief operational officer was the state forester. As Poole's administration began, the state forester asked the Clemson Extension Service for help in its first effort to distribute seedlings. David Watkins, extension director, hesitated to be-come involved until some confusion and uncertainty in USDA about the two federal acts cleared. The concerns soon resolved themselves, and by December 1940, Marlin Bruner, Clemson extension forester, worked to distribute 179,000 pine seedlings in Aiken County alone. The seedlings were provided by the ex-panding pulp and paper industry in the state.[24] However, the multiple layers of federal, state, and extension authority caused confusion, particularly at the local level.[25]

Athletics

Besides the changes in personnel toward war-readiness and *The Tiger* notices of alumni being moved to active duty, much of the college's life went on as usual. The great successes in intercollegiate sports at the end of Sikes's administration had raised the hopes of most Clemson supporters. Football was the leader. Since 1934, its fortunes had been on the upswing, climaxing in the 1938 and 1939 seasons in which Clemson accumulated a 16–1–1 record, including two second place finishes in the Southern Conference, winning the Cotton Bowl, and achiev-ing a twelfth place ranking in the nation.[26]

The number of alumni (not graduates) had exceeded 12,000, the cadet corps had reached 2,300 (or triple the number when Riggs Field was built), and the

Aerial photograph of campus with Memorial Stadium as it appeared during a 1943 game. Clemson University Photographs, CUL.SC.

old playing field, with its small 3,000-permanent-seat capacity (expandable with wooden bleachers and stands to create a "wooden O" for several thousand more), obviously was inadequate to meet the demand. Discussions had begun to build a larger football facility. In fact, when he bid Frank Howard goodbye, departing Coach Jesse Neely cautioned the newly hired athletic director and head coach not to rush into adding more than a few thousand seats. It was no surprise, then, when the Board of Trustees received from President Sikes (without comment) proposals from Clemson's Athletic Council calling for the relocation of the facility, to provide more seating and better parking for the increasingly more mobile public.[27]

The general assembly, basking in the reflected lights of Clemson's year-old Cotton Bowl win and the recently won 1940 Southern Conference football championship, authorized the issuance of $100,000 in bonds (Act 180) to build a new facility. These were to be redeemed by a portion of the admissions fee to future Clemson games. By July 1941, notice of the bond offering ran in the *State*.[28]

The site chosen was a western campus ravine just southwest of the newly dedicated Field House. It was below Fort Hill house, and, prophetically, to the north of Woodland Cemetery, where lay the remains of some of the Calhouns and of President Walter Merritt Riggs. The body of President Enoch Walter Sikes was added during the stadium's construction. During the spring of 1941, football play-

Engineering faculty from the 1941 edition of the Clemson College annual, *Taps. Front row, left to right:* D. H. Shenk, John Logan Marshall, Elwyn Lorenzo "Will Rogers" Clarke, Dean Samuel Broadus Earle, Rudolph "Pop" Edward Lee, Bernhard Edward Fernow, Howard Emmitt "Pop" Glenn, Samuel Roseborough "Slim" Rhodes. *Second row, left to right:* F. T. Tingley, A. B. Credle, G. N. Gaylord, A. M. Quattlebaum, L. A. King, G. E. Hoffman, J. E. Shingley, S. M. Watson. *Third row, left to right:* Edwin Jones Freeman, J. B. Downs, R. L. Anderson, D. W. Bradbury, D. D. Curtis, C. D. Philpot. *Fourth row, left to right:* W. M. Wachter, G. C. McMakin, W. D. Stevenson, Williston Wightman "Wee Willie" Klugh, E. B. Therkelson. *Fifth row, left to right:* W. F. D. Hodge, L. R. Ambrose, D. L. Parrott, D. N. Harris.

ers cleared the hillsides, and the upper level civil engineering students undertook the preliminary surveying under the direction of Prof. H. E. "Pop" Glenn. Glenn, along with Carl Lee, a 1908 Clemson graduate in engineering, designed the stadium and made the construction drawings. Because of the lay of the land, the field ran east-west, while most outdoor fields lie north-south. The seating rose on the north and south banks to the top of the ravine (and thus stopped at grade level with no portals.) When completed, the stadium seated about 20,000 spectators.[29]

During the summer of 1941, Coach Howard, his small staff (none including Howard received extra compensation), and the returning football team prepared the playing surface. And on September 5, 1941, the C. Y. Thomason Construction Company of Greenwood won the contract and construction commenced.[30] Because of the terrain and to minimize costs initially, the stadium had no team dressing rooms or spectator restroom facilities. These were located in the new Field House. Nor was there plumbing or electricity. Plans developed to move the press box over from Riggs Field. The stadium was first used on September 19, 1942, in a 32–13 victory over Presbyterian College. To that point, Frank Howard's Tigers had compiled a 13–4–1 record. For the duration of the era (1940–1945), the football record was twenty-two wins, twenty-one losses, and two ties.[31]

The winter sports, boxing and basketball, found their home in the nearly completed Field House, and on April 11, 1941, the multipurpose facility, built in three stages during the past twelve years, was finally dedicated. The two gyms provided space for intercollegiate, intramural, and "free-play" sports. And they served as the venue for cadet dances and for concerts where many rising stars of classical music, opera, and drama performed for students, faculty, community, and out-of-town guests. The Field House also had a two-story balconied lobby with trophy cases, ticket office, staff offices, and some twenty-three dormitory rooms with group bathrooms that frequently accommodated visiting teams. Below were team dressing rooms and bathroom, and equipment rooms. For the last football season on Riggs Field (1941), the players walked from the new dressing rooms east across the baseball field to the gridiron.

The big gym in the Field House could present a real challenge for visiting teams (not football) because of its "special features." With the interior tapestry brick, high windows placed to accommodate "roll-away" bleachers, and incandescent lights, the gym was rather dark. In addition, the gym had no reserved or even marked spectator seats. The cadets and the community squeezed in on each other and pressed closely in on the Tiger team, their opponents, the coaches, the timer, and the scorer. But the crowded space was not much different from the gymnasiums in comparable Southern Conference institutions.[32]

The basketball team in the years 1940–1942 did not finish as strongly as it had between 1938 and 1940. In two years, the Tigers won only eleven of forty games. Boxing, coached by Bob Jones and Walter Cox, won one-third of their matches. Track fared much better, garnering four state event records and winning the state track championship once. Swimming, tennis, riflery, and baseball all had winning records from 1940 to 1942.[33]

Although the students, many parents, faculty, and alumni appeared pleased with Clemson's sports teams' performance, Poole was uneasy. He perceived that intercollegiate athletics had started drifting toward professionalism rather than "developing health-mindedness" among student athletes. Although he found no blame at Clemson, he contended that the student athlete should meet the same academic standards as any other student.[34] This issue had emerged nationwide almost since the beginning of competition and at Clemson since Walter Merritt Riggs had urged rules keeping "gypsy athletes" out of intercollegiate play.

"Tiger Rag"

Between 1940 and 1942, Clemson College gave birth to another tradition. This would also be musical. Robert Dean Ross, cadet bandmaster of the Clemson Corps band, with another cadet, hitchhiked on a 1941 September Saturday to Atlanta, Georgia, to look for new music for the band. Rummaging through different scores, the cadets found sheet music for "Tiger Rag." The Louisiana State University and A&M College Tigers, or "Bayou Bengals," had occasionally used the tune, but more often than not they played "Fight for LSU" (usually known as "Like Knights of Old"). Ross bought the band score for $1.50 from the Old Southern Music Company and brought it back to Clemson. Paul Yoder had done the arrangement. The eighty-three-member band learned it quickly and, with the connivance of the head cheerleader, used it after every touchdown during the 7–2–0 season in 1941. Ross recalled, "The cadets warmed up slowly to the tune." But it stuck and eventually proved wildly popular.

Robert Dean Ross, the cadet bandmaster who introduced "Tiger Rag" as a Clemson fight song. Taken from the 1943 (his junior year) edition of the Clemson College annual, *Taps*.

Ross was drafted in 1943 and served in the U.S. Third Army under Patton. He returned and graduated from Clemson in 1947.[35] After World War II, "Tiger Rag" became so closely associated with Clemson's Tigers, that of its two mentions in *The Guide to United States Popular Culture*, one references lyrics developed for the Mills Brothers in the 1930s, while the other notes "Clemson anonymous tune for 'Tiger Rag' (1917)."[36]

Over There

Even before Japan attacked the United States, and America declared war on Japan, Germany, and Italy, Clemson alumni in the military services along with other troops had moved into areas where the War Department had grave concerns. These men ranged from veterans of World War I to newly awarded baccalaureates.

One of Clemson's World War I veterans was Frank Johnstone Jervey (1893–1983). A native of Summerville, he attended Porter Military Academy and enrolled at Clemson to study electrical and mechanical engineering. While at Clemson, Jervey played intramural football for his class and was a cheerleader, athletic editor for *The Tiger*, active in the YMCA, in a number of dance clubs, and recipient of the R. W. Simpson Award in 1914 for the best cadet. After graduation, he worked in engineering at the Charleston Navy Yard and then moved to the Winchester Repeating Arms Company in New Haven, Connecticut. Jervey entered World War I in 1917, served as a captain in the Fourth U.S. Infantry Regiment in the Third Infantry Division, and suffered a near-killing wound near Chateau Thierry in France. The "Captain," as all his Clemson friends knew him, lost a leg there. Among his many military honors, he received the U.S. Distinguished Service Cross and the Italian Merito di Guerra for his valor. Following recuperation, he returned to the Army Department as an ordnance engineer. Advancing in position because of thoroughness, accuracy, and timeliness, he became one of the armed force's most respected authorities on small arms.[37]

A second Clemson alumnus who served in the U.S. Army in World War II was Floyd Lavinius Parks. Born in Louisville, Kentucky, he came to Clemson from Anderson. As a student, he played on his class tennis and basketball teams. Active in the Calhoun Literary Society, he served as class editor for *Taps*, literary editor of the *Chronicle*, and editor-in-chief of *The Tiger*. He graduated in mechanical and electrical engineering and reached the rank of major in the cadet corps.[38] After graduation, he joined the U.S. Army, serving in the first Tank Corps unit under the command of Capt. Dwight D. Eisenhower (1918–1923). He earned an MS in engineering from Yale in 1924. By 1935, he had graduated from the Army Command and General Staff School (Fort Leavenworth, Kansas) and by 1940 from the Army War College. In March 1942, he received appointment as deputy chief of staff under Lt. Gen. Lesley J. McNair. Then in June 1942, Parks was promoted to brigadier general. He served as chief of staff of the First Allied Airborne and succeeded as commander with the First Airborne Army. He served as military governor of Berlin from July to October 1945. Until his retirement in 1956, he continued in executive capacities in the army. Parks received the Distinguished Service Medal (twice), the Legion of Merit, the Bronze Star, and the Air Medal. He also received the Soviet Order of Kutuzov and was invested with the British Order of the Bath. Parks and Eisenhower were frequent golfing partners. Twice married, Parks had four children with his second wife, Harriet Marie Appleby-Robinson.[39]

Floyd Lavinius Parks, Clemson 1918, was promoted to brigadier general in 1942, served as chief of staff of the First Allied Airborne, and served as military governor of Berlin from July to October 1945. Taken from the 1918 edition of the Clemson College annual, *Taps*.

A Clemson man who died very early in the European war was William B. Inabinet. Born in Bishopville in September 1918, he entered Clemson in 1937 to study animal husbandry. He spent his first year in First Regiment Company H, led by Otis Morgan from Laurens. Inabinet was a member of the rifle team and in his second year joined Alpha Zeta honorary society. In September 1939, when Stalin's and Hitler's armies coordinated their attack on Poland, Inabinet went to Canada and joined the Eagle Squadron with other Canadian and American young men. They shipped out to the United Kingdom and were inducted into the Royal Air Force. The Germans shot his plane down over the coast of England, whereupon he was buried in Surrey and was one of Clemson's first eleven war casualties remembered in a memorial service on December 7, 1942, on campus.[40]

Other alumni already served in the areas of conflict. Ben F. Robertson Jr. (1903–1943), son of a Clemson faculty member, had been an active student. "Millie," as he was called, had served on the *Taps* staff and in his senior year served

Ben Franklin Robertson Jr., Clemson 1923, authored the book *I Saw England* and wrote for many newspapers and news bureaus in the U.S. and in Europe, including heading the New York *Herald Tribune*'s London office. Clemson University Photographs, CUL.SC.

as editor-in-chief. In addition, he edited the *Chronicle*, sang in the glee club, played in the orchestra, played the piano, and held membership in the Palmetto Literary Society. In 1923, he graduated with a BS degree in horticulture and went on to the University of Missouri for an MS degree in its famed school of journalism. From there, he served on the staff of the Adelaide, Australia, *News* until 1929, when he returned to be a reporter for the New York *Herald Tribune*. In 1934, he spent a year with the Associated Press, first in Washington, D.C., and then in London. After a year, he joined the United Press, staying for two years. Most of 1937 was spent working in the flooding of the Ohio and Tennessee rivers and then as a seaman on a voyage to Australia. Back in Britain, he worked for *PM*, a privately funded newspaper that accepted no advertisements. He watched the opening of Germany's blitzkrieg of London in the city and from Dover.[41] His significant book *I Saw England* played a role in helping move Americans away from isolationism. Edward R. Murrow interviewed him on his international radio programs. A stint with the Chicago *Sun* took him to Guam, Midway, India, Russia, and Egypt. Then in December 1942, Robertson headed the New York *Herald Tribune*'s London office. He flew to Europe to assume the new post in February 1943 on the *Yankee Clipper*. As the airplane approached the Lisbon, Portugal, airport, it crashed in the Tagus River, killing Robertson.[42]

Four young Clemson graduates served in the Philippines as U.S. Army officers. They, with some 24,000 other Americans, helped to build the new Philippine National Army.[43] Among them was Marion "Manny" Lawton, Clemson

1940, from Estill. After his graduation from Clemson, Lawton, who had served as an executive officer in the Clemson cadet corps, took a "crash course" at the Army Infantry School. Now he advised the Philippine Army's First Battalion.[44] Henry D. Leitner, who graduated in textile engineering in 1937, had worked for Sirrine and Company in Greenville and was married.[45] Otis Morgan, Clemson 1938, hailed from Laurens. He had served as associate editor of *The Tiger* and president of the Central Dance Association, gained membership in Alpha Chi Psi social fraternity, and received recognition in the national student *Who's Who*.[46] Beverly N. "Ben" Skardon, Clemson 1938, one of four sons of an Episcopal clergyman, was born in St. Francisville, Louisiana, but grew up in Walterboro. His older brother had already graduated from Clemson by the time Ben enrolled. A younger brother graduated a year after Ben, and the youngest was due to graduate in June 1942.

Four Clemson men who served in World War II and were imprisoned in the Philippines. *Left to right*: Manny Lawton, Clemson 1940, advised the Philippine Army's First Battalion; Henry D. Leitner, Clemson 1937; Otis R. Morgan, Clemson 1938; and Beverly N. "Ben" Skardon, Clemson 1938. Unfortunately, only Lawton and Skardon returned from service, as Leitner and Morgan died aboard sinking Japanese transport ships or "hell ships." Photos taken from each cadet's senior class edition of the Clemson College annual, *Taps*.

Although he began in engineering, Skardon moved to general science with a major in English. He soon joined *The Tiger* staff and in his senior year served as managing editor at the same time that Leitner served as associate editor. Skardon also joined the student regional club the Colletonians, composed of young men from Colleton County; Beta Sigma Chi, more a social fraternity but limited to cadets whose homes were within fifty miles of Charleston; the Central Dance Association; and Tiger Brotherhood. In the college military, he served as battalion commander and in his senior year was also listed in *Who's Who in American Colleges and Universities*. Graduating in June 1938, he was too young to be commissioned. He spent the next years teaching school, first at Riverside Military Academy (Gainesville, Georgia) and then in the Yemassee Consolidated School.

After being commissioned in the army and detailed to Fort Benning, Georgia, Skardon asked for an overseas assignment. A cross-continental automobile drive with Manny Lawton got them to San Francisco, from where they shipped out to the Philippines. A twenty-day crossing brought them to the islands on October 23, 1941. Their work with the Philippine infantry let him observe quickly that the young men were armed with obsolete, late nineteenth century British rifles. Skardon and Lawton had separate assignments. Skardon's Philippine unit moved to Manila, entering Manila Bay on December 6, 1941. The next day, while Skardon and his men remained on board the steamer *Le Gaspé*, another American, 1ˢᵗ Lt. George Coburn (State University of Iowa), who was on the bridge, received word that the Japanese Air Force had bombed the U.S. Naval Base at Pearl Harbor, Honolulu, in the American territory of Hawaii. It was the morning of Sunday, December 7, 1941. Skardon and his unit moved to block a feared and expected Japanese invasion of the Philippines.[47] For the United States, "it" had begun.

Home at Clemson

That day and moment struck hard in Clemson. The townsfolk, cadets, and college faculty, with their families, had settled in after church and their Sunday dinners for the remainder of the "day of rest and gladness." For the faculty, this provided a break from the Monday to 1:00 p.m. Saturday classes and the 200 to 250 students each taught. A number of the young, single faculty lived in the large, white-frame Clemson College Hotel, which overlooked Bowman Field. One of them, Penn Brewster, a mathematics professor, whose nickname "Speedy" marked his reputation for erasing his chalk notations nearly as fast as he marked them on the blackboard, invited three other young men to his room to play bridge. As one of them dealt the cards, Ernest "Whitey" Lander, an instructor in history, political science, and economics, asked Brewster to turn on music. Brewster dialed the radio to Sammy Kaye's "Sunday Serenade." As the music played, a newscaster interrupted to say, "We interrupt this program to bring you this news flash. The Imperial Japanese Air Force has bombed the United States Naval Base at Pearl Harbor...." The news left the faculty stunned.[48]

At the same time, Morris Cox, assistant professor of English, was walking from his campus home to the Main Building (now Tillman Hall), and he heard the news when an automobile slowed down and the driver shouted it to him. Cox turned in his tracks and headed back to his wife, Irene Todd Cox, and to his home, called "Radio House" because it had earlier served as the studio for the first commercial radio station in the Upstate. They turned on the radio and heard the news commentator H. V. Kaltenborn suggest that the attack must have been made by a renegade group within the Japanese military.[49]

It took only a few hours to dispel that thought. By the morning, the campus, like the rest of the nation, understood what it meant, and radios everywhere tuned to the broadcasting networks to hear President Roosevelt tell a quickly assembled joint session of the U.S. Congress, "Yesterday, December 7, 1941, a date which will live in infamy, the United States of America was suddenly and deliberately attacked by naval and air forces of the Empire of Japan."

After giving a few details of prior diplomatic efforts with Japan and the hours leading to the unexpected attack, Roosevelt noted that "very many American lives have been lost. In addition, American ships have been reported torpedoed on the high seas between San Francisco and Honolulu." Then he quickly counted off other targets, American and otherwise, that had been attacked: Malaya and Hong Kong (British Empire), Guam, the Philippines, Wake Island, and Midway Island (United States). And, he concluded, "With confidence in our armed forces, with the unbounding determination of our people, we will gain the inevitable triumph. So help us God." Both houses of Congress swiftly declared war on Japan. Four days later, Hitler's Germany declared war on the United States. America found itself at war in both the Pacific and Europe.

For the student body in the Clemson community, December 1941 and the winter and spring of 1942 did not change matters appreciably, although anxiety rose. Few were called into service. Sports continued as before. *The Tiger* appeared regularly, and *Taps* made its annual appearance. The student enrollment fell from 2,349 in the autumn of 1941 to 2,139 at the high point of the winter and spring terms of 1942. And an additional seventy-one cadets left for military service between January and June 1942.[50] To meet the immediate possibilities, the Board of Trustees gave the faculty permission to determine which of those cadets had successfully completed no less than seven semesters and, if acceptable to the faculty, to grant those students their diplomas. In addition, on consultation with the deans, each of whom headed an academic division, the board moved graduation date to May 25, 1942.[51]

Besides the decrease in students, younger faculty and professional staff whose reserve commissions were activated disappeared. By mid-March 1942, thirty-two of the faculty and staff had gone on military leave. The draft cut deeper as manpower became increasingly in shorter supply, so that by the spring of 1944, 105 faculty and staff were on military leave. Covering suddenly vacated classroom lecterns, merging classes into larger sections, or increasing the number of classes a faculty member taught fell to the deans and the department heads, who also had to convince former colleagues to return from retirement to the classroom. If the replacement was over sixty-five years old, Board of Trustees approval was needed. Eventually, the top age of the faculty rose from the board's set age of sixty-five to seventy-seven.[52]

Overseas

But the winter news from the two major war fronts continued to worsen. The news from Asia was grim. The Japanese had begun the invasion of the Philippines on December 10, 1941, and under Gen. Douglas MacArthur, the small band of American military moved toward Bataan as Japanese pressure grew. By February 15, British forces surrendered Singapore; two weeks later the Japanese sank both the United States carrier *Langley* and the largest American warship in the Pacific, the *Houston*. Equally as threatening to Americans was news that in late February, a Japanese submarine shelled an oil refinery at Santa Barbara, California. On March 18, 1942, the United States began moving about 120,000 Japanese-Americans into barbed-wire internment camps in the U.S.

The Japanese had two strategic goals, to gain control of the oriental race parts of Asia and to establish a defensive perimeter in the western Pacific Ocean. Included were the Solomon Islands, New Guinea, the Philippines, along with Thailand, Malaya, Singapore, the Gilbert Islands, the Netherlands East Indies, and Wake Island, all of which Japan attacked in early 1942. The Japanese captured Tulagi that spring, but they were repelled in May at the Battle of the Coral Sea, which was followed in June by the American victory at Midway Island. The next major step in the Allied offensive was the recapture of Tulagi. One of the Marine officers directing that campaign was Lt. Col. O. K. Pressley.[53]

Orin Kirkpatrick Pressley, from Lowrys, Chester County, had graduated from Clemson in animal husbandry in 1929. He had attained the rank of second lieutenant and served as junior class vice president and captain of the football team. He was named a third team All-American, Clemson's first for the honor.[54]

Aquilla James "Jimmie" Dyess (1909–1944), Clemson 1931, received America's highest military decoration. A redhead from North Augusta, he was educated at First Presbyterian Church and at Richmond Academy, a public boys military school, and was an active Boy Scout in the Augusta Sea Scout troop in Augusta, Georgia. He played football and worked in his father's lumber company. The latter probably influenced his desire to become an architect. Dyess likely chose Clemson for several reasons: its military, its football, and its architecture program. At Clemson he perfected his riflery marksmanship, serving on the regional team and rising to the rank of cadet major and commander of the first battalion. During the summer after his initial year at Clemson, while at the beach on Sullivan's Island, Dyess risked his life to save separately two young ladies who were being swept out to sea. When he reached shore with the two, he successfully gave one artificial respiration, while the other, after gagging, recovered. He received the Carnegie Medal for bravery, given by the Carnegie Hero Fund Commission.

Dyess returned to Clemson and in 1931 received his BS degree in architecture. A varsity football letterman, he was also active in Minarets, the student

Aquilla James "Jimmie" Dyess (1909–1944), a major in the U.S. Marine Corps, received the Medal of Honor after his death in the Battle of Roi-Namur on February 1, 1944. Clemson University Photographs, CUL.SC.

architectural society, and served as president of Kappa Phi, his local fraternity.[55] After graduation, Dyess returned to Augusta and started at the bottom of the family business. He married in 1934, and a baby girl was born to the couple some ten months later.

By 1936, upon the formation of a Marine Reserve battalion, Dyess received permission for an interservice transfer from the Army Reserve. His Marine unit was activated in November 1940, then split up, and Dyess was sent to Norfolk, Virginia, and from there, in March 1941, to the barrage balloon unit. By November 1942, Maj. Dyess had transferred to a Marine Infantry battalion and to the Pacific Ocean campaign. In July 1943, the United States moved onto offense against the Japanese. The first objective would be to conquer the Marshall Islands, which the Japanese had seized from Germany in World War I when Japan had been an ally of the British Empire. In the attack on the Marshalls, Adm. Chester Nimitz, commander-in-chief of the Pacific Fleet, elected to bypass the outer island and focus on Roi-Namur, where a major Japanese air base and supply facility were located, and on Kwajalein, the larger of the two islands. This dual island operation, which involved the U.S. Army, Navy, and Marine Corps, was risky because its plans involved several innovations. The United States used underwater demolition swimming teams to clear the way for the armada, and attack airplanes were fitted with air-to-ground, high-velocity rockets to assault the Japanese entrenched in fortified positions. Third, the American forces had new, better-armored, and heavily armed but untested landing craft.

Col. Jimmie Dyess boarded such a vessel on the morning of February 1, 1944. Although not overly fatalistic, the Clemson graduate, a husband, father, and Presbyterian, signed his will, saying to his lawyer friend, "…I'm going to be killed on this operation." Heavy American air attack had begun on January 29, and naval destroyers moved in close to pound the ground. At 1:30 a.m. on February first, the 54,000 U.S. combatants arose to dress, eat, and arm. The conflict lasted two days, with Dyess serving as de facto regimental commander. He was killed directing the fire ahead of himself. His roles of being on the front line of an assault, assuming leadership without command, and personally moving behind the enemy lines to rescue four wounded and about-to-be-killed men in his unit were more than brave. Dyess's men recovered his body and carried it back to the landing beaches for transport back home. Later, he received the Medal of Honor posthumously.[56]

For the American forces on the Philippines, Ben Skardon and his Clemson colleagues with their Philippine men-in-arms, the final Japanese assault on

Bataan began on April 3, 1942. The small army, unsupplied and unreinforced, held out until April 9, when they had to surrender unconditionally. About 64,000 Philippine nationals and 12,000 Americans were taken prisoners. The Japanese called them "captives" rather than "prisoners of war" (POWs). The Japanese then marched them—with quickly diminishing food supplies, few, if any, medical supplies, tattered uniforms, and with more and more captives shoeless—through blazing heat. Skardon found two of the other Clemson men, Henry Leitner and Otis Morgan, and together they struggled with their Philippine and American comrades, some carrying friends too sick and weak to continue walking. The enemy offered no transport, although most of the Japanese forces not guarding, beating, and taunting their prisoners, rode. When the prisoners arrived at their internment camps, Skardon was racked with malaria, so Leitner and Morgan fed him, bathed his face, and worked with his pustule-ridden feet. They carried him to the latrines and cleaned him. To get ever more meager food, they arranged for him to trade his Clemson ring for food.

Years passed, and as American forces started liberating islands from the enemy, the Japanese moved the imprisoned Americans from the coast and eventually to Manila. From Manila those still alive were loaded into the hulls of ships for evacuation. Because the ships had no marking, U.S. aircraft attacked them often. In the debris falling from the hits, Morgan was killed and Leitner was badly injured. After being in route since December 13, 1944, the ship, with only 400 of the 1,600 American prisoners, arrived at Moji in Japan, where they were separated. Leitner later died in a prison camp from his injuries, and Skardon was liberated from a Japanese prison camp by the Soviet Army.[57] Meanwhile, the Japanese had captured Manny Lawton on April 9, 1942. After the Japanese had stripped the prisoners of all valuables, Lawton still retained his Clemson ring. Then the prisoners marched about 25 miles a day. By the time the Japanese herded the prisoners into Camp O'Donnell, the living had dropped from 12,000 to 9,000 across seven weeks. In June, the captors moved 7,000 prisoners, leaving 2,000 more dead and buried. Eventually, Lawton sold his ring for food that reversed his starvation-induced illnesses and was selected for an agriculture camp at Davao.[58]

By October 1944, the American armed forces under the command of Gen. Douglas MacArthur prepared to invade the Philippines. On October 20, Col. Aubrey S. Newman commanded the Thirty-Fourth Infantry Regiment of the Twenty-Fourth Infantry Division, which was pinned down by Japanese artillery and infantry as the Americans attempted to take Leyte. Newman rose up and cried out to his men, "Follow me!" The men rallied and rushed forward. They overwhelmed the defenders and were followed by others. Newman received the Distinguished Service Cross for his bravery and, unfortunately, after leading his men through seventy-seven days of fighting, was wounded in the stomach. He recovered and returned to service after the war, attaining the rank of major general before he retired in 1960.[59] Newman had more than a passing Clemson attachment. His maternal grandfather, Henry Aubrey Strode, was Clemson's first president, and his paternal grandfather, James S. Newman, was Clemson's first active director of the experiment station. His father was Prof. C. C. Newman of Clemson's horticulture unit. Aubrey S. Newman (1904–1994) enrolled as a first-year ROTC student in 1919 at Clemson. After two years at Clemson, he took up an appointment to USMA, graduated in 1925, and received a commission in the infantry.[60]

The European War was equally as arresting to the Clemson community. There, the United States, following the collapse of France, agreed to supply Great Britain with war material, and by the end of June 1940, about a half million American-made rifles, machine guns, and field guns, along with ammunition, had arrived in Great Britain. Fifty U.S. destroyers were transferred to Britain, which in turn leased British bases in Newfoundland, Bermuda, the Caribbean, and South America to the United States. German bombing of Britain reached its heaviest in the summer and autumn of 1940 and only lessened after June 22, 1941, when Germany, with an army of some three million troops including a half million from their allies, invaded Russia, penetrating to Leningrad by September 4. A siege commenced. By mid-September, the Germans had reached Moscow, and by November 15, they had laid siege to Sevastopol on the Black Sea. Simultaneously, Nazi forces moved into the Mediterranean, thrusting through Yugoslavia into Greece and North Africa, while stirring up many Arabs against the West by encouraging anti-Semitism among them and playing on their anti-imperialist sentiments against Britain.

On December 11, 1941, four days after the attack on Pearl Harbor by Japan, Germany's ally, Hitler declared war on the United States. Now, with the fighting actively pursued in both hemispheres and on most continents, the world was truly at war.

Over Here

Limited as it was to males aged twenty to thirty-six, the existing American manpower pool simply could not sustain the country's wartime military and economic needs. In February 1942, the upper age limit for the military draft increased to forty-five, and in April to sixty-five. The summer of 1942, with the Axis military advances nearly everywhere in the war, pressed the U.S. to lower the draft age to eighteen. However, the actual induction, training, and service did not immediately include males aged eighteen and nineteen, so younger men were able to continue on farms, in college, and in industry until November 13, 1942.[61]

Thus, during the fall of 1942, the Clemson College student population increased slightly, but by 1943–1944, student enrollment had fallen to 752, the smallest number since 1920–21. And the student body would be that small and smaller yet through 1945. Much of the work on the local selective service board fell on Prof. Marion Kinard, in Arts and Sciences, and P. S. McCollum, the town pharmacist.[62] Gustave Metz, who assumed the post of registrar in 1940, and his small staff handled the registration of cadets as each student reached age eighteen. His office also prepared the necessary forms and affidavits that attested to students' special considerations for deferment from the draft such as occupation, hardship, or other issues that ranged from age, citizenships other than U.S., or physical limitations.[63]

Although not required, the Registrar's Office also received hundreds of transcripts of credits awarded for young Clemson men who had completed course work through other accredited institutions as part of their military training. Many received credits in mathematics, science, and engineering, while others received them in languages of countries the United States prepared to help rebuild. At the same time, the registrar issued transcripts for young men assigned to Clemson. Of course, these were not couched in the standard "credit hours" but were in actual "seat time." Art Spiro, a Clemson alumnus serving overseas, was amazed to open a letter at "mail call" informing him that "having completed all requirements and having received the recommendation of the faculty," he had been awarded his BS degree in textile engineering and chemistry.[64]

Back at the Front

An increasing number of Clemson students, from seniors to freshmen, enlisted, and their ranks swelled by the day. One was freshman Absalom Snell, a promising and bright cadet from Elloree. In November 1942, having just turned eighteen, he answered the call of the Army Air Corps team of recruiters visiting the college, volunteered, and took the entrance test. He passed and went the next day to the Field House to take the physical portion of the exam. Again, he passed and, because he was under twenty-one, received papers to get his parents' approving signatures. These they gave, and, on December 14, 1942, he entered the United States Army Air Force as an aviation cadet enlisted reserve. He remained in school until he received his orders to report for duty, which came in February 1943.

Snell went home and then by bus and train to the Army Air Force base near Miami Beach for basic training. He was moved to an ever-intensifying flight training, then to Great Britain, and finally, during the latter half of 1944, to France to fly the new C-46 aircraft. There his group bunked in hastily abandoned German barracks featuring rough, outdoor improvised showers and latrines. By comparison, the fifty-two-year-old Clemson Agricultural College barracks looked luxurious. From his base at Achiet, France, he co-piloted his plane with a full load of armed paratroopers, taking off from a steel mat runway to cross the Rhine River into the well-defended German homeland. As the formation of seventy-two airplanes began falling in altitude in the drop zone, Snell remembered, "All hell broke loose." Flak and bullets whizzed; the planes dropped further in altitude and speed until the troops aboard could parachute out. Then with all levers forward, they climbed as quickly as they could to return to France. The formation had long separated; only thirteen of seventy-two planes made it back undamaged. Snell's craft was classified as such, although the immediate ground inspection report recorded otherwise. And he flew more missions before the German capitulation on May 7, 1945.[65]

Over Here

Two groups of U.S. Army trainees took the places of many of the young cadets at Clemson in 1943–1945: the Army Student Training Program (ASTP), divided into Basic ASTP, Advanced ASTP, and ASTP-ROTC; and the Army Air Force. The Basic ASTP men, at least eighteen years old, usually had some high school education; the Advanced ASTP group had completed the basic courses; while the ASTP-ROTC men had completed high school. The Air Force cadets were young men, many with some college background, selected for this relatively new unit. By September 1943, 490 Basic ASTP and 598 Air Force trainees had arrived at Clemson. The high point was reached in December 1943, when basics numbered 492, advanced 180, ASTP-ROTC 249, and Air Force cadets 598. The regular undergraduates totaled 685, resulting in a total enrollment of 2,204. The total for all groups, including regular students, dropped to 428 by May 1, 1945.[66] Besides South Carolina, the regular student body hailed from eleven other states, the District of Columbia, Puerto Rico, and Costa Rica, the only foreign country. Of these, 330 were freshmen.[67]

World War II's presence in the community showed itself in a large number of ways. An undated article from the *Philadelphia Inquirer*, which one member of the branches of Thomas Green Clemson's family clipped in early 1943, noted that Clemson Agricultural College had at the time 3,448 men in uniform, out of 11,200 who had attended the college since it opened in 1893. The only higher education institutions that had more men in service were USMA and Texas A&M. By the war's end in 1945, of all the 12,500 cadets at Clemson since its founding, 6,475 had worn the military uniform of the United States in World War II.[68]

Those killed or missing were remembered each December 7 in a service attended by the cadets, the U.S. Army and Air Corps trainees, the bereaved and worried families, the faculty, staff, and their families, and many others. The Memorial Chapel was filled above capacity. The service each year was organized by the YMCA, led by P. B. Holtzendorff, and the churches of the community, the leader of which was the Rev. Dr. Sydney J. L. Crouch of Fort Hill Presbyterian Church. The first service, held in 1942, commemorated eleven Clemson men killed, and the congregation prayed for the safety of six missing in action. A number of the dead perished in flying accidents, although most who died as a result of enemy action were killed in the Pacific. All but one of the missing had fought in the Pacific. By the service of December 7, 1945, the known dead had reached 301.[69] But of course, some had suffered such terrible wounds that they died after the guns had long ceased. The best roster, compiled nearly sixty years later, listed 390 Clemson men killed as a result of World War II.[70]

Student Life in Wartime

For those still on the campus, life did not go on as usual. *The Tiger* reduced its issues to once a month, and, with support from the YMCA and President Poole's office, sent a copy to every Clemson serviceman for whom the college had an address. At one point, a different editor served for each issue. Partially because of a severe shortage in photographic film, chemicals, and high quality paper, no *Taps* appeared in 1944, 1945, or 1946. The local social fraternities, social clubs, county clubs, and a large number of student branches of academic clubs also ceased their activities, some for the duration of the war, while others never reappeared. On the other hand, the national academic groups that had strong faculty support, such as Phi Kappa Phi, Phi Eta Sigma, Tau Beta Pi, Alpha Zeta, and others, continued on, although with diminished membership.

Intramural athletics remained active, fueled by the influx of the army trainees. But intercollegiate athletics took an odd turn. The 1942–1943 football season was very much like the years of the mid to late 1930s. The first game in the new stadium was played on September 19, 1942. After considering a variety of names for the stadium, the trustees decided on "Memorial Stadium," commemorating all Clemson men, graduates, other alumni, faculty, and staff who died for the nation. The board rejected all other suggestions, even "Clemson Memorial Stadium." It reasoned that some unknowing folks might think the stadium was another memorial to Mr. Clemson.[71] The Tigers reached another high point in the season by claiming their two-hundredth football victory, made sweeter because the win came over South Carolina 18–6, and, as ever, it happened in Columbia.

The third major feature of the season was the appearance on the schedule of the Jacksonville Air Station, to whom the Tigers lost. Clemson had last met a noncollegiate team on November 9, 1918.[72] During the latter years of the war, many colleges played such teams. In the final national football rankings beginning in 1943, five of the top twenty teams included unusual appearances by Colorado College, the College of the Pacific, and three military bases. The Department of the Army made the situation even more strange by deciding that its trainees on college campuses could not play intercollegiate sports. All land-grant colleges had U.S. Army and Army Air training units on their campuses. The Department of the Navy, whose V-12 units more frequently lodged at public and private liberal arts colleges, allowed their trainees to play. Thus, the student pool available to coaches and their colleges shifted radically in all sports and not by a conscious decision on the part of the colleges.

Clemson basketball compiled a winning record from 1942 through May 1945. The sports that were not as dependent on recruiting had reduced schedules because of increasing travel restrictions. Baseball continued to produce strong teams. The 1943 season ended with a 12–3 season (.800), one of the best in Clemson's history. Frank Howard served as head coach for the amazing year. Baseball continued to have winning seasons in 1944 and 1945. No record survives for track or swimming.[73]

On another important level of campus culture, the concert series played a number of vital roles during the war years, especially for the young men assigned as U.S. Army and Army Air Force trainees. Many of the numerous military camps, stations, bases, and other encampments formed orchestras, bands, drum and bugle corps, and a large variety of singing groups. Troop transport also moved by rail engines powered by plentiful coal. And the touring service musicians moved that way also, as did the large number of professional musicians who had migrated to America from around the world, particularly Europe. Clemson provided a nearly perfectly placed overnight stop, and even with trainees could offer bed space, three or four performing stages, of which two were enclosed, and a substantial capacity to feed large groups. It also had a young audience.

Many groups stopped and performed. These became part of the Clemson College Concert Series, which has grown, changed, and continues today. It is the oldest of such series in colleges in the fifteen-state South. Although many of the groups were associated with the military, the lineup included the Southern Symphony, the National Symphony (Washington, D.C.) directed by Hans Kindler, several ballet companies, choruses, and famous opera singers including Helen Jepson, Richard Crooks, Bidu Sayao, and Lawrence Tibbett. A highlight for the students (at least, according to *The Tiger*) was a full scale production of Puccini's *La Boheme*. James Melton, a tenor with the Metropolitan Opera, came to Clemson as part of the troop entertainment program of the government to produce the opera and sing the lead of Rudolfo. Faculty from several Upstate institutions took the other lead and secondary roles, while the chorus, which is significant in the second act, included Clemson students, the other young military trainees, and women from area colleges. It was what some called a "learning experience."[74] Virginia Earle Shanklin in President Poole's office managed the Concert Series. All such musical, athletic, and theatrical activities continued to enrich the lives of young Clemson students, military trainees, and local families.[75]

Experiment and Extend

The state-wide work of the college had a sense of urgency as well. As they had in droughts and depressions of the 1930s, both the experiment and extension divisions received extraordinary tasks. One significant problem was that 42 percent of all American families were not landowners. Their land was held either by lease or by tenancy (sharecropping). Sixteen states, including South Carolina, ranked above the national average in these arrangements, and in ten states, again including South Carolina, half or more of all farmland was held by such arrangements. This was greatest in the South and the Midwest. The farming enterprise in the West also had grave, but different, agricultural labor problems. These issues had been a long time in the making. They negatively affected both income and yield.[76]

Part of the strategy was the home "Victory Garden" for all households. Extension offices prepared and distributed local monthly information on home food gardening, wild food harvesting, good food preservation, and storage charts. The education in gardening fell to the extension agents and their assistants. Home demonstration agents taught home canning, while in many counties canneries supervised by extension agents were built and operated by the service.[77] Thrift in food consumption, both in rural and urban areas, was also instituted in the protein-rich foods, particularly meat and beans. The government quickly rationed various food categories, and extension urged meatless days in a program called "Share the Meat for Victory." The purpose stated, "To meet the needs of our armed forces and fighting allies, a government order limits the total amount of meat for civilians." The government program also encouraged the use of cheese, eggs, beans, peas, peanuts, and soy for protein as the main course for meals.[78]

Each of the forty-six counties had neighborhood groups. The county extension agents, as advisors, convened the 889 South Carolina neighborhoods, but the neighborhoods elected their own leaders. County, regional, and state meetings (frequently held at Clemson) disseminated regular production reports and the latest in crop and meat production techniques, while new breeds, strains, and cultivation techniques were announced and demonstrated. Aid in marketing, regional farmers' markets, and distribution was given. And in the counties, the vocational agricultural schoolteachers (almost all of whom were Clemson, SC State, and Winthrop graduates) operated farm, kitchen, and sewing machinery repair schools out of the public school vocational facilities. Special attention was paid to cotton, so critical for uniforms, medical supplies, and mattresses. Through earlier efforts and the research of the experiment stations, the cotton yield per acre and staple length had greatly improved. Efforts by extension, the experiment station, the State Nutrition Committee, the Home Economics Association, and the Dietetic Association helped urge the legislature to enact bills requiring enrichment of all flour and oleomargarine. At the same time, research commenced on the enrichment of corn meal. D. W. Watkins, the director of extension, served as chair of the State Nutrition Committee.[79]

The Clemson Extension Service, strengthened by the Bankhead-Flannagan Act, added forty men and ninety women, both black and white, to serve as food administrative assistants.[80] By the end of 1943, the efforts of South Carolina farmers yielded record production in oats, peanuts, soybeans, sorghum syrup, sweet potatoes, cattle, calves, hogs, chickens, eggs, and turkeys, while the preserving of fruits, vegetables, and meat also expanded. Despite the work of the salaried agents, the 7,825 volunteers, and the families, South Carolina remained a food-importing state throughout the war. [81]

The Pacific Front

Slowly, the tide of the war in Asia and the war in the Pacific turned. An early sign was the U.S. victory at the Battle of Midway, June 4–5, 1942, in which U.S. aircraft carriers launched torpedo and dive-bomber planes, successfully destroying four Japanese carriers and a cruiser, and damaging two destroyers and another cruiser. The U.S. Navy lost the *USS Yorktown*. The Japanese launched a counterattack in Burma in late September 1942. By the end of May 1943, the United States had recaptured almost all of the Aleutian Islands. But the defeat of Japan, and the freeing of its vast conquered lands in the southwest Pacific and Asia, had only begun. On October 26, 1943, the Emperor Hirohito stated that Japan's situation was "truly grave."

The Atlantic Front

On the African front, Italy's 1940 declaration of war on Great Britain and France and its subsequent invasions of British Somaliland and then Egypt changed that war just as the fall of France had brought German influence in France's holdings in North Africa. In early January 1941, the British began a strong counteroffensive in East Africa. To support Italy, Germany dispatched divisions led by Gen. Erwin Rommel to North Africa. These were successful until Hitler's surprise invasion of Russia, with the enormous manpower needs there, made it impossible for Germany to send Rommel more troops and supplies. The British stopped Rommel at El Alamein in Egypt in November 1942. By the end of 1942, British forces, led by Gen. Bernard L. Montgomery, forced Rommel and his troops into a long retreat west through Libya and into Tunisia.

On November 8, 1942, British and American forces, led by Gen. Dwight D. Eisenhower, made the largest amphibious landing to that point in the war, "Operation Torch," in northwest Africa. Only in slow and difficult fighting—the first for American troops in the European theater—did the Allied forces overcome Vichy French, and especially the German, resistance. A number of Clemson men, including Roy Pearce, Clemson 1941, received their baptism in combat in the fighting. By May 1943, the Axis had been swept from North Africa, and the "soft underbelly" of Europe was exposed. Allied invasions of Italy began shortly. Important to the success of the invasions of Sicily and Italy were the growing and relentless Allied bombings of Nazi-held northern "Fortress Europa," and many Clemson men participated in the air assault. Among the many who flew out of the British airstrips was Henry Grady Way, Clemson 1942, from Ridgeland. He flew as a bomber pilot twenty-five times before his fatal bombing run over Berlin on June 21, 1944. His bombardier had just released the load on the order of "bombs away" when the B-17 was hit by enemy fire and crashed. Slightly over twenty-two years old and a graduate in dairy science, 1st Lt. Way died along with four of his crew. Four survived as prisoners of war.[82]

One of the biggest obstacles to the Allies' air war against Germany was the distance of the mission flights of bombers with their fighter airplanes to targets deep in Germany. The larger bombers had fuel tanks with enough capacity to make the round trip, but the smaller, more maneuverable fighters did not have the capacity. An Army Air Corps officer, Mark Edward Bradley (December 10, 1907–May 22, 1999), who had graduated from USMA in June 1930 and then from the engineering school at Wright Field, Ohio, designed an auxiliary tank that fit behind the pilot's seat and provided the gas necessary for the round trip mission. Eventually, this developed into the "drop-down" tanks, but for the moment, it gave the Allies the ranges they needed to disrupt German production. Bradley was the son of Mark "Prep" Bradley of the Clemson English faculty and a cousin of Mrs. Poole. The Army Air Corps engineer had attended Clemson from 1925 to 1926. Besides his fuel tank innovation, he flew six combat missions during World War II. His campaign ribbons, all with battle stars, included the European-African-Middle Eastern Campaign Medal and the Asiatic-Pacific Campaign Medal. Also he received the Philippine Liberation Ribbon. His decorations include the Distinguished Service Medal, Legion of Merit, Bronze Star with the oak leaf cluster, Air Medal, and Croix de Guerre.[83]

During the summer of 1943, Soviet Russia, reinforced by American and British supplies, airplanes, and food, mounted a massive offensive. Imported U.S. airplanes helped Russia gain air superiority, and a slow, costly reconquest of European Russia began. British Prime Minster Winston Churchill later wrote, "The tide had turned."

Earlier in 1943, the Allied leaders of the Free French (Charles de Gaulle and Henri Giraud), the British Empire (Winston Churchill), and the United States (Franklin Roosevelt) had met in Casablanca. In closed session, they agreed on nothing less than "unconditional surrender" of the Axis powers.

On June 6, 1944, the Allied forces, under the overall command of Gen. Eisenhower, fought their way ashore on the beaches of Normandy and fought for every blade of grass between Pointe du Hoc and Honfleur. That day and during the next days and weeks—under withering fire from the German defenders of the coast and inland France, but supported by some 10,000 airplanes from the U.S. Air Force, the Britannic Royal Air Force, and the Royal Canadian Air Force and coastal pounding by more than 800 ship-to-shore cannons on warships—4,000 ships and landing craft unloaded 2.2 million men, a half million vehicles, and four million tons of war supplies onto the Norman coastal plateau. Many Clemson men, including Robert Grigsby, Clemson 1944 (although he graduated several years later), and Roy Pearce participated in the D-Day invasion. From an airplane flying above the massive amphibious landing operation on its first day, Clemson alumnus Wright Bryan broadcast to the waiting free world that the invasion of Adolf Hitler's Fortress Europa was moving forward. His report was a first.

Ernest H. Carroll Jr. from Rock Hill came ashore in the invasion. He had entered Clemson as a "rat" in 1941, and the army called him to duty in the spring of 1943. His father, Ernest Carroll, was already in the army. Young Carroll died in the invasion. His father received the news in the Pacific.[84]

But this was a war the western Allied leaders had declared they would pursue to an "unconditional surrender," which meant chasing "the jackal to his lair." That included spending the winter of 1944–1945 in Europe during one of the coldest in modern times. Among those who broke through Hitler's Siegfried Line, Sam Putnam returned to Clemson after World War II and elected to stay past his graduation year (1948) to receive the college's first bachelor of architecture degree a year later. Already a skilled artist, Putnam created a water color of the heavily damaged Remagen bridge and of the destroyed rail yards and warehouses of Köln (Cologne) with the barely touched cathedral rising up from the rubble in March 1945.[85]

Also on the western front, many other young Clemson men had roles to play. One was "Abe" (Albert Neill) Cameron. Born in Fort Mudge, Georgia, where his father worked with the Atlantic Coast Line Railroad, Abe, along with his family, moved to Waycross, where Abe began school. When he was eight years old, the family moved to Savannah, staying until Abe finished high school there. He had been industrious and worked hard, saving his money for college. When that time came, he applied to Georgia Tech and Clemson and received acceptance at both schools. Selecting Tech, he arrived at the school's admissions office, found the staff so "clumsy and snooty" (his words) that he picked up his suitcase and caught the Southern train to Clemson. By this time, his family had moved to Rocky Mount, North Carolina. Cameron enrolled in civil engineering and had his Clemson experiences, including a summer at Camp Clarke, near Batesburg. Cameron served as manager of the football team his junior and senior years and in his senior year was elected to Tau Beta Pi, the engineering academic honor society. He went to the ROTC encampment at Fort McClellan, Alabama, and (in his words) "received my diploma from President Poole and my commission from Commandant Poole."

During the 1944–1945 armed forces drive into Germany, his unit was assigned to break the Siegfried Line, the highly fortified German defense zone that ran along the German border with France. Cameron and three other men were detailed as spotters. They made their way cautiously into a large, recently emptied monastery. Scrambling up the inner spiral stair, they entered a crawl space that lay between the gothic ceiling and steep pitched roof and wriggled their way forward. Cameron, the smallest, moved to a viewpoint and served as lookout, helping to position Allied artillery. At 11:30 p.m. the battle commenced, but by daylight the Germans surrendered, sparing the town and monastery from destruction.[86]

"They Also Serve..."

The fierce German resistance and counterattacks required unbelievable courage from the Allied forces. One of Clemson's young faculty, George Dunkelberg (1913–1970), an agricultural engineer from Rockford, Iowa, who held BS and MS degrees from Iowa State College, joined the Clemson faculty in the autumn of 1938. Married to Dorothy Stuart, who remained in Iowa to bear their first child, he arrived at Clemson alone. George Nutt, the head of Clemson's Agricultural Engineering Department, met Dunkelberg at the Clemson-Southern Railways station and got him settled at the Clemson Hotel, which then was managed by Mrs. Freeman, sister-in-law of Prof. Edwin Freeman in engineering. (Of her home-cooked meals, he described them as "bounteous and good.") Dunkelberg's wife and infant son, John (later a Clemson track star), arrived from Iowa by train at the end of October and moved into a recently vacated cottage. From there, "Dunk" left in mid-March 1942 to join a war that called forty-three professors (a quarter of the entire faculty) to service, the younger ones to combat and many of the older ones to scientific or research duties related to the war.[87]

The 82nd Division to which Dunkelberg belonged became one of the first two airborne divisions in the U.S. Army. Shortly thereafter it merged into the 101st Airborne, the "Screaming Eagles." The men were separated into paratroopers and gliders, with Dunk in the gliders. As the fateful June 1944 approached, his unit, along with the British Sixth Division, moved to Wales and boarded there. They set sail for several days before they learned that D-Day had come. As they debarked into landing craft off the continental coast, the ship struck a mine and began sinking. The men, the uniforms, field packs, and their weapons made it to safety. All other light supplies sank. The heavy-duty equipment traveled separately. So the 101st Airborne arrived on the Normandy beach by boat.[88]

After the initial landing and ferocious fighting, the unit prepared for a second assault, this one against the Germans entrenched in the Netherlands. Dunkelberg was part of a 6,000-airplane-and-glider armada in a massive air invasion of the Nazi-held Dutch nation on September 17, 1944. By October 10, his wife received a dreaded "missing in action" telegram from the War Department. At the campus Armistice Day ceremony on November 11, however, Dorothy told all with happiness that Dunk was a POW. The airplane towing his glider had been hit by enemy fire. Dunkelberg, in charge of the cadre of men and the glider that carried them,

George Dunkelberg, a faculty member in agricultural engineering, was shot down as a glider with the "Screaming Eagles" and taken as a German POW. He escaped and safely reached the United States on April 10, 1945. Photo courtesy of George Dunkelberg Jr.

had to choose whether to stay tethered to the aircraft, thus lessening the chance for any survivors, or cut free so the "mother ship" might limp back to Britain and the glider to fly wherever. He chose to cut loose and glide. The tow plane returned home. Dunkelberg guided the glider down and into a German anti-aircraft battery. A frantic search produced a utility rag to signal surrender of the hopelessly out-gunned Americans to the Germans, who moved them and others eastward into Oflag 64 (a POW camp in Poland, about one hundred miles south of Gdansk [then Danzig]).

However, the Russian counteroffensive moved into Poland, and the Germans began retreating west. Dunkelberg and some others escaped, briefly joined a Red Army unit, and then, "put off" by the brutal Russian mode of "liberation," left the unit. With a companion, Dunkelberg made his way to Odessa in the Black Sea and traveled through Port Said, Egypt, to Italy. The two reached Boston on April 10, 1945, and Dunk's wife picked him up at Fort Bragg, North Carolina, for a trip home to Clemson on April 25, 1945. It was almost V-E (Victory in Europe) Day.[89]

However, other horrors awaited the Allied forces. As they moved into the ever more heavily fortified areas, the soldiers began reaching "concentration" camps, where the Nazis had systematically murdered millions of Jews, gypsies, mentally and physically handicapped, and homosexual people. Charles P. Gordon, a 1935 Clemson graduate in textile chemistry, had been called into service on February 14, 1942, and trained at Fort Knox, Kentucky, as a reconnaissance officer. He was in the lead of his unit when it broke in upon a "death camp" in western Czechoslovakia. Very few of the prisoners were alive to tell what they and the others had suffered. Gordon and his unit called in transport for the broken women, children, and men and arrested the remaining guards and other perpetrators. Gordon did not return to his wife and family until late in 1946.[90]

Those Who Stand and Wait

Just sixteen days after D-Day (June 6, 1944), President Roosevelt signed the Servicemen's Readjustment Act. This document changed the face of America just as assuredly as the Constitution and Bill of Rights, the Morrill Land Grant Act of 1862, and the Thirteenth Amendment had earlier. Four provisions of the GI Bill of Rights applied to men and women who served in the active forces of the U.S. Army, Navy, Marine Corps, or Coast Guard between September 16, 1940, and through the war's end: Veterans received medical, educational, housing, and employment aid. While all have since been significant, educational assistance and aid for acquiring property seem to have been the greatest agents of that change. For a veteran's education, the federal government paid $500 per year for tuition, fees, books, supplies, and equipment; $50 per month for living expenses for a single person; and $75 per month for persons with one or more dependents. There were no stipulations on types of schools (public, private, undergraduate, graduate, professional, trade school, or two-year school) for the veterans to attend.[91]

At Clemson, President Poole and Jim Littlejohn had anticipated some sort of opportunity for the college's expansion, not dissimilar from the approval of new programs that had occurred during the Depression. Thus, in 1943, they had prepared an immediate building and equipment list to make ready for the coming wave of new students. As they saw it, Clemson needed sixteen new major buildings. The total cost proposed reached $4 million, of which the top priority was a new chemistry building; a new sewage disposal plant and power plant ranked second and third; and fourth they proposed new barracks and a women's dormitory. High on the list also were a hotel (the old frame structure housed many unmarried faculty) and a larger, modern infirmary. Poole also put forward requests for new equipment and especially for library books.

Two of Poole's most significant recommendations were that returning veterans should have a revolving loan fund against which they could borrow, the repayment of which would come from federal benefit checks, and that veterans be exempted from reveille, drill, and "certain other formations." But, at least initially, the veterans had to wear uniforms. Books, equipment, the revolving loan funds, and military issues were very much in the trustees' authority to grant. But all such students needed external funding.[92]

Recognizing that Clemson's own students would be returning from military service, along with many other veterans, probably within the year, Poole also pointed out to the trustees the gravity of the faculty shortage. The trustees neither offered nor accepted any strategy except salary raises. The class that entered in 1944 contained 553 freshmen, which included twenty-three veterans. An additional seventeen veterans were classified as upperclassmen. Further, to meet these new needs, the federal government offered most colleges surplus housing to accommodate veterans, who, in many cases, would arrive with wives and frequently with children. Littlejohn set to work immediately.

First, the college contacted Jimmy Byrnes's office. Byrnes, when a U.S. senator, had been elected a Clemson College life trustee in April 1941 to fill the seat left vacant by the death of Trustee Frank Lever.[93] On June 12, 1941, Byrnes had received unanimous confirmation as an associate justice of the U.S. Supreme Court by the U.S. Senate, barely eleven minutes after President Roosevelt's nomination had been received by the chamber.[94] Byrnes continued as a Clemson life trustee. In October 1942, he resigned the court seat to assume the post of director of economic stability for the United States. Within months, Roosevelt, by executive order, created the Office of War Mobilization and named Byrnes its director. The powers of his new job were broader than any placed into a single person's hands previously.[95] Byrnes, in response to "Mr. Jim's" request for federal help in Clemson's housing, directed Littlejohn to contact the Federal Public Housing Administration (FHA). At the FHA's direction, Littlejohn, along with David J. Watson, Clemson's buildings and grounds director, visited a variety of suggested sites, including Charleston, South Carolina; Brunswick and Atlanta, Georgia; Wilmington, North Carolina; and Radford, Virginia. Then to begin the process, and armed with Watson's estimates, Littlejohn traveled to Washington, D.C., to talk with Byrnes and the FHA. Clemson was approved, according to Littlejohn, "as the first college needing houses."[96]

A representative from the FHA, John Hobart Gates, visited Clemson, and in considering the costs of housing, the men (Littlejohn, Poole, Gates, and Watson) agreed that the best houses for Clemson (given Clemson's weather history) were a number of dormitory units to accommodate about 200 single veterans. Clemson already had army housing for 100 single males left from the army and army air force training programs. For married veterans (the congressional allotment was space for 300), Littlejohn, Poole, Gates, and Watson decided to use a single unit called the U.K. type. The FHA agreed, and in October 1945, the trustees concurred. Fortunately, federal regulations allowed a percentage of the space for assignment to faculty. Eventually, the college also placed side-by-side double houses on campus.[97]

Victory in Europe

The spring and summer of 1945 brought great news. On Friday, May 7, 1945, Gen. Alfred Jodl, chief of the operations staff in the German High Command, signed the unconditional surrender document in Reims, France, and, two days later, German Field Marshall Wilhelm Keitel surrendered in Berlin. The Allies had won victory in Europe. The Clemson community—college students, trainees, and town—gathered in Memorial Chapel to give thanks, read scripture and sing hymns. Prof. D. W. Daniel spoke about the occasion, and following the benediction, the congregation rose and sang "Old One Hundredth," ending with "Praise God from Whom all Blessings Flow."

Less than one month earlier, the congregants meeting in the same chapel had remembered the life of Franklin Delano Roosevelt upon his death. The corps of

The funeral train of President Franklin Delano Roosevelt as it moved through Clemson, journeying from Warm Springs, Georgia, to Washington, D.C., on the Southern Railway line. Clemson cadets stood at attention as the train, which did not stop at Clemson, passed by the station. Photo courtesy of the Pendleton Historical Commission.

cadets and army men marched through the town to the railway station to present arms to their commander-in-chief as his funeral train passed through from Warm Springs, Georgia, to Washington, D.C. A Clemson man served as the engineer.[98]

Victory Over Japan

But the war was not yet over. Many of the American forces in Europe prepared to occupy those lands for the new peace. Other combatants and support staff were to be moved to Asia, where the American and other Allied forces prepared for a bitter struggle to defeat the Japanese. By the first of April, the U.S. Army invaded Okinawa. Its conquest took nearly three months, ending in great loss of life. American strategists dreaded the anticipated invasion of the Japanese home islands. After Japan's emperor rejected a July letter from the U.S. requesting Japanese surrender, President Harry Truman, the successor to Roosevelt, reached the painful decision to use a new weapon, the atomic bomb, to shorten the war and greatly reduce American casualties. This weapon had been tested successfully, and its awesome power was known.

Thus, on August 6, 1945, the U.S. dropped the first atomic bomb on Hiroshima. The death and destruction were enormous. Two days later, Soviet Russia declared war on Japan and invaded Manchuria. On August 9, 1945, the U.S. dropped a second atomic bomb, this one on Nagasaki. By August 14, the emperor agreed to unconditional surrender. On September 2, 1945, the official articles of surrender were signed by the Japanese officials on the *USS Missouri* in Tokyo Bay, and President Truman declared Victory in Japan Day. World War II had ended.

Notes

1. Bourret, *Clemson Football 2003*, 288–289 and 352–353. Bourret notes that Dobson had been a professional baseball player for the Pittsburgh Nationals. The first coach to work at Clemson on a school contract, he also coached Clemson's first basketball team and the baseball team. Williams had coached at Clemson in 1906 and 1909; he returned to coach from 1913 through football 1915.
2. CUL.SC.CUA. S 38 f "Bradley, M. E., Sr."; and S 30 ss 1 f "Bradley."
3. These paragraphs are based on Clemson *Announcements*, 1916–1917, 50–51; Anderson *Daily Mail*, January 12, 1942; Bryan, *History*, 121; and Hite, "The Gentleman Manager: Robert Franklin Poole, 1940–1958," in *Tradition*, 160–166.
4. The data are from *Records* of 1894–1895, 1915–1916, 1940–1941, and 1946–1947.
5. *The Tiger*, October 5, 1939.
6. Http://en.wikipedia.org/wiki/conscription_in_the_United_States#World_War_II. The article is based on work by Dr. Stetson Conn of the Office of the Chief of Military History.
7. Springs, *Selective Service in South Carolina*, 61.
8. McKale, *Destined for Duty*, 41.
9. CUL.SC.CUA. S 30 ss iii b 8 f 1.
10. *Taps*, 1940–1941; *The Tiger*, May 15, 1959; and CUL.SC.CUA. S 37 f "Agricultural Fair." For Davidson, see *Clemson World*, Winter 2004, 24–25.
11. CUL.SC.CUA. S 30 v 5, 285–290, 347, 383–386, and 417–430.
12. Ibid., *President's Report to the Board of Trustees*, 1942, 1–2; and S 15 f 204.
13. *Record*, 1942.
14. CUL.SC.MSS 255 b 2 f 6.
15. *Greenville News*, August 24, 1941.
16. CUL.SC.CUA. S 30 *President's Report to the Board of Trustees*, 1942, 23.
17. Atlanta *Journal*, June 23, 1944.
18. CUL.SC.CUA. S 32 b 152 f 17.
19. *A History of 4-H in South Carolina*, CU Extension Service, 1985, 6–21.
20. CUL.SC.CUA. S 32 b 159 ff 485.
21. Ibid., S 15 f 127; S 32 b 116 ff 1, 8, and 12; b 122 f 8; and b 159 f 9.
22. *Record*, 1940–1943; and *The Tiger*, December 5, 1940, November 27, 1941, and December 10, 1942.
23. Dunn and Holliday, "A History of Forestry at Clemson University," Clemson University Forestry, Technical Paper 7, 1977.
24. CUL.SC.CUA. S 41 b 1 ff 10 and 13.
25. Ibid., S 32 b 95 f 4.
26. MacCambridge, *College Football Encyclopedia*, 223 and 1177.
27. CUL.SC.CUA. S 30 ss iii b 8 f 1.
28. Columbia *State*, July 17, 1941.
29. CUL.SC.CUA. S 304 A. N. Cameron to J. V. Reel.
30. Ibid., S 30 v 5, 334–340; ss iii b 69 f 13; and MSS 66 b 1 f 3.
31. Bourret, *Football 2003*, 354; and *Football 2009*, 42–43, 204.
32. Jacobs, "Fike Field House," in Blackman, Bradley, and Kriese, *Clemson*, 36–38.
33. *Taps*, 1941, 316–337 and 1942 unpaginated.

34. CUL.SC.CUA. S 30 v 5, 299–300.

35. Seneca *Daily Journal* and Clemson *Daily Journal*, November 16, 2002; Wilson and Ferris, eds., *Encyclopedia of Southern Culture*, 1025–1027; and MacCambridge, *College Football Encyclopedia*, 416–425.

36. Studwell, "College Fight Songs"; and Foran, "The Mills Brothers," *The Guide to United States Popular Culture*, ed. R. B. and P. Browne, 185–186 and 536–537. All that can be said about the origins of "Tiger Rag" with certainty is that its first recording was August 17, 1917, by the Original Dixieland Jass [*sic*] Band for Aeolian-Vocalion Records. Because of the reproduction format, the recording did not sell well. The Original Dixieland Jazz (they had changed the spelling in the late autumn of 1917) issued a second recording March 25, 1918, and Victor Records copyrighted it with Dominic James "Nick" La Rocca as the leader. The other members were Eddie Edwards, Henry Ragas, Tony Sbarbaro, Larry Shields, and Harry Da Costa. La Rocca, a main contender for the title of composer, in his recorded interviews (Tulane University: Joseph Jones Special Collections: Jazz Archives) noted that the first section is a traditional eighteenth century French quadrille, but the second section was, he claimed, his contribution. It is a countermelody to John Philip Sousa's "American Emblem March." La Rocca stated that he learned how to compose countermelody by attending performances at the New Orleans French Opera House with his parents. While many standard works on jazz history credit La Rocca and/or the Original Dixieland Jazz Band as the "creators" of the piece, all I have seen note that section "A" is an eighteenth century quadrille. Others who have claimed authorship include Ferdinand Joseph Le Menthe (a.k.a. Jelly Roll Morton), Achille Baquet, Jack Carey, Johnny DeDroiet, "Papa" Jack Laine, and Ray Lopez. The major recordings are legion and include ODLJS's 1917, the New Orleans Rhythm Kings 1922, Jelly Roll Morton 1938, and the Mills Brothers (vocal edition 1931 Decca).

37. CUL.SC.MSS 72 gives a brief glimpse of his war career. While the captain was a very involved Clemson student, alumnus, administrator, and then trustee, I was fortunate to have known him, and with my wife to have shared the friendship of him, his wife, Anne, and their daughter, Mary, and her husband, Ed Kilby. For Capt. Jervey's Clemson career, also see *Taps*, 1915.

38. *Taps*, 1918, not paginated.

39. Http://en.wikipedia.org/wiki/Floyd_Lavinius_Parks (accessed June 20, 2010).

40. *Taps*, 1938 and 1939; and *The Tiger*, December 3, 1942.

41. *Taps*, 1923. In 1940, Robertson wrote *I Saw England*, a book that expressed strong support for the besieged United Kingdom.

42. CUL.SC.MSS 77 ff 1 and 3.

43. Lawton, *Some Survived*, xiii.

44. Ibid., 2.

45. *The Tiger*, March 1944.

46. *Taps*, 1938.

47. Beverly "Ben" Skardon in two oral interviews January 25 and 26, 2007, and a DVD interview with Jerry Reel in 2010.

48. Lander, *From Clemson College to India in World War II*, 1–5.

49. H. M. Cox to Jerry Reel, January 30, 2007. DVD interview with Sterling Eisiminger, 2010.

50. CUL.SC.CUA. S 30 *President's Report to the Board of Trustees*, March 1942, 1–2.

51. Ibid., v 5, 369.

52. Lander, *World War II*, 5; CUL.SC.CUA. S 30 v 5, 301, 304, 362–364, 398, 404–405, 422–423, and 447; and S 30 *President's Report to the Board of Trustees*, 1943, 1.

53. Http://www.history.navy.mil/photos/events/wwii-pac/guadlcnl/guad-1c.htm (accessed July 21, 2010).

54. *Taps*, 1929, not paginated.

55. Ibid., 1931.

56. Smith, *A Hero Among Heroes: Jimmy Dyess and the Fourth Marine Division*, 3–74 and 117–175.

57. Skardon, "This My Ring," a regular presentation made by Col. Skardon, professor emeritus of English and Clemson 1938, to students in anticipation of receipt of the university ring, the students having achieved senior status.

58. Lawton, *Some Survived*, 32–95.

59. *New York Times*, January 22, 1994. I owe all this information on Newman to Robert L. Mc-Garity, colonel, U.S. Army (ret), security affairs advisor, U.S. Department of State.
60. Http://www.cgsc.edu/carl/resources/ftlvn/postww.asp. The dates of Clemson enrollment were provided by Clemson Registrar Stanley Smith, August 27, 2010.
61. Springs, *Selective Service in South Carolina*, 40.
62. Ibid., 166.
63. Ibid., vi.
64. Arthur Spiro to Jerry Reel DVD.
65. Snell, *My Air Force Experience: February 13, 1943–June 1946*, iii–iv and 1–38.
66. CUL.SC.MSS 68; and CUL.SC.CUA. S 6 "Annual Report of the Registrar's Office, June 1, 1943–May 1, 1945."
67. *Record*, 1942–1945.
68. American Philosophical Society, MSS 76 (Smith Family Papers.) S 50: Ogden papers.
69. CUL.SC.MSS 118 b 2 f 31.
70. CUL.SC.CUA. S 37 f "Clemson War Dead."
71. Ibid., S 13 f 7; and S 30 *President's Report to the Board of Trustees*, October 26, 1942, 17.
72. Bourret, *Football 2003*, 352–354.
73. *The Tiger*, 1942 through May 1945.
74. CUL.SC.CUA. S 39 f 6; *The Tiger*, 1940–1945: and Edwin Freeman to Jerry Reel DVD.
75. Edwards to Reel, personal conversation.
76. CUL.SC.CUA. S 32 b 152 f 9; and USDA: Farm Tenure Improvement, May 1940.
77. CUL.SC.CUA. S 32 b 71 f 4.
78. Ibid., b 159 f 9.
79. Ibid., f 8.
80. Ibid., b 71 f 5 and b 126 f 4.
81. Ibid., b 141 f 12.
82. *Taps*, 1942; and http://www.303rdbg.com/358way.html (accessed April 20, 2010).
83. Http://www.af.mil/information/bios/bio.asp?bioID=4768 (accessed November 3, 2010).
84. *Taps*, 1942 and 1943; and *Clemson World*, Summer 2004, 11.
85. Sam Putnam narrative, the Putnam scrapbooks, and the Putnam CDs, all in cataloging in CUL.
86. Albert N. Cameron Sr. to J. V. Reel, DVD.
87. Dorothy S. Dunkelberg Boulware, *The Name May Change*, 47–52, 60; and *Record*, 1942, 1943, 1944, and 1945. These last data fluctuated widely.
88. Ibid., 69.
89. Ibid., 70–78.
90. CUL.SC.MSS.
91. CUL.SC.MSS 147; and CUA. S 32 b 160 f 2.
92. CUL.SC.CUA. S 32 b 126 f 2.
93. CUL.SC.MSS 68 b 7 f 141.
94. Anderson *Independent*, June 12, 1941.
95. *Greenville News*, May 29, 1943.
96. CUL.SC.MSS 68 b 7 f 141; duplicate in CUA. S 6 b 2 f 1.
97. CUL.SC.CUA. S 6 b 2 f 1.
98. CUL.SC.MSS 68 f 286.

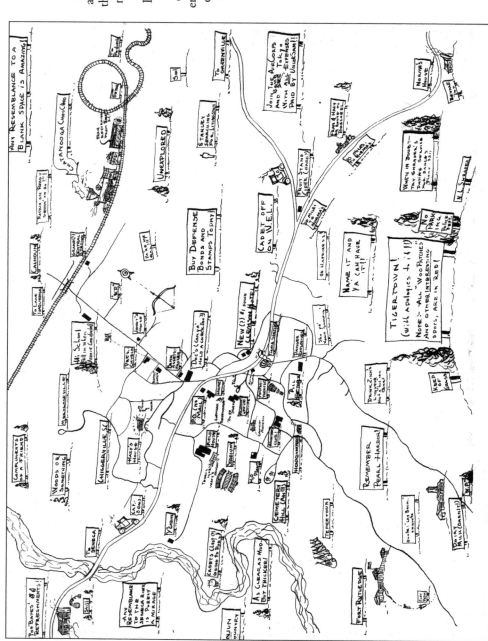

A humorous map of Clemson drawn by GIs and returning veterans in the years 1943–1947. The map is a gift of the Hon. Judge Hazel Collings Poe, wife of Vernon Poe, professor emeritus of electrical and computer engineering, and daughter of Prof. Gilbeart "Lord" Collings (1895–1964), longtime professor of agronomy and soils.

CHAPTER XII

Trustees Don Hard Hats

1945–1955

The Board of Trustees, chaired by W. W. Bradley, approached the opening of Clemson Agricultural College in September 1945 with both anticipation and caution. The trustees knew that Clemson had been sustained through the war years, in part, by being selected to serve as one of the military officer training campuses. They could only thank the federal government for the influx of young men preparing for the war. And they could only thank the skills of now-deceased President Enoch Sikes, his astute business manager, Jim Littlejohn, who handled the sheaf of paperwork, and the dedicated service of Rudolph Lee, who designed buildings almost to order in the 1930s, using federal "Depression emergency funds" to help underwrite the bonds and construction of the five new barracks, Long Hall, and much of the Physical Education Building. A small group of men, including James Byrnes, then a U.S. senator, and Frank Lever, who died in 1940, both with close knowledge of Washington, D.C., and strong Democratic Party ties, had kept the "way clear" for the college's miracle of growth during the Depression.

Byrnes, the newest of the life trustees elected in 1941, filled the vacancy on the board created by the death of Lever. He had been a friend of Clemson College for years. Bradley, the oldest board member, had replaced his father, J. E. Bradley, in 1907. Having served as president of the board since 1935, W. W Bradley began his service when Richard Wright Simpson, B. R. Tillman, and J. E. Wannamaker, all named life trustees in Mr. Clemson's will, were still active. Bradley served as board president until his death in 1948. In fact, the thirteen trustees in 1945 collectively supervised the college for a combined total of more than 220 years, or an average of twelve and a half years per person.

Like most institutions of higher education, Clemson, its trustees, and other leaders braced for three major challenges: increased enrollment, facilities that needed enlarging, and replacing aging faculties. Of course, each challenge had been created and made worse by the Depression decade and a half of material shortages and then the demands of war. For all schools, some common answers existed, but each college faced unusual hurdles and specific combinations.

The Enrollment

Preparation for the expected war's end continued at Clemson since late 1943 or early 1944. President Frank Poole and Littlejohn had made reasoned estimates of what the male enrollment might reach because eighteen-year-olds were no longer drafted and Clemson men now in service were demobilized and returned to domestic life via the GI Bill of Rights. The initial increase of students in September 1945 numbered 296, or about 40 percent since the close of the college the past June. While some were veterans, others included the hoped-for new high school graduates. But in South Carolina, the number graduating from high school remained lower than originally expected because the legislature had authorized the addition of the twelfth grade, which obviously reduced the availability of new high school graduates.

The addition of the twelfth grade had resulted from two decades of efforts by State Superintendent of Education James Haskell Hope (1874–1952), who served in that office from his election in 1922 until 1945. From Hope Station, Newberry County, he had graduated from Clemson in the Class of 1896 and received his master's degree from Newberry College. He is noted for a number of major reforms and gifts, including his donation of land in his county to the Rosenwald Fund to help create the Hope Rosenwald School. It was built to a Rudolph Lee plan and continues today to serve the community. Hope is also noted for helping open the way for African Americans to receive high school diplomas from South Carolina public schools. During his twenty-three years as superintendent, his best-known achievements included the creation of the public school teachers' retirement plan, the passage of a state school attendance law, and the previously noted addition of twelfth grade.[1]

Poole had made it quite clear that Clemson welcomed all academically (and legally) qualified male veterans who applied, while some neighboring schools chose to admit any veteran. But in schools everywhere, pockets of resistance existed to the intrusion of the much older and more worldly men into the academic community, and some institutions took in many more students than they could accommodate.[2]

Some schools opened special parts of their campuses, separating the veterans with a *cordon sanitaire* from the traditional students. Clemson's challenge was a bit different. For the trustees and administration, three other problems loomed: the relationship of the veterans to the cadet corps, housing, and the teaching capacity. The first involved Clemson's military regimen. The small number of veterans who enrolled in late 1944 and 1945 had remained in regular service uniforms until the end of hostilities in August, as generally required by the War Department. They were excused from regular cadet formations, training, and duties. And the administrators assumed the veterans wished it that way and planned to continue that mode. But not all wanted to remain "military." In early 1946, John Evans remembered that when he returned to Clemson to enroll and heard that full military regimen would continue for veterans, he picked up his baggage and planned to catch the bus out of town. His next choice was Auburn, also a land-grant college. But before he arrived there, a group of veterans, returning Clemson students led by Robert Grigsby, met with Poole to state firmly the veterans' case. Clemson's administration reversed itself, setting aside military participation for returning servicemen. John Evans returned to Clemson to finish in agriculture in 1948 and then join the college's staff. Other veterans did likewise.[3]

The second semester of 1945–1946, the student population rose by 403, and the growth continued until fall of 1949, when the student number leveled off and even turned down once more. But the new men were very different students. Many were older, war-toughened individuals. By the second semester of 1945–1946, enrollment reached 1,644, the largest since 1942–1943. But 917 (or 56 percent) were freshmen (although a number were not of the more usual younger age), a percentage only surpassed by the college's opening Class of 1893, and the mean age of the freshman class had risen from seventeen in 1940 to twenty-one. The men twenty-five and older numbered 181 (11 percent), with four over thirty-five. These were neither the young striplings who had arrived at the school in 1893 nor the young men who returned from World War I, following the nineteen-month participation in battle. Nor were they almost completely southern with more traditional attitudes toward the land, race, religion, and any other characteristics that had marked the earlier "new boys."[4]

Emergency Housing

The immediate housing of students posed no serious problem. Through the influence of U.S. Senator Burnet R. Maybank, the financial juggling of Littlejohn, and the attention of John Hobart Gates in the Federal Housing Administration, surplus military housing began rolling on trucks into the campus. Over 300 additional single men could be squeezed into existing buildings by adding 84 beds in Barracks One, housing 120 in the upper floors of the Physics (originally Textiles and now Godfrey) Building, putting 94 beds in the little gym (the western part of the Field House), and picking up additional space in Barracks Seven and the firehouse. The cost to the college, including war surplus beds and enhancing the bathrooms, amounted to $16,600. A survey indicated that another hundred could be housed in the small town of Clemson.

Fifty prefabricated homes were moved onto the campus. These houses, with two bedrooms, one principal room, a bath and a kitchen, and called "U.K." homes, soon received the name "prefabs" from locals. Eventually, 300 of these were placed in two campus communities: one on the south campus in an area, according to Poole, "suitable for the development of our future Agricultural building program";

Housing the influx of returning veterans following World War II led to the move of single and double prefabricated homes, called "U. K. homes" or "prefabs," onto campus. Clemson University Photographs, CUL.SC.

and the other along the Greenville Highway (now Walter T. Cox Jr. Boulevard), in an area later developed into athletic buildings and fields. In addition, two-story frame barracks housed 196 single veterans, and other surplus buildings found use for classes. A large group of these lay in the field west of the baseball diamond and north of the Field House. Clemson was prepared for 2,700 students.

Thus, that enrollment limit was set not by administrative choice, but by crowding and stretching existing facilities, by the Federal Housing Administration, and by the very nature of the small, isolated community. Just one year proved the federal government's prediction for housing needs was inadequate. Flooded with applications from more recently demobilized veterans and by a record number of the newest high school graduates, the college administration, nudged by Registrar Gustave Metz (Clemson 1927), stepped, perhaps belatedly, into action. Littlejohn took inventory, not just of living space, but also of faculty and their teaching fields, of the college's capacity for teaching and laboratory space, and of the library and its holdings. A series of faculty committees assisted. The mess hall and the infirmary also had increasing problems. And the long-term faculty housing problem still needed resolution. Fortunately, federal regulations permitted a modest percentage of government surplus housing to be occupied by faculty.

Gustave Ernest Metz (1907–1996), Clemson 1927, served Clemson from 1929 to 1964, first as an associate registrar and mathematics instructor, then as chief registrar, and finally as secretary to the Clemson Board of Trustees and assistant to presidents Poole and Edwards. Taken from the 1951 edition of the Clemson College annual, *Taps*.

Student Growth Continues

The 1946 freshman class of 1,477 included many students who had enrolled at February registration or had enrolled in a very full summer session, and the 1945–1946 freshman-to-sophomore retention rate (cohort to cohort) reached an unbelievable 91 percent. It was even higher for sophomores-to-juniors, which increased from 141 in 1945–1946 to 510 in 1946–1947. And the senior class grew from 85 to 394. The Registrar's Office carefully maintained firm standards for new students, whether freshmen or transfers, while it admitted returning "old boys" on prior eligibility. And the faculty, many back from duty, had every bit as rigorous demands in the classroom as before the war. Overall, the student body, including special students, postgraduate students, and graduates, numbered 1,863 by June 1946. Also by then, women again enrolled in summer school for graduate course work in various vocational education programs, and one woman, Judith Haulbrook, began undergraduate work in education during summer sessions only.[5] By the end of 1947, the total student body had reached 3,350, an increase of nearly 80 percent.[6]

Throughout the summer of 1946, more temporary wooden barracks arrived, but the trustees, on the suggestion of Charles Daniel, not a trustee but an informal advisor to the board, hired the architectural firm of Lyles, Bissett, Carlisle and Wolff of Columbia to study the situation and make a thorough recommendation about the existing old barracks.[7] The college's Building and Grounds Committee, headed by David Watson, had undertaken an inventory of the lands and properties of the college, both on the campus and around the state. Excluding the large property leased from the federal government for ninety-nine years, the campus contained 1,610 acres, of which the teaching buildings and athletic fields occupied 400, the farms 463, and forest, meadow, and other uses 747. The estimated value of the acreage amounted to $198,562 (2009 equivalent $2,158,417.50). The real properties around the state were worth approximately $168,144 (2009 equivalent $1,827,739). On campus, the Main, Chemistry, Trustee, and Barracks One buildings, and a few of the original faculty homes, survived from their construction between 1890 and 1893, while the most recent new facility was the football stadium. All the campus buildings collectively had a value of $3,717,751 (2009 equivalent $40,412,250.32), including contents. The buildings and contents off campus were estimated at $305,859 (2009 equivalent $3,324,711.76). The total value of everything at Clemson, including land, buildings, equipment, and supplies, was $6,146,716 (2009 equivalent $66,815,293.88), while everything away from Clemson had a value of $677,347 (2009 equivalent $7,362,815.99), for a grand total of $6,824,063 (2009 equivalent $74,178,109.87).

The same committee estimated that Clemson's immediate campus needs in buildings and renovation reached $8,465,000 (2009 equivalent $92,015,226.13). The renovation and addition of student dormitories cost twice everything else. The college also needed a new student hospital, the existing one having been built in 1893 in anticipation of the first class that entered. Porches had been added and equipment upgraded since then, but the examination and treatment rooms remained unchanged.[8]

A Master Plan

Confronted with this list of needs, the trustees determined that they should establish a master plan for such growth. A new chemistry building, renovation of the Main Building as a classroom structure for general studies, and renovation of the old Textile Hall for physics, raised questions of what could be done with the old Chemistry Building. Concern about the placement of four new engineering buildings, an architectural building, a new graduate studies building, and six new agricultural buildings bothered the faculty and the trustees. Rudolph Lee proposed massive renovation of Barracks One, Two, and Three; the erection of more brick barracks between One, Two, and Three and the stadium; and the use of the tract bordered by Fort Hill house, Textile Hall, and the cemetery for the additional engineering buildings. The agricultural expansion would continue around Long Hall, the old extension building, and the Dairy Building to the east of the outdoor theater. No indication existed whether or not the pre-war Lee exterior style would be continued. John Gates, the new head of architecture in 1947, conducted a thorough analysis of faculty and staff (as apart from employees) housing condition and needs. In the planning of the new Clemson, existing faculty committees, all of which reported to the president, along with new committees that also reported to the president, assisted in the process.[9]

The next year (1947–1948), student enrollment continued to rise, but more slowly, reaching 3,756. It then declined very slowly as the veterans graduated and the freshman class returned to the traditional sixteen- to eighteen-year-olds. All the counties of South Carolina were represented in the student body; however, students from the five most urban counties now comprised more than one-third of all the students. That alone, mirroring the change in South Carolina, helped dictate the shift from agriculture to more general studies. And 575 (15 percent) students came from other U.S. states and territories, with the remainder hailing from the Western Hemisphere.

Enrollment in major fields of study hastened the move away from agricultural and related areas (22 percent in 1946, down from 44 percent in 1919) toward more industry-related programs such as engineering, which included architecture (43 percent) and textiles (8 percent). The subjects preparatory for medical, teaching, legal, and commercial professions comprised the remaining growth. This continuing shift reflected both changes in society hastened by the more practical bent of the land-grant movement in the middle of the nineteenth century and by the strong movement toward general public high school education that had swept America near the last century's end. This was not unique to Clemson or South Carolina or even the South. America was no longer basically a rural, agricultural society. The newer age of the towns and suburbs dedicated to commerce and industry received support from a more efficiently produced, preserved, and transported food supply.

Besides rapid shifts in educational needs and goals, other national problems existed. They would be part of the problems that confronted many colleges and universities and would not be settled quickly, cheaply, or easily. These included equal opportunities for women and African Americans. In 1945, race represented the deepest and most pressing of America's domestic problems. These two and others would haunt the nation and all its institutions, including Clemson, for decades to come.

For Clemson Agricultural College, another pressing question involved teaching the swelling group of students seeking an education for the postwar world. Many of the younger prewar faculty remained away on military leave—whether in Japan as with English Prof. H. Morris Cox, in India as with history Prof. E. M. Lander Jr., in Europe as with several faculty in agriculture, or in the U.S. as with faculty on loan to science and technology pods. Thus, much of the teaching fell on older faculty, some summoned from retirement, others whose retirement was delayed, and still others who taught out of their academic field, particularly in the freshman and sophomore courses. New faculty were difficult to find at first because the salaries had remained unusually low, not having recovered from shortages brought on by the Depression and World War II, and many of the brightest young people were attracted to higher paying industry and just-emerging research complexes.

Clemson had to face the issue of gender, which although as important as race, did not have as vocal proponents or opponents as did the other question. Women had worked as part of the nonprofessional staff since the college's opening in 1893, as librarians since 1905, and on occasion as faculty since 1918. But during the 1930s, there had been none in the faculty until World War II created the shortage of available men.[10] Of the 208 faculty, two were women who had joined Clemson in World War II. One, Elizabeth Epting, taught the French language and introductory European history. The wife of Carl L. Epting, a professor in social sciences, she joined the faculty in 1943 and served through the early postwar years. When the opportunity came to replace her with a male, President Poole wrote her a letter, thanking her for her service and noting that she had been the best Clemson could find during the war.[11]

Faculty and Staff

Of the 208 faculty at the college in 1946–1947, thirty-two held PhD's (15 percent), three others held earned doctorates in veterinary medicine and surgery and in theology, and one held an honorary doctorate. Two others held terminal master's degrees in architecture and one a master's degree in fine arts, for a total of 16 percent of the faculty with terminal degrees. President Poole remained concerned about the number who held only master's degrees. The situation could not be remedied until state funding improved, the supply of new faculty increased, and Clemson developed strategies to give promising younger faculty the time and resources to secure terminal degrees. The fifty-person administration (25 percent the size of the faculty) contained persons with earned doctorates (10 percent of the administrative staff). In addition, in 1946, thirty-two staff worked at the five experiment stations; fifty-one were at the "home farm" at Clemson, with much of the research taking place on "land-use" property.

The Clemson regulatory commissions had eighty-six staff, many of them housed in Columbia. At the same time, the extension service employed fifty-five professional and support staff based at Clemson, Winthrop, and South Carolina State. There were three district agents and forty-six county agents. Twenty-nine African American agricultural agents, none with full county responsibilities, worked with the county agents. In addition, the home demonstration agents, located at Winthrop by an agreement between the earlier presidents of Clemson (Riggs) and Winthrop (Johnson), but directed from Clemson, were assigned to the counties. African American agents worked under an African American assistant director, who received direction from Clemson but was housed in Orangeburg at South Carolina State. Although exceptions had existed very early in extension history and later in the human resource shortages during World War II, the county agents were required to hold bachelor's degrees at the minimum. Home demonstration agents and assistant agents (both agricultural and home) had no such requirement. In the years immediately after the war, the number and percentage of African American agents without bachelor's degrees remained unchanged, and the salary disparities were, though present, not great. But as the decade progressed and the effects of the GI Bill emerged, the disparities were perceived to have grown steadily. In their separate annual meeting in 1947, the Association of Negro Agents petitioned the Clemson administration for relief, not because the gap in wage scales with white assistant agents had grown (which it had), but because the African American wage scale had not kept pace with the rapidly escalating cost of living.[12]

Although the student housing shortage had received brief attention, long-term housing for students awaited the report of the Lyles architecture firm. Housing for faculty and staff was also poor. Erecting needed homes was beyond the immediate capability of the college. The town lay between the concentration of classrooms, dormitories, other principal buildings, and the older campus faculty homes and the Southern railway tracks. Some residential development, mostly west of College Avenue, the artery that connected the campus with the Southern line as it passed close to the small but growing business district, had occurred. College Avenue crossed the Southern rail line into the village still known as Calhoun and on through some of the Clemson College-managed land-use property. The property most conducive to residential growth lay east of College Avenue and north of the Greenville road that bordered the campus, creating an east-west axis.

Individual younger faculty built homes in that section, and gradually the community grew. Unlike the older neighborhood with the five churches (Presbyterian, Episcopal, Methodist, Baptist, and Catholic, in order of founding), where only a few streets had names of persons and the rest for trees and plants, the newer streets were named for former faculty such as Strode, Riggs, Daniel, and Martin. The new neighborhood barely met the need of younger faculty and their families. Littlejohn and faculty leaders realized this shortage of housing was so acute that it seriously limited the college's ability to recruit new professors.

The New Accommodations

The Gates-led study provided a large amount of population data and estimates of the availability of potential faculty in the fields that Clemson emphasized. President Poole received the report on April 13, 1948; it called for a mixed-use apartment house-hotel complete with meeting rooms, a large lounge, and other features more common to upscale urban hotels to replace the rambling frame hotel that had overlooked the parade ground for over a half century. The hotel-apartment house, the committee reasoned, would appeal to more transitory faculty, staff, and retired members of the faculty. The committee also recommended a large complex of attached two- and one-story residences set on a park-like hill overlooking older faculty homes located on the college grounds. The residences would help attract new young faculty and their families. The report also noted the need for a private building project sponsored in some way by the college.[13] When the Board of Trustees received this report, Edgar A. Brown (July 11, 1888–June 26, 1975), a legislative trustee from 1934 to 1947 and elected a life trustee on March 20, 1948,[14] had the state bond bill amended to permit Clemson's trustees to issue $1 million in bonds to proceed with construction immediately.[15] (The break in Brown's tenure on the board resulted from a new state law that prevented legislators from holding two state posts simultaneously.)

Unencumbered by a large state bureaucracy, the bonds were issued, architects and engineers were selected, and the vital construction project began. In the meantime, the prefabricated housing units vacated by veterans and their families were pressed into service.[16] Housing for African American staff was also in short supply, and, through careful tending of the bond money and other savings, a series of apartments was erected on the eastern border of the campus between the new faculty units and the African American residential neighborhood. These were named the Tom Littlejohn Apartments by the trustees in honor of a long-serving African American cook in the mess hall.[17] The rental price was generally higher than many families felt able to pay, and this effort went for nothing.

The apartment houses and hotel proposed by the Lyles firm's study were opened for bidding, with plans for the college to issue bonds under state authority for $1 million. In case that was not sufficient for covering the building costs, Poole and Littlejohn intended to approach the FHA for a loan at 4.5 percent interest. The bids were opened, and Daniel Construction Company of Greenville had the lowest. Once he signed the contract, the firm's owner, Charles Daniel, proposed to begin immediately, bypassing the FHA and returning to the state for authorization to issue sufficient bonds at a lower interest rate. During the wait, his crew began the work and the company paid the cost without interest until the state issued the bonds. If that did not happen, then the college planned to turn to the FHA. The FHA concurred. The trustees and Littlejohn leapt for joy. The massive building project began.[18]

Daniel's crews and machinery remained on campus for the next decade. As it arose from the hill overlooking the campus, the new hotel-apartment house drew interest from the community similar to that shown during the creation of the campus in the early 1890s. The complex had a slate-paved porch and entrance hall, a large open lounge that soon became a community center and would be the site of regular tables of bridge and other games, a lower level "nonalcohol-selling" club, and a pair of elevators that whisked folks up the seven stories of rooms and apartments to a fully equipped three-bedroom penthouse.

The luxurious penthouse on a gracious, but utilitarian, campus was Charles Daniel's special gift (for which he paid) to Clemson. The terraces of the penthouse still give glorious views over the rolling college acreage against successive vistas of lakes and the Blue Ridge. And the penthouse has served special Clemson guests, including a number of S.C. governors, U.S. senators, U.S. Secretary of State Dean Rusk, and some of the world's greatest performing artists, such as violinist Yehudi Menuhin and world-renowned opera singer Beverly Sills. On the main floor, a large dining room named the Sabre Room was furnished with famous Charles Eames wooden tables and chairs and featured a large mural by Gilmer Petroff. The largest mural in the state (forty-by-seven-foot), it received a superb description from Louis Wolff, a member of the architecture firm that designed much of the campus that emerged in the next decades:

> The mural will represent a sort of cavalcade of cadet activity beginning on the right (the viewer's left) with a lonely freshman hiding behind a signal corps insignia and progressing from Pfc. through sergeant to the coveted 'pie plates' as the officer's collar insignia is known. Infantry symbols join allusions to the Clemson-USC rivalry, and a foaming beer mug leads to a student contemplating military or civil life.

The mural was a gift from the partners of the architecture firm of Lyles, Bissett, Carlisle and Wolff, all four graduates of Clemson's architecture program.

A fountain beside the main entrance to the hotel, named the Clemson House, contained a freely mounted stainless steel tiger sculpture done by Charleston artist Willard Hirsch. Water play and the breezes caused the tiger to move and "roar." The hotel had a staff of five chefs, and students earned money as waiters and lug-

The Clemson House, built in 1950, was known as "Carolina's smartest hotel." The hotel-apartment house complex included a large dining room (the Sabre Room) featuring a mural by Gilmer Petroff, a club (Tiger Tavern), seven stories of rooms and apartments, and a three-bedroom penthouse overlooking the rolling college acreage. Clemson University Photographs, CUL.SC.

Top: the Clemson House on the crown of its hill. *Middle*: the Clemson House's Sabre Room. *Bottom*: the famous Tiger Tavern.

gage carriers. Its Sunday luncheons attracted guests from around the area, and the Clemson House was called "Carolina's Smartest Hotel."[19]

Campus Changes

In the midst of this eruption of modern art and architecture at the college, two memories of the past were added to Clemson's campus. The first was one of South Carolina's oldest "European" houses. Thomas F. Waterman, an architect with the U.S. Department of the Interior, had surveyed all the properties in the path of the Santee-Cooper hydroelectric project along with many other remnants of colonial life. He concluded that "Hanover (the name it was given by its builder, Paul de St. Julien, in 1714) is the only house in the proposed region of inundation, the loss of which can be considered of national importance." Clemson, through Rudolph Lee, had shown interest in helping to save this early relic and, with the work of Watson and Littlejohn, successfully applied to the Santee-Cooper Authority for a grant to move the house to the campus. J. B. Lee, Clemson 1940, photographed the entire removal project, supervised the dismantling and labeling of each shingle, board, stud, joist, beam, and brick, and loaded all carefully on trucks for hauling 250 miles to Clemson. Stored, it awaited the end of

HANOVER HOUSE   CLEMSON, SOUTH CAROLINA

A drawing of Hanover House by Joseph L. Young, A.I.A. Young was a professor of architecture at Clemson from 1950 until his retirement. This presentation drawing is used with the kind permission of the Joseph Laurie Young estate.

World War II for Watson to supervise the careful reassembly near the sheep barn in an area Watson hoped to turn into a "colonial restoration district." The work on reassembly began in 1945. The Spartanburg Committee of the Colonial Dames of America furnished the house, which the committee accomplished over several years. The home opened on June 7, 1962, and among the Colonial Dames most involved were Mrs. M. A. Owings and Mrs. James Sams, both faculty wives.[20] Hanover House has since attracted unusual gifts, including a 1694 Huguenot Bible printed in London and two 1771 hand-colored bird prints by Mark Catesby, a gift of Mr. and Mrs. Charles N. Gignilliat.[21] Unfortunately, Hanover House found itself directly in the path of progress again as the Clemson campus grew. Although a volatile issue, the house was moved in 1994 to a new campus site in the S.C. Botanical Garden.[22]

The second memory from the past involved the placing of two cannons on campus. Sculptor Abe Davidson had accepted the cannons on behalf of the college in the 1930s from Charles Gerald, the secretary to Governor Ira C. Blackwood. Gerald, knowing that Davidson was searching for metal from which to cast Thomas Clemson's statue, suggested, "In the basement of the Capitol there are some Civil War cannons. Would you like to have these cannons to use for the casting of the Clemson statue? If you don't get them something will happen to them and they will get lost." Davidson accepted but then promptly dismissed the offer as a mere courtesy. Half a year went by, and Davidson received a phone call from his brother in Greenville, "What in the hell are you doing bringing cannons to my back yard? A highway truck is here with two cannons. Get them out of here as soon as you can. I don't want any cannons laying [sic] around here." Davidson had the truck rerouted to the campus and the cannons delivered to the shop, where Prof. Ed Freeman stored them.[23]

Forgotten again, they resurfaced only in 1951, by which time the story of how the cannons got to Clemson was lost. John D. Jones Sr., Clemson 1915, contributed to a fund to mount them on Bowman Field. His son, Lt. Col. James B. Jones, and Watson supervised the construction.[24] The cannons took the place of the World War I howitzer, originally a gift of the Class of 1926, which the college had donated to the scrap metal drive in 1942.[25] Years later, an artillery historian concluded that the 1842 Ames cannon is one of sixty-two made and is either No. 11 or No. 24. The second is the Alger 1861 and is probably No. 178 or No. 206. Students call the cannons "Tom and Jerry."[26]

Academic Expansion

The teaching and research missions required an entirely new heating plant and system; buildings for chemistry, general engineering, ceramic engineering, plant science, animal science, and agricultural engineering; and 690 additional two-person student bedrooms. The cost was estimated at $7 million.[27] The money would come from a combination of housing bonds, state-secured bonds, federal grants (particularly in agricultural research money), and various other sources. Edgar Brown proved extremely helpful with the legislature in getting bonding permission for much of the financing.

Among the most desperately needed was a new chemistry building. The original building, marked "1890," had been enlarged in 1900 at a time when all students took some chemistry, but the building had long ago been strained far beyond capacity. In 1946, the building caught fire. Area fire departments responded quickly and contained the fire, limiting the loss to the upper floor interior and the large, Romanesque hipped roofs. The state acted quickly, finding money to stabilize and rebuild the landmark. Of course, insurance money, paid by college funds, provided a basis on which to expand. While the rebuilding provided a stopgap measure, it would not be the larger, up-to-date chemistry building needed for post–World War II teaching and research. Daniel Construction Company did the work.[28]

The larger, desperately needed chemistry building now awaited a master plan. The college hired the firm of Perry, Shaw and Hepburn, Kehoe and Dean of Boston to develop the long-desired master plan for the campus. The firm assigned it to J. F. Larson, who had already provided such plans for Dartmouth, Lehigh, Bucknell, and Wake Forest. When the plan was presented, it designated logical areas for programmatic enlargement and circulation schemes for pedestrians and vehicles given Clemson's long-term goals, enrollment models, topography, and environment. Building perspectives were in a generic red brick style. Nothing alarmed Poole or the older trustees.

Trustee Changes

Between the years 1945 and 1950, the changes in Clemson board membership accelerated. The S.C. Legislature amended the state code in the spring of 1947 to bar public officials from holding two state positions simultaneously. The new law affected four Clemson legislative trustees. In the face of the change, Clemson's six surviving life trustees elected Edgar A. Brown, one of the four affected legislative trustees, to the open life position. When officially asked, the state attorney general issued an opinion that life trustees were not public officials, which only confirmed the importance of the intention of the Clemson will. Brown, needing no time for "learning," joined the life trustees.

On the legislative side, trustees ousted by their colleagues in the general assembly included W. C. Graham, a nine-year veteran; J. P. Mozingo III, elected in 1941; and S. H. Sherard, who had served since 1930. Among those who took their place was W. A. Barnette of Greenwood (1886–1962), a 1910 Clemson

T. Wilbur "Buddy" Thornhill (1892–1978), Clemson 1914, the owner of the Charleston Oil Company and a Clemson trustee from 1947 to 1960, was a proponent of moving Clemson into the future rapidly, especially in the enrollment of women students. Clemson University Photographs, CUL.SC.

graduate in agriculture and a veterinary science faculty member from 1914 to 1918.

Another addition, John McLaurin of Bennettsville (1901–1959), came from Marlboro County and attended elementary and high schools in McColl. He enrolled briefly in North Carolina State College before serving in the U.S. Army during World War I. When he returned, he attended Clemson and received a BS degree in textiles in 1922. He spent four years raising cotton with his father, then he married Leila Kirkpatrick, moved to Bennettsville in 1931, and became a "large scale farmer," according to the *News and Courier* of Charleston (September 21, 1959).

The third new legislative trustee, T. Wilbur "Buddy" Thornhill (1892–1978), graduated from Clemson with a degree in electrical and mechanical engineering and married Anna Van Noy Smith from Summerville, Thornhill's birthplace. After serving in Panama and France during World War I, he and his family settled in Charleston, where he served as the principal director of the Charleston Oil Company. He had a close friendship with Poole, whom he addressed privately as "Sarge." Thornhill strongly supported opening Clemson to women.[29] He was already irritated that Poole had not really pushed the trustees on the issue and the legislature on permission to offer bonds for women's housing.

The fourth new legislative trustee was Ben Tillman Leppard (1892–1957) from Greenville. After graduating from Greenville High School, he studied agriculture at Clemson, interrupted his education to serve in the army in World War I, and upon his discharge received his BS degree in 1919. From there he studied law at Furman University, was called to the bar, and joined the Greenville firm of Leppard and Leppard with his brother James Ernest. Leppard had served in the S.C. House (1933–1934) and then the S.C. Senate (1937–1940). In between, he worked as an aide to Governor Olin D. Johnston (1934–1938) and participated actively in state and national Democratic Party affairs. He had also been a legislative trustee for Clemson from 1934 to 1938.[30]

But change on the board had not yet run its course. Besides claiming J. E. Sirrine, death laid its shroud on Life Trustee W. W. Bradley, who had served as a member of the board for forty-one years and as board president since Wannamaker's death in 1935. For the new board president, the remaining legislative and life trustees selected Christie Benet (1879–1951), who had served as a life trustee since 1929. Born in Abbeville, Benet was nine years old when his father played a leading role in moving the bill to accept Thomas Green Clemson's will through the general assembly. Benet initially attended South Carolina College, transferred, and earned a BS degree from the College of Charleston. He earned a law degree from the University of Virginia, where he played football and was awarded a Phi Beta Kappa key. While in Columbia, he worked as a volunteer coach for South Carolina's football team. In the aftermath of South Carolina's upset victory over Clemson in 1902, he is credited with holding up the brewing confrontation between the students long enough for police to arrive and halt the trouble.

Benet had filled the U.S. Senate seat left vacant by B. R. Tillman's death in 1918. He had served as chair of the S.C. War Finance Committee in World War II. An active Episcopalian, he was involved with the Episcopal retreat Camp Kanuga and the Diocese of Upper South Carolina. Married and father of a daughter, he strongly urged higher education for women. In his papers is a report in which he wrote, "It is the glory of this century that now a woman may acquire the highest education without being decided as a blue stocking."[31]

Of course, the life trustee post made vacant by Bradley's death needed filling. In 1949, the remaining six life trustees elected Charles Ezra Daniel (1895–1964), the Greenville construction magnate, to join the board. Daniel, born in Elberton, Georgia, had grown up in Anderson, South Carolina, where he attended high school. He entered the Citadel in 1916 and after two years there began working with Townsend Lumber Company, where he had also worked while in high school and where he continued to work until 1935. In 1924, he married Homozel Mickel of Elberton, Georgia; they had no children.

Charles Ezra Daniel (1895–1964), a U.S. senator and co-founder of Daniel Construction Company, served Clemson as a builder, planner, forward thinker, and life trustee. Clemson University's Charles E. Daniel Center for Building Research and Urban Studies in Genoa, Italy, is named in his honor. Clemson University Photographs, CUL.SC.

Upon leaving Townsend, Daniel organized Daniel Construction Company of Greenville. He was a close friend of A. C. Crouch, the founder of Piedmont Engineers, Architects, and Planners, Inc., whose father, the Rev. Dr. Sydney Crouch, served as pastor of Fort Hill Presbyterian Church in Clemson. Under Crouch's leadership, the congregation, whose primary ministry was to Clemson students, faculty, staff, and their families, joined by Presbyterians across South Carolina and Clemson alumni everywhere, had constructed a new building in 1931 to accommodate the rapidly growing Clemson cadet corps. A year later a fire broke out and destroyed the sanctuary, the pastor's study, and a large room designated for college students. Daniel endorsed, by letter, a petition to the state office of the Reconstruction Finance Corporation (an agency of the federal government) for financial help for the church. The petition also had the support of regional Boy Scout executives (the church was the host institution for the little community's scout troop along with the local town fellowship club for men) and had the signatures of over a third of the cadets. The RFC contributed the amount necessary to pay the salaries of the skilled workers who rebuilt the church.[32]

Daniel Construction Company next built the barracks, known then as Barracks Four, Five, Six, Seven, and Eight, and the Textile (Sirrine) Building, along with smaller textile plants before the approaching military conflict turned the company's attention to war needs, which included the construction of the Charleston Naval Yard.[33]

When Daniel received the invitation from the six life trustees of Clemson to join the board, he did not accept until he had assurance that his company could still bid on construction for the college. Benet posed the question to the attorney general, who replied that so long as the bidding was open and the low bid was taken or rejected with good reason, no conflict existed. There was also an internal problem; Section 14 of the bylaws of the Clemson Board of Trustees prohibited the board from entering into a contract with the business of a fellow member. Before Daniel received the offer to join it, the whole board clarified the relationship of the section when the transaction was by open bid. In his prior dealings with Clemson College in the five barracks and the Textile Building, Charles Daniel had always submitted the lowest bids, saving Clemson an estimated $115,000 during the Depression. It would be to Clemson's good fortune in matters much broader than money alone that Daniel took his place as a trustee.[34]

The board had changed greatly. The life trustees, who ranged in age from fifty-two (one) to seventy-five (two), were considerably younger on average than the group five years earlier. The same held true for the legislative trustees, whose age spread was narrower, from forty-six to sixty-three, averaging fifty-five, or ten years younger than their life colleagues. The board service for the life trustees averaged fifteen and a half years, but the average of those elected by the legislature numbered only five and a half, with most of that credited to F. E. Cope and J. B. Douthit Jr.

If the life trustees' multiple careers are considered, three had strong agricultural backgrounds, two had longtime industrial ties (one close to textile interests), one had a legal and financial background, and two had major political careers. Four were primarily farmers of large properties, although one of them, R. M. Cooper, had powerful industrial connections. Byrnes was on his way to becoming a political icon. The legislative trustees had greater homogeneity in occupation. One was an urban lawyer; another was an urban businessman with strong agricultural interests. The others were also in agriculture. But then, all life and legislative trustees were community leaders who had served or did serve in public life. All were Protestants (Baptist, Episcopalian, Methodist, or Presbyterian), although Byrnes was born into a Catholic family, and all were active churchmen.

Residentially, men from the Lowcountry (including the Pee Dee), where eight of the trustees had primary residences, dominated, while three came from the Upstate. Only Board President Benet called the Midlands home. While Byrnes had a geographic attachment to the whole state, he really had national interests at heart. Politically, all were progressive or "New Deal" Democrats.

They had practical educational interests. Three had not attended college. Board President Benet had personal ties to the College of Charleston, then a quasi-municipal, private college more in the tradition of the classical liberal arts. But Benet also had familial ties to Clemson, educational ties to the University of Virginia, and an affection for the University of South Carolina. Among the life trustees, only T. Benton Young held a Clemson degree, but all the legislative trustees had Clemson degrees, and of them, Leppard had also received a law degree from Furman University. As a whole, they were sensible political and economic progressives and realists, with deep affection for Clemson College, and they were committed to steering the school's course in the best interests of South Carolina of the future.

Architectural Revolution

To this board, Lyles, Bissett, Carlisle and Wolff Architects brought their housing report. It was not really what Poole wanted to hear. Barracks One, Two, and Three, built from the 1890s to 1907, were wooden-frame structures whose appearance of stability resulted mainly from the two-ply brick. All wiring, electrical equipment, and plumbing, along with almost all the sinks, toilets, showers, and tubs, had to be replaced. Further, the placement of windows and exterior doors was such that the option of retaining the brick shells and creating new interiors would yield only a slight increase in capacity. Further, Barracks One held the primary kitchens and the mess hall, which, while kept clean, contained outmoded equipment. And the space was (and had been for years) simply too small to serve the traditional "one seating" Clemson College meals. Furthermore, the county health department had placed the YMCA small dining room on notice for significant improvement or closure, while the only local café had received a health warning. Simply to fix Clemson's housing and feeding problem would cost about $4,250,000, with no increase in capacity.[35] Daniel, whose engineering firm had estimated the cost, noted that a new, modern design for well-built and safe housing and an adequate dining facility would cost less than half, and some increase in capacity would be achieved relatively inexpensively.

After much discussion, the board decided to raze the three old barracks, and it directed the Lyles firm to begin sketch plans. While the records do not speak to the issue, the architects must have understood that they could abandon the older, dark red brick that had more or less brought an aesthetic unity to the campus. Meanwhile, the Florence firm of Hopkins and Baker worked on the new Chemistry Building. It was located directly north of the old Chemistry Building, which made the removal of the old greenhouse necessary. While this older metal and glass structure was lovely in its late Victorian and early Edwardian style, it had been isolated from the group of agriculture buildings since the original Agricultural Hall destroyed by fire had been rebuilt as the library between 1925 and 1927.

The new Chemistry Building continued the use of red (but now cherry) brick in combination with fieldstone, slate, and limestone, and it had a flat roof. Its footprint, a "C," continued the Lee tradition of avoiding quadrangles (probably for fire safety and ventilation). Inside, the north wing had a large lecture laboratory with modern audiovisual equipment and a seminar room. However, it did not take advantage of the northern sky's even, reflected light. The south wing had a range of smaller (approximately one-hundred-seat) lecture halls and lecture laboratories. The center or west unit included student laboratories, faculty office laboratories, the chemistry library and faculty lounge, and the departmental head/dean's reception and office. The interior was surfaced in ceramic tiles. One of the college's first permanent modern buildings, it was well constructed. Industrial Builders of Anderson, the low bidder, received the contract for $514,731. The laboratories con-

The new Chemistry Building shortly after its completion in 1951, later named Brackett Hall in honor of Richard Newman Brackett, eminent Clemson professor of chemistry. Clemson University Photographs, CUL.SC.

tained the finest equipment available, thanks to a $50,000 grant from the Rockefeller Foundation. Poole personally presented the faculty-authored application.[36]

At almost the same time, the area south of the main cluster of buildings, where the southern "prefabs" were placed, was prepared for Poole's dream—a new center for agricultural sciences. These facilities ranged along the eastern ridge, as were Long Hall, the Dairy Building, and a few others. The first of the buildings designed was for agricultural engineering, which had survived in the sheep barn. The new building continued the use of cherry red brick with a modest amount of limestone. C. Hardy Oliver of the Oliver and Dickson of Columbia firm served as the architect, and Daniel Construction Company was the builder. This much construction required a large amount of furnishings and a prior major expansion of the heating, water, electric, and sewer systems, not to mention new streets and landscaping. The immediate and foreseeable building costs amounted to a staggering $3,875,000. Managing and facilitating these projects were J. C. Littlejohn, Edgar Brown, and Charles Daniel.[37]

Shortly thereafter, Lyles, Bissett, Carlisle and Wolfe presented the firm's plans for the new barracks. The plans were audacious. The overwhelming, low-slung range of modern buildings was designed to hold 2,200 cadets in reasonably sized double rooms. The units took advantage of the hillside sloping west toward the football stadium and the Seneca River, which made the relocation of the laundry and a smattering of other smaller support structures necessary. While each of the seven units functioned separately, they were interconnected so that the entire complex formed a large quadrangle. In basic scheme, it owed much to the Walter Gropius-designed Harvard-Harkness Graduate Center featured in *Architectural Record*.[38] The Clemson plan was three times as large and, like the Gropius design, included a modern series of kitchens and a single dining room capable of holding the entire corps in one sitting or, with dates, for all-student dances. The quadrangle had multiple entries, with covered openings suitable for moving cars and trucks in and out. The public entry was to the east through an open-air "loggia" (an Italian word meaning a covered but open-air entrance or passage), above which was a series of enclosed floors that included a lounge, administrative offices, rooms for student radio broadcast and the various publications, a nondenominational chapel, counseling offices, and meeting rooms. Also the central facility had a barbershop (an absolute necessity for an all-male military college), a lounge, and restrooms. The lower level (the main entry to the dining room) housed a canteen, dining room, kitchens, and a good-sized separate dining room that could serve as an athletic training table or banquet hall for clubs and societies.

But the real wonder was the construction. It used a new, but not untried, method known as "lift-slab," a system that required the erection of towering columns of reinforced concrete that had steel connectors protruding from all four sides at each level. Then, using metal forms, construction engineers and workers set the metal reinforcements and some utilities and poured concrete into the forms, all at ground level. When the concrete had hardened and cured, the slabs were slowly jacked to the appropriate level and fastened to the steel connectors on the load-bearing columns. It was a giant assembly line that minimized the need for concrete forms and teams of carpenters and laborers pushing wheelbarrows. Further, work crews were relatively small and specialized, and the scheme minimized the time and expenses of lifting concrete blocks, tiles, plumbing, and heavy materials because those could be ground-loaded before the slab was lifted. Interestingly, Buck Mickel, a relative of Mrs. Charles Daniel and a future life trustee of Clemson College, served as the site engineer for this huge complex.[39]

The new barracks, only a portion of which remains in today's Section A of Johnstone Hall, as it was being built. *Below:* an aerial view of one of the massive building's wings. *Right:* a closer photo of men engaged in raising the slabs that formed the floors of the building, a revolution in building construction. Clemson University Photographs, CUL.SC.

Concrete ledges that extended past the exterior walls emphasized the horizontality of the structure and were designed to serve as sun baffles in the not-air-conditioned South. Of course, they served as unintended sun decks and galleries for surprise sallies on the unwary. Long bands of glass, some panels of which opened for ventilation (and egress or entrance) and others fixed, emphasized the sense of horizontality. Inside the building, designed for young men, each floor had gang showers and toilets at intervals, while every room had lavatories and mirrors for shaving and grooming and built-in rifle racks. Halls wide enough for units to be formed and stairs wide enough to march down and for steamer trunks to be hauled from the car to the room fit the military life. Those who lived there also remembered kegs of beer and tubs of ice hauled in and impromptu (or arranged) contests of touch and tag football waged in the halls.

The massive complex, elegantly designed for a male military college before the age of air conditioning and ubiquitous electronic sound amplification, also captured the attention of *Architectural Record* and would reemerge in dormitories, apartment housing, and motels around the nation. It was a great improvement over the old barracks, even if it did break away from the red brick tradition of a campus that seemed to have sprung from the Piedmont's red hills. But within a very few years, the trustees would render the building much less functional when the board changed policies on military and women. Also, with glass on four sides, the complex could be very hot or very cold, depending on the weather.

While housing and the space for chemistry (and geology) were solved for the foreseeable future, and Old Chemistry would soon be occupied first by education and then by history—which was required of everyone, as it had been since the first year, and was grouped with government and economics as "social sciences"—there were still major classroom needs for the other fundamental fields of mathematics, English, and physics. And while textiles was generously housed in the textile building recently dedicated to the memory and honor of Life Trustee J. E. Sirrine, engineering had nearly burst the walls of Riggs Hall. In fact, engineering had spilled over into a specially designed brick building that housed industrial and some civil engineering classes and into several "growing more permanent" temporary wooden buildings. Classes and offices in the older fields of mechanical, electrical, and chemical engineering and architecture found themselves badly crowded. If Clemson expected to house over 3,000 (for which chemistry and the new barracks were built), then the college needed classrooms and laboratories for most fields and a much larger library. Also Daniel Construction Company undertook the construction of the new laundry and the new water filtration plant. Both were sited between the new barracks and the football stadium, as called for in the master plan being overseen and updated by Lockwood, Greene and Company of Greenville.[40]

President Poole asked the Building and Grounds Committee to recommend names for some of the principal buildings on campus. The pressures for this came from the fact that a new chemistry building replaced the near sixty-year-old original building, which had the legend "Chemistry" in the stone arch over one door. The college leaders sought to maintain traditional academic attachments. A second impetus was coming from Benjamin Ryan Tillman Jr., who visited in the community awaiting the fiftieth anniversary of his graduation, and he had written several articles on his father's role in establishing the college. His writings paid little attention to the work of other men and proposed that something should be done to keep his father's name alive.[41]

In the past, only the trustees had given names to buildings and spaces. They had named the main building "Agriculture," the fertilizer and chemistry building "Chemistry," and the old engineering and physics building "Mechanics." But then in 1904, they called the new building "Agricultural Hall," and although they did not specifically change the main building's name, most people referred to it as "Main."[42] The trustees also named the playing fields behind the YMCA "Riggs" in honor of the then president. Ten years later, they named the new engineering building "Riggs" for the just-deceased president.[43] Their next naming came with the opening of the new agriculture building, which they named for the recently deceased extension director, W. W. Long.[44]

Poole turned to the Building and Grounds Committee for its advice. David Watson, Clemson 1915, who was responsible for buildings and grounds, chaired the committee. The members were S. R. Rhodes, R. A. McGinty, A. M. Musser, G. B. Nutt, H. E. Glenn, J. H. Gates, J. H. Sams, and H. J. Webb.[45] They grappled with the problems and recommended that the old chemistry building become Hardin Hall; the new chemistry building to be named for Richard Brackett, the second chemist on the faculty; old Barracks One for R. W. Simpson, the first president of the board; old Barracks Two for Alan Johnstone, the second board president; and the main building for B. R. Tillman, one of the seven will life trustees. Curiously, the committee did not suggest a name for old Barracks Three. Poole took the committee's recommendations to the trustees, who approved them.[46] Regardless, just a few years after naming the two barracks, the trustees voted to raze all three old barracks. So Simpson and Johnstone disappeared from the physical portion of the campus.

Then, a fortuitous event for Clemson occurred. Frank Johnstone Jervey (Clemson 1914), a retired U.S. Army captain, returned "home" to Clemson from the Washington, D.C., area, where he had been with the Army Ordnance Corps for thirty-one years. Jervey, through his Clemson education, military service, and diligence, had become one of a handful of persons in America who were experts on side-arms munitions. One of the major manufacturers, whom he judged to produce the highest and most reliable of products, had a large endowed foundation, the Olin Foundation. Jervey had brought Clemson's work to the foundation's attention in the 1930s, and it had helped support the Clemson 4-H summer camps through the Depression.[47]

Frank Johnstone Jervey (1893–1983), Clemson 1914, captain in the U.S. Army, ordnance engineer for the Ordnance Corps of the Department of the Army (1922–1953), president of the Clemson Alumni Corporation, vice president for development at Clemson (1959–1963), and Clemson life trustee (1965–1976). Jervey was instrumental in working with the Olin Foundation to procure funds for two campus buildings. Clemson University Photographs, CUL.SC.

Jervey understood better than most the links between the ores explored carefully by faculty in Clemson's rapidly emerging ceramic engineering program and chemical engineering, another field of research for Clemson's younger faculty. He brought the laboratory and teaching space needs to the attention of the Olin Foundation's trustees and particularly to that of Charles L. Horn, the president, and James A. Wynn, the secretary-treasurer. After a few exploratory trips to Clemson, Horn announced a gift from the Olin Foundation of $421,871 for a building and $180,000 for equipment for a new ceramic engineering building for Clemson. During the visits, Horn had developed a warm friendship with Poole, who also presented Clemson's need very well. Olin reserved the right to name the builder.

What would almost immediately become a real team, the ceramic and chemical engineers and the architects in Clemson's School of Engineering, led by Gates, developed the plans and specifications for the building. Daniel Construction Company, with the lowest bid, a guarantee to absorb any overruns, the shortest promised date to completion, and much of its heavy equipment already on site, won the job. The state's engineers approved state construction and safety standards, and because the building needed no state funds for construction, Columbia provided no delay for it. The agreement between the foundation and the college was reached in the autumn of 1952, construction began on January 2, 1953, and the building's doors opened on September 24, 1953. The Clemson trustees had enthusiastically named the buff brick structure, which occupied the site south of Hardin Hall where the Fertilizer Building had stood, Olin Hall.[48] With the building of Brackett, the new barracks, and Olin Hall, the problem of a logjam of space on campus began to loosen.

In the field of natural resources, internal and public pressure had grown for Clemson to involve itself much more in the issues of water and soil, because every South Carolinian who had experienced the eroded land and the drought of the 1930s knew the importance of these substances for life. One of the most outspoken of South Carolina's citizens on these subjects was Buddy Thornhill of Charleston, who donated money to Clemson to carry on research and to pay for student trips into the hills and river basins of the region, hoping to impress upon the young men the necessity of thoughtful reconstruction of nature.[49] But the most pitifully housed of all Clemson's disciplines was agricultural engineering. Housed in one of Clemson's older barns, the faculty was led by George Nutt (1908–2007). Nutt, born in the farming town of Enterprise, Mississippi, received his BS degree in agricultural engineering from Mississippi State College in 1930. He joined the Clemson faculty in 1932, using the Depression summers and the academic leave encouraged by President Sikes to earn an MS degree in agricultural engineering from Iowa State College in 1940. He returned to Clemson and in 1941 became head of the department, a position he held until 1950, except for a period of service in the U.S. Army.[50]

In his budget request to the 1946 legislature, the first after World War II, Poole asked for, and received, permission to issue bonds up to $250,000 to build an agricultural engineering classroom and laboratory building. He formed a building committee with two tasks: write the building program and recommend a site. David Watson chaired the group, which included Gates, the head of architecture, Sams and two others from engineering, and Nutt, McGinty, and Musser from agriculture. Hamilton Hill, from the Business Office, was on the committee to watch over the fiscal aspects.[51] The architectural firm of Oliver and Dickson served as the design team. The chosen site for the building lay to the west of the three oldest barracks on the slope toward the stadium and the Seneca River basin.[52] Perhaps the building committee considered the slope for experimentation. However, it was far removed from the agricultural buildings to the east, only marginally closer to Riggs Hall, the center of the engineering world, and the attendant wooden "temporary" buildings behind it, and a good distance from

Olin Hall, longtime home to Clemson's Ceramic Engineering Department, shortly after its construction in 1953. Clemson University Photographs, CUL.SC.

the newer agricultural fields in the "bottoms" to the west. A number of faculty from engineering and agriculture complained vigorously to Poole. These reactions helped move Clemson toward hiring the master planning team noted earlier, while Littlejohn insisted that these decisions belonged to the trustees alone.[53]

After the Perry firm developed a master plan that fit well into the terrain, the almost entirely new agricultural complex was placed on the southeast side of campus, stretching out south of Long Hall. A site was chosen where the land began flattening as it sloped southward to the fields and pastures. The plans for the Agricultural Engineering Building showed a building of four large blocks. The center block was a two-story class and office unit surrounded on three sides by a large "C," a one-and-a-half-story set of laboratories equipped to study and test problems of water and soil of different types, water fall, and drainage, and allowed the study of agrarian mechanization on soils. Of cherry red brick and limestone, the new building sported aluminum-framed, ventable windows, large truck entrances, and a water-cooling tower. Money was also found to build a new seed laboratory and steam plant. The Agricultural Engineering Building was eventually named McAdams Hall for Prof. William U. McAdams, Clemson 1938, and a faculty member from 1939 to 1959.

The Clemson House, the faculty homes behind it, and the Tom Littlejohn staff homes were completed in 1950 at a cost of $2,925,000. The steam plant had cost $510,000, while the seed laboratory was only $25,000. The Agricultural Engineering Building would cost $275,000. Within two years, the new Chemistry Building was finished, equipped, and in use, and the equipment for the newly

The new home for Clemson's Agricultural Engineering Department in 1950, which stands today much changed as McAdams Hall. Clemson University Photographs, CUL.SC.

dedicated textile building, named Sirrine Hall; all was accomplished at a cost of $920,000. The very next year, 1953, the Olin Foundation paid $653,000 for Olin Hall and its special equipment. Moving the laundry and fitting it with new equipment, finishing the power, heat, and electricity enhancements (all which Gates designed), and new facilities for the 4-H camp at Pinopolis brought the total building cost up to $6,286,000.[54]

The remainder of the agriculture group consisted of two other buildings, the first the large Plant and Animal Sciences Building. The upper two floors held faculty offices, classrooms, laboratories, and student lounges. The basement had a ground level entry and loading dock on the south. Much of the basement space was given over to mechanical equipment and storage. The southwest quarter of the basement had small research, laboratory, and office space, while a goodly portion of the eastern side had space for the ever-increasingly important agricultural communications. The latter included space for producing and storing extension bulletins, an early form of outreach for agricultural extension, and for the radio, a medium in which Clemson had been an early leader.[55] And for the immediate future, considerable space provided for television. The exploration of this new mode of communication had been advocated by Poole almost since he arrived as president at Clemson in 1940.[56] Now a younger Board of Trustees and younger faculty were agreeing with him. Lyles, Bissett, Carlisle and Wolff designed the immense P&A Building of 205,515 square feet, and Daniel Construction Company built it. The façades were of buff brick with small inset glass windows. The north front had a beautiful green slate protrusion that held a large lecture hall. Willard

The Plant and Animal Sciences Building around the time of its completion in 1955. It was later renamed for Clemson's first alumnus-president, Robert Franklin Poole, after his death. Clemson University Photographs, CUL.SC.

Hirsch of Charleston, who also created the Clemson House tiger sculpture, created a symbolic stainless bas-relief that combined a bull, a beaker, and a plant.

The next and, for the time being, last of the major buildings in the agriculture group was the Food Industries Building, planned for instruction in meats and dairy. Besides the various types of meat laboratories and offices, it contained an adaptable auditorium designed for a variety of levels of instruction. A retractable curtain screened off a large open room suitable for preparing and butchering animal carcasses or having fruit, vegetable, or flower judging. The auditorium proved useful for student and community theater, partially because of its adaptability and its desirability, but also because of ample close-by parking. It also became increasingly popular as a site for smaller parties that frequently took place on big dance weekends. The building also contained dairy facilities, complete with a dairy bar that sold rich Clemson ice cream, milk, eggs, and the signature product, Clemson Blue Cheese. There is no wonder that the Food Industries Building welcomed steady streams of traffic. However, it rendered Lee's old Dairy Building useless, and it was destroyed. The two stories plus basement in the Food Industries Building contained 71,048 square feet, and Daniel was the builder. It continued the use of buff brick, slate, and aluminum, keeping a harmony with the Plant and Animal Sciences Building.[57]

A number of individual efforts produced this amazing feat of planning, design, and construction: the juggling abilities of J. C. Littlejohn; Charles Daniel's

The Food Industries Building, the new home to, among other programs, Clemson's Dairy Science Department, rendering Rudolph Lee's Dairy Building obsolete. It was later renamed in honor of Charles Carter Newman, Clemson 1896 and professor of horticulture (1899–1946), and in memory of his father, Col. John Stanley Newman, Clemson's first professor of agriculture (1892–1905). Clemson University Photographs, CUL.SC.

"gifts" as an aggressive builder whose bottom line was the economic and, thus, social progress of South Carolina; and a board under the direction of Christie Benet and then R. M. Cooper, about whom more will appear shortly. Alumnus Frank Jervey, whose deep loyalty to Clemson moved the college forward at a time when the state had other concerns, brought business friendships that provided two buildings. The transformation was hastened by the great desires of Buddy Thornhill, who occasionally chided President Poole, his old school chum. Poole wanted progress for Clemson, but he had his own dreams of Clemson primarily as a major agricultural research and teaching center.

The final cost for all the physical changes exceeded $16,130,000. State appropriations for planning, utilities, roads and walkways, the 4-H camp improvements, several regulatory facilities, and seed building amounted to $3,129,500. Charles Daniel's contributions in financing and the ability of Frank Jervey to involve Charles Horn and the Olin Foundation added $1,476,000 to Clemson's need. The remaining $10,500,000 came from the sale of bonds, the payment of which was pledged on anticipated dormitory room and rent, board payments, and by future tuition. An additional $316,000 was available from collegiate savings, again thanks to Littlejohn.[58]

However, a majority of the trustees had little patience with the seemingly endless discussions that Poole held with his administrative staff and with the desire of every branch of the college to be involved in every decision. Secondly, Poole's unhappiness with the architectural decisions that were leading Clemson away from its red brick, Bruce and Morgan and Lee styles, was pointed. Since the end of World War II, several trustees had urged Poole to recommend a management consulting team to study the Clemson administrative structure, but Poole had not done so. Perhaps some of the trustees had grown weary of the wait.

Notes

1.   Http://en.wikipedia.org/wiki/James_Haskell_Hope.
2.   Edgar, *South Carolina*, 516.
3.   Martha Grigsby to J. V. Reel and John Evans to J. V. Reel.
4.   CUL.SC.CUA. S 30 *President's Report to the Board of Trustees*, June 28, 1946.
5.   *Record*, volumes for the years 1945–1955. Data on enrollments and faculty throughout this entire study are derived from *Record*.
6.   CUL.SC.MSS 91 f 211.
7.   Ibid., 68 b 11 f 212.
8.   CUL.SC.CUA. S 7 f 10.
9.   CUL.SC.MSS 68 b 11 f 211.
10. Reel, *Women and Clemson*, 10–11.
11. Rebecca Epting, in organizing her mother's correspondence, came across the letter.
12. CUL.SC.CUA. S 7 f 208. I have used the word "perceived" purposefully, because salary differentials, to be demonstrated to be valid, require careful analyses of a number of factors and then studying all the results, position by position. However, the African American agents' argument that salary increases for them as a group were not "keeping up" with the rise in the cost of living was accurate.

13. Ibid., f 10.
14. Ibid., S 30 ss i, f "Brown."
15. CUL.SC.MSS 91 b 15 f 208.
16. CUL.SC.CUA. S 30 v 6, 47–51.
17. CUL.SC.MSS 68 b 11 f 211.
18. SCHS 1231, 00/25/26/10.
19. Columbia *State*, September 29, 1951. After the Clemson House was converted from a hotel-apartment house into a student dormitory, the mural was not seen. Whether it remains intact under the covering, was removed, or was simply destroyed awaits discovery. For the tiger sculpture, see CUL.SC.CUL. S 11 f 286.
20. *The Tiger*, "Freshman Issue," August 28, 1978; Columbia *State*, December 31, 1972; and Clemson *Messenger*, July 16, 1970.
21. CUL.SC.CUA. S 37 f "Hanover House."
22. Mrs. David J. Watson, the widow of the house's first mover, wrote a well-expressed objection to the move in Clemson *Messenger*, January 8, 1992. The story of the second move is in *Greenville News*, March 31, 1994, and June 22, 1994.
23. A. Wolfe Davidson's unpublished autobiography, 380–382, photo pages of which are filed in CUL.SC.CUA. S 37 "Monuments-Cannons on Bowman Field."
24. *The Tiger*, October 11, 1951.
25. *Clemson World*, Summer 1995, 18–19.
26. CUL.SC.CUA. S 37 "Monuments-Cannons on Bowman Field."
27. CUL.SC.MSS 91 b 15 f 210; and SCHS 30–04 and MSS Benet 43/0219.
28. Canup and Workman, *Charles E. Daniel*, 19–22; and CUL.SC.MSS 47 f 10.
29. CUL.SC.MSS 47 ff 10, 14 and 15.
30. *Greenville News*, August 18, 1957.
31. SCHS MSS Benet 43/0219.
32. McMahon, *Fort Hill Presbyterian Church*, 101–106.
33. Canup and Workman, *Charles E. Daniel*, 23.
34. CUL.SC.MSS 91 b 15 f 210 and 211; and CUL.SC.CUA. S 87 I B 22.
35. CUL.SC.CUA. S 87 I b 14 f 7.
36. Ibid. *Greenville News*, April 21, 1950; and RAC.RF.28 S 2 ss 1 3 b 406 f 4254.
37. CUL.SC.CUA. S 87 I b 13 f 10.
38. Ibid., S 37 f "Buildings-Johnstone Hall."
39. Reel conversation with Buck Mickel.
40. CUL.SC.CUA. S 7 f 9.
41. Ibid., S 5 f 7.
42. Ibid., S 37 f Buildings "Tillman Hall."
43. Ibid., "Long Hall."
44. Ibid., S 7 f 7.
45. Ibid., S 30.
46. Ibid.
47. Ibid., ss i, "Jervey." He was a great conversationalist whose dreams of the past were vivid, but who always saw visions of the future clearly.
48. Ibid., S 87 ss i b 19 f 13 and b 49 f 1.
49. Ibid., S 30 ss i "Thornhill."
50. Ibid., S 28 "Nutt."
51. CUL.SC.MSS 68 f 244.
52. CUL.SC.CUA. S 87 ss i b 13 f 10; and CUL.SC.MSS 44 f 7.
53. CUL.SC.CUA. S 87 ss i b 14 f 6.
54. Ibid., S 30 *President's Report to the Board 1948–1953*, 15; and S 87 ss i b 30 f 24.
55. *The Tiger*, December 16, 1948.
56. CUL.SC.CUA. S 30 v 6, 167.
57. Ibid., Facilities Documents – Building 0040, 5 sheets.
58. Ibid., S 87 ss i b 30 f 24; S 30 v 6, 177; and CUL.SC.MSS 91 b 15 f 210. Not all dreams were realized. Poole's request to the Rockefeller Foundation for money for a 2,500-seat auditorium was denied. RAC.GEB.SC103 S 1.1b 129 f 1179.

As Clemson would change from an all-male military school to a large, all-purpose school, a lone cadet views the old Main (Tillman Hall) Building. Clemson University Photographs, CUL.SC.

CHAPTER XIII

Academic Changes

1945–1955

T he Board of Trustees continued to experience change, although it would not be "wholesale" after 1950. The first alteration, however, surprised everyone. Board President Christie Benet, who had served as president only since 1949, died unexpectedly on March 30, 1951. A life member since 1929, he had proved a wise and stabilizing counsel across the Depression and World War II, and his two short presidential years had major importance for the college's future.

First, Benet long recognized the importance of Robert M. Cooper to South Carolina and to Clemson. Cooper, a farmer, had served as president of the S.C. Livestock Association, the State Dairyman's Association, and the S.C. State Fair Association. Then he became general manager of the S.C. Public Service Authority, which the general assembly had created in 1934 primarily to bring modern electric power to much of the state. After five years of delay, construction had begun on the massive dam and lock project at Pinopolis, and when completed it became the source of power for Charleston's wartime industries.[1] He also chaired an informal board on planning, research, and development that would become the S.C. Development Board (1954). A confidant of most of the governors during the 1940s, 1950s, and until his death in the mid-1960s, Cooper, with Edgar A. Brown, counted as one of Clemson's major advocates to the state government. Thus, it was no surprise when the other eleven trustees unanimously elected Cooper as president of the board.[2]

Second, with Cooper and Brown, Benet had recognized the value of Charles Daniel to Clemson and to all of South Carolina. Those three had used their influence with the other three life trustees to secure Daniel's election to the life seat left vacant by J. E. Sirrine.

Benet's third legacy was to keep the "public face" of the board united, a style that lasted until the mid-1980s. But some among the trustees and influential alumni seemed restless and worried that President Poole had neither the forcefulness nor vision to make Clemson a major contributor to South Carolina's newly emerging economy. Benet never expressed his own views on Poole but differed with him, as did some other trustees, on architectural developments in campus buildings. There were also differences, some expressed in writing, over the opportunities for women to become a permanent part of the teaching and learning enterprises at Clemson. The last point of difficulty with a few trustees and a small cluster of alumni involved the role that military discipline should play on the campus. Each of the above issues carried with it the weight of a half-century of tradition. The easiest burden to lift was that of architecture. And cost spoke so persuasively that the decision would come surprisingly quickly.

Peabody Report

In some ways, the most complex of the decisions involved a combination of academic issues. In 1945, the Peabody Foundation completed and published a study of "consolidation and coordination" in colleges and universities around the nation as the multiple layers of America's governments, along with foundations

The much-changed Board of Trustees convening in June 1953. *Seated, from left to right:* Edgar A. Brown, Joseph B. Douthit, T. Wilbur "Buddy" Thornhill, John F. McLaurin, William A. Barnette, Charles E. Daniel, Benjamin T. Leppard, Andrew J. Brown (secretary of the board and college treasurer), Robert M. Cooper (president of the board), and Robert F. Poole (president of the college). *Seated by the window:* James C. Littlejohn. *Standing, from left to right:* Thomas B. Young, Paul Sanders, and Frank E. Cope. Clemson University Photographs, CUL.SC.

and associations, jostled to help redirect American life after nearly three decades of hand-to-mouth "emergency life" survival (World War I, the drought, the Depression, and World War II). The Peabody report noted the unusual structure of Clemson's governing board. The report also cited Clemson's three separate sets of charters, which made the college nearly unique. To the report's authors, Mr. Clemson's will was paramount, with its board composed of a majority of self-perpetuating and a minority of legislatively selected trustees. A number of court decisions and several rulings of the S.C. attorneys general had confirmed and reconfirmed that the Act of Acceptance (1889) created a charitable trust that made the state's continued possession of Mr. Clemson's bequest dependent on full acceptance of the terms of the will.

The second set of charters was a series of S.C. statutes that claimed a growing collection of federal laws for the people of South Carolina that were applicable to one or more designated or created institutions. The best known, the Morrill Land Grant Act of 1862, assigned the federally supported teaching of agriculture, mechanics, and military strategy to each state's designated school. The S.C. General Assembly had moved and divided that designation several times, but not since November 27, 1889. The U.S. Hatch Act of 1887 assigned continued federal funding and research authority to whichever institution(s) had been the designated "1862" land-grant institutions. The S.C. General Assembly, understanding that term, had closed and sold properties designated for this purpose and transferred the revenue to the Clemson board following the Act of Acceptance. The third federal law, not nearly so often cited, was the Morrill Second Land Grant Act of 1890, which allowed (but did not require) states to accept African American students at existing land-grant schools or to establish specific land-grant colleges for the teaching of African Americans and to fund the teaching mission of previously designated institutions more thoroughly. Because the S.C. state government had done that much earlier, its institutions simply gained increased endowment. It is important to note that the 1890 law did not speak to any mission except teaching. The fourth law, the Smith-Lever Act of 1914, created the Cooperative Extension Service and assigned it to the land-grant college, which the S.C. General Assembly again awarded to Clemson. Given the collection of experts in material and academic subjects at land-grant schools, it was no wonder that as the federal and state governments expanded their roles in internal safety and defense, the various governments frequently attached regulatory responsibilities to land-grant institutions. For Clemson, this meant that at varying times the trustees and officers of the institution have had responsibility for fertilizer inspection and analysis, crop and pest management, livestock quarantines and sanitation, and many other similar obligations. In addition, the Peabody report, funded by the Rockefeller Foundation, noted the expensive (to the state) tripling of engineering at Clemson, USC, and the Citadel. It wondered whether or not the state could afford it. Commenting on the report, the Rockefeller consultant expressed surprise to "learn that USC also offers engineering with four options."The Peabody report concluded that the Clemson board had consistently acted and operated for the public good.[3]

Textiles

The public good, of course, changed with the times, and the needs in 1945 were as great as they ever had been. The board had already proved its foresight when it created the textile program in 1898. It was the first collegiate textile program in the South. For nearly fifty years, the program provided the engineers who improved the old and developed the new textile machinery, just as the agricultural scientists improved the fibers and worked on fertilizers, irrigation, and field machinery. The heavy exposure to basic studies in grammar and mathematics, along with history and literature, sent many a textile graduate into the mill towns of the South equipped to manage and improve the mills and to teach younger mill workers the three "r's" of reading, 'riting, and 'rithmetic. Of course, the passage of the federal Smith-Hughes Act of 1917 institutionalized this concept in a variety of vocational education programs that, with the Clemson-managed youth programs, played, and continue to play, an important part in adjusting the direction of South Carolina and other parts of the country to meet changing times. Generally, these programs were housed in the land-grant universities and colleges.

Clemson's textile program was led by Hugh M. Brown, a noted research scientist who had earned advanced degrees from the University of California (Berkeley) and who had spent most of the war years on loan to MIT working with a team of other

Hugh Monroe Brown (1895–1991) was a professor of physics at Clemson from 1928 to 1942, during which time he also assumed directorship of the department, and was dean of the School of Textiles from 1946 to 1957. Clemson University Photographs, CUL.SC.

leading scientists in radiation research.[4] The textile faculty of thirty-two were a mixture of practical and theoretical men, most of whom had been hired from industry and six of whom were working toward advanced degrees. Further, when industry progress seemed ahead of collegiate teaching and research, Brown sent faculty to major industries to catch up. When synthetic fibers appeared as a major upcoming trend, for example, Joseph Lindsay spent time in some of the foremost textile chemistry industries and laboratories, such as Tennessee Eastman in Kingsport, Tennessee.[5]

Most of the textile and connected industries contributed to Clemson's research program. The J. E. Sirrine Foundation, in one year alone (1947), funded nine major research projects at Clemson, while Charles E. Daniel in 1949 gave $100,000 personally to Clemson for textile research. Several other donors added $40,000, and the chair of the board of M. Lowenstein and Sons of New York gave another $25,000. By 1951, Poole reported to the S.C. Cotton Manufacturers Association that over the past few years, various friends donated another $250,000, of which most went for undergraduate education, while equipment manufacturers had discounted new equipment, saving Clemson an additional $150,000.[6]

Students enrolled in textiles composed about 25 percent of the entire student body, and Clemson's School of Textiles was the largest in the nation. In fact by 1954, 2,035 men had graduated from Clemson in one or another of the branches of textiles.[7] The formal dedication of the textile building, named Sirrine Hall in memory of J. E. Sirrine, was accompanied with the awarding of honorary doctoral degrees and hoods to twenty-eight national textile, cotton, and industrial executives.[8]

Engineering

Despite the size and growth of the textile program, engineering was 20 percent larger and enrolled about 34 percent of all the undergraduate students. But some of the faculty taught in surplus buildings moved from closings on shrinking military bases and that had limited useful service. The engineering program was still led by Samuel B. Earle, the director and then dean of engineering since 1910, except for the break in 1919 when he acted for the president while Riggs had gone to Europe on educational duty, and then from Riggs's sudden death in January 1924 to the arrival of Sikes in 1925. Earle held a deep desire to help diversify the economy of South Carolina and the South. He could note with satisfaction that 44 percent of all Clemson's engineering graduates worked in South Carolina and 77 percent in the South. Most of the graduates working beyond the region were in Earle's and Riggs's specialty in electrical engineering, where Clemson men had made significant contributions to hydroelectrical power and aeronautical sciences. In fact, Earle must have regretted that in the 1920s and 1930s the trustees had ignored his and Prof. James Sams's suggestions that Clemson institute a formal program in aeronautical engineering.[9]

But Earle was an imaginative leader, and as soon as the war ended, he and a small group of younger faculty and alumni created a program in ceramic engineering. South Carolina had a small ceramic industry that dated from the first European settlements and generally operated on techniques introduced from Europe and Africa. The most advanced work had been done in the mid-1700s when men from Great Britain's Josiah Wedgwood firm had worked the kaolin veins in South Carolina for export to the British midlands. In addition to local brick manufacturing companies, a local art industry had developed in the Savannah River basin. Begun in the 1810s in the Edgefield district, the Edgefield pottery, or stoneware, was used for storage and was enhanced by the alkaline glaze that contained no lead and thus was not poisonous.[10]

The field of ceramic engineering was relatively new. Earle and his small group found a twenty-six-year-old graduate of North Carolina State College who had served in World War II to begin the program. Gilbert C. Robinson, born in 1920 in Lykens, Pennsylvania, had attended the Episcopal School of Alexandria, Virginia.[11] Robinson joined the Clemson faculty in August 1946 and set out immediately with "Doc Rock" Calhoun to undertake a sweeping mapping of South Carolina's mineral resources.[12] Robinson also collected a small, energetic group of faculty. Together they analyzed the samples. "Gil" met with clay product executives and managed to upgrade and slowly and quietly change this cottage industry into a fast-growing and significant South Carolina industry.[13] The program was strengthened through the friendship shown it by Frank J. Jervey and Charles Horn, president of the Olin Foundation. Horn enjoyed the companionship and sportsman's interests of Poole and Earle and the industry and thoroughness of Robinson. Soon the Olin Foundation, with its strong interests in American mineral and ore deposits, began planning to fund for Clemson Agricultural College its own ceramic building with laboratories and a ceramic engineering library, including

Gilbert C. "Gil" Robinson (1919–1996) came to Clemson in 1946 to help create and chair the Department of Ceramic Engineering. Robinson, who also owned and operated a round kiln brick plant north of Gaffney with his wife, Barbara, retired in 1985. Clemson University Photographs, CUL.SC.

a set of the *Transactions of the British Ceramic Society.*[14] The first graduates received their rings and diplomas in June 1950.

However, space remained a great problem in the School of Engineering. While a new ceramic engineering building, dedicated to the memory of F. E. Olin, provided a great addition to the overall mission of Clemson, it did not relieve the overcrowding in Riggs Hall and adjacent laboratories. Some programs were taught in the temporary buildings, others in temporary space in other buildings. The problems existed most acutely in chemical engineering, civil engineering, and architecture.[15]

Architecture

In architecture, the problems were even more critical than elsewhere. The architectural professional accrediting board withheld accreditation from Clemson primarily because of the college's inadequate and scattered space for the program's 225 undergraduates. The minimum space the National Accrediting Board (NAB) required was 37,000 square feet, while Clemson could squeeze out only 11,500. As a result, Clemson graduates could practice their profession only in South Carolina, while no architecture schools existed at all in Tennessee and Mississippi for student alternatives. The S.C. Branch of the American Institute of Architects (AIA) and the State Board of Architecture urged Governor James Byrnes to support the inclusion of an architecture building in his recommendations to the legislature.[16] Albert Simons, a prominent Charleston architect and onetime (1915–1916) Clemson faculty member, wrote Edgar A. Brown, chair of the Senate Finance Committee, also urging the legislature to finance the needed space.[17] Also a letter from the S.C. Chapter of the AIA in 1948 strongly urged a separate School of Architecture be created in two years (1950). Poole took the letter to the Board of Trustees as information.[18] The board disagreed, instructing him to have the program separate and functioning by 1949. He replied that he could not accomplish it so quickly. They then directed him to have it done by the end of the fiscal year 1950.[19] It did not happen until 1955, which caused more irritation among some trustees.

Nonetheless, the students won regional and national honors. In 1949, Kirk Craig of Greenville finished second nationally in the competition for the Beaux Arts Institute of Design scholarship for international study. Three years later, another Greenvillian, Edward H. Shirley, won first place in the same competition. This prize paid for eighteen months' study and travel in Europe.[20] John Gates, the architecture head since 1947, continued in a dual role, helping to alleviate the housing shortage at Clemson and working to secure accreditation by the NAB. He had success with the former but not the latter.

In the case of accreditation, Gates wrote Trustee Thornhill, identifying two major impediments: faculty and space. Among the new young architecture faculty that Clemson had begun to hire were Antonio Paul de Albuquerque, a Brazilian, and Robert St. Hubert, a Frenchmen. Both had been educated in a more traditional *beaux-arts* style, which was no longer generally taught nor practiced. St. Hubert immersed himself in campus work and spent time planning the murals for the large reading room in the college library. One of the three can still be seen today with difficulty because of the manner of insertion of a mezzanine floor in the southern section of Sikes Hall. A second fresco, done by St. Hubert and his wife, Martha Van Deriken, on the third floor of Riggs, was unveiled by Rudolph E. Lee and the artists in late spring of 1949. It was dedicated to the memory of fourteen Clemson architecture graduates and students killed in military service in World War II.[21] Accreditation obviously depended on acquiring much more space for architecture and perhaps on the program becoming a separate school within the college.[22] Also it might have depended on faculty whose designs were not so eclectic as the previous generation's designs had been.

But no new building had even made it to the planning stage, and salaries across the whole college remained quite low, especially in numerically (by student majors) small fields such as architecture and the liberal arts. Gates thought he saw a glimmer of hope for a building when a Permanent Improvements Bill was introduced in the general assembly. But by June 1954, the Board of Trustees became frustrated because it had received a large number of letters from architects in South Carolina, many who were Clemson graduates, complaining about the issues of building, school, and accreditation. Gates and, less frequently, Poole received the blame.[23] The matter reached a climax at the board meeting of June 18, 1954, when it was agreed that Gates be asked to resign and Poole was directed to inform Gates. The vote later that day in the board's open meeting provided "that the resignation of Professor J. H. Gates, Head of the Architectural Department, be accepted...."[24] Poole did nothing about the directive for nineteen days. Finally on July 7, Cooper ordered him to carry out the board's wishes. He did, but board frustration with Poole had increased.[25]

Earle Retires

Probably no other event in the School of Engineering was so momentous as the decision of Samuel B. Earle to retire from the college and the deanship of engineering. Earle had come to Clemson in 1902, and upon Riggs's succession to Clemson's presidency in 1910, he became director of engineering. No trustee, nor almost anyone else at Clemson, could remember the college's engineering program without Earle. The branches he inherited were mechanical, civil, and electrical. In the forty years as director and dean, Earle had added architecture, established as a department in 1933, and then in 1917, chemical engineering, which lasted until 1924. It was revived in 1933 to help develop the emerging pulp industry in South Carolina and has played a major role in the region's developments since that time. Ceramic engineering was a post-World War II addition.[26] Although the trustees knew of Earle's imminent retirement, they read his dignified resignation letter with great regret and respect. The letter included memories such as

...I had begun to be interested in the work here, and when Dr. Riggs went in as President in 1910, and I was put in charge of the School of Engineering, I made up my mind that I would devote the rest of my life to the work here at Clemson if the Board wanted me....I can always be ready to help in any way I can toward the further development of any of the work at Clemson.[27]

The dedication of Earle Hall in 1959, the new home of the emerging chemical engineering program. It was built with funds procured from the Olin Foundation and named in honor of Samuel Broadus Earle, recently retired engineering dean and former acting college president. Clemson University Photographs, CUL.SC.

James H. Sams Jr., who graduated from Clemson in 1924 and then served on the faculty prior to World War II, was appointed acting dean. When the United States declared war in 1941, Sams joined the Army Air Corps, served in the European theater, and received several medals and commendations before he left military service in March 1949 with the rank of colonel.[28] Sams resumed his post at Clemson and served as vice-dean when Earle resigned. He became dean of the school in 1951 and was aggressive and innovative in strengthening relations between Clemson's students and faculty with industrial leaders, which led to a better

James Hagood Sams (1903–1970), the man who inherited the leadership of the School of Engineering from the long-time dean, Samuel Broadus Earle. Sams, Clemson 1924, joined the faculty in 1927, teaching until service with the Army Air Corps in World War II interrupted in 1941. He returned to Clemson a colonel in 1946, became acting dean in 1950, full dean in 1951, and resigned his post in 1960, becoming dean emeritus to take the post of executive secretary for the National Council of State Boards of Engineering Examiners. Clemson University Photographs, CUL.SC.

understanding of industries' needs and probable future direction for Clemson. During Sams's first year, McAdams Hall for agricultural engineering opened, moving the fast-growing program from the unheated barn in which it had been housed. The schools of Engineering and Agriculture jointly supervised agricultural engineering, one of the early interdisciplinary programs. Real space relief occurred with the opening of Earle Hall, a second gift of the Olin Foundation.[29]

Agriculture

McAdams Hall was also the first move the School of Agriculture made into the south section of campus, formerly devoted to fields, sheds, barns, and some of the "prefab housing." That made the movement of those support buildings even farther south but opened up more meadowland that allowed for growth in animal husbandry. Clemson's researchers and extension agents worked with the dairy farmers to increase the quality of the herds through scientific insemination, improved feed, and careful selection of cattle best suited for the different conditions of the region. "Big Ben" Goodale, long active in South Carolina's dairy industry, along with Joseph P. LaMaster, demonstrated that, in combination with livestock and poultry, these industries had annual sales of $122 million a year, while the herds had a value of $93 million. The addition of new faculty such as Victor Hurst moved the programs forward rapidly.

Hurst had been an undergraduate at Rutgers, by then the state land-grant university of New Jersey and the only land-grant school built on a colonial collegiate foundation. After earning his PhD at the University of Missouri, he came to Clemson. The housing shortage found him rooming at the home and boarding house of Margaret Morrison, a much-beloved local public schoolteacher and principal. His scholarly research and experimentation focused on the improvement of dairy cattle.[30] One of the newer dairy industries had begun in 1940 when the college, with the permission of the Blue Ridge line (a division of Southern Railway), experimented with curing blue cheese in nearby Stumphouse Tunnel. When the college had the wartime training of army and Army Air Corps men, the milk was needed for the war effort. Production of the cheese gradually slowed and halted in 1944. After the war, some confusion arose between the rail corporation and heirs of the onetime owners. When settled, Clemson purchased the tract[31] and reached full production of cheese in 1953. With the completion of the Agriculture Center, now Newman Hall, the entire process was moved to the new agricultural complex emerging on the southern side of the campus.[32]

Forestry

A second major area of expansion in agriculture halted by the Depression and the war was in forestry, which the college discontinued in 1936. Koloman Lehotsky, an Austro-Hungarian-born PhD in forestry, joined the faculty to restart the teaching of forestry, heighten public service, and carry on research in moving the state forward in this new land-based economy. A two-year curriculum, transferable to an accredited program, began in 1947. In the meantime, Marlin Bruner of the Forestry Service supervised the developing forests growing rapidly on the "land-use" properties assigned to Clemson by the federal government, as the result of a proposal created by Prof. George Aull.

The state's forestlands and their produce had increased since the turn of the century. At that time, the softwood yield, which accounted for slightly more than two-thirds of the annual output for South Carolina, amounted to about 20 million cubic feet, while hardwood production reached about 5.5 million in 1936. The yields increased to 210 million and 95 million cubic feet, respectively, by the 1945–1946 USDA Forest Service survey. The increase over the ten years from 1945 to 1955 was slight (about 3 percent) until the seedlings planted by the Civilian Conservation Corps in the 1930s would be ready for harvesting. As best as can be discerned from the same survey data, a spike occurred in the percent of forestland in federal and state ownership in the 1930s as a result of resettlement of farmers from marginal land. From the war's end in 1945, that acreage remained a stable 10 percent through 1955. Besides the increase in total acreage, the major shift had been the decline in private forests (usually not managed for commercial purposes) as a part of private farms and the growth of commercial plantations by individuals (the greatest single share) and industry. The state's total forest acreage increased from about 10.5 million acres to about 11.9 million acres (13.3 percent).

At the same time, the continued expansion of the textile industry and the emergence of the strong southern population belt (running from Atlanta, Georgia, through the South Carolina Upstate and deep into the North Carolina Piedmont), coupled with the continued movement of the three states' midlands toward a few urban areas (most notably the North Carolina Raleigh-Durham metropolis), added urgency for these states to take more aggressive stances toward the new forest industry. South Carolina chose not to move as vigorously as did the other two, and it was not until 1956 that the Board of Trustees and President Poole had the money needed to open a four-year forestry curriculum and a forestry department for the campus.[33]

Agricultural Experiment Station

The S.C. Agricultural Experiment Station attracted much of Poole's personal interest. He worked carefully with the general assembly on the improvement of the experiment stations around the state. In the 1945–1946 budget, the stations received nearly half of the state funds designated for Clemson. The college invested most of the money in research on new or improved crops, crop and animal diseases, and in pest control. That remained constant in percentage across the decade.[34]

In crop improvement, the number of successes included the work of Rupert McGinty, the vice-director of the experiment station between 1936 and 1951. He developed the spineless okra, which began the rise of that vegetable from one that required very early picking because of the toughness of its spines to a digestible and more popular vegetable. W. C. Barnes, the superintendent of the Coast Station since 1937, a Clemson graduate and Cornell PhD, developed the Cherokee waxbean, listed as one of eight All-American new vegetables in 1948 in *New York Times*. Barnes assembled a team of industrious scientists at the Coast Station who worked together to adapt vegetables to flourish in South Atlantic climates. One of the most successful team members, William Epps, led in breeding mildew-resistant cucumbers, mosaic-resistant lettuce, winter cabbage, winter broccoli, and several excellent strains of tomatoes resistant to blossom end-rot. At the Edisto Station in Blackville, asparagus culture had led the region into a major export industry. These vegetable improvements, together with the abundant coastal seafood, played a significant role in the rise of South Carolina's tourist industry.

Aside from vegetable crops, the Pee Dee Station in Florence focused much research on lice and pests on tobacco.[35] In 1955, at the "home farm" at Clemson, Poole and the cotton specialists, with strong support from J. F. McLaurin of Florence and U.S. Senator Barnwell Rhett Maybank, brought the Southern Regional Cotton Ginning Laboratory to Clemson. This served as the catalyst for research in cotton staple in Alabama, Florida, Georgia, South Carolina, North Carolina, and eastern Tennessee.[36]

The research unit also received funds from alumni to increase research. W. B. "Bill" Camp, a Gaffney native who had served in the federal government and was a major California agriculturalist, gave the agricultural experiment unit a sizeable gift to work with large-volume irrigation. The early results increased corn yield 50 percent per acre. On the very same day as Camp's gift, August 5, 1949, 150 specialists from Central America, South America, India, and the United States gathered at Clemson to exchange research information on growing, harvesting, and extracting valuable oil from sesame seeds.[37]

Cooperative Extension

The extension service, like the entire nation, had adjusted to issues as South Carolina returned to a semi-peace mode. Fourteen professional extension agents remained on military active duty in February 1946. While their Clemson positions were secure, that did not help David Watkins, extension director.[38] With little help from the legislature and no aid or encouragement from Poole, the problem of covering the temporarily vacant positions worsened.[39]

Watkins and the extension service faced another drought that led to a food and grain shortage by the spring of 1946. It was made more difficult by returning veterans who wanted to continue raising cotton, ignoring the greater need for food supplies for humans and animals.[40]

But for the S.C. Cooperative Extension Service, new opportunities existed. The 4-H program, which focused on youth from nine to nineteen years of age, experienced a growth from 26,000 to 34,000 members between 1945 and 1947.[41] The influx of about 30 percent more members was accommodated by the opening of 4-H Camp Bob Cooper, named for the president of the Clemson Board of Trustees and chairman of the Santee-Cooper power authority. Made possible by the state and surreptitiously urged by Cooper, the new camp took over buildings originally built for the massive Santee-Cooper hydroelectric construction project.[42] Donations from federal surplus goods furnished the camp.

Thomas Morgan, for the extension service, and Hamilton Hill, assistant business manager for the college, worked together on the federal surplus goods project that benefited not only the youth of South Carolina at camps Bob Cooper and Long (the 4-H camp in the Aiken area), but also helped the experiment stations and the educational and research programs in sciences, textiles (acquiring advanced laboratory equipment and basic surplus), and engineering (receiving heavy duty equipment). Also, the college library added much-needed tables, chairs, desks, and bookcases, along with some basic reference works.[43]

Farm and Home Weeks

Not only were the Clemson camps, campus, and research centers enriched, but the S.C. Department of Wildlife Resources, in conjunction with Clemson and Dartmouth College naturalists, used surplus material to begin family summer camps in the relatively new state parks.[44] And, although entering the "Indian summer" of its life, Farm and Home Week was revived. In 1948, 2,500 farmers and their families came to campus for the weeklong event.[45] Besides the practical seminars on agricultural management and food preservation issues, the program included 4-H competitions and talent shows, along with displays of new, large, and "shiny" farm machines, equipment, and implements. Potential owners and children, both of the farm families and the communities that surrounded the college, could climb aboard some of the gigantic machines arrayed on Bowman Field.[46]

Broader American and world politics also received attention at these events. For example, at Farmer's Week on August 18, 1950, the main speaker for the affair was Assistant Secretary of State Dean Rusk, who discussed U.S. foreign policy, including the "police action" in Korea. Several seminars discussed the role the farmers could play, particularly in light of U.S. President Harry S. Truman's 1948 request for all of the agricultural community to prepare for another military effort that might be greater than the "Berlin air-lift" to relieve the pressures of South Korea facing hostile actions from Communist North Korea.[47]

Postwar readjustment also called on the extension service to improve the communities in which South Carolinians of all races lived. The Federal Housing Act of 1949 allocated some funds for the construction of better homes and other needed farm buildings for the agricultural communities and assigned the work to the extension service, but designated little money for the task. Similar legislation also encouraged the building of fishponds to increase the sources of protein.[48] As part of Clemson's program to improve dairy cattle, the extension service opened artificial insemination laboratories in five major dairy-producing counties. Clemson laboratory directors, educated at the college, supervised each laboratory. Much the same effort was expended on the improvement and enlargement of the state's poultry flocks.[49] And the U.S. Department of Defense called upon the Clemson Extension Service, through USDA, to aid in the resettlement of families dislocated by the construction of the Savannah River hydrogen power and bomb facilities constructed in the 1950s between the Savannah River basin and Aiken, Williston, and Barnwell.[50]

But as farm families, faced with changing transportation and labor costs, continued moving from commercial agricultural production to town and community work, they frequently did not abandon the home place, but kept milk cows, chickens, and maintained fewer acres in fields, gardens and crops. The mission of the extension service went with them. The service as a model was attractive in rebuilding and developing communities and counties. The land-grant colleges, like Clemson College, sent out faculty to assist the people and hosted visitors from other countries, some emerging from centuries of foreign rule.[51]

Radio and Television

In fact, general outreach, beyond the rural community, continued a long American tradition that harkened back far earlier than the famous Clemson trains that took staff to the countryside at the turn of the century. Clemson, quick to realize the possibilities of the radio in its early days, had operated one of the state's first stations from a brick bungalow on campus, called by many local residents "Radio House." Radio broadcasting would move around the campus. When the Clemson House was built in 1950, it contained a radio studio and broadcasting facility that stayed there until the early 1980s. The Clemson station broadcast regular early morning weather reports, general and local news, and programming usually focused on home, farm, and domestic concerns. Toward the end of the day, agricultural commodity market reports, stock market summaries, and occasionally talk shows and prerecorded music led to the station's fairly early sign-off each evening.[52]

President Sikes used the radio effectively before Poole became president. Thus, it is no wonder that with the advent of television as a public medium (although not yet widespread), Poole pressed Clemson administration, faculty, staff, and trustees to create a television filming and transmitting center on the campus. It was hard to generate a lot of enthusiasm, but in this he was determined. He assembled short-lived committees on several occasions. The technical knowledge of most of the committee members and the steep costs of building before broadcasting could begin represented major hurdles. However, with the prospect of the new agricultural center on the south campus, Poole insisted that television studios and workspaces be included, along with photography laboratories and storage for printed materials of an educational nature and quality.

With that settled with the trustees and with their advice on its membership, Poole charged a staff and faculty committee to develop a television planning document. The large report, which appeared in draft circulation in early 1952, called for locating a 400-foot tower on Six Mile Mountain, a prominent landscape feature ten miles north of Clemson and ten miles west of Easley. This would make the entire structure (including the mountain) about 1,000 feet above local grade and 1,700 feet above sea level. The proposed ultra-high-frequency transmitter radiating at 1 million watts would broadcast in top-grade television service at a radius of forty-three miles and the next grade (B) for an additional sixteen miles. In sheer distance, the proposed top service would exceed the power of WBTV in Charlotte, North Carolina, and WSB-TV in Atlanta, Georgia, the only stations then operating in the area. Three much smaller stations were contemplated in Anderson and in Greenville. The cost of the equipment for it all ran an initial $220,000, and equipment for remote filming, including such events as sports, church services, concerts, and the like, an additional $67,000. Annual operating costs amounted to another $60,000, while the plan called for each program sponsor to bear filming costs. Leading the committee was John W. Gillespie, a veteran who had received a BS degree in chemistry from Clemson in 1948. After graduation and time in Korea, he returned to study for a chemistry master's degree before joining the faculty.[53]

With only the Six Mile transmission radius of forty-three miles, service included all the communities from Hendersonville, North Carolina, to Royston, Georgia, and in South Carolina, Honea Path to Greer, including Anderson and Greenville. A booster transmitter at Paris Mountain, just north of Greenville, would somewhat enlarge Grade A's population market, but the B level added the desirable Spartanburg market.

The market also proved favorable to the venture. The previous year (excluding the fifteen network-owned and -operated stations nationwide), income to the major stations increased 33 percent in one year, while total expenses grew by 28 percent. In fact, the average profit for television stations with the same population market and similar competition had, from 1951 to 1952, increased 70 percent, and none reported a loss in 1952. The proposed market reached 22 percent of the state's population with a buying income of 24.5 percent. Advertising revenue potential was not as great as about half the compared areas because of the less-concentrated nature of the population. All in all, the faculty and staff report on a television station at Clemson was a most fair and positive one.[54]

Delivered to the trustees at their spring 1953 meeting, the report was sent to a committee of trustees, alumni, and staff chaired by William Augustus Barnette. A Clemson graduate of 1910 and later a veterinary science faculty member, he came from Greenwood. Other members were Ben Leppard, L. W. Riley, J. R. Mattison, and Walter T. Cox, who served as director of public relations after several years' experience in the Athletic Department. At the second meeting in June, Barnette's committee recommended that Clemson build a large television studio along with a visual aids studio. It was added to the new agriculture complex. The committee urged that the trustees and key administrators continue to study the remainder of the report.[55] By the October meeting, Poole advised that the college immediately purchase equipment to produce television programming, including mobile filming and transmitting equipment, and that programs be distributed to regional stations for their use. The cost amounted to $70,000 for the equipment, plus the annual costs for salaries and supplies. Acquiring a license, a channel, and the transmitting capabilities had to await state funding of the $200,000 (2009 equivalent $1,586,092). The trustees approved it all, providing the state helped to finance it, but the state government did not move on doing so until 1961.[56] By that time, regional competition and costs had increased considerably.

Arts and Sciences

The School of General Science was renamed Arts and Sciences in 1946, and the deans had begun filling the faculty openings, caused by the war, in physics (one), history (two), and mathematics (one). Some faculty members in military service had returned. H. Morris Cox returned from service in Japan to the English Department and began working on his PhD degree at the University of Pennsylvania, which he completed in 1958. Marion Kinard, dean of the School of Arts and Sciences, named Cox head of the English Department.

Historian E. M. Lander, who had served in India, remembered on his return that after arriving back in America and some brief "mustering out," the returning GIs boarded trains in various directions. Those who got off the train in Raleigh to split up for their local train journeys home decided to share a bottle or two of beer to honor their surviving the war. So they entered a local beer hall. The bartender quickly told them that only white people could be served in the saloon. Lander and his travelling companions in their service uniforms forewent the beer, turned, picked up their duffle bags, left the bar, shook hands, and separated forever. Several of the soldiers were African Americans.[57]

Still a separate school, Chemistry and Geology had four faculty positions open, along with positions open for four student laboratory assistants. Among those who returned to the School of Chemistry and Geology was Howard L. Hunter. He had received his PhD degree from Cornell in 1928 and immediately joined the Clemson faculty. When World War II began, Hunter joined the U.S. Army and was named chief administrator of the Division of Chemical Warfare Service Development Laboratory of MIT in Boston. He returned to Clemson in 1945 as a lieutenant colonel and professor of chemistry. Hunter led the faculty study team that wrote the projected needs analysis for the new chemistry building. Then, in 1947, upon the retirement of F. H. H. Calhoun, "Footsie," as Hunter was

Howard Louis "Footsie" Hunter (1904–1975) joined the Clemson faculty in 1928, teaching chemistry until he entered the U.S. Army in 1941. Hunter returned to Clemson a lieutenant colonel in 1945, and in 1947 he became dean of the School of Chemistry and Geology. He held this position until he assumed the position of dean of the School of Arts and Sciences in 1955. Hunter retired as dean emeritus in 1969. Clemson University Photographs, CUL.SC.

called for his Tom Clemson-sized feet, received the appointment as dean of the School of Chemistry and Geology.[58] Further, a separate list of anticipated retirements of faculty who were, or soon would be, over seventy years of age (of whom six had each taught at Clemson for more than forty of the college's fifty-four years) forecast ten retirements within two years. These represented nearly one-third of the Arts and Sciences faculty and 60 percent of all the anticipated college faculty retirements.

Poole received board permission to hire faculty to replace this large number along with some additional faculty to replace the retirees. Faculty such as Lander taught across various fields and recalled "burning the midnight oil" to prepare for the additional assignments. Another returning faculty member in social sciences, Frank Burtner, a sociologist, had completed undergraduate and some graduate work at the universities of Texas and North Carolina. Having continued his study and then served in the Army Medical Corps during the war, Burtner had made contacts invaluable to Clemson students planning to go on to medical, dental, or pharmacy schools. Both Burtner and Lander earned PhD degrees during the decade using the GI Bill. Each had a significant impact on their students' lives, Lander as an outstanding lecturer and highly regarded, well-published author, and Burtner as an advisor to academic and leadership societies and to pre-professional students.

Others joining the faculty of the Social Sciences Department included Waldron Bolen, "Uncle Remus," who had served in the European theater. While Lander married Sarah Shirley, a librarian who had lived at the old wooden Clemson Hotel as had "Whitey" (E. M. Lander's nickname, which derived from his hair color), Bolen came to Clemson with his young wife, Eleanor, and his PhD degree in German history from Duke University. As historian Alester G. Holmes, nearing retirement, finished lecturing to a class of cadets one day, Bolen remembered walking in a hall while classes changed, ahead of two of Holmes's young cadets. One quipped to the other, "Well, 'Old Misery' [Holmes's nickname] has just started on the Civil War for the third time this semester." His comrade-in-arms chuckled, "Yep, but I think the South is gonna win this time!" Bolen had served in the army in Europe, which, added to his European history degree, led him to contemplate the "tragedy" of the students' verbal exchange. Another newcomer, Robert Lambert, with his field in American colonial history, and his wife, Edythe, lived in the "prefabs" near the Bolens. The Lamberts left Clemson, then returned, settling for their careers.[59]

Another of the large departments in Arts and Sciences was English. It offered classes in grammar, literature, modern language, speech, and music. Francis Marion Kinard, dean of the School of Arts and Sciences (then General Science) in 1943, continued in that capacity until August 1955. Educated at Wofford College, with his MA degree from UNC in 1929, he understood the importance of faculty receiving doctoral degrees for advanced teaching and research and to raise the reputation of Clemson. He slowly produced such a faculty.

Mark Bradley served as the English Department head until his retirement on June 30, 1950. H. Morris Cox replaced Bradley as head. Because of his rich educational background, Cox added studies in linguistics and etymology to the curriculum in the late 1950s and 1960s. Cox's wife, Irene, from Laurens County, was a relative of President Poole.[60] Some of the faculty, such as Jordan Dean and Orestes "P. Doggie" Rhyne, taught both English and foreign languages.

Given the large teaching loads (200 students per faculty member each semester with five, or occasionally six, classes each term) and the determination to teach excellent communications through writing, in-depth reading, substantial amounts of parallel readings, and essay examinations, these teachers had little time for research, writing, and publication. Nonetheless, some did publish and built good reputations for themselves and for Clemson's School of Arts and Sciences. The other big unit in Arts and Sciences, the Mathematics Department, with a faculty of sixteen, also continued as teachers and as leaders in the craft of teaching.

...Angels Unawares

The mind for this sort of teaching and research wanted neither the laboratory nor the pasture, but rather the stuff of the library. Although the library had been housed in fine space since 1926, it shared the building from time to time with agricultural extension, with a few classrooms for the faculty whose offices were in Tillman Hall, and with the Thomas Green Clemson collection of visual art and other artifacts. Thanks to Poole and his great interest in the role a good library should play in a student's education, by war's end the library subscribed to 600 periodicals, including newspapers and some popular magazines, but also an increasing number of scholarly journals, and with the addition of over 21,000 volumes across the war years, the holdings were becoming respectable. In addition, after more than a year of discussion and preparation at Clemson, the Rockefeller Foundation contributed $30,000 for new books and reference works. However, during that same period, the salaries for the professional staff were among the lowest in the South.[61]

Poole kept the library needs of the "Clemson family" always before him. Many of the finest volumes in the collection were given to Clemson during his first fifteen presidential years. When he arrived in 1940, he had found a 49,000-volume collection,[62] to which nearly 21,000 volumes had been added by 1945. In 1936, the Carnegie Foundation gave Clemson (and other colleges) good phonographs and 900 recordings of classical music. Having no other place for the use of these, Sikes had added the collection to the library reading room, where they were heavily used until 1951. At that time, the college moved the collection to the radio broadcasting station in the Clemson House.[63] The biggest coup, however, began in 1938 when the highly regarded engineering laboratory of Bernard A. Behrend, a native Swiss engineering pioneer, came to the attention of Engineering Dean S. B. Earle. Several private eastern schools sought to purchase the laboratory, which contained a large number of unique or unusual instruments and equipment. Behrend's widow, Margaret, had no plans to sell until she decided to move "down South" to Aiken and accidently befriended Earle. On one of her drives south, she met two Clemson cadets, both extremely courteous, so she undertook to visit the campus. Driving onto it, she stopped a gentleman walking and asked for directions. The gentleman, Dean Earle, offered to give her a campus tour. Although the laboratory had been appraised at $100,000, after meeting Earle and visiting the campus as his guest, she offered it to Clemson for $25,000. Earle and then-President Sikes were excited, but Business Manager J. C. Littlejohn, mainly concerned about finding the money, opposed acquiring it. But both trustees Edgar Brown and R. M. Cooper urged acceptance of the offer. The trustees acted. Sikes and Earle told Mrs. Behrend that she had a deal. Brown negotiated a special bill through the legislature to pay for the laboratory, while Cooper urged his many legislative contacts to support the project. All were more than pleased. Then Mrs. Behrend paid to have everything crated and shipped. Later, she donated the $25,000 to Clemson to maintain the laboratory. But what did this mean to the library?

Mr. and Mrs. Behrend also collected rare and first edition books. And the Behrends had filed and saved their correspondence with scientists and others worldwide. During the next quarter of a century, Mrs. Behrend regularly gave much of this collection to the Clemson library. A second edition *De Revolutionibus Orbium Coelestium* (1564) by the Polish mathematician Nicholas Copernicus was among the important works in science. In it, under the guise of a mathematical exercise, Copernicus posited the sun, rather than the earth, was the center of the universe.

Bernard Arthur Behrend (1875–1932), inventor, electrical engineer, and avid collector of rare first-edition works of science. His wife, Margaret Plummer Chase Behrend (1895–1982), through her meeting with Dean Samuel Broadus Earle, gave a large portion of the couple's rare book and manuscript collection to Clemson. Clemson University Photographs, CUL.SC.

His work called into question the accepted ancient Greek view of a geocentric, or earth-centered, universe. However, it did not challenge the concepts of finite universe or of motion. Those would await the publication of two other Behrend gifts, the Italian Galileo Galilei's *Dialogo 1632 (Dialogue Concerning the Two Chief World Systems 1632)* and Isaac Newton's *Opticks* (1704), and then Michael Faraday's, Charles Darwin's, and Albert Einstein's studies, which are among the most important (and sometimes controversial) works of modern science.

Besides these, other rare (including first editions) and beautiful books given the library by Mrs. Behrend ranged from Edward Gibbon's multivolume history, John Ruskin's philosophical and architectural musings, John James Audubon's *Birds* (1840–1844) and *Quadrupeds* (1846–1853), a large collection of the works of William Makepeace Thackeray, and hundreds of other volumes. Mrs. Behrend's gift of books occupied one-half mile of shelving. The Behrend collection was marked by bookplates, with separate designs for each of the two owners. Greenville junior Phifer Byrd drew Mr. Behrend's bookplates, and Sam T. Earle, also a Greenville junior, created Mrs. Behrend's. Both were architecture students. Each received a monetary gift from Poole.

Friends of the Behrends, from Illinois, California, Massachusetts, and South Carolina, also gave books. In addition, Mrs. Behrend gave the library the correspondence of her husband and some of his friends, such as Thomas Huxley and Oliver Wendell Holmes. From her collection, she also added first editions by Jonathan Swift, Alfred Tennyson, Thomas Hardy, J. J. Audubon, E. White, and noted South Carolina author Julia Peterkin (along with personal letters between Peterkin and Mrs. Behrend), Thackeray's well-regarded aquatints, and one of a set of three bronze statuettes of Thackeray.[64] Mr. Behrend's portrait, done by Mrs. Fernow, the wife of a faculty member, still hangs today in the University Special Collections.

The library also received 140 volumes of general reading from the shipboard library of the *S. S. Ben Robertson* when it was decommissioned on January 13, 1946.[65] Librarian Cornelia Graham began a library of great authors' works from the Carnegie Foundation and received a substantial grant from the General Education Fund (the Rockefeller Foundation) in 1947, by which time the collection had reached 86,000 volumes.[66] At the same time, given the size of the student body and the academic fields taught, the college possessed only half the reference works and periodicals recommended by the American Library Association. But by 1955, the library's holdings had reached 108,000 volumes, 977 periodical titles, and 745,000 government documents.[67] This was one of Poole's major achievements.

Knowing that librarian Cornelia Graham intended to retire soon, Poole convened a faculty committee to search for her replacement. It included several young, research-oriented faculty as well as several senior faculty, including department heads and school deans. The committee looked through a number of

John Wallace Gordon Gourlay, a native of Lancaster, Ontario, Canada, with training in history, economics, English, and library science and a veteran of the Royal Canadian Air Force and the Royal Air Force during World War II, was the first director of the Clemson College Library, taking the position in 1954 and retiring in 1980 as director emeritus. Clemson University Photographs, CUL.SC.

applications it had received, resulting from advertisements in major newspapers and library associations' publications. In late 1953, the committee recommended John Wallace Gordon Gourlay, a Canadian. Gourlay had received his BA degree in English, history, and economics from Queen's University, Ontario, in 1940, a bachelor of library science (BLS) from McGill University in 1941, and an MLS degree from the University of Michigan in 1942. During the height of World War II, he served as a combat pilot in both the Royal Canadian Air Force and the Royal Air Force. After the war, Gourlay had worked in the libraries of two major universities, Brown and Indiana, and in the collection at Louisiana Polytechnic Institute (Louisiana Tech at Ruston, Louisiana). He and his wife joined the Clemson academic staff in the summer of 1954.[68]

Research

Outside of the field of agriculture, which received funds from the federal government through USDA and in some states through privilege fees (such as the fertilizer tag sales in South Carolina), most money for research came from corporations for developing specific solutions to problems. A few colleges and universities (large private schools in the main), and a very few public universities, had created separate research foundations or corporations designed to receive gifts, grants, and copyright or patent revenues to hold, invest, and use to fund worthy faculty projects. The land-grant schools had made a number of efforts before World War I to push engineering research and dissemination of it into the federal budget, but to no avail.

In the past, Clemson had been able to accumulate money from the fertilizer tag sales revenue that could be used for one-time expenses, particularly for buildings such as the old textile building and additional barracks. The individual agricultural experiment stations sold excess produce and used the revenue to improve stock, update equipment, and add to supplies. However, during the gubernatorial administration of J. Strom Thurmond (1947–1951), the state required that all public money not expended by the end of the fiscal year be returned to the state treasury. The oversight authority passed to the South Carolina Budget and Control Board, established in 1948 (Act 621) to centralize fiscal activity. This, in effect, caused all public research institutions to turn to private sources for research.[69]

The first major support for Clemson's nonagricultural research program was in the form of a bequest from Claude W. Kress, who left Clemson one-sixtieth of his residual estate, most of it invested in S. H. Kress Company stock. The trustees accepted (happily) the gift in stock and a small amount of cash. The value totaled about $560,000; the cash was invested in U.S. bonds. Throughout the early years, unexpended income was carefully placed in the bonds, but, because the donor had placed no restrictions on its use, the trustees spent time debating what to do with it. Urged by Poole, they eventually decided to use it to underwrite research. Poole then appointed a committee of faculty active in research and some deans and department heads to recommend rules for faculty application for research funds. The committee's work took time, and Poole then presented its recommendations to the trustees.

The trustees then adopted the rules for use of the Kress fund revenue. Six principles guided its use. Of them, four provided certain limits: primarily, the revenue was to be used for scientific projects, except for projects eligible for USDA funds; second, funds could be used to design and construct specific research equipment; third, research should be favored that had economic importance; and fourth, publication of results of the funded projects could be supported financially. The two loopholes included the permission to use income to bring to campus "outstanding personalities to enhance the cultural aspect of students and to fund community life," and to fund "miscellaneous worthwhile projects not covered by the above items." Clearly, research in the liberal arts was not encouraged. In a long paragraph urging scientific experimentation, a sentence stated, "Projects involving surveys and those consisting of 'library research' will be considered, but a specially critical analysis of proposals for such projects will be made before support is granted."[70]

Other bequests and memorial gifts given to support research added to this fund. Also, a large number of industries, recognizing the rapid strengthening of research capabilities of state universities, particularly those that emphasized engineering, began funding research at those institutions and a few selected private schools. Schools that moved to advance their research agenda included Clemson neighbors Georgia Tech and Duke. Georgia Tech had a strong advantage, a well-established and state-funded engineering experiment station that attracted new industries to Atlanta. Duke, on the other hand, a private institution with Methodist connections, involved itself in tobacco research funded by the Duke family, whose tobacco-derived wealth had essentially bought, renamed, and rebuilt Trinity College as Duke University in Durham, North Carolina. During 1953–1954, Textiles was the major departmental recipient at Clemson of nonagricultural federal and private research grants, receiving $95,000 in private funds, while Chemistry received $5,500, Arts and Sciences, $6,750, Engineering $22,000, and Agriculture $14,000. Roger Milliken, a major textile entrepreneur, worked eagerly for Clemson to develop a research center for textiles and gave stock worth $30,000 to begin the planning.[71]

Graduate Work

But there the research stalled, in part because of the college's lack of a strong graduate program. While some graduate work had been done in agriculture and in textiles with success, most such work was at the master's level in education. Initially, it focused on vocational (agricultural and industrial) education, although as early as May 5, 1945, a faculty committee led by F. H. H. Calhoun had recommended that master's programs be established in agricultural economics, agricultural engineering, animal husbandry, plant physiology, entomology, and horticulture, all in the School of Agriculture. The committee also urged the creation of master's programs in textiles (in which Clemson had given some degrees earlier), chemistry, and in all fields of engineering, education, and architecture.[72]

After considering the committee's report, Poole recommended to the trustees that graduate work should begin in chemistry and in all education fields except elementary education, but he mentioned nothing about Clemson's two original "mission" fields, agriculture and engineering.[73] His overlooking of agriculture, at a time when other southern land-grant schools were moving into such work, led those schools to attempt to recruit some of Clemson's better-known younger faculty. Particularly targeted was the program in agricultural economics and its kin field of rural sociology, both of which Poole had expressed "animus" toward shortly after accepting the presidency in 1940. The prospect of several faculty losses caused him to reconsider and recommend one year later that a master's degree be offered in agricultural economics. The trustees approved, and in the fall of 1946, six graduate students enrolled.[74]

One year later, the USDA proposed the opening of graduate programs at all of the 1862 land-grant colleges because they received Hatch Act funds. Approved at the cabinet level in 1948, and in states with a combined land-grant school and a liberal arts state school, the 1862 land-grant institutions had a strong outside mandate to begin graduate education.[75]

Thereafter, the master's program at Clemson slowly took root in engineering and in the sciences.[76] By 1948, W. H. Washington, dean of education, proposed the master's degree for that school's advanced work in six specific fields, most in forms of vocational education, but also a few in more traditional fields.[77] Shortly thereafter, Clemson received admission to the Conference of Deans of Southern Graduate Schools, and the college placed its graduate organization under a Graduate Council composed of a graduate dean and committee of faculty that approved new master's and proposed doctor of philosophy degrees. By 1951, H. J. Webb served as dean and chair of the Graduate Council. The council's faculty members, all holders of the PhD degree, were G. M. Anderson (Agriculture), M. D. Farrar (Agriculture), O. B. Garrison (Agriculture), E. M. Lander Jr. and W. G. Miller (Arts and Sciences), and W. T. Rainey Jr. (Textiles, Chemistry). The council answered to Poole. But apparently, the trustees' concern remained that Poole's flat and slow management style would not change.[78]

To compound the trustees' anxiety, Littlejohn, whose health since 1948 had been very poor, at which time he had asked his life insurance company to settle his policy because of his total disability,[79] announced that he would retire effective September 30, 1954.[80] Faced with all these changes and the managerial problem, the trustees, led by Daniel, contacted the New York management firm of Cresap, McCormick and Paget (CMP) requesting that it make a thorough study of Clemson Agricultural College. Much of the cost of the study would be borne by the trustees, with Daniel paying the major share.[81]

Notes

1. Edgar, *South Carolina*, 503.
2. CUL.SC.CUA. S 30 ss ii f "Cooper"; CUL. SC.MSS 68 f 140; and MSS 91 b 4 f 408.
3. CUL.SC.MSS 68 f 146. Rockefeller comments are in RAC.GEB.SC 103 S 1.1 b 129 f 1179.
4. CUL.SC.CUA. S 6 f 2; S 15 f 232; and S 37 f "Textiles in the 1950s."
5. Ibid., S 15 f 232.
6. Columbia *State*, clipping with no date in CUL.SC.CUA. S 37 f "Textiles in the 1950's"; CUL. SC.CUA. S 30 v 6, 156; Anderson *Independent*, June 3, 1951; *Greenville News* July 1, 1951; SCHS 1231.06/25/36/10; CUL.SC.CUA. S 11 f 446; and S 30 v 6, 156.
7. Lancaster *News*, June 3, 1952; and *Greenville News,* November 7, 1954.
8. Anderson *Independent*, November 3, 1951.
9. CUL.SC.MSS 47 f 8.
10. Baldwin, *Traditional Stoneware of South Carolina;* and Koverman, "Edgefield Pottery" in *South Carolina Encyclopedia*, 285–286.

11. Anderson *Independent*, February 25, 1996.
12. Ibid., September 4, 1946.
13. CUL.SC.MSS 47 f 5.
14. CUL.SC.CUA. S 11 f 480.
15. CUL.SC.MSS 47 f 7.
16. Ibid., f 10.
17. SCHS 1231.00/25/36/10.
18. CUL.SC.CUA. S 30 v 5, 754.
19. CUL.SC.MSS 47 f 6.
20. *Greenville News*, April 28, 1949; and CUL.SC.CUA. S 37 f "Architecture 1950–1970."
21. The problem is the placement of a mezzanine floor and the creation of a viewing space that forces the looker into an unusual posture. For the missing Riggs Hall fresco, see *Clemson Alumni News*, Spring 1949, no pagination.
22. CUL.SC.MSS 47 f 12.
23. Ibid., 91 f L 454.
24. Ibid., 47 f 17.
25. Ibid., 91 f L453.
26. Benjamin, *Clemson University: College of Engineering*, 26, 27, 30, 37, 52–57, and 81.
27. CUL.SC.MSS 47 f 8.
28. Benjamin, *Clemson University: College of Engineering*, various; and Anderson *Daily Mail*, November 11, 1970.
29. Benjamin, *Clemson University: College of Engineering*, 80, 88, and 89.
30. Victor Hurst to Jerry Reel, February 2007, a personal conversation.
31. CUL.SC.CUA. S 30 v 5, 608; and Anderson *Independent*, February 6, 1951.
32. Seneca *Daily Journal* and Clemson *Daily Messenger*, July 21, 2004.
33. These data have been gathered by A. C. Land, history master's student, from a number of sources. The most useful has been the USDA's Economic Research Services, which has assembled acreage in forest-use land in approximately five-year intervals. Data from the U.S. Census Bureau, the University of Virginia's Geostat Center, and the Clemson University Division of Public Service Activities have been invaluable. Thanks to the many specialists in these centers who replied to Land's requests and my sometimes confusing pleas.
34. CUL.SC.CUA S 87 ss i b 8 ff 2, 3, 4, 7, and 8.
35. Anderson *Independent*, March 18, 1953; *New York Times*, January 4, 1948; and Anderson *Independent*, December 9, 1953.
36. Anderson *Independent*, January 11, 1955.
37. Ibid., August 5, 1949.
38. CUL.SC.CUA. S 32 b 126 f 5.
39. Ibid., b 76 f 3.
40. Ibid., b 153 ff 6 and 7.
41. Ibid., f 1.
42. Ibid., S 37 f "Camps."
43. Ibid., S 32 b 150 ff 2 and 3; and *The Tiger*, January 13, 1946.
44. CUL.SC.MSS 281 f 12.
45. CUL.SC.CUA. S 37 f "Farmers' Institutes."
46. *Greenville News*, June 15, 1952; and Anderson *Independent*, April 27, 1953.
47. CUL.SC.CUA. S 32 b 154 f 4; and *Greenville News*, August 18, 1950. Rusk, who visited Clemson on a number of occasions, occasionally stopped at the grave of his ancestor, John Rusk, a stonemason whose remains rest in the historic churchyard of Old Stone Church (Presbyterian). The old church, built by John Rusk, still stands.
48. CUL.SC.MSS 281 f 24; and CUL.SC.CUA. S 32 b 125 f 1.
49. CUL.SC.CUA. S 32 b 126 f 7 and b 128 f 7.
50. CUL.SC.CUA. S 32 b 134 f 4.
51. Ibid., b 127 f 9, b 153 f 6 and 73; S 6 f 12; and Anderson *Independent*, April 29, 1953.
52. H. M. Cox to Jerry Reel, a personal conversation, February 2007.
53. *Record*, 1948–1956.
54. CUL.SC.CUA. S 87 ss i b 59 f 18.

55. Ibid., S 30 v 6, 322.
56. Ibid., 342.
57. Lander, *From Clemson College to India*, 111–113.
58. CUL.SC.CUA S 37 "Agricultural Experiment 1945–1955."
59. Lander and Lambert, with their spouses, kindly met with my wife and me to discuss their careers and their lives in Clemson during the decade. I appreciate their openness. Bolen and his wife died far too early, but we were very close friends. My wife's and my memories are vivid. Data are from *Record*.
60. Cox to Reel, February 2007.
61. CUL.SC.CUA. S 15 f 159; and RAC.RF 2B S 2 ss 1.3 b406 f 4255. The correspondence of Mark Bradley, chair of the Clemson Library Committee, reinforces the fact that the facility could take no more books. A. Mann of the Rockefeller Foundation suggested that before a major grant could even be considered, readers' space had to be increased. He recommended a large "stacks" building connected to the south wing of the then-library. One year later, Cornelia Graham hired a new professional assistant cataloger and moved long out-of-date U.S. government reports to the basement of the old Chemistry Building to make room for newer volumes. The Rockefeller Foundation then made the appropriation.
62. *The Tiger*, August 5, 1939.
63. CUL.SC.CUA. S 15 ff 157, 158, and 159; *The Tiger*, April 23, 1936; and Carnegie Foundation Archives, Columbia University, New York, NY.
64. CUL.SC.CUA. S 87 ss 1 b f I; CUL.SC.MSS 240 b 12 f 12, b 14 f 41, and b 15; CUL. SC.CUA. S 15 f 158; *The Tiger*, January 16, 1947; *Greenville News*, March 8, 1959; and Augusta *Chronicle*, April 25, 1963.
65. *The Tiger*, January 13, 1946.
66. CUL.SC.CUA. S 6 f 15 and S 15 f 160 and 161.
67. Ibid., S 7 f 737 and S 30 *President's Report to the Board of Trustees, 1948–1953*, 19.
68. Ibid., S 28 f "Gourlay"; and *The Tiger*, February 11, 1954.
69. Edgar, *South Carolina*, 518.
70. CUL.SC.MSS 68 b 5 f.
71. CUL.SC.CUA. S 30 *President's Report to the Board of Trustees, 1953–1954*, October 25, 1954, 3 and S 87 ss i b 48 f l.
72. Ibid., S 7 f 27; and CUL.SC.MSS 255 b 2 f 6.
73. CUL.SC.CUA. S 30 *President's Report to the Board of Trustees*, June 15, 1945, 7.
74. Ibid., S 7 f 27; and CUL.SC.MSS 255 6 2 f 64.
75. CUL.SC.CUA. S 7 ff 28 and 29.
76. CUL.SC.MSS 255 b 2 f 7; and CUL.SC.CUA. S 7 ff 28, 29, and 30.
77. CUL.SC.CUA. S 7 f 31.
78. Ibid., 7 f 33; and RAC.GEB.SC 103 S 1.1 b 129 f 1179.
79. CUL.SC.MSS 47 f 6.
80. CUL.SC.CUA. S 87 ss i b 52 f 15.
81. CUL.SC.MSS 90 S 7 b 11 f 16 and MSS 68 f 125.

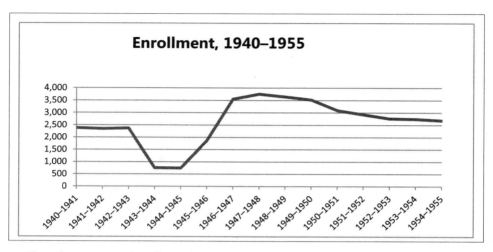

Enrollment, 1940–1955

Chart demonstrates the effects of World War II, the return of veterans to Clemson, and the continuation of the college's all-male, all-military policy on enrollment. Data and chart prepared by graduate research assistant Paul Alexander Crunkleton.

Year	Enrolled
1940–1941	2,381
1941–1942	2,349
1942–1943	2,370
1943–1944	752
1944–1945	745
1945–1946	1,863
1946–1947	3,550
1947–1948	3,756
1948–1949	3,645
1949–1950	3,522
1950–1951	3,093
1951–1952	2,926
1952–1953	2,764
1953–1954	2,749
1954–1955	2,690

CHAPTER XIV

GIs Return

1945–1955

T he swell in enrollment at Clemson caused by the end of World War II and the arrival of veterans at the college in the school year 1949–1950 reached an apex of 3,522. However, the number of returning veterans dropped from 1,943 in 1947–1948 to 1,672 in 1948–1949. The commencements for those years bore witness to the beginning of the decline. The June Class of 1948 received 303 undergraduate diplomas and one postgraduate degree. A year later, the Class of 1949 received 490 undergraduate and three graduate degrees. In June 1950, undergraduate degrees dropped to 369 while graduate degrees increased to 9.[1] While most colleges and universities showed a slight decline, few land-grant schools had sharp downturns.[2]

One obvious reason was the supply of GIs. Many who enrolled had some college credits when they arrived. While no records of either the number of veterans or the average amount of transfer credit for the veterans are available, traditionally Clemson had received a small number of transfer students, beginning with the first entering cadets in 1893. But the entire influx of veterans bringing transcripts from a great variety of institutions produced a new situation for Gustave Metz, the registrar. He assembled teams of experienced faculty from several academic fields with advisors from the professional fields. The core members included Marvin Owings (English), Gaston Gage (Textiles), and K. N. Vickery (assistant to the registrar). With diligence they sat and mulled over transcripts, frequently working with little more than a course title to make the decision whether to accept the course or not, and if so, for which degree-granting curriculum. They sent complex issues to the deans of the schools.

Many of the returning veterans were former Clemson students. Ab Snell from Elloree had enrolled in Clemson in the autumn of 1942 and enlisted in the Army Air Corps, having already begun training as a pilot. Stationed in the United Kingdom, and following the success of the Normandy invasion in 1944 in France, he served in the occupation army detailed to Oberfaffenhofen, Germany. In June 1946 with other American military, he shipped out from Le Havre, France, and returned to the States in time to enroll with the new student group in September.[3] With his own interests in "how things work" and the knowledge he acquired in the Army Air Corps, Snell graduated from Clemson in 1949 in agricultural engineering. He was a member of Phi Eta Sigma, Alpha Zeta, and the Wesley Foundation. From Clemson he attended Iowa State College for his master's degree and then North Carolina State College for his doctorate. Snell returned to Clemson and joined the experiment station, from which he retired years later.[4]

Snell and other returning Clemson veterans received the highest priority for entrance. Second came other veterans. Then priority was given to nonveterans, usually young men between the ages of seventeen and nineteen who had finished the eleventh grade and enrolled, but not in the numbers as before because South Carolina had added the twelfth grade in 1945–1946, and finally to those who had completed the twelfth grade.

The flood of applications caught Metz shorthanded. Fortunately, Kenneth N. Vickery, who had graduated from Clemson in 1938, was back in 1946. He had begun working with Metz in the summer of 1938 and interspersed that with graduate study in educational statistics at the University of North Carolina. As a Clemson graduate with the rank of second lieutenant, he was called to active duty and was deployed to the United Kingdom. He remained overseas until mid-1946. Upon demobilization, he returned to Clemson to the Registrar's Office, where he served as assistant (the only other professional staff) and concentrated on admissions.[5] In that capacity, he kept statistics on many different things, among them the reasons accepted applicants decided not to enroll. He had a particular interest in the applicants coming straight from high schools. Slowly, he discerned a pattern among those who did not enroll at Clemson. He also surveyed the students who did matriculate, asking them about the effectiveness of Clemson's recruiting materials. And he asked especially if any had friends who ap-

Kenneth Notley Vickery (1917–2006), 1938 Clemson graduate and early assistant to the registrar. After service in World War II, he returned to Clemson in 1946 and successively served as the school's chief registrar, director/dean of admissions and registration, and assistant vice president of student affairs. He played a key role in the establishment of the Atlantic Coast Conference's academic eligibility standards for student athletes, the reason for Clemson's current student-athlete enrichment center's being named Vickery Hall in his honor. He retired in 1982, having a role in the assigning of approximately 90 percent of Clemson's diplomas up to that time. Clemson University Photographs, CUL.SC.

plied, were offered admission, but chose to go elsewhere, and why the friends made that decision. Three answers clearly emerged: narrow curricular choices, no women, and the four-year military requirement. These were major problems for the trustees to study and resolve.[6]

The trustees turned to Poole to develop solutions. He willingly agreed to broaden the curriculum. From his contacts with other land-grant colleges and his consultation with the Clemson school deans, he decided to build a program in business with a strong bent toward industrial management. Because Poole and the deans were gradualists, they began by creating programs in economics and industrial management to differentiate the Clemson thrust from USC's emerging business program. They recognized that the industrial management area would also draw support from the existing fields of agriculture, engineering, and textiles. In the latter, textile management was already operating.

President Sikes had raised the question of female students years earlier, following what he felt had been a great success with women enrolling as full-time (nonresidential) undergraduates during the 1932–1933 Depression school year. Upon reporting that the experiment had succeeded, Sikes had recommended that female undergraduates be added permanently to the student body. But the Board of Trustees rejected the president's proposal.[7] Later, toward the end of World War II, Poole, Littlejohn, and the Buildings and Grounds Committee had begun an analysis of Clemson's construction needs. Among the recommendations they made to the board was a residence hall for female students. By taking the entire building phase of the recommendations upon advisement and further review, the board effectively killed the female issue. Poole, therefore, resorted to a gradual approach to the issue.[8]

Women had also attended summer sessions since the establishment of the federal-mandated vocational education teacher preparation programs at the time of World War I. Some women came to the campus for classes, but generally the Clemson faculty traveled to "centers" in the surrounding counties to teach women and other vocational education students, and the Clemson director traveled the wider state in a move reminiscent of the earlier Clemson extension trains. However, the costs of such travel had increased greatly. Consequently, in 1945 Poole requested that the trustees set aside one of the smaller dormitories (Barracks Four, Five, Six, or Seven) for summer female student occupancy. They complied.[9] Nine months later, and in order to shorten the time required for women to obtain a master's degree, Poole recommended that female graduate students be allowed to enroll across the entire year in response to the requests and needs of women, many of whom were veterans' spouses. The trustees decided in favor of Poole's recommendations, but they still refused to permit fall and winter term enrollment for undergraduate females.[10]

The Korean Conflict

To add to the erratic enrollment trends that gave problems to Metz and his staff was the unexpected attack of North Korea on South Korea (June 25, 1950). Emboldened by communism's recent successes in Czechoslovakia (1948) and in the Chinese Communist Party's mainland victories (1949) over the Chinese Nationalists, a very large, well-trained, and well-armed North Korean army launched its attack south across the border. Under the orders of U.S. President Harry Truman, a contingent of United States forces was shipped from Japan to bolster the underarmed forces of the Republic of Korea (South Korea), a United States ally. One of the contingents contained William H. Funchess, Clemson 1948, who was with the Twenty-fourth Division of the Nineteenth Infantry. It set sail from Japan with armaments Funchess described as "a few small tanks, some corroded hand grenades, old vehicles, and weapons left over from World War II. In addition, South Korea had made no preparations to fight a war. We were in a desperate plight."[11]

By July 7, 1950, the United Nation's Security Council, having resolved that North Korea must withdraw, asked Truman to name the commander of the U.N. forces in Korea. The next day Truman named Gen. Douglas MacArthur as commanding general of U.N. Military Forces. The pale blue and white U.N. flag joined those of the two nations that were part of the very early operations against North Korea. But it took time to move men, arms, and equipment from around the globe to Korea, and by August 3, 1950, the U.N. forces were hemmed in the small southeastern corner of South Korea guarding the Port of Pusan. At that point, the United Kingdom and Australia had joined the United States at the port. The U.S. draft was also re-energized, reducing the number of young high school graduates available for college and calling back young veterans.

As men and supplies became available, the consolidated U.N. command planned a counterattack. By September 15, 1950, nearly 85,000 U.N. troops were in the "Pusan Perimeter," equalizing the forces on both sides. Then, new U.N. troops carried by ships attacked the Korean peninsula on September 15, just south of the South Korean capital of Seoul, far north of the invading North Korean Army. The area was called Inchon. In the Pusan Perimeter, the penned-up U.N. forces began attacks at all points of the front. Within a matter of days, most U.N. forces simultaneously were in pursuit of the rapidly retreating North Koreans. The Inchon invasion, surely one of the boldest military strikes in recent western military history, was successful.[12]

When the U.N. forces reached the border between North and South Korea, they held up, uncertain of what to do. Funchess remembered, "We departed Taejon (South Korea) the next day and continued our march north. We met very little resistance. We held up near Kaesong just south of the 38th parallel, the negotiated division between the two Koreas. We didn't know if we were going into North Korea, but before the day ended, orders came for us to continue north."[13]

By September 30, 1950, South Korean troops crossed the 38th parallel and, on October 9, led by the U.S. Cavalry, the U.N. forces crossed the parallel. The People's Republic of China warned the United Nations to withdraw to the 38th parallel. Five days later, a massive P.R.C. Army entered North Korea, crossing the Yalu River at Andong under cover of night. MacArthur and his staff were shocked when they became aware of the Chinese counteroffensive.[14]

By this time, sixteen U.N. countries took part in the combat. In addition, five others sent medical units.[15] But as the U.N. forces moved deeper, the P.R.C. forces increased. Funchess's unit received orders to halt north of the North Korean capital. On November 4, 1950, Funchess was taken prisoner along with other American and South Korean soldiers. Funchess had been wounded in the foot, and enemy soldiers would not allow captured U.N. medics to help him.[16]

Even though cease-fire negotiations began on July 10, 1951, brutal fighting continued until a cease-fire was finally signed by July 27, 1953. Only then would the exchange of prisoners of war begin by both sides. The United Nations, led by the United States, had achieved its original objective to defend the territory of South Korea. Most Clemson men came home, including Funchess after nearly three years in captivity in dreadful conditions.

Among those who never returned was William C. Fowler Jr., who would have been in the Class of 1952. A South Carolinian, he was born in 1927 and entered the service in the last winter of combat in World War II. Upon entering Clemson, he remained in the reserves until President Truman called the reserves into readiness. He died in fighting in South Korea on January 30, 1951. By the time the widespread fighting had ended, seventeen Clemson men had been killed, adding to those who died in earlier wars.[17]

Student Campus Life

The series of long and costly wars had many effects in the United States and certainly at a military college such as Clemson. In spite of the fears of President Poole, few faculty or staff were called for duty to Korea, but some other phases of life did change. First, student involvement emerged in nonacademic collegiate government. Of course, the process unfolded gradually. Students had class officers from the very early years. Much of the class officers' duties, in such free time as they had, included organizing social activities, interclass sports, and rare trips to follow intercollegiate teams on the road. But as nonacademic disciplinary power lessened, first under Riggs and then under Sikes, social life grew.

Dance clubs, county clubs, and regional clubs took their place alongside the original literary societies. The professional clubs were first local societies open to all and supported by most students studying in a general field. In the years between the World Wars, most of the local Clemson groups converted into national student preprofessional associations. The honor societies emerged next in each academic field. The honor societies usually required a high academic grade average and class standing for members and occasionally a membership vote of something greater than a simple majority. Arching over this were the general academic societies. Membership again was selective.

Immediately after World War II, most of the clubs and societies attached to professional honorary national societies quickly reawakened. The academic societies, such as Phi Kappa Phi, the all-fields honorary society in which faculty participated and served as one or more of the lead officers, never "went to sleep" but continued receiving new student members. The revival of local academic societies depended upon their advisors. Thus, Gamma Alpha Mu, a society for students who excelled at writing, reactivated through the strength of John D. Lane, Clemson's highly regarded teacher of English. A clutch of alumni who had gone on to brilliant careers in journalism and writing—men such as (Octavus) Roy Cohen, Wright Bryan, George Chaplin, Earl Mazo, and Harry Ashmore—helped renew interest. Other less-fortunate societies did not revive.

Few, if any, of the county and regional clubs seem to have been active after 1943. But by November 11, 1946, two quickly activated. Beta Sigma Chi, which included men from the coastal counties of South Carolina, and Gamma Kappa Alpha, composed of North Carolina men, operated and received a reminder that they might have only the students' place of primary residency as a condition of membership.[18] Other such groups gradually revived or formed. Most of the regional clubs took Greek-letter names, usually indicating their region. So, for example, the students from the counties of Marlboro, Dillon, and Marion became the Mu Delta Mu Club.[19] The idea of Greek-letter national social fraternities fascinated many students, and some who had been members of one of the local social groups begun during Sikes's administration asked Poole to allow them to affiliate with national fraternities. Poole carried the request to the Board of Trustees, which quickly answered "No." The local groups simply diminished; some died.

But special-interest groups were easily formed and open to all, and they attracted the youngest freshmen as well as the seasoned veteran. One of the more popular was the Clemson Aero Club, revitalized in 1947 by Robert R. Russell Jr. A nonveteran freshman in 1946, Russell had built his first model airplane as a ten-year-old. No doubt the heroics of airmen in World War II had fascinated him. With his father's permission, he began flying lessons in the summer before his freshman year in college and continued at the local airport when Clemson started anew in September. His enthusiasm stirred up others, and the club formed. The twenty members agreed to buy shares in the club, which they could sell upon leaving school or leaving the club. The founding money was used to buy a Piper J-3

Cub. Each member agreed to pay two dollars per month for hangar rental space, maintenance, a "bit" toward a club savings account, the cost of his own fuel, and the instructor's fee. Another Clemson student, James M. Jackson from Rock Hill, who had served in the U.S. Army Air Corps as a flight instructor, joined the club and served as the instructor. So the Tigers were off and flying, using the new Clemson-Central Airport that Leonard Meldau of Seneca had just built.[20]

The many other special-interest clubs that came and went across the years included the Amateur Radio Club and the Clemson Little Theatre, which had townsfolk and faculty as members. The latter performed in a number of makeshift venues until it settled in the demonstration auditorium of Newman Hall.[21]

As a mark of the college's growing diversity, one of the most stable of the regional clubs was Nu Epsilon, a society for students who came from the northeastern states. Good-natured teasing went on between the students who were from the southern states and the others. One of the true "Yankees" (in the New England use of the word) was an architecture student from Augusta, Maine. Ward Buzzell, ever a champion of his home state, wrote Governor Frederick G. Payne of Maine and complained that he was forever losing the argument over the superiority of Maine lobsters to Carolina and Georgia shrimp. Amused by the problem, Payne enlisted the state's commissioner of Sea and Shore Fisheries, and they airshipped a dozen live lobsters to Buzzell, who invited his southern comrades to test the product. The lobsters were cooked in the Clemson House kitchen and served with bibs, drawn butter, and claw crackers. At the end of the experiment, all twelve students representing Georgia, South Carolina, and North Carolina signed a "lobster confession," attesting that the State of Maine lobster is "the best I have tasted; and that I will uphold and defend the State of Maine lobster as the most distinguished and flavorful food of its kind." Buzzell, an active student, returned to his drafting table but found time to serve as editor of the architecture publication *Minaret* and resumed his hobby of broadcasting over the campus radio station.[22] After a long and successful architectural career, Ward and Beverly, his wife, returned to Clemson, first to bring their two sons to Clemson and then for Ward to teach in architecture.

In fact, most students from outside the South got involved quickly in student life. The two wars had carpeted over much of the old sectional animosity, and the growth of national radio networks also played a role in the development of a more national culture. *Taps*, in 1949, quipped about the "northernness" of the Nu Epsilon men, "Those 'Damn Yankees' have once again invaded the Southland, but this time they are more than welcome."[23]

Also foreign students found in Clemson a home away from home. When he graduated on January 28, 1951, H. Islam, a student from Pakistan, wrote President Poole, "Your kind and sympathetic treatment together with that of all the faculty members will…keep afresh the map of Clemson College in my mem-

Mian Mohammed Rafique Saigol (*left*), winner of the Trustee Medal for public speaking, applied his schooling in Clemson's textile management and economics programs with great success in Pakistan's emerging business world during the 1950s and 1960s. During his career as an industrialist, Saigol was director of six business ventures, on seven national industrial advisory boards, managing director of the Kohinoor Textile Mills in Lyallpur, chairman of the All-Pakistan Textile Mills Association, a founding member of the Lahore Stock Exchange, and on the Board of Directors for the State Bank of Pakistan. Clemson University Photographs, CUL.SC.

ory for all times to come as the holy shrine...."[24] Only a year later, Mohammed Rafique Saigol, a sophomore textile and economics double major from Pakistan, received permission from Poole to return home and assume the leadership of his 800,000-member tribe. He returned to Clemson, won the Trustees' Medal for the best speaker in the student body, and earned his baccalaureate degree.[25]

Diversity: Not for All

But all males were not so welcomed. When, in June 1948, the registrar received applications from Spencer M. Bracey and Edward Bracey desiring to transfer from South Carolina A&M (now South Carolina State), each listed "Negro" as his race. The trustees met to ensure that Clemson's correspondence with the applicants conformed to the letter of the state's law. Not surprisingly, the board directed Poole to respond that Clemson was full and that it was "the well established policy of this state to furnish separate and comparable facilities for the education of white and Negro races within the state."[26] Five years later, Freddie C.

Fortune, a graduate of SCA&M, applied to Clemson to enroll in the architecture program, writing on his application that because architecture at SCA&M was not accredited, he wanted to attend Clemson. Fortune received the same rejection and reasons as stated before.[27] There the matter of African Americans at Clemson rested for the time being.

Community

Koloman Lehotsky (1906–1975), a professor of forestry at Clemson from 1947 to 1969 and dean of the college's Department of Forestry beginning in 1956. The World War II veteran created Clemson's first arboretum in 1951 and a master's degree program in forestry in 1965. Clemson University Photographs, CUL.SC.

Among the traditional college-aged students, the denominational-based collegiate groups had as strong an appeal as before World War II. The Lutheran students and community members realized their hopes when their fellowship and congregation were organized and a Rudolph Lee-designed deep red brick church building was erected on downtown Sloan Street. California-based Clemson alumnus Wofford "Bill" Camp gave money for the organ. The new church joined St. Andrew's Catholic, Fort Hill Presbyterian, and Clemson First Baptist to create one of the two church "precincts" in the community. A small fellowship of Unitarians met also, using the campus YMCA as their regular meeting place.

The Jewish students organized into the Hillel Society and met in the YMCA. Even though there were few Jews in the faculty or community, the students had no trouble finding supporters and an advisor. The Rev. Dr. Sydney Crouch, pastor of Fort Hill Presbyterian Church, continued to serve as a "moral advisor" to the young men, while Koloman Lehotsky, a forester and member of the Presbyterian congregation, served as Hillel faculty advisor. Born in 1906 in the then-Austro-Hungarian Empire, Lehotsky received his education at the Bohemian Technical University, Grenoble Institute, and the University of Michigan, from which he earned a PhD in 1934. In the years after his PhD, he headed the Forestry Department in Escola Superior de Agricultura e Veterinaria, Brazil. Lehotsky had fluency in sixteen languages. After his service in the U.S. Army from 1942 until 1946, Clemson recruited him to build a forestry program.[28]

Student Governance Emerges

All of these changes weakened the monolithic cadet corps. To be certain that all their myriad voices were adequately heard, the students created several new groups. Veterans formed a Veterans Council, which included representation for single veterans living in the temporary barracks set in the field to the north of the gymnasium (now Fike Recreation Center) and for the married veterans residing in the clusters on the north and south sides of the central campus. The clubs that were recognized by the faculty committee on student organizations, the local religious groups, the class presidents, and the corps-elected officers constituted the Council of Club Presidents. In all, the council had seventy-three student organizations, each with its own faculty advisor. The college, allowing clubs for the first time a greater-than-majority vote requirement for membership, permitted a no-more-restrictive vote than approval of three-fourths of the members.[29]

Nonetheless, the idea of student involvement and government as an attractive alternative to the club council resulted in several experiments. But the basic structure that came into existence in 1950 would last with internal expansion and some modifications, changes, and development for half a century. Austin Mitchell, a junior, created the concept of the new plan with executive, judicial, and legislative branches. The faculty committee on student organizations studied the proposal recommended by the Council of Club Presidents. The faculty devoted a great amount of time and thought, both to the student government's recommended structure and the suggested jurisdiction. Plainly, the faculty wanted to minimize the types of "inter-branch" struggles that characterized that form of government, and by implication, they reserved academic matters to the faculty, which included department heads and academic administrators, the president, and the Board of Trustees. After the faculty concurred, the document was submitted to a student referendum. It passed. Then President Poole consulted with the deans, all of whom were the heads of the schools. With their agreement, Poole took the proposal to the trustees. They also considered the issue carefully and with the understanding that the approval, in accordance with Mr. Clemson's will, was always conditional.[30] This step represented one of the major ones taken during President Poole's eighteen-year presidency.[31]

Student Behavior

Besides desires for greater liberty in general social matters, marked change had occurred in student attitudes toward *public* behavior. The near disaster of the federal government's constitutional amendment of 1919 prohibiting alcoholic beverages seemed to make public drinking of distilled liquor more widely accepted upon the amendment's repeal in 1933. The economic dislocation caused by the Depression, coupled with the rise of "statism," whether in fascist or socialist form, and then the horrible atrocities of the Second World War had major effects on the public social behavior of Clemson students, whether veterans or traditional college students.

Also the rise in the entrance age of freshmen contributed to the change. As a result, the graduation rate climbed from the 1939 figure of approximately 40 percent of the entering freshmen in five years or less to 64 percent in the graduating Class of 1954. Of all students who had entered as freshmen from 1893 to 1953 (31,625), a third (11,072) had graduated through the summer of 1954.[32]

Disciplinary issues also changed. The personal, and sometimes vicious, hazing that had permeated the lives of the fourteen- through sixteen-year-old freshmen had lessened and become more a token, a rite of passage. Surviving were the pranks, such as the announcements in the mess hall or dining hall that the refrigeration in the Dairy Building had broken and the soon-to-melt ice cream

One of Clemson's prank traditions, the freshman rush on the Dairy Building for melting ice cream at the instigation of upperclassmen. Clemson University Photographs, CUL.SC.

was free "for the taking." That sent freshmen galloping to get handy buckets and bowls. The stampede across the ravine, past the outdoor theater, and on up to the Dairy Building usually halted when "rats" returned with empty buckets and embarrassed in face. But the vestiges of personal servitude, such as running errands for soft drinks, sandwiches, and cigarettes, or the polishing of shoes and boots remained. Public displays of inferior status, such as wearing special symbols, found widespread acceptance in the various student groups. These were not considered hazing or humiliation, but matters of pride.

Some clubs, particularly the regional societies, interest groups, and a few others, had risky initiation practices, usually in the evenings. On a very few occasions, bodily injury required infirmary attention. One death not related directly to hazing occurred when a just-returning initiate, standing in a road talking with a person in a car, was struck by an oncoming vehicle and killed. The leadership societies and scholastic honoraries reported no such incidents with their initiations.[33]

The greatest increase in problems involved those related to alcohol consumption. Automobile accidents appeared minor because the number of cars owned by students, faculty families, and other folk was low in comparison to later years and also because the students who had automobiles generally did not use them on campus. So accidents, even those associated with alcohol, received almost no mention in disciplinary reports. However, public use of alcohol on campus, possession of alcohol in dormitory rooms (veterans' "prefabs" were not subject to regular room inspections), and public drunkenness accounted for a bit more than half of the disciplinary reports.[34]

The age maturity of the seniors, both veterans and students who entered Clemson directly from high school, in combination with alcohol led to one of the unfortunate social discipline decisions of the era. Student leaders had promoted a free day of no class attendance for seniors in the late spring shortly before final examinations, and in 1949 President Poole granted what was called "Senior Day."[35] During the official lifetime of Senior Day, some students organized for the upcoming exam ordeal, some slept late and then lolled or played games or pick-up sports, and some left campus for other activities. But some made themselves more than campus public nuisances.

Probably the most infamous Senior Day happened in that first spring of 1949. The activities became particularly ugly late that evening. The signal for the revelry was a spilled bottle of ink on the post office steps. However, a diligent janitor cleaned it up so fast that the signal giver had to repeat the "sinister sign." Some students, supposedly led by unmarried veterans, broke into the motor pool of the college and the military unit transport lots and started up equipment such as bulldozers, tractors, and tanks. They rumbled through the campus pushing over garbage cans and signs. The tractors "drag-raced" across Bowman Field, and the front loaders extracted a concrete pad, once the site of the town's gas pump. It had

Three instances of humorous hazing at Clemson: "rats" pushing eggs up a grassy hill without the use of their hands while onlookers enjoy the show (*top*); a "rat" being prepared for shearing (*center*); and "pooling" in process (*bottom*).

Taken from the 1950 and 1951 editions of the Clemson College annual, *Taps*.

The hijinks of Senior Night, 1949, as
recorded in that year's edition of the Clemson College annual, *Taps*.

jutted out into the (Old) Greenville Highway in front of Mr. Sloan's commercial building and was a driving nuisance. When a storeowner in a neighboring town refused to sell some drunken students more beer, he was struck.

One group of students, not part of the mayhem, returned to campus late from a trip to Atlanta to attend a touring Metropolitan Opera production and were quite surprised. The faculty member who had driven them there and back, Frank Burtner, a sociologist and advisor to several student societies, was called to President Poole's office at 6:00 the next morning, along with several other faculty group advisors, to discuss Senior Day and what should be done. The police chief presented the toll. Of course, one could plainly see most of the chicanery and mess, but according to the chief, a relatively small number of students were involved.[36] Other universities and colleges experienced something of the same rowdiness that year.[37] The faculty group decided to substitute more productive activities for future Senior Days, frequently confined to the stadium.

Senior Day officially lasted a few more years. At the spring 1952 faculty meeting, that body withdrew its approval of Senior Day. After lengthy consideration of it, the trustees officially abolished Senior Day. But more than a decade passed before the vestiges of that unfortunate "new" tradition died. One diversionary tactic had graduation candidates spend a day impressing their names in newly poured concrete walkways. So the custom of senior sidewalks began. They were soon abandoned because of lack of permanence of the concrete and the cost.[38]

Music

Music of all types also played roles in student interest and activities. Clemson's sports competition made it quite clear that the music used as the Clemson alma mater and other songs was hardly unique. The fight songs were "Tiger-Rag" and occasionally "Caissons Go Rolling Along," while the alma mater was sung to the tune that Cornell University (and a large number of other schools) used. Tiger Brotherhood, which emphasized Clemson's uniqueness, announced in January 1946 a contest for an original tune. Entries had to be original, well pitched, setting the 1919 words in a fashion that could be sung. The records of the competition do not survive, but the winning entry does.[39]

Robert Farmer, a student from Greenville who could neither read nor write music, created a tune in his head. He "dee-dah-dah-dee-ed" it for his roommate, who picked out the melody on his guitar. When Farmer was satisfied with the tune, it was set down as a melody single line score. The judges, composed of alumni, faculty, and students, thought Farmer's melody the best. It was given to music professor Hugh McGarity, a new faculty member. He orchestrated and arranged the tune, making some changes in the musical logic, and then he dis-

Robert Farmer, an architect major from Anderson, submitted a tune in the Tiger Brotherhood competition to create a new score for the Clemson alma mater in 1947. Taken from the 1949 edition of the Clemson College annual, *Taps*.

tributed it to the college chorus. Time passed, more adjustments to the harmony were made, and finally the finished product emerged.

A record was cut, distributed to students, and sold to alumni. It featured both the words set to Cornell's "Far Above Cayuga's Waters" (or "Amici" or "Anna Lisa," other traditional names of the tune) and to Farmer's melody as developed by McGarity. The alumni in reunion and the students' votes overwhelmingly supported Farmer's melody in McGarity's arrangement. Based on the response, the Board of Trustees adopted it and had it copyrighted. The alma mater remains synonymous with the words "Clemson" and "Dear Old Clemson" to this day, thanks to students A. C. Corcoran and Robert Farmer, to Prof. Hugh McGarity, and to Tiger Brotherhood.[40]

Hugh Harris McGarity (1919–1977), the director of the Clemson band and glee club from 1947 to 1954 and the first paid professor of music at the college, joined the faculty in 1946 and taught until his retirement as professor emeritus of music in 1968. He orchestrated the Robert Farmer tune, creating the alma mater—with A. C. Corcoran's original words from 1919—we know today. Clemson University Photographs, CUL.SC.

Musical groups, some informal and some formal, were popular. And the groups varied widely in what styles they performed and in whether or not the college sponsored them. One band, the Brigadiers, an eleven-piece brass band, played throughout the region. Its predecessor and better-known student group, the Jungaleers, also had eleven instruments including horns, trombones, and saxophones. Both served as alternate musical outlets to the college regimental band, which served both athletics and military.[41]

While these student musical organizations were (and in the case of the Jungaleers, remain) popular, a change had emerged in dancing music. There is no certainty where or how the new movement began. Without a doubt, it had roots in jazz and in blues. At the same time, the dancing style had similarities to the jitterbug, greatly slowed down. For the Clemson cadets, however, the origin appeared in Myrtle Beach. By the early 1950s, although the music was broadcast from out-of-state stations, the performers and dance style became associated closely with the Grand Strand, from which the local name "beach music" arose. The "shag" became the better-known name. Among many observers, it raised the spectre of interracial socializing and dancing. Nonetheless, the style dominated dancing at Clemson and Winthrop in the late 1950s and continued thereafter.[42]

However, the cadets also desired and enjoyed "high art," particularly the styles of the twentieth and nineteenth centuries. Prof. McGarity presented the first post-World War II student concert with the glee club in December 1946.[43] And by 1952, Robert E. Lovett, also a faculty member in music, directed the Clemson Community Choir's presentation of several Easter concerts. Students made up a portion of the choir.[44]

The presentation of concerts and programs, called the Lyceum in the 1900s and on, had gained additional student revenue in 1940 and received a new name, the Clemson Concert Series. From time to time, Poole also used income from the Kress Fund for this purpose. The series continued during the war years, and afterward it kept offering the Clemson cadets, veterans, and community some of the world's greatest performers, including Swedish tenor Jussi Bjorling, violinist Fritz Kreisler, and the Wagnerian tenor Lauritz Melchior. The last offered were "In fernem land" (*Lohengrin*) and "Siegfried's Forging Song" (*Siegfried*), both by Richard Wagner. The famed ballerina Alicia Markova danced in 1948. And in 1952, Eugene Ormandy and the Philadelphia Orchestra performed in the basketball gymnasium (now Fike Recreation Center).[45] The group returned several years later.

Also with the slow deregulation of military life begun under Riggs, hastened by Sikes, and continued by Poole, intramurals, frequently the seedbed of intercollegiate sports, expanded significantly. The presence of students from far-flung places across the rapidly dissolving European empires brought games such as cricket and rugby, which never had enough interest to field more than one team of foreign and American students, and they competed with some visiting clubs. The usual sports of baseball, basketball, and touch football, along with tennis, swimming, and golf, were also popular. Others, such as soccer, came and went.

Student publications remained important to Clemson's students. *Taps* had stopped publication after the 1943 issue, partially because of manpower but especially because of the growing scarcity of some photographic supplies. It restarted in 1947 and has appeared continuously. *The Tiger* continued to report and comment on campus news and, as had been its custom since the 1920s, on the events that affected the college in the growing hamlet of Clemson. Advertisements carried the movies shown in the YMCA and the new theater on College Avenue, noting with joy that the first movie shown there was "Scudda Hoo! Scudda Hay." Of course, the cadets had access to regular movies at the YMCA for many years. But the off-campus theater was a place for the men, particularly the veterans, to take their families. Although *Tiger* advertisements still appeared occasionally for pipe tobacco, cigarette ads and photographs in its pages demonstrated their widespread use.[46]

The academic-discipline publications, such as the *Bobbin and Beaker* in the Textile School, *The Agrarian* in Agriculture, and the *Slip-Stick* in Engineering, along with the already-noted *Minaret* in Architecture, demonstrated scientific and technical work and the value of thorough rhetorical and logical skills instilled by the humanities faculties.[47]

Athletics

Hardly surprising, however, intercollegiate athletics loomed ever larger in the minds of the cadets, the veterans, their families, and the now far-flung alumni. And football remained the most popular of all sports. For the student-veterans and alumni whose connections extended beyond the geographic reach of the southern collegiate athletic conferences, football became their school's battle for respect. For Clemson, high moments occurred in 1945. The season record, 6–3–1, was marked by a victory over a weak but nonetheless Southeastern Conference (SEC) member, Tulane, a team the Tigers had not beaten since 1938. The victory came in New Orleans, always a great city in which to be victorious. The next week the Tigers won 21–7 over Georgia Tech, a Clemson rival since 1898. It was all the more sweet because Tech, also an SEC school, had a first-year coach, Bobby Dodd. And for the decade beginning in 1945, the season's 6–3–1 was fourth best.

But Frank Howard's Tigers had one of their greatest seasons in 1948. Co-captains Bob Martin and Phil Prince led the team, which had four wins, no losses, and no ties as it rolled into Columbia on October 21 for the traditional clash

Key members of the second perfect season in Clemson's history, one that ended with a 24–23 Clemson victory over the University of Missouri on January 1, 1949.

Fred Cone, All-State fullback

Ray Matthews, All-State wingback

Bobby Gage, All-America tailback

Oscar Thompson, end

Sterling Smith, guard

Co-captains Bob Martin, blocking back (*left*), and Phil Prince (*right*), All-State tackle

with the Gamecocks. USC, led by freshman Steve Wadiak, held a 7–6 lead with 4:15 left in the contest. At that point, the Gamecocks had to punt from their 28-yard line. Prince smashed through the line to block the punt, whereupon Oscar Thompson scooped up the ball to carry it across the South Carolina goal line for a 13–7 Clemson win. The regular season ended with Clemson undefeated, untied, and ranked eleventh in the nation. The Clemson Tigers played the Missouri Tigers in the January 1, 1949, Gator Bowl game in Jacksonville, Florida. At the time, only five significant bowls existed in postseason play. Ultimately, Clemson won the two-Tiger match on a fourth-quarter field goal kicked by Jack Miller. Clemson ended its second perfect season in football ranked ninth in the country. The year produced outstanding players, including the tailback Bobby Gage, backs Ray Matthews and Fred Cone, and receiver John Poulos, who joined the others mentioned previously.

The 1949 football team ended its season 4–4–2. Then the 1950 team also produced something exceptional: The undefeated, but one-tie (with USC), Clemson Tigers won an Orange Bowl bid to face Miami of Florida in the latter's home stadium. Both teams sported undefeated but one-tie records. With only six minutes to go in the bowl game, Miami led 14–13. Deep in its own end of the field, Miami ran a pitch-out play. Clemson's Sterling Smith "nailed" Miami's Frank Smith in Miami's end zone for a two-point safety, giving Clemson a 15–14 victory.[48]

The spring and summer of 1951 produced a period of sports soul-searching by the Southern Conference, created in 1920 by a number of schools that were either independents or members of the Southern Intercollegiate Association. At its founding, the Southern Conference had twenty-two institutions as members. The secession of the Southeastern Conference from the Southern Conference in 1933 removed thirteen schools. By 1950, the Southern Conference had expanded again to seventeen colleges and universities and was certainly a crowded field. Further, with the post-World War II enrollment growth, which affected public universities mightily, the conference tilted askew in the size differentials of the various schools. In addition, other problems included cost concerns arising from travel and the increasing number of coaches and support staff. A host of other issues, such as the lengthening (in all college sports) of sports seasons and the effect that such matters had on academics, also were being debated.[49]

The Clemson *Football Guide* for 1950 noted Coach Frank Howard had six assistants, of whom one was Dr. Lee Milford, titled "team physician." Another was Howard's secretary, and others on the staff all had other athletic coaching assignments. A test of Howard's commitment to Clemson occurred when Wallace Wade announced his retirement as Duke's athletic director and head football coach early in January 1951. The Southern Conference appointed Wade commissioner almost immediately, and the Duke administration invited Howard to Durham to discuss the coaching position.[50] He went, but whether or not he was offered the job, there is no record. Poole's correspondence notes that after the Gator Bowl of 1949, a number of alumni wrote him urging a significant increase in Howard's salary. Poole answered each, pointing out that all salaried employees of Clemson earned well below the average for the type of institution (small land-grant school in the South) and that "true Clemson men do what is necessary for the College, regardless." Years later, when asked about the outcome of his visit to Durham, Howard quipped, "I decided not to go. It's hard enough to be a Methodist once a week, but not for all seven days."[51]

But even more than the number of coaches or costs of head coaches, much of the concern about money for football involved the bowl games. Certainly, the costs had grown. For any school there were bands, trustees, administrators, and other officers to take as guests, while state institutions usually also invited governors and other select public officials. Consequently, at the 1951 annual spring meeting of the presidents of the schools in the Southern Conference, the members voted to forbid member institutions to accept postseason bowl invitations, effective immediately. It passed thirteen to four. Clemson had voted in opposition to the measure, but little arose regarding the issue until the football season of 1951 began.[52]

The cadets eagerly anticipated the September 22 season opener, which resulted in a 53–6 romp over Presbyterian College. Before the game, Lonnie MacMillian, the Presbyterian head coach, was asked how he felt taking his team year after year (an annual occurrence since 1930) to Clemson for the opener. Noting that Clemson had won all but three of the games (one loss in 1943 and ties in 1931 and 1933), the coach cracked, "It's like going into Death Valley." The name has stuck, even though there is no indication whether the coach's reference was to the California desert or the much more familiar Psalms 23. Of course, the former is now reinforced by "Howard's Rock," taken from the desert and placed at the site of the Clemson football team's dramatic field entry. There was no rock there in 1951, but the stadium, then only twenty-six rows, sat in a valley. The Woodland Cemetery, resting place of many of the Calhouns and hundreds of deceased Clemson faculty, presidents, a few trustees, some staff, and their families, was then clearly visible from many parts of the stadium. So, indeed, it was a "valley of death."

When the season drew to a close, Clemson held a 7–2 record, and rumors spread of a bowl bid for the Tigers. The same was true for Maryland, also in the Southern Conference. The Terrapins had a perfect 9–0 record and ranked third in the nation. The Sugar Bowl selection committee hoped to match Jim Tatum's Maryland against Robert Neyland's unbeaten and also first-ranked Tennessee. Clemson received an invitation to play Miami of Florida in the Gator Bowl, and both Clemson and Maryland appealed to the conference for permission to accept the invitations. Both were denied. The Clemson trustees asked Poole and Milford about the consequences if the Tigers played. They responded that it likely meant expulsion from the conference. The trustees decided to leave the decision to the president, and Clemson accepted the invitation.[53] So did Maryland, who upset Tennessee 28–13, but made no gain in the final rankings. Clemson lost a rematch with Miami in the Gator Bowl and fell in ranking from nineteenth to twenty-third. Rather than expel both schools as promised, the Southern Conference suspended the two, forbidding them to play other teams in good standing in the conference. Shortly thereafter, the S.C. Legislature inserted itself into the athletic scheduling business and required USC and Clemson to play in 1952.[54]

The bowl scheduling issue led soon to the breaking away from the Southern Conference of seven schools to form the Atlantic Coast Conference. Those leaving included the two penalized schools, plus USC, UNC, Duke, North Carolina State, and Wake Forest.[55] The Southern Conference never really recovered. The University of Virginia, an independent, joined the Atlantic Coast Conference for the 1954 season.

As the football season ended, Frank Howard's Tigers could look back on a decade with fifty-five victories, thirty-six defeats, and six ties, or about a 56 percent success rate. Further, Clemson had won two of three postseason games. And Clemson had ranked nationally as high as tenth at the conclusion of a regular season. But the games with USC produced a much less successful story. Two ties, seven losses, and only one victory demonstrated that the Rex Enright-coached Gamecocks had the Tigers chasing their own tails. Clemson's faithful renewed the complaint that playing the game every year in Columbia during the State Fair placed Clemson at a decided disadvantage.

The other sports, although zealously followed by the students, did not have the fan base among alumni and others that football did. Basketball had only two coaches during the decade, Rock Norman and Banks McFadden. The 1945–1946 season was the last year for Norman, who had taken the position in 1940–1941. McFadden, Clemson's only basketball All-American to that point, followed him as coach. During the ensuing eight years, McFadden had a stretch of success during 1949–1950, then a break-even season, followed by two winning seasons. The high point, the 17–7 season of 1951–1952, included a Christmas trip to the Gator Bowl basketball tournament.

Rock Norman, an alumnus of Roanoke College, was a far more effective track coach, leading the Tigers to state championships in 1949 and 1951. Further, W. J. Brown won the Southern Conference pole vaulting championships in 1948 and 1949. Baseball during the decade posted seven winning seasons, one Southern Conference and one Atlantic Coast Conference Championship, the NCAA Southern Championship in 1946–1947, and two other trips to the NCAA District Tournaments. In that era, Randy Hinson coached for two years, Walter Cox for four, and Bob Smith for three. The coaches recruited most players from the student body, and the coaches had other coaching duties. The three other sports, golf, tennis, and swimming, had mixed success. Their coaches were faculty volunteers, and the students brought from home such equipment as they needed.[56]

Administrative Unease

Despite the pride most Clemson families and many other Clemson admirers felt in all the positive steps the school had taken and the sacrifices made by its sons and their families in the wars in which America had found itself, not everything went smoothly at the institution. First, concern had grown among the trustees and close Clemson watchers that the administration was not functioning well. As early as May 1951, the board directed Poole to approach either, or both, the Carnegie Foundation and the Ford Foundation for funds to hire a management-consulting firm. Nothing apparently happened.[57] J. C. Littlejohn, the college's business manager, provided what central direction existed in the sprawling administration, and he could not keep up with the sources of income much less the expenses. He proposed to Trustee Charles Daniel that Clemson needed to move to a centralized purchasing system. After thought, and perhaps consultation with his own company's financial officer, Daniel brought the idea to the board. The board unanimously adopted the concept.[58]

In addition, Littlejohn was not in good health. Dr. Rupert Fike, founder of IPTAY, had worried about him for some time, and in an effort to provide the business manager some rest, took Littlejohn on an extended fishing trip to Florida. Littlejohn went but stayed in touch with his office, the registrar, and President Poole. Suggestions and concerns moved back and forth. Some ran day to day, but a few were of the utmost importance. In March 1953, Littlejohn alerted Poole that USC was planning PhD programs in biology and chemistry, two fields central to Clemson's land-grant charge.[59] There is no sign that Poole was aware of the development, nor is there an indication that he worried about any of the news.

When the board met in March 1954, the matters coalesced. The trustees had read the responses from their inquiries to some colleges and other institutions that had used management consultants. One particularly important response came from the head of the consolidated University of North Carolina, and the trustees contacted the New York firm of Cresap, McCormick and Paget (CMP), which had made recommendations previously to UNC.[60] The firm accepted the task and, by early summer, had prepared a list of Clemson documents it wanted to study. From those, it developed a series of questionnaires for key faculty and alumni located in selected parts of the nation and in a series of professions and occupations. CMP also submitted a preliminary sketch of the parts and functions of Clemson for study. The sketch came to the board on June 15, 1954, and when it analyzed the document, its members were dismayed to discover that none of the public service functions, such as the experiment stations, regulatory agencies, or extension service, nor intercollegiate athletics, were scheduled for scrutiny. There is no record whether or not someone connected with Clemson had set that restriction. The trustees then directed the consultants to include in their study all parts of the college.[61]

The second issue that hit the table at the meeting was Metz's long-range enrollment report and projection prepared by Kenneth Vickery. The projection ran from autumn 1954 through 1964. The registrar detailed first the recruiting activities recently used to attract more applications. These included personalized letters to male high school seniors who held membership in high school academic societies in North Carolina, South Carolina, Georgia, Florida, and Tennessee and who had ranked Clemson their first or second choice. This amounted to 2,000 letters yearly. Second, Clemson's one admissions counselor accepted and attended all in-state high school college days. A special day at Clemson brought some 500 high school students to spend a day on campus. The report also noted the gradual lightening of the military regimen and that the share of South Carolina high school students who then continued their education at Clemson had increased from 8.3 percent in 1936–1937 to 9.4 percent in the autumn of 1949 and remained there for four years. The report concluded that Clemson had growing interest from women who wanted to study more scientific subjects and wanted to attend Clemson.[62]

The second major report concerned the choices that future and enrolled students made in fields of study. During the past four years, the choice by freshmen for the School of Chemistry had declined 50 percent, Arts and Sciences 25 percent, and Textiles 27 percent, while Education increased 10 percent and Engineering slightly over 40 percent. But if one subtracted agricultural engineering and textile engineering from their home schools of Agriculture and Textiles, respectively, and added them to Engineering, then its enrollment, which still included Architecture, amounted to 60 percent of the student body.

If military, females, and fields of study were indications of the need to change and if the administrative structure was, in the minds of some trustees, not working, then the next announcement, while not a surprise, merely added a "timetable" for the trustees. Littlejohn announced to the board that he would retire as of September 30, 1954. He had worked for the college for fifty years and served as Clemson's business manager for over a quarter of a century. He was the hub around which the Clemson wagon wheel turned.[63]

The Gender Break

The trustees sorted through the avenues open to them. The next buildings, planned for chemical engineering and structural engineering, would include space for civil engineering, engineering mechanics, and architecture. Together, these would provide academic room for an enrollment increase. The hoped-for results of the CMP report provided indications of major organizational change and direction. Thus, the principal questions involved the nature of the student body. Should it remain all-male military or move toward two-year ROTC required and at the conclusion of the two years give students a choice of whether or not to continue in it, which was the general land-grant college style everywhere except Texas A&M, Virginia Polytechnic, and Clemson agricultural colleges? And if Clemson did the latter, should the board open all fields to women? After all, women had been in the graduate program for nine years and enrolled in undergraduate education programs since the immediately preceding September 1953.[64]

Recognizing that the legislature had not funded the new dormitory requests for women and that the college, with a slightly declining enrollment, could make no special plea for any housing, even conversion of one of the existing barracks to female use, the trustees determined that the most workable approach was to continue the corps for upperclassmen who were already in ROTC and to require new students to take ROTC for the two years customary in land-grant colleges.[65] By May, the decision was being announced, and although some anger and concern were expressed over this truly major shift in Clemson's military and student life tradition, a bit of which surfaced at the annual alumni reunion, most were very pleased with it.

But Paul Quattlebaum, an alumnus and a former state legislator, wrote Poole, pointing out that two of his daughters, unable to enroll at Clemson, had to attend Auburn (Alabama Polytechnic Institute) to study their desired courses, which only Clemson offered in South Carolina. He ended his letter, "Women are entering technical fields. Many are leaving the state to acquire their education. There should be a place for them at Clemson. Clemson cannot fulfill its full obligation to the state of South Carolina until its doors are opened to girls as well as boys. Let me urge that you give the matter your serious consideration."[66]

The immediate concern focused on the autumn opening of Clemson. Many eyes watched, none more anxious than those of President Poole, Registrar Metz, and his admissions officer. The work of admissions, matriculation, and registration was by hand, so the final count of the autumn enrollment remained uncertain for several days after classes began. The results were not good. The number of students enrolled, 2,690, had dropped by fifty-nine from the previous year. The all-time high enrollment only six years earlier had stood at 3,360. That amounted to a decline of some 20 percent from the figure used in the planning of the new barracks (Johnstone).[67] It appeared to the trustees that lightening the military requirement had not succeeded in drawing more students.

The October meeting of the trustees received the report from Vickery's study "Why Students Choose Clemson." The primary thrust of the report, however, asked why friends chose to go elsewhere. The results said "required military" and "no women."[68] With the enrollment data set before them, and Vickery's document indicating the reasons for the enrollment decline, the trustees agreed that Clemson must admit women to all its programs, not just limited fields in education. Thus, on October 25, 1954, the sixty-one-year-old tradition of Clemson—an all-male military college—ended. Frank Jervey, Clemson 1914, an invited observer at the meeting, returned home to his wife and commented, "There are empty beds in the barracks and empty desks in the classrooms. So the trustees have voted to let girls in."[69]

Looking back on the twin decisions of 1954, reducing the military requirement and admitting women to the college, Wright Bryan, Clemson 1926, wrote, "Wiser heads realized that continuation of military life and government would result in dwindling enrollments and thus curtailed resources. Clemson would be less effective in the prime purpose set forth by Thomas Green Clemson to provide scientific and technological education."[70] The question now was, "What kind of Clemson would emerge?"

Notes

1. *Record*, 1943–1946 combined and 1947–1955 individually.
2. Conklin, *Gone With The Ivy*, 460–462; and Ballard, *Maroon and White*, 119.
3. Snell, *My Air Force Experience*, 2–3 and 89–94.
4. *Record*, 1954.
5. CUL.SC.CUA. S 28 f "Vickery."
6. CUL.SC.MSS 91 f L 451.
7. Reel, *Women and Clemson University*, 20.
8. Ibid., 21.
9. CUL.SC.CUA. S 30 v 6, 24.
10. Ibid., 95.
11. Funchess, *Korea P.O.W.*, 4.
12. Http://www.koreanwar.com (accessed August 28, 2010).
13. Funchess, *Korea P.O.W.*, 13.
14. Ibid., 14–15.
15. Http://www.koreanwar.com (accessed August 28, 2010).
16. Funchess, *Korea P.O.W.*, 21.
17. CUL.SC.CUA. S 37 f "Scroll of Honor."
18. *Taps*, 1948, 372–380. This is the section on clubs from which the material in the three paragraphs was drawn.
19. Ibid.
20. Vaughan, "There's Something in the Air," 6–8.
21. CUL.SC.MSS 68 f 245; and *Taps*, 1954.
22. Buzzell to Reel, a personal conversation.
23. *Taps*, 1949, 361.
24. CUL.SC.CUA. S 5 f 8.
25. Anderson *Independent*, May 11, 1952.
26. CUL.SC.MSS 47 f 6; and CUL.SC.CUA. S 30 v 5, 754–756.
27. CUL.SC.MSS 68 f 201.
28. CUL.SC.CUA. S 28 f "Lehotsky."
29. The administration had moved from a no restrictions by membership vote in 1946 (see CUL. SC.CUA. S 7 f 65) to a membership negative vote of no less than 25 percent (see CUL. SC.CUA. S 37 f 66).
30. CUL.SC.CUA. S 7 f 64.

31. *Greenville News*, April 16, 1954.
32. CUL.SC.CUA. S 11 f 117.
33. Anderson *Independent*, March 17, 1953.
34. CUL.SC.CUA. S 7 f 64.
35. Ibid.
36. CUL.SC.CUA. S 87 ss 1 b 34 f 13; and *Clemson World*, February 1987, 29. The narrative is, in part, from a reunion paper from the Class of 1949, who were the perpetrators, given to me by Tommy Thornhill, Clemson 1949, one of the two sons of Trustee "Buddy" Thornhill. The paper and other memories are in Special Collections in the Historian's Series.
37. Douthat, *Privilege*, 196.
38. *Greenville News*, September 14, 1966; Cox to Reel; and a letter from T. Thornhill to Reel in CUL.SC.CUA. S 367.
39. CUL.SC.CUA. S 37 Student Organizations f "Tiger Brotherhood."
40. Ibid., f "Alma Mater."
41. *Taps*, 1948, 339–341.
42. Bass and Poole, *The Palmetto State*, 140–142; and Beacham, "This Magic Moment," in Moore and Burton, *Towards the Meeting of the Waters*, 119–141. These treatises were predated by the writings of John Hook of Myrtle Beach.
43. CUL.SC.CUA. S 37 "Concerts, 1940s."
44. Ibid., "Concerts, 1950s."
45. Ibid., "Concerts, 1940s."
46. *The Tiger*, 1942–1945; and *Taps*, 1943, 1947.
47. Most copies of the publications are collected in Special Collections; however, few collections of this type are complete.
48. *Tips on the Tigers*; Charlotte *Observer*, January 2, 1949; and Blackman, Bradley, and Kriese, *Clemson*, 43–45.
49. MacCambridge, *College Football*, 1165. The thirteen schools were Alabama, Auburn, Florida, Georgia, Georgia Tech, Kentucky, LSU, Mississippi, Mississippi State, Tennessee, Tulane, University of the South (Sewanee), and Vanderbilt. Sewanee withdrew after the 1940 season.
50. Atlanta *Journal*, January 2, 1951.
51. CUL.SC.CUA. S 103 b 1 f 9 and S 105 b 1 f 9. The Howard remark was made to a Tiger Brotherhood dinner, spring 1974.
52. Ibid., S 37 f "Football 1951" and S 30 v 6, 234–237.
53. *The Tiger*, November 29, 1951.
54. CUL.SC.CUA. S 37 "Football 1952."
55. Ibid., f "Football 1953" and S 7 f 54.
56. Ibid., ff "Basketball" and "Baseball"; and *Taps*, 1947–1954.
57. CUL.SC.MSS 68 f 217.
58. CUL.SC.CUA. S 87 ss 1 b 52 f 15.
59. Ibid., S 5 f 11.
60. CUL.SC.MSS 47 f 18.
61. Ibid.
62. CUL.SC.CUA. S 87 ss 1 b 52 f 15.
63. Ibid., S 30 v 6, 336.
64. Ibid., v 6, 368–369; and *President's Report to Board of Trustees*, 1954–1956, 6.
65. *President's Report to Board of Trustees*, 1954–1956, 5–7.
66. CUL.SC.MSS 76 f 23.
67. *Record*, 1949–1954.
68. CUL.SC.MSS 47 f 18.
69. CUL.SC.CUA. S 30 v 6, 408. Jervey's daughter, Mary Jervey Kilby, remembered the comment well.
70. Bryan, *Clemson: An Informal History*, 131.

The night before the first women enrolled as general students at Clemson, the young men of Clemson erected this sign on Bowman Field, an expression of their delight. Adapted from a 1955 photo appearing in *The Anderson Independent*.

CHAPTER XV

Crucible, A New Formula

1955–1958

When the spring semester began on January 30, 1955, the returning students, mostly men and a small number of women in the graduate programs along with a few women in undergraduate education courses, were greeted by large cutout letters standing on Bowman Field. They read "W-E-L-C-O-M-E C-O-E-D-S." Without uproar or complaint, eleven new young women matriculated and enrolled. Six were transfer students, each at a different point on her way to a college degree, and five were women at the beginning of the college career. Because no housing for women existed (the legislature had ignored the college's requests for funding for it, which neither the president nor the trustees had strongly pushed), the women were limited to commuters and day students. Most resided in the recently incorporated town of Clemson.[1] The numbers of enrolled women rose very slowly until the college built and opened the first women's dormitory in 1963.

Other changes also contributed to the total reshaping of the Clemson Agricultural College of South Carolina into a modern university. No one change was most significant, but the crucible had a number of streams flowing into it. The long-evolving organization of Clemson had been a "worry" from the moment the trustees selected Henry Strode as the president. A strong tension, inherent in Mr. Clemson's will, on the line between policy and administration, or between the trustees and the president, alternately proved to hasten or impede the school's development. The very words of the will could have been read as helping to create the tension:

> I desire to state plainly that I wish the trustees of said institution to fix the course of studies, to make rules for the government of the same, and to change them, as in their judgment, experience may prove necessary, but to always bear in mind that the benefits herein sought to be bestowed are intended to benefit agricultural and mechanical industries.

Though many have read and understood that passage as conjoining the roles of policy-making and administration, the remainder of the same paragraph in the will strongly suggested that Mr. Clemson had more concern about interference in the trustees' authority by the state legislature than by an overly ambitious college president.[2]

Nonetheless, partially because of the problems encountered by the first four Clemson presidents and grave fears present among the trustees about the fate of the college, particularly at the hands of the legislature, interventions and reversals of administrative decisions had occurred that led to changes in the presidency. But that had not happened since before the lengthy terms of Riggs, Sikes, and now Poole.

Reorganization

Because Poole was the first alumnus to serve as president and because his own academic discipline provided the organizational center around which the college of his youth revolved, Poole was deeply attached to the image of the Clemson of his younger years. And after the great change in the composition of the board occasioned by the legislative ban on legislators holding other state offices, the newer members expected more immediate action on board decisions than Poole, a careful and cautious research scientist, wished to give.

However, the Board of Trustees on June 15, 1954, had reached an agreement with Cresap, McCormick and Paget (CMP) through David Boefferding, their on-site representative. CMP's proposed management study would deal with Clemson's total administration, including the internal functioning of the board, the entire administration, the academic structure (but not the curriculum), faculty organization, research, experiment stations, extension, all aspects of student life, athletics, alumni, and support staff.[3] CMP and the board agreed on a fee of $40,000 (2009 equivalent $320,690) for the firm's work. Charles Daniel paid half the cost, and the State Budget and Control Board provided the remainder. The CMP staff stayed at Clemson much of the remainder of 1954, conducting interviews, studying financial issues, grasping organizational patterns, and developing, circulating, receiving, and collating various surveys.

The autumn season afforded opportunities also to discuss the school with alumni, students' parents, students, county and state officials, and other people interested in Clemson and in South Carolina.

However, without waiting for any outcomes of the CMP study, Board of Trustees President Robert Muldrow Cooper had formed in July a committee to search for a new head of the Architecture Department. The committee, itself a rather unusual signal that someone from the outside would receive the most consideration, included James Sams, a few members of the department's faculty, several architects in South Carolina, and Cooper as the chair. By October 25, and on Poole's recommendation, the board set the salary for the position 30 percent higher than John Gates had received.[4] This step alone indicated that the board, particularly Cooper, had assumed control of what it perceived to be a drifting

Clemson. Later in the spring meeting, Cooper presented the name of Harlan Mc-Clure as head. The board unanimously approved him.[5]

McClure would not join the faculty until July 1, 1955. He came to Clemson from the University of Minnesota, where he had served as a professor since 1946. He earned the bachelor of architecture (the five-year professional degree) from George Washington University and his master's degree from MIT. He also received an advanced diploma from the Royal Swedish Academy in Stockholm. He saw World War II service in the navy as an operations officer on an aircraft carrier and was demobilized as a lieutenant commander. His wife and three children joined him in Clemson.[6]

On March 18, 1955, Cresap, McCormick and Paget presented a preliminary report to the board, President Poole, and Board Secretary A. J. Brown. The observations presented, and then briefly discussed in the report, follow (quoted in order listed):

1. The role of the trustees is not specifically defined.
2. The span of supervision of the president is excessive.
3. The lines of authority have not been clearly established.
4. The number of committees is excessive.
5. The faculty organization is not effective or used.
6. The board of visitors is not performing its intended function.
7. Necessary central services are not provided.[7]

After much discussion, the CMP group recessed for a week to consider further its preliminary report based on the trustees' comments. The board apparently discussed the first observation about the role of the trustees privately because it soon issued a trustee manual. It modified both custom and practice. For at least the next few years, the correspondence of each trustee, as best as can be determined from what is publicly available, seemed to flow to and from the president of the board and among the other trustees. Letters to other campus leaders generally were congratulatory in nature or were in response to questions. In the latter, replies were noncommittal or vague. Apparently, the main correspondence ran between Cooper, as board president, and Poole, as college president, until the next step, reorganization, occurred. Very few references exist to telephone or casual conversation.

The second observation (along with points three, four, and five) held the key to the management revision. Sixteen units reported directly to Poole. This included the six schools and the graduate program, the library, the commandant, registrar, treasurer, business manager, athletic director, medical head, YMCA director, and director of alumni affairs. In most administrative matters, the president did not always consult all the units. For example, academic issues, such as curricula, new courses, academic and military calendars, graduations and commencements,

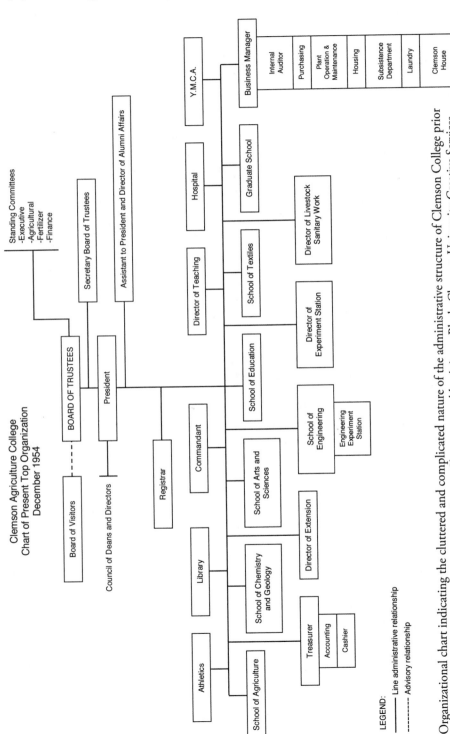

Clemson Agriculture College
Chart of Present Top Organization
December 1954

BOARD OF TRUSTEES

Standing Committees
-Executive
-Agricultural
-Fertilizer
-Finance

Secretary Board of Trustees

Assistant to President and Director of Alumni Affairs

Board of Visitors

President

Council of Deans and Directors

Registrar

Y.M.C.A.

Hospital

Director of Teaching

Commandant

School of Education

Graduate School

School of Textiles

School of Engineering

Engineering Experiment Station

Director of Experiment Station

Director of Livestock Sanitary Work

Business Manager

Internal Auditor

Purchasing

Plant Operation & Maintenance

Housing

Subsistence Department

Laundry

Clemson House

Library

School of Arts and Sciences

Director of Extension

School of Chemistry and Geology

Athletics

School of Agriculture

Treasurer

Accounting

Cashier

LEGEND:
——— Line administrative relationship
------- Advisory relationship

Organizational chart indicating the cluttered and complicated nature of the administrative structure of Clemson College prior to the Cresap, McCormick and Paget streamlining. Chart prepared by Arizona Black, Clemson University Creative Services.

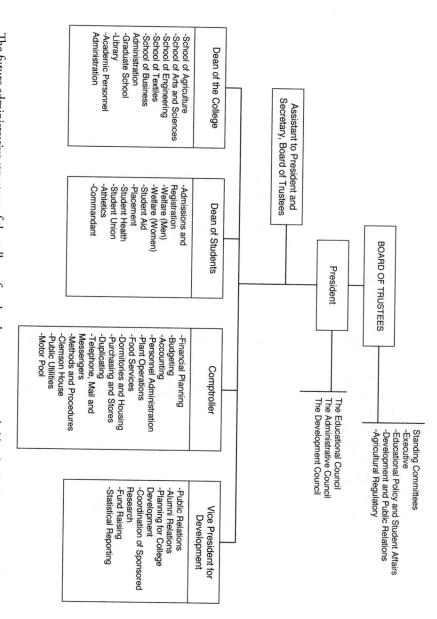

The future administrative structure of the college after the changes recommended by the Cresap, McCormick and Paget firm were to be implemented. Chart prepared by Arizona Black, Clemson University Creative Services.

BOARD OF TRUSTEES

Standing Committees
-Executive
-Educational Policy and Student Affairs
-Development and Public Relations
-Agricultural Regulatory

President

The Educational Council
The Administrative Council
The Development Council

Assistant to President and Secretary, Board of Trustees

Dean of the College

-School of Agriculture
-School of Arts and Sciences
-School of Engineering
-School of Textiles
-School of Business Administration
-Graduate School
-Library
-Academic Personnel Administration

Dean of Students

-Admissions and Registration
-Welfare (Men)
-Welfare (Women)
-Student Aid
-Placement
-Student Health
-Student Union
-Athletics
-Commandant

Comptroller

-Financial Planning
-Budgeting
-Accounting
-Personnel Administration
-Plant Operations
-Food Services
-Dormitories and Housing
-Purchasing and Stores
-Duplicating
-Telephone, Mail and Messengers
-Methods and Procedures
-Clemson House
-Public Utilities
-Motor Pool

Vice President for Development

-Public Relations
-Alumni Relations
-Planning for College Development
-Coordination of Sponsored Research
-Fund Raising
-Statistical Reporting

graduation standards, and the like, involved the six school deans, dean of the graduate program, commandant, director of the libraries (by this point the library had a branch in the new Chemistry Building and another in Sirrine Hall), and directors of the experiment station, agricultural teaching, extension, livestock, and sanitary work. Poole always brought Littlejohn as business manager in on meetings until "Mr. Jim" retired in September 1954.

Besides all this, twenty-three committees reported to Poole. Some were very significant. The Building and Grounds Committee, directed by David Watson and comprised of the deans (all were faculty), a few senior faculty, and Littlejohn, remained continually busy and reported to the president regularly. On the other hand, the Concert Series Committee met annually to hear the financial report from the previous year and recommend the series for the next year. Virginia Shanklin, President Poole's secretary, handled the committee's reports, selection of the annual series, and all the arrangements. She reported her decisions to him, although no evidence exists of his concern about who or what performed. In between, myriad committees ranged from the Faculty Alumni Athletic Committee to the Faculty Committee on Student Social Events. This whole "flat structure" did not function smoothly or in a timely fashion.

The CMP overhaul was drastic. First, the Board of Trustees now had four standing committees: Executive, Educational Policy and Student Affairs, Development and Public Relations, and Agricultural Regulatory. The full board considered nothing without receiving the positive recommendation of the appropriate board committee. The board president and the college president served as ex officio, nonvoting members of the four committees. Of course, the college president was not a board member and had no vote in any trustee action. The board secretary, relieved of any judiciary or fiscal responsibility, would serve as the nonmember (and nonparticipating) secretary to the committees and as the college president's assistant.

Based on the CMP recommendation, the institution's functions were divided into four large divisions: Academic Affairs, Student Affairs, Business Affairs, and Development. Academic Affairs brought together the six school deans and directors of the library and graduate school. The dean of the college, a new post, headed the unit, and through that post all issues had to be recommended to the president. Student Affairs grouped together admissions and registration, conduct and welfare (different because of place of residence and by custom for men and women), student aid, placement, student health, the student union and YMCA, intercollegiate and intramural athletics, and nonacademic military matters. A dean of students headed the division. A comptroller oversaw all Business Affairs operations, including financial planning, budgeting, accounting, personnel supervision, physical plant operations, food services, housing (student, faculty, and staff), Clemson House, purchasing, stores and storage, printing and duplicating services, communications (by any technique other than face to face), all administrative procedures (hiring, terminating, ordering, etc.), public utilities, and all motor vehicles owned or leased by the institution. Those that were paid for with nonpublic money (e.g., food services and housing) were called Auxiliary Services. The fourth unit, to be headed by a vice president for development, was new, not organized, and not yet as complicated. Its components included public relations, alumni activities, statistical development and reporting, long-range planning, fund-raising, and coordination of sponsored research.[8]

Of course, this massive reorganization changed the access to the board and to the president. It also threatened the numerous small "kingdoms" that existed in the college, while creating potential new frictions between units. And it would take years to sort out relationships. Next, the board had to choose the four leaders of the divisions. The trustees turned back to CMP for its advice, which it gave in closed session. CMP reported that, in the process of meeting with so many campus leaders, it had a good sense or feeling for persons who would be excellent candidates for some, but not all, the leadership posts.

The New Leaders

The board selected Francis Marion Kinard, who had served as dean of arts and sciences (formerly general science) since 1943, as dean of the college. Born in 1902, he had received an AB degree from Wofford College and an MA degree from

UNC before joining the English faculty at Clemson. Wofford College had awarded him an honorary doctorate of literature degree for his excellent teaching and disciplinary leadership.[9] He had already proven himself a skillful leader and negotiator and was highly respected for his integrity. His greatest concern was for his faculty (particularly the younger of them) to have time to complete their doctoral degrees.

Francis Marion Kinard (1902–1960), a professor of English from 1924 until his sudden death in 1960, became dean of the School of Arts and Sciences in 1943 and then dean of the college in 1955. The new home to Clemson's Department of Physics, Kinard Laboratory of Physics, was dedicated to his memory and in honor of his service to Clemson in 1961. Clemson University Photographs, CUL.SC.

The board, on CMP's advice, chose Walter Thompson Cox Jr. to hold the post of dean of students. Born in Belton in 1918, Cox received his bachelor of science degree in arts and sciences from Clemson in 1939 and immediately joined the Athletic Department as a football coach while continuing his academic work in education. He had served as a coach with the January 1, 1940, Cotton Bowl championship team. During the summer of 1940, Cox was summoned to West Point for advanced army officer training. When World War II exploded, he entered the regular army and served in Fiji, New Caledonia, New Zealand, and Guadalcanal, where he contracted beriberi. After recovery, he received a medical discharge and returned to Clemson, where he held a variety of positions in the Athletic Department. In 1950, Poole appointed him alumni director and head of public relations. He had an excellent memory for people and details, and was especially respected for his integrity.[10]

The board did not fill the other two top leadership posts with existing Clemson personnel. The searches for the comptroller and for the vice president for development, though undertaken at the same time, were a bit more difficult. The board selected as comptroller Melford A. Wilson. Born in Dunn, North Carolina, Wilson began college at UNC in 1928, but when the Depression struck, he withdrew from Chapel Hill and enrolled in Newberry College. He left school to work with the federal government in Columbia on unemployment issues in South Carolina. While there he enrolled part time at USC and graduated in 1937 *summa cum laude*. During World War II, he served in the U.S. Navy. After military service, he became executive director of the S.C. Employment Commission. He served in that post when CMP recommended him for Clemson's comptroller. The trustees concurred and offered Wilson the post. He accepted and brought his years of experience and government connections to the college.[11]

The position of vice president for development remained unfilled for a year. As in the case

Melford Alonzo Wilson (1911–1992) was the executive director of the S.C. Employment Security Commission before joining Clemson's staff as comptroller in 1955. During his twenty-two-year Clemson career, he saw Clemson's budget increase tenfold—$8.8 million to $86 million—and more than $90 million of construction projects on campus. Clemson University Photographs, CUL.SC.

of the comptroller, CMP recommended a search, which indicated that the consultants felt no one they had encountered at Clemson fit the multifaceted position. Eventually, CMP recommended Clemson alumnus Robert Cook Edwards. Born on March 25, 1914, in Fountain Inn, he entered Clemson without finishing high

Robert Cook "R. C." Edwards (1914–2008) was undoubtedly one of Clemson's favorite sons. A nineteen-year-old textile engineering graduate of the Class of 1933, Edwards enjoyed a textile career that ultimately led to his serving as treasurer and general manager of the Abbeville Group of Deering Milliken Mills. For his alma mater, Edwards served as president of IPTAY in 1954, Clemson's first vice president for development in 1956, and acting college president after the death of Robert F. Poole in 1958. He was formally named the college's eighth president in 1959 and retired from the presidency in 1979. Clemson University Photographs, CUL.SC.

school and graduated in 1933, at the age of nineteen, in textile engineering. While a student, he belonged to Phi Psi, Clemson's oldest chapter of a national academic disciplinary honorary society. He also served as the football team's student manager and would remain highly involved in Clemson athletics for most of his life. Two years after his graduation, he married Louise Odom of Red Springs, North Carolina. World War II found him serving in the Far East. Most of his career, until he accepted Clemson's call, he had spent with the Milliken Corporation, where he had developed a close relationship with its president, Roger Milliken. At the time the board offered Edwards the Clemson vice presidency in June 1956, he also served Clemson as the second president of IPTAY, a volunteer post, succeeding Rupert Fike. He accepted the position of vice president and shortly became the "trash mover" (according to him) in the new, very streamlined senior administration.[12]

The four principal officers met regularly with the president in the Administrative Council. The council also included the budget director and personnel director. Its role was very limited. In academic matters, student issues, or development issues, it developed costs and possible sources of revenues for the information of the Educational Council, and then it oversaw the implementation of any decision recommended by the Educational Council to the president, who, in turn, had the choice whether or not to present the recommendation to the appropriate committees of the board.

Academic Concerns

In Dean Frank Kinard's academic territory, the Educational Council was the guiding group. The president, as the chief academic officer, presided. Its membership included the dean of the college, school deans, librarian, comptroller, dean of students, and vice president for development. But there were changes both in its structure and management. In principle, the dean of the college was "the first among equals," not stopping access by school deans or faculty to the president, but learning in advance the nature and business of any such meetings. However, the dean of the college had to "evolve and recommend" the long-range plans for educational development. Further, the dean directed the work of what was essentially an office of "institutional research," at this time a very new idea. And the dean of the college had sole responsibility for determining the standards for hiring all academic personnel (that is, any person holding academic rank regardless of where the majority of the person's work lay). That task extended to titles, promotions, tenure, and salaries.

The school deans were reduced to five. The dean of the School of Agriculture, Milton Farrar, supervised all three aspects of its mission—teaching, research, and extension (the relationship of the last two to each other needed clarification)—and each mission area. Further, the federally funded research and extension work was to be centralized at Clemson as envisioned in the Hatch Act of 1887 and the Smith-Lever Act of 1914. Farrar, who would oversee this massive amalgamation, had joined the Clemson faculty in 1949. He earned his PhD degree in entomology

Milton Dyer Farrar (1901–1977), a research entomologist for the Illinois Natural History Survey and associate director of the Crop Protection Institute in Durham, New Hampshire, before coming to Clemson to be the head of the Department of Entomology-Zoology in 1949. He became dean of the School of Agriculture in 1953 and remained in that position until 1962, when he resigned to become senior scientist on the Clemson and S.C. Experiment Station staff. Farrar, seen here with the Harllee Egg Collection, retired in 1966. Clemson University Photographs, CUL.SC.

from Iowa State College, where as an undergraduate he had joined Theta Chi Fraternity. He had served as dean of the School of Agriculture for two years. Because of his experience in that administration, he recommended (and it was adopted) that a fourth school mission, regulatory services, be added. He remained school dean until 1962, when he retired to become a senior scholar in agriculture.[13]

James Sams remained dean of the School of Engineering, which continued to include architecture. The issue of the separation of architecture from engineering worried Poole for the rest of his life. Chemistry and education merged into the School of Arts and Sciences, and the CMP consultants recommended Howard Hunter, who headed chemistry, as the new dean.

The Board of Trustees envisioned separate schools for textiles and business, although in fact the new Department of Industrial Management joined the existing School of Textiles. After the board made several efforts to name this unit, it chose the title School of Industrial Management and Textile Science. Dean Hugh Brown of textiles returned to research, and Prof. Gaston Gage became the dean. The graduate school, which showed signs of expansion, was placed under Dean Kinard, who tackled the program vigorously.

Gaston Gage (1898–1983), Clemson 1921, joined the college's staff in 1932 after working for the Aragon-Baldwin textile mill in Chester. He was appointed acting dean of the School of Textiles in 1957 and full dean in 1958, a post he held until the School of Industrial Management and Textile Science was formed in 1962. Gage, a charter member of IPTAY and of the Clemson Athletic Council since 1935, retired in 1964. He is pictured here in a textile classroom, surrounded by his students and his wife. Clemson University Photographs, CUL.SC.

The college library also reported to Kinard. The new librarian, J.W. Gordon Gourlay, had arrived at Clemson in 1954 to replace Cornelia Graham, who had come to Clemson in 1922.[14]

As part of his responsibility, Kinard supervised all personnel issues that affected faculty. In this, he, his successors, and the comptroller developed close business and personal relationships that allowed the split authority to function well. The dean of students and the vice president for development did not have much potential cause for discord because all of their employees were members of the recently created state classification system.

But amid the extensive reorganization of the college, potential opportunities for problems still existed. CMP had placed IPTAY and all other fund-raising under the vice president for development. This posed a problem for athletics. Because the new vice president for development was Edwards, then the president of IPTAY, no difficulty existed in shifting IPTAY to Student Affairs, whose head, Walter Cox, had been involved in athletics almost all of his twenty years in Clemson's service. That produced no public comment. Edwards even recommended the move. In other examples of potentially competing jurisdictions, the comptroller had responsibility for housing and food services, but students were the vast number of consumers, and their welfare was the responsibility of the dean of student affairs. This also presented no problem, partially because so many of the facilities were so new that the users (students) had little excuse to complain. A final example of crossed jurisdictions was on admissions and registration. In this, the Educational Council set the admissions and graduation standards, which CMP insisted be raised. This became an issue only in individual cases, which normally found a fair resolution in everyone's best interests. Problems emerged in larger, general questions of preferences, such as offspring of alumni or potential athletes gaining admission over others.[15]

Graduate Studies

Even in overcoming the potential difficulties in cooperative or competing jurisdictions, the CMP plan left several questions of organization unanswered. Three would be resolved within the next few years. The first involved a college-wide graduate studies program. Clemson, whose graduate requirements had conformed to the standards of SACS and the Conference of the Deans of Southern Graduate Schools since 1949,[16] had laid out requirements for the PhD degree in June 1954. Considered the pinnacle of academic degrees, it was the only one requiring extensive original research.

Few southern schools offered anything beyond the baccalaureate and master's degrees (including business and professional degrees) other than medical, veterinary, and ministerial doctorates before 1925, when Vanderbilt University began its programs. As a few more programs emerged in late 1944, the Conference of the Deans of Southern Graduate Schools was formed. It proposed critically needed standards for graduate work. Major funding foundations, some with full treasuries, gave large grants to strengthen programs in the humanities and social sciences. But the more scientific subjects, in part because of their enormous laboratory and research costs and in part because of the scarcity of research faculty, were slower in being funded. Vanderbilt, Duke, UNC, Texas, and Tulane received large gifts from the General Education Fund (Rockefeller) and the Carnegie Corporation in the years before 1955.[17] Poole had hoped that the GI Bill and "the acute shortage of teachers, research scientists, and leaders in the fields of agriculture, engineering, and textiles" would lead to a "scientific 'GI' style" approach.[18] Despite the slow beginning, this offered the land-grant schools real opportunities.

Kinard developed a plan, and the Educational Council and the president agreed to it. He asked a visiting team of faculty—prominent in graduate studies in the fields that he and the council felt had the best opportunities considering the resources, regional needs, and potential support—to make recommendations about graduate work at Clemson.

Led by the chair of the Conference of Deans of Southern Graduate Schools, the committee saw great potential advantages in the region, pointing to traditional fields such as soil conservation, forestry, and agriculture. The committee also proposed newer fields, including nuclear energy and water conservation. To prevent extreme compartmentalization of the programs, the committee recommended a free-standing dean and a graduate council (both of which Clemson once had). And they joined CMP in pointing to the poor state of most of the college's research facilities, such as the library and laboratories, with the exception of chemistry, ceramic engineering, agricultural sciences, and textiles. But the committee worried, as did CMP, about the large teaching loads and poor compensation of the faculty. Federal studies indicated that in the past fifty plus years (1900–1954) at land-grant institutions, the faculty had "not...fared as well as many other groups, including both professional and skilled and unskilled labor groups." Even with members of other groups that had "similar training and experience," the purchasing power of the faculty remained less in 1957 than it had been in 1900. If South Carolina and the Clemson trustees really wanted, or needed, a graduate program at the college (and the visiting team clearly indicated that South Carolina did), then priorities and/or the state method of funding needed reordering.[19]

The Graduate Dean

Kinard then consulted with the school deans about the choice of a graduate dean. Ultimately, he recommended that the trustees name to the position Jack Kenny Williams, a professor of history. Williams, born in Galax, Virginia, had

(*Front to back*) Jack Kenny Williams (1920–1981) joined the Clemson faculty in 1947 as a professor of history and government. During his almost twenty-year career at Clemson, he also became chairman of the Graduate Council and dean of the Graduate School in 1958, dean of faculties and acting dean of the college in 1960, and vice president for academic affairs in 1963. Claud Bethune Green (1914–1979) worked as a professor of English at Clemson from 1940 to 1979. He also served as director of summer sessions and chairman of the Honors Council (1962–1967), assistant dean of the university (1968–1970), and dean of undergraduate studies (1970–1979). Marvin Alpheus "Jake" Owings (1909–2004) joined Clemson's faculty as a professor of English in 1946, became head of the Department of English in 1969, and retired in 1975. Clemson University Photographs, CUL.SC.

received his BA degree from Emory and Henry College in 1940. When World War II began, he joined the Marine Corps, attaining the rank of captain. After his discharge at war's end, he attended Emory University. Upon receiving his MA degree, he joined the Clemson faculty and continued work on a PhD degree, which he received from Emory in 1953. Active in most of the major history societies, he published in American southern and frontier history. The trustees confirmed the nomination.[20]

Williams was skillful in placing the graduate program on a firmer foundation. He addressed three problems almost immediately. The first concern of many faculty who held PhD degrees was the poor quality of some theses presented for the completion of the master's degree. Several of the members of the Graduate Council argued vociferously that the level of work must equal that of the other land-grant schools. Their position prevailed.[21] Second, graduate enrollment had to increase. In January 1955, sixty-four graduate students had enrolled, representing 2.4 percent of the total student body. Only one land-grant college that offered graduate work had a smaller percentage. Lincoln University (the Missouri 1890 land-grant school) had eleven graduate students (1.6 percent of the total student body), while the University of Alaska (an 1862 land-grant school) had twenty-four (2.6 percent). Ten of the seventeen 1890 land-grant colleges had no graduate enrollment.[22]

By working with the individual school deans, Kinard and Williams moved what money they could scrape together and strengthened the fundamental sciences, moving each into a niche position in hiring and lightening undergraduate teaching loads for a few younger professors with research promise. This allowed those faculty to apply for grants, some of which they received, and then travel to recruit graduate students to join them in their funded research. The same process was followed in agriculture and engineering. Weaker graduate programs slowly ended, taking student needs and progress into account. In choosing the favored fields, two questions needed answering. First, did the field fit squarely into Clemson's economic mission to South Carolina? If so, then the college undertook a deliberate process of strengthening library resources and laboratory facilities. Second, was the field essential to strong undergraduate excellence? If so, then fields such as English, mathematics, economics, and history, which would be prepared to assume graduate work soon, received funds to recruit and to help the department heads search for new doctorally qualified faculty to fill spaces made vacant by retirement or faculty who left the college. This also required the creation of new positions to meet the anticipated enrollment growth, particularly with the entry of females and the lessening of military obligations.[23]

Development

This dramatic change required financial resources far beyond those South Carolina would, or even could, provide. The job of finding those resources fell to Robert "Bob" Edwards, the vice president for development. And he wasted no time. Because of his willingness to work at a killing pace, he never was still. A trusted member of South Carolina's textile inner circle, he already knew, usually on a first-name basis, most of the public figures of the state and the region. It did not hurt that his degree in textile engineering gave him access to, and friendship with, the rapidly emerging engineering sector of the Southeast. Further, his passion for Clemson athletics (football in particular), witnessed by his serving as IPTAY's second president, had already placed him in favor with Clemson football loyalists, whose number exceeded that of Clemson's alumni.[24]

The first task he faced was raising funds for Clemson. The approach to governmental funding had long been focused in the school's president, partially because of the land-grant charter. Therein President Poole had been, and would remain, the significant figure at the federal agricultural level. His support of research and of extension, particularly youth and family programming, had won high regard both within and beyond South Carolina. But Poole's captains in other federal arenas had been J. C. Littlejohn, now retired, and James Byrnes, still a life trustee but with political strength now only in South Carolina. Trustees Cooper, Daniel, and Brown were, and would be, instrumental in South Carolina. At first, Edwards stayed out of the South Carolina arena, but he kept in touch with those people he knew. He traveled with Daniel nationally to enlarge the circle in banking, construction, and manufacturing.[25]

Financial Needs

After a study of projected needs related to enrollment growth and funding capacity, the Administrative Council, headed by Poole, but quickly dominated by Edwards, laid out a building plan. The plan took into consideration estimated enrollment growth trends that Kenneth Vickery, assistant registrar, provided through Walter Cox; tuition and bonding capacity from Wilson; and a reasonable estimate of five-year academic needs focusing on the short supply in space in the disciplines Kinard thought had the most growth potential in the next five years.

In academic space (offices, classrooms, and laboratories), the School of Industrial Management and Textile Science and the School of Agriculture were in the best shape. The lack of space existed in the School of Engineering (including architecture) and in Arts and Sciences. Short-term projections required teaching space in physics, English, and mathematics. Biological sciences expanded in Long Hall in space made available by the move into new spaces and offices for agricultural engineering, food industries, and plant and animal sciences. The engineering needs included space for mechanical, civil, and chemical engineering and architecture, which would give over Riggs Hall to first-year engineering students and to all of electrical engineering. And Clemson needed student housing for married students and for women (space for the latter required more than merely demonstrating the fact to the legislature and to the public and private women's collegiate establishments).[26]

Edwards and Wilson proposed approaching the legislature for planning money and permission to fund the construction via bonds secured by increased tuition resulting from a projected student population increase, anticipated from the potential addition of many more female students and the lightening of military requirements. The 1955–1956 applications, acceptances, and enrollments bore out the expectations. When the Administrative Council presented the package plan to the trustees, few questions or delays arose. Poole then presented this refined Edwards and Wilson proposal to the state.

Construction

By the summer of 1956, with Life Trustee Edgar A. Brown, chairman of the S.C. Senate Finance Committee, making the way clear, the State Budget and Control Board approved a proposal for four of the Clemson buildings. Those would be civil, including structural, engineering (Lowry), architecture (Lee), physics (Kinard), and mathematics and English (Martin). After brief negotiations, the

The new engineering building, built in 1958 for the departments of Civil and Industrial-Structural Engineering, was named for Walter L. Lowry Jr., head of civil engineering from 1949 to 1961. Clemson University Photographs, CUL.SC.

Clemson's Physics Department gained a new home in 1961 with the construction of the Kinard Laboratory of Physics, named for the recently deceased dean of the college and professor of English, Francis M. Kinard. Clemson University Photographs, CUL.SC.

The departments of Mathematics and English also moved in 1961 into a three-building complex now known as Martin Hall, named for the venerated mathematics professor Samuel Maner "Major" Martin. Clemson University Photographs, CUL.SC.

firm of Hopkins, Baker, and Gill of Florence won the bid for the physics, mathematics, and English complex, while Lockwood-Greene of Greenville contracted for the structural engineering unit. Harlan McClure, head of the Architecture Department, served on the program committees for both structures. His fine sense of proportion was demonstrated best in the structural engineering complex, built with the adjustable vertical sun louvers and the transitional sets of courtyards. The engineering building was finished in one year with Boyle Construction of Sumter as the general contractor.[27] The other complex (four buildings connected by breezeways at every level) was delayed because of the death of the senior partner in the design firm. General Construction of Columbia won the construction bid and worked in stages. The buildings were not completed until 1961.[28]

Further teaching space was made possible by the CMP recommendation that the School of Education, which remained small, be divided with vocational industrial education moving into engineering, agricultural education remaining with agriculture, and the education methods faculty merging into a composite Department of Social Sciences. The social sciences faculty, which included historians, economists, and several behavioral scientists, joined their new department mates in education in the old Chemistry Building, now Hardin Hall.

That effectively left Tillman Hall with the offices of the president, the dean of the college, the registrar, the comptroller, and a few classrooms on the main floor. The second floor provided space for a few other administrators and senior faculty in English, a department that also included the languages faculty. Classrooms were dotted through the building, with business functions such as the bursar and housing located in Tillman basement.

The dean of students and his small staff occupied the central (Student Union) section of Johnstone Hall, along with publications offices, student government space, the student radio station, and a small chapel. No meeting space existed for clubs, but in an era when night police and/or watchmen checked and locked every classroom building late each evening (11:00 p.m.), students used the classroom buildings for meetings and for overflow study space. The new Development Office was located in the old Trustee House (built in early years as a faculty home). And a fast-growing problem involved the near frenetic growth of automobiles driving through and parking on campus.

Encouraged by the success of the legislative proposals of 1955–1956, the administration, with the guidance of the politically well-placed trustees, along with Edwards and Wilson, developed its proposal for 1957–1958. The package presented to the State Budget and Control Board requested $1.35 million for a new women's dormitory (the same board had turned down a similar proposal at least once before), new married student housing, a new home for the president, and a home for the vice president. The Budget and Control Board removed the women's dormitory from consideration and reduced the other amounts by half a million dollars. It might have been worse, but Charles Daniel used his influence and reason to pressure the legislators. The most telling figures were that, according to Daniel, since 1946 North Carolina had appropriated $18 million for NC State, Georgia $15 million for Georgia Tech, Alabama $12 million for Auburn, Mississippi $15 million for Mississippi State, and South Carolina $500,000 for Clemson. Daniel indicated that many of these funds were teaching and research appropriations.[29]

Clemson and Cooperative Extension

There were other dimensions to Clemson's efforts to achieve the results proposed by CMP. The latter's report had considered the Clemson Cooperative Extension Service far too expensive, in part because of a multiplication of its administration. This occurred in two ways. First, the operation of a separate division of African American outreach centered at the 1890 college in Orangeburg produced a duplication of administration, secretarial services, and communications, not to mention time lost. CMP merely alluded to the issue because of segregation barriers caused by state laws and regulations. Separating the home demonstration portion of the extension service at Winthrop College in Rock Hill produced the second extra expense. The cost factors were the administrative duplication, particularly in youth services, and time lost in communications. Double sets of accounting records, personnel papers, and records and the routing (or detouring) of decisions through Winthrop's president(s) were expensive and were paid by Clemson's allotments. The Winthrop replication resulted from an agreement between Winthrop's President David Johnson and Clemson's Walter Riggs and approved by the boards of the two schools before World War I. No state law or regulation required it. From time to time, the Clemson board noted the cost but elected to let it lie.

In the early years of the extension service, a number of states used this split arrangement, but by 1955, it remained only in South Carolina. To confirm the basic unity of the extension service (and perhaps to counter a possible separation-ist feeling at Winthrop or within the home demonstration service), the Clemson Board of Trustees stated publicly that the extension service worked in a unified fashion and with all farming families and individuals, whether farming was their sole occupation or part time, or whether the clients were black or white, male or female, children or adults.[30]

By the mid-to-late-1950s, South Carolina was well along the process of trans-formation from an agricultural to an industrial state. The primary source of in-come for the majority of South Carolina households came mostly from industry and commerce, but many still tilled the soil, kept cattle and poultry, and bartered or occasionally sold surplus produce locally. Most still preserved vegetables and fruits. The children did farm chores and joined rural church youth leagues, Fu-ture Farmers of America, Future Homemakers of America, or 4-H (all part of the cooperative extension service or agricultural education). But the children no longer "walked two miles through the snow" to school unless they were African American, and then, depending on the district, they might. Nor were the schools the one-, two-, three-, or even four-room schoolhouses based on Clemson archi-tectural designs supervised by Rudolph Lee, unless they were African American. In spite of Governor Byrnes's efforts, many African Americans still attended the older schools. Now, rural and suburban white young people rode yellow school buses or, if they were teenagers, drove pickup trucks to consolidated schools of brick, concrete, and aluminum.

Clearly, extension planned to follow its clients and continue the education processes. A few states, particularly those with unified land-grant/liberal arts uni-versities, moved to establish urban extension services. The University of Florida had done so. The University of South Carolina, ignoring the fact that Florida was a combined liberal arts/land-grant institution, planned an urban extension office; however, it did not happen.

Acting on the directions of the Board of Trustees, Poole wrote Winthrop's president on October 29, 1955, noting that the Clemson board was moving all the home demonstration agents from Winthrop to Clemson as of January 1, 1956 (two calendar months shortened by Thanksgiving and Christmas holidays). The letter, best described as curt and peremptory, produced an angry response from Winthrop's President Henry R. Sims, himself a former legislator.[31] Sims contact-ed his governing board, urging it to fight "this action to the last ditch." His board supported him. One Winthrop trustee, a former state home demonstration agent, responded urging Sims to "use every legitimate means at his disposal to prevent this change." At an even more emotional level, state Senator W. Lewis Wallace of York warned, "There won't be any transfer as long as I'm senator."[32]

As the date for the consolidation of home demonstration at Clemson came closer, Sims directed the state home demonstration agent, Juanita Neely, and all the personnel in her department, to ignore Poole's letter informing them to transfer to Clemson by January 1956. He also wrote Edgar A. Brown, his former senatorial colleague, arguing, "This division was based upon a definite contract between the two colleges and the approval of the Department of Agriculture in Washington."[33]

Then the question was posed to S.C. Attorney General T. C. Callison, who stated that the issue was not one of law involving the state, but rather a policy matter involving the two schools.[34] Sims charged that the extension agents at Clemson, supported by the Clemson publicity services, had actively worked to move the program from Winthrop to Clemson. Sims then began efforts to establish the home demonstration service totally separate from Clemson,[35] but the USDA, in response to an inquiry in May 1955 from Melford Wilson, Clemson's comptroller, stated plainly, "By law the program is a mutual responsibility of the Department of Agriculture and the Land-Grant institutions of the States and Territories."[36] Winthrop was not the land-grant school.

The home demonstration staff accepted this and began to move, which the Clemson board affirmed on June 21, 1957. Questions continued to arise. The president of the S.C. Home Demonstration Association asked for the opinion of the agents. McNeely had resigned, and Sallie A. Pearce, the new state home demonstration agent, and her staff at Winthrop agreed with the move, saying, "There was not and cannot be the coordinated program that is desired." She continued, "…the feeling of all who are directing the program is that we can and will service the public more efficiently and economically with a unified staff located here at Clemson."[37] Resolutions supporting the move came from the home demonstration clubs of Anderson, Beaufort, Clarendon, Colleton, Dillon, Fairfield, Florence, Jasper, and Richland counties. As soon as the personnel move was completed, Sims replaced all the locks to the doors, rendering the back files temporarily inaccessible.[38]

"Land-Use Land" and the Lake

The extension controversy, which Poole seems to have wanted to avoid and did not handle well, had created another heavy burden for him. Still another issue, which he tried also to avoid but which simply would not "go away," was the question of the land-use properties. These were among many abandoned and nonproductive acres purchased by the federal government. By 1940, this included about 29,000 acres in tracts either contiguous to each other or to the Clem-

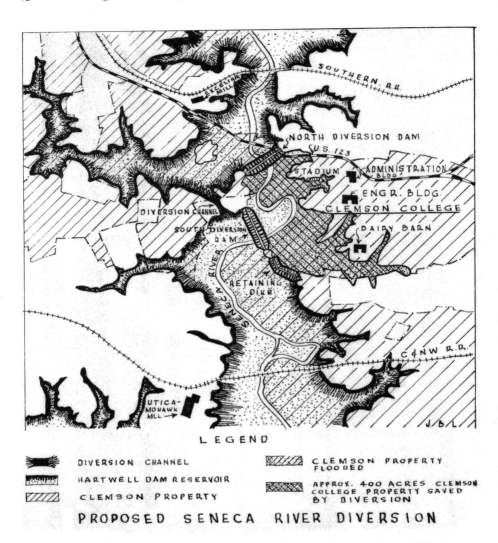

LEGEND

DIVERSION CHANNEL		CLEMSON PROPERTY FLOODED	
HARTWELL DAM RESERVOIR		APPROX. 400 ACRES CLEMSON COLLEGE PROPERTY SAVED BY DIVERSION	
CLEMSON PROPERTY			

PROPOSED SENECA RIVER DIVERSION

This map, one of the final proposals developed by the U.S. Army Corps of Engineers, shows the placement of the dikes, the land that Clemson College sat on, the land flooded by the proposed lake, and the land that Clemson saved through the work of Life Trustee Charles E. Daniel and the negotiations of R.C. Edwards. Clemson University Photographs, CUL.SC.

son holdings in Oconee, Anderson, and Pickens counties and drained by the Keowee-Seneca-Twelve Mile systems. Neither the Clemson Board of Trustees nor the state of South Carolina owned these lands; the United States of America did by purchase, usually through the "just and prior indemnity" clause of the U.S. Constitution.

Congressional consideration of the long-term best use of the land had begun in 1938, but preparation for World War II had turned the politicians' attention elsewhere until 1944, when Congress directed the U.S. Army Corps of Engineers to begin careful studies of the hydroelectric capacities of the Savannah River basin into which the Seneca system flowed.[39] The first indication that Poole had heard of the possible construction of such a dam and an impoundment and what the potential changes to the Clemson campus might be appeared in a letter he sent the trustees on October 1, 1949. He dismissed the effects as minimal.[40]

However, a new lake, whose "full pool" surface would be 665 feet above sea level, would flood the entire low-lying fertile land on the Seneca River, where Clemson regularly raised crops, besides some of the meadows used for livestock, for a total of about 430 lost acres. It also would flood almost completely the seven-year-old football stadium. The board, when it realized what would be lost, recommended that Poole negotiate a new and lower water level of 640 feet instead of the water level of 665 feet. But Poole never seemed to be "tough enough" to negotiate with such a powerful force as the Corps of Engineers. Perhaps Trustee Byrnes sensed that Poole did not have the "rough and tumble" nature for such serious negotiations, or perhaps Byrnes had spent enough time in Washington, D.C., to know that a unified federal "juggernaut" really did not negotiate but merely out-waited the other side. He suggested that Poole propose embanking those parts of the campus that contained the most buildings and accede to the basic federal plan.[41]

In hindsight, that approach might have saved seven to eleven years, many work hours assessing potential losses and devising strategies, and the expense of lawyers' fees, but the trustees elected to wage a series of moves that resembled a "rear guard" action and resulted in a real achievement for the board and the administration. But even the trustees were not unified in their approach to the matter. Certainly Edgar A. Brown, chair of the state Senate Finance Committee, had concluded that the huge capacity to generate hydroelectric power could only help the entire Savannah River basin, including his home of Barnwell and, in the long run, Clemson. In that opinion, he joined the majority of the combined congressional delegations of South Carolina and Georgia.[42] Nor would one imagine that the trustees who had helped to make Clemson Agricultural College a foundation pier of South Carolina's forward progress—men like Cooper, Daniel, and Byrnes—would be in total opposition. Whether the delaying defensive strategy that Clemson College trod in opposing the Corps of Engineers was planned or fortuitous is uncertain, but the approach appears to have been on two fronts: to acquire a clear assessment of the damage that would be incurred by the corps' project, and at the same time to make a substantial change in the odds against Clemson.

First, the college made an assessment of the loss for Clemson if the dam were built and the lake flooded the campus. Rather than waiting for an offer from the federal government, Poole asked Charlotte engineer A. C. Lee (Clemson 1908) to serve on a committee chaired by Prof. H. E. Glenn to assess such costs. Two months later (March 27, 1951), the committee's charge publicly broadened to consider alternative solutions. By 1955, the Clemson Alumni Association set up its own committee dealing with the matter.[43]

By this point, Clemson had ascertained that the football stadium would be flooded up to the twenty-sixth row. The Corps of Engineers proposed tearing down the stadium and rebuilding it close to the (then) intersection of the Greenville highway and Anderson highway (roughly where the S.C. Botanical Garden is now located). But a portion of the site had long been used as a garbage dump, and much of the surface was unstable and would have to be excavated. A second problem was that forestry Prof. Koloman Lehotsky had recently established a large arboretum with a substantial variety of trees on this same site. A third issue involved the feeling of the students, who did not want the stadium so removed from the campus.[44]

No one of these objections to the corps' plan appeared insurmountable, but the state highway department also opposed it. The department had developed plans to reroute the two federal highways running through Clemson and to widen them from two to four lanes. The new path would move the roads from the campus farther north and east and closer (in the case of the Greenville road) to the Southern Railway mainline. Those plans had been known since at least 1949, when J. C. Littlejohn and H. E. Glenn had visited the highway department to urge that a connector be placed through the south and the west of the student part of campus, diverting the Anderson-Clemson-Seneca through-traffic in a shortcut through that side of campus. The department agreed and made plans for the road. During the career of highway department head Silas Pearman (Clemson 1927), the road was named Perimeter Road, but when he retired, the name was changed to Silas Pearman Boulevard.[45]

The "lake issue," as many called it, came down to two options: lower the water level of the proposed lake or build dikes. Clemson's trustees preferred it lowered, but that option would not generate enough electricity to meet the needs projected by the corps. With dams or embanking, Clemson would still lose over 7,000 acres, mainly consisting of fertile river bottomland, roads, research buildings, and other improvements. Much discussion appeared in newspapers about alternate dams farther north (eventually some of these would be built), but the Corps of Engineers was determined to carry out its project. With less than a month to go before the November 1952 presidential election, President Harry S. Truman signed the army civil functions appropriations bill that provided $40 million for the building of Hartwell Lake. The bill protected a small amount of the lands (much of it "bequest land") and Memorial Stadium.[46]

Clemson proceeded, however, with its "second front," changing the "rules of the game." The hidden issue was the one of title. There was no question that the federal government (as a corporation) owned the land and "leased" it to Clemson. But the agreement was long-term (ninety-nine years) and required only that the land be used for educational or other public functions. Given the length of the lease, Clemson faculty in agriculture, forestry, and some fields in engineering had initiated long-term research projects based on that land. Very little of these projects was transportable, and the time already invested was not redeemable. This threat represented serious challenges to a number of academic careers and ventures. Thus, there was sympathy for Clemson's plight in many circles (including the USDA and others in Washington, D.C.).[47]

Clemson Life Trustee Charles Daniel, named U.S. senator by Governor James Byrnes, also a Clemson life trustee, to fill the vacancy occasioned by the death of Senator Burnet R. Maybank, introduced a bill in the U.S. Senate. The bill granted the trustees of Clemson Agricultural College "use restricted possession" of the 27,469 acres. William Jennings Bryan Dorn, representative for the S.C. congressional district in which the land lay, introduced an identical bill in the U.S. House.[48] It passed both houses of Congress. Daniel served in the senate only from November 8 until December 24, 1954.[49] He resigned Christmas Eve to give J. Strom Thurmond (Clemson 1923) a bit more valuable seniority in a legislative body in which both houses revered it. President Dwight D. Eisenhower, whose presidential election both Byrnes and Daniel had actively supported, then signed the bill. Now, no question remained that the Board of Trustees owned the land.[50]

The "rules of the game" had changed, and the magnitude of "just and prior indemnity" was increased. As a result in the change in ownership, the federal government now could be expected to pay in "just and prior indemnity" not only for the college's land, which Clemson owned in the name of the Board of Trustees, or that land, such as Thomas Green Clemson's bequest, which was in the name of the state of South Carolina, but also for the land the board had just received from the United States. And the federal government could be expected to compensate for buildings, improvements, and functions (such as power and water) lost as a result of the federal changes. However, all would not be finished until 1961. Cooper directed that the "dam-lake" issue after 1956 was to be negotiated by Edwards. The negotiation remained uphill involving the indemnification and would occupy much of Edwards's time.

Faculty Involvement

The CMP report also noted that the faculty had not received any of the traditional guarantees of position or recognition of service. President Poole, with the advice of deans Kinard and Williams, appointed a select faculty committee to make recommendations. Headed by Prof. John D. Lane, the committee proposed a faculty constitution that would establish a faculty senate composed of representatives elected by the schools' faculties. Such a senate, bound by a constitution, required general faculty approval. In a college faculty meeting, the faculty approved the proposed constitution, which had received much discussion in the departments and schools. The board approved the document on April 9, 1956.[51] The faculty had access to a great gathering of materials on tenure, program, appointment, and promotion policies so that when the Faculty Senate met, it had substantive conversation on those and other issues, once it selected its officers and committees. The Faculty Senate chose John Lane as its first president, and soon the senators placed policy proposals on the above issue before the whole faculty. Of course, the usual amount of debate ensued. After minor changes, the policy proposals were recommended forward. The package went before the board, which approved the proposal, along with a policy on student class attendance, on August 29, 1955.[52] At that point, 372 persons held faculty rank, and 27 percent had the PhD degree. The highest percentage of earned research doctorates was in agriculture, with arts and sciences next.[53]

While the Faculty Senate spent much of its time on what are classified as welfare concerns, such as annual leave and sick leave, by its second year, it demonstrated a genuine interest for the school's academic stance. Among its notable achievements in its first seven years, especially during "Big Ben" Goodale's presidency, were the conception, planning, and even helping to raise funds for Clemson's first academic recruiting scholarships. The scholarships, named for Poole, expanded in number and value during the next autumn term. A succession of strong senate presidents—Claud Green, George Meenaghan, and then Victor Hurst—obtained the first named professorships, the Alumni Professorships, along with approval by the Educational Council and trustees of a strong academic freedom statement and a statement on academic responsibilities and ethics.

Retirement

The trustees and CMP consultants also worried about the lack of a mandatory retirement benefits plan (South Carolina had been working on one for some time) and a mandatory retirement age. At Cooper's request, CMP consultants delivered a retirement age proposal, setting it at June 30 immediately after the administrator, faculty member, or any other employee reached the age of sixty-five. The proposal reserved the right for the trustees to grant exceptions on a year-by-year basis through their executive committee. Most likely, the trustees' debate was protracted. In a letter to other trustees, "Buddy" Thornhill supported the concept and urged that such include the trustees also. But the policy adopted did not mention the trustees. It became effective on June 30, 1957.[54]

Facing the future with fewer and fewer new faces around him and now with this looming new retirement policy, Poole became even more concerned when the board executive committee removed A. J. Brown as the board's secretary and treasurer and assigned him and the treasurer's functions to Melford Wilson in Business and Finance.[55] To fill the newly redefined position of board secretary, the trustees selected the registrar, Gustave Metz. In turn, that opened the increasingly important position of registrar. The new dean of students, Walter T. Cox, appointed as the new registrar Kenneth Vickery, who had begun immediately after World War II to use the newest data collections and statistical analyses in admissions.[56] Vickery, in turn, recognizing emerging needs, named D. G. Hughes to the newly created position of director of student aid and career placement. All these changes led Thornhill to write a fellow trustee, "Clemson laid dormant for twenty years and as soon as we wake up the sleeping giant, attention is focused on the institution and everybody wants to ride the wagon."[57]

Poole's Concerns

But these changes were not the sum of Poole's concerns. He had written about the whole CMP recommendation:

> To follow the report in its entirety would be a mistake....It would be wrong for me to be restricted in making recommendations to the Board on any college matters....If we use the report the needed changes can be made without undue frustration to those who do not deserve to be frustrated....If we treat the report unwisely we can also do Clemson much harm.[58]

The new retirement plan also bothered him. His correspondence about it with Cooper raised questions as to whether or not the plan applied to those who had been hired before the policy was announced.

After announcement of the retirement policy in 1957, academic administrators in other land-grant institutions began to wonder about Poole's future. After all, he was a visible academic leader whose advice on graduate studies was sought by other schools' officials. He had served as president of the Association of Land-Grant Colleges and Universities during 1951. Further, he was at the forefront of the youth education movement, leading the drive to build the 4-H Conference Center in Washington, D.C. And as a scholar he had written and published over one hundred articles in scholarly journals, a number of extension bulletins, and thirty-six general agricultural history articles. During the spring of 1956, Governor George Bell Timmerman (1912–1994; governor 1955–1959) appointed Poole South Carolina's representative to the Southern Regional Education Board, which was at once a data collection, regional program collaborative, and graduate student access agency.

The rumor of Poole's impending departure from Clemson's presidency appeared publicly in early 1958. In response to a letter from an old friend, a faculty member at Wisconsin, Poole replied, "I have not completely made up my mind in regard to retirement." At about the same time, Solomon Blatt, speaker of the S.C. House (and one of a group called "the Barnwell Ring," which included Clemson Trustee Edgar A. Brown), wrote Poole that he had read in the newspaper that some members of "your Board are going to attempt to cause you to retire." Blatt then promised Poole his full support. Almost immediately, Poole wrote R. M. Cooper expressing his displeasure and deep concern about the entire matter and its appearances in the press.[59]

Graduation and the alumni reunion in 1958 fell seven days apart. For Poole, the week began on May 31, when he drove to North Carolina to give an address at a high school commencement. The Saturday itinerary took him to graduation at the Citadel, from which he received an honorary doctorate. Receptions that involved standing and handshaking followed both events. The Pooles left Charleston late Saturday afternoon to get back to Clemson for the baccalaureate service on Sunday, June 1. A luncheon for most of the Clemson platform party and commissioning of the new army and air force officers followed the service, and then Poole was allowed a short rest in his office in Tillman Hall. Clemson commencement followed. Each of the candidates shook Poole's hand. Finally, the day concluded with one more reception. Graduates, their parents, siblings, alumni, kinfolk, and friends needed attention, and the ever-genial Poole disappointed no one.

The Administrative Council met on Monday. During the next two days, Poole consulted continually with Kinard, Wilson, and Cox. Edwards came in and out of these meetings as time allowed because his staff was preparing for the alumni reunion. They expected a large crowd along with most of the trustees. The Clemson House was packed, and the cleaning staff prepared several of the dormitories for use by young, single alumni. Some guests likely stayed on after commencement, awaiting reunion.

The alumni began arriving on Thursday, June 5. Class parties filled the early evening, and the Jungaleers provided the dance music later Thursday night. Friday morning, the alumni officers met to discuss the restructuring of the Alumni Association. Wright Bryan, serving as the Alumni National Council president, ran the meeting with the gracious efficiency that he had displayed through his entire career. Besides working on new organization, the alumni officers rearranged the order in which classes reunited to ensure that classes met in clusters of alumni who had been in school together. Recognizing, however, that the pre-Depression classes were fast thinning because of age and the two World Wars, they decided that after a class reached its twenty-fifth anniversary, it could reunite annually if it chose. Such were merely suggestions, however, brought about because of the

Robert F. Poole (*center*), nearing the end of his presidency of Clemson and his life, at the spring 1958 graduation of the Citadel, during which ceremony he received an honorary degree. He died in office on June 6, 1958, the second Clemson president to do so. The strain of the presidency of Clemson had clearly taken its toll on the once robust Poole. Clemson University Photographs, CUL.SC.

limits of suitable facilities for lodging. Edwards, as the vice president for development, attended only his second reunion in that role, and he listened and participated in the discussions. Poole also attended, but was very quiet. Several people (including Bryan) commented that Poole did not look well.

Most alumni walked around the campus, and more than a few appeared amazed at the new buildings, many erected since World War II. Much conversation dealt with the lake issue; however, now that the board had directed Edwards to serve at their direction as their liaison to the involved branches of the federal government, the mood was no longer one of despair but of hope.

Poole felt discomfort. He went home to rest, but by the time he should have returned for the alumni banquet, he notified Joseph Sherman, the alumni director, and Bob Edwards that he would not be able to be present. His pain in his chest grew worse, and, at about 9:30 p.m., Dr. Lee Milford, both the campus physician for the students and the Poole family's personal physician, was called to Poole's home. President Poole was admitted to Anderson Memorial Hospital at 11:15 p.m. He died of a heart attack at 11:55 p.m. His sixty-fifth birthday would have been reached December 2, 1958.[60]

Notes

1. Reel, *Women and Clemson University*, 22.
2. McKale and Reel, *Tradition*, "Appendix: The Will of Thomas Green Clemson," Introduction, paragraph 4.
3. CUL.SC.MSS 91 f L451.
4. CUL.SC.CUA. S 30 v 6, 407.
5. Ibid., 413.
6. *The Tiger*, May 5, 1955.
7. The Cresap, McCormick and Paget report is detailed and fills several boxes in CUL.SC.CUA. S 30 ss vii *Periodic Reports to the Board of Trustees*, bxs 27–28. It also is filed in the Archives as an entity.
8. Ibid., v 6, 431, 436–438, 444–453, 468–471, 473–475, 489–490, 504–505, 511, 524, and 529.
9. Ibid., S 11 ff 419–421.
10. Ibid., S 28 f "Cox"; Cox with McKale; and Reel personal interviews with Cox 1979, 1986, 1988, and 1999.
11. CUL.SC.CUA. S 28 f "Wilson."
12. Ibid., f "Edwards"; and Edwards to Wainscott, DVD.
13. CUL.SC.CUA. S 28 f "Farrar."
14. Ibid., f "Gourlay."
15. CUL.SC.CUA. S 30 ss vii bxs 27–28. *Cresap, McCormick, and Paget Report to the President of the Clemson College Board of Trustees*, March 1955. This document is the foundation of Clemson's organization through Edwards's administration.
16. CUL.SC.MSS 47 f 7.
17. Conklin, *Vanderbilt*, 292–295; and Dyer, *Tulane*, 252–256.
18. *The Tiger*, October 19, 1945.
19. Bohelman, D'Amico, and Hollbrook, *A Half-Century of Salaries and Land Grant Institutions*, 1–3. The trend turned upward in 1957–1958 and would remain so until at least 1964.
20. CUL.SC.CUA. S 28 f "Williams"; and CUL.SC.MSS 91 b 15 f 210.
21. Lander interview with Reel. Lander was a member of the Graduate Council. See also CUL. SC.CUA. S 367.
22. *Report on Graduate Education in American Public Colleges and Universities*, U.S. Department of Education, 1956.
23. CUL.SC.CUA. S 30 v 6, 494; and S 37 f "Graduate School."
24. Ibid., S 28 f "Edwards."
25. Ibid., S 30 v 6, 503–504; and CUL.SC.MSS 47 f 26.
26. CUL.SC.CUA. S 30, v 6, 503–505.
27. Ibid., S 87 ss i b 17 ff 19 and 20.
28. Ibid.
29. Ibid., b 44 1 and 5.
30. Ibid., S 30 v 4, 606–607.
31. Sims Correspondence, Dacus Library, Winthrop University.
32. Winthrop College Trustee Minutes, November 2, 1955; and Webb, *The Torch is Passed*, 158–160.
33. CUL.SC.MSS 91 f L 446; CUL.SC.CUA. S 30 ss vii ff 1; and S 30 v 6, 430 and 483–484.
34. CUL.SC.CUA. S 32 b 162 f 6.
35. CUL.SC.MSS 91 f L 446. On Sims and his effort to establish a separate USDA program at Winthrop, see the Charleston *News and Courier*, January 30, 1956.
36. CUL.SC.CUA. S 32 b 162 f 6.
37. Ibid.
38. CUL.SC.MSS 91 f L 446.
39. Anderson *Independent*, July 2, 1949.
40. CUL.SC.MSS 67 f 301.
41. CUL.SC.CUA. S 30 v 6, 69–70.

42. Anderson *Independent*, April 2, 1952; Sorrells, *Clemson Experimental Forests*, 18–21; and CUL. SC.CUA. S 37 f "Hartwell Dam #1."
43. CUL.SC.MSS 281 b 2 f 3.
44. *Greenville News*, March 27, 1951.
45. CUL.SC.MSS 68 f 301.
46. CUL.SC.CUA. S 37 f "Hartwell Dam #1." A cynic might suggest Truman was punishing Byrnes for the 1948 Philadelphia "secession."
47. CUL.SC.CUA. S 5 f 56.
48. CUL.SC.MSS 100 Correspondence b 5 f 48.
49. Hollings, *Making Government Work*, 36–38; and Bass and Poole, *Palmetto State*, 106–107.
50. CUL.SC.MSS 100 Correspondence 1955 b 5 f 48. The deed is dated December 22, 1954, and approved by U.S. Congress August 4, 1955. Clemson accepted the conditions April 9, 1956 (see CUL.SC.CUA. S 30 v 6, 499). However, ownership was not in "fee simple." There were permanent restrictions on use in resale and mineral rights. The latter were later conferred to Clemson's trustees.
51. CUL.SC.CUA. S 30 v 6, 490.
52. Ibid.
53. CUL.SC.CUA. S 11 f 544.
54. CUL.SC.MSS 90 S 8 b 8 f 5; and CUL.SC.CUA. S 30 v 6, 526.
55. CUL.SC.CUA. S 6 f 1.
56. Ibid., S 11 f 117.
57. CUL.SC.MSS 47 f 24.
58. Ibid., 90 S 8 b 8 f 4.
59. CUL.SC.CUA. S 5 f 15.
60 Ibid., S 30 v 7, 87–88.

The Edwards family around the time of his selection as college president. *Seated, left to right:* daughter Nancy Edwards, son Bob Edwards Jr., his wife Sandra, and their daughter Elizabeth Louise. The new president, Robert Cook "R. C." Edwards, and his wife, Louise Odom "Moon Pie" Edwards, are standing. Clemson University Photographs, CUL.SC.

CHAPTER XVI

Crucible, Transformation
1958–1961

On Saturday, June 7, 1958, the trustees not already in Clemson received telegram or telephone notification of President Poole's death and were urged to be in Clemson on Sunday for the funeral and for an emergency board meeting. The trustees, some with their spouses, called on Mrs. Poole to express their sorrow as the Poole and Bradley families gathered at the President's home. William, the youngest of the Pooles' four sons and a student at Clemson, along with Margaret Poole Cuttino and Marsha Poole Everett, the Poole daughters, greeted the stream of folk arriving to express their sorrow and bring flowers and food.

Meanwhile, the trustees discussed informally the steps they needed to take as a result of the president's death. They faced numerous questions: What to do about living and financial arrangements for Mrs. Poole? Who would serve as interim chief administrator for the college? Who might best serve on a search and screening committee for a new president? The Rev. Dr. Sidney Crouch, Presbyterian pastor to students, and the Rev. Mr. Charles Raynal, pastor of Fort Hill Church, had called on the Pooles and made arrangements for the funeral to be held in Memorial Chapel.

Of course, the state's newspapers carried accounts of the happenings in Clemson, while many of the alumni in town for reunion made plans to extend their stay. Other alumni and students began returning to Clemson on Saturday afternoon and Sunday. Meanwhile, Clemson College's dining hall manager and his staff planned for an unexpected number of meals on Sunday and Monday morning. The mess hall (now Harcombe Commons) was still set up for the reunion and needed only cleaning and straightening, more provisions brought in, and other details made ready. Further, the staff shuttled a steady stream of light food, coffee, and iced tea from the kitchens of the Clemson House Hotel to the Poole home.

On Sunday, the pastors of the town churches and many in surrounding towns told their congregations the details of the service scheduled for the college's chapel at 3:00 p.m. Their morning prayers asked for comfort for the Poole family, direction for the trustees, and continued mercy and favor for the college. President Poole's body was placed in the chapel by 1:00 p.m. Flowers were brought to the chapel and the grave at Woodland Cemetery, now being prepared to receive Clemson's seventh president.

An estimated 2,000 people filled the chapel beyond its 1,250-seat capacity. At 3:00 p.m., the congregation stood as all the town pastors, vested according to custom, took their places on the podium. Mrs. Margaret Bradley Poole, on the arm of William, was followed by her other children, and with their families, took their seats. Next came other Pooles and the Bradleys. In the Bradley family were her uncle Mark, longtime Clemson English professor, his wife, and others. The governor, the lieutenant governor, the speaker of the house, and a large number of other state and college officials then entered. Eleven of the thirteen trustees completed the official mourners. Raynal presided, and Crouch gave the homily. The other town clergy offered prayers and Scripture readings. After the benediction, the family filed out to waiting automobiles while the casket was borne out and down the granite steps that had been set in place sixty-six years earlier. The bell from the clock tower tolled the sixty-four years of Poole's life as the faculty formed the honor attendants. Slowly, the recession of cars and walkers moved past some of the college's oldest buildings—buildings in which Poole had studied and from which he had planned and directed.[1]

The eighteen years of Poole's presidency constituted the longest administration at Clemson to that moment. Also, it represented the era of the greatest change. However, Poole, because he held dear the Clemson of his college days, did not lead the changes; others did. Modern architecture did not repel him. He approved of the new chemistry, agricultural engineering, ceramic engineering, and chemical engineering buildings. However, he disliked the lift-slab dormitory that replaced Barracks One, Two, and Three. Possibly, his support of John Gates as head of the architecture program centered on the similarity of their artistic sensibilities. In the question of women as students, Poole knew the reality that Clemson had taught and would continue to teach women. When he proposed a women's residence hall toward the end of World War II, he faced and accepted change. But when the trustees turned the request down, he failed to pursue the need. Even when federal energy plans threatened the campus, he approached the situation with placid acceptance. Simply, Poole did not aggressively champion a "bigger and better Clemson."

But Poole had another side. He supported academics and, from his early days in the presidency, especially research. His own publication record remained strong. He knew Clemson's research in agriculture, though strong, needed strengthening if South Carolina's crops, flocks, and herds were to improve. He approved and strongly supported Clemson's movement into ceramic engineering. And he believed in libraries. The library collection more than doubled during his administration, and that began the support for strengthening the humanities. And his sense of fairness and proportion was such that he turned aside the occasional request from alumni to raise the salaries for selected coaches.

All this having been stated, Robert Franklin Poole was a very conservative leader whose vision for Clemson followed closely the thinking of men who lived a generation earlier. His values remained unimpeachable, but his vision was thought by many too narrow for the needs of the people of America's South Atlantic community.

The Acting President

With Poole's funeral concluded, the work of the trustees began. Across the rest of Sunday, Cooper called on each of the four "seconds in command"—Kinard, Wilson, Cox, and Edwards—to hear thoughts and to ask questions.[2] The next day, June 9, Cooper presided over the Board of Trustees members present: W. A. Barnette, Edgar A. Brown, James T. Byrnes, Robert S. Campbell, J. F. McLaurin, A. M. Quattlebaum, Winchester Smith, Robert L. Stoddard, T. Wilbur "Buddy" Thornhill, and T. B. Young. Because no official record of the meeting exists, it is impossible to know whether Secretary to the Board Metz or anyone else attended. What is known is that when Cooper spoke, he reported that he and each of "the four" had met separately. He then recommended the board ask Bob Edwards to serve as acting president. Further, Cooper noted that Edwards understood that he was not to be considered for the permanent presidency. There might have been discussion. The board then named Edwards acting president of Clemson. He would remain vice president for development. The college released the news the next day.[3]

The trustees of Clemson College assembled in 1957. *Seated, left to right:* Thomas B. Young, Paul Sanders, Robert M. Cooper, Winchester Smith, and T. Wilbur "Buddy" Thornhill. *Standing, left to right:* William A. Barnette, Robert S. Campbell, John F. McLaurin, Robert L. Stoddard, and Charles E. Daniel. *Not pictured:* James F. Byrnes, Edgar A. Brown, and the outgoing Ben T. Leppard. Clemson University Photographs, CUL.SC.

Ten days later, the trustees gathered for their regularly scheduled meeting. Their first business was to help the Pooles through the transition. The trustees had already begun the process of building a new home for the president and another for the vice president for development, so they offered Mrs. Poole continued use of the president's home in which she lived. In addition, with the number of female students increasing, the trustees saw a need for someone to serve as a counselor to them. They offered Mrs. Poole the post with pay, and she accepted.[4]

Then, the trustees heard Edwards's first report. He began, "I am at the service of the Board of Trustees and will carry out its desires to the best of my ability." Time would demonstrate that Edwards's energy and judgment allowed the board to stop "hovering" over him as they had done with Poole since World War II. Edwards reported that he and his three colleagues (Kinard, Wilson, and Cox) had spent two days meeting first with the faculty, including school deans and the professional librarians, and second with the staff. Some faculty recalled that Edwards clearly recognized faculty primacy in all academic matters. His actions made it clear that faculty included all teachers, researchers, deans, and directors who were part of the dean of the college's operations. That position assured most faculty of academic freedom, an idea of concern particularly in the 1950s, the era of national political "loyalty hearings and oaths." Others, of course, were not so sure. However, all faculty were more than pleased when Edwards said that Clemson's greatest need was a larger and much-better-stocked library.[5] That, he recognized, could only come about during his "acting" presidency if private sources provided funding.

Finding those sources fell to Edwards as the vice president for development. There were problems. First, with the great amount of work that Edwards faced serving in two capacities, some things had to move before others. The library, as pressing as it was, paled to that of the desired enrollment growth. (But the biggest involved gaining a women's dormitory, according to Kinard, Cox, and Vickery.) As was his style, Edwards decided to visit the opponents and listen to their objections. (The three formidable "foes" were Henry Sims, president of Winthrop College; Solomon Blatt, speaker of the house who seemed to be the roadblock in state finances; and parts of the press.) Edwards approached each in turn.

So Edwards went "calling." First, he visited Rock Hill and Sims. Edwards did not intend to provoke a confrontation, but rather encourage an exploration of areas of cooperation, and he knew that he must invest a number of trips. The first meeting occurred in the late summer of 1958. Edwards knew Sims faced declining enrollment, a trend common to most women's colleges in the country, except for those that had a special academic niche (such as Smith College in Massachusetts) or a strong relationship with a traditionally male school (such as Radcliffe College with Harvard University or Newcomb College with Tulane

University). Thus, for Clemson to have something to offer Winthrop that would guarantee its viability, Edwards had to make strong suggestions and promises. First, inasmuch as Clemson's School of Education focused on secondary work in agriculture, industries, and the secondary level mathematics and sciences, he proposed to Sims that perhaps Winthrop use the opportunity to enhance the fine arts, humanities, social sciences, and elementary education (a field with potential growth). But Sims's worst fear was the possible loss of home economics. Edwards listened, took notes, and returned to Clemson in time for the September 26, 1958, trustees' meeting. While the meeting minutes are not full transcripts, it seems that Edwards ("The Administration") urged the board to state clearly that "adequate courses in this field are offered by several other colleges in the state and that there is no demand or need that Clemson offer this curriculum." The trustees, after discussion, adopted the statement. Sims received the news first, then the governor, the legislators, and the S.C. Department of Education. Newspaper announcements came last.[6]

Besides keeping close ties with Sims, Edwards strengthened the presidential ties with the state's other college presidents, particularly at the independent schools. It may have been nothing more than courtesy, or a gesture simply to ensure no objections to Clemson's desire for women's housing. But the next obstacle involved Blatt and his allies in the legislature. The wooing was subtle and involved much more personal contact. On one occasion, Don Richardson, a member of the S.C. House of Representatives from Georgetown and an alumnus of the University of Virginia, introduced legislation that would bar women from the freshman and sophomore years at Clemson and at the University of South Carolina. An editorial in *The Tiger* pointed out that most Clemson degree programs required one full year of a science and two years of mathematics, which most other schools in South Carolina did not require, and that a large number of Clemson degree programs were not offered in other institutions, a combination that Richardson's bill did not foresee. The result would cause female students and their parents extra expenses and extra years. This egalitarian rebuff drew support from a number of quarters.[7] While these positions did not turn Blatt's economic (and perhaps "protectionist") opposition to support of women at Clemson, his strong public opposition disappeared. Slowly and gradually, the sentiment grew that women should be allowed to attend Clemson. By late 1960, Clemson issued a request for bids for construction of a women's residence hall, and by the autumn of 1963, women enrolled as regular residents on campus, some nineteen years after Poole first noted the need.

The second nagging problem was adequately staffing the Development Office. Before Poole's death, Edwards had begun hiring new development officers. An early appointment brought Joe Sherman (1912–1990) back to the college as director of alumni affairs and public relations. Sherman had grown up in

Joseph Edgar Sherman (1912–1990), Clemson 1934, began the Clemson News Bureau and became Clemson's public relations director in 1956. He also developed the Clemson Loyalty Fund, the Alumni Association's Distinguished Service Award, and Tigerama before retiring in 1977. Sherman, a key figure in Clemson's "integration with dignity" in 1963, is depicted announcing the school's acceptance of its first African American student, Harvey Gantt. Clemson University Photographs, CUL.SC.

Clemson. While he was a Clemson student, he served as the only publicist for Clemson athletics beginning in 1934. Later he worked for seven years at the University of Florida as director of public relations for athletics. Then he spent two years as general editor for the public relations bureau of the NCAA before Edwards beckoned him home. Like a number of other Clemson men who had, or would, reach prominence in the 1940s through the 1970s, he had worked for the college's student newspaper, *The Tiger*, and was a member of John Lane's informal "Clemson school of journalism."[8] Sherman's assignment included all Clemson publicity: academic, students, athletics, and alumni.[9] He had a small staff, mostly recruited by Walter Cox when he served as director of public relations. Sherman added a few other staff in the limited space of the Trustee House. In that group was a young, brilliant Clemson graduate, Robert Bradley, a former staffer of *The Tiger*, a Gamma Alpha Mu, and another of John Lane's "boys." Bradley began at the bottom, but his genius for data and his passion for sports led him to athletics.[10] With the strong support of Edwards and the guidance of Wright Bryan, who was serving as the president of the Clemson Alumni Association, Sherman and his staff created an annual alumni fund-raising campaign called the Loyalty Fund. With the Development Office now well-staffed, Edwards directed his attention to his acting presidential duties.

Meanwhile, the Board of Trustees, after much thought, had appointed a committee to search for candidates to become the president. Cooper asked Frank Jervey, who held no college post but who had retired to live in the Clemson House, to chair the presidential search committee, and Jervey accepted. Board members who served on the committee were Cooper (ex officio), Buddy Thornhill, probably the most outspoken of the legislative trustees, and Robert L. Stoddard, chair of the board's influential Educational and Student Affairs Committee.

To the September 26, 1958, board meeting, Jervey brought the first report. He presented the report during the board luncheon, which was open to the press. He explained that the committee had sent letters seeking nominations to the Association of Land Grant Colleges and Universities, the American Council on Education, the Southern Association of Colleges and Secondary Schools, and a number of foundations interested in higher education. They also sent requests for nominations to the Clemson College Alumni National Council, Educational Council, Faculty Senate, and academic schools. The committee had already received nominations and suggestions and met for a multiple-day session of reading, working, and ranking the candidates. Jervey oversaw the correspondence, acknowledgments, and updates to others on the committee. And he compiled a monthly updated list of the nominees available for trustees to study at his temporary campus office.[11]

In the meantime, Edwards went about the president's job with great energy. He knew the state's officials very well. And he was everywhere, or so it seemed. He moved well socially and was punctilious in attention to his duties. Campus concerts, sporting events, student theatrical performances, alumni, IPTAY, foundation, or legislative committee meetings found him there representing Clemson's interests. Further, he read widely in newspapers and news and opinion magazines and seemed to absorb everything that came across his desk. His correspondence was voluminous. And the search committee, especially Robert Cooper, could not help comparing the "noncandidate" at the helm of Clemson to the résumés and references of candidates they studied.

The President

There is no indication who moved first or when, but by January 13, 1959, Edwards was clearly in command. Efficient assessments of every issue with well-reasoned suggestions and step-by-step solutions flowed from Edwards to the Executive Committee and on to the full board for its emendations and action. Compared to the indecision (and occasional confusion) of the past few years, the movement seemed easy, precise, and clear. Sometime in the very late winter, Cooper and Edwards met. Given the frequency they both were in Columbia, it is possible that their discussion happened there. Cooper, when he had met with the campus leaders (again, Edwards, Kinard, Cox, and Wilson) the past June, had elicited a statement as to the intentions each had toward the office. There is no record of the other campus leaders' answers, but Cooper, upon putting Edwards forward for acting president, stated that Edwards was not interested in the job of president. Edwards later said the same thing. At some point (given the committee and Cooper correspondence sequence), however, Cooper, Jervey, and the search committee agreed, and Edwards's name appeared as a presidential candidate in the search committee files.

Cooper then called an executive session of the board, which by the board's definition excluded the board secretary and acting president. The board convened on April 9, 1959, at the Wade Hampton Hotel in Columbia at 10:00 a.m. T. B. Young, ill and physically absent, was connected to the meeting via telephone. Cooper asked Jervey to come in and read his nominating committee report. Carefully setting forth its reasons, Jervey stated that the committee recommended that Robert Cook Edwards be invited to assume the vacant presidency of the Clemson Agricultural College. After answering questions, Jervey excused himself. Senator Edgar A. Brown moved that the board ask Edwards to accept the post. The other trustees who had served on the search committee seconded the motion, and the "yeas" were unanimous. Charles Daniel moved to offer Jervey the position of vice president for development as of May 1, 1959. Seconded, the motion passed unanimously. The trustees invited each man in to the meeting and offered him the designated post. Each accepted, and the board adjourned. After World War II and when meetings were not on campus, senior administrators usually joined members of the press waiting outside the doors of the room where the trustees deliberated. The presence of Edwards close by was thus to have been expected. Jervey was available by invitation.[12]

Since that time, many have questioned whether or not Edwards accepted the acting presidency with the plan to become president. Others have wondered if Edwards had initially accepted the vice presidency of the Development Office with the goal to succeed Poole when he retired. Edwards always publicly claimed that both suppositions were wrong and that he was surprised when Cooper talked with him about his name being added to the presidential candidates' list.

Of the possibilities, the most likely seems that Edwards gave up his excellent position with Roger Milliken's corporation with the idea of becoming Clemson's president. Edwards's attachment to Clemson was genuine. As a freshman (at age fifteen), he joined the football team. When his dairy farmer father heard it, the father told the son that if he had time to play "games" at the college, he could come home and return to milking cows. Edwards withdrew from the team, thus obeying his father. But Edwards's attachment to Clemson led him to become a football manager, a position that furthered Clemson's interests while it "ducked under" public and newspaper attention.[13] Second, Edwards was always in a hurry. He left high school early to enter Clemson on an academic scholarship. He graduated at age nineteen, met the young lady he would marry at twenty, and married her two months after his twenty-first birthday. His military career began in July 1942 and concluded with his achieving the rank of major in 1946. Upon his honorable discharge, he joined the Deering-Milliken organization and in two years rose from a single plant manager to treasurer and general manager of six related enterprises. He obviously learned rapidly, worked diligently, and moved himself forward relentlessly. But, even though he appeared relentless, he had two goals beyond his family—at least from the early 1950s on—and those were to be Clemson's leader and to guide Clemson firmly into a leadership role among American schools.

The Lake Again

Edwards had promised to work hard for Clemson. And because as vice president for development he had been the leader of the college Hartwell Lake team since September 1956, he continued in that task as president. In 1955, the federal government transferred the deed in fee restricted with an initial reservation of mineral rights to the government.[14] The "fee restricted" title granted the Board of Trustees ownership of the "lease use" land. Now, the U.S. Army Corps of Engineers would have to buy the land at a reasonable market price, offered and accepted or court-adjudicated before the United States could possess and use the land. Prior to the board's receipt of the title, the United States (the holder of the "fee") was obligated only to pay Clemson College for its "improvements to the land." Other compensation, for example, for lost, unfinished research, could be requested but not required. However, the deed carried the "restriction" that the land could be used only for educational or eleemosynary purposes as judged by the U.S. government. Further, the deed stated that mineral rights, which encompassed minerals such as natural gas, oil, gold, and others, but not including those trace minerals found in the surface soils, were reserved for the federal government. The Board of Trustee continues to operate within the "restriction," but the federal government has since transferred the mineral rights. However, how much land the federal government would purchase was still being debated. That was the challenge that awaited Bob Edwards.

The college turned to its alumni and encouraged them to ask their congressmen to help move the negotiations forward in Clemson's favor. Thurmond, after a host of such letters, wired the White House, urging that because agreements had not been reached, contracts on Hartwell Dam not be let. Sherman Adams, White House chief of staff, wired back the next day that no contract would be concluded until the Corps of Engineers, the Clemson trustees, and the South Carolina delegation had conferred (not necessarily concurred). To be sure his point had struck home, Thurmond then wired the corps, "I strongly urge you not to award contract to construct Hartwell Dam on Savannah River until this matter has been considered further." On the very same day that Edwards had been offered the vice presidency, Lockwood Greene, through its Spartanburg office, delivered an extensive independent report to the Board of Trustees on the damage the Corps of Engineers' plan would do to Clemson. It confirmed that 400 acres of the Fort Hill estate of 1,100 acres would be flooded. All were the same fertile bottomland that had caused the original dike-building six decades earlier. In addition, another 1,200 acres of riverfront meadows would be destroyed. Slightly higher land totaling 7,400 acres on either side of the Seneca would also go underwater.[15] It shocked even Brown and Byrnes.

Construction of one of the dikes impounding the Seneca River. Clemson University Photographs, CUL.SC.

As Clemson's negotiator, Edwards brought the trustees, President Poole, the three principal administrators, and the S.C. congressional delegation to meet with the assistant secretary of the army for civil-military affairs, Gen. Emerson C. Itschner, chief of the army engineers.[16] The meeting was on December 20, 1956, in the penthouse of the Clemson House. All the Clemson group were in the principal sitting and dining room except Cooper, Edwards, and Poole, who accompanied the guests and their aides up the elevator. Edwards remembered that as the guests stepped into the elevator foyer, Gen. Itschner looked straight through the glass doors, across the campus, and to the mountains, dazzling in the winter sun. He commented to Edwards and Poole, "This is so beautiful...."[17]

In the meeting, Gen. Itschner presented the corps' "Short Diversion Plan." He asked Clemson to study the plan, which included engineering drawings and specifications, and to respond to it in three months' time. A number of questions about details in the plan ensued. Itschner answered each as fully as he could. The meeting ended. Edwards turned the "plan" over to Lockwood Greene for an analysis, which he quickly received.

Using Lockwood Greene's analysis and expertise, Clemson developed its response, labeled "Plan X." Its study was rigorous and to the point of the plan offered by the government. Clemson wasted no time with any new proposals. The plan proposed three dikes to an elevation of 675 feet above sea level (or 15 feet above the corps' "full pool" of 660 feet). These would save 497 acres of the campus-contiguous bottomland, almost all in regular agricultural use, holding for Clemson most of the original estate land, including the land south and east of the present Pearman Boulevard, Memorial Stadium, the dairy barns, pastures, married student housing, and many support facilities. There were omissions that the Clemson team set forth in detail, including the water intake, needed sewer lines, replacement of Memorial Bridge (a lovely piece of Art Deco work that spanned the Seneca River on U.S. Route 123, now S.C. Highway 93 and named Walter T. Cox Boulevard as it progresses through the campus), and a number of other smaller structures.[18] Plan X was a major step forward for Clemson. Now the issue centered on what responsibilities the Corps of Engineers would accept, because Clemson's stated loss included a number of features not contemplated by the corps. The Lockwood Greene/Edwards response was based on a much larger student body and educational program. Because that did not affect the corps' physical plans but did affect the cost, the corps could begin heavy construction, which it did.

Six months passed before the corps presented to Clemson its reconsidered compensation of $465,655 for the corps' taking of the 7,964 acres (or $57.30+ per acre). Clemson could also remove or harvest anything on the land that it wished.[19] Clemson responded to the offer on July 11, 1957, noting first that it understood that the offer was for the land alone and not for the costs of the diversion plan with all engineering, material construction costs, and the costs of water intake, treatment, and disposal along with connecting sewers and roads. Nor did the offer cover the differences in cost between the low-valued land the engineers wanted and the replacement land Clemson would be required to seek. Legal counsel William L. Watkins (Watkins, Vandiver, and Freeman of Anderson) presented a counteroffer of $2.25 million, or quadruple the corps' offer. When the corps responded negatively, Clemson, through Watkins, suggested U.S. court condemnation hearings. Gen. Itschner concurred in October.[20]

In the meantime, construction on the dikes continued, using 250,000 cubic yards of rock and 3,500,000 of dirt. The dam at Hartwell was nearly finished, and the numerous new bridges, whether large, such as the one that stretched from Cherry's Crossing to the Seneca side, or small were completed.[21] The U.S. District Court for Western South Carolina issued the decisions. On the facilities' rebuilding, the court ruled that the Army Corps of Engineers had to pay for the entire water intake purification, waterlines, power lines, sewage system, water treatment, water return system, and replacement of the facilities, mostly with new structures and equipment. In addition, the corps had to locate land comparable in quality and amount and purchase it for the college.[22] Apart from that, the corps had responsibility for costs of all activities, that is of the land surveying, $4,194; the various appraisals, $9,335; engineering, $21,000; and legal fees stretching from March 1956 to August 26, 1961, $51,750. The corps paid these along with internal expenses for travel from the U.S. Army's "Clemson Land Use and Condemned Lands Account."

Clemson had also retained Watkins to obtain land to replace some of the land the college had lost. He negotiated with the successors of Richard Wright Simpson—Clemson's first board president, Mr. Clemson's lawyer, and executor of Clemson's will (and one of the college's founders, with Clemson, Tillman, and Norris)—to purchase the 1,000-plus-acre Simpson farm southeast of Pendleton. He negotiated also with the estate executor of Joe Douthit, a later Clemson trustee, to purchase his large farm, which lay between the Simpson property and Lebanon Road. Clemson also gained free and clear title to the smaller farms located between the two large tracts to form the Simpson Research and Education Center. The new property included the Queen Anne-style Douthit home and the Simpson burial grounds. Ultimately, the federal government paid in excess of $1.2 million to Clemson Agricultural College, besides the additional college-related construction.[23]

As the lake rose, other lake-related problems surfaced. Watkins and Edwards sent each to the Corps of Engineers, with copies to many public officials. Slowly, the new campus bypass roads opened. A four-lane extension of U.S. Route 76 linked into a new path of U.S. Route 123, bypassing the town of Clemson on the east and north. Perimeter Road ran along the west of the campus and joined U.S. Route 76 with the old Greenville highway. Sorrow attended those who watched the plaques being detached from the bridge that connected the Clemson shore over the Seneca River to the Ravenel lands on the west side. One of the plaques, commemorating the World War I Clemson College war dead, was given over to the care of the state highway department and the other to the college. As the water rose, the Art Deco bridge slipped beneath the surface. Another monument of Clemson's past disappeared (only to resurface during times of extreme drought).

That was in the name of progress. But the lake claimed another victim. On April 25, 1961, Joe Henry Derham, a sophomore from Green Sea and a pledge to one of the college's recently formed local fraternities, drowned in the lake in an attempted late-night initiatory prank. Hazing, which had haunted Clemson's military "rat" system since 1894, had continued among the freshman rats and in many club and society initiations.[24]

Academic Increase

Clemson's newfound ability to attract new faculty and students hastened with the broadening and enriching of academics, streamlining of the administration, continued enhancement of student opportunities in new or improved fields, and a more plentiful social life. Clemson's circumscribed degrees were a most significant aspect that needed upgrading. Two glaring omissions existed. The first centered on the absence of the arts degree at every level. Clemson did not award the two oldest degrees—the master and bachelor of arts—nor the ultimate doctor of philosophy, the degree that represents original research and is as appropriate for animal husbandry as it is for Grecian epigraphy. In fact, among the faculty, the School of Agriculture held the most PhD's, followed by the faculty in Arts and Sciences. With fields and scientific laboratories enriched by the work of Poole and the board and with the steady leadership of deans Farrar and Hunter, Clemson stood ready to take the step of awarding the doctoral degree, which would bring it into line with most other land-grant universities and colleges.

Graduate Studies

The honor fell to agriculture. With the research capacity of the Agricultural Experiment Station, the unification of the three missions of teaching (the Morrill Act of 1862), research (the Hatch Act of 1887), and practical field-testing (the Smith-Lever Act of 1914) under one dean of agriculture, the parts were in place. Further, Clemson had offered the master of science degree in agricultural economics, agronomy, dairy science, chemistry, and physics, along with the science master's degree in engineering (no field specified), and textile chemistry since the late 1940s.[25] Right after Edwards became president in the spring of 1959, Jack Kenny Williams, the graduate dean, announced that the trustees had approved offering the PhD degree in agricultural economics, entomology, plant pathology, and chemistry. Within a short period of time, Williams, Edwards, and Farrar placed the large doctoral hood with its dark blue philosophy velvet border and the startling orange and purple silk lining over the head and onto the shoulders of D. H. Petersen, then a new doctor of philosophy in plant pathology.[26]

A little over a year later, the National Defense Education Agency awarded money for Clemson to establish fifteen three-year doctoral fellowships in

Donald H. Petersen, a plant pathology student from Ludington, Michigan, the recipient of Clemson's first PhD degree. Taken from the 1960 edition of the Clemson College annual, *Taps*.

chemistry, entomology, and plant pathology.[27] And Clemson announced that it had awarded 161 master's degrees in the School of Agriculture, 126 in Arts and Sciences (which included Education), fifty in Engineering, and seventeen in Textiles.[28]

Death, illness, and retirement that began with Poole's unexpected death in 1958 were followed in two years by the unexpected death of Francis Marion Kinard, dean of the college, on May 25, 1960. President Edwards called the individual members of the board and recommended that they name Williams acting dean of the college; he would also continue as graduate dean. The board, in its June 6 meeting, confirmed Williams as college dean. It was not long until Edwards and the board named Hugh Macaulay, a brilliant professor of economics, the new graduate dean. The pace of growth in graduate degrees increased.

Clemson announced graduate programs in chemical engineering and physics and counted 304 full-time graduate students actively working, with eighty-eight in Agriculture, 109 in Arts and Sciences, ninety-two in Engineering, and fifteen in Textile Sciences. Much of the growth resulted from the successful launching of an unmanned satellite, *Sputnik*, by the Union of Soviet Socialist Republics (U.S.S.R). An alarmed federal government began pumping money into graduate programs in relevant sciences, mathematics, and critical foreign languages, producing a nationwide expansion of graduate education. Clemson, in part because its development had been slow to

Hugh Holleman Macaulay (1924–2005), a professor of economics on Clemson's faculty from 1949 to 1983, when he retired as Alumni Professor of Economics. From 1961 to 1965, after returning to Clemson from work as a U.S. Treasury Department economist (1959–1960), he also served as dean of the Graduate School. Clemson University Photographs, CUL.SC.

that point, grew at three times the national average.[29] By Christmas of 1962, Governor Ernest Hollings's Advisory Committee on Higher Education recommended that Clemson's graduate programs in most sciences and engineering receive all, or almost all, of South Carolina's state funding for graduate studies in those fields.[30]

Liberal Arts

Clemson needed at least two other degrees to fill its offerings: the bachelor and master of arts. Williams, Macaulay, and School of Arts and Sciences Dean Howard Hunter met to consult on steps that could and should be taken. They appointed a faculty committee chaired by Robert S. Lambert, professor of history, to study and make recommendations. Lambert moved the faculty with "deliber-

Robert Stansbury Lambert (1920–) arrived at Clemson in 1949 as an instructor of history and government. Except for teaching at other schools from 1952 to 1956, Lambert was a Clemson mainstay, eventually becoming a full professor of history and government (1959), head of the Social Sciences Department (1963–1972), and head of the Department of History (1972–1974). He retired in 1985 as professor emeritus of history. Clemson University Photographs, CUL.SC.

ate speed." He had prepared BA and MA curricular materials from eight respected land-grant universities, including Wisconsin, Georgia, North Carolina State, and Virginia Tech, along with some public liberal arts universities, including North Carolina, Virginia, and South Carolina. The committee reached decisions relatively quickly. First, it recommended a bachelor of arts curriculum with major field minimum requirements. Components included two semesters of basic writing and one of advanced writing, two semesters of literature, two semesters of collegiate level mathematics, two semesters of one laboratory science, two semesters of American history, two semesters of western civilization, ten semesters of advanced courses in the major field, five in the minor field, and a spread of cross-disciplinary subjects and foreign languages. In the last field, the student would take six semesters of the same foreign language or four semesters each of two foreign languages. Faculty within disciplines were free to specify the literature sequence, science sequence, and mathematics groups and could limit minors. Inasmuch as the education degree had been eliminated (the education faculty were members of the Department of Social Sciences in the School of Arts and Sciences), education would be the specified minor for students planning to meet S.C. State Department of Education requirements. Harold F. Landreth, professor of education who held a bachelor's degree from Clemson, master of arts in history from Vanderbilt, and doctorate in education from Houston, served on the committee. The committee report made its way through various councils and was approved by the board, which also authorized the granting of the MA degree with the conditions that it be thesis-based and require written proof of foreign language competence whenever the Educational Council deemed it appropriate.

Lambert's committee advised that both the faculty and library holdings were sufficient for the degrees proposed in the fields of chemistry, English, botany, history, and mathematics. These faculty were also working to define their internal requirements. The board approved the concept of the new degrees on November 10, 1961, and the Educational Council approved the major and minor requirements on February 12, 1962. The college first offered the curriculum in the autumn of 1962.[31] The thoroughness of the report, the apparent faculty consensus, and the rapidity of its internal approvals are tributes to the committee members' commitment, Lambert's adroit leadership, and the highly streamlined central administration structure.

Forestry

Although not connected with the expansion of degree types the college offered, the second great growth area in academics was in forestry. Clemson had offered courses in that field since the early 1900s. South Carolina had created the State Forestry Commission in 1927.[32] And Clemson county agents, with the backing of the commission, had begun a forestation program in the 1930s, but the wartime needs for fruit, grain, and vegetables forced the college to focus on those products during World War II.[33]

The Clemson forestry program began during World War II when, at Poole's direction, the agriculture school hired William J. Barker from the North Carolina Extension Service to become Clemson's full-time forest extension agent in 1942. He had received his forestry education at NC State, where his skills in applied research had attracted the attention of Poole, then dean of NC State's graduate school. E. I. DuPont de Nemours Company lent Clemson a second extension forester, Marlin H. Bruner, to assist in applied research. He became a full-time extension agent with Clemson in 1953.[34] In between, Poole and the trustees agreed that Clemson, with or without large state support, needed to start a two-year pre-forestry curriculum. To do so, they, with the agriculture dean, identified, recruited, and hired Koloman Lehotsky to begin designing the curriculum, which would take great discussion among Lehotsky, the Society of American Foresters (the professional accrediting board), the S.C. Forestry Commission, and deans of the seven forestry schools, to ensure that Clemson's program would meet standards and be transferable.[35]

That did not change the need to deal with the barren hillsides of the Midlands and the Upstate. The forest agents went to work encouraging people to convert those hillsides into stands of trees. The foresight in planting much of the "land-use" land to serve as tree nurseries and to distribute seedlings aided in the effort. In many places, small farmers (who held 71 percent of the farmland) were happy to cut the stands but hesitant to replant. However, both the forest and agriculture agents were successful. They had identified areas that needed immediate attention. As an example, on land-use land, they planted 150,000 loblolly pines. Over a period of seven years in Aiken County alone, county extension agents distributed 6,235,000 pine, cedar, and cypress seedlings for planting by local landowners, by FFA members under the supervision of their high school agriculture teachers, or by 4-H members directed by 4-H leaders, most educated or trained at Clemson, South Carolina State, or other land-grant colleges.[36]

Of course, with the arrival first of Clemson's deed to the land-use land and with the lake rising, many people had ideas on how the college should use the "surplus" lands. Land developers, or would-be developers, both outside and in the college, had visions for it, ranging from sales of new lakefront lots, which was hailed as a possible source of a ready endowment for Clemson, to holding it as intact research land for so long as Clemson would exist. Most of the agricultural and forestry interests held to the latter proposition.[37] Many within the Clemson academic community were on the side of "mixed-use" concept. Bruner pointed out that while the federal and state governments were primarily concerned with generating "cheap power" and secondarily with "flood control," the general public was interested in forestry, wildlife improvements, and recreation. Obviously, Clemson and the appropriate state agencies fulfilled the first two. To a great extent, limited and yet generally open wildlife and recreation would be real opportunities for Clemson to develop.[38] Edwards's presidency demonstrated his commitment to that opportunity.

However, opposition had emerged to Clemson's interest in moving toward a degree program in forestry. It came first from the Southern Regional Education Board (SREB), an interstate coalition of states with advisory capacity whose interests focused on improvement of education opportunity in the South. Its intent from its establishment in 1948 was to increase the bases of southern education by improving both the quality and availability of basic southern baccalaureate education and to increase funding first for those needs. It noted that the South did not possess an abundance of exploitable natural resources, other than those of its citizens, and that the states were not teeming with taxable assets. Therefore, it adopted a position that duplication of advanced or specialized curricula was a waste and that sharing the resources would be better. Later, it expanded its interests and became involved in many other phases of education.[39]

In the case of forestry, the SREB, based on reports begun in 1949, had considered "the region's needs for forestry training and research" and concluded that there was already enough capacity in the seven existing, accredited programs "to provide the South its needs in the foreseeable future," since each school could take care of at least 50 percent more students than it enrolled at the time. However, in Poole's request for comments on the SREB statement, Bruner noted that "capacity" did not account for soil, climate, or material differences among the southern regions, nor did it account for out-of-state tuition differences. On those issues, South Carolina's state forester agreed with Bruner.[40]

Poole moved ahead. Probably the rate at which South Carolina was being reforested (as were other southern states) influenced him. But he would not live to see a forestry degree program established. However, this was also a concern dear to the heart of a number of the college's trustees, particularly Buddy Thornhill. The role of forestry was key to his interests in soil conservancy and water management. Therefore, when Koloman Lehotsky reported his recommendations for a two-year pre-forestry curriculum to the Educational Policy and Student Affairs Committee of the board, Thornhill did not flinch at the costs. Lehotsky noted that creating a forestry program would require a bit over $33,000 for teaching equipment, a recurring annual budget of $40,000 for instruction, and $30,000 for faculty research. In spite of the sums, the trustees agreed for the program to begin.[41]

Lehotsky, with permission of Kinard and Edwards, recruited new faculty to join his small staff. He was fortunate to have Norbert Goebel, a graduate of Colorado State College, whose master's degree was from Duke University, already on the research faculty. He knew also that Goebel could help with teaching assignments. A major recruit Lehotsky brought to Clemson was Davis McGregor. A South Carolina native, born in Florence and reared in Greenville, McGregor entered Clemson in 1944 and on turning eighteen, in March 1945, joined the U.S. Navy. In the summer of 1946, McGregor returned to Clemson, all the while remaining in the Navy Reserve. After suffering with service-contracted tuberculosis in a veterans' hospital for two years, he returned to Clemson and graduated in 1951 with a bachelor's degree in biological sciences. After graduation, he and his young family moved, and he enrolled at the University of Michigan for the bachelor's program in forestry, which he followed with a master of forestry degree. McGregor returned to the Southeast, working as a research scientist with the U.S. Forest Service. Recognizing his scientific skills, the Forest Service sent him to Duke, where he earned his PhD degree in 1957. He moved on with the service to Lakeland, Florida. Lehotsky brought him back from there to Clemson as associate professor and leader of the research team in 1961. Along with outstanding teachers like Bing Cool and Robert Allen, these men created Clemson's (and South Carolina's) Forestry Department.[42]

Enrollment Growth

The growth of all the new programs, the elimination of the mandatory corps of cadets, and the slowly expanding number of women in the student body had the salutary effect of turning the college's general enrollment around. Between January 15, 1956, and June 15, 1964, the student numbers grew by 1,600 to 4,400. Further, Ken Vickery encouraged the trustees, president, Educational Council, and faculty to raise the minimum standards for enrollment. Like most persons involved in the business of admissions, he knew the pitfalls of comparing a grade of A in a subject from one high school with an A in the same subject from a different school. Because of Vickery's background in educational statistics, he was convinced that Clemson needed to improve the mathematics abilities of its entering students. First, he urged the use of standardized (statewide) entrance examinations. After several years, Clemson noticed the effects. It began using the national leader in testing, the Scholastic Aptitude Test (SAT). Through careful research, observation, and work with the professional societies in admissions and registration, Vickery and his staff developed a multivariable formula involving the applicant's high school class rank (understood as an indicator of work values), academic record (using only academic courses), and quality of the school (if Clemson had enough recent experience with students from the particular school) to calculate a reasonable expectation of an applicant's first-year collegiate performance. Certainly, the process was time consuming, but it laid a basis for evaluation before other variables, such as the subject the student wished to study or nonacademic considerations such as school activities, athletics, or other issues, were added. The process, of course, took years to develop and to adjust. But Vickery had the confidence and support of Walter Cox (his supervisor), Frank Kinard, Jack Williams, and the Faculty Senate leadership. The effect was stunning, particularly in the percentage of entering freshmen who returned for the second year and the percentage who persisted to graduation.[43]

Slowly, Clemson's academic quality and reputation began to increase, a process that has continued unabated to the present. Of course, the change added challenges. Some were continual expansion and improvement in learning opportunities, learning facilities, and academic support. The Faculty Senate and the school deans began informal talks that led in 1962 to the creation of the college's honors program. As conceived, the program was in two phases: junior and senior division. The junior division consisted of special sections of courses in the subjects required of all students for graduation, such as freshman mathematics or sophomore literature. In order to qualify for junior division honors, a student had to maintain a high academic average and successfully complete at least one honors class each of four semesters. Senior division honors requirements were designed by the department offering the program and recommended to the Educational Council by the Clemson-wide Honors Council, composed of faculty representatives of departments that offered honors courses. The best students participated in the program and benefited from extra intellectual stimulation, but they were not separated from the rest of the student body, as was frequently the case at other institutions.[44]

Academic Facilities

Learning facilities had been the primary building priority for all of Clemson's boards of trustees since the first meeting after Governor Richardson signed the Act of Acceptance. The Morrill Land Grant Act of 1862, by explicitly prohibiting the use of its revenue for facilities, implicitly expected the cost of buildings and attendant expenses to come from state revenues. In most states, however, that would not be the case. South Carolina had attempted to support Clemson through the fertilizer inspection tag fees. Those fees were ample for about twenty years, then Clemson had to turn to the legislature and tuition for needed revenue. By the governorship of Strom Thurmond (1946–1950), when the flow of *all* state revenues had to go to the state treasurer, that ended completely. After that, the state assumed by default obligations made by its institutions. The state of South Carolina had begun to build many state-owned structures on bond issuance, thus passing the costs, interest, and upkeep on to the people of the future. Dormitories were financed on pledges of future rent, academic needs on pledges of future tuition. The obvious results could only be increased tuition and fee structures.

For some fortunate schools, friends, alumni, and foundations were sources of money. For Clemson's School of Engineering, the Olin Foundation and Charles Horn had helped with funds to build the ceramic and chemical engineering buildings. But the two remaining buildings, Riggs and Industrial Engineering, still had far more students than capacity. Easing the overcrowding in engineering continued to be a priority. The college had secured funding for the structural engineering complex. The northern wing was to be named for Walter Lowry Jr., who had served as department head of civil engineering from 1951 to 1960 and dean of engineering from 1960 until his untimely death at age fifty-four on September 14, 1961. He had received his undergraduate education from Virginia Military Institute and earned his master of civil engineering degree from Rensselaer Polytechnic Institute. He had taught at VMI and, from 1942 to 1946, served in the European theater in Britain, France, Belgium, and Germany. He had returned to civilian life at VMI. When he separated from service, he held the rank of major and had received five combat medals.[45]

Engineering mechanics and laboratories occupied the east wing of this new complex, which connected Lowry Hall to the architecture quadrangle. The quadrangle was named for Rudolph Lee, the founder of Clemson's architectural pro-

Lee Hall's quadrangle has been a haven for budding architects on Clemson's campus since 1958. The building is named for alumnus Rudolph Edward "Pop" Lee, longtime head of the Architecture Department and designer of many Clemson buildings standing today, including Sirrine, Riggs, Long, and Holtzendorff halls, Fike Recreation Center, and the Fraternity Quad. Clemson University Photographs, CUL.SC.

gram and principal designer of Clemson buildings from 1910 to the early 1940s. After several expansions that led to a southern quadrangle, a library, an auditorium, and an annex tower of studios, this cluster, the design of which Architecture Dean Harlan McClure carefully supervised, remains the best example of the international style on the campus.

A New Library?

The oft-repeated goal for Edwards in academic facilities was a purpose-built library, designed not for the Clemson of the present but for the Clemson of the foreseeable future. For Edwards, three major issues stood out: the long-term needs, the major impediments, and funding. Not yet beset with layers of state bureaucracy, the first was a matter for experts: librarians, faculty, and architectural designers experienced in library construction. The second dealt with location and the master plan. And the third was, as he saw it, his job. The first was done in stages. The group involved for stage one was relatively small: Kenneth Vickery projected the student population and the fields most likely to be in demand for the next quarter century. While Clemson certainly had space to create any size campus the people of South Carolina desired and could afford, Vickery and his advisors (faculty, the dean of the college, the dean of students, the school deans, and a few business executive alumni), after taking the infrastructure into consideration, arrived at an enrollment figure of 10,000 on-campus, full-time students.[46] The committee estimated that the full-time teaching faculty eventually needed would number about 700. The committee gave guidelines concerning fields thought to be needed in South Carolina and degrees and asked them to consider the appropriate ones for Clemson. A library committee used these variables to estimate required library space. Many members of the college community took part in informal discussions urging special needs.

At the June 26, 1959, board meeting, Edwards presented the report from the Library Committee, which brought the many hopes, dreams, and projections together into a single set of specifications. Gray Dinwiddie from chemistry headed the committee, which included one school dean, Harlan McClure; one department head, J. C. Cook; two professors, J. E. Miller, physics, and R. W. Rutledge, botany; one associate professor, G. E. Bair, English; and J. W. G. Gourlay, director of the library. The report called for a 150,000-square-foot library building, designed for easy reorganization. Collections should be readily available to all users and provide comfortable and quiet spaces for reading, searching, and study. Noise-tolerant spaces were proposed for group work, typing, and staff work. In addition, graduate students and faculty needed carrels (assigned study desks with cupboards to secure personal study items), and a music room was also thought to be needed, along with a rare books room and college archives (although the committees hesitated to guess on the size needed). The proposed building was ambitious. The trustees doubted that the state would appropriate the money for it. Edwards countered with the statement that obtaining the money was the job of the development vice president (now Jervey), the president, and all the trustees.[47]

This became, for Jervey and Edwards, the new major priority. Jervey worked on a list of potential donors both for materials and for money. Part of the strategy seemed to be to make the space problem more obvious. Campus spaces such as parts of the 1900 basement section of Hardin Hall received rarely used back issues of U.S. government documents to make space for newer additions. Edwards, Kinard, and Jervey approached significant people with strong Clemson ties, such as trustees Byrnes, Cooper, and Daniel, about giving their papers to Clemson's new library. All showed interest, but in the cases of Byrnes and Cooper, they had already received requests from other sources. Yet, all agreed to consider the request. Jervey and his Development staff asked alumni to consider aiding by contributing to a rare books fund. Gourlay, for example, announced that he had received ten works on South Carolina history, while an anonymous alumnus added a series of documents on "First Nations" (American Indian or Native American) affairs and an autographed score of the opera *Wuthering Heights*, composed by South Carolina native Carlisle Floyd.[48] J. A. Milling, another alumnus, sent fifty-six new volumes in science and technology and another fifty-eight titles of contemporary humanities. This followed a long pattern of his giving to the library.[49]

As the first year of his presidency ended in the summer of 1959, Edwards carefully noted a reasonable surplus of funds and with Wilson assigned each school, Student Affairs, Development, and Business Affairs a share of it, but the library received double.[50] And in the first four years, the library's professional staff nearly doubled.[51] The search for major private support was not so successful. Charles Horn informed the college that the Olin Foundation would not fund major building projects for public institutions any longer. Another prominent "friend" responded vaguely. It soon became obvious that Clemson would have to look to the state for at least half of the anticipated cost of $3 million for the library building. Edgar Brown, on the inside of the legislature, and Board President Cooper, with his legislative connections, took over the leadership and began the negotiations. Combining Clemson's needs with those of USC into a joint finance bill to permit each institution to issue special bonds for academic construction, they pushed the legislation. It took several years to hammer together the package, but by the end of the 1962 session, the authorization was signed. On April 17, 1963, the board selected Lyles, Bissett, Carlisle, and Wolf to begin work, using the faculty analysis and a respected library consultant.[52]

The site for the new library had appeared on the master plan as far back as the Perry plan of 1948 as lying "between the new physics building and the Olin

Ceramic Engineering building." The plan also stated that to build there would require that the motor pool be moved, and it made reference to the "old print shop." Long memories would recall that the space had been a ravine with a small stream piped at the time of the construction of the Outdoor Theater. From there, it fed the poplar-lined reflection pool before continuing in its culvert. It emerged again as a stream flowing south to Hunnicutt Creek. Then again, much longer memories recalled that the site had been the convict stockade during the first decade and a half of the college's existence. The few students and faculty who discovered that nugget found an amusing irony. The location of the library turned out to be a brilliant focusing of the campus on the intellectual mind and soul of Clemson's true business.

The Students in Transition

American colleges and universities had always been in the business of educating the whole person, and, therefore, in the business of teaching leadership, service, and collaborative work. Historically, this had been the responsibility of the corps of cadets at Clemson. However, the nonacademic and nonmilitary time had increased steadily ever since Clemson opened. The formation of the literary societies represented the first "diversion." But their importance faded with the rise of alternative forms of communication and with the growth of other nonmilitary activities.

Communication had grown most rapidly and, by the late 1950s, had grouped around the twin popular styles of print and broadcast media. Clemson had three publications of strength. The *Chronicle*, which had ceased publication during the Depression, began again in 1961. Published two to three times a year, the magazine depended on advertisements and individual purchases to meet expenses. *Taps*, the yearbook, had spun out of the *Chronicle* in 1908. It had matured into an award-winning annual, the release of which each spring was a major anticipated event. The students on the *Taps* editorial staff came from all academic fields. They sharpened their skills through a gradual progression from their first to senior years. They also remained active in numbers of other ways on campus. For example, one head editor in the mid-1950s, a mechanical engineer, had served on the staff since his freshman year. He had served as president of the freshman honorary fraternity, Phi Eta Sigma, and held membership in Blue Key and Tiger Brotherhood. The remainder of his senior staff came from diverse academic fields such as animal husbandry and textiles. They included a few varsity athletes, several students involved in religious organizations, and others participating in a variety of co-curricular activities such as the American Society of Mechanical Engineers. The students ran photography studios, and an architecture student directed the overall book design. The advisor was a senior faculty member, and the dean of student affairs oversaw the entire operation.[53]

By 1963–1964, the *Taps* editor was an economics student also active in student government, Blue Key, Tiger Brotherhood, and the Kappa Sigma Nu (local) fraternity. Another member of his staff, a biology major, belonged to a (local) social fraternity, Kappa Delta Chi, and two preprofessional fraternities, Alpha Zeta and Delta Sigma Nu. The design editor was an architecture major. From Binghamton, New York, he held a position on the Central Dance Association and membership in Sigma Alpha Zeta (local) fraternity. The junior staff had several women students, including Nancy Miller. Miller, from Westminster, was active in women's residence hall issues and in Sigma Beta Chi (local) sorority. The students involved came from across the campus and, just as their predecessors in the fifty-year history, participated in many campus activities. The advisor, another senior faculty member, served, as did his predecessor, voluntarily. Student Affairs, which now had three professionals and one secretary, oversaw these and all other extracurricular activities. By this point, the American Collegiate Press Association had named four consecutive editions of *Taps* All-American.[54] Through this era, and continuing a long tradition, *Taps* was an almost complete and accurate "annual" of student life, including photos of a very high percentage of the entire student body, all college-wide dances and weekends, classical and semiclassical concerts, registered student organizations, intercollegiate and intramural athletics, clubs, co-curricular clubs, faculty organized by schools, and military activities.

The weekly newspaper, *The Tiger*, also dated from 1907. Unlike *Taps*, it had not suspended publication during World War II, although it appeared biweekly and for a brief period monthly from 1943 to 1946. As the student body grew in size, *The Tiger* diminished coverage of faculty social activities, but continued its broad coverage of student life. Of course, it covered intercollegiate and intramural sports and featured lists of new members in the clubs, social societies, honorary organizations, and the new faculty. *The Tiger* publicized and reviewed college-wide classical and popular concerts, and reported on exceptional news, including student government and state government (particularly as it related to education), frequently discussing it on the editorial page.

Just as for *Taps*, *The Tiger* staff came from across the student body and diverse fields of study. Freshmen were generally recruited openly through receptions and were self-selecting through their sophomore year. Students for whom the extra work was not rewarding simply stopped being a part of it, while those whose writing, photographic, editorial, or business skills failed to develop did not receive new assignments. As with *Taps*, rising fast on *The Tiger* staff were women like Rebecca Epting, who, after graduation, built a rich career in public service. The Edwards era opened for *The Tiger* with it being advised by longtime English faculty member John Lane. He had long nurtured the craftsmanship of *The Tiger* staff while not attempting to censor their thoughts. Through his many years, he also helped absorb the occasional efforts of J. C. Littlejohn to rein in youthful zeal. But he did insist on concision, accuracy, and clarity. On gaffes of that nature, he came down hard, but always after the issue containing such had been circulated. By the time students had survived his "school of journalism" for two years, they had become concise, accurate, and clear. Sadly though, John Lane's health declined in the late 1950s, and he retired early in 1960 after thirty-six years of service to, and nurturing of, the many students who came into his domain.[55] Fortunately for his students, he had selected his successor—Claud B. Green.

Many Clemson students (and faculty) had long held the dream of establishing a radio station operated by the students with a modicum of faculty guidance. Following a number of efforts in the late 1920s and 1930s and following the development of radio use by the Clemson Cooperative Extension Service, a team of three students—David Suggs of Columbia, Harry Bolick of Kinards, and Van Fair of Gastonia, North Carolina—constructed a long-term plan. Located in the Student Center, over the loggia in the sprawling lift-slab dormitory, they built a station that was initially a closed-circuit broadcasting system. Suggs served as program director, Bolick as business manager, and Fair directed the eight-member engineering crew. The call letters "SBF" represented the initials of the three student founders' last names. They had no trouble recruiting the engineering staff of the seventeen-member programming group. When the station aired its first programs on May 1, 1958, it broadcast popular music, Clemson athletics, and news.

After three years on the air, by which time the staff had added regular classical music and educational programming, the Federal Communications Commission granted the Clemson station an FM license that allowed a fifteen-mile radius broadcasting range. Among the faculty involved in operating the station were J. N. Thurston (electrical engineering), George Bair (English), and Hugh McGarity (music). As with the campus print media, the senior staff generally recruited from the freshman class, and interest and ability decided which students moved on to the junior (third year) and then senior (fourth year) staffs.[56]

Fraternities—Again

One of the frequent requests of Clemson students involved their wish to form Greek-letter social fraternities. In fact, the experiment with local fraternities during the 1930s had proved helpful to the social life of the campus. Walter Cox, dean of students, had been a member and, in his senior year, president of Sigma Phi local fraternity (not to be confused with the older national fraternity, established in 1827 at Union College in New York). The Clemson experiment had not included housing, which remained based on military organization. As men returned to Clemson after World War II, the administration quickly squelched efforts to reorganize the local societies.

However, several of the regional clubs functioned much like traditional local fraternities. As much fun as these could be, they excluded students from other areas, unfortunately encouraging "localism" to continue. A few groups formed and called themselves "service fraternities," but in fact they functioned as traditional "social fraternities." The most successful of these, the Numeral Society, was the creation of Joseph Laurie Young, a faculty member in architecture and a member of Phi Kappa Sigma Fraternity while a student at the University of Texas.

But that did not fill the students' desires. Thus, after Edwards assumed the acting presidency in June 1958, a small group of students visited Cox to discuss the issue. Led by Bill Schachte of Charleston, it emphasized that, with the announced ending of the corps and its final disbanding, dormitory life was almost totally unstructured and that a fraternity structure could help fill that void. Cox discussed the matter at length with Edwards. They decided to form a committee of faculty, students, and alumni to study the issue through the spring of 1959 and to write a report for Cox, Kinard, and Edwards to consider. If these thought it wise, they would present the report (amended if necessary) to the Board of Trustees for its June meeting.[57] This was a timely decision. Earlier in September, the student body president, Joe Fox, a textile chemistry major and an officer in Army ROTC, had stated in *The Tiger*, "The role of student government is to increase the value of the college and also to deal with the social problems of a college community so that the students would be as free as possible from administrative supervision."[58]

And Cox had already done his homework. He consulted with his counterparts at somewhat similar southern schools to understand the role of social organizations such

Walter Thompson "Dean" Cox Jr. (1918–2006), Clemson 1939, began his career at the college as a football coach. He went on to serve as assistant to the president, alumni director, head of public relations, vice president/dean of student affairs, interim university president (1985–1986), and vice president of institutional advancement. He ended his nearly fifty-year career at Clemson in 1987, retiring as president emeritus and as one of the most dedicated and beloved figures in Clemson's history. He is pictured here (*right*) in 1959 as dean of student affairs with Bill Schachte, one of the founders of Clemson's fraternity movement. Clemson University Photographs, CUL.SC.

as fraternities on other campuses. Only one male, all-military college had long experience with fraternities, Norwich University. Interestingly, it had grown out of the Norwich Academy that Thomas Green Clemson attended in his youth. Its first Greek-letter group had begun in 1856, and by 1958 Norwich counted six men's groups. But Norwich's board considered closing its fraternities in part because all six had residences and the fraternities owned the land, which made it difficult to maintain military discipline. Ultimately, the board determined that other values imparted by the fraternities were more beneficial.

The closest comparable institution to Clemson was Mississippi State University. It had an underground chapter of Sigma Alpha Epsilon in the late nineteenth century and a local club ostensibly tied to Kappa Alpha Order around the same time. The decision to open the campus to fraternities in 1927 brought onto it chapters of Pi Kappa Alpha and Kappa Alpha Order legally. By 1958, the school had nine fraternities and two sororities.[59] Its experience had been positive. Cox dispatched sociology Prof. Frank Burtner, heavily involved with students since his return to Clemson in the 1940s, to Mississippi State to ask questions of, and learn from, its officials and students about their Greek program. Burtner, like Young, was a graduate of the University of Texas, which had a large, flourishing fraternity system.

Frank Alan Burtner (1914–1990) came to Clemson in 1939 to teach sociology and economics. He also served as director of fraternity affairs (1970) and coordinator of pre-professional health education during his 45-year career at Clemson, which ended when the dedicated counselor and teacher retired in 1984. Clemson University Photographs, CUL.SC.

The Clemson student representative body passed a resolution calling for the creation of fraternities, which indicated that strong support existed for establishing the organizations. In fact, when women numbered slightly over twenty, they too formed a Greek-letter, nonsecret society to give them a sense of belonging to the community. And *The Tiger* published columns examining the appropriateness of fraternities at Clemson.[60]

With data from all these sources available, Cox named the members of the advisory committee to study the question and make recommendations to the president and the board. The student members included Frank E. Abell of Lowrys; Alan Elmore (junior class officer and member of the swimming team) of Charlotte, North Carolina; Miles Powell of Mullins; William A. Shirley of Honea

Path; and William Wysong of Florence. Faculty serving on the committee included Ben Goodale of dairy science, William A. Speer of architecture, Hugh H. Wilson of ceramic engineering, and George E. Bair of English. The alumni members represented the Clemson Alumni Association: Tom Millford, president; Jess Jones, vice president; Frank Jervey, past president; and Joe Sherman, director.[61]

The committee met frequently, using the auditorium in Olin Hall as its base. Bair served as the chairman of the group. The committee soon reached the conclusion that with the ending of the mandatory four-year military life in companies, the campus was growing and diversifying rapidly. The large, modern lift-slab barracks built in the 1950s provided either for a very regimented life or for a totally individualistic and isolated existence. The committee recommended that the student community needed careful study. Student living, it said, should encourage small interest-group formation and, with the goal of breaking down the "hometown" attitude and moving toward geographic diversity, social interest groups were critical. Those clubs that wished to ally with national fraternities should do so "under careful administrative control."

The committee focused on one critical issue: the inadequacies of the existing dormitories. In the old dormitories (those called "the barracks" or "quad"), almost no social space existed. This was needed. For the newer dormitory (by this point called the "Tin Cans"), the social space remained entirely too meager and too central to help create a sense of a smaller, personal community. Finally, the committee recommended that student interest groups, including social clubs, be encouraged. And of fraternities, the report said,

> As for these social clubs that develop, some of them may desire eventually to affiliate with national fraternities. If, as one outgrowth of a planned re-organization of the student community at Clemson, a fraternity system develops under administrative care and control of the student community at Clemson, then it is to be assumed that fraternities under these circumstances would be an asset to Clemson. If a fraternity system does not develop, then the question will have proved to be academic.[62]

The report was thoughtful. It pointed out that the trustees' 1954–1955 decisions on admissions and the military formed the single great break that delineated the old from the new Clemson. The thinking of the past had been cast away; a new age had dawned. The trustees received the report on June 26, 1959, and Cox and Edwards gave their strong, positive support. The trustees adopted the report and charged Cox to begin the process of preparing the way for social fraternities, which they added should include a social club governing council. The trustees also informally instructed Edwards and Cox, along with Henry Hill, director of auxiliary enterprises (whose oversight included the dormitories), to survey the dormitories and determine the most suitable of them for this new style of living and to develop staged plans for the transformation.[63] This project would occupy Cox and Hill for a good bit of the summer.

News releases in early June announced the change, and a number of students began planning for it. Cox talked with Burtner, Wilson, Young, and a small number of faculty who had belonged to fraternities. Basic planning for the transition suggested that the "quad barracks" would be the most adaptable to small-group living if lounges were created in each of the eight subunits. This would provide an opportunity to update the bedroom furnishings and make other cosmetic improvements. Most renovations could be completed during the summer of 1960. Planning included the hallmarks of membership. First, a student could join a fraternity only after successfully completing the first semester, defined as having passed four courses (twelve credit hours) with a grade average of 1.4 (a measure of the ratio of hours taken divided into the quality points earned). A grade of D would carry the value of 1; a C, 2; a B, 3; and an A, 4. Thus, in a freshman English course assigned three credit hours, if the student earned a C in the course, the student's quality points would be 3x2 or 6 points. The sum of all the quality points earned for the semester, divided by the sum of all credit hours attempted (or enrolled in after some arbitrary date), produced the grade average. (Sometimes this is called GPA, or grade point average, or GPR, grade point ratio.) Thus, a 1.4 was a D, enough to continue studies, but not sufficient to graduate. To move the student ever closer to graduation, the continuing-education requirement increased at regular intervals measured by hours attempted. In addition, the plan created minimum membership and officer requirements for the fraternities.

When the fall semester of 1959 opened, students began forming a few groups. The first fraternity accepted was the group Schachte and a friend, Winston Fowler, organized. On November 6, 1959, Cox proposed to the Student Organizations Committee (composed of faculty, Cox, and his assistant) that Sigma Alpha Zeta, Clemson's first social fraternity (it had originally been called Sigma Zeta), be recognized. The committee agreed. Within four weeks, it also approved two women's fraternities (called sororities), named Omicron and Chi Chi Chi. In the new year, other men's groups were formed and approved. The Numeral Society successfully applied to change from a service to a social fraternity. Quickly the groups formed into the Inter Fraternity Council (IFC). Cox appointed Burtner to serve as the IFC advisor. As required of all student organizations, each fraternity and sorority had an advisor, usually a faculty member.[64]

By the fall of 1960, the fraternities, now seven in number, resided in the quad. Because Clemson had no women's housing, this impelled the school to press harder at the state level for women's facilities. The groups also stepped forward to engage themselves in a variety of activities, most of them positive, on and off campus. Because they recruited members from emerging student leaders in publications, academics, athletics, and religious societies with no particular interest in home states or majors or religions, they proved in their early years to have both an energizing and unifying effect. By 1964, eight men's groups and three women's groups existed, all housed in college dormitories. Of course, all was not perfect. The men's groups inherited the hazing that still lingered in the freshman class, a holdover from the "rat" system that had dogged every commandant and every president since the second class entered in 1894.

Athletics

The larger "spirited" unification of the Clemson community was its athletics. Baseball, Clemson's oldest intercollegiate sport, emerged from a long period of average success on the diamond. Although many claimed a hand in hiring the new baseball coach, the credit goes to Frank Howard, who occupied the dual roles of head football coach and athletic director. Knowing that he needed Bob Smith, the present baseball coach, to concentrate his efforts on football, Howard began looking for a person to take over both baseball and the intramural program. The baseball team had eight winning seasons in the first nine years after World War II. Three coaches had served as baseball's mentors during that period, but, in the last three years, Clemson had only seventeen wins. Howard found a new baseball coach in a University of North Carolina assistant, Bill Wilhelm.

Coach Billy Hugh "Bill" Wilhelm (1929–2010), legendary skipper of Clemson's baseball teams from 1958 to 1993, accumulated a record of 1,161 wins, 536 losses, and 10 ties. His winning record ranks first among all sports and coaches in Clemson's history and in the top 20 in the history of Division I baseball. Wilhelm, pictured here (*right*) with star pitcher Harold Stowe, never had a losing season as head coach at Clemson while guiding the Tigers to 11 ACC Championships and to the College World Series six times: 1958, 1959, 1976, 1977, 1980, and 1991. Taken from the 1959 edition of the Clemson College annual, *Taps*.

The change was amazing. The team won twenty of thirty games in Wilhelm's first year. It also captured the ACC championship with twelve victories and three losses. Representing the conference, Clemson won the NCAA District III tournament. The last two games were a double-header victory over the University of Florida on June 9, 1958. George Bennett, a Clemson graduate of 1955 and later IPTAY executive secretary, remembered that Harold Stowe pitched the first game against Florida. Stowe started twenty-one games (the national record for the year) and received credit for fourteen victories. In the bottom of the ninth, a hit for a single by second baseman Bailey Hendley brought Larry Wilson home for a 15–14 victory over Florida. The second game began at 11:30 p.m. and finished with Clemson's 3–1 victory. Stowe later played for the New York Yankees. Clemson advanced to the NCAA College World Series in Omaha, Nebraska, for the first time in the school's history. During the next six years, Wilhelm's teams went to Omaha one more time and never had a losing season.[65]

Clemson's second oldest intercollegiate sport, football, during the 1955–1963 seasons almost reached its competitive best in its sixty-seven-year history. Since the formation of the Atlantic Coast Conference, the team had ended the season second or third in the conference five times and first, three times. Further, the Tigers had finished ranked in the top-twenty four times, reaching eleventh (Associated Press) in 1959. The team amassed fifty-nine victories, thirty losses, and two ties. Seven of the victories were over old rival South Carolina.

On three occasions, Clemson appeared in postseason bowls. The first was in the Orange Bowl in 1956 against the University of Colorado Buffalos. The Clemson quarterback was Charlie Bussey, an all-ACC player, and the running back was Joel Wells. The cheerleaders and the band occasionally accompanied the team, which traveled frequently to away games by bus. With Clemson now no longer an all-male military college, the band was no longer a regimental unit. Although the band had elected to continue its all-male tradition, it did have its first female, Phyllis O'Dell, as drum majorette. When the band traveled (usually on chartered buses), O'Dell and subsequent majorettes rode along with the female cheerleaders with the chaperones. The next year she was joined by Carolyn Willis. Both were award-winning majorettes. Women would remain as majorettes until Anne Barnes joined the band in 1970 as a trumpeter. One of Tiger Band's special moments was a visit to the White House as part of an away-game trip. Arranged by faculty member and Band Director John Butler, the tour ended in the Rose Garden with a surprise visit by President John F. Kennedy. When Kennedy asked for a tune, Butler reminded him that instruments and cases were left behind for security reasons. But he offered that the all-male group could sing. He began the alma mater to forestall the bawdy bus-ride songs. As the hymn petered out to a close, the president whispered to Butler, "I hope they play better than they sing."[66]

A photo taken during President Kennedy's surprise inspection of the
Clemson marching band. Clemson University Photographs, CUL.SC.

The Orange Bowl, which since 1953 had matched the champions of the Big
Eight and the Atlantic Coast Conference, now pitted Colorado against Clemson.
Even though Clemson was the favored team, Colorado led 20–0 at halftime. At
the break, Howard berated his team, and behind Bussey, the Tigers took the field
in the second half and played well. Sticking to Howard's traditional game strategy
of running the ball, with Rudy Hayes or Charlie Horne as blocking backs, Bussey
alternately handed the ball to Bob Spooner or Joel Wells to move Clemson into
the lead 21–20 in the fourth quarter. Clemson then tried an onside kick. Colorado recovered at its 46-yard line and scored to win 27–21.[67]

Clemson played in two other bowl games, the January 1, 1959, Sugar Bowl
in New Orleans, Louisiana, and the December 19, 1959, Bluebonnet Bowl in
Houston, Texas. The Sugar Bowl pitted the No. 1 ranked and undefeated Louisiana State University Tigers against Clemson's eight-win and two-loss Tigers. LSU
was heavily favored, and Clemson, although it had played Tulane in New Orleans
a number of times during the 1930s and 1940s, had faded from the view of
many New Orleanians. A New Orleans radio announcer, discussing the upcoming game in November 1958, described Clemson as a "small, co-ed, liberal arts,
church-related college in North Carolina."[68] Most of Louisiana's "raging Cajuns"
dismissed Clemson as a pushover, but that was not to be the case. Clemson played
its best. Lou Cordileone held the line as Billy Cannon, a Heisman winner, found
little space to run for LSU. Clemson quarterback Harvey White *almost* connected
with George Usry for a touchdown. Usry was open, as was the field to the goal.

But White's pass was low and uncatchable. In the end, LSU escaped with a hard-fought 7–0 victory. But Clemson folks left proud of their Tigers.

"Wait till next year" proved a good adage. Frank Howard had successfully converted his team from the "wing" to the "T" offense. A large number of football lettermen returned. Clemson's defense, as usual, proved strong, holding five of Clemson's eleven opponents scoreless. The Bluebonnet Bowl matchup ended with a 23–7 Clemson victory. However, the South Carolina game was remarkable on several counts. Clemson's victory margin of 27–0 almost made up for South Carolina's upset of Clemson the previous year.

The real upset, however, was that the 1959 game was the last "Big Thursday." Clemson had desired, since at least 1907, for the game to be a "home-and-home" rivalry with the University of South Carolina. They had met for the first time in 1896 and met almost every successive year (except 1901 and 1903 to 1908), always in Columbia. The near bloody confrontation between partisans of the two schools (mainly students), provoked by the actions of the Clemson cadets (see Chapter VII) following the October 30, 1902, Clemson loss, had caused officials of the two schools to break off the rivalry. When USC in 1907 asked to revive the attractive game, Clemson officials suggested a home-and-home arrangement. For a variety of reasons (including Clemson's lack of adequate stands and local accommodations), USC refused. The schools renewed the series in 1909. But the matchup was always held in Columbia and was fairly even until 1945, when South Carolina had a victory run of seven wins, one loss, and three ties.

With the formation of the Atlantic Coast Conference and its first full football schedule in 1953, the games Clemson played at home became nationally attractive. Maryland, a recent mythical national champion, played at Clemson. The crowd that filled the 20,500-seat Death Valley (at that point, the nickname was one year old), and the subsequent traffic jams on the two-lane highways, gave impetus for improved highways and an enlarged stadium. At that point, when USC erected temporary stands, its 1934 New Deal-built Carolina Stadium (seating about 17,700 normally) nearly reached the size of Memorial Stadium at Clemson. Having both schools in the ACC justified larger stadiums. USC supporters argued that the state did not need two large facilities, and inasmuch as Columbia lay in the center of the state, it could be used for more gatherings than just USC games.

After much back-room and closed-door wrangling and compromises involving state politicians partisan to one or the other institution, a compromise bill in the legislature, drafted with the blessing of Solomon Blatt, speaker of the state house and a member of the USC board, and Edgar A. Brown, chairman of the state Senate Finance Committee and life trustee of Clemson, proposed to allow each school's board to issue bonds to enlarge their two stadia. The issue of the home-and-home or always-in-Columbia game was not a major concern in the struggle. The bill moved through both government chambers, and both sets of trustees made preparations for the stadium expansions.

At Clemson, Prof. H. E. Glenn oversaw the enlargement plans for Memorial Stadium. He had designed and supervised original plans and construction of the stadium just as World War II had begun to involve the United States. Bob Edwards, at the time acting president and vice president for development, successfully corralled donors to contribute to various parts, such as the electric scoreboard.[69] General Construction Company of Columbia won the contract, which added about 17,500 seats to make a 37,500-seat Memorial Stadium. As a campus facility in the ACC, it fell in the middle range in size.[70]

With a larger stadium from which to negotiate, the Clemson Board of Trustees reopened the question with USC of the home-and-home series. Perhaps because of the presence of a number of state officials ex officio on the USC board (and perhaps realizing that whatever was decided, half the state would be angry), it gave USC's Athletic Council the duty of negotiating for the Gamecocks. After all claims were heard about tradition and statewide accessibility of the game in Columbia, the negotiators agreed that the 1958 and 1959 games would be held in Columbia, and that beginning in 1960, the game would be held in Clemson, and thereafter on a home-and-home basis. Happy Clemson students put up signs chuckling, "UP ON EVEN, DOWN ON ODD." There was a second part to the agreement: The rivalry game moved to the last one of each school's regular season as soon as advanced scheduling would permit. Clemson would accomplish this in 1960, but it took USC until 1963.[71]

Thus, Big Thursday ended in the 1959 season. Many spectators remembered various Big Thursday stories. A number were collected and published in the October 22, 1959, game program, and James F. Byrnes saved a copy from it of Wilton Garrison's "Recollections of Big Thursday." Garrison was a sports editor for the Charlotte *Observer*. One of his stories recounted a player on the field taking a drink of water. As the player glanced up into the stands, he saw a fan "crown another with a bottle and knock him about three rows of seats." The player sputtered, "I'm glad I'm down here on the field. It ain't safe up there in the crowd."

But Byrnes had marked another Garrison memory. This was of the 1946 game, "when the fans broke down the gates and ringed the playing field. James F. Byrnes, then U.S. Secretary of State, watched the game from between a player's legs as subs and coaches had to stand all during the scrap."[72] Clemson won the last Big Thursday 27–0 with quarterback Harvey White passing to George "Pogo" Usry and handing the ball to Bill Mathis.[73]

But the new seating in Memorial Stadium seemed insufficient, so in the fall of 1959, the Clemson trustees elected to add 6,000 more seats, placed on the western end of the field. This new section added team dressing rooms, restrooms, and more concession stands. The seating capacity increased to 40,000.[74] Crosland-Rood Construction of Columbia won the contract for the addition and began construction during the late spring of 1960. The various sides cautiously approached the first Clemson-Carolina game in Clemson. Angus McGregor, Clemson's student body president, and Mike Quinn, his counterpart at South Carolina, had met on several occasions to help prepare for the day, which they dubbed "Solid Saturday." And in keeping with a ten-year-old tradition, the two schools' Blue Key chapters sponsored the game dance, "The Tea Cup Dance." But the Clemson rank and file students were sure their Carolina counterparts were planning a raid on the campus. It, of course, was their bounden duty to protect the place from potential threats. So as the traditional ring of drummers gathered around the fifty-five-gallon metal barrel placed in front of Mr. Clemson's statue to spend Wednesday, Thursday, and Friday tattooing "BEAT CAROLINA" on the oil drum head and into the brains of all passersby, younger students "camouflaged themselves as all sorts of beasts of the jungle, Confederate battle flags and what have you to guard the Tigers' lair." No marauders came,[75] but the "guards" had fun. Was this the first Clemson football "face painting" tradition?

Clemson expected another exceptional season in the autumn of 1963. Predicted to have a football powerhouse, Clemson opened the season against Oklahoma in Norman. It was swelteringly hot. Howard's men jumped to a 14–0 lead before the sun overtook them and the larger, deeper Sooners ground them down, 31–14. Thirsting for revenge, Clemson then traveled to Atlanta, hoping to best Bobby Dodd's Georgia Tech. Again the weather won, in a deluge of rain so great that the radio announcers called attention to a floating football. Tech won 27–0.[76]

After a home-opener victory over NC State, Clemson faced Georgia. The game was in Death Valley on a bright sunshine-drenched Saturday. But during the second quarter, with Georgia leading 7–0, the sky grew dark; first thunder, then rain, and then hail drove the faithful out of the concrete seats and under the stands. Concession stands, restrooms, toilet stalls, all became sanctuaries. The game? It was halted, and when the skies settled to a steady, cold rain, Clemson returned to slog out a tying touchdown. The Charlotte *Observer* noted, "'Hail to the Victors,' but nobody won."[77] The season that began with so much hope ended sadly. The Carolina game was moved from November 23 to November 28, 1963, because of the assassination of President John F. Kennedy on the twenty-second.

The decade also saw the beginning of new customs during the football season. With the passing of the corps, the presentation of the "Mother of the Year" traditionally held at the Mother's Day Parade on Bowman Field in May was transferred to the football season. Tiger Brotherhood always selected the honored lady, who received a corsage and usually an engraved silver tray. One overwhelmingly common characteristic dominated the event: The "Mother of the Year" was almost always a person important to more than a small handful of students. Over the years, this has remained one of Clemson's special moments.

A 1959 photo of the first Homecoming display at Clemson built by a fraternity. Pictured in front of Brackett Hall (*left to right*): Sigma Alpha Zeta brothers Vance Lippard, Steve Long, Mike Britt, Bill Ellerbe, and Luther Anderson. Photo courtesy of Winston Fowler.

The end of the corps also changed Homecoming customs. Clemson's custom had been to hold a full military review, and then the entire corps marched behind the regimental band down past Fort Hill and into the stadium. The cadets' dates followed the corps and awaited the cadets as they filed into Memorial Stadium. In 1954, the students not in the corps erected chicken wire screens with brightly colored crepe paper slogans urging the team to annihilate the opponents. Thus, a tradition of Homecoming displays began. Then when Joe Sherman returned to Clemson from New York, he imported a University of Florida activity, a combination student variety show blended with a pep rally in Memorial Stadium, held the night before Homecoming. The activity ended with a large, professionally managed fireworks display. Sherman asked the student leadership society, Blue Key, to coordinate the project. Its first showing was held on November 8, 1957, and individual students, along with student clubs, musical groups, the band, several military teams, and all manner of events, worked to entertain the crowd, estimated at 5,000. The very first Tigerama was a success. All three customs have survived, been reshaped, and improved to become part of Clemson's post-corps tradition.[78]

Even basketball was unusual during the decade. Banks McFadden served as head coach during the 1955–1956 season, his final year. Although the Tigers beat both Tennessee and LSU, they managed only one win in the conference play. McFadden resigned to devote more time to football. Press Maravich took over as coach in 1956–1957. In his seven years at the helm, Clemson had no winning seasons, producing sixty-seven wins and 109 losses. And in the conference, the

Tigers had only thirty wins against sixty-eight losses. However, the surprise season was in 1961–1962 when the Tigers reached the final game of the ACC tournament. Other schools took note of Maravich's talent, and Everett Case, NC State's legendary coach, hired Maravich as his assistant and to prepare to take over when Case retired. Maravich took with him his young and talented basketball son, Pete (later dubbed "Pistol Pete"). Bobby Roberts, Maravich's assistant, became Clemson's coach and inherited a good team and superb freshman class.

The basketball Tigers continued to play home games in the "big gym," built with alumni contributions in 1930. It served as Clemson's concert series hall, a place for school dances until the new mess hall was built, a registration hall, and most anything else. The lighting was dim, the ventilation nonexistent, and smoking permitted. At game time, when packed with 3,300 loud and boisterous college men, it could prove more than a challenge for visiting teams. Roberts's first years certainly benefited from such support. His 1963–1964 season opened with Clemson victorious over North Carolina, a feat repeated in February 1964, 97–90 in Charlotte. The ACC tournament opened in Raleigh with Clemson's convincing 81–67 victory over Maryland, before the team lost 68–64 to Wake Forest. The record was 13–12 overall, the first winning season since 1951–1952, and Clemson enjoyed its first winning ACC season.[79]

But there were a few troublesome signs in intercollegiate sports, not all of which affected Clemson immediately. These might be summarized as cost and control. A number of factors, including salaries, travel, and participants' costs, affected the expenses of the Athletic Department. Few coaches commanded or demanded salaries very different from those of other institutional leaders, but the coaches asked for more assistants. Football squads were growing. Freshman teams, an early insistence of Walter Merritt Riggs as an insurance against "tramp athletes," combined with the increasing length of playing seasons, were among the culprits. And the division of squads into offense and defense, the addition of specialty players, and the growing emphases on position depth required specialty coaches. With them came trainers and team managers. Of course, it must be remembered that the number of students enrolled in colleges and universities (and their percentage of the total population) had increased greatly since World War II. But good evidence exists that nonteaching or nonresearch staff of higher education grew much faster than teachers and researchers. And the salaries, particularly at the upper level, advanced much more quickly.

The second rapidly increasing cost involved student-athlete grants-in-aid. While not a new expense in many schools, the open awarding of grants-in-aid to potential athletes was little different from other reward systems based both on past performance and future expectations.[80] Clemson, which had long used its semi-external fund-raising arm, IPTAY, relied on grants-in-aid to even the ability of private schools to "adjust tuition and fees." And Clemson's faculty, Board of Trustees, and administration had sought eagerly to raise the school's recognition. Winning athletics, built on Clemson's solid academic tradition, seemed a strong way of accomplishing that. Of course, among Clemson's most devoted supporters were some who quietly objected to IPTAY. Some faculty, even those who contributed to it regularly, had mixed feelings about IPTAY. One faculty leader, a regular giver, observed that, to him, IPTAY meant "I Play Tennis All Year!"

The entourage that accompanied the football team, coaches, trainers, managers, and team physicians to away games included the trustees, president, and other dignitaries. And then there were the bands, cheerleaders, and other student groups. The band served as a good example of increasing costs. Clemson's first all-military band members wore military uniforms and furnished their own instruments, but slowly the college began to provide instruments. After the corps was dissolved, the band members needed uniforms. The costs for these plus travel and a portion of the salaries of the various music instructors were usually assigned in one way or another, but paid for from Athletic Department revenues.[81]

Control was connected with cost. Ever since the formation of collegiate athletic conferences, members had made conference-wide agreements. Generally, the agreements related directly to the rules of playing, leaving such questions as player eligibility to the colleges. In fact, efforts to make or enforce such rules on eligibility were seen as an attack on the honor of the school. Some schools frequently rejected Walter Riggs's Southern Intercollegiate Athletic Association rule of "no freshman players" for that reason. The formation of the Atlantic Coast Conference was as much tied to the Southern Conference's effort to regulate post-conference play and cost as to anything else.

The National Collegiate Athletic Association (as opposed to "conference"), or NCAA, formed to bring uniformity to rules of play, including equipment used, but its early authority did not extend much beyond that. Further, it only had the authority to sanction an institution because it had no power (that is, "threat of physical force") to bring to bear. And membership in it remained purely voluntary, as its apologists were (and are) quick to remind critics.

Athletic grants-in-aid provided the first step toward the power the NCAA needed. The second step was the interest of the major television networks in broadcasting the four big football bowl matchups (Rose, Orange, Sugar, and Cotton). While the bowl sponsors delighted in the prospect of focusing attention on their shows and communities, few local organizers had interest in the inner workings of the industry. They were happy the NCAA would serve as the portal. Slowly the idea of televised sporting events took hold. Feared at first by athletic directors, who worried about the loss of gate revenue, television coverage actually seemed to increase seat demand at the larger and more successful schools. College publicity agents saw another side, the public relations freely gained, if they could fill some of the dead time with appealing film of happy students cavorting on lovely campuses. It was enough to make school admissions officers and institutional fund-raisers ecstatic.

The possibilities seemed overwhelming. National exposure required bowl appearances because that commanded the largest audience. Considering that only four bowls really mattered, invitations to them required superior seasons, which, in turn, required superior student athletes. And considering that only eight schools would be the "winners," then getting the "right student athletes" was an old goal elevated far above the northeastern "tramp athletes" who had bothered Walter Merritt Riggs a half century earlier. Some uniform standard for eligibility beyond the institutional certification was needed. The conference seemed to be the logical body. And when the Pacific Coast Conference caught three football giants in California in the web of overzealous partisans who privately, or through athletic support organizations, rewarded teenaged stars for agreeing to play for the desired school or for performing very well, it slapped penalties on the three schools. After some soul-searching, the NCAA ruled the penalized schools ineligible to appear on any NCAA-televised contest. Truly, a new age had emerged. By the time the issue ended, three West Coast teams from well-respected universities had been shamed.[82]

By 1957, the NCAA moved to the next level: greater regulation of the grants-in-aid that could not exceed "commonly accepted educational expenses." To attempt to control (or, as was said, "level") the process, the NCAA set forth regulations limiting the amount of time and where a prospective student athlete could be "encouraged" to attend a school. The penalty, again, involved regulation of television appearance. The NCAA's executive director succeeded in getting a "big stick" for the association in such matters.[83] So, a television revenue stream could help with the institution's cost, and the creation of the NCAA's "power" might be the control. At this stage of development, the questions of student-athlete eligibility for play and culpability of college officials, individual supporters, and coaches had not received serious attention. The furnace fire was banked.

Notes

1. *Greenville News*, May 31–June 28, 1958; and CUL.SC.CUA. S 63, June 7–June 11, 1958.
2. Edwards to Reel with W. T. Cox and Joey Delaney.
3. CUL.SC.CUA. S 30 v 7, 89.
4. Ibid., 87–89.
5. Reel with H. M. Cox, R. S. Lambert, E. M. Lander, and T. L. Senn, Spring 2007 variously.
6. CUL.SC.CUA. S 30 v 7, 114–115; and Winthrop University, Sims Correspondence, 1955–1958.
7. *The Tiger*, February 13, 1959. This unsigned editorial was probably by Ronnie Ellis, the newspaper's editor.
8. CUL.SC.CUA. S 38 f "Sherman."
9. For example, see his article in the Anderson *Daily Mail*, August 15, 1933.
10. Sherman, *Clemson Tigers: A History of Clemson Football 1896–1977*; and Bradley, *Clemson: Where the Tigers Play*, 48–55.
11. CUL.SC.CUA. S 30, v 7, 119. The committee files are available in the sub-series. These do not contain names of the nominees because some of the most prominent are still living. I have also consulted with the Jervey (MSS 72) and the Thornhill (MSS 47) files in the Special Collections

in the Clemson University Libraries. A collection of relevant correspondence in the Thornhill collection (1231.00) in the South Carolina Historical Society has also been studied.

12. CUL.SC.CUA. S 30, v 7, 10.
13. The story was related by Edwards's grandson at Edwards's funeral.
14. See the earlier discussion of the question of ownership. This is a fascinating issue, worthy of its own study. See the Congressional Record-Senate, vol. 101, Part 2, 84th Congress, February 15, 1955, 1534 (by Thurmond and Johnston) and July 22, 1955, 11239; House, February 22, 1955, 1912 (by Dorn), February 23, 1955, 1955 (by Riley), February 24, 1955, 2072 (by Ashmore), February 25, 1955, 2184 (by Rivers); and Public Law 237 Chapter 559, 496.
15. Wainscott, "A Take-Charge Businessman: Robert Cook Edwards, 1958–1979," in *Tradition*, 190–194.
16. CUL.SC.MSS 100 Subject Correspondence Series 1956, b 3 f "Hartwell Dam."
17. R. C. Edwards to Donald McKale, DVD.
18. CUL.SC.MSS 47 f 30.
19. Ibid., f 31.
20. CUL.SC.CUA. S 11 f 382; and S 30 ss ii b 4 f 1.
21. *The Tiger*, December 19, 1966.
22. CUL.SC.CUA. S 87 ss ii b 42 f 4.
23. Ibid., ff 1, 2, and 3.
24. *The Tiger*, April 28, 1961.
25. CUL.SC.MSS 280 b 1 f 12.
26. CUL.SC.CUA. S 11 f 673.
27. Ibid., S 30 ss ii b 4 f 5.
28. Ibid., S 7 f 27.
29. Ibid., S 30 v 7, 195 and 203; and S 11 f 277.
30. *The Tiger*, November 16, 1962.
31. CUL.SC.CUA. S 30 v 8; and *Clemson College Announcements*, 1962–63.
32. CUL.SC.CUA. S 19 f 282; S 49 b 20 f 13; and Maughan, *Guide to Forestry Activities*, 202.
33. CUL.SC.CUA. S 63 August 14, 1962.
34. Ibid., S 30 v 6, 339.
35. Ibid., S 41 b 38 f 4.
36. Ibid., S 4 b 3 ff 7 and 10.
37. The presidential correspondence of Poole and Edwards was full of "land sale" propositions. A paper by Koloman Lehotsky, written in 1955 and found in CUL.SC.CUA. S 6, is an example of the "conservancy" concept.
38. CUL.SC.CUA. S 41 b 12 f 11.
39. Http://www.sreb.org/page/1304/academic_common_market (accessed January 11, 2011).
40. John E. Ivey Jr., SREB director, to R. F. Poole, February 2, 1956, in CUL.SC.MSS 91 f L 442. The seven schools noted were Alabama Polytechnic Institute, Duke University, Louisiana Polytechnic Institute, Louisiana State University, North Carolina State College, University of Florida, and University of Georgia.
41. CUL.SC.CUA. S 30 ss ii b 5 f 3.
42. McGregor to Reel, Fall 2007.
43. W. T. Cox to Reel, 2001; and H. M. Cox to Reel, Spring 2007.
44. C. Sawyer to Reel, letter on file with Reel.
45. CUL.SC.CUA. S 28 "Lowry."
46. Major considerations were the size and accessibility of the community, which had about 2,000 inhabitants; the highways, including the federal interstate whose construction in Atlanta was well underway while the remainder as far as Charlotte was in the early stages; public transportation and particularly the to-be-built Greenville-Spartanburg Airport; housing for additional faculty and staff; and on-campus sewage capacity. Another reason that the planners reached the figure of 10,000 was an emerging national standard that a full-time student was enrolled in twelve credit hours at a PhD-granting institution or fifteen credit hours at a lesser-degree granter for undergraduates. For faculty, instructors of all ranks in PhD departments were calculated at nine credit hours of instruction on average and twelve in non-PhD departments. The emerging standard had yet to take into account student enrollment in the hour, credit for contract, courses

in laboratory work, number of graduate students in thesis preparation, use of teaching assistants, and other such variables. Obviously, such quantification works to the disadvantage of the scientific and technological institutions and probably to the rigor of assignments and examinations.

47. The report is in CUL.SC.CUA. S 30 ss ii b 4 f 3. The board action is reported in S 30 v 7, 160.
48. Anderson *Independent*, May 21, 1959.
49. CUL.SC.CUA. S 11 ff 269 and 271.
50. Ibid., f 678.
51. Ibid., S 12 f 333.
52. Ibid., S 30 v 98.
53. *Taps*, 1958, 310–312.
54. *The Tiger*, April 17, 1964.
55. Louis Henry to Reel. Henry had been an editor of *The Tiger* and, after receiving the PhD, joined the Clemson faculty and succeeded Green as advisor. Also Epting interview with Reel.
56. CUL.SC.CUA. S 61 February 18, 1958; April 4, 1961; *The Tiger*, September 3, 1961; and *The Tiger*, October 18, 1962.
57. *The Tiger*, February 15, 1959.
58. Ibid., September 25, 1958.
59. Ballard, *Maroon and White*, 114.
60. *The Tiger*, February 15, 1959. For an early column on fraternities, see Frank Anderson's essay in *The Tiger*, December 15, 1955.
61. CUL.SC.CUA. S 61, April 30, 1959; and informal conversation with Alan Elmore in 2008.
62. CUL.SC.MSS 147 b 2 f 24.
63. CUL.SC.CUA. S 30 v 7, 147–148.
64. *The Tiger*, November 6, 1959, December 4, 1959, January 15, 1960, February 26, 1960, and March 11, 1960.
65. Bourret, *Clemson Baseball 2007*, 179–181; and George Bennett, "This is the Way I Remember It," *Orange and White*, April 22, 2008, 5.
66. Reel, *Women and Clemson University*, 34–36; and Butler to Eisiminger, DVD.
67. Bourret, *Clemson Football 2006*, 122–123; and Charlie Bussey to Reel, December 2007.
68. Edmee Franklin Reel, an LSU student, 1957–1961, recounted the announcement. George Chaplin, a Clemson graduate and then editor of the *New Orleans Item*, laughed when he remembered that misstatement, commenting that the announcer was right on two points, "small and co-ed, but just barely."
69. CUL.SC.CUA. S 105 b 2 f 6.
70. Ibid. The seats cost a total of $17.10 each. Besides the construction costs, electric power cables, row and seat markers, concession stands, and walkways would add a bit more to the cost.
71. Bourret, *Clemson Football 2006*, 205.
72. CUL.SC.MSS 90 b 8 f 9.
73. *The Tiger*, October 28, 1959.
74. CUL.SC.CUA. S 63 b 4 f 23.
75. Ibid., f 24. Webster P. Sullivan of Norfolk, Virginia (now of Portsmouth, Virginia), was a freshman that year. The question was his.
76. Bourret, *Clemson Football 2006*, 205.
77. Charlotte *Observer*, October 12, 1963.
78. *Taps*, 1958, 156.
79. Bourret, *Clemson Basketball 2005–2006*, 201–202.
80. Defenders of grants-in-aid pointed to examples such as academic scholarships, musical grants, leadership awards, or any other past performance-based awards. While some opponents discredit all forms of monetary inducements, others tout financial need as reasonable. At issue is whether to reward the grantor (the institution) or the parents for misfortune (financial aid). Even the middle position runs the risk of heightened economic stratification.
81. Walter T. Cox Jr. to Reel.
82. Watterson, *College Football*, 283–284.
83. Ibid., 284–286.

This landmark era, notable especially for the ending of legal inequities regarding the composition of Clemson's student body, represented the ushering in of a new, more "modern" Clemson, shown here with a key driver of that movement, President R. C. Edwards, ca. 1965. Clemson University Photographs, CUL.SC.

CHAPTER XVII

Crucible,
End of Legal Inequities
1955–1964

Regardless of how well Clemson's reorganization was progressing, or the ending of Clemson's military discipline was being accepted, or the way women were being received in the Clemson student body, the international and national developments on race, civil rights, and equity certainly indicated that some South Carolina public institutions or services would have to decide how to proceed. The surprise was not that the question of civil rights arose, but where and how it arose. Most challenges to racial segregation that attracted great attention came in public issues—education, employment, and accommodations. For Clemson, the challenge arose in research.

When it came to research, Clemson trustees had been of two minds. They had been very supportive of agricultural research, but they were very hesitant about major commitments to fields in which they could not see return value for South Carolina.

Thus, the utility of urging active work in forest industries made immediate sense to the trustees. Their inability to get legislative attention to focus on forests in the 1920s and 1930s may have been the long-term investment necessary for the legislature to see income benefits in forest research. By the same token, in a state without much in the way of mineral deposits, the trustees had little interest in the fields of automotive or aeronautic research, despite faculty and student interest in such areas, nor in the strides young Clemson alumni made in those fields in the same two inter-war decades (1919–1940).

The Second World War had become, among many other things, a race for sources of power and for increased firepower. In the 1930s, 1940s, and into the early 1950s, the search for exploitable and renewable resources had focused on the ability to find oil and gold deposits. Now the new power source was atomic or nuclear energy. While the European conflict had been brought to an end by slowly amassed and armed traditional weaponry, a major factor in the end of the Asian war was the unleashing of nuclear might. Although it raised the terrifying specter of human annihilation, nuclear energy held out a glittering promise of a utopia in any industry that required any form of animal or mineral power.

Nuclear Energy

Shortly after Bob Edwards was appointed vice president for development, an opportunity for the college in the arena of nuclear energy presented itself. On September 5, 1956, the U.S. Atomic Energy Commission (AEC) announced that it would grant to a small number of accredited universities and colleges equipment, advanced faculty training, and (later) money to offer graduate education in nuclear science and technology. With personal visits, phone calls, and letters, Edwards urged the trustees to seize this chance immediately. Clemson, he pointed out, could be very attractive for developing a program in the field. It was reasonably close to two centers of atomic research at Oak Ridge, Tennessee, and Huntsville, Alabama. The emerging power and water availability in the planned Savannah River plant added to its appeal, and the large amount of underdeveloped land that Clemson held in the Savannah Valley was a special component. In October 1956, the trustees voted to pursue the possibility of work in such a field.[1]

James Sams, engineering dean (and, ironically, the man who years earlier had urged Clemson's entry into automotive and aeronautic engineering), gathered a team of men in physics, mathematics, and engineering to consider the AEC request for proposals; to recommend to him, Hunter, Kinard, and Williams whether or not to enter the fray; and, if so, to suggest what researchers should be added to the team to write the proposal. A positive recommendation came quickly, and the expanded committee formed, comprised mainly of faculty who had spent time working at one of the U.S. nuclear facilities.

By December 4, 1956, Sams had gained institutional approval, and Clemson submitted a request for $99,050 to the AEC for establishing a research program in nuclear energy. Within five months, the AEC had granted Clemson's request. Ultimately, the $99,050 could have been used to garner about $350,000 worth of valuable laboratory equipment. Edwards also forecast the need to send some faculty and staff for extensive (perhaps two years) training at AEC installations. Then the big expense would come. A critical reactor large enough to meet all the teaching and research activities cost about $1.5 million. Edwards had already arranged a meeting with USC President Donald Russell to discuss full cooperation and to avoid duplication.[2]

Edwards then sent the AEC documents to William L. Watkins, Clemson's lawyer, for review. Watkins wrote back on May 20, 1957, noting a possible conflict between the AEC contract and a one-year-old provision in the S.C. Appropriations Act of 1956. The AEC contract required nonracial discrimination in admission of qualified persons to have access to, or use of, the facility. Watkins reminded Edwards that the Appropriations Act made the use of state-appropriated money dependent on racial segregation in state facilities. However, the restriction applied only to "collegiate" activities (thus avoiding extension work), and the act used the word "pupil" in connection with admissions, limiting the action to students admitted to Clemson. Watkins warned that he would have to research the issue further, but he thought the possible state restrictions could be overcome. Nonetheless, he recommended getting the advice of the general assembly's Special Segregation Committee, and that Clemson pay attention to what Georgia, Alabama, and Mississippi were doing.[3]

William L. Watkins (1910–1999), a native of Anderson and a product of Wofford and the University of Virginia's School of Law, practiced law with the Watkins, Vandiver, Kirven, Gable, and Gray firm in Anderson. He served as Clemson's counsel from the 1940s to 1960s, representing the college's interests in cases concerning Hartwell Lake, integration, the university status change, and the issue of outside access to the campus. Watkins (*far right*) is pictured with (*left to right*) S.C. Attorney General Daniel R. McLeod, Assistant Attorney General William L. Pope, and Clemson President R. C. Edwards. Taken from *Greenville News*, August 23, 1962, edition.

Edwards and Watkins met first with S.C. Governor George Bell Timmerman Jr., who recommended that Clemson not sign the AEC contract. They also met with Senator Marion Gressette, chair of the Special Segregation Committee, who concurred with the governor, although he seemed reluctant to involve himself or the committee in the work of the trustees. With advice from Cooper and Daniel, Edwards asked Watkins to redraft the wording in the AEC contract of Condition 8, which gave Timmerman and Gressette pause. The original statement read: "(8) The recipient agrees that no person shall be barred from participation in the educational and training program involved or be the subject of unfavorable discrimination on the basis of race, creed, color, or religion."

Clemson offered the following revision: "(8) The grantee agrees that no legally enrolled student or member of its faculty and staff shall be barred from participation in the education and training program involved, or be the subject of other unfavorable discrimination on the basis of race, creed, color, or religion."[4] Before Clemson mailed the suggestion, Watkins contacted an unidentified South Carolinian on the staff of the AEC who suggested such a modification might be accepted.

As Edwards prepared for the June 1957 Clemson board meeting, Watkins wrote Timmerman, explaining the recent developments. Further, he reminded the governor that Clemson, relying on the federal telegram, had ordered the equipment requested. A delay would set Clemson back a crucial year and further handicap

South Carolina's quest to attract new industry. Watkins called attention to Timmerman's statement, basically affirmed by the Gressette committee, that "if Federal money should not be available except at the cost of sacrificing the great principles involved…state funds should be made available." Watkins added, "We wonder if you will express to the Free Conference Committee a request that the amount of the grant be made available to the College if the AEC does not modify the condition of the grant."

On June 11, 1957, William Mitchell, the AEC general counsel, responded. Mitchell pointed out that Clemson's stated reason for requesting the rewording was to ensure that the institution did not lose control of its prerogatives to select its students and faculty and to discipline them as the school considers appropriate. Mitchell dismissed that argument, stating bluntly that the federal language was to guarantee equal access to all such facilities and instruction if they were members of the group selected for participation in the program. It was "to prohibit discrimination because of race, creed, color, or religion among the student body." The counsel ended his letter, requesting that Clemson accept the contract as had thirty-three other schools.[5]

Edwards placed all the information before the Board of Trustees at its June meeting. Apparently, the trustees discussed the entire issue at great length, but that can only be inferred. By a split vote, the board instructed the administration to sign the agreement, which was the first clear indication that a number of trustees were not rigid segregationists. Edwards executed the document and returned it to Washington on June 22, 1957. Watkins informed the governor and Senator Gressette on June 25.[6]

Governor Timmerman was away at a governors' conference when Watkins's letter arrived. When he read it, he was not happy. He replied to Watkins stating,

> It is with grave concern that I learn from your letter that, on the day following *sine die* adjournment of the General Assembly, the Board of the Trustees of Clemson College voted to accept a grant of $99,000.00 from the Atomic Energy Commission upon the terms of condition (8). This action is contrary to the advice which you previously had sought from the Gressette Committee and from me as Governor.

He set forth three objections (in no stated priority). On the issue of "race," he rejected Watkins's and Edwards's argument that in this context it did not apply to admissions. Second, he interpreted "creed" to open entrance to Clemson for persons with political "creeds" such as communism. Third, he objected to a state institution accepting financial aid from the federal government while the state was perfectly able to provide the support.[7] The governor closed by asking the Clemson board to rescind its action of June 21. The Governor's Office sent a copy of the letter to every board member.[8]

The trustees' reactions varied. One indicated that he could see the governor's concern and would ask Board President Cooper to reopen the question. Several thought the governor overreacted and that a trustees' committee should meet with the governor to convince him of such. No one commented on the issue of "creed." Further, the governor seems to have done nothing to address the request that the state move to supply Clemson the funds it would forego by turning down the federal grant. Senator Gressette's reply of July 6, 1957, was even stronger. He added an implied threat:

> But I am not convinced that we should not consider legislation at the next session of the General Assembly whereby no governing body of an institution shall be permitted to enter into an agreement with the Federal Government or any of its sub-divisions until such time as the subject agreement has been approved by some legally constituted agency of the State for that purpose.

Although this represented an unusual statement, the direction of his thought was there. Gressette addressed the letter to Watkins, but he also copied it to Timmerman, R. M. Jefferies, each Clemson trustee, and R. C. Edwards. No records show it sent to President Poole.

Timmerman's letter drew a number of replies. On behalf of the board, Watkins wrote the governor on July 2, 1957, acknowledging receipt of the governor's letter and telling him that the board had not met to take action on his request. Watkins noted that the date for the meeting of the board had been set "almost three months ago," and with no relation to the general assembly's *sine die* adjournment.

Watkins's subsequent letter to the board raised two relevant questions about Timmerman's communication. First, he noted that the federal offer could not be considered a violation of states' rights because the federal government had a monopoly on fissionable materials and products. He wrote, "It is no more possible to conduct a nuclear science course at the College without signing a contract with the Commission than it is to conduct an ROTC program without signing a contract with the Army or the Navy." And Watkins also pointed to his letter of June 4 to the governor, asking for funding for the program as the governor and Gressette had both suggested Clemson do. The governor had not replied.[9]

Byrnes had misgivings about the entire application. Cooper, who had a close relationship with Byrnes, wrote him after the exchanges and attempted to ease his concerns by pointing out that in conversations with Mitchell, AEC's general counsel, Cooper had received assurance that the use restriction to Clemson students and faculty was satisfactory to Mitchell and was close to the same limitations that the Department of Agriculture used with the Cooperative Extension Service. Nonetheless, Cooper told Byrnes that Clemson would "comply with the governor's request."[10]

Interracial Developments

But this did not deter Edwards from his long-range plan to enhance Clemson's research posture in all parts of the college. A plan that Edwards and Sams had developed to reopen the never-well-funded Engineering Experiment Station had been built on the premise that Clemson was to receive the AEC grant in 1957; it came to naught because of the governor's objection. But governors change, and the election brought to the state Governor's Office Ernest Hollings, a man determined, as were Cooper, Daniel, Edwards, and younger public leaders, to improve South Carolina economically. It would be hard to label them as "liberals" on a national scale, but in the minds of many white southerners, they seemed so. These men, like most of the Clemson faculty, had lived through the Depression and had served in World War II. Nor were their thoughts far out of step with moderate southern white leadership. James Coleman, governor of Mississippi (1956–1960), had expressed this well in his statement, "I believe in preserving segregation, but I don't believe in waging war. In the first place, I am a loyal American, and in the second place, you can't win." Earlier, he remarked, "Mississippi will be a state of law not of violence."[11]

While this position might not satisfy all modern critics, it was the gradualism whose roots lay in the utterances of Abraham Lincoln, the practical progressivist notions of Walter Merritt Riggs, the strategies of Franklin Roosevelt, and many who combined morality with practicality. But the crucial question was, "When was the time?" For long-suffering African Americans, and representative groups such as the NAACP, the answer was, "Now," as it was for American liberals of other races. But a reaction to gradualism began erupting shortly after World War I. The signs of "resistance to change" materialized in many ways. In some quarters, it appeared in personal actions, such as those of "Cotton" Ed Smith, South Carolina's senior senator who stormed out of the 1936 Democratic national convention when an African American minister came to the podium to deliver the invocation. Some of the South Carolina delegation followed Smith. Byrnes and the other South Carolina progressives stayed in the convention hall.[12]

But by 1948, the opposition to racial integration hardened, and again the focus fell on South Carolina. Once more, the setting was Philadelphia and the occasion the Democratic Party convention. This time the issue was not a prayer, but a platform plank in which the platform committee proposed the use of all federal power to end segregation, both de facto and de jure, everywhere in the United States. On the vote on the plank, the convention chairman Sam Rayburn of Texas, perhaps concerned that the debate had been more fierce and even more widespread than anticipated, called for a voice vote. He ruled that the affirmative had won and the "civil rights platform" was adopted. There were immediate demands for "Division" and "Roll Call." Rayburn ignored the calls and moved the convention agenda forward. Some southern states' delegations left the hall. A political revolt was in the making.

The immediate upshot resulted in the formation of one more "third party," the States' Rights Party, called by most the "Dixiecrats." Its Birmingham convention nominated Strom Thurmond, then South Carolina's governor (and a Clemson alumnus), for president, and Mississippi's Governor Fielding Wright for vice president. They attempted to focus the issue on the concept that the federal government had consistently violated the U.S. Constitution by ignoring the Tenth Amendment (the "reservation of power" or "states' rights" amendment). Whatever their spoken positions may have been, much of the national conversation focused on continued segregation, and while support (even tacit) was greater than the popular vote indicated, it did not appear as one of the major political issues for most white Americans. The States' Rights ticket gained only 2.41 percent of the popular national support confined to the southern states. People also cast a negligible number of votes for the ticket in Missouri, California, and North Dakota. Thurmond and Wright received a total of thirty-nine electoral votes. President Harry S. Truman received 57.1 percent of the Electoral College and won 49.55 percent of the popular vote.[13]

Antigovernment sentiment (if there was much) showed up in the South and in a few other places. National magazines noted the surprising outcropping of Confederate symbols such as the Confederate battle and naval flags (frequently erroneously called the "stars and bars"); the playing of "Dixie" by southern college and school bands also became commonplace. Clemson was not immune. One of the student clubs gave the cheerleaders a Confederate battle flag, which became an object for stealing by students from other schools. But this was neither the first nor the last time the battle flag presented a problem for Clemson students.

In the 1948 presidential election, 71.97 percent of South Carolina voters cast their ballots for the States' Rights ticket. Among the voters who did not, a portion was a large majority of African Americans able to vote. But there were some liberals and moderates, Democratic and Republican, who formed the basis of the new progressives. They held differing views on many points, but they knew that the transformation of South Carolina lay in education, which held the key to economic and social improvement. South Carolina remained an educational backwater. Its work force was in large part unskilled, while the efforts to upgrade the quality of the public school teaching facilities begun by Governor Byrnes were just beginning to work. The improvement of the ability and value of the teaching force depended on an improved teacher pay scale. To make matters worse, many of the schools, particularly above the primary grades, had neither been designed nor fitted for much vocational education beyond agriculture. To improve lives required will and money. But South Carolina, well blessed with resolve, never had hard money in abundance.

Public Education

One of the earliest states to create a public institution of higher education, South Carolina founded its first state college in 1801. Earlier states that had founded colleges included North Carolina (University of North Carolina) and Georgia (University of Georgia). In each case, the governing boards contained many churchmen from the denominations that required a "learned clergy," a group that represented a large portion of the highly educated males in the state.

As early as 1811, the S.C. General Assembly had passed a free school act based (roughly) on population. The schools were opened only to white children, received very poor funding, and carried the stigma of being known as "paupers' schools." While the evidence of basic literacy and the skills of addition and subtraction indicate a higher rate of attendance, by 1860 about half the whites had some formal education. African Americans had none. The state constitution provision of any education was the result of the Republican reconstruction government, but because the requirements were neither mandatory nor segregated, most white families shunned the schools. Further, to a great extent because of the agricultural base of the economy, school terms fit around local agricultural needs. Thus, school session periods varied.

With the inauguration of Rutherford B. Hayes as U.S. president and the end of Reconstruction (1877), those schools not already segregated quickly did so. South Carolina's government, faced with large debts, was fiscally conservative. And in keeping with a strong attitude of "individual responsibility," the leadership understood education to be the responsibility of the child's parents. By 1880, white literacy (at the most basic level) reached nearly 75 percent, while among African Americans literacy was 22 percent.

The Constitution of 1895, whose writing was dominated by Tillmanites, did not close the public school system. But the law imposed a segregated system of education, making "de jure" that which was "de facto." It did not, as might have been anticipated, close South Carolina College, the name of the University of South Carolina at the time. And it separated the South Carolina Agricultural and Mechanical Institute (established by the general assembly in 1872), then a state institute attached to Claflin University, which was built by the Methodist Episcopal Church (North), and raised the institute in status to the Colored Normal, Industrial, Agricultural and Mechanical College of South Carolina. But the school could not grant degrees.

Only in 1907 did the S.C. General Assembly provide state revenues for high schools. Twelve years later (1919), the state enacted its first compulsory school attendance law, requiring eight- to fourteen-year-olds to attend school four months a year. But the law was not well enforced. By 1927, 279 high schools for white students and ten for black students existed. After World War II, some progress was made to boost the "equal" part within the "separate but equal" concept, spelled out in the U.S. Supreme Court 1896 *Plessy v. Ferguson* ruling, which had been foreshadowed in the Morrill Land Grant Act of 1890.

South Carolina Higher Education

Further, South Carolina had not developed regional schools, normal schools, vocational schools, or two-year colleges as had many other southern states, such as Mississippi, Georgia, and North Carolina. Students who excelled in vocational studies had few options. After World War II, for example, the lack of opportunity for higher education in Horry County led local citizens to form the Coastal Educational Foundation. Rather than attempting to create a new school requiring a large investment in land and buildings and having to face immediately the question of SACS accreditation, the foundation received support from the extension division of the College of Charleston as a junior college extension. It opened on September 20, 1954. Two years later, citizens in the Florence area began a similar process. Their affiliation with the University of South Carolina led to the opening of the first USC regional campus in 1957. The success of that venture prompted USC to open regional campuses in Aiken and Beaufort. When the College of Charleston closed its extension office, the Coastal Carolina Junior College lost its accredited "parent" institution, so its officers sought a tie with Clemson. But because Edwards had just begun his presidency and faced the issues of that transition, Clemson did not respond positively. Led by President Donald Russell, USC accepted the overture and added the Horry venture to its growing "system."[14]

Ernest Frederick "Fritz" Hollings (1922–), lieutenant governor of South Carolina from 1955 to 1959 and the 106th governor of the state from 1959 to 1963. During the waning days of his governorship, Hollings, a dedicated advocate of public education improvements in South Carolina, helped to ensure that Harvey Gantt's entrance, and therefore Clemson's integration, would be peaceful. He later served as a U.S. senator for his home state from 1966 to 2005, the eighth-longest serving senator in U.S. history. Clemson University Photographs, CUL.SC.

However, these schools did not offer the much-needed "shorter term" vocational education. Governor Ernest F. "Fritz" Hollings, already a recognized advocate of improved education at all levels, began his term of office in 1959. He created a joint house and senate study committee led by John C. West. The committee recommended that South Carolina fund special schools created to work with the State Development Board and to provide training for workers for industries considering locating in the state. Coordination came from an advisory committee supported by the S.C. Department of Education. To help fund the new venture, legislators used existing federal laws [e.g., 1917 (30 42); 1932 Code Section 5283; 1942 Code Section 5 5394; 1952 Code Section 21–691]. The legislation created no new bureaucracies, gender qualifications, or statements about race. In many ways, this marks a major turning point—a turning away from "massive resistance" to segregation. Further, the lengthy Special Types of Schools of Instruction Act allowed, in Article 8, certain school boards to begin establishing junior colleges.[15]

The Clemson administration was wary of a junior college system. Although no "statements" were issued, Clemson preferred efforts to create "community colleges," a combination of two-year junior colleges offering the first two years of course work that, while never defined, had come to be thought of as "general education," with a wide array of technical and vocational courses tailored to the needs of the areas served by the schools. Broadly constituted local advisory boards kept themselves fully aware of their area's opportunities and needs and recommended the best local technical and vocational choices to a state advisory board. The latter board was to consider possible duplication of curricula and then recommend truly long-term attractive programs to the State Development Board. Recognizing the issue of local pride, the state board might restrict or forbid costly, unnecessary duplication.[16]

However, as important as the issue of expanded educational opportunity appeared for the future of all the people, most political, social, and religious leaders focused on the efforts to break or protect the state's legally instituted policy of racial segregation. Ever since 1938 in the Gaines case, the U.S. Supreme Court had ruled that whether a state provided higher educational opportunity in a racially unified or separated system, the opportunities had to be of precisely the same quality to all races. To James F. Byrnes, that goal became the clarion call and a major point of emphasis during his gubernatorial term.

In fact, the direction of the nation toward an "open society" was clearly marked in July 1946 when President Harry Truman created the President's Commission on Higher Education. When the commission finished its work in 1948, its report addressed a number of higher education issues. Its major recommendations were two. First, increased research at America's most capable higher education institutions was critical for the long-term health of the nation. But the focus did not always meet the regional characteristics, and vast duplication of efforts proved wasteful. Because the cost of new scientific and technological research likely exceeded the capacity of any single institution or state, the commission placed the obligation to fund such research on the federal government for the "general welfare" of the nation. That move was in the tradition of the Hatch Act of 1887. And when the issue was agricultural, the "land-grant delivery system," which took the regional characteristics of climate and soil into account, was appropriate. Further, the land-grant schools gathered an excellent collection of scientists and technologists. That was not necessarily true in the other fields that the federal government deemed necessary for the "general" (as opposed to "individual") welfare. Thus, according to the commission report, the federal government, as the "fount of funds," must select those institutions that were to be the research centers. That approach proved most effective in war efforts such as the famous "Manhattan project."

The second recommendation of the President's Commission on Higher Education was, to many, much different. The report stated that access to education (particularly higher education) must be available for all races and religions. Therefore, where federal money went, the Fourteenth Amendment followed. The Supreme Court's Gaines decision could play an extended but clear role in accomplishing this "open access" concept. Therefore, threatened were not only the states with the de jure racial, but also all the de facto exclusions in the nation based on religion or ethnicity.[17] While no effort was made immediately to require anything like that, it is not hard to recognize the longer influences in Clemson's and Edwards's disappointment with the rebuffing of the school's Atomic Energy Commission effort.

Within two years of the presidential commission's educational report, the U.S. Supreme Court ruled that a state that practiced de jure segregation must open to African American students programs that were hitherto available only to white students at both the graduate and undergraduate levels.[18] Louisiana complied. South Carolina chose to consider some duplication in areas potentially in demand by African Americans. The field that came to mind was law, and the state completed preparations to open a second law school at South Carolina State College.

To that point, the only legal change vis-à-vis racial separation was Truman's executive order racially desegregating the armed forces. The stunning unanimous 1954 decision by the U.S. Supreme Court in a case called *Brown v. Board of Education of Topeka* (Kansas) ruled that "separate was inherently unequal." While that ruling covered only the small group of school districts in the suit, it included one South Carolina district that provided public school bus transportation for whites but not for African Americans. Further, some legal experts argued that the ruling applied only to elementary and high schools because they were the schools in which attendance was mandatory. The court, however, clearly indicated the potential difficulties throughout the country in its phrase, "with all due deliberate speed."[19]

Even if the ruling applied only to primary and secondary public schools, the higher education state institutions in Maryland, West Virginia, Kentucky, and Missouri ended racial restrictions. After a Supreme Court implementation ruling in 1955, Oklahoma and Arkansas ended legal racial segregation in their state post-secondary institutions. The last major case on school segregation in higher education heard by the Supreme Court was *Frasier v. North Carolina*, when the court upheld the decision of the Fourth Circuit Court of Appeals that persons should be admitted to public colleges and universities on the basis of ability not race.[20]

In the Atlantic Coast Conference, only the state of South Carolina's public colleges remained completely segregated by law. In October 1957, North Carolina State's football team and band arrived for the scheduled game. The band, which included two African Americans, ate in Clemson's dining hall. A complaint was filed with South Carolina's attorney general, but the state took no official action. In the spring, President Poole wrote the North Carolina State president asking him to keep two African American varsity tennis players from traveling to Clemson for the match. NC State ignored the request.[21]

A more troubling issue for Clemson's trustees regarding segregation had occurred a year earlier, on July 17, 1956, when John L. Gainey, an African American veteran, inquired about admission to the college's textile chemistry program. Clemson sent him the usual admissions forms and information, but Gainey proceeded no further.[22] Later, the University of Georgia faced possible racial integration. Some public officials urged that the school be closed, and some students distributed a public declaration, "We will NOT welcome these intruders. We will NOT associate with them. We will NOT associate with white students who welcome them."[23]

A Request from Charleston

On July 19, 1959, Harvey Gantt, a rising senior at Burke High School in Charleston, wrote Clemson, requesting materials for applying to Clemson's School of Architecture. On July 21, Reginald Berry, the admissions director, promptly sent the materials and offered to answer any questions Gantt might have. But Gantt's application was not completed. Had it been and had Gantt been admitted, then under South Carolina law, enacted in 1956, which gave the State Budget and Control Board authority to withhold state funds from institutions that were integrated, funds could have been withheld from South Carolina State at the same time.[24]

Gantt was also interested in Tuskegee Institute, Iowa State College, and Howard University. Gantt remembered that his Burke High guidance counselor encouraged him to go to Iowa State (as opposed to Tuskegee or Howard) because "99 percent of the architects practicing in the United States were white, and he needed to be trained where they are."[25] So Gantt selected Iowa State and enrolled at Ames in the autumn of 1960. However, several things bothered him. Most of the other students were from the Midwest. Gantt planned to practice in the Southeast; thus, he would not meet his potential colleagues while in school. He also noted that a ranking of schools of architecture placed Clemson's program quite a bit above Iowa State's. The weather provided another concern for

Gantt. As the winter approached, the days grew shorter, the wind blew colder, and mounds of snow accumulated. Gantt remembers that as he trudged through deep snow in below-zero weather, he knew he wanted to return home. Back in his dormitory, he began the transfer process to Clemson. He recounted later that he shortly received his application back, along with a letter from Kenneth Vickery noting that South Carolina law provided that for African Americans who desired fields not available to them in South Carolina, the state would pay the out-of-state differential. Of course, this did not compensate for the lost opportunity or for the other possible limitations that weighed on Gantt's mind.[26]

In the meantime, Edwards had notified the trustees that the college had received two transfer applications, one from Gantt and a second from Cornelius Fludd, also an African American Charlestonian. Fludd's interest was electrical engineering, which South Carolina State did not offer.[27] Whatever the attitude the other trustees held, Senator Brown let a number of his state senatorial colleagues know about the applications. Among them was Senator Marion Gressette, chair of the Segregation Committee.[28]

Senator T. Allen Legare of Charleston also received notice of the applications. He informed Brown that Gantt and Fludd, while home from their colleges on Christmas vacation, had met with local leaders of the National Association for the Advancement of Colored People (NAACP). They also conferred with lawyer Matthew Perry, a graduate of the South Carolina State College Law School. They wanted advice about their applications. Legare also noted that both Gantt and Fludd had a "blemish." Both, when seniors at Burke High School, had been arrested along with twenty-seven other young people for trespassing when they "sat in" at a lunch counter. Found guilty, they paid their fines on April 1, 1960.[29]

Through Gantt's exchange of letters with Vickery, the latter set forth the transfer requirements. Gantt submitted an Iowa State transcript that indicated a "B-plus average" and also a statement of Gantt's eligibility to return to school. There must have been some delay in the report on Gantt's College Board examination scores because it did not arrive at Clemson until August 1961. Gantt had taken the test during his senior year in high school, some eighteen months earlier. Gantt scored 7.5 percent higher than the average of Clemson's freshman class of 1961. Gantt also notified Vickery when he would be available in June to complete whatever remained of the transfer process.[30]

Imagined and Real Impediments

Meanwhile, on July 11, 1961, the presidents of the five state institutions (the Citadel, Clemson, South Carolina State College, the University of South Carolina, and Winthrop) met informally in Columbia. Although they met regularly, this was not a scheduled business meeting; there are no surviving minutes. All that can be deduced is from subsequent correspondence among the participants. Because other schools had also received "other race" applications, that appears to have been their discussion topic. The consensus seems to have been that whatever else, each leader's primary duty was to his college or university, to its survival, and its reputation.[31]

At Clemson, several other issues existed regarding admissions: housing and standards. Because of its military heritage, and because of its small surrounding community (the not-yet-available 1960 census reported a population of 1,154 for the recently incorporated town), Clemson College aimed to be fully residential. The state had made that difficult for women students, but a solution for it was in hand, thanks to Edwards's diplomacy. For men, unless they lived with parents or nearby relatives, were older, or were married, living on campus was obligatory. Thus, the college needed no new accommodations for an African American male.

Also, academic entrance standards had increased. A long, slow trend in this regard reached back to Hartzog's administration (1897–1902). Nonetheless, the CMP report stated that admissions standards had to rise even more. Edwards had firmly supported the move because he perceived that improved academic standards meant the long-term economic development of the state and region. The process to increase admission standards, guided by Vickery, the registrar and the admissions director, at the dictate of the Board of Trustees, had the goal of admitting only students who showed a reasonable chance of graduation in the field selected. A great amount of data needed analyzing. Admissions and Registration collected reams of statistical and other information, such as entrance test scores, high school grade average, quality of the high school, applicants' high school rank, the field students wanted to study, and other measurable factors. Once Vickery developed the process, he gained a regional and then national reputation as a leader in this analytical race. As these data were compared to and correlated with graduation performance, the field became statistically more and more dependable.[32]

Clemson's attractiveness to prospective students grew wider. As demand for entering Clemson crept up, space became increasingly critical, whether measured in beds, laboratory tables, architecture drafting tables, or books in the library. Thus, room for entering students depended on sleeping and study space. Even that had its problems. The addition of females, so far as it concerned housing, represented a much greater problem than the addition of an African American male. But the addition of an upper-division architecture student, who required a twenty-four-hour-a-day dedicated drafting table, was much more difficult than a biology student, who shared laboratory space with a dozen other students.

As the summer of 1961 wore on, there remained a cadré of prospective students with incomplete applications. In most cases, the fault lay with the student's not having submitted something required. In Gantt's case, he had requested the College Board scores, but they were slow in arriving. Gantt's incomplete application also involved the required interview and inspection of his earlier drawings and designs. He had made a number of efforts to schedule the interview, which proved unsuccessful. Then Gantt, along with other applicants, received the letter saying that all places in the freshman and transfer groups were taken.

So, for Harvey Gantt, the trip was "back to Ames." At Iowa State, Gantt's experience (apart from the weather) was good. He had pleasant relationships with the other students; his teachers were attentive. But Gantt knew he would not be designing buildings for that environment; thus, many elements of design such as materials, window placements, heating and air handling, and insulation differed from those used for the South. He exchanged a bit more correspondence with Vickery, and on November 13, 1961, he wrote requesting that his earlier application be considered as a new and current application to Clemson. If that were not possible, he asked Vickery to send a new transfer application form. Clemson mailed the materials on November 22, 1961. By December 6, 1961, Gantt sent in his application and, over the winter and spring, such other materials as Vickery requested.

On June 13, 1962, Gantt, Fludd, and Matthew Perry arrived at Clemson to meet with Vickery; his supervisor, Walter T. Cox Jr., dean of students; and Clemson's legal advisor, William L. Watkins. Gantt asked that the meeting serve as his architectural interview. Vickery stated that Dean Harlan McClure of the Architecture School had to conduct the architectural interview and that Dean

Matthew James Perry (1921–), a product of the South Carolina State College School of Law, was Gantt's lead attorney in the eventually successful suit to integrate Clemson in 1963. Perry was named to the U.S. Military Court of Appeals in Washington, D.C., in 1976 and was later appointed to the U.S. District Court for the South Carolina District in 1979, the first African American to hold a federal judgeship in the state. Perry (*far left*) is pictured with Gantt and attorney Constance Baker Motley. Taken from *Greenville News*, January 28, 1963.

McClure was not available. Only Gantt and Fludd attended the meeting; Perry had remained off campus.[33]

On June 26, Gantt telegraphed Vickery: "Informed transcript of my grades forwarded to your office June 13 1962. Request my application to Clemson be favorably considered and I be given interview reply within 48 hours please."

Vickery responded on June 28: "Transcript received. Your application along with all others pending completion is being processed in manner we advised during your visit to this office on June 13. You will be advised date for interview as soon as other details to your application have been completed." Perry felt keenly that Vickery did not move with speed in all stages of Gantt's admissions process.[34]

Gantt's Lawsuit

The exact timing of the events during the next two weeks is unclear. McClure wrote a detailed letter dated July 2 that carefully laid out what would be needed for the interview. Further, he advised Gantt to make his portfolio as complete as possible. But on July 7, Perry, along with Willie T. Smith, an associate, filed suit in behalf of Gantt in the Western District of the South Carolina Division of the U.S. Fourth Circuit Court of Appeals in Greenville. The suit named as defendants the thirteen Clemson trustees (even though Robert L. Stoddard, a legislative trustee, had resigned when elected mayor of Spartanburg, and W. A. Barnette had died), Vickery, registrar, and J. T. Anderson, the superintendent of the S.C. Department of Education. Gantt's lawyers included Perry and his law partner, Lincoln C. Jenkins Jr.; lawyers Donald James Sampson and Willie T. Smith Jr. of Greenville; and Jack Greenberg and Constance Baker Motley of New York, New York. Greenberg and Motley belonged to the NAACP Legal Defense Fund.[35] The summons, complaint, and motion asked for a preliminary injunction requiring the college to admit Harvey Gantt. On the instructions of Clemson's Development Vice President Frank Jervey, Joe Sherman, director of alumni affairs and public relations, notified the Associated Press and the United Press International news bureaus of the lawsuit.[36]

By Monday, July 9, 1962, the *Greenville Piedmont* headlined, "Negro Youth Files Suit For Clemson Admission" and reported that the legal action "marked the initial suit brought in South Carolina for admission on a college level to a hitherto-segregated institution."[37] The next day, the *Charlotte Observer* pointed out that "a similar suit was brought in an attempt to integrate the University of South Carolina Law School or require the state to provide a law school for Negro students. The state adopted the latter course, setting up a law school at State College for Negroes in Orangeburg."[38]

The Clemson news office also noted that the court papers had been delivered to South Carolina's Attorney General Daniel McLeod. But Watkins and Edgar Brown had kept McLeod fully informed about the lawsuit and every other controversial issue that had occurred. While South Carolina's government had forestalled integration by opening a second law school in 1947, the demand for places in law far exceeded that in architecture. To business-minded folk, it would have been difficult, no matter how "great the issue," to justify such an expense for architecture.

William Watkins, a University of Virginia Law School graduate and an excellent lawyer, had worked with Clemson's leadership to bring the Hartwell Lake issue to a satisfactory conclusion, including helping the college acquire replacement land. Noted for his gentility, Watkins never failed to treat every witness with respect, every opposing counsel with courtesy, and every judge with good manners. Consequently, he provided a contrast to many in his profession who, on occasion, mounted strident postures that only attracted attention. Perry later described Watkins as "a fine gentleman. He and I had a very fine relationship."[39]

Watkins built his case on two points. First, South Carolina law did not forbid racial integration of public colleges and universities. Second, Gantt had not completed his application; therefore, it had neither been considered nor denied. The law, however, was fraught with potentially devastating penalties for any white state higher education institution that enrolled an African American and for South Carolina's only public African American college. Were the S.C. Budget and Control Board to decide so, the two schools could lose all state funding.[40] Including South Carolina State in the severe penalty was a design of the Gressette committee and legislature to discourage African Americans from applying to the currently all-white schools.

Rumors surfaced in South Carolina (and probably elsewhere) that the NAACP had persuaded Gantt to apply to Clemson. The presence of Greenberg and Motley on Gantt's legal team added weight to the rumor, although nothing improper existed if that had been the case. Perry remembered that he had met Gantt in the spring of Gantt's senior year at Burke High School. Gantt had been arrested for taking part in a "sit in" at a lunch counter in downtown Charleston. Perry recalled, "Gantt came up to me, and he said, 'Hello! My name is Harvey Gantt. I'm going to be an architect. I want to go to school at what I understand is one of the finest schools of architecture in the country… Clemson College. But I understand there might be a problem; and they tell me that I might not qualify because of the color of my skin.'" Gantt then asked Perry if he would help him get admitted should Clemson deny his application. From this exchange, one can infer that Gantt sought out Perry because he wanted to study architecture at Clemson; he was not recruited to apply by anyone.[41]

The lawsuit contained eight pages. Watkins responded correctly for Clemson that Gantt had not completed his application. But Perry pointed out that Gantt had attempted "to comply variously with the requirements of the registration office, which invariably informed [Gantt and Fludd] that your applications are incomplete in that you did not do thus and such...."[42] Each defendant had reviewed the Clemson response written by Watkins while at a conference in McLeod's office. McLeod, Gressette, and lawyer David Robinson, who counseled the legislature's segregation committee, also attended. According to Watkins's draft of Clemson's response, the school could legally admit Gantt if the completed application warranted it. Further, Watkins wrote that Clemson did not agree that the state's legislation imposing penalties for admission of an African American was constitutional. Every defendant read it and agreed to it. Gressette initially objected but, after consulting with Robinson, withdrew his position.

What, then, did Clemson hope to achieve? Watkins suggested, "Time." In Alabama and Georgia, efforts to admit African Americans to public "no Negro" institutions had encountered raucous and even violent reactions. Clemson's leadership, particularly President Edwards and Walter T. Cox, dean of students, knew the college needed time to prepare for the entrance of the first African American into a hitherto "no Negro" South Carolina public college since Reconstruction.[43] During the football season, a visiting conference team fielded an African American player, who, when he came onto the field, was heckled and booed. Edwards left his seat at the top of the stadium, made his way to the sidelines, and using the cheerleaders' microphone told the crowd, students and others, to behave in a polite and civil manner. The crowd went silent and obeyed.[44] While Edwards and Cox felt sure student leadership would not be the locus of trouble in the admission of Gantt to Clemson, they could not be certain of other groups.

Clemson submitted its response on July 30, 1962, and Federal Judge C. C. Wyche set the date of August 22 to hear both sides on Gantt's request for relief and admission to Clemson that autumn term. Charles Wickenberg, the Columbia-based reporter for the *Charlotte Observer,* wrote that both sides thought it "the strongest integration case" filed in South Carolina since the 1954 *Brown v. Topeka* ruling.[45]

After hearing both sides, Wyche, on September 6, 1962, stated that no evidence existed that Clemson had either created or used the "portfolio-interview" entrance requirement for architecture simply to bar African Americans. He based this on an examination of all applications for admission to Clemson for 1961–1962. Therefore, he did not find for Gantt in the case.[46] Perry immediately petitioned to the Fourth Circuit Court of Appeals. The chief judge designated a three-magistrate panel to hear the appeal: Simon Sobeloff of Baltimore, Maryland (himself the chief justice), retired Judge Morris Soper, also of Baltimore, and Clement F. Haynsworth Jr. of Greenville. The hearing lasted two days, September 25 and October 4, at which time the justices withheld their decision, stating "assurance having been given by counsel for the college that the case can be conveniently heard on the merits in the District Court at an early date" and requiring that the case be heard no later than the first term date in January so that the final decision came in time for spring semester.[47]

Respite for Preparation

Clemson had gained the valuable preparation time Edwards and his advisors sensed they needed. Edwards dispatched Joe Sherman to visit campuses that had experienced court-ordered integration, both those that occurred quietly and others that were contentious. Sherman was a direct man, not given to unnecessary words or flourishes. He submitted a straightforward report. In each instance of violence at schools, blame could be laid at many feet.

He pointed toward five groups. First, state political figures, mainly elected, usually inserted themselves into the action and overrode the school's officials. The goals of the two were not always similar. Second, communication between those in institutional control (whether the school, civil, or police authorities) and the plaintiff and her or his party (legal counsel, family, national or local organizations, friends, etc.) had broken down. Third, the emotions of students, given their ages and backgrounds, could be volatile. Fourth, the press's goal seemed more often to get photo shots, "creative" video footage, or a special article angle or activity rather than functioning as good witnesses for a wider public. And fifth, frequently state and regional "outsiders" initiated incidents.[48]

Sherman's five "findings" guided the actions of Clemson's leaders throughout the autumn of 1962. Edwards, in a way so characteristic of his leadership style, had strong and close relationships with many of the state's leaders. In the business world, his most influential connections existed through Clemson's own Board of Trustees, with men like Jim Self in the textile industry, Charles Daniel in construction, and Bob Cooper in power. To them could be added Edwards's own personal relations with Roger Milliken, whose involvement in agriculture, industry, and textile and chemical research was worldwide, or John Cauthen, the acknowledged leader of the state's textile manufacturers.[49] Edwards's ties to state government were no less formidable, and again existed in part through the board. As chair of the state Senate Finance Committee, Edgar Brown—an old new-dealer and southern progressive, who, like most southern politicians, preferred integration's "cup not to have come"—had close ties to the influential "Barnwell Ring" of South Carolina politicians, which included Solomon Blatt and Winchester Smith of Williston. Some charged that this small coterie ran the state government. Edwards's economic and educational alliance with Governor "Fritz" Hollings, who held a strong place among southern moderates, and his successor apparent, Donald Russell, strengthened the ties. The relationship between Edwards and Russell, while Russell served as president of USC, had been marked by amity and cooperation.

On the issue of communications, all of Clemson's leadership had kept such lines wide open. Watkins, although not pleased at dealing with the NAACP legal team, treated Motley and Greenberg with courtesy. With Perry, however, the relationship developed into one of mutual and genuine respect. Watkins and Edwards both admired Perry's honesty and manners. All three collaborated on plans that helped keep peace and calmness. Communications also meant the college's leadership maintain openness toward the press. Logically, this role fell to Sherman, who handled it brilliantly. This proved effective as the day of change came closer. Further, Sherman had a close working relationship with Jim Strom, the chief of the State Law Enforcement Division, and Silas Pearman, head of the State Highway Commission. Together, they worked to develop a precise plan for the day of change. Later, the media received the final timetable, thus removing the necessity of its frenetic scouting for stories.

Walter Cox received the dual task of working with students and alumni. Cox was an extraordinary person who rarely forgot anyone or anything. More so, he remembered the nuances of familial relationships stretching back through the years. His unflinching loyalty to Clemson fell second only to his love of his family, and in 1962 his oldest son was an accomplished Clemson junior and member of the Tiger football team. Dean Cox, as almost everyone knew him, and his assistant, George Coakley, visited with as many student groups, clubs, and fraternities as possible. Even when met by angry, hostile, or bitter students, their message touched many. In a meeting with one of the YMCA subdivisions, an out-of-state student with no family ties to Clemson commented to Coakley, "I don't like this, I think it wrong, but I would never do anything to hurt the honor and integrity of Clemson."[50]

Several years earlier, in 1959, one of *The Tiger* columnists had written,

> May we hope and pray, too, for amity between the races as we successfully ride out the storm. May demagoguery and agitation from without be damned. May the ominous connotations of the terms "segregation" and "discrimination" be forgotten and the beauty of these words returned.
>
> May the United States of America remain one nation indivisible....Thus was our legacy. Certainly we owe this to posterity.[51]

Those words expressed the thoughts of a patient, moderate young man who saw the race issue from a historical perspective and based on his nation.

Two years later, in September 1961, as the possibility of integration "by-passed" Clemson, another *Tiger* columnist, Zalin "Zip" Grant, had written, "Can South Carolina, along with Mississippi and Alabama, continue to sashay merrily on its way down a path which is contrary to the Constitution?" Grant continued by setting before his readers two men as examples of racial extremism. One was an African American whose rhetoric advocating violence toward whites led to his

Zalin P. "Zip" Grant from Cheraw was a pre-law student and editorial columnist for *The Tiger* during the 1963 integration process. Taken from the 1963 edition of the Clemson College annual, *Taps*.

removal from the NAACP; the other, a white calling for nothing short of racial warfare. Grant ended by asking Clemson students to choose as to whether the students preferred one of those paths or integration.[52] As Clemson opened in September 1962, Grant again wrote an editorial column that set out President Edwards's recent talk to some 200 student leaders in which Edwards "unfolded step by step the fight to integrate Clemson and declared strongly that he would keep the student body informed about the issue."[53]

Sorrow in Mississippi

But the eyes of South Carolinians were not fixed on Clemson. Rather, they, black or white, segregationist or integrationist (or somewhere in between), watched the situation unfolding in Mississippi. Just a week before Grant's editorial in *The Tiger* and in response to a judicial stay on the admission of James Meredith to the University of Mississippi (Ole Miss), Supreme Court Justice Hugo Black, an Alabaman, set aside the stay and ordered that Meredith be admitted. Three days later, on September 13, 1962, Mississippi Governor Ross Barnett read a message on the radio and television to his fellow citizens:

> In the absence of constitutional authority and without legislative action, an ambitious federal government, employing naked and arbitrary power, has decided to deny us the right of self-determination in the conduct of the affairs of our sovereign state.... The Kennedy Administration is lending the power of the federal government to the ruthless demands of these agitators.... The day of expediency is past. We must either submit to the unlawful dictates of the federal government or tell them no.[54]

Three days passed, and on September 16, 1962, the closest major southern newspaper to Oxford, Mississippi, the *Commercial Appeal* of Memphis, Tennessee, responded:

The issue arouses the emotions of the people of both sides. It has disrupted the processes of education in many localities. We can sympathize with the strong feelings of many Mississippians in this crisis. But we hope that in this confrontation they will let reason and temperance prevail, that they will place law and order above the frustrated anger which can lead to violence....[55]

Shortly thereafter, the Mississippi Board of Trustees of State Institutions of Higher Education ceded to Governor Barnett full power as registrar. By the morning of September 27, the day Meredith expected to enroll at Ole Miss in Oxford, Barnett proposed to Robert Kennedy, President John F. Kennedy's brother and U.S. attorney general, that if the U.S. marshals accompanying Meredith drew weapons, Barnett would back away, thus allowing the governor to "save face." Kennedy agreed to the public sham. However, as the day progressed, the crowds milling around the university campus convinced the governor he should negate the agreement. On September 30, South Carolina senior senator and Clemson alumnus Strom Thurmond wired the president, urging him not to use troops, calling the action "unconstitutional, abominable and highly dangerous."[56]

By 4:30 p.m., U.S. marshals were in place on the university campus, and at 6:30 p.m. Meredith arrived. Some in the large crowd threw rocks, bricks, bottles, and lead pipes, hitting the federal marshals. In less than fifteen minutes, President Kennedy broadcast by television to the nation, "Mr. James Meredith is now in residence on the campus of the University of Mississippi. This has been accomplished thus far without the use of National Guard or other troops...."[57] But at almost the same moment, a foreign journalist was killed. By 10:00 p.m., the violent crowd had wounded two state troopers and a U.S. marshal. Slightly after 2:00 a.m. on October 1, units of the U.S. Army arrived on the Ole Miss campus and restored a semblance of order. No positive evidence places Ole Miss students among the fighters, although hostile behavior against Meredith continued for a good while longer.[58]

Clemson's Preparations

Certainly, the elements of the problems Joe Sherman had identified seemed present at Oxford. But the resolve of Edwards, the actions of Clemson's board, and all the planning for Clemson's integration would prove effective. However, before that happened, Edwards and Governor Hollings showed themselves more than equal to the task that faced South Carolina.

Edwards continued what he had already done so well—communicating with the students. He met regularly with student leaders who played a very important role in the Clemson system of communications. In addition, he conferred often with *The Tiger* staff. On October 19, Edwards talked with Dave Gumula, the paper's chief editor for 1962–1963. The resulting published article made no reference to cases, issues, or violence on any other campuses. Instead, it set out the chronology of Gantt's case and quoted Edwards explaining from his perspective why Clemson had taken its actions in the matter. Much of the article dealt with the dates of the arrival of Gantt's transcript from Iowa State, or Architecture Dean McClure's request to see Gantt's portfolio, and how that request and the filing of Gantt's suit by Matthew Perry, his legal counsel, had crossed each other. Edwards also stated that when Gantt wrote McClure and offered to present his portfolio, on the advice of Watkins, Clemson "took the position, through its attorney, that since the college's administrative procedures were under attack, it would not be proper to do anything further on this matter until the case had been disposed in the courts."[59] Such regular, open communications helped keep troublesome rumors to a minimum.

But *The Tiger* also took a risky step in the same issue. The staff interviewed students, asking them, "How do you feel about the admission of Harvey Gantt to Clemson?" Some students refused to answer. The paper printed a selection of responses. They ranged from "Being from the Deep South, I have associated with 'niggers' all my life. I cannot say that I hate them but…" to "I see no reason why Harvey Gantt should not be accepted into Clemson if, as an individual, he is qualified for admission." The staff summarized, "The general feeling seemed to be that students personally did not like the idea but that they, as individuals, would do nothing which would downgrade the high reputation of Clemson College or impede his admission." The main editorial concluded, "The tragedy that was Mississippi must not become the tragedy that is Clemson. We, as students, don't want it; the faculty doesn't want it; and we hope, no sane person that has considered the matter rationally would want it."[60]

The attention of Clemson leaders continued to focus on Sherman's report. His fourth point, concerning the press, fell to him to solve. He surmised that in every case in which problems existed at other schools, the latter kept the press wondering about the time of the arrival of the plaintiff to register. Thus, the press, following local radio and television, chased every rumor up and down the highways and around the campus, eventually producing widespread confusion. Sherman drafted a plan that provided the press with an accurate and specific, minute-by-minute schedule. In this, he worked with college Police Chief Jack Weeden, whose small forces received help from officers of the Highway Patrol. With those logistics cared for, Sherman and Weeden, armed with enlarged road maps and detailed campus maps, went to Columbia to consult with Chief Strom and Director Pearman and with Attorney General McLeod on issues of law and campus access. The approval (or in some correspondence, "understanding") was necessary if Sherman's plan were to succeed fully.

With those approvals, or understandings, in hand, Sherman set up a meeting with Edwards, the four principal college officers, and Watkins to consider the plan. The first principle was that on the day slated for Gantt to register, the college would close the campus to all people except students, faculty, staff, and others issued written permission by President Edwards. This was presented with the authorization of the attorney general, and the advisors assembled recommended that enforcement for students, faculty, and staff would be through the use of identity cards. Students had used such cards since the autumn of 1954, first for meals, then for borrowing books from the library, and later for campus events. Jim Burns, who served as the campus photographer, set up a studio and began photographing the staff and faculty. The photos were used to create identity cards for everyone from the trustees through the president to the farm workers and to the professors.

The most likely contentious issue was restriction on the press. Sherman's plan granted limited access to a number of regional media. He organized the national press by corps (AP, Reuters, etc.) and medium (print, broadcast, etc.) and allowed each to dispatch a small team, with special certification, to a restricted campus area. The area included the entrance from the Old Greenville Highway (now Walter T. Cox Boulevard) to Tillman Hall and access to the latter's first floor, the location of the Office of Admissions and Registration. The rest of the campus, at least for the days immediately before and after the expected arrival of Gantt, was open only to people with college ID cards. In addition, the college, which maintained (and still does) its own police, fire, and power, stockpiled extra supplies for most eventualities. Sherman's staff notified all groups involved of the decisions and restrictions. Rental space for telephone and Teletype, and for hotel bedrooms, was available by reservation and advanced payment. After a great deal of questioning and other discussion among his advisors, Edwards traveled to Columbia to present the plan to Governor Hollings, the constitutional officers, and the governor's staff. Then the trustees approved the plan.[61]

The Day Draws Nigh

During November 19–21, 1962, the Federal Court for South Carolina (Western Division) reheard the case "on its merits." Judge Wyche presided over all hearings. At Perry's request, Wyche took special note of "certain statutes and Acts of the State of South Carolina." Wyche ruled on December 21 that there was no fault or racial bias on the part of Clemson, its trustees, or the registrar.[62] Immediately, Gantt's counsel appealed the decision back to the Fourth Circuit Court of Appeals in Richmond.

On the Clemson campus, communications remained open. *The Tiger* published, with editorial comments and historical analogies, a selection of the mail from the public (including alumni). A letter from a Charleston-based group titled "Concerned Clemson Alumni," mailed to some individual students, labeled the integration effort part of a Communist ploy to "weaken our country's resistance." In the November 9 edition, Zip Grant delighted in taking the letter apart to dispute its logic. On December 14, Frank L. Gentry, the paper's managing editor, published an editorial that reduced the issue for the students to two questions. First, regardless of what you think about segregation or integration, when integration comes, how will you, the individual, react? Will it be with peace or with violence? Regardless of how you feel about segregation or integration, if you, the student, "believe in constitutional government," you must choose peace, wrote Gentry. Second, recognizing that each person has the constitutional right to advocate either position, does that presume to give each or any of us the right "that would endanger the lives and principles of others?" An answer leading to physical resistance or verbal abuse could itself only lead to "killing." And a riot would be to "kill our way of life, kill the school as a university, kill the value of each Clemson diploma, and kill the growth and progressive spirit of this state, and above all, it would kill our self-respect."[63]

The Fourth Circuit Court of Appeals met on January 9, 1963, to hear Gantt's case. In its ruling issued on January 16, the three justices (Sobeloff, Soper, and Haynsworth) dismissed the position that South Carolina did not prohibit the integration of the races but merely discouraged it with a caustic remark that the argument was "a novel one in legal literature, and we must hold it unacceptable." With this statement, the court destroyed the foundation of the state Segregation Committee's legal maneuvering. Further, the court turned its eye on Clemson's negative response to Gantt's post-suit request for a review of his portfolio. It ruled that here the fault was procedural, in that the college should have accepted the portfolio and examined it in the same way that it had all others since the school had instituted such a review in 1961. The court held that "officials of a college ought to be allowed to pass upon applications free of the coercive effect of a pending action against them...." And in conclusion, the court ordered "Gantt's admission to Clemson College, beginning with the opening of the next semester."[64]

Edwards had a statement ready for the media, prepared and taped for release the next day. He stated that Clemson would appeal the decision to the U.S. Supreme Court. The speed with which the statement was ready suggests the college, its attorney, and the state government had already concluded that such a ruling was imminent, but that Clemson and the state government must, for political reasons, follow the path through to its conclusion. However, the message contained a deep and sincere request. The Clemson students were taking final semester examinations, and faculty were immersed in making judgments that affected the 4,000 students. After all, this was "Clemson's first mission—that of education." Clemson's officers wanted no disruption or disturbance.[65]

The appeal to the U.S. Supreme Court would have delayed enforcement of the court order, but would not overturn it. When presented to Chief Justice Earl Warren by his clerk, Warren wrote, "Denied. E.W." While at least one scholar concluded, "Clemson had lost," that view referred to the suit brought against

Clemson, its trustees, Vickery, and the state superintendent of education.[66] What that did not take into account, however, was that just as Thomas G. Clemson's will had not mentioned gender, it also did not specify race; the justices of the Fourth Circuit Court of Appeals in fact rejected the argument that a difference in substance existed between the state's concept of "deny" and "discourage."

Regarding the court's decision, Governor Hollings addressed the legislature in his last speech to it as governor. That day, he reminded the legislators that South Carolina had a tradition of respect for the law, and he told them and their constituents, "We are running out of courts, we are running out of appeals and time." The speech, coupled with public statements from state Senator Edgar Brown, from South Carolina's revered statesman James Byrnes, and from Marion Gressette defused almost all lingering potential for violence. To add to the weight of opinion, the bishops, chairmen, moderators, and secretaries of eight of the larger religious denominations issued a joint statement calling for all to follow the "love of God and neighbor to avoid every form of violence and hatred in our relations among ourselves and to use peaceable means to reach conclusions founded on justice and order...."[67]

As the day for Gantt's arrival on campus to register drew nearer, local physicians offered their services to President Edwards. Given the small population of the little town of Clemson, several addressed him in their correspondence as "Dear Bob." Edwards's response, also on a first-name basis, thanked each for the offer but closed, "At the present time I do not believe there will be any need for such steps."[68] The day Gantt was scheduled to enroll at Clemson College now arrived.

Integration with Dignity

The Clemson College campus awoke early on the morning of January 28, 1963. Campus police and deputized officers, all in distinctive garbs, patrolled the perimeter of the campus as they had since noon the day before. And each Clemson student received a letter early that morning from Dean Cox in which he stated, "The faculty and administration of Clemson College have confidence in the intelligence and integrity of our students and expect them to exercise good judgment." Cox reminded the students "to carry their identification cards at all times. Student government officers, student hall supervisors and members of the college faculty and staff have the authority to ask you to exhibit it." The letter addressed the possibility of disorder and instructed the students that should trouble begin, for all to stay inside, or if outside, to return immediately to the student's residence hall. He further cautioned them not to "let idle curiosity allow you to become involved in a situation in which you have no connection or responsibility."[69]

Slightly under three hours' driving time away from Clemson, Matthew Perry met in Columbia, first with the attorney general for McLeod's briefing, and then

Harvey Bernard Gantt (1943–), shown here exiting the Registrar's Office on the day Clemson integrated, became Clemson's first African American student on January 28, 1963. He went on to receive a master's degree in city planning from the Massachusetts Institute of Technology. The Charleston native is a partner in the architectural and city planning firm Gantt/Huberman Architects and served two terms as the first African American mayor of Charlotte, N.C. Clemson University Photographs, CUL.SC.

Harvey Gantt meeting with his coordinating dean, Harlan Ewart McClure, FAIA (1916–2001) of the School of Architecture. McClure was head of the Department of Architecture from 1955 to 1957 and became the first dean of the newly created School of Architecture in 1958. A proponent of international architecture and its introduction into South Carolina, he helped create Clemson's Charles E. Daniel Center for Building Research and Urban Study in Genoa, Italy, in 1972 and helped the school's architecture program climb to national prominence. McClure retired as dean emeritus of the College of Architecture in 1985. Clemson University Photographs, CUL.SC.

with SLED Chief Strom for his advice. With Perry were Harvey Gantt, his father, Christopher Gantt, and their minister. They then went to the Governor's Office. There Perry received the Clemson plan for the day. He noted the careful details, including a single car escort one-half mile ahead, a single car rear guard one-half mile behind, and a SLED helicopter monitoring from the air. As the four drove westward toward Clemson, they could see their escort-guardians, and along the roads, units of county law officers watched. Every overpass across the highway had an armed small detachment of state officials. Just this side of Greenville, an old friend of Perry's caused Perry to stop his car. The man wanted to wish Gantt well on his history-making ride. Before almost any words were exchanged, air surveillance notified the rear guard, which raced forward, and the lead, which swung sideways to block the highway. With external speaker blaring, the rear car quickly arrived within hearing distance and kept repeating, "Mr. Perry, Mr. Perry! Keep moving, keep moving!" Perry pulled away, reached Greenville, and dropped Gantt's father and the cleric at the arranged spot. Perry and Gantt then were off again. But it suddenly dawned on Gantt that his suitcase was in the car trunk. His checkbook, needed to pay his tuition, was in the suitcase, and he and Perry and suitcase would part company once they reached Clemson. They made another stop to retrieve the checkbook, and again the police urged them to "Keep moving." The towns rolled by—Easley, Liberty, Norris, and Central—as they moved closer to the campus. Along the road, the crowd thickened, and reporters seemed to be everywhere. Then they entered the long tree-lined way past President Edwards's home, past the Library (Sikes), and up to the statue of Thomas Green Clemson. Perry stopped the car, Gantt got out, a police guide slipped into Gantt's seat, and Perry drove on to Gantt's dormitory. A student took the belongings and moved toward the dormitory. Perry and the guide drove off campus to await the notice that all was well.[70]

With several college policemen walking beside him, Gantt entered Tillman Hall (the irony was not overlooked) and went to the Registrar's Office, where he completed the necessary forms and wrote a check for his tuition, room, and board. Then, he and his guides walked out of the old brick building and across campus to the stylistically cool, clean architecture complex. Dean Harlan McClure greeted Gantt, and they sat to evaluate his transcript from Iowa State. Usually, a transfer student's advisor undertook this task, but Edwards, Academic Vice President Jack Kenny Williams, and McClure wanted no mistakes. When the evaluation process was complete, Gantt and his escort crossed campus to his room in Johnstone Hall, where he would room alone, with a police agent in the room next to him.[71]

Did the day, the semester, or the other sessions pass without incident? Of course not. Walter Cox told of a student who was marching to and fro on the quadrangle of Gantt's dormitory, carrying a large Confederate battle flag. Cox asked him to his office and reasoned with him. The student retorted that he was within his First Amendment rights. Cox agreed but reminded him of Clemson's honor, which he must protect. The student relented, put away the banner, and went to his dormitory. During the winter months, a mimeographed circular called "Rebel Underground" appeared on campus. An almost identical tract had appeared at Ole Miss.

Another reported incident was in the college dining hall, which could serve 2,300 at one sitting. Early in Gantt's first semester, he went to meals accompanied by his guard. The first few visits were greeted with silence. However, once, when without the escort, Gantt was waiting in the cafeteria line to be served, two students seated at a table close to the line began making mean and insulting comments in "stage whispers." After a few moments, Gantt asked the student behind him to hold his place in line. The student agreed; Gantt walked over to the commentators' table. With a pleasant countenance on his face, Gantt told the two that they had better say nice things about him because if they didn't, when he got his meal, he would return, sit down, and eat his lunch with them. Perry, upon hearing of this later, said, "Just like Gantt!"[72]

And the press? To the greatest extent they also obeyed Clemson's plans. On one occasion, however, men with press equipment and credentials approached several students and asked them to participate in interviews at Dan's Café, the most popular off-campus student "hangout." The men attempted to set up "informal man on the street" interviews, something Dean Cox had urged the students not to do and something Sherman had also asked the press to avoid. One student's reaction was a simple, "No!" A second retorted, "Ask a federal marshal!" There were none; the federal offer of such help had been rejected by the governor. A third lectured the newsmen on honor and integrity. One of Clemson's student leaders, aided by a resident hall supervisor, removed a news reporter/photographer from Gantt's dormitory ledge and turned him over to the police, who revoked his credentials and expelled him from campus.[73]

Slowly, Gantt ceased being an issue. Architecture consumed him, just as calculus, Shakespeare, and thermodynamics diverted others. Finally, the semester ended. Of course, the national press was amazed! Early on *The New York Times* printed an editorial (January 31, 1963) that began by pointing out that Gantt was not wanted at Clemson and that the school's lawyers were petitioning the Supreme Court for relief. Nonetheless,

> Clemson and its sponsors and the authorities of South Carolina faced up to the issue honorably....On the decisive day the student body itself behaved admirably. Resentment and reluctance there may have been; but there was none of the violence, none of the open flaunting of racial hatred, none of the rowdyism wearing the mask of white supremacy that have characterized events of this land elsewhere. Instead, there was an encouraging display of order and restraint.... What a contrast to Mississippi.[74]

And the editorial was titled "Bravo, Clemson."

Harvey Gantt receives his diploma during the 1965 spring commencement from President R. C. Edwards, the man who personally assured the young architect two years earlier, "You're a Clemson student now, and I promise that you will be treated just like any other student." Clemson University Photographs, CUL.SC.

Everyone asked, "Who was the hero in this? Who made it happen?" And everyone had or has her or his own answer. In the courts, the heroes were clearly William Watkins, with his abundant courtesy, and Matthew Perry, with his towering intelligence. In South Carolina, credit goes to the Clemson trustees, the business and manufacturing executives, governors Hollings and Russell, and the attorney general and those in his command. On Clemson's campus, peaceful integration would not have occurred without the efforts of President Edwards, Dean Cox, the hundreds of faculty and staff who encouraged restraint and courtesy, and without fail, *The Tiger* staff: Dave Gumula, Zip Grant, Frank Gentry, and Cecil Huey, whose editorials spoke of honesty, true courage, and integrity, virtues frequently in short supply in emergencies. And there's the subject—Harvey Gantt, a young man who early exhibited a quiet righteousness, who through a three-year travail showed remarkable patience and good humor. And who was the victor? All of the above, but equal to them all, Clemson College. More than any other, that year set Clemson apart.

What was next for both Gantt and Clemson? In the autumn of 1963, Clemson enrolled a new student in mathematics, a young lady named Lucinda Brawley, the first African American female. She and Harvey began to see each other—at the football and basketball games of 1963 and 1964 and the school dances—and they fell in love. At the end of spring 1965, in Clemson's Outdoor Theater, Gantt strode across the stage and clasped President Edwards's hand, as a grinning Edwards welcomed Gantt into the "Clemson family." Brawley and Gantt married, and Gantt enrolled at MIT for the master's in city planning degree.

As beneficial as the year opened for South Carolina, the comity that could have developed was still slow in coming. Two days after Gantt came to Clemson, the S.C. House Education Committee introduced a state tuition grants bill that would provide indirect support to private schools. *The Tiger* editorial cartoonist depicted it as blatant robbery of an already impoverished program (HR 1155). One of *The Tiger* staff, Jerry Gainey, a junior from Hartsville who was active in the Baptist Student Union and served as assistant chaplain in the YMCA, was also an active member of the S.C. Student Council on Human Relations. With other Clemson students, including Stephen Ackerman from St. George and Emmitt Bufkin from Port Royal,[75] Gainey circulated a petition among Clemson students opposing the tuition grants bill. When he presented the petition with 180 signatures to the House Education Committee, a committee member asked if he supported integration. Gainey answered, "Yes, I do believe in integration."[76] In addition, the state conference of the American Association of University Professors and the Spartanburg PTA opposed the idea as injurious to the general public; nonetheless, the house passed the amended bill 78–24 on to the state senate on May 14, 1963. The bill also passed the senate fifteen days later, with house reconciliation on June 5, 1963. After final approval, the state Board of Education issued guidelines for this new program. In Clemson's case, the state of South Carolina on May 15, 1963, filed a petition to overturn the "class-action status" of the Gantt case. The U.S. Supreme Court denied the petition on October 14, 1963. In the meantime, other South Carolina racial segregation statutes, ordinances, and regulations continued to fall, although public vestiges would remain into the 1970s.[77]

As Attorney General McLeod had promised, regardless of the outcome, the state of South Carolina reimbursed the expenses that Clemson incurred in the admission of Gantt. The three greatest expenses were (in order of magnitude descending) the S.C. Highway Patrol, the law firm of Watkins, Vandiver, Freeman and Kirvin, and the State Law Enforcement Division. And the bill totaled $32,697.21. Some (not many) public officials complained, and newspapers carried a few complaints. But the state paid the bill. *The Saturday Evening Post*, in an article entitled "Integration with Dignity," written by editor George McMillan, hailed the entire process a "conspiracy for peace."[78]

A New Status and a New Name

There was more on Clemson's agenda—Clemson's name, "The Clemson Agricultural College of South Carolina." Although the public name derived from the Clemson will and the state in the Act of Acceptance, customary and institutional use had shifted the style of the name frequently. The Main Building carried the words "Clemson College."—the period indicating that the style was an abbreviation. On occasion, the name used was "Clemson College, the Agricultural and

Mechanical College" or "Clemson A + M." From the moment Edwards became permanent president, he undertook a campaign to change Clemson's name. Immediately, and with trustee consent, he had the school use the name most appropriate to the college's status—"Clemson College." Stationery, publications, the school ring, all the marks carried that name. But in the minds of most people in the "higher education business" in the United States, the title "college" indicated institutions that granted only bachelor's degrees or bachelor's and master's degrees. The title "university" belonged to institutions in which faculty carried on original research and directed "research doctoral students," whose accomplishments were rewarded with the doctorate of philosophy. Nowhere was such an idea codified. There were exceptions in the United States; the British usage was more restrictive, while Europe also remained different. In fact, as early as March 17, 1956 (before Edwards had come on the campus), the S.C. Fiscal Survey Commission criticized Clemson for policies that "at least give the impression of a trend to a second university." After Edwards took over as acting president, the Board of Trustees Development Committee asked the registrar to determine the original and current legal names of all 1862 "stand-alone" land-grant institutions.[79] "Stand alone" was a colloquial term for institutions not attached to existing state liberal arts colleges or to institutions that, when created, were to function as the sole state institution combining both the liberal arts and land-grant colleges.

The move toward doctoral degrees awarded by Clemson began early in the 1950s, and the logical place for it was in the School of Agriculture. Its faculty had the highest number and percentage of PhD degrees, and its faculty had engaged in research since shortly after the college began and before the students had even arrived. It had accredited faculty, the reputation, and, ever since the opening of the three-building Poole Agricultural Center, the facilities to conduct a doctoral program. Consequently, George H. Aull proposed that the Graduate Council recommend that Clemson offer a PhD degree in agricultural economics. The proposal was approved on March 4, 1958.[80] Several other agriculture departments followed suit and admitted doctoral students in the summer of 1958. In two years, in August 1960, the first doctoral candidate, D. H. Petersen, was awarded Clemson's first such degree.[81]

Edwards was not ready to approach the name change, which he judged might cause a serious uproar. Further, his biggest concern was getting the legislature's permission to issue dormitory bonds to build a residence hall for women. He also was keeping a watchful eye on Harvey Gantt's and Cornelius Fludd's applications for admission. Only when those issues concluded successfully did he feel the time to propose university status was right. He turned again to attorney Watkins for advice. After considerable research, Watkins brought an in-depth report. First, the immediate prerogative to change the name belonged to the state, through action of the legislature and approval of the governor. But second, the will of Thomas Green Clemson specified the name as "The Clemson Agricultural College of South Carolina." It might be possible that the heirs of Thomas Green Clemson could file suit against the college, the state, or both and gain possession of the property and the Clemson portion of the endowment.

So it became necessary to trace Mr. Clemson's descendants and secure their permission for the change. Holmes's and Sherrill's study of Clemson, although only twenty years old, ended their analysis with Mr. Clemson's granddaughter, Floride Isabella Lee, married to her second cousin, Andrew Pickens Calhoun II. Efforts to locate her descendants led to Texas and a large collection of Calhouns. Williams, the graduate dean, suggested asking "Whitey" Lander of the History Department, an expert on southern history and on the Calhouns, for help. Edwards did, and in less than twenty-four hours, using gravestones in Woodland Cemetery and records in the college archives, Lander concluded that the only heir was an army captain currently studying for a master's degree in bacteriology at the University of Wisconsin.

Watkins wrote Capt. Creighton Lee Calhoun on December 4, 1963, explaining the issue in careful detail. Calhoun replied on January 4, 1964:

> I am in complete accord with the proposed name 'Clemson University' since Clemson College is, today, a university in everything but name. Certainly it would be a travesty for someone considering graduate study to turn away from Clemson College because of a misunderstanding caused by its name. It is significant that the name 'Clemson' would be retained in recognition of Thomas Clemson's foresight and generosity in those dark days following the Civil War.

Calhoun then traced his descent from Mr. Clemson, concluding that his (Calhoun's) only child, Andrew Duff Calhoun, had been adopted in 1960. He ended, "I am acquainted with the physical and scholastic growth of Clemson College only in a general way, but I am well aware of the great expansion of both in recent years. I hope in the years to come circumstances will allow me to be closer to the institution which was founded by my honored ancestors."

Armed with the powerful letter, Watkins and Edwards filed suit for declaratory judgment in the S.C. Court of Common Pleas on February 3, 1964. The four-page complaint was accompanied by a document that was developed by Watkins from material provided by J. K. Williams, dean of the college, addressing the differences between universities and colleges in the United States. It noted the changes in Clemson's size and complexity and the liberty of the trustees to make changes in order to continue the institution's usefulness to the people of South Carolina. Further, it would bring Clemson's name into harmony with what was already in effect being done on the campus. The complaint also noted that it would bring Clemson into "line with all other land-grant institutions which have changed their names to reflect enlarged services in their states." Calhoun, in his

The signing of the document that changed Clemson from college to university status by the Honorable Donald Stuart Russell (1906–1998), the 107th governor of South Carolina, with President Robert Cook Edwards (*right*) and Senator and Clemson Life Trustee Edgar Allan Brown (1888–1975) looking on. Clemson University Photographs, CUL.SC.

letter, joined the request, permitting the legislature to change the name and not incur objections from Mr. Clemson's only heir. As required, the attorney general's response indicated that his office wished to hear or see the evidence.[82]

Judge James B. Pruitt studied the documents presented by Clemson and the statutes, decisions, and case law that pertained to legal matters dealing with "trusts founded on valuable consideration" and "trusts founded on donation or will." The judge's decree concurred with the complainant, and he commented, "The Will of Thomas G. Clemson is a most interesting document. Few papers can be found which have affected the history of this section of the United States more drastically for good." Further, Judge Pruitt recognized that the administrative side (i.e., the state), for carrying out the true purpose of the trust (the dispositive side), "should give way." And obviously Mr. Clemson's will gave to the trustees "full authority 'to fix the course of studies…and to change them as in their judgment, experience may prove necessary.'" Because the beneficiaries were South Carolina and "the thousands who would benefit from instruction received at the institution if the new name eliminated that of its founder, Mr. Clemson," Judge Pruitt, on February 28, 1964, decreed that a "change of the name of the plaintiff to 'Clemson University' will not constitute a breach of any of the provisions of the Will of Thomas G. Clemson or the trusts imposed thereby…."[83]

The appropriate legislation had already made its way through both houses of the general assembly. From the senate, its president, Lieutenant Governor Robert McNair, who, although a graduate of the University of South Carolina, had spent his first semester at Clemson, signed it. Solomon Blatt, speaker of the house and a trustee of the University of South Carolina, signed the bill from the house. Governor Russell, formerly the president of the University of South Carolina, invited a party of Clemson faithful to join him for the final signing held on March 11 in the Secretary of State's Office. Besides Edwards and Watkins, a number of trustees (including Board of Trustees President Robert Cooper and James Byrnes, former governor and Clemson life trustee), students (including the student body president and the editors of *The Tiger* and *Taps*), the president of the Faculty Senate, the president of the Alumni Association, the foundation president, and the four major administrators watched as Russell signed Law No. 803 of 1964. The deed was done.[84]

However, the actual effective date implementing the name change would be July 1, 1964. Clemson had requested such timing in order to cast the new seal and dies for printing stationery and other communications to all the associations that accredited Clemson, to associations to which Clemson belonged, to the various learned and honorary societies that had chapters on Clemson's campus, to the counties, and to the other higher education institutions with which Clemson had regular contacts. Also, leading alumni in many walks of life would receive early notification.[85]

But the state's newspapers already broadcast the news. The *Greenville Piedmont's* editorial of February 3, 1964, carried the headline, "Clemson is a University and Should Be Called It." On the same day the Columbia *Record* wrote, "Changing the name of Clemson College to designate the institution as a university will be a long overdue recognition of an accomplished fact." A week later Charleston's News *and Courier* agreed.[86]

Some young graduates in the June 1964 class felt a bit sorry that their diplomas and rings did not carry the new name, and they made reasonable arguments for that. Some alumni wrote asking (and indicating a willingness to pay) for replacement diplomas and rings. The answer, very gently couched, was that to do such would be misleading to the future and, at worst, dishonest.[87]

Notes

1. CUL.SC.CUA. S 30 ss 2 b 3 f 15; Orlans, *The Non-Profit Research Institute*, 13–14; and Mohr and Gordon, *Tulane*, 112–113.
2. CUL.SC.MSS 91 b 1 f 19.
3. CUL.SC.MSS Watkins Papers, 1956–1957.
4. Ibid. Both quotations are from papers within this citation.
5. CUL.SC.MSS 91 b 1 f 19; and b 16 f 213.
6. CUL.SC.CUA. S 30 ss ii b 4 f 1; and CUL.SC.MSS 91 b 16 f 213.
7. CUL.SC.MSS 91 b 16 f 213. The quotation is taken from the letter in this collection.
8. Ibid., 90 S 8 b 8 f 7.

9.   Ibid., Watkins Papers, 1956–1957.
10. Ibid., 90 S 8 b 8 f 7.
11. Ashmore, *Hearts and Minds*, 340–341.
12. Baker, *What Reconstruction Meant*, 89, 96–97.
13. Http://uselectionatlas.org (accessed August 30, 2008). For South Carolina see Edgar, *South Carolina*, 297–299, 389–394, 519–529, which gives a most judicious account of the segregation struggle.
14. Walker, Richardson, and Parks, "Organization of Public Education in South Carolina"; Morris, "Coastal Carolina University," 194–195; Switzer and Green, "Education," 287–289; Rotholz, "Francis Marion University," 340; Hine, "South Carolina State University," 905–906; and Frocke, "Technical Education," 961; in Edgar, ed., *The South Carolina Encyclopedia*.
15. *South Carolina, Code of Laws, 1962*, 5, Title 21, 268–278.
16. Morris, *South Carolina Technical Education System*, 58–61.
17. The published report is titled *Establishing the Goals*. See Wallenstein, ed., *Higher Education and the Civil Rights Movement*, Appendix 4, 253–256. On de facto segregation see Ashmore, *Hearts and Minds*, 140–145.
18. Conklin, *Vanderbilt*, 539.
19. Wallenstein, *Higher Education*, 17 and ff.
20. Ibid., 17–32.
21. Charlotte *Observer*, October 19, 1957; and Blackman, Bradley, and Kriese, *Clemson*, 48–55.
22. *Greenville News*, July 17, 1956.
23. Pratt, "Rhetoric," *Georgia Historical Quarterly*, 2006, 246.
24. CUL.SC.CUA. S 10 f 99.
25. Gantt to Reel, 2008.
26. Ibid. See also Ira Berlin, *The Making of African America*.
27. CUL.SC.MSS 90 S 8 b 8 f 9.
28. Ibid., 91 b 16 f 213.
29. Ibid., b 30 f 383.
30. CUL.SC.CUA. S 61 b 128 f 1212.
31. Ibid., S 11 f 673.
32. Ibid., S 30 ss ii b 4 f 5.
33. The Hon. Justice Matthew Perry to Michael Allsep, LLB and MA history graduate student, and Jerome V. Reel Jr., March 14, 2002; and Reel in Eisiminger, *Integration with Dignity*, 48.
34. Suggs in Eisiminger, *Integration with Dignity*, 28; telegram reproduction in Eisiminger, 67. The Perry conclusion was told to Allsep and Reel (see note 33).
35. Watkins, *Clemson Agricultural College of South Carolina et al., petitioners, vs. Harvey B. Gantt, a minor, by his father and next friend Christopher Gantt, respondent*, 1–24a.
36. *Greenville Piedmont*, July 9, 1962.
37. Ibid.
38. Charlotte *Observer*, July 10, 1962.
39. Perry to Allsep and Reel; and Watkins, "Harvey Gantt Enters Clemson: One Lawyer's Memories," in *Carologue*, Autumn 1998, 10.
40. Watkins, "Harvey Gantt," 11.
41. Perry to Allsep and Reel.
42. Ibid.
43. Watkins, "Harvey Gantt," 12. During the Reconstruction government in South Carolina, the public college open during that period had been integrated in both race and gender.
44. Eugene M. Klein, at that time a Clemson freshman, to Reel, Klein's wife, Violet (a Clemson alumna), and Edmee Reel, September 5, 2008. Several people remembered that it happened in the 1963 season.
45. Charlotte *Observer*, July 31, 1962.
46. Wyche, "Findings of Fact in Civil Action 4101, December 21, 1962" in CUL.SC.MSS Watkins Papers.
47. Watkins, "Harvey Gantt," 12.
48. CUL.SC.CUA. S 11 f 189.
49. Durham, "Integration With Dignity," Clemson University Communications Center, 2003. DVD filed in CUL Special Collections.

50. The alumnus, W. P. Sullivan, who related this very personal comment, agreed to being quoted; however, he noted that like Paul, he has come to see this issue "face to face."
51. *The Tiger*, February 20, 1959.
52. Ibid., September 15, 1961.
53. Ibid., September 21, 1962.
54. Http://www.jfklibrary.org/meredith (accessed September 19, 2008).
55. Ibid.
56. CUL.SC.MSS 100, Subject Correspondence Series 1954–1976, b 3 f 3.
57. Http://www.jfklibrary.org/meredith (accessed September 19, 2008).
58. Ibid.
59. *The Tiger*, October 19, 1962.
60. Ibid.
61. Manning N. Lomax to J. V. Reel; Walter Cox to J. V. Reel; and James Burns to J. V. Reel.
62. U.S. District Court for the Western District of South Carolina: Findings of Fact, Conclusions of Law and Opinion, CA/4101 in CUL.SC.MSS Watkins Papers.
63. *The Tiger*, October 16, 1962; November 9, 1962; and December 14, 1962.
64. United States Court of Appeals, Fourth Circuit, No. 8871 in CUL.SC.MSS Watkins Papers.
65. CUL.SC.CUA. S 11 f 19A.
66. Burton, "Dining with Harvey Gantt: Myth and Realities of 'Integration with Dignity,'" in Burke and Gergel, *Matthew J. Perry: The Man, His Times, and his Legacy*, 184–219 and specifically 192. The comment in the text is mine. Burton's article is based on excellent research and is very well written.
67. The famous Hollings quote was, in this instance, taken from Suggs in Eisiminger, *Integration with Dignity*, 36–37. The ministerial reference is in CUL.SC.CUA. S 11 f 194. See also CUL. SC.MSS 91 f L397.
68. CUL.SC.CUA. S 11 f 194. The exchanges took place between January 23 and 26, 1963.
69. Ibid.
70. Perry to Allsep and Reel.
71. Gantt to Reel.
72. CUL.SC.CUA. S 11 f 194; and Perry to Allsep and Reel.
73. Webster P. Sullivan to Reel; and Frank Gentry to Reel.
74. *New York Times*: Western edition, January 31, 1963.
75. *Taps*, 1963, 130, 244, 247, 302, and 499.
76. Wisconsin Historical Society, MSS 540 f 2.
77. Cox, *1963—the Year of Decision: Desegregation in South Carolina*, ix–xxvi. A chronological journal for the year 1963.
78. McMillan, "Integration With Dignity," in *Saturday Evening Post*. The cost figures are summarized June 26, 1963, in CUL.SC.CUA. S 30 ss vi b 22 ff 6 & 7.
79. Charlotte *Observer*, March 15, 1956; and CUL.SC.CUA. S 30 ss 4 f 3.
80. CUL.SC.MSS 255 f 1.
81. CUL.SC.CUA. S 11 f 673.
82. The letter from C. L. Calhoun is in the Watkins papers as are the documents with Clemson's statement "Basic Reasons for Changing the Name of Clemson College to Clemson University" and an "Extract from the Minutes of October 4, 1963, Meeting of the Board of Trustees of the Clemson Agricultural College of South Carolina," along with a letter of March 20, 1963, from J. K. Williams, dean of the college, March 20, 1963.
83. Ibid., County of Oconee, State of South Carolina: Court of Common Pleas, Judgment Roll No. 11,077.
84. General and Permanent Laws of South Carolina, 1964, no. 803, 1885. The narrative is drawn from my interview of Frank Gentry, then *The Tiger* editor, and from Watkins, "How Clemson University Got Its Name," *Carologue*, Spring 1997, 20–21.
85. CUL.SC.CUA. S 30 v 9, 23.
86. *Greenville Piedmont*, February 3, 1964; Columbia *Record*, February 3, 1964; and Charleston *News and Courier*, February 10, 1964.
87. CUL.SC.CUA. S 11 f 82.

The last quarter of Clemson's existence as a college saw much change—in the architecture and in the gender and the ethnicities of the students. And as this volume illustrates, change can be very good, indeed!

Epilogue
1889–1964

The College Era Ends

Seventy-six years had passed since Thomas Green Clemson died at Fort Hill, and the seventy-fifth anniversary of South Carolina's acceptance of Mr. Clemson's gift that led to the establishment of the Clemson Agricultural College of South Carolina rapidly hastened to the forefront. In three-quarters of a century, eight presidents guided nearly 22,000 students to various college degrees and achievements. Well over a thousand faculty patiently (usually) taught subjects as diverse as differential calculus or nouns and verbs. Cadets studied the intricacies of European history, while female students learned and taught organic chemistry. Three of the four oldest college buildings still stood; by their sides, modern buildings fit closely to the red hills.

Clemson served the state. Hundreds of Clemson graduates taught in schools and colleges across the state and beyond. Others worked as community leaders with women, youth, men, and children in small communities and towns of size. In addition to the many thousands Clemson College served directly, Clemson's sons and daughters had improved the food on almost every person's table, upgraded rural sanitation, and helped build schoolhouses, roads, and communications systems for all South Carolinians.

Furthermore, Clemson served the nation and the world. In several legislatures and congresses, Clemsonians helped make decisions that propelled civic governments. They helped build America's power plants, businesses, hospitals, and homes. And they helped supply and speed food to the tables of America.

Yet, within this glow of triumphalism, flecks of difficulty could be seen. The apparent harmony of the contemporary American age, forged in the difficulties and compromises of the 1920s and 1930s and tempered in World War II, showed signs of coming apart. Some Americans were not "buying in" to this age of the white middle class. The gender gap was not closed by admitting a few women or even by building a women's residence hall, although that was a hopeful start. Nor could America's racial divide be crossed by letting a few students enter a door. Not even the issues of social or economic disparity could be eliminated by imposed uniformity.

Economic prosperity, attainable by any, lay at the base of Mr. Clemson's charge. And that would take tolerance, patience, and change if the institution he called "the high seminary of learning" would achieve his charge.

First page of Thomas Green Clemson's Last Will and Testament, November 6, 1886. Probate Court Records of Walhalla, S.C. Will Book: 234-244.

APPENDIX A

Last Will and Testament of Thomas G. Clemson

State of South Carolina, County of Oconee.

Whereas I, Thos. G. Clemson, of the county and State aforesaid, did, on the 14th day of August, 1883, execute my last will and testament wherein I sought to provide for the establishment of a scientific institution upon the Fort Hill place, and therein provided what sciences should be taught in said institution; and, whereas, I am now satisfied that my intention and purpose therein may be misunderstood as intending that no other studies or sciences should be taught in said institution than those mentioned in said will, which was not my purpose or intention. Now, desiring to make my purpose plain as well as to make some other changes in the distribution of my property, than made in said will, I do now make, publish and declare this instrument as and for my last will and testament, hereby revoking all previous wills and codicils by me made, especially the will above referred to, dated August 14th, 1883.

Feeling a great sympathy for the farmers of this State, and the difficulties with which they have had to contend in their efforts to establish the business of agriculture upon a prosperous basis, and believing that there can be no permanent improvement in agriculture without a knowledge of those sciences which pertain particularly thereto, I have determined to devote the bulk of my property to the establishment of an agricultural college upon the Fort Hill place.

This institution, I desire, to be under the control and management of a board of trustees, a part of whom are hereinafter appointed, and to be modeled after the Agricultural College of Mississippi as far as practicable.

My purpose is to establish an agricultural college which will afford useful information to the farmers and mechanics, therefore it should afford thorough instruction in agriculture and the natural sciences connected therewith — it should combine, if practicable, physical and intellectual education, and should be a high seminary of learning in which the graduate of the common schools can commence, pursue and finish the course of studies terminating in thorough theoretic and practical instruction in those sciences and arts which bear directly upon agriculture, but I desire to state plainly that I wish the trustees of said institution to have full authority and power to regulate all matters pertaining to said institution—to fix the course of studies, to make rules for the government of the same, and to change them, as in their judgment, experience may prove necessary, but to always bear in mind that the benefits herein sought to be bestowed are intended to benefit agricultural and mechanical industries. I trust that I do not exaggerate the importance of such an institution for developing the material resources of the State by affording to its youth the advantages of scientific culture, and that I do not overrate the intelligence of the legislature of South Carolina, ever distinguished for liberality, in assuming that such appropriation will be made as will be necessary to supplement the fund resulting from the bequest herein made.

Item 1. I therefore give and devise to my executor, hereinafter named, the aforesaid Fort Hill place, where I now reside, formerly the home of my father-in-law, John C. Calhoun, consisting of eight hundred and fourteen acres, more or less, in trust, that whenever the State of South Carolina may accept said property as a donation from me, for the purpose of thereupon founding an agricultural college in accordance with the views I have herein before expressed, (of which the Chief Justice of South Carolina shall be the judge), then my executor shall execute a deed of the said property to the said State, and turn over to the same all property hereinafter given as an endowment of said institution to be held as such by the said State so long as it, in good faith, devotes said property to the purposes of the donation; provided, however, that this acceptance by the State shall be signified, and a practical carrying-out be commenced within three years from the date of the probate of this my will. During this term of three years, or as much thereof as may elapse before the acceptance or refusal of this donation, my executor shall invest the net produce of the land and other property; such invested fund awaiting the action of the legislature, and to form a part of the endowment of said institution if accepted, or to form a part of the endowment of the college or school hereinafter provided for, should the donation not be accepted by the State.

Item 2. The following named gentlemen, seven in number, shall be seven of the Board of Trustees, to wit:

R. W. Simpson, D. K. Norris, M. L. Donaldson, R. E. Bowen, B. R. Tillman, J. E. Wannamaker and J. E. Bradley, and the State, if it accepts the donation, shall never increase the board of trustees to a number greater than thirteen in all, nor shall the duties of said board be taken away or conferred upon any other man or body of men. The seven trustees appointed by me shall always have the right, and the power is hereby given them and their successors, which right the legislature shall never take away or abridge, to fill all vacancies which may occur in their number by death, resignation, refusal to act, or otherwise. But the legislature may provide, as it sees proper, for the appointment or election of the other six trustees, if it accepts the donation. And I do hereby request the seven trustees above named, or such of them as may be living, or may be willing to act, to meet as soon after my death as practicable, and organize, and at once to fill all vacancies that may have occurred, and to exert themselves to effectuate my purposes as herein set forth, and I hereby instruct my executor to notify them of their appointment herein as soon after my death as practicable. The name of this institution shall be the "Clemson Agricultural College of South Carolina."

Item 3. Should the three years expire without the State accepting the donation, in manner as herein before provided, and if accepted, at the expiration of three years from my death no practical beginning has been made to carry into effect the purposes of the donation, or, if before the three years expire the legislature shall refuse to accept said donation, then the donation to the State is hereby revoked, and my executor shall execute his trust by conveying the said Fort Hill place, and the accumulated fund arising therefrom, together with all other property, real or personal, hereinafter disposed of and intended to be given to the said agricultural college, as an endowment, to the seven trustees named above, or their successors, who shall erect upon the Fort Hill place such a school or college for the youth of South Carolina as, in their judgment will be for their best interest; provided, that said school or college shall be for the benefit of the agricultural and mechanical classes principally, and shall be free of costs to the pupils, as far as the means derived from the endowment hereinafter provided and the use of the land may permit. The trustees shall securely invest the funds hereinafter provided and given to said institution and hold them as a perpetual endowment, and shall only use the interest derived therefrom and the income of the land to support and maintain said school or college, except that the accumulated fund derived from the land, and the interest derived from the fund hereinafter given said institution, from the time of my death, and as much as five thousand dollars of the principal fund may be used if, in the judgment of the trustees, it may be necessary to erect suitable buildings for said school or college. The name of this institution shall be the "Clemson Scientific School" or "College."

Item 4. It is my desire that the dwelling house on Fort Hill shall never be torn down or altered, but shall be kept in repair, with all the articles of furniture and vesture which I hereinafter give for that purpose, and shall always be open for the inspection of visitors, but a part of the house may be used by such of the professors as the trustees may direct.

Item 5. I give and bequeath to my granddaughter, Floride Isabella Lee, all of my silver plate and table silver, also all of the family pictures, except the large picture of John C. Calhoun, now hanging in my sitting room, also any one article in my present residence which she may select as a memento of me, also my decorations, and also the sum of fifteen thousand dollars ($15,000), to be paid to her on the day of her marriage, or when she becomes twenty-one years of age, if unmarried; provided, that if my said granddaughter should die unmarried, and before she is twenty-one years of age, then all of said property mentioned in this item shall revert to and become a part of the residue of my estate, and become subject to the trusts and conditions of Items 1, 2, and 3 of this my will.

Item 6. I give and bequeath to my faithful housekeeper, Mrs. Jane Prince, one year's provisions for her and daughter, and furniture and bedding, suitable to her condition, sufficient to furnish two rooms, and the sum of three thousand dollars ($3,000), to be paid to her at the expiration of one year after the probate of this my will, and I also desire my executor to permit her to live at Fort Hill until he disposes of the property as herein directed.

Item 7. I give and bequeath to Hester Prince, the daughter of my faithful house-keeper, as aforesaid, the sum of three thousand dollars ($3,000) to be paid to her, or such person as may be selected by her and appointed her guardian, at the expiration of one year from the probate of this my will.

Item 8. I give to my executor, James H. Rion, as a memento of my friendship, the antique entaglio Marcus Aurelius Antonius sealing which I habitually wear, and also such one of my pictures as he may select, if the same is not selected by myself.

Item 9. I give and bequeath to my executor, or to be held by him subject to the trusts and conditions of Items 1, 2, and 3 of this my will, and for the purpose of adorning the Fort Hill residence as provided in Item 4 of this my will all of my permanent furniture, relics and articles of vesture, pictures and paintings, including the large painting or picture of John C. Calhoun, now hanging in my sitting room, and not otherwise disposed of herein, and all of my books.

Item 10. I direct my executor to sell, at public or private sale, as he may deem best, all the balance of my personal property upon my Fort Hill place, not herein disposed of, and to sell and convey all of my real estate lying and situate outside of the State of South Carolina, either at private or public sale, as he may deem best, and to hold the proceeds derived therefrom, together with the proceeds of the personal property, herein directed to be sold, subject to the trusts and conditions of Items 1, 2, and 3 of this my will.

Item 11. All the residue and remainder of my property of every kind and description whatsoever, after paying off the legacies above provided for, together with the property which may revert to my estate, should it revert thereto, and the proceeds of all my real and personal property herein directed to be sold, and all accumulated funds derived from the Fort Hill place and interest on my investments, I give and bequeath to my executor, to be held by him subject to the trusts and conditions of Items 1, 2 and 3 of this my will.

Item 12. I nominate, constitute and appoint my friend, James H. Rion, the executor of this will.

In witness whereof I have hereunto subscribed my name and affixed my seal before the witnesses below subscribing, the 6th day of November, A. D. 1886.

Thomas G. Clemson, L. S.

The above written instrument was subscribed by the said Thos. G. Clemson in our presence and acknowledged by him to each one of us, and he, at the same time, published and declared the same to be his last will and testament, and we, at his request, and in his presence, and in the presence of each other, have signed our names as witnesses hereto.

James Hunter
T. O. Jenkins
E. L. C. Terrie

Codicil to the Will
of Thomas G. Clemson

State of South Carolina, County of Oconee.

I, Thos. G. Clemson, of Fort Hill, in the State and county aforesaid do make this my codicil to my last will and testament, dated the 6th day of November 1886, hereby confirming my said last will and testament, so far as the same is not inconsistent with this, my codicil.

Item 1. I will and direct my executor to pay my debts and funeral expenses as soon after my death as practicable out of the proceeds of any part of my estate that is the most available.

Item 2. I hereby revoke the 12th item of my last will and testament as aforesaid, in which I appointed James H. Rion as executor of my will, he having recently departed this life, and I now do nominate and appoint my trusted friend, Richard W. Simpson, of Pendleton, South Carolina, my executor of my said last will and testament and of this my codicil thereto, and in my said last will and testament the name of James H. Rion, wherever it appears, shall be stricken out, and Richard W. Simpson shall be inserted in place thereof.

Item 3. I revoke the 8th item of my said last will and testament, in which I gave to James H. Rion my sealing ring and one of my pictures, which he may select, and I do now give and bequeath to R. W. Simpson my sealing ring, which I habitually wear, and such one of my pictures as he may select.

Item 4. I do hereby revoke Item 6 of my said last will and testament, which contains a bequest to my faithful housekeeper, Mrs. Jane Prince, she having been otherwise provided for.

Item 5. It is my will and I do direct that neither the legacy to my granddaughter in the fifth item of my said last will and testament, or the legacy to Hester Prince in the seventh item of my said will, shall bear any interest until the same are due and payable, as provided in said items of my said will.

Item 6. I authorize my executor to purchase that portion of the original Fort Hill tract of land which set off to Gideon Lee, guardian of Floride Isabella Lee, and the same if so purchased shall become a part of the Fort Hill tract of land, and shall go with and be disposed of as I have in my said will disposed of the Fort Hill tract.

Item 7. I will and direct my executor to sell either at private or public sale, and for cash or upon a credit, both as he may think best, all the real estate of which I may die seized and possessed, except the Fort Hill tract of land, whether the same be situate in the State of South Carolina or outside of it.

Item 8. Should the Chief Justice of South Carolina decline to decide when the State of South Carolina has or has not accepted the donation given to it in the first item of my said will, then I give to my executor the same power as I in the said first item of my will gave to the said Chief Justice, and his decision shall be final.

Item 9. I hereby authorize and direct my executor to employ such persons he may deem necessary to take charge of the Fort Hill dwelling house and the articles therein donated, and to manage the farm and to pay the said persons such a sum of money for their service as he may deem right and proper.

Item 10. In the view of the great responsibility and labor which my executor will encounter in managing the affairs of my estate, as directed in my said will, and in consideration of the great kindness he has shown to me, and of the assistance in taking care of my business when I have no other friend to help me, I will and bequeath that he, my said executor, shall have, take and receive in addition to the usual commissions allowed by law to executors as commissions for receiving and paying out money, five percent of the appraised value of my entire estate, both real and personal.

Item 11. I desire to state here that my granddaughter, Floride Isabella Lee, has received the one-fourth part in value of the original Fort Hill tract of land, the part which her mother, under the will of Mrs. John C. Calhoun, was entitled to, the same having been appraised and set off to her by commissioners appointed by Mrs. Clemson, and by Gideon Lee, her father and guardian, and she has also received through Gideon Lee, her said guardian, her mother's share of the estate of my son, John C. Clemson. Notwithstanding this fact, from a letter received by me some time ago from Gideon Lee, I am led to believe that as guardian of my said granddaughter, he will make claim to my estate a large balance alleged by him to be due my said granddaughter by me. I therefore desire and direct my executor to examine closely into such claim if so made, and if he, my said executor, is satisfied that the claim so made is justly due by me, to my said granddaughter to pay the same; but on the other hand, if he is not satisfied that the said claim or claims are justly due by me, then he shall not pay it or them unless compelled by law to do so, in which case I hereby revoke so much of the bequest of fifteen thousand dollars given in the fifth item of my said last will and testament to my said granddaughter as will be equal to the amount which my said granddaughter may recover against my estate.

Item 12. The desire to establish such a school or college as I have provided for in my said last will and testament, has existed with me for many years past, and many years ago I determined to devote the bulk of my property to the establishment of an agricultural school or college. To accomplish this purpose is now the one great desire of my life. I have not been unmindful of the interest of my said granddaughter, nor have I acted in this matter through any prejudice to anyone. It may be possible that the disposition of my property as herein made may not give satisfaction to my said granddaughter or to Gideon Lee, her father and guardian, but I trust that neither the one nor the other, or any other person lawfully authorized by law to represent my said granddaughter, will ever attempt to frustrate or defeat the purpose which I have herein sought to accomplish, but will respect the settled desire of my life as contained in this my will, but should my desire and request as herein expressed be ignored, and should Gideon Lee, as guardian of my said granddaughter, or should my said granddaughter herself, or any other person lawfully authorized by law to represent her, or any person as heir, legatee or distributee of my said granddaughter in their right as such, attempt to contest my will or attempt to invalidate it, or attempt to change or alter it in any particular whatever, then it is my will and I do direct that such attempt or attempts to contest, alter, change or invalidate my said last will and testament, or codicil hereof, shall as soon as commenced work an absolute revocation of my entire and of all my bequests to my said granddaughter, Floride Isabella Lee, as made in fifth item of my said last will and testament, and then and in that case, my said granddaughter, Floride Isabella Lee, shall receive no part of my estate whatever, and the money and articles mentioned in the fifth item of my said will shall go to my executor and be held by him subject to the trusts and conditions contained in Items 1, 2, and 3 of my said last will and testament; provided, that my executor shall sell in manner as to him may seem proper any of the articles mentioned in the said fifth item of my said last will and testament, except the family pictures. These shall be held by my executor subject to the trusts and conditions of Items 1, 2, and 3 of my said last will, and kept with the other articles mentioned in the eighth item of my said last will and testament, to adorn the Fort Hill house.

Item 13. It is my will and I direct that my executor shall not be held liable for, or responsible for any losses to my estate by reason of my errors of judgment or mistakes, as I am fully aware of the varied and responsible duties I herein have required of him. This codicil is written in part on the fourth page of my last will and testament to which this sheet is attached, and which is dated November 6th, 1886.

Item 14. I authorize and empower my executor to expend such sums of money as he may deem necessary to keep the Fort Hill dwelling house and premises in repair, and the Fort Hill farm in good condition.

In witness whereof I have hereunto subscribed my name and affixed my seal before the witnesses below subscribing, this the twenty-sixth day of March, in the year of our Lord one thousand eight hundred and eighty-seven (1887).

Thos. G. Clemson, L. S.

The above written instrument was subscribed by the said Thos. G. Clemson in our presence and acknowledged by him to each one of us and he at the same time published and declared the same to be his codicil to his last will and testament, and we, at his request and in his presence, and in the presence of each other, have signed our names as witnesses hereunto.

R. M. Jenkins
C. W. Young
J. H. Mounce

The foregoing paper bears this endorsement:
"This will was admitted to probate in common form on the 20th day of April A.D. 1888, and recorded in 'Will Book,' pages 234-244."

Richard Lewis,
"Judge of Probate"

*Reprinted from Alester G. Holmes and George R. Sherrill, *Thomas Green Clemson: His Life and Work* (Richmond, VA: Garrett and Massie, 1937) 193-201.

APPENDIX B

Clemson Historical Enrollment
1893–1964

Clemson historical enrollment numbers have been taken from *The Clemson Catalog/Record* for each year, the registrar's reports to the college president from each year, various presidential reports to the Board of Trustees of Clemson College, and the Historical Enrollment chart compiled by registrar G. E. Metz in 1988, available online at

http://www.clemson.edu/oirweb1/fb/factbook/Historical%20Enrollment/ Enrollment1893topresent.htm.

Prepared by graduate research assistant Paul Alexander Crunkleton.

Academic Year	Enrollment
1893–1894	446
1894–1895	635
1895–1896	370
1896–1897	348
1897–1898	449
1898–1899	446
1899–1900	461
1900–1901	483
1901–1902	500
1902–1903	539
1903–1904	605
1904–1905	674
1905–1906	652
1906–1907	658
1907–1908	687
1908–1909	648
1909–1910	653

(Table continues on p. 536)

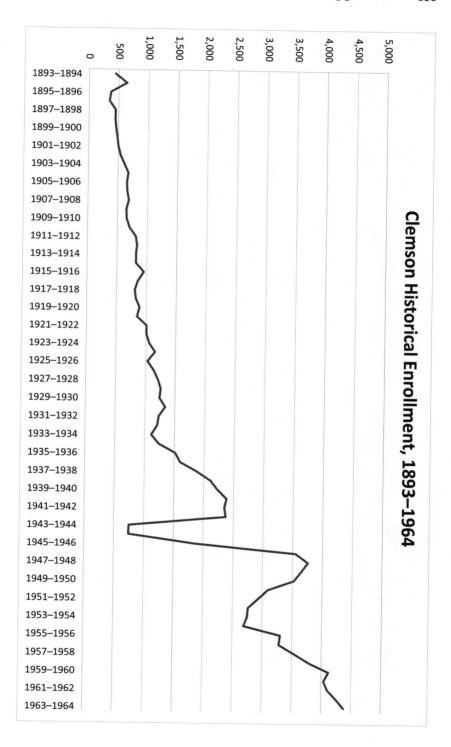

Clemson Historical Enrollment, 1893–1964

Academic Year	Enrollment	Academic Year	Enrollment
1910–1911	703	1942–1943	2,370
1911–1912	811	1943–1944	752
1912–1913	834	1944–1945	745
1913–1914	818	1945–1946	1,863
1914–1915	819	1946–1947	3,550
1915–1916	951	1947–1948	3,756
1916–1917	853	1948–1949	3,645
1917–1918	804	1949–1950	3,522
1918–1919	825	1950–1951	3,093
1919–1920	886	1951–1952	2,926
1920–1921	847	1952–1953	2,764
1921–1922	1,007	1953–1954	2,749
1922–1923	1,008	1954–1955	2,690
1923–1924	1,057	1955–1956	3,305
1924–1925	1,155	1956–1957	3,283
1925–1926	1,032	1957–1958	3,540
1926–1927	1,137	1958–1959	3,793
1927–1928	1,212	1959–1960	4,119
1928–1929	1,258	1960–1961	4,040
1929–1930	1,238	1961–1962	4,104
1930–1931	1,336	1962–1963	4,252
1931–1932	1,228	1963–1964	4,376
1932–1933	1,207		
1933–1934	1,108		
1934–1935	1,234		
1935–1936	1,516		
1936–1937	1,599		
1937–1938	1,877		
1938–1939	2,108		
1939–1940	2,227		
1940–1941	2,381		
1941–1942	2,349		

BIBLIOGRAPHY

Clemson University Libraries, Special Collections, Clemson, SC

Manuscripts (CUL.SC.MSS)
Aull, George Papers MSS 255.
Behrend, Bernard A. MSS 240.
Boggs, H. B. MSS 21.
Brown, Edgar A. Papers MSS 91.
Byrnes, James F. Papers MSS 90.
Calhoun, Noble, and Pickens Family Collections MSS 0225.
Camp, W. B. MSS 165.
Cannon, F. W. Scrapbook MSS 150.
Clemson, Thomas Green MSS 002.
Crouch, Sydney MSS 118.
Davidson, Abraham Wolfe 82–7.
Edwards, Robert Cook Papers MSS 285.
Fifth Regiment, South Carolina Volunteers MSS 44.
Forestry, S.C. Division MSS 301.
Gordon, Charles Pierce in process.
Holman, Harriet R. MSS 0215.
Holmes, Alester G. MSS 1.
Holtzendorff, Preston B., Jr. MSS 0290.
Husbandry, Patrons of MSS 38.
Jervey, Frank Johnstone MSS 72.
Johnson, F. D. MSS 94.
Johnson, W. B. MSS 254.
Klugh Scrapbook MSS 64.
Lambert, R. S. MSS 159.
Lander, E. M. MSS 280.
Lane, J. D. MSS 79.
Lawton, M. R. MSS 260.
Lee, Rudolph E. MSS 41.
Lemon, C. C. MSS 67.
Lever, Asbury Francis MSS 95.
Littlejohn Family Papers MSS 304.
Littlejohn, James Corcoran MSS 68.
Martin, Furman Hovey MSS 294.
McClain Family Papers MSS 71.
McKale, Donald MSS 292.
Mills, William Hayne MSS 88.
Mitchell, Ethel B. MSS 5.
Mott, K. J. MSS 284.
Norris, Daniel Keating MSS 22.
Poe Family Papers accession 07–117.
Poole, Robert Franklin MSS 73.
Quattlebaum Family Papers MSS 76.
Red Shirts, Pendleton, SC, 1876–1880 MSS 8.
Robertson, Benjamin F., Jr. MSS 77.
Thornhill, T. Wilbur MSS 47.

Thurmond, J. Strom MSS 100.
Simpson, R. W. MSS 96.
Simpson, W. N. MSS 268.
Sitton, Benjamin Gaillard Scrapbook MSS 271.
Stafford, Donald MSS 166.
Tillman, B. R. MSS 80.
Traynham-George W. Carver Correspondence accession 10–41.
Watkins, William L. Legal papers relating to Clemson University.
Williams, B. O. MSS 86.
Young, E. L. MSS 70.

Oral Interviews
Town of Calhoun, South Carolina Oral History Collection by James Megginson.
Bradbury, Douglas (alumnus, faculty engineering) by Laura L. Benjamin.
Curris, Constantine (thirteenth president) by J. V. Reel.
Gantt, Harvey (alumnus; mayor of Charlotte, NC) by J. V. Reel.
Greenlee, William (a witness to the first 80 years) by J. C. Littlejohn.
McHugh, James H. (a witness to the first 40 years) by J. C. Littlejohn.
Putnam, Samuel (member, first class) by J. C. Littlejohn.
Turnipseed, B. R. (member, first class) by J. C. Littlejohn.

Oral Video Interviews
TTE-Through Their Eyes: A Project of the Strom Thurmond Institute

Bennett, George (alumnus, IPTAY director) by Donald McKale.
Cox, Walter T., Jr. (tenth president, vice president, student affairs) by Donald McKale.
Edwards, Robert Cook (eighth president) by Stephen Wainscott.
Macaulay, Hugh (faculty, economics) by Donald McKale.
McClure, Harlan (dean, architecture) by Donald McKale.
Prince, Philip (twelfth president) by Donald McKale.
Rich, Linvill (dean, engineering) by Donald McKale.
Vickery, Kenneth (dean, admissions and registration) by Donald McKale.
Webb, Bud (vice president, agriculture) by Donald McKale.
Willimon, Tilla (staff) by J. V. Reel.
Young, Joseph L. (faculty, architecture) by Donald McKale.

Emeritus College Interviews and University Historian Interviews

Abernathy, Larry (alumnus; mayor of Clemson) by J. V. Reel.
Aucoin, C. (faculty and head, mathematics) by Farrell Brown.
Barker, James F. (fourteenth president; dean, architecture; alumnus) by J. V. Reel.
Bishop, Gene (faculty, engineering; fraternity advisor) by J. V. Reel.
Brawley, Joel (faculty, mathematics) by Farrell Brown.
Briscoe, I. C. (faculty, education) by Richard Klein.
Butler, John (faculty and head, music) by Sterling Eisiminger.
Cameron, Albert Neill (alumnus and veteran) by J. V. Reel.
Cameron, Albert Neill, Jr. (vice president, advancement) by J. V. Reel.
Caskey, Claire (faculty, English) by Sterling Eisiminger.
Cheatham, Harold E. (dean, health, education, and human development) by Richard Klein.
Clark, Bobby (alumnus; staff) by J. V. Reel.
Cox, H. Morris (faculty and dean, liberal arts; veteran) by Sterling Eisiminger.
DiSabatino, Gail (vice president, student affairs) by J. V. Reel.
Dodson, Eliot (alumnus) by J. V. Reel.
Dunning, Deborah (alumna; staff) by J. V. Reel.
Durham, Harry (staff, public affairs) by J. V. Reel.

Efland, Thomas (associate dean, research; faculty, textile science) by J. V. Reel.

Elrod, Alvin (faculty, mechanical engineering; modifier of camshaft) by J. V. Reel.

Freeman, Ed (alumnus; faculty, music; veteran) by J. V. Reel.

Fuller, Elizabeth (patron) by J. V. Reel.

Fulmer, Pat (alumnus; faculty, horticulture) by J. V. Reel.

Gantt, Nat (alumnus) by J. V. Reel.

Goswami, Dixie (faculty, English) by Sterling Eisiminger.

Harder, Byron (alumnus; physician, university health center) by Donald McKale.

Harder, Lillian "Mickie" (faculty, music; director, Brooks Center) by J. V. Reel.

Hare, William (faculty, mathematics) by Richard Klein.

Heavner, Christopher (pastor, city of Clemson) by J. V. Reel.

Helms, Doris (provost) by J. V. Reel.

Hobson, J. Harvey (faculty, chemistry) by Thomas Wooten.

Hubbard, Julius "Mike" (faculty, textile science) by J. V. Reel.

Jacks, Almeda (vice president, student affairs) by J. V. Reel.

Johnstone, Alan McCrary (alumnus) by J. V. Reel.

Jones, Joe K. (faculty, agricultural extension) by Elaine Richardson-Burrows.

Kay, Mark (alumnus) and Edna by J. V. Reel.

Kelly, John (vice president, agriculture and economic development) by J. V. Reel.

Lambert, Robert (faculty and head, history) by Donald McKale.

Lander, E. M. (faculty, history) by Rameth Owens.

Lennon, Max (eleventh president) by J. V. Reel.

Lomax, M. N. (vice president, student affairs; vice president, administration) by Farrell Brown.

Lovelace, Fred (alumnus) by J. V. Reel.

Martin, Campbell (civil engineer; advisor to Greenville programs) by J. V. Reel.

McKenzie, Jack (alumnus; staff) by J. V. Reel.

Mullins, Joseph (faculty, chemical engineering; president, Faculty Senate; volunteer tennis coach) by J. V. Reel.

Nicholas, Stanley (vice president, development) by J. V. Reel.

Phillips, Terry Don (athletics director) by J. V. Reel.

Przirembel, Christian E. G. (vice president, research) by Sandra Woodward.

Poole, Randy (alumnus) by J. V. Reel.

Pyles, Vern (alumnus) by J. V. Reel.

Reamer, Larry (manager, Clemson Forest) by Thomas Wooten.

Sams, James (alumnus) by J. V. Reel.

Schwartz, Arnold (dean, graduate school) by J. V. Reel.

Senn, Tazewell (faculty and head, horticulture; founder, SC Botanical Garden) by J. V. Reel.

Skardon, B. N. (alumnus; faculty, English; POW veteran) by J. V. Reel.

Skove, Malcolm (alumnus; faculty, physics) by J. V. Reel.

Smith, Joy (alumna; dean of students) by J. V. Reel.

Smith, Junius (alumnus) by J. V. Reel.

Smith, Sandy (town citizen; head nurse, university health center) by J. V. Reel.

Spiro, Art (alumnus) by J. V. Reel.

Steadman, Clayton (alumnus; university legal counsel) by J. V. Reel.

Steadman, Mark (faculty, English; author) by Sterling Eisiminger.

Trapnell, Jerry (alumnus; dean, commerce and industry) by J. V. Reel.

Turk, Don (faculty, poultry science) by J. V. Reel.

Turner, Joseph J. (alumnus; executive secretary, IPTAY) by J. V. Reel.

Wannamaker, Patricia (faculty, German) by J. V. Reel.

Washington, Joel (alumnus) by J. V. Reel.

White, Charlie (faculty, PRTM; director, Outdoor Laboratory) by Thomas Wooten.

Wilhelm, Bill (baseball coach) by Farrell Brown.

Wilson, T. V. (faculty, agricultural extension) by J. V. Reel.

Young, Art (faculty, communications) by Richard Klein.

Zielinski, Paul (faculty, engineering; director, Water Resources Institute) by J. V. Reel.

Oral Video Programs

Clemson University Foundation: 75th Anniversary.
Gantt Day: 1:48:00 program with talks by Harvey Gantt, Hon. Matthew Perry, and Clemson University students.
Thomas Green Clemson: A Life and a Legacy.
Welcome Coeds: 50 Years of Women at Clemson.

Personal Interviews

(Notes in the possession of the author)
Berry, Ronald (alumnus; IBM executive) by J. V. Reel.
Bostic, James (alumnus; member, Board of Trustees) by J. V. Reel.
Cox, Headley Morris (faculty and dean emeritus) by J. V. Reel, February 3, 2007.
Cox, Walter Thompson, Jr. (alumnus; president emeritus; athletic coach) by J. V. Reel, August 3, 1999.
Edwards, Robert C. (alumnus; president emeritus) and DeLaney, Joey (sophomore member, Student Alumni Council) by J. V. Reel at Seasons, Madren Center, January 10, 2003, a transcript survives.
Elmore, H. Alan (alumnus) by J. V. Reel, Clemson, S.C., 2008–2009.
Gantt, Harvey (alumnus, Class of 1965) by J. V. Reel, March 3, 2008.
Gentry, Frank (alumnus, Class of 1964; editor, *The Tiger*) by J. V. Reel, March 3, 2008.
Grigsby, Mrs. Robert L. (relict of Robert L. Grigsby) by J. V. Reel, August 12, 2007.
Hurst, Victor (vice president emeritus, academic affairs) by J. V. Reel, February 7, 2007.
Jones, Champ (alumnus; faculty emeritus) by J. V. Reel, February 10, 2007.
Keller, Leonard, Jr. (alumnus; community leader) by Farrell Brown.
Lambert, Edythe (Clemson community leader) by J. V. Reel, March 18, 2007.
Lambert, Robert S. (faculty and head emeritus) by J. V. Reel, March 18, 2007.
Lander, Ernest M. (alumni professor emeritus) by J. V. Reel, March 12, 2007.
Lander, Sarah (Clemson College librarian) by J. V. Reel, March 12, 2007.
Lomax, Manning N. (alumnus, Class of 1963; vice president, student affairs; vice president emeritus, administration) by J. V. Reel, February 9, 2009.
Massey, Larry (alumnus; Clemson extension) by J. V. Reel, March 10, 2003.
McLellan, Hensley "Bill" (athletic director) by J. V. Reel, February 16, 2009.
Reid, Mrs. Lawrence (Clemson community leader) by J. V. Reel, August 8, 2007.
Senn, Tazewell (alumnus; head emeritus, horticulture) by J. V. Reel, March 27, 2007.
Skardon, Beverly N. "Ben" (alumnus; faculty emeritus, English) by J. V. Reel, Clemson, S.C.
Sublette, Mark (alumnus; band member 1974–1980) by J. V. Reel, March 5, 2009.
Turner, Joseph J. (alumnus; staff, alumni office; executive secretary, IPTAY; CHE) by J. V. Reel.
Willis, Samuel (alumnus; dean emeritus, extension) by J. V. Reel, February 16, 2007.

Clemson University Archives (CUL.SC.CUA.)

Series 1	E. W. Sikes Correspondence 1925–1931.
Series 2	E. W. Sikes Correspondence 1931–1941.
Series 3	E. W. Sikes Speeches and Writings 1926–1941.
Series 4	E. W. Sikes Reference and Research Materials.
Series 5	Robert F. Poole Correspondence 1940–1958.
Series 6	Robert F. Poole Administrative Files 1926–1957.
Series 7	Robert F. Poole Committee Files.
Series 8	Robert F. Poole Speeches and Writing 1918–1958.
Series 9	Robert F. Poole Biographical 1917–1958.
Series 10	Admissions 1902–1970.
Series 11	Robert C. Edwards Presidential Correspondence 1959–1965.
Series 12	Robert C. Edwards Presidential Correspondence 1966–1970.
Series 13	Robert C. Edwards Presidential Correspondence 1971–1975.
Series 14	Robert C. Edwards Presidential Speeches 1956–1979.
Series 15	Reports to the President 1940–1955.
Series 16	Samuel B. Earle Presidential Records 1924–1925.
Series 17	Walter M. Riggs Presidential Records 1907–1925.

Series 18   Patrick H. Mell Presidential Records 1902–1909.
Series 19   Bill L. Atchley Presidential Correspondence 1971–1986.
Series 20   Bill L. Atchley Presidential Papers Restricted Access.
Series 21   IPTAY 1935–1983.
Series 22   Cadet Discipline Files.
Series 23   Henry A. Strode Presidential Records 1890–1892.
Series 24   Edwin B. Craighead Presidential Records 1895.
Series 25   Henry S. Hartzog Presidential Records 1897–1902.
Series 26   Clemson University Athletic Council 1929–1985.
Series 27   Bill Atchley Speeches.
Series 28   Office of Publications Biographical File 1909–1976.
Series 29   B'nai B'rith Hillel Student Organization.
Series 30   Board of Trustees Records 1888–1991.
Series 31   Cooperative Extension Service Programs 1930–1984.
Series 32   Cooperative Extension Service Administration 1918–1987.
Series 33   Cooperative Extension Service Field Operations 1909–1985.
Series 34   Clemson University Athletic Council 1983–1992.
Series 35   Walter T. Cox Presidential Records 1970–1989.
Series 36   Clemson University Faculty Senate 1897–1988.
Series 37   Clemson University Subject Files 1893–2005.
Series 38   Clemson University Biography Files.
Series 39   Clemson University Performing Arts Department 1903–1990.
Series 40   Athletic Department Records 1947–1996.
Series 41   Department of Forestry 1931–1985.
Series 42   Animal Science Department Records 1924–1995.
Series 43   Commencement Programs 1896–1995.
Series 44   Athletic Department Publications 1939–1992.
Series 45   Cooperative Extension Service Publications 1931–1995.
Series 46   News Services Publications 1939–1992.
Series 47   School of Textiles, Dean's Office Records 1927–1963.
Series 48   Office of Admissions Publications 1923–1963.
Series 49   College of Forest and Recreation Resources 1940–1994.
Series 50   Office of the Treasurer 1891–1959.
Series 51   Cooperative Extension Service Photographs 1880–1979.
Series 52   Textile Research Department 1955–1966.
Series 53   Commencement Programs 1996–.
Series 54   News Services Publications 1993–1998.
Series 55   School of Industrial Management and Textile Sciences 1951–1975.
Series 56   College of Industrial Management and Textile Sciences 1947–1982.
Series 57   Department of Textiles 1936–1982.
Series 58   Department of Industrial Management 1952–1980.
Series 59   Department of Parks, Recreation, and Tourism Management.
Series 60   Department of Biological Sciences Harllee Egg Collection.
Series 61   A. Max Lennon Presidential Records 1939–1993.
Series 62   Professional Development Office Records 1951–1998.
Series 63   News Services Releases 1956–1985.
Series 64   Vice-President for Administration 1982–1994.
Series 65   Agricultural Business Office Personnel Records 1920–1963.
Series 66   College of Commerce and Industry Administrative Files 1969–1990.
Series 67   Institutional Self Study Reports 1955–1994.
Series 68   Department of History Records 1956–1986.
Series 69   Student Government Records 1962–1996.
Series 70   Department of Accountancy Records 1974–1995.
Series 71   Department of Management Records 1973–1985.
Series 72   Department of Finance 1982–1995.
Series 73   University Research Office 1941–1993.

Series 74   University Libraries 1893–1995.
Series 75   Computer Science Master's Theses 1980–1999.
Series 76   College of Agricultural Sciences Dean's Office 1953–1990.
Series 77   Communications Center Audio Recordings 1965–1980.
Series 78   University Relations 1965–1996.
Series 79   YMCA 1911–1975.
Series 80   Chemistry Department 1909–1993.
Series 81   College of Liberal Arts in process.
Series 82   College of Agriculture Resident Instruction 1957–1988.
Series 83   College of Architecture 1940–1988.
Series 84   Plant Industry Department in process.
Series 85   Marketing Department 1950–1997.
Series 86   Textiles Theses and Senior Papers 1904–1972 in process.
Series 87   Vice-President for Business and Finance.
Series 88   Horticulture Department 1939–1989.
Series 89   Student Housing 1932–2001.
Series 90   College of Nursing 1967–1995.
Series 92   Department of News Services 1943–1996.
Series 93   Office of Undergraduate Studies.
Series 95   Office of the Commandant 1927–1952.
Series 97   Campus Recreation Department 1969–1996.
Series 98   Communications Center: Audio Recordings.
Series 99   Communications Center: Film Library.
Series 100   Clemson University Photographs.
Series 101   Athletic Council 1899–1996.
Series 102   Philip H. Prince Presidential Records 1991–1996.
Series 103   A. Max Lennon Presidential Records 1978–1994.
Series 105   W. T. Cox Papers 1930–1986.
Series 140   4-H and Youth Development 1926–2004.
Series 367   University Historian.

Other Archives

American Philosophical Society, Philadelphia, PA
Ogden Papers.

Columbia University Library, New York, NY
Carnegie Foundation Archives.

Georgia Institute of Technology, Atlanta, GA
Georgia School of Technology Board of Trustee Minutes, vol. 1 1886–1906. No extant minutes
    from 1906–1916.
Georgia School of Technology Faculty Minutes, vol. 1 to 1910.
Georgia School of Technology Announcements, 1888–1906.
Lyman Hall Correspondence, vol. 1 1896–1899 and vol. 2 1900–1902.

McCollum-Lindsay Papers
(in possession of Pickens Lindsay)

Mississippi State University: Mitchell Memorial Library, Starkville, MS
John Crumpton Hardy Correspondence.
Stephen Dill Lee Correspondence.
Annual Catalog 1880–2006.

Rockefeller Archives Center, Tarrytown, NY
Family Fund.
General Education Board.
Rockefeller Fund.

South Carolina Historical Society, Charleston, SC
Manuscripts
26.8.09   Albert Simon Correspondence.
28.5.6   Anne King Gregorie Correspondence with Schools.
28.5.7   Anne King Gregorie Correspondence with Schools.
30.04   Christie Benet Miscellany.
30.04   Thomas Green Clemson Miscellany.
30.04   Quattlebaum file in Hutson Collection.
30.8.139   Clemson University Miscellany.
30.9.19   Clemson University Miscellany.
34/0491   M. L. Radcliffe, European and American Genealogies.
43/1004   Aldrich Affidavit.
43/0219   William Christie Benet Papers.
43/2034   Katy Austin Crouch, The Ravenel Research Center, Clemson, SC.
43/0234   A. J. Batson, Jenkins Family History.
0152.01/02/03/04/05/06   Mitchell and Smith Law Firm Records 1839–1925.
0202.00   SC CCC Camps Correspondence.
0259.00   George B. Buell Papers.
0386.00   B. H. Rutledge, Jr. Family Papers.
0417.00   Jenkins Family Papers.
1022.02.04/11/21/16   De Saussure Correspondence.
1048.00/11/238/03   Holmes Family Correspondence.
1071.01.01.01   Petrona Royall McIver Correspondence 1900–1970.
1176.03.01   A. T. Smythe Papers in John Bennett Collection.
1195.02   Charles Richardson Miles 1879–1904 (part of Arthur Mazyck Collection).
1209.03   A. T. Smythe Papers 1888–1914.
1218.00   J. E. Colhoun Property Records 1830–1855.
1231.00   T. W. Thornhill Papers 1914–1978.

South Carolina State University, Orangeburg, SC
Presidential Papers.
Robert Shaw Wilkinson 1911–1932.
Benner C. Turner 1950–1967.

Tulane University of Louisiana: Joseph Merritt Jones Library of the Howard-Tilton Library, New Orleans, LA
Jazz Archives
Dominick James LaRocca Transcripts of taped interviews.

Special Collections
Deutsch, Hermann Correspondence: Series 130.

Tulane University Archives
Edwin Boone Craighead Manuscripts 1903–1912 Series 4.

University of South Carolina, Columbia, SC
Manuscripts
Colhoun, John Ewing (1750–1802) 10.
De Saussure, Henry William Papers (1763–1839) 10.
Norris-Thomson Papers 11.

Winthrop University, Dacus Library, Rock Hill, SC
Johnson Correspondence.
Sims, Henry Correspondence.

Wisconsin Historical Society, Madison, WI
Shirah, Samuel C., Jr. Papers.

Legal Documents and Abstracts

United States of America
Cases Argued and Decided in the Supreme Court of the United States in October 1889. Washington, DC: Government Printing Office.
Congressional Record. Washington, DC: Government Printing Office.
Federal Reporter. Washington, DC: Federal printer. Various.
Report on Graduate Education in American Public Colleges and Universities. Washington, DC: U.S. Department of Education, 1956.
U.S. Army Corps of Engineers, Savannah District. *Lands of Clemson College: Hartwell Reservoir, Savannah River, Georgia and South Carolina: Real Estate Appraisal Study.* Savannah, GA, 1957.
Watkins, William L. *Clemson Agricultural College of South Carolina et al., petitioners, vs. Harvey B. Gantt, a minor, by his father and next friend Christopher Gantt, respondent.* Washington, DC: B. S. Adams, 1963.

State of South Carolina
Acts and Joint Resolutions of the General Assembly of the State of South Carolina. Columbia, SC: State Printer.
Journal of the House of Representatives of the General Assembly of the State of South Carolina. Columbia, SC: State Printer.
Journal of the Senate of the State of South Carolina. Columbia, SC: State Printer.
Reports and Resolutions of the General Assembly of the State of South Carolina. Columbia, SC: James H. Woodrow. Session 25 November 1890 until Spring 1964.
Report of Superintendent of Education. Columbia, SC: State Printer, 1893 and following.
Report of Board of Trustees, President and Officers of Clemson Agricultural College, 1890 and following.
Report of Superintendent of Penitentiaries, 1893 until 1912.
Legislative Manual: South Carolina. Columbia, SC: State Printer, 1916 to present.

Counties of South Carolina

Anderson County, South Carolina. Clerk of Court:
   Deed Book
   Plat Book
   Probate Records

Pickens County, South Carolina. Clerk of Court:
   Deed Book

Epitomes

South Carolina in 1888. Charleston, SC: *News and Courier,* 1888.
Alexander, Virginia, Colleen Morse Elliott, and Betty Willie. *Pendleton District and Anderson County, S.C.: Wills, Estates, Inventories, Tax Returns and Census Records.* Easley, SC: Southern Historical Press, 1980.
Cheek, Linda Gale Smith. *Families of Old Pendleton District, South Carolina.* Greenville, SC: Southern Historical Press, 2006–2007.

Ellison, Carl G. *Will Abstracts: Anderson County, S.C., 1789–1839*. Anderson, SC: Anderson County Genealogical Society, 2000.
Willie, Betty. *Pendleton District, S.C., 1790–1806*. Easley, SC: Southern Historical Press, 1982.
Worley, James E. *A Collection of Upper South Carolina Genealogical and Family Records*. 3 vols. Easley, SC: Southern Historical Press, 1979–1982.

Published Papers

Meriwether, Robert L., W. Edwin Hemphill, and Clyde N. Wilson, eds. *The Papers of John C. Calhoun*. Columbia, SC: University of South Carolina Press, 1976.

Reference

Bailey, N. Louise, Mary L. Morgan, and Carolyn R. Taylor. *Biographical Directory of the South Carolina Senate*. 3 vols. Columbia, SC: University of South Carolina Press, 1986.
Browne, Ray B., and Pat Browne. *The Guide to United States Popular Culture*. Bowling Green, Ohio: Bowling Green State University, 2001.
Edgar, Walter, ed. *The South Carolina Encyclopedia*. Columbia, SC: University of South Carolina Press, 2006.
Fryde, E. B., et al. *Handbook of British Chronology*. London, UK: Published for the Royal Historical Society by Cambridge University Press, 1986.
Garlington, J. C. *Men of the Time: South Carolina*. Spartanburg, SC: Garlington Press, 1902.
Lee, Sidney. *Dictionary of National Biography*. Oxford, UK: Oxford University Press, 1990.
Hemphill, J. C. *Men of Mark in South Carolina*. Washington, DC: Men of Mark Publishing Co., 1907–1909.
MacCambridge, Michael. *ESPN. College Football Encyclopedia*. New York, NY: Hyperion, 2005.
Reynolds, E. B., and J. R. Faunt. *Biographical Dictionary of the Senate of South Carolina*. Columbia, SC: Department of Archives, 1964.
Robson, John. *Baird's Manual of College Fraternities*. 18th edition. Menasha, WI: Collegiate Press, 1949–1991.
Wilson, Charles Reagan, and William Ferris. *Encyclopedia of Southern Culture*. Chapel Hill, NC: University of North Carolina Press, 1989.
Withey, Henry F., and Elsie Rathburn Withey. *Biographical Dictionary of American Architects (Deceased)*. Los Angeles, CA.: Hennessey and Ingalls, Inc., 1970.
Workers of the Writers' Program. *Palmetto Place Names*. Columbia, SC: Work Projects Administration, 1941.

Dissertations and Theses

Andrew, John, Jr. "Clemson Agricultural College and the Southern Military Tradition: 1889–1926." MA thesis, Clemson University, 1993.
Boggs, H. A. "A History of the Calhoun-Clemson School." BS thesis, Clemson Agricultural College, 1934.
Brookover, Robert Shelton, IV. "An Assessment of Organizational Commitment among Faculty at Clemson University." PhD diss., Clemson University, 2002.
Burdette, Robert McPherson. "The Class of 1929 of Clemson Agricultural College." MA thesis, Clemson University, 1974.
Burton, O'Neil B. "The Impact of Participation in a Cooperative Education Program on the Academic Performance of Certain Engineering Students at Clemson University." PhD diss., Clemson University, 2000.
Clayton, Frederick Van. "The Settlement of the Pendleton District: 1777–1800." MA thesis, University of South Carolina, 1930. Subsequently published by Southern Historical Press, Easley, SC, 1988.

Cox, Maxie Myron. "1963—The Year of Decisions: Desegregation in South Carolina." PhD diss., University of South Carolina, 1996.

DeSpain, Raymond Earl. "An Historical Analysis of the Life and Professional Career of John William Heisman, 1869–1936." EdD diss., Texas A & M University, 1991.

Doss, Eric Hayden. "War Classes: Social and Institutional Change at Clemson College and the Citadel, 1937–1947." MA thesis, Clemson University, 2005.

Hale, Rebecca McKinney. "Clemson Agricultural College: Years of Transition, 1925–1929." MA thesis, Clemson University, 1984.

Hall, Ricardo D. "An Analysis of Student Perceptions of Clemson University's Parental Notification Policy." PhD diss., Clemson University, 2003.

Harris, Carmen V. "Blacks in Agricultural Extension in South Carolina." MA thesis, Clemson University, 1990.

———. "A Ray of Hope for Liberation: Blacks in the South Carolina Extension Service, 1915–1970." PhD diss., Michigan State University, 2002.

Howser, Zachary D. "He Roars for a Better Clemson: The Clemson University Student Newspaper and the Legacy of Desegregation, 1963–1988." MA thesis, Clemson University, 2006.

Karns, Daniel Page. "The Impact of Residence Halls on First Year Students' Academic Success." PhD diss., Clemson University, 2002.

Krause, Lois Breur. "An Investigation of Learning Styles in General Chemistry Students." PhD diss., Clemson University, 1996.

Lesesne, Joab Mauldin, Jr. "A Hundred Years of Erskine College, 1839–1939." PhD diss., University of South Carolina, 1967.

McKown, Bryan Forrest. "Fort Prince George and the Cherokee-South Carolina Frontier, 1753–1768." MA thesis, Clemson University, 1988.

Miller, James Cleo, Jr. "South Carolina Legislators' Perceptions of the Clemson University Cooperative Extension Service." EdD diss., Clemson University, 1986.

Morris, Kevin J. "A History of the South Carolina Technical Education System, 1961–1991." PhD diss., Clemson University, 1997.

Njagi, Kageni Omisda. "Students' Attitudes Towards Web-Based Learning Resources." PhD diss., Clemson University, 2003.

Peeler, Jodie. "The Life and Works of Ben Robertson, South Carolina Journalist and Author." PhD diss., University of South Carolina, 2001.

Russell, Nancy Ann. "Legacy of a Southern Lady, Anna Calhoun Clemson, 1817–1875." PhD diss., University of South Carolina, 2003.

Skinner, Leslie Wallace. "Sibling Institutions, Similar Experiences: The Coeducation and Integration Experiences of South Carolina's Clemson and Winthrop Universities." PhD diss., University of South Carolina, 2002.

Smith, Joy Shuler. "The Relationship between Involvement in Extracurricular Activities and the Psychosocial Development of Clemson University Students." PhD diss., University of South Carolina, 1990.

Weaver, Kenneth Allen. "Operationalizing Predictive Factors of Success for Entry Level Students in Computer Science." PhD diss., Clemson University, 2004.

Newspapers and Serial Publications

National
USA TODAY

Georgia
Atlanta Journal
Atlanta Journal and Constitution

Mississippi
Meridian Star

New York
New York Times

North Carolina
Charlotte Observer

South Carolina

Aiken County
Williston Way

Anderson County
Anderson Daily Mail
Anderson Independent

Charleston County
Evening Post
News and Courier
Sentinel
Sunday Budget
Sunday News
World

Edgefield County
Edgefield Monitor

Greenville County
Greenville (Daily) News
Greenville Mountaineer
Greenville Piedmont

Laurens County
Laurensville Advertiser

Oconee County
Seneca Daily Journal

Pickens County
Clemson Commentator
Clemson Daily Journal
Clemson Messenger
Clemson News
Keowee Courier (published at Pickens Courthouse until February 28, 1868, when its operations were transferred to Walhalla, the county seat of Oconee County.)
Pickens People's Journal
Pickens Sentinel

Richland County
Columbia Record
Columbia State

York County
Rock Hill Herald

Unpublished Typescripts

Boatright, Sherry L. "The John C. Calhoun Gold Mine: An Introductory Report on Its Historical Significance." State of Georgia: Department of Natural Resources: Historic Preservation Section, June 15, 1974.

Davidson, Abraham Wolfe. Autobiography. Unpublished in CUL.SC.

Doggett, C. V. "History of the Textile Department at Clemson." Unpublished in CUL.SC.

Leemhuis, Roger. "The Liberal Arts at Clemson Agricultural College." Unpublished in CUL.SC.

Marrett, Keels W., et al. "History of Cotton Production in the Old Pendleton District." Pendleton, SC: Memoirs Pendleton Farmers Society, vol. 1, no. 3, April 11, 1945. Unpublished in CUL.SC.

Miles, James F. "Tour of Historic Places Near Clemson." Clemson, SC, August 14–18, 1961. Unpublished in CUL.SC.

Office of Research and Information, National Association of State Universities and Land-Grant Colleges. Engineering Research at State and Land-Grant Universities. Washington, DC, 1985.

Roper, L. David. "Bruce Family of Pendleton District SC." Blacksburg, VA, 1996.

Vaughan, Otha, Jr. "There's Something in the Air: Clemson Aviation and Space Heritage." Lent to J. V. Reel by Vaughan, 2005.

Watson, David Joseph. "Historical Sketch of the Calhoun-Clemson School." Clemson, SC, 1951. Unpublished in CUL.SC.

Clemson University Publications

Unless otherwise noted, published at Clemson, S.C.: Clemson Agricultural College of South Carolina until June 1, 1964, after which Clemson University, and filed in CUL.SC.

Annual Report of the Board of Trustees: Clemson Agricultural College to the General Assembly of South Carolina, 1890 to present.

Clemson Agricultural College Record, 1905–1963. This is issued annually with a first title for tentative statements and is called *Clemson Agricultural College Announcements.* Informally the two are referred to as "the Catalog." The series continues as *Clemson University Record.*

Clemson Alumni News. Clemson College News Bureau, 1947.

Clemson Alumni Review. Clemson Alumni Association, vol. 1, 1930–1931.

Clemson Alumnus. Clemson Alumni Association, vol. 1–2 (1921–1922); new series vol. 1–3 (1925–1929).

Clemson Baseball. Published yearly by the Athletic Department.

Clemson Basketball. Published yearly by the Athletic Department.

Clemson Football. Published yearly by the Athletic Department. Supersedes the older mimeographed press guide.

Clemson News. Department of Media Relations. Originally duplicated; now distributed by Internet: http://www.clemson.edu/media-relations.

Clemson Track and Field. Published yearly by the Athletic Department.

Clemson World. Division of Advancement, 1947 to present.

Clemson Y.M.C.A. Handbook. Young Men's Christian Association, 1917 to 1964.

Dunn, B. Allen, and Elizabeth M. Holladay. "A History of Forestry at Clemson University," Department of Forest Resources. Technical Paper no. 7, 1977.

Exchange. College of Business and Behavioral Science, 2010.

Extension Work in South Carolina. Clemson Agricultural College, 1919–1964.

(A) History of 4-H in South Carolina. Clemson Extension Service, 1985.

Inside Clemson. Department of Media Relations, 1991 to present.

Memorial to Walter Merritt Riggs: President of The Clemson Agricultural College. Private Printing, April 16, 1926.

Morgan, Thomas W. *Clemson University Extension Service: Graphic Summary of South Carolina Agricultural Statistics and Certain Extension Activities,* 1946.

Orange and White. Athletic Department and IPTAY, 1980 to 2009.

Perry, Jim. "The Farmer Takes a Wife – to a Convention." Cooperative Extension Service, 1948.

Prospectus of Clemson Agricultural College. Fort Hill, SC: Board of Trustees, 1893.

Seeing Orange. Division of Advancement, 2006.

Sorrells, Robert T. *The Clemson Experimental Forest: Its First Twenty Years.* College of Forest and Recreation Resources, 1984.

South Carolina Agricultural Experiment Station Publications.

Tiger Insider, 1999–2001.

Tiger Net, 1999. Absorbed into *Tiger Insider.*

Tips on the Tiger. Athletic Department, 1947–1952.

Clemson University Student Publications

Chronicle, 1898–1927; new series 1961–1964.

Clemsonian, 1901.

Oconeean, 1903–1906.

Slipstick, 1954–1964.

Taps, 1906–1964.

Tiger, 1907–1964.

Articles

Abbott, Kathryn A. "Review of *Two Landmark Decisions in the Fight for Sovereignty.* Norman: University of Oklahoma Press, 2003" (by Jill Norgren). *South Carolina Historical and Genealogical Magazine* 106, no. 4: 261–263.

Abbott, Martin. "The Freedman's Bureau and Negro Schooling in South Carolina." *South Carolina Historical and Genealogical Magazine* 57: 65-81.

Ali, Omar. "Standing Guard at the Door of Liberty: Black Populism in South Carolina." *South Carolina Historical and Genealogical Magazine* 107, no. 3: 190–203.

"Aubrey S. Newman, 90 Colonel Famed for 'Follow Me!' Battle Cry." *The New York Times,* January 22, 1994.

"Bernard H. Rawl." *Journal of Dairy Science* 8, no. 1 (January 1925): 1–3.

Booker, L. R. "Textile Education in South Carolina." *Bobbin and Beaker* (May 1947): 13, 18, and 21.

Bruner, Marlin H. "Clemson Management Stresses Wildlife Values." *South Carolina Wildlife* 2, no. 3: 8–9 and 19.

Coclanis, Peter A. "Global Perspectives on the Early Economic History of South Carolina." *South Carolina Historical and Genealogical Magazine* 106, nos. 2 and 3: 130–146.

Davis, John Martin. "Coosaw Rock Alchemy." *South Carolina Historical Magazine* 109, no. 4: 269–298.

Easterby, J. H. "The Constitution of the Winyah and All Saints Agricultural Society." *South Carolina Historical and Genealogical Society* 44: 52–54.

Edgar, Walter B. "South Carolina Historical Society: Sesquicentennial Address." *South Carolina Historical and Genealogical Magazine* 106, nos. 2 and 3: 102–116.

Foscue. "J. S. Newman." *Highlights of Agricultural Research* 9, nos. 2 and 4.

Gage, Gaston. "History of the Textile School at Clemson College." *Textile History Review* 4, no.1 (January 1963).

Goldstein. "Washington and the Network of W. W. Corcoran." *Business and Economic History On-Line,* 2007.

Heiser, David C. R. "Scepters of Academe: College and University Maces in the Palmetto State." *Carologue* 10, no. 4 (1994).

Henderson, A. Scott. "'Building Intelligent and Active Minds': Educational and Social Reform in Greenville County during the 1930s." *South Carolina Historical and Genealogical Magazine* 106, no.1: 34-58.

Hine, William C. "South Carolina State College: A Legacy of Education and Public Service." *Agricultural History* 65, no. 2 (Spring 1991).

Lakes, Arthur. "The Haile Gold Mines" (of South Carolina). *Mines and Minerals,* September 1900: 55–57. (Provided by Michael Kohl, Special Collections librarian, Clemson University Libraries, May 23, 2005.)

Longley, Mary B. Robertson. "Benjamin Franklin Robertson: Fifty Years a Clemson Man." *South Carolina Magazine* 37 (Winter 1973): 6–9.

McMillan, George. "Integration with Dignity: The Inside Story of How South Carolina Kept the Peace." *Saturday Evening Post*, March 16, 1963.

Michel, Gregg L. "It Even Happened Here: Student Activism at Furman University." *South Carolina Historical and Genealogical Magazine* 109, no. 1: 38–57.

Pratt, Ralph. "Rhetoric." *Georgia Historical Quarterly*, 2006.

Quattlebaum, Paul. "Quattlebaum: A Palatine Family in South Carolina." *South Carolina Historical and Genealogical Magazine* 48, no. 1: 1f; no.2: 84; no.3: 167; no. 4: 219.

Salley, A. J., Jr. "The Calhoun Family of South Carolina." *South Carolina Historical and Genealogical Magazine* 7: 81–85

"South Carolinians at the Partridge Military Academy, 1826." *South Carolina Historical and Genealogical Magazine* 61: 11–12.

Sweet, Julie Anne. "A Review of *The Invention of the Creek Nation, 1670–1763.* Lincoln: University of Nebraska Press, 2004" (by Steven C. Hahn). *South Carolina Historical and Genealogical Magazine* 106, no. 4: 261–263.

Watkins, William L. "Harvey Gantt Enters Clemson: One Lawyer's Memories." *Carologue* 14, no. 3: 8–16.

Webber, Mabel. "Historical Notes: Calhoun Burial Ground Inscriptions." *South Carolina Historical and Genealogical Magazine* 27: 184–187.

West, Stephen A. "A Review of *Never Surrender: Confederate Memory and Conservatism in the South Carolina Upcountry*" (by F. Scott Poole). *South Carolina Historical and Genealogical Magazine* 106, no. 1: 59–60.

Pamphlets

Cauthen, John K. *Edgar A. Brown. Clemson University, 1970.* Clemson University: Privately printed.

Garvin, Noel. *The Tiger Paw of Clemson University: Its Birth and Adoption.* Clemson, SC: Privately Published, 2006.

Hemphill, J. C. *A Short Story of the South Carolina Inter-state and West Indian Exposition.* Charleston, SC: Walker, Evans & Cogswell, 1903.

Lever, Asbury F. *Cotton Futures.* Washington, DC: House of Representatives, 1910.

———. *The Cotton Question.* Washington, DC: House of Representatives, 1910.

Richards, John Gardiner, Jr. *Biography of Rev. John Gardiner Richards.* Privately printed, 1934.

Roberts, Daniel M. *Presbyterian Home of South Carolina: 1952–1984, The Tapp Years.* Privately published, 1985.

Tierney, William G., and James T. Minor. *Challenges for Governance: A National Report.* Los Angeles, CA: University of Southern California, 2003.

Websites

http://encyclopediaofarkansas.net/encyclopedia
http://en.wikipedia.org/wiki/conscription_in_the_United_States#World_War_II
http://en.wikipedia.org/wiki/Floyd_Lavinius_Parks
http://en.wikipedia.org/wiki/James_Haskell_Hope
http://en.wikipedia.org/wiki/nation_forest_service
http://en.wikipedia.org/wiki/Theodore_Roosevelt
http://en.wikipedia.org/wiki/william_henry_perkin
http://en.wikipedia.org/wiki/yellowstone_national_park
http://www.af.mil/information/bios/bio.asp?bioID=4768
http://www.bbc.co.uk/history/historic_figures/cartwright_edmund.shtml

http://www.cgsc.edu/carl/resources/ft.lvn/postww.asp
http://www.csrees.usda.gov
http://www.earlyamerica.com/earlyamerica/milestones/ordinance
http://www.environment.yale.edu
http://www.fs.fed.us
http://www.georgiaencyclopedia.org
http://www.history.army.mil/books/AMH_V1/ch16.htm,381–383
http://www.history.navy.mil/photos/events/wwii-pac/guadcnl/quad-lc.htm
http://www.jfklibrary.ord/meredith
http://www.koreanwar.com
http://www.lib.unc.edu/mss/inv/w/wiggins
http://www.millerschool.org
http://www.sciway.net/hist
http://www.state.sc./schdah/guide
http://www.sreb.org/main/HigherEd/higheredindex.asp
http://www.sreb.org/page/1304/academic_common_market
http://www.303rdbg.com/358way.html
http://www.uscensus100.
http://www.uselectionatlas.org

Monographs

Anderson, Robert. *British Universities: Past and Present.* London: Hambledon Continuum, 2006.

Andrew, Rod. *Long Gray Lines: The Southern Military School Tradition, 1839–1915.* Chapel Hill, NC: UNC Press, 2001.

———. *Wade Hampton: Confederate Warrior to Southern Redeemer.* Chapel Hill, NC: UNC Press, 2008.

Arbena, Joseph L., Aurora B. Arbena, Robert C. Bradley, Harper S. Gault, Joseph J. Jackson, Jr. *IPTAY 50th: The First Fifty Years.* Clemson, SC: Clemson IPTAY Club, 1984.

Arrington, Charles. *A Brief History of Clemson Baptist Church, 1907–1957.* Clemson, SC: Privately printed, 1957.

Ashmore, Harry S. *Civil Rights and Civil Wrongs: A Memoir of Race and Politics, 1944–1996.* Second Edition. Columbia, SC: University of South Carolina Press, 1997.

———. *Hearts and Minds: The Anatomy of Racism from Roosevelt to Reagan.* New York: McGraw-Hill Book Company, 1982.

Bailey, J. Wendell. *The Mississippi Agricultural and Mechanical College and the War.* Nashville, TN: Brendon, nd.

Baker, Bruce E. *What Reconstruction Meant: Historical Memory in the American South.* Charlottesville, VA: University of Virginia Press, 2007.

Ballard, Michael B. *Maroon and White: Mississippi State University, 1878–2003.* Jackson, MS: University Press of Mississippi, 2003.

Baldwin, Linda K. *Great and Noble Jar: Traditional Stoneware of South Carolina.* Athens, GA: University of Georgia Press, 1993.

Banister, Robert A. *The Jungaleers, 1922–1963.* Privately published, 1999.

Barry, John M. *The Great Influenza: The Epic Story of the Deadliest Plague in History.* New York, NY: Viking Press, 2004.

Bass, Jack, and W. Scott Poole. *The Palmetto State: The Making of Modern South Carolina.* Columbia, SC: University of South Carolina Press, 2009.

Benjamin, Laura L. *Clemson University, College of Engineering: One Hundred Years of Progress.* Clemson, SC: College of Engineering, Clemson University, 1989.

Bennett, Alma, ed. *Thomas Green Clemson.* Clemson, SC: Clemson University Digital Press, 2009.

Berlin, Ira. *The Making of African America: The Four Great Migrations.* New York: Viking (Penguin), 2010.

Betterworth, John K. *People's University: The Centennial History of Mississippi State.* Jackson: MS, 1980.

Blackman, Sam, Bob Bradley, and Chuck Kriese. *Clemson: Where the Tigers Play.* Champaign, IL: Sports Publishing L.L.C., 1999.

Bleser, Carol. *In Joy and In Sorrow: Women, Family, and Marriage in the Victorian South.* Oxford, UK: Oxford University Press, 1992.

Boulware, Dorothy Stuart Dunkelberg. *The Name May Change but the Song Goes On.* Clemson, SC: Privately published, 1991.

Brackett, Richard Newman. *Old Stone Church, Oconee County, South Carolina.* Pendleton, SC: Old Stone Church and Cemetery Commission and Pendleton Historical and Recreational Commission, 1972.

Brubacher, John S., and Willis Rudy. *Higher Education in Transition: A History of American Colleges and Universities, 1636–1976,* 3rd edition. New York: Harper and Row, 1976.

Bryan, W. Wright. *Clemson: An Informal History of the University, 1889–1979.* Columbia, SC: R. L. Bryan Co., 1979.

Burke, W. Lewis, and Belinda Gergel. *Matthew J. Perry: The Man, His Times, and His Legacy.* Columbia, SC: University of South Carolina Press, 2004.

Calhoun, Orval O. *Eight Hundred Years of Colquhoun, Colhoun, Calhoun, and Cahoon: Family History in Ireland, Scotland, England, United States of America, Australia and Canada.* Baltimore, MD: Gateway Publishing Co., 1976.

Calhoun, Robert S. *The Calhoun Family: Origin and Activities.* Privately published, 1977.

Canup, C. R., and W. D. Workman, Jr. *Charles E. Daniel: His Philosophy and Legacy.* Columbia, SC: R. L. Bryan Co., 1981.

Cassels, Louise. *The Unexpected Exodus.* Aiken, SC: Sand Hill Press, 1971.

Cheves, Wallace R. *Snow Ridges and Pill Boxes.* Miami, FL: Privately published, 1957.

Conklin, Paul K. *Gone With the Ivy: A Biography of Vanderbilt University.* Knoxville, TN: University of Tennessee Press, 1985.

Cross, Coy F., II. *Justin Smith Morrill: Father of the Land-Grant Colleges.* East Lansing, MI: Michigan State University Press, 1999.

Couch, W. T., ed. *Culture in the South.* Chapel Hill, NC: University of North Carolina, 1934. (Particularly H. Clarence Nixon, "Colleges and Universities" and Edgar W. Knight, "Recent Progress and Problems in Education.")

Dabney, Virginius. *Mr. Jefferson's University: A History.* Charlottesville, VA: University Press of Virginia, 1981.

DeVane, William Clyde. *Higher Education in Twentieth Century America.* Cambridge, MA: Harvard University Press, 1965.

Dodson, Robert, et al. *Pickens District: Eastern Division; 1850 Census.* Central, SC: Old Pendleton Genealogical Society, 1995.

Douthat, Ross G. *Privilege: Harvard and the Education of the Ruling Class.* New York: Hyperion, 2005.

Dundas, Francis de Sales. *The Calhoun Settlement: District of Abbeville, South Carolina.* Staunton, VA: McClure's Printers, 1949.

Dyer, John P. *Tulane: The Biography of a University, 1834–1965.* New York: Harper and Row, 1966.

Dyer, Thomas G. *The University of Georgia: A Bicentennial History, 1785–1985.* Athens, GA: University of Georgia Press, 1985.

Easterby, J. H. *A History of the College of Charleston: Founded 1770.* Charleston, SC: The Trustees of the College of Charleston by the Scribner Press, 1935.

Edgar, Walter. *South Carolina: A History.* Columbia, SC: University of South Carolina Press, 1998.

Edmond, J. B. *The Magnificent Charter.* Hicksville, NY: Exposition Press, 1978.

Eelman, Bruce W. *Entrepreneurs in the Southern Upcountry: Commercial Culture in Spartanburg, South Carolina, 1845–1880.* Athens, GA: University of Georgia Press, 2008.

Eisiminger, Sterling, ed. *Integration with Dignity.* Clemson, SC: Clemson University Digital Press, 2003.

Fite, Gilbert C. *Cotton Fields No More: Southern Agriculture, 1865–1980.* Lexington, KY: University Press of Kentucky, 1984.

Fosdick, Raymond B. *Adventures in Giving: The Story of the General Education Board.* New York: Harper and Row, 1962.

Funchess, William H. *Korea P.O.W.: A Thousand Days of Torment.* Clemson, SC: Privately published, 1999.

Gilmore, Leroy H. *Two Great-Grands: A Factual Story.* Charleston, SC: Walker, Evans, and Cogswell, 1955.

Grant, James. *Bernard M. Baruch: The Adventures of a Wall Street Legend.* New York: Simon and Schuster, 1983.

Green, James L. *Our Honoured Relation: John Ewing and Floride Bonneau Colhoun and the Unification of South Carolina.* Greenville, SC: Southern Historical Press, 2009.

Griffin, John Chandler. *Carolina vs. Clemson: Clemson vs. Carolina: A Century of Unparalleled Rivalry in College Football.* Columbia, SC: Summerhouse Press, 1998.

Grose, Philip G. *South Carolina at the Brink: Robert McNair and the Politics of Civil Rights.* Columbia, SC: University of South Carolina Press, 2006.

Hagedorn, Ann. *Savage Peace: Hope and Fear in America, 1919.* New York: Simon and Schuster, 2007.

Hamer, Fritz P., and John Daye. *Glory on the Gridiron: A History of College Football in South Carolina.* Charleston, SC: History Press, 2009.

Hollings, Ernest F. with Kirk Victor. *Making Government Work.* Columbia, SC: University of South Carolina Press, 2008.

Hollis, Daniel W. *The University of South Carolina.* 2 volumes. Columbia, SC: University of South Carolina Press, 1951.

Holmes, Alester G. *Fiftieth Anniversary of Holy Trinity Church, Clemson College.* Clemson, SC: Privately printed, 1949.

Holmes, Alester G., and George R. Sherrill. *Thomas Green Clemson: His Life and Work.* Richmond, VA: Garrett and Massie, 1937.

Hofstadter, Richard, and Walter P. Metzger. *The Development of Academic Freedom in the United States.* New York: Columbia University Press, 1955.

Horowitz, Helen Lefkowitz. *Campus Life: Undergraduate Cultures from the End of the Eighteenth Century to the Present.* New York: Alfred A. Knopf, 1987.

Horton, J. Wright, and Victor A. Zullo. *The Geology of the Carolinas.* Knoxville, TN: University of Tennessee Press, 1991.

Howard, Frank, with Bob Bradley and Virgil Parker. *Howard.* Lincoln, NE: Privately published, 1990.

Kale, Wilford. *Hark upon the Gale: An Illustrated History of the College of William and Mary.* Norfolk, VA: Donning Co.,1985.

Kantrowitz, Stephen. *Ben Tillman and the Reconstruction of White Supremacy.* Chapel Hill, NC: UNC Press, 2000.

Katz, S. M., John M. Murrin, and Douglas Greenberg, et. al. *Colonial America: Essays in Politics and Social Development.* New York: McGraw-Hill, 1993.

Kean, Melissa. *Desegregating Private Higher Education in the South: Duke, Emory, Rice, Tulane, and Vanderbilt.* Baton Rouge: Louisiana State University Press, 2008.

Keefer, Louis E. *Scholars in Foxholes: The Story of the Army Specialized Training Program in World War II.* Reston, VA: COTU Publishing, 1988.

Kerr, Clark. *The Great Transformation in Higher Education.* Albany, NY: State University Press, 1991.

Kerr, Norwood A. *The Legacy: A Centennial History of the State Agricultural Experiment Stations, 1887–1987.* Columbia, MO: University of Missouri-Columbia, Missouri Agricultural Experiment Station, 1987.

Kinnear, Duncan Lyle. *The First Hundred Years: A History of the Virginia Polytechnic Institute and State University.* Blacksburg, VA: Virginia Polytechnic Institute Educational Foundation, 1972.

Koverman, Jill Beute. *Making Faces: Southern Face Vessels, 1840–1990.* Columbia, SC: University of South Carolina Press, 2001.

Lambert, Robert S. *South Carolina Methodists in Mission: A History of the Clemson United Methodist Church, 1908–1998.* Clemson, SC: Clemson United Methodist Church, 1998.

Lander, Ernest M., Jr. *The Calhoun Family and Thomas Green Clemson: The Decline of A Southern Patriarchy.* Columbia, SC: University of South Carolina Press, 1983.

———. *Few Would Listen: A Clemson Professor's Memoir of Dissent.* Clemson, SC: Clemson Printers, 1997.

———. *A History of South Carolina, 1865–1960.* Columbia, SC: University of South Carolina Press, Second Edition, 1970.

————. *From Clemson College to India in World War II*. Spartanburg, SC: Reprint Company, 1992.

————. *Tales of Calhoun Falls*. 2 volumes. Milledgeville, GA: Boyd Publishing Co., 2004.

Lander, Ernest M., and Charles McGee. *A Rebel Came Home*. Columbia, SC: University of South Carolina Press,1989.

Lawton, Manny. *Some Survived*. Chapel Hill, NC: Algonquin Press, 1984.

Lee, Stephen D. *The Agricultural and Mechanical College of Mississippi: Its Origin, Object, Management and Results*. Jackson, MS: Clarion-Ledger Publishing House, 1889.

Lemmon, Thomas W. *South Carolina Corporation Law*. Columbia, SC: R. L. Bryan Co., 1939.

Lomax, Alan. *Mister Jelly Roll*. New York: Duell, Sloan and Pearce, 1950.

Major, David, and Betty Monahan. *New Index to History of Old Pendleton District with a Genealogy of the Leading Families of the District, by R. W. Simpson*. Greenville, SC: Greenville County Library, 1996.

Mancini, Matthew J. *One Dies, Get Another: Convict Leasing in the American South, 1866–1928*. Columbia, SC: University of South Carolina Press, 1996.

Matalene, Carolyn B., and Katherine C. Reynolds. *Carolina Voices: Two Hundred Years of Student Experiences*. Columbia, SC: University of South Carolina Press, 2001.

Matthews, Edgar M., ed. *Clemson's Foot Ball: An Historical Sketch of Foot Ball at Clemson College*. Clemson Agricultural College of South Carolina: Foot Ball Aid Society, 1900.

Maughan, William. *A Guide to Forestry Activities in North Carolina, South Carolina, and Tennessee*. Asheville, NC: Appalachian Section Society of American Foresters, 1939.

McCandless, Amy Thompson. *The Past in the Present: Women's Higher Education in the Twentieth-Century American South*. Tuscaloosa, AL: University of Alabama Press, 1999.

McFall, Pearl Smith. *So Lives the Dream: History and Story of the Old Pendleton District, South Carolina, and the Establishment of Clemson College*. New York: Comet Press Books, 1953.

McInerney, Rev. Michael, O.S.B., A.I.A. *The Catholic Chapel of Saint Andrew, Clemson College, South Carolina*. Clemson, SC: Privately printed, 1935.

McKale, Donald M. *Destined for Duty: The Clemson Class of 1941*. Clemson, SC: Clemson University, 1990.

McKale, Donald M., and Jerome V. Reel, Jr., eds. *Tradition: A History of the Presidency of Clemson University*. Macon, GA: Mercer University Press, Second Edition, 1998.

McMahon, Sean. *Country Church and College Town: A History of Fort Hill Presbyterian Church*. Clemson, SC: Privately published, 1995.

McMath, Jr., Robert C., Ronald H. Bayor, Lawrence Foster, August W. Giebelhaus, and Germaine M. Reed. *Engineering the New South: Georgia Tech, 1885–1985*. Athens, GA: University of Georgia Press, 1985.

Miller, Annie Elizabeth. *Our Family Circle*. Hilton Head Island, SC: Lawton & Allied Families Association, 1931.

Miller, John J. *A Gift of Freedom*. San Francisco, CA: Encounter, 2005.

Miller, K. A., Arnold Schrier, Bruce Boling, and David Doyle. *Irish Immigrants in the Land of Canaan: Letters and Memoirs from Colonial and Revolutionary America, 1675–1815*. Oxford, UK: Oxford University Press, 2003.

Mills, Robert. *Mills' Atlas of South Carolina*. Greenville, SC: A Press, 1979.

Mohr, Clarence L., and Joseph E. Gordon. *Tulane: The Emergence of a Modern University, 1945–1980*. Baton Rouge, LA: Louisiana State University Press, 2001.

Moore, Winfred B., Jr., and Orville Vernon Burton. *Toward the Meeting of the Waters: Currents in the Civil Rights Movement in South Carolina during the Twentieth Century*. Columbia, SC: University of South Carolina Press, 2008.

Murray, Chalmers. *This Our Land: The Story of the Agricultural Society of South Carolina*. Charleston, SC: Carolina Art Association, 1949.

Myers, Craig A. *Greenville Railroad History Since 1853: An overview of Greenville's railroads, streetcars, buildings and businesses*. Greenville, SC: privately printed, 2002.

Newman, C. L., and J. C. Stribling. *Pendleton Farmers' Society*. Atlanta, GA: Foote and Davies Co., 1908.

Niven, John. *John C. Calhoun and the Price of Union: A Biography*. Baton Rouge, LA: Louisiana State University Press, 1988.

Orlans, Harold. *The Non-Profit Research Institute*. New York: McGraw-Hill, 1972.

Parker, William Belmont. *The Life and Public Service of Justin Smith Morrill.* Boston: Houghton-Mifflin Co., 1924.

Peterson, Merrill D. *The Great Triumvirate: Webster, Clay, and Calhoun.* Oxford, UK: Oxford University Press, 1987.

Phillips, James Edmund, Jr. with Ken Tysiac. *Still Roaring: Jim Phillips's Life in Broadcasting.* Champaign, IL: Sports Publishing L.L.C., 2005.

Pollard, James C. *Military Training in the Land-Grant Colleges and Universities.* Columbus, OH: Ohio State University, nd.

Poole, W. Scott. *Never Surrender: Confederate Memory and Conservatism in the South Carolina Upcountry.* Athens, GA: University of Georgia Press, 2004.

Potts, John F., Sr. *A History of South Carolina State College, 1896–1978.* Columbia, SC: R. L. Bryan Co., 1978.

Quattlebaum, Alexander McQueen. *Clergymen and Chiefs: A Genealogy of the MacQueen and MacFarlane Families.* Charleston, SC: South Carolina Historical Society, 1990.

Quattlebaum, Paul, Jr. *Ancestors and Descendents of Paul Quattlebaum and Sue Martin Quattlebaum.* Columbia, SC: South Carolina Historical Society, 1984.

Reel, Jerome V. *Women and Clemson University.* Clemson, SC: Clemson University Digital Press, 2005.

Reznek, Samuel. *Unrecognized Patriots: The Jews in the American Revolution.* Westport, CT: Greenwood Press, 1975.

Russell, Ann Ratliff. *Diary of a Southern Lady: Anna Calhoun Clemson.* Clemson, SC: Clemson University Digital Press, 2007.

Sanders, Albert E., and William D. Anderson, Jr. *Natural History Investigations in South Carolina from Colonial Times to the Present.* Columbia, SC: University of South Carolina Press, 1999.

Schurman, Rachel, and William A. Munro. *Fighting for the Future of Food: Activists versus Agribusiness in the Struggle over Biotechnology.* Minneapolis, MN: University of Minnesota Press, 2010.

Seaborn, Margaret Mills, ed. *Andre Micheaux's Journey in Oconee County, South Carolina in 1787 and 1788.* Columbia, SC: R. L. Bryan Co., 1976.

Sheriff, G. Anne, and Lavina Moore. *Pendleton District, S.C.: 1810 Census; Present-Day Anderson, Oconee, and Pickens Counties.* Central, SC, 1994.

Sherman, Joseph. *Clemson Tigers: A History of Clemson Football, 1896–1977.* Columbia, SC: R. L. Bryan Co., 1976.

Simpson, Richard Wright. *A History of Old Pendleton.* Easley, SC: Southern Historical Press, nd.

Skardon, Beverly. *A Brief Informal History of Holy Trinity Episcopal Church, Clemson, South Carolina, 1889–1999.* Privately printed, 1999.

Sloan, Dave U. *Fogy Days and Now: Or the World Has Changed.* Atlanta, GA: Foote and Davis, 1891.

Smith, Perry M. *A Hero among Heroes: Jimmie Dyess and the 4ᵗʰ Marine Division.* Quantico, VA: Marine Corps Association, 1998.

Snell, Absalom W. *Growing Up in Elloree: August 1928–September 1942.* Elloree, SC: Privately printed, 2001.

———. *My Air Force Experiences: February 1943–June 1946.* Privately printed, 1997.

South Carolina American Institute of Architects. *The Clemson Architectural Foundation.* Clemson, SC: Privately printed, 1956.

Sperber, Murray. *Beer and Circuses: How Big-Time Sports is Crippling Undergraduate Education.* New York: Henry Holt and Company, 2000.

Springs, Brig. Gen. Holmes B. (Ret.). *Selective Service in South Carolina, 1940–1947: An Historical Report.* (Delivered to Hon. J. Strom Thurmond, Governor of S.C.) Columbia, SC, 1948.

Stewart, William C. *1800 Census of Pendleton District, S.C.* Washington, DC: National Genealogical Society, 1963.

Thelin, John R. *Games Colleges Play: Scandal and Reform in Intercollegiate Athletics.* Baltimore and London: The Johns Hopkins University Press, 1994.

Tucker, Andrea, ed. *Agriculture in America: 1622–1860.* New York: Garland Publishing Co., 1984.

Turner, Jeffrey A. *Sitting In and Speaking Out.* Athens, GA: University of Georgia Press, 2010.

Tysiac, Ken. *Tales from Clemson's 1981 Championship Season.* Champaign, IL: Sports Publishing, L.L.C., 2006.

Umphlett, Wiley Lee. *Creating the Big Game: John W. Heisman and the Invention of American Football.* Westport, CT: Greenwood Press, 1992.

Walker, Melissa. *Southern Farmers and Their Stories: Memory and Meaning in Oral History*. Lexington, KY: University Press of Kentucky, 2006.

Wallenstein, Peter, ed. *Higher Education and the Civil Rights Movement: White Supremacy, Black Southerners, and College Campuses*. Gainesville, FL: University Press of Florida, 2008. (Especially Wallenstein, "Black Southerners and Nonblack Universities: The Process of Desegregating Southern Higher Education, 1935–1965" and Synnott, Marcia, "African American Women Pioneers in Desegregating Higher Education.")

Washington-Williams, Essie Mae with William Stadiem. *Dear Senator, by the Daughter of Strom Thurmond*. New York: HarperCollins, 2005.

Watterson, John Sayle. *College Football: History, Spectacle, Controversy*. Baltimore, MD and London, UK: Johns Hopkins University Press, 2000.

Webb, Ross A. *Winthrop University: The Torch is Passed: A History*. Mansfield, OH: BookMasters, Inc., 2002.

West, Stephen A. *From Yeoman to Redneck: in the South Carolina Upcountry, 1850–1915*. Charlottesville, VA: University of Virginia Press, 2006.

Williamson, Joel. *A Rage for Order: Black and White Relations in the American South since Emancipation*. New York: Oxford University Press, 1986.

Wolmer, Christian. *Fire and Steam: A New History of the Railways in Britain*. London: Atlantic Books, 2007.

Woodruff, Nan Elizabeth. *Rare as Rain: Federal Relief on the Great Southern Drought of 1930–31*. Urbana, IL: University of Illinois Press, 1985.

Yarmolinsky, Adam. *The Military Establishment: Its Impact on American Society*. New York: Harper and Row, 1971.

Yearbook: Epsilon Sigma Phi, The National Honorary Extension Fraternity. Washington, DC: Judd and Detweiler, Inc., 1934.

INDEX